Take Two

Other Books by Frank Manchel

Exits and Entrances: Interviews with Seven Who Reshaped African American Images in Movies
Every Step a Struggle: Interviews with Seven Who Shaped the African American Image in Movies
Film Study: An Analytical Bibliography. 4 Vols.
An Album of Modern Horror Films
Great Science Fiction Films: Revised Edition
Great Sports Movies
The Box Office Clowns: From Bob Hope to Woody Allen
Gangsters on the Screen
Women on the Hollywood Screen
An Album of Great Science Fiction Films
The Talking Clowns: From Laurel and Hardy to the Marx Brothers
Yesterday's Clowns: The Rise of Film Comedy
Film Study: A Resource Guide
Cameras West
Terrors of the Screen
When Movies Began to Speak
When Pictures Began to Move
Movies and How They Are Made

Take Two

A FilmTeacher's Unconventional Story

FRANK MANCHEL

Washington, DC

Copyright © 2016 by Frank Manchel

New Academia Publishing, 2016

All rights reserved. No part of this book may be reproduced or transmitted in any form or by any means, electronic or mechanical, including photocopying, recording, or by any information storage and retrieval system.

Printed in the United States of America

Library of Congress Control Number: 2016914790
ISBN 978-0-9974962-7-7 paperback (alk. paper)
ISBN 978-0-9974962-8-4 hardcover (alk. paper)

New Academia Publishing
4401-A Connecticut Ave. NW, #236, Washington, DC 20008
info@newacademia.com - www.newacademia.com

Unless otherwise noted, all visuals are from the Frank Manchel Cinema Collection at the University of Vermont or at Burlington College.

Cover Illustration: Don Quixote (Peter O'Toole) rides against his imagined demons. Arthur Hiller, *Man of La Mancha* (1972). From the core collection production photographs of the Margaret Herrick Library, Academy of Motion Picture Arts and Sciences.

To my grandchildren Harrison and Benjamin
Whom I love and treasure

Lest We Forget

Olga and Lee Manchel, Pearl and Harry Wachtel, Barton Bereck, Arnold Gunar, Lucille Jarvis, Professor Littleton "Tiny" Long, Professor Errol Hill, Dr. H. Lawrence McCrorey, Prof. Albert Johnson, Jack Barry, Jason Robards Jr., Walter S. Tevis, Sylvia Silvano, Sy Gomberg, F. Loretta Coons, John T. Donovan, Anna M. Barnett, Dugan Foley, Maggie Mae Hathaway, Professor T. Alan Broughton, Leroy Bowser, Professor Worth McDougald, Albert Murray, Dr. Alfred Rollins, Dr. James Welsh, Professor Lawrence A. Fink, Dr. Peter C. Rollins, Professor Alan P. Wertheimer, Professor Laura T. Fishman, Professor Robert L. Allen, Professor Robert A. Bone, Professor Louis C. Forsdale, Dr. Muriel J. Hughes, Dean Joan Smith, Bonnie Christensen, Ambassador John E. Reinhardt, William Greaves, Esther J. Urie, Tom Devine, Lucille White, and Lester Glassner.

If I am not for myself, who will be
If I am only for myself, what am I?
If not now, when?¹

Rabbi Hillel

That's all we are: amateurs. We don't live long enough to be anything else.

Charles Chaplin

If you would have your son to walk honourably through the world, you must not attempt to clear the stones from his path, but teach him to walk firmly over them—not insist upon leading him by the hand, but let him learn to go alone.²

Anne Bronte

Things which matter most must never be at the mercy of things which matter least.

Johann Wolfgang von Goethe

Centuries ago, an artist scribbled on a wall, 'Let something of me survive.'³

George Stevens

The only thing necessary for the triumph of evil is for good men to do nothing.

Edmund Burke

I've seen things you people wouldn't believe. Attack ships on fire off the shoulders of Orion. I've watched C-beams glitter in the dark near the Tannhauser Gate. All those moments will be lost in time…like tears in rain…Time to die.⁴

Roy Batty (Rutger Hauer)

For me, the movies are like a machine that generates empathy. It let's you understand hopes, aspirations, dreams, and fears. It helps us to identify with people who are sharing this dream with us.[5]

Roger Ebert

The most essential gift for a good writer is a built-in, shock-proof, shit detector.[6]

Ernest Hemingway

In my walks, every man I meet is my superior in some way, and in that I learn from him.

Ralph Waldo Emerson

Notes

[1] Pirke Avos (*Ethics of the Fathers*, Chapter I (Saying 14).
[2] Anne Bronte, *The Tenant of Wildfell Hall*. London: Wordsworth Classics, 1994. 24-5.
[3] George Stevens, Jr. *George Stevens: A Filmmaker's Journey*. USA: Castle Hill Productions, 1984.
[4] Ridley Scott, *Blade Runner*. USA: Warner Bros, 1982.
[5] Qtd. in Steve James, *Life Itself*. USA: Magnolia Films, 2014.
[6] "The Art of Fiction: Interview with Ernest Hemingway" by George Plimpton, *The Paris Review* (Spring 1958): 18.

Contents

List of Illustrations — xii
Acknowledgments — xiii

1. Getting Ready — 1
2. Paradoxes — 19
3. Crossroads — 37
4. Don Quixote, Alive and Well — 55
5. From Mediocrity to Excellence — 83
6. Where Have All the Heroes Gone? — 97
7. Dystopia — 111
8. Interpretations — 149
9. War and Peace — 179
10. Hilberg's Dilemma — 213
11. History Redux — 277
12. Now That the Buffalo's Gone — 321
13. Nickel Psychology — 353
14. Far From the Lonely Crowd — 373
15. Laugh and Learn — 399
16. My Zip Code — 425
17. Different Agendas — 449
18. Looking Backwards, Gratefully — 525
Epilogue — 545

Appendix I — 552
Appendix II — 561
Bibliography — 565
Index — 586

List of Illustrations

1. The author's parents, Olga Fluhr and Lee Manchel — xviii
2. Gregory Peck and Celeste Holm in *Gentleman's Agreement* — 18
3. Ivan Dixon, Julius Harris and Gloria Foster in *Nothing But a Man* — 36
4. David Franzoni and the author — 54
5. Two pictures from La Mancha faculty — 72
6. The author with Clarence Muse, The Dean of Black Character Actors during the first half of the Twentieth Century — 82
7. Silvester Stallone in *Rocky* — 96
8. Billy De Williams and James Earl Jones in *The Bingo Long Traveling All-Stars and Motor Kings* — 109
9. Marcel Ophuls — 110
10. Stephen King, Mick Garris and the author — 148
11. Geoffrey Holder — 178
12. Liam Neeson and Ben Kingsley in *Schindler's List* — 212
13. Jessica Lange and Armin Mueller-Stahl in *Music Box* — 276
14. James Stewart and Jeff Chandler in *Broken Arrow* — 320
15. Paul Muni and Vladimir Sokoloff in *The Life of Emil Zola* — 352
16. Robert De Niro and Dana Andrews in *The Last Tycoon* — 370
17. Marlon Brando and Al Pacino in *The Godfather* — 372
18. Charles Chaplin and Buster Keaton in *Limelight* — 398
19. Spike Lee, Jon Kilik, Sheila Manchel and the author — 424
20. H. Lawrence McCrorey — 448
21. Cicely Tyson — 466
22. James Earl Jones in *The Man* — 498
23. Heavyweight Boxing Champion Jack Johnson and former Heavyweight James L. Jeffries — 520
24. Robert B. Richardson, Oliver Stone, and Jon Kilik — 524
25. Robert B. Richardson — 544

Acknowledgments

I wish to thank the following publishers for the permission to quote from published works.

"A War Over Justice: An Interview with Marcel Ophuls," *LFQ* Volume 6:1 (1978): 26-47. And "What Does It Mean, Mr. Holmes? An Approach to Film Study," *LFQ* Volume 31:1 (2003): 69-76. Reprinted with permission of *Literature/Film Quarterly* @ Salisbury University, Salisbury, MD 21801.

"Talking Pictures," *Vermont Quarterly* Winter 2005: 28-31, 61-2. And "Friendship in Film," *Vermont Quarterly* Summer 2012: 30-1. Reprinted with permission of Tom Weaver, editor of *Vermont Quarterly*.

"Introduction," *Film Study: A Resource Guide*, Fairleigh Dickinson University Press (1973). "Preface," *Film Study: An Analytical Bibliography*, Fairleigh Dickinson University Press Volume I (1990): 26-27. And "The American Dream and The Hollywood Inquisition," *Film Study\: An Analytical Bibliography*. Fairleigh Dickinson University Press Volume 2 (1990): 1067-1076. Reprinted with permission of Julien Yoseloff and the Fairleigh Dickinson University Press.

"What About Jack? Another Perspective on Family Relationships in Stanley Kubrick's *The Shining*," *Discovering Stephen King's The Shining*, edited by Tony Magistrale. LQ Evans Studies in the Philosophy and Criticism of Literature MCMXCVIII (1998): 82-94. Reprinted with permission of Tony Magistrale.

"A Reel Witness: Steven Spielberg's Representation of the Holocaust in *Schindler's List*," *The Journal of Modern History* Volume 67, Number 1 (March, 1995): 83-100. Reprinted with permission of the University of Chicago Press.

"Cultural Confusion: Broken Arrow," *Hollywood's Indian: The Portrayal of the Native American in Film*. Edited by Peter C. Rollins and John E. O'Connor. Lexington: The University Press of Kentucky, 1998. Reprinted with permission of The University Press of Kentucky.

"Introduction," *Great Sports Movies*, New York: Franklin Watts, 1980. Reprinted with permission of Scholastic, Inc.

"Film Study: Nothing But a Man," *Media & Methods*, 1965. The magazine is defunct, and all efforts to contact a possible copyright holder have proven fruitless.

"Book Review: 'Projecting the Holocaust into the Present: The Changing Focus of Contemporary Holocaust Cinema,' *Journal of Popular Film & Television* 34:1 (Spring 2006). Reprinted with permission of Heldref Publications.

I wish to thank as well the following people who in various ways made this project possible.

Let me begin by expressing my gratitude to the artists and colleagues I have interviewed over the years and are present in this book. Without their kindness in sharing their stories with me, my tale would not have been as rich as it is.

To my pupils from New Rochelle High School up through Southern Connecticut State University and concluding with my students at the University of Vermont, I express my deep appreciation for countless and unforgettable memories. You are very special to me. I would just like to add how touched I was by my former student and now friend Sabin Gratz who provided the photo of me for the cover. Both he and it were and are perfect.

My gratitude also extends to the many friends and colleagues, who over sixty years have shared their wisdom and time with me. Their names, too numerous to list here, are mentioned in footnotes throughout the various chapters; but I would like to acknowledge them in general on this page. In particular, I would like to thank Mr. Tom Weaver, Ms. Kristine Krueger, Ms. Ula Klein, Ms. Leslie Wells, and Ms. Shelley Barbour for their generosity in helping put together this book.

The next set of well wishers is easy. Drs. Paul S. Unger and Jonathan Hayden, and Ms. Michelle Paschelle have kept me alive for the past twenty-one years. I encourage them to keep up the good work.

Acknowledgments xv

A word of thanks also goes to Merrill Jarvis and the late Lucille Jarvis for making it possible for me to see so many movies for so many years. Without their support and friendship, my career and my life would be less rewarding.

Another group of persons I wish to thank are the various UVM librarians, who for many decades have built and maintained a superb book and film collection. Nothing I have done at the University of Vermont would have been possible without their help. The essential individuals include William Dunlop, Albert Joy, Lori Holiff, Chris Burns, Erin Doyle, and Martha Day.

Add to the forefront of these people, the dependable and gifted Peter H. Spitzform. If my research meets your standards, it is thanks to him. If it falters, that's me! Standing shoulder to shoulder with him is Hope Greenberg, who does the formatting, indexing, and handholding. Without her skill, I wouldn't even attempt writing a book. She is extraordinary.

There are certain personalities, however, whose contributions have been so vital to the crafting of *Take Two: A Film Teacher's Unconventional Story* that they too require special mention. Dr. Richard Sugarman, a very special man, was invaluable in polishing several chapters; as was my longtime colleague, Professor Tony Magistrale. Surpassing any of my expectations were two friends: Dr. Alfred Rosa and Mr. Ernie Cabrera. Although Al has always had my back, I want him to know I have never taken him for granted. Ernie has long been an acquaintance, but only now has been moved into the status of friend. Both men patiently, sensitively, and carefully read almost every word of the manuscript. Without their wisdom, this book would not have seen the light of day.

Dr. Denise Youngblood merits still more special recognition, since she has been my editor, my guide, and my friend for many years. Her countless insights jump out at me on every page. Moreover, she remains the role model for what I consider a trusted and irreplaceable colleague!

Not to be ignored is my publisher, Anna Lawton. Her support, encouragement, and talent make me never want to stop broadcasting my ideas. It is a privilege and a joy to have her at my side through the long journey to gaining the public's attention.

Of course, if not for my family—Gary, Steven, Sharon, Harrison,

Benjamin, Rose, Barbara, and Louis — the effort, the challenges, and the results would matter little to me.

Finally, there is my wife Sheila. No one knows better than she what I have invested in this book. No one has paid a greater price so that I may indulge my wants; no one rates more apologies for my foolish neglect and my unforgivable behavior. Most importantly, there is no one I love more or who merits greater praise for making me human, wise, and content. Thank you, my dearest, for putting in the infinite time to make it all happen! Sorry it's taking so long.

1. My beloved mother, Olga Fluhr Manchel and my father, Lee Manchel, who not only brought me into the world, but also set me on an idyllic road to happiness.

1

Getting Ready

When you wake up in the morning, tell yourself: The people I deal with today will be meddling, ungrateful, arrogant, dishonest, jealous, and surly. They are like this because they can't tell good from evil. But I have seen the beauty of good, and the ugliness of evil, and have recognized that the wrongdoer has a nature related to my own—not of the same blood or birth, but the same mind, and possessing a share of the divine.[1]

Meditations of Marcus Aurelius

Art is something that comforts us, reassures us, tells us about life in terms that are extremely positive. It makes us think about life which otherwise would only amount to a heart that beats, a stomach that digests, lungs that breathe, eyes that are filled with senseless images. I believe that art is the most successful attempt to instill in mankind the need to love a religion, a feeling; that's what any kind of art expresses....[2]

Federico Fellini

Let me introduce the theme of this book with an anecdote. Years ago, The Roman Opera House mounted a production of Giuseppe Verdi's masterpiece, *Aida*. Antonio Ghislanzoni's libretto, set in ancient Egypt, focuses on an epic love triangle involving a military officer, a captured Ethiopian slave, and a princess. In the new stage adaptation, playing the central role of Radames, captain of

Pharaoh's army, (a difficult part even for a seasoned performer), was a young tenor making his operatic debut.

Soon after Act One began, the novice sang the opening aria, the beautiful "Celeste Aida" ("Heavenly Aida").

The audience roared enthusiastically, "Encore! Encore!"

Excited by what he perceived to be a triumph, the tenor repeated the aria for his adoring fans.

And the spectators shouted even louder, "Encore! Encore!"

Worried he might strain himself if he continued to indulge the audience's wishes, the humble but happy artist stepped to the footlights and said, "Much as I would love to please you, I need to move on if I am to preserve my voice for four acts."

And out of the darkness a patron screamed, "You will continue to sing the aria until you get it right!"

In many ways, I am that tenor, no longer young, but still trying to get my career right. I have had a full and ideal life teaching and studying stories from the tales of Agamemnon and Medea to those of Lemuel Gulliver and Hamlet reaching to those of Alan Turing[3] and Stephen Hawking.[4] Now seems a good time to revisit my journey. This book is the means to do that. It probes my professional life, why I wanted to teach, how I taught, the lessons I learned, the challenges I met, what keeps me afloat these many decades, and why it's taken so long to accept the fact I will never be anything other, then as Charlie Chaplin correctly states, "an amateur." And I will never live long enough, as he pointed out, to be anything else.

Let me be clear on this point. By "amateur," I do not think of myself as incompetent, or lacking analytical skills and relevant information. I have had more than enough transient trappings to get by. I also do not consider my scholarly efforts a waste of time. I loved my experiences, honored those whose shoulders I stand on, and I believe these efforts contributed to benefitting my generation. What I mean by "amateur" is I never became an expert at what I did, never mastered my discipline, or felt totally satisfied with the courses I taught, the books I wrote, or the causes I championed. Most of all, I never felt I gave my students enough knowledge. Not that I didn't try; and not that they complained.

I want to stress that this admission is no ruse to win the reader's favor with false modesty. Those who know me even slightly understand that is not my style. Nor should my sincerity with the reader be misconstrued as a defensive device. Rather, it is a belief I have that "humility" is a prerequisite for personal growth. Unless one recognizes his failings, it's hard to see why or how he would change. Moreover, my self-deprecation is not a rarity among reflective people. The great philosophers, theologians, and writers—e.g., Aristotle, the authors of the *Bible*, Thomas Aquinas, Fyodor Dostoyevsky, Mahatma Gandhi, and Martin Luther King, Jr.— often found value in seeing themselves in relation to others; in knowing their shortcomings were not always weaknesses. Flaws might also be seen as spurs encouraging them to become better human beings.

In retrospect, it is clear I had personal doubts about my values and behavior, but few if anyone noticed them. For the most part, I always thought people perceived me as confident and passionate. There were, however, other attitudes clearly visible to all. I rarely showed complete respect for authority, often challenged my colleagues' controversial positions, and proved to be a tough teacher. I believed then and now I was given an important trust to educate present and future generations; it was a charge I took seriously.

Of course, I knew many people with similar obligations to fulfill. But surprisingly, many such individuals I encountered abused their responsibilities, and they were not trustworthy teachers. Wherever I went from childhood to old age, I saw the need to rail against incompetence, indifference, and corruption. And I did not turn the other cheek when challenged, nor was I ashamed of what I did or believed. Some painted me as a self-righteous, arrogant, and pretentious. Some encouraged me (often like Nicodemus in the night) to fight the good fight. In truth, many of my battles were not of my own choosing. I just happened to be at the right place at the right time. What matters to me now, however, is whether I could have or should have done things differently.

These doubts resurfaced in designing this book. They affected the selections chosen to fashion my narrative, and they signify the issues troubling me this late in life. I assume you will have no trouble recognizing my unresolved problems in your analysis.

It is not a big deal, and I do not want to overstate my anxiety. (Thanks to my family and friends I consider myself blessed.) You have your limitations; I have mine. We just need to be clear I know better than anyone, except my wife and my severest critic, just how flawed I am and have been; and, at this stage in the journey, there is no way and no reason to mislead you as to my strengths and weaknesses.

That said, *Take Two: A Film Teacher's Unconventional Story* is not a confessional or an apologetic memoir, nor is it a methods book on teaching. Neither is it a chronology on film history, industrial patterns, famous performers, movie masterpieces, or academic dogmas. My deeply felt views on such subjects already exist in prior publications and are readily accessible. As film prologues often state, this work before you is based on a true journey. The eighteen chapters and two appendices that collectively make up the text emphasize what I am just beginning to understand about the past sixty years from being a high school English teacher to becoming a professor emeritus of English and Film Studies.

Although I am a familiar figure to the world I live in, my true thoughts are known only to a relatively few people. I suspect that criticism relates to my colleagues as well. Rarely does the world see us as we truly are. Jim Jarmusch, the marvelous and sadly underrated independent film director, once explained my situation by putting his arm around me, and saying very kindly, "Frank, you and I have a lot in common. I make movies that nobody sees, and you write books that nobody reads."

The obvious questions, therefore, are why should you read this book? What makes it any different from my other publications? What do I hope to achieve? Who is my intended audience?

As is my nature, let's start with the last question first. There is no intended audience. I am and always have been a populist. I consider all the brows—high, middle, and low—as potential readers. I have no favorites. I am committed to diversity. How could I spend so much of my life studying and teaching about the movies, what the film intellectual Garth Jowett aptly describes as "The Democratic Art," and feel anything else?

Equally, the book's eclectic chapters go beyond itemizing obscure data, sentimentalizing specific events, and glamorizing personal concerns. Each selection, in its own way, reflects not only the time in which it was written, but also my educational growth. As a result, even the most skeptical reader should find more than enough scraps and crumbs to justify a quick read. Accordingly, I share the insight voiced by another film scholar, critic Jonathan Rosenbloom: "To assume something is good for everybody, or bad for everybody, is insulting to everybody."[5]

Continuing in the order of complexity, I admit to having several goals in this clearly self-serving but hopefully helpful exercise. First, at eighty-one years of age and with the benefit of hindsight, I am intrigued by how my past positions look today. Is what I said then still what I believe now? How true was I to the great film critic Pauline Kael, who admonished me and other likeminded educators at a 1965 Dartmouth College film conference? "Don't do to movies," she pleaded, "what you did to literature." (The late blacklisted filmmaker and teacher Maurice Rapf also remembers her telling us, "If you think the movies can't be killed, you underestimate the power of education."[6]) Secondly, I genuinely believe my intellectual activities have value not only for me, but also may be useful to other pilgrims in the present and beyond. For example, I argue in the following pages nothing is more important to a teacher than self-confidence, the courage to fail, irreverence, a passion for your subject matter, and fairness. In addition, nothing is more satisfying than relating to your students, understanding their dreams as well as their misperceptions, and helping them with their journeys. Moreover, I strongly believe that if my audience can relate to the movies they study, then they will benefit from the mistakes of the past and be more capable of behaving better in the present and the future. Lastly, nothing is more deadly than equating education with knowledge, teaching with learning, and passion with substance.

Shortly, I will describe why my roots act as a guide to exploring this book. But now it is imperative you understand this chronicle concerns my experiences alone. Any resemblance, as we say in the underworld, to other teachers living or dead is purely coincidental. Considering I am a Professor Emeritus of English and Film Studies, I am surprisingly neither excessively vain nor foolishly humble. *Take Two: A Film Teacher's Unconventional Story*, nonetheless, reminds its readers of my early and lingering strengths and weaknesses. They summarize what I almost overcame to get where I am today. (I suspect the major difference between my colleagues and me is not which of us had flaws, but merely how many we had.)

Oddly, I found rigidity and misunderstanding the most dangerous enemies in my passage. With all due respect to Cyrano's crushing list of life's rational dangers—Dishonesty, Compromise, Prejudice, Ignorance, and Corruption—,[7] nothing in the past seventy years tops the paranoia I encountered championing popular culture against its severest critics. While some readers may dismiss many of my *mea culpas* as a lack of common sense, I find few nations, institutions, and communities any wiser in meeting their daily daunting challenges. Compared to many of them, I am a candidate for sainthood. For that matter, I also find the concept of "reasonableness" much overrated. Far too often it is a weakness exploited by those in power to abuse the powerless. Thus my conclusion about the world after a lifetime living with the dogs of war is similar to that of Jonathan Swift's deductions: "I have ever hated all nations, professions, and communities, and all my love is toward individuals...."[8]

Let me offer one caveat to this admittedly harsh but deeply felt verdict. I have never abandoned hope that things could be better, that Nature intended things differently; and that in each generation there are artists, scientists, politicians, statesmen, business leaders, and innovative individuals who through their imagination and influence will make a significant contribution to fighting "man's inhumanity to man." But far too often these irreplaceable humanists exist in cultures and in climates corrupted by apathy, hypocrisy, ignorance, mistrust, ambition, and greed.

A descriptive case is Akira Kurosawa's magnificent film *Ikiru*. Based on a story by Leo Tolstoy, the screenplay focuses on Kanji Watanabe (Takashi Shimura), a minor public servant, who after thirty years of toil, felt he had wasted his life and wanted to do one meaningful deed before he died. While the heartbreaking bureaucrat's actions inspire many of us, they also remind us of the obstacles and cynicism he faced.[9] Maybe, as some optimists insist, today's technology that allows for faster messaging and downplays age or experience or class or connections will result in a great age of reform and compassion. Maybe! Until then, I share William Wordsworth's difficulty: "Have I not reason to lament/What man has made of man?"[10]

As for what is different here from my other publications, *Take*

Two: A Film Teacher's Unconventional Story revisits a pilgrim's predictable problems and explains what I feel I learned from rejecting the status quo. It is also my rationalization for my rebellious behavior over six memorable decades. Let's have no misunderstanding on this subject. Rarely have I seen anything in the material you are about to read that runs contrary to my current thinking. The presentations may lack distinction but the content stands my test of time.

From the advantage of hindsight, however, I see how contact with famous people, or praise for my former students' films have blindsided good judgment. Some movies I have judged too harshly; others not sternly enough. Thanks to recent film documentaries and scholarly discoveries, I am embarrassingly aware of many film treasures I have missed or never even knew existed. In such cases, my oversights may help present and future pilgrims make more sophisticated choices on their journey. By that I mean, what films you choose to teach, the strategies you use with your students, how you interact with colleagues, and even the schools and departments you select for employment. I am also talking about where I put my intellectual emphases, the battles I took on, and what I chose to write about. Of course, not all the juicy stories are told (my wife wouldn't let me), but there are more than enough exposés to make the reading ahead provocative and informative.

Now to the last but key query: why should you read this book? That is the trickiest question of all. Other than my inflated ego and the lessons you may learn from exploring my extensive teaching experiences, I have no satisfactory answer. Hopefully, the subject matter will speak for itself. This book is about an unruly child from the tough streets of New York whose hard-working parents found him difficult to control and to understand. A synopsis of my early days explains how educators first raised me up and then almost destroyed my love for learning. You discover how my dependence on the three I's—insubordination, independence, and imagination—served me well on my difficult and uncharted road. At the same time, I identify certain defining moments in my life when chance encounters produced intellectual tsunamis, which took me to places I never intended to be and for reasons I never fully understood. Because of what I have learned, as well as how I experienced it, I have faith much of my story might benefit others.

Let me now describe how knowing about my childhood proves meaningful to the reader's understanding of almost every page of *Take Two: A Film Teacher's Unconventional Story*. Being aware of who I was provides the keys to knowing who I am and what I did with my opportunities.

My story begins on New York's Lower East Side. The mythologized setting has been immortalized in such films as William Wyler's *Dead End*, King Vidor's *Street Scene*, Alan Crossland's *The Jazz Singer*, Abraham Cahan's *Hester Street*, Sergio Leone's *Once Upon a Time in America*, Milos Forman's *Ragtime*, and Michael Curtiz's *Angels With Dirty Faces*. Thoughts on my early years—1938 to 1942—appear reflected in these aforementioned cinematic narratives; and, up to a point, I very much identify with the legendary Dead End Kids such as Spit (Leo B. Gorcey) and Dippy (Huntz Hall). Even now, three-quarters of a century later, I remember quite well the poor neighborhoods, the concrete playgrounds, the poverty, the dirt, the smells, and the crowded living conditions. I make no claim I was Oliver Twist's cousin, but those were tough times. Other storytellers may say they never knew they were poor, because everyone around them faced the same problems. Not so for me. I knew I was lower middle class and was never allowed to forget it!

There are, however, powerful differences between the films' fictional characters and me. I belonged to no gang and had no special friends; I benefitted from no benevolent relatives, friendly shopkeepers, or supportive neighbors. My exceptional mother, who bore the major responsibility for bringing up my incomparable sister and me, had to work everyday of her life as a salesperson in women's clothing stores to make ends meet.

Because there were no daycare centers or nannies for us, the chief safe houses to deposit her children were third-run movie theaters. In those days, most theaters had a children's section and a matron who watched over the youngsters left in her care. New York's Loews Delancy, later replaced by Flatbush's The Elm and The Midwood, opened its doors at ten a.m. and remained open until late in the evening. By the time I was four, that's where I stayed most days watching cartoons, short subjects, documentaries, newsreels, (serials on the weekend), and double features. On special occasions, the theaters repeated screenings of popular films from the past. And since my protective and loving mother worked tirelessly on her feet until seven at night, I often saw the programs over and over.

Today, people in my generation matter-of-factly describe those unassuming but intense times with a throwaway line, "I used to go the movies regularly." It won't do here. Let me quickly name some of my pre-public school viewings: Victor Fleming's *Captains Courageous*, Norman Taurog's *Boy's Town*, Michael Curtiz's *Angels With Dirty Faces*, Busby Berkeley's *They Made Me a Criminal*, William K. Howard's *Knute Rockne: All American*, William A. Wellman's *A Star is Born*, Frank Capra's *Lost Horizon*, William Wyler's *Dead End*, John Ford's *The Adventures of Marco Polo*, Victor Fleming's *Gone With the Wind*, John Ford's *The Grapes of Wrath*, Zolton Korda's *The Four Feathers*, George Stevens' *Gunga Din*, William A. Wellman's *Beau Geste*, Charlie Chaplin's *The Great Dictator*, Frank Capra's *Mr. Smith Goes to Washington* and *Meet John Doe*, Sam Wood's *Goodbye, Mr. Chips*, John Ford's *Stagecoach*, William Wyler's *Wuthering Heights*, George B. Seitz's *Andy Hardy Meets Debutante*, King Vidor's *Northwest Passage*, Zolton Korda's *Elephant Boy*, Lewis Milestone's *Of Mice and Men*, Ludwig Berger's *The Thief of Bagdad*, and John Ford's *How Green Was My Valley*. In musicals like W. S. Van Dyke's *I Married an Angel*, Roy Del Ruth's *DuBarry was a Lady*, W. S. Van Dyke's *Sweethearts*, H. C. Potter's *The Story of Vernon and Irene Castle*, Norman Taurog's *The Wizard of Oz*, Busby Berkeley's *Babes in Arms*, Gregory Ratoff's *Rose of Washington Square*, Vincente Minnelli's *Cabin in the Sky*, Norman Taurog's *Little Nellie Kelly*, Robert Z. Leonard's *New Moon*, Victor Schertinger's *Road to Singapore*, Norman Taurog's *Broadway Melody of 1940*, and Victor Schertinger's *The Birth of the Blues*, I was introduced to the hit tunes of Irving Berlin, Richard Rodgers and Lorenz Hart, George and Ira Gershwin, Cole Porter, Nacio Herb Brown, Arthur Freed, Jerome Kern, Yip Harburg, Duke Ellington, Louis Armstrong, Richard Rodgers and Oscar Hammerstein II, and heaven knows how much jazz and how many classical scores underpinning the genre films, documentaries, serials, and cartoons.

Films like these molded my tastes in movies, music, behavior, and social values. Of course, other profound influences would be added with the passing years, but this was the beginning. By the time I entered the first grade, I may not have understood most of what I saw and heard in these mainly anti-intellectual, anti-authoritarian fantasies, but I took what I saw very seriously. I found movies, like books, definitely more than just entertainment. They were the stairways to the stars.

Nonetheless, I recognized the differences between the exploits of Roy Rogers, Gene Autry, and Johnny Weissmuller; and the adventures shown in the highly touted "A" films. The former were for fun, the latter were for personal growth. In addition, early on I became comfortable with controversial ideas about people, places, institutions, and presumed notions of respectability. Unlike many of my peers, however, I never became "house broken." Having been drawn into an idyllic world, I never abandoned it.

The late film critic Roger Ebert ingeniously labeled movies, the "empathy machine."[11] It is no wonder then, why I found movies so meaningful to my intellectual curiosity. Because of films, I was able to compare and to contrast my feelings and my life with viewers around the world. The empathy machine also allowed me a chance to escape my drab surroundings. But it is important to recognize I fled to something meaningful! (A lovely film illustrating how movies provided Depression audiences with escape is Woody Allen's *The Purple Rose of Cairo*.[12]) Right or wrong, good or bad, helpful or not, I was dealing with complex issues and complicated situations far beyond my years. Keep in mind, these were the days when you defined an intellectual as someone who could listen to the William Tell Overture and not think of The Lone Ranger.

America's "National Theater," as Pauline Kael branded the movies,[13] inspired me in a thousand different ways, and it showed in my attitude towards public school. I loved learning. And because of my vicarious experiences in multiple theaters offering riveting images of our national life, I was far ahead of my more conventional classmates. My teachers certainly felt that way; and at the end of the first grade, they skipped me to the third grade. But that summer the family moved from the callous sidewalks of New York to Brooklyn's fabled Flatbush area. The passage dramatically altered my life forever.

The first days in my new school led to an emotional tidal wave. P.S. 193 (now called the Gil Hodges Elementary School) had no program for gifted children. Worse, the teachers thought me stupid, ill prepared, and a major discipline problem. Nothing in my life prepared me for what followed. I was bullied, ridiculed, disciplined, and isolated; in short, traumatized. If growing up in those "prison years" taught me anything about public education, it was how irrelevant, unjust, and out-of-touch educators could be for challenging students. Not surprisingly, such an unjust system taught me to despise conformity, bureaucracies, and rigidity. George Bernard Shaw explained the situation perfectly: "Never let school interfere with your education."

No disrespect to the late Mr. Shaw, public school, not the movies, did teach me, admittedly unintentionally, to be irreverent. I refused to respect or to trust or to follow "educators" who because of their status or authority or degrees mistreated and misled me every day, every week, and every year of my elementary school education. From the start of my Flatbush days, I considered anyone a fool if he believed that just because someone in a position of authority said something it should automatically be accepted. Years later, many people in my generation would need the McCarthy era, the Civil Rights Movement, the Vietnam War, and the Watergate Investigation to question the "wisdom" of the Best and the Brightest. I had a head start in 1942.

Thankfully, the popular arts not only reinforced my counterculture attitudes but also offered me a lifeline. I found in the mass media what many marginalized children like me saw as valuable options. Paraphrasing the words of Andrew Keen, the English Internet critic: "[They] offered me [then and now] some of the best qualities we can possess as human beings: irreverence, vitality, and youthful excitement."[14] I have been applying those lessons first learned in the darkened auditoria ever since.

Because I discovered the hard way there are consequences for going against Society's "norms," I needed defense mechanisms. One useful tool proved to be what Ernest Hemingway called a "bullshit detector." Here, I cannot overstate how much a literary hero this great American novelist proved to be in my journey. As *New Yorker* film critic David Denby noted, the classic writer expounded on why "life is hard, fulfillment mysterious, contentment never without a cost.[15] Like Hemingway, I too grew to recognize and to rail against the yahoos, the philistines, and the phonies among us.

Another useful defensive tool was humor. I learned early on in life, that thinking differently from the general public—administrators, colleagues, family, friends, and enemies—could be dangerous, divisive, and destructive. Joking, making someone laugh, and being irreverent became invaluable weapons when disagreeing with other people's points of view. The trick was using humor tastefully and intelligently. Thankfully, I've done that more often than not.

Thus relying on instinct, a well-developed bullshit detector, and comedy became my primary means to intellectual survival for more than three-quarters-of-a-century. Certainly, these tools helped me survive my childhood. I also credit them with my success in life. Few remarks describe my intellectual and emotional feelings better in those bygone days than H. L. Mencken's one-liner, "School teachers, taking them by and large, are probably the most ignorant and stupid class of men in the whole group of mental workers."[16]

As the movies shifted from the war years to the Eisenhower and Kennedy eras, there was a noticeable change from conservative themes toward iconoclastic motifs. This Modernist swing reinforced my progressive leanings. Now, artists from around the world imaginatively introduced brilliant film narratives filled with revolutionary values that had a profound impact on me. Ironically, the more I was drawn to the foreign films, the more I became increasingly confused about everything and everyone. It had all been so clear before the 1950s. Now I questioned the status quo even more than before. One only has to read David Riesman's *The Lonely Crowd*,[17] or Charlie Reich's *The Greening of America*[18] to place me in my time. Almost everything I would write and teach would stem from the first eighteen years of my life. Fortunately, I met a remarkable English teacher in my senior year in high school and had a second major life change (the subject of Chapter 18).

At Ohio State University, I became an English major and for the first time found value in scholarly studies. Using an imposing but subjective list of great imaginary works, required to master by the time I graduated, I spent the next four years feverishly cramming into my head western civilization's "major" literary writings. My only problem was the list didn't satisfy my intellectual curiosity. For example, if I read Thomas Hardy's *The Mayor of Casterbridge* and liked it, then I wanted to read Hardy's other novels. If I read

Shakespeare's tragedies and liked them, then I also devoured his comedies and histories.

By the time graduation arrived, I had compiled a subjective list of my favorite books, which have been added to over the years but never replaced the irreplaceable Buckeye choices of the fifties: the *Bible* as literature, Homer's *Iliad* and *Odyssey*, Virgil's *Aeneid*, Thomas Malory's *Le Morte d'Arthur*, Jonathan Swift's *Gulliver's Travels*, Miguel de Cervantes' *Don Quixote*, Mark Twain's *Huckleberry Finn*, Leo Tolstoy's *War and Peace*, George Bernard Shaw's *Saint Joan*, Edmond Rostand's *Cyrano de Bergerac*, Nathaniel Hawthorne's *The Scarlet Letter*, William Somerset Maugham's *Of Human Bondage*, Herman Melville's *Moby Dick*, William Shakespeare's plays and poetry, Charles Dickens's complete novels, Joseph Conrad's *Lord Jim*, plus the poetry collections of the Romantic and Victorians authors, as well as the verse anthologies of Emily Dickinson, T.S. Eliot, Dylan Thomas, and W.B. Yeats. I can truly say without qualification, it is a list I treasure to this day.

These overwhelming books also made me appreciate Geoffrey Chaucer's writings even more than before. That is, in his Prologue to *The Canterbury Tales*, the Father of English literature had given me a Clerk upon which to model my career, one who was "Filled with moral virtue…And gladly would…[I] learn and gladly teach."[19] By the time I left Columbus, Ohio, making money was never a priority for me, nor was ambition or fame or being with the right people.

However, I did have three main objectives: I wanted to be a better teacher than the ones who taught me, I wanted security—like Scarlett O'Hara "I never wanted to be poor again—," and I wanted a home and family similar to the ones I had seen romanticized in the movies but never experienced in life. These three pursuits shaped my entire career. They form the spine of what you will read in *Take Two: A Film Teachers Unconventional Story*.

We turn now to methodology. In the eighteen chapters and two appendices that follow, there are essays, interviews, and anecdotes on teaching innovations, how the motion picture industry historically operates, how gifted teachers turned my life around, my meetings with famous personalities like Marcel Ophuls, Cicely Tyson, James Earl Jones, Jon Kilik, David Franzoni, and Robert B. Richardson, thoughts about how movies manipulate our collective consciousness, the serious problems propagated by the mass media, judgments on what makes for good teaching, recommendations on favorite books and movies, and instances describing how one is able to defy the system and still survive. It is also a book that challenges myths that assume one can predict the future. I found no guarantees or shortcuts to achieving what I discovered on my journey. Thus, my best advice to my dear reader is to expect the unexpected and to be open to wherever the Chapters lead.

Deciding on what pieces adequately represented my journey posed no problems. Some articles immediately jumped to mind because of the treatment they received on publication. Others less known only added to my desire to include them in the collection. No one piece is more noteworthy than another when it comes to charting the course of my career. Each is republished here almost as it appeared. The only change might be in making titles of films and publications consistent with other material throughout the book. Collectively, they document my intellectual and emotional growth, the times in which they were written, and provide an opportunity for me to comment on the past.

Furthermore, my published footprints refreshed my memory about key landmarks and influences. The following selections, shaped inadvertently by David Denby's thoughtful writings, illustrate my challenges in tracing significant threads hidden in my work, as well as how movies and literature intersected in my life.[20] They signify meaningful swings in my academic priorities and views. Placed together, the material showcases my rational vacillations, as Dorothy Parker might say, from A to B.

Additionally, you encounter the range of film study issues faced in my professional career: the nature of screen adaptations, industrial practices, censorship, the birth of screen education, the importance of genres, varieties of film criticism, the composition of motion picture audiences, and suitable teaching strategies. But no one variable proved more meaningful to me than the overarching questions about the role of film in our society and in my life. While I am satisfied my journey was both useful and valuable, you the reader might be frustrated if you expect a closure to my investigations. Possibilities yes; answers, no.

Each chapter begins with a modest introduction relating to the subject matter presented. That is, in Chapter 2 concerning my experimental book/film program at New Rochelle High School, I provide a framework as to what led me to the novel approach itself. I also offer some thoughts about the emotional experience resulting from academic innovation. In Chapter 10 on *Schindler's List*, I provide material not only on my relationship with the distinguished Holocaust scholar Raul Hilberg, but also about the origins and reactions to the article itself. In essence, the introductory material provides a context by which to understand and to interpret the material.

Still further, my collected writings reveal no partiality toward subject matter or intellectual status. There is no smoking gun that appears and defines what I thought from the first grade to my Vermont sanctuary. Let me be clear on this point. Contrary to the professional paranoia of various misguided colleagues, I never rejected classical values or meaningful traditions. I never had any intention of abandoning those cherished ideas first learned in my basic academic studies. It was only the limited imagination of my print-oriented adversaries that made things confusing to them. From the very start of my career, what I wanted to do was to extend, not to restrict, the humanities in our lives. Teaching, for me, became sharing valuable past experiences in order to create new and equally meaningful ones for present and future generations. To do that, I believed people at all ends of the human landscape had to abandon territorial positions and stereotyping; they must become more inclusive and open to fresh interpretations and perspectives. Specifically, they must reject discredited notions about the mass media being lowbrow, simplistic, and their exclusive property. In the end, what works best for me always are locating what I consider works of art in the mass media and benefitting from their constructive criticism.

Finally, we would not be discussing any of this adventure today if not for a single, life-altering moment. In the summer of 1954, I met and fell in love with a beautiful fifteen-year-old girl. Four years later, we were married. A week after our honeymoon, we were called into my in-laws' New Rochelle living room. These two exceptional individuals, unimaginable even in Hollywood terms, were worried that my salary for my first teaching job, which began in September, amounted to only $5000. Thus, my generous father-in-law offered me a place in his retail business with a starting salary of $20,000.

Before I could answer, my exceptional bride jumped up and said, "My husband was born to be a teacher, and that's what he's going to be."

To this day, I wonder what I would have answered, given the chance!

Notes

[1] Quotations: Meditations - (II. 1, trans. Gregory Hays). *Wikipedia, The Free Encyclopedia.*
[2] Federico Fellini, *I Am a Born Liar.* France: Arte, 2003.
[3] Morten Tyldum, *The Imitation Game.* USA: The Weinstein Company, 2014.
[4] James Marsh, *The Theory of Everything.* USA: Focus Features, 2014.
[5] Qtd. in Steve James, *Life Itself.* USA: Magnolia Films, 2014.
[6] Maurice Rapf, *Back Lot: Growing Up with the Movies.* Latham: The Scarecrow Press, 1999. 177.
[7] Edmond Rostand, *Cyrano de Bergerac.* Translated by John Murrell. 1897. Loc 4114-45.
[8] Jonathan Swift, *The Correspondence of Jonathan Swift.* 1725.
[9] Akira Kurosawa, *Ikiru ("To Live").* Japan: Toho, 1952.
[10] William Wordsworth, "Lines Written in Early Spring," *English Romantic Poets.* Edited by James Stephens, et al. New York: American Book Company, 1952.
[11] Qtd. in Steve James, *Life Itself.*
[12] Woody Allen, *The Purple Rose of Cairo.* USA: Orion Pictures, 1985.
[13] Pauline Kael, "Author's Note," *Deeper into Movies.* Boston: Little, Brown and Company, 1973. Xv.
[14] Andrew Keen, *The Cult of the Amateur: How Today's Internet is Killing Our Culture.* New York: Doubleday, 2007.
[15] David Denby, *Do The Movies Have a Future?* New York: Simon & Schuster, 2012. 202.
[16] H. L. Mencken, *The Philosophy of Friedrich Nietzsche* (1908). 217.
[17] David Riesman et. al., *The Lonely Crowd.* New Haven: Yale University Press, 1950.
[18] Charles A. Reich, *The Greening of America.* New York: Random House, 1970.

[19] Geoffrey Chaucer, "The Prologue to the Clerk of Oxford's Tale," *The Canterbury Tales*.
[20] Denby, *Do The Movies Have a Future?* 134.

2. Reporter Phil Green (Gregory Peck) explains to fashion editor Anne Deffrey (Celeste Holm) why he changed his name in order to write a series of articles on anti-Semitism. Elia Kazan, *Gentleman's Agreement* (1947). From the core collection production photographs of the Margaret Herrick Library, Academy of Motion Picture Arts and Sciences.

2

Paradoxes

If we just take people as they are, ...we make them worse, but if we treat them not as they are but as they should be, we help them to become what they can become.[1]

Johann Wolfgang von Goethe

What I must do is all that concerns me, not what the people will think.[2]

Ralph Waldo Emerson

One does not have to adhere to middle – or upper-class etiquette — to live a civilized life. One does not have to speak the English language correctly to lead a civilized life. One does not have to be financially well off to impart civilized values to one's children. The ability to live a civilized life is not determined by believing in a special religion or coming from a particular branch of the human family. To believe otherwise is to be a racist or given to religious or class prejudice.[3]

Stanley Crouch

September 1958 and the first day of teaching! Even now, fifty-eight years later, I sense my excitement starting a career as a New Rochelle High School English instructor, "45 Minutes from Broadway" according to George M. Cohan, and the closest I ever came to an academic Camelot. Like Maurice Chevalier sings in Vincente Minnelli's *Gigi*, I remember it well.

I was only a few months out of Brooklyn, a time beautifully described in an HBO documentary, as a place where "people...talked a certain way, and never felt as if they were better in anything. We always considered ourselves underdogs in a blue-color borough."[4] Predictably, falling in love with an extraordinary woman who also had an affable brother, and both coming from a caring family made my move from Flatbush to Westchester painless. Not that there couldn't have been problems. For example, Larry Peerce's romantic screen adaptation of Philip Roth's novel, *Goodbye, Columbus*, in the film of the same name,[5] sympathetically touches on the hiccups possible in such a transition. Now, however, I was in what James Agee called "the land of the safe."[6]

I'm not sure what about NRHS is dearest to my heart: the principal who took me under her wing, the assistant principal who always had my back, the English Department chairwoman who encouraged me to grow, the students who made my classes so rewarding, or the colleagues who shared my passions. But what I do know is that I had no idea what was about to happen to me.

To simplify my steps from 1958 to 1963, let me set the stage by suggesting some stereotypical Hollywood teachers,[7] and what I innocently thought back then about my profession heading into an unknown and unpredictable future. Of all the prized films from Sam Wood's *Goodbye, Mr. Chips*, Stephen Herek's *Mr. Holland's Opus*,[8] Richard Brooks' *The Blackboard Jungle*,[9] James Clavell's *To Sir, With Love*,[10] John G. Avildsen's *Lean on Me*,[11] John Hughes' *The Breakfast Club*,[12] John Hughes' *Ferris Bueller's Day Off*,[13] Peter Weir's *Dead Poet's Society*,[14] John N. Smith's *Dangerous Minds*,[15] Ramon Menendez' *Stand and Deliver*,[16] Steven Zaillian's *Searching for Bobby Fisher*,[17] Alexander Payne's *Election*[18] Brian De Palma's *Carrie*,[19] Gus Van Sant's *Finding Forrester*,[20] Richard LaGravenese's *Freedom Writers*,[21] Michael Hoffman's *The Emperor's Club*,[22] Amy Heckerling's *Fast Times at Ridgemont High*,[23] Mimi Leder's *Pay It Forward*,[24] to Damien Chazelle's *Whiplash*,[25] only one movie comes close to what I recall of those first days: Robert Mulligan's *Up the Down Staircase*.[26]

Based on Bel Kaufman's insightful 1965 book about life in an inner-city high school, Mulligan's 1967 movie, to me, realistically transformed the novel's memo style into a "real-life" narrative. "Be serious," the reader might sensibly ask. "How can you compare

New York's 'problem schools' with NRHS, a powerful and prestigious institution that prides itself on meeting the needs of every student? The faculty at the fictional Coolidge High School was cynical and demoralized; the students unruly, the dropout rate depressing; and the building should have been condemned way back when. So what if Sylvia Barrett (Sandy Dennis) is a young, idealist English teacher who shares some of your literary heroes and values? You were teaching college-bound, grade-conscious, privileged students, not undisciplined, poorly educated, diverse teenagers from working-class homes. Moreover, why would you cite an unremarkable film to bolster a problematic academic argument? Most people today possibly have never seen the movie or read the book. Aren't you a responsible scholar who is supposed to defend film as art?"

Okay, let's start with the last issue first. While here is not the place to layout a treatise on film aesthetics, a few random comments should suffice. Since childhood, I have always found movies mainly a social art, not primarily an art form for art's sake. Knowing what you do about my growing up, you understand why I value movies best as helping us become human. And not just human! That is, if you can study the poor decisions made by foolish characters depicted in significant movies in previous generations, it is possible, even probable, you will make better decisions in the future. At least, that's my theory. And more often than not, what brings about those changes is the impact the movie has on the audience.

Let me be clear on this essential point. I love the art of the film. I believe great movies must have both an intellectual and an emotional quality. Clearly, profound ideas don't go very far if the cinematic mechanics prove prosaic. Nor does great technique matter much to trite thoughts and clichéd themes. I have consistently argued that evaluating films is a difficult process. While many individuals strive to create noble works, critics and academics struggle to identify the good, the bad, and the ugly. The results are not always successful. I realize part of my job is to report the consensus of what are considered film masterpieces.

But because a movie lacks depth or vision, it does not, in my eyes, disqualify it from being influential, engaging, or entertaining. No less an authority than the fabled director Martin Scorsese makes a similar argument. Often, he insists, "I found obscure films more inspirational than the prestige movies of the day. I can only talk to you about what moved me, intrigued me; and thus I cannot be objective."[27] In short, I believe any movie, depending on its chemistry with the viewer, can make a difference, and do either good or harm in society. A key caveat is context. What is the spectator's relationship to the film at the time of contact? That belief is central to how I see films and teach about them.

One last detail. Because I have spent so much of my time talking about movies and exchanging opinions with people across the intellectual landscape, I have adapted several specific defensive stances. First, I make a distinction between liking and appreciating a film. If you say you enjoy a movie, no one can say you are wrong. It is a psychological reaction. But if you say, you value a movie, then we are talking about standards. Here is the place for the disagreements.[28] Secondly, I find Gene Siskel and Roger Ebert's labeling certain films as "guilty pleasures," extremely useful. We all like films that we're embarrassed to admit to publically. I freely admit my weak choices, get bashed, and then move on. Finally, just as helpful is my belief some movies you should not examine closely. Poorly acted, lacking striking production values, and containing thoughtless messages, they nonetheless may have a sentimental and blind appeal. For example, despite all their silliness, I have always liked but felt embarrassed by Johnny Weissmuller's Tarzan movies, Randolph Scott and Joel McCrea westerns, Tom Tyler playing Captain Marvel,[29] and Buster Crabbe appearing as Flash Gordon.[30] Great villains like Ming the Merciless (Ray Middleton) and The Scorpion (Harry Worth) are priceless. *Up the Down Staircase* falls into the category of "Don't look too closely."

Now back to the relevance of Mulligan's film to this chapter. On the surface, there appears to be little reasonable correlation between the movie and my career. My college-bound classes could not have been more successful and enjoyable. Rarely if ever did they pose a problem. Even though the curriculum was insane—teaching on any one day, the history of English or American literature—I had all sorts of study guides to keep me one step ahead of the students. Even better, I was learning more than anyone. And not just about literature. I studied writing, taught reading comprehension, and experimented with different teaching techniques. Not to be discounted in the mix, I learned to love dramatic readings on long playing records. Listening to Dylan Thomas or Robert Frost read their work, or hearing Hal Holbrook impersonate Mark Twain remains for me an irreplaceable pleasure.

Because I had mastered the basic rules of public school teaching—get your teenagers to like and to respect you, as well as be prepared for each class—I was successful. They saw me as authentic! They even rewarded me with several plaques that to this today adorn my office. In addition, my gifted colleagues enjoyed sharing my success. We fed off each other's ideas. Few, if any of us, bought into the status quo system that takes the fun out of teaching: middle school teachers are higher up the prestige ladder than elementary school teachers; high school teachers are the most important. But it is even more ludicrous than that. At the high school level, we were emotionally ranked in order of what classes we taught: topping the list were those who qualified for advanced placement courses, followed by those who were assigned ordinary college-bound classes. But at the bottom of the rung were those given the non-regents students (the undisciplined, ignored, and overlooked youngsters who were at the end of the educational spectrum.) You didn't teach them; you babysat them, and made sure they didn't destroy the school!

Here's the rub. I cared next to nothing about this pecking order. I went merrily along teaching all my classes. Unlike some of my peers, then and now, I taught the students assigned me. I never schemed to get "the top" classes or the "best" students. It was like listening to music. I preferred the software to the electronics. You walk into a classroom, find out what the challenges are, and then motivate the kids to learn. Simple as that! And just as magnificent an experience.

Up the Down Staircase illustrates effectively what inner-city students were like, while also emphasizing how important learning was to their future. It shows Sylvia Barrett using books from the school storeroom—e.g., *Macbeth*, *Silas Marner*, and *A Tale of Two Cities*—and distributing them to the disorderly teenagers. It shows how creative she was in using the Socratic method, getting the youngsters involved, and in the end proving to be a very impressive teacher.

There the ties between Mulligan and Manchel take a different road. While I was using those same titles in my required non-regents classes, I failed miserably, in part because I was buying into a suffocating educational system. So what if the texts were hand me downs. So what if the adolescents didn't learn anything. I kept them quiet, filled their time with busy work, and made the school safe for the teachers and other students.

Then one day it all changed. I wish I could tell you why. I wish I could explain why even someone so naïve as I would give up his hard-earned status in the teaching chain for students no one cared about or who could not advance your career or bring you any apparent academic rewards. It may have been no more than I chose morality over self-interest.

But I did. One day in 1962 (four years into my career), I don't even know when, I changed. I didn't feel right about what I was doing with the non-regents students. So I broke the rules. Simple as that! According to school policy, no one was permitted to require students to buy their books. I did. No one was allowed to venture too far from the established school curriculum. I did. No one expected you to work overtime with discipline problems. You turned the hard cases over to the assistant principal. I turned my back on the land of the safe and entered an educational wasteland for no other reason than I wanted to. It wasn't that tough a decision since no one cared about the non-regents students. No one even paid attention so long as things were calm and quiet.

The essay that follows tells the story of what happened. While it would take years before the full impact of what I had done registered with me, I obviously still had a lot to learn. As you will see, my goals clearly outstripped my skills and my knowledge. My writing is weak, my ideas are untested, and there really is no appropriate measurement to evaluate the experiment itself. All that being true, it remains one of the great adventures in my career. It was like the old World War II song, "Coming in on a wing and a prayer." Or better still is the comment by Paul Boray (John Garfield) in Jean Negulesco's *Humoresque*: "It all seemed so simple once. You live your life. You do your work. As simple as all that. Then you find out that it's not so easy. Nothing comes free. One way or another you pay. You pay for what you are."[31]

Two anecdotes I do remember from those paradoxical times. First were the students' reactions to *Gentleman's Agreement*. The class—all male, exclusively white, and no Jews—had a hard time with Laura Hobson's book about Phil Green, the fictional reporter who decides to pose as a Jew in order to write a series of articles on anti-Semitism for a major New York magazine. Not only didn't the teenagers care about the issues, but also they blamed the Jews for America's "current" civil rights problems. But when they saw the movie, they became enraged at what was happening not to Phil Green, but to Gregory Peck, his family, and his friends. Now they had a lot to say about racism and bigotry. The second anecdote had to do with James Hilton's *Goodbye, Mr. Chips*. The class had no feel for what an old-fashioned private school teacher like Chipping was about, nor did they see any relevance between his life and theirs. After all, these macho teenagers never dared show a sentimental bone in their makeup. Then they watched Robert Donat[31] describe through flashbacks what teaching was about. As the film concluded, and Chips, near death, tells us that his students were "all his children," I went to put the lights on. And one of the toughest kids in the class, with tears streaming down his face, grabbed my hand, and said, "Don't touch that switch." In the discussion that followed, I taught them the difference between young and old teachers: the former know all the rules; the latter know all the exceptions.

In all my years, I have received my share of flattering letters and touching e-mails from former students sharing their memories. Only one non-regents student ever said anything to me. It was at a NRHS class reunion. A person I didn't recognize with a name I had long forgotten said, "Thank you, Mr. Manchel. If not for you, I would be long dead!"

Notes

[1] Johann Wolfgang von Goethe, *Wilhelm Meister's Apprentice*. Translated by Eric A. Blackall. *Goethe's Collected Works* Vol. 9. New York: Suhrkamp, 1989. 326.

[2] Ralph Waldo Emerson, "Self-Reliance: Essay II," *The Collected Works of Ralph Waldo Emerson*, Volume II. Introduced and edited by Joseph Slater. Cambridge: Harvard University Press, 1979. 131.

[3] Stanley Crouch, *Always in Pursuit: Fresh American Perspectives*. New York: Vintage Books, 1998. 25.

⁴ Major League Baseball, *Brooklyn Dodgers: The Ghosts of Flatbush*. USA: Major League Baseball Productions 2007.
⁵ Larry Peerce, *Goodbye, Columbus*. USA: Paramount Pictures, 1969.
⁶ James Agee and Walter Evans, *Let Us Now Praise Famous Men*. Boston: Houghton Mifflin Company, 1941.
⁷ I'd like to acknowledge a debt to K. Krugelis' "Best movies about teachers," IMDB (August 2011), and Nicholas Provenzano's "20 Movies Every Educator Should See," *Edutopia* (August 26, 2011). Both these helpful lists are readily available on your web browser.
⁸ Stephen Herek, *Mr. Holland's Opus*. USA: Buena Vista Pictures, 1965.
⁹ Richard Brooks, *The Blackboard Jungle*. USA: MGM, 1955.
¹⁰ James Clavell, *To Sir, With Love*. USA: Columbia Pictures, 1967.
¹¹ John G. Avildsen, *Lean on Me*. USA: Warner Bros., 1989.
¹² John Hughes, *The Breakfast Club*. USA: Universal Pictures, 1985.
¹³ John Hughes, *Ferris Bueller's Day Off*. USA: Paramount Pictures, 1986.
¹⁴ Peter Weir, *Dead Poet's Society*. USA: Buena Vista Pictures, 1989.
¹⁵ John N. Smith, *Dangerous Minds. USA:* Buena Vista Pictures, *1995.*
¹⁶ Ramon Menendez, *Stand and Deliver*. USA: Warner Bros., 1988.
¹⁷ Steven Zaillian, *Searching for Bobby Fisher*. USA: Paramount Pictures, 1993.
¹⁸ Alexander Payne, *Election*. USA: Paramount, 1999.
¹⁹ Brian De Palma. *Carrie*. USA: United Artists, 1976.
²⁰ Gus Van Sant, *Finding Forrester*. USA: Sony Pictures Entertainment, 2000.
²¹ Richard LaGravenese, *Freedom Writers*. USA: Paramount Pictures, 2007.
²² Michael Hoffman, *The Emperor's Club*. USA: Beacon Communications, 2002.
²³ Amy Heckerling, *Fast Times at Ridgemont High*. USA: Universal Pictures, 1982.
²⁴ Mimi Leder, *Pay It Forward*. USA: Warner Bros., 2000.
²⁵ Damien Chazelle, *Whiplash*. USA: Sony Pictures Classics, 2014.
²⁶ Robert Mulligan, *Up the Down Staircase*. USA: Warner Bros., 1967.
²⁷ Martin Scorsese, *A Personal Journey with Martin Scorsese Through American Movies*. England: British Film Industry, 1995; USA, 1996.
²⁸ Frank Manchel, "Movies and Man's Humanity," *Teaching the Humanities: Selected Readings*, Ed. By Sheila Schwartz. New York: Macmillan. 1970. 192-200.
²⁹ William Whitney, *The Adventures of Captain Marvel*. USA: Republic Pictures 1941.
³⁰ Frederick Stephani and Ray Taylor, *Flash Gordon*. USA: Universal Pictures 1936.
³¹ Jean Negulesco, *Humoresque*. USA: Warner Bros., 1946.
³² This was the role that won Robert Donat the 1939 Best Actor Award over Clark Gable in *Gone With the Wind*.

The Universal Classroom[1]

Did you ever stop to analyze what your students will remember most from this past year? Did you ever stop and ask yourself why students remember some things more than others? Have you examined your relative position to the student as regards the knowledge he is exposed to? I wonder for instance, what has made a greater influence on him: the textbook account of World War II or the television coverage of programs about war, the motion pictures like *The Longest Day* and *Judgment at Nuremberg*, and recordings such as *I Can Hear It Now*. I wonder which has had a more lasting effect: the textbook accounts concerning scientific development or the television coverage of rocket adventures into outer space; what has had a more profound influence on our young people: the provisions of the 14th Amendment or the mass media coverage of the Civil Rights movement?

  As a teacher of literature, I find myself involved very often with theories concerning the psychology of learning and causal relationships. With your indulgence, this talk will encompass several hypotheses to be tested. (1) I believe that in the comprehensive schools of our country the term "slow learner" is not justified in referring to students with I.Q.'s ranging from 75-95. Rather, based upon an admittedly limited observation, these children should be called "The Tolerated". They have been conditioned to accept 2nd class citizenship in a society sometimes governed by grade-conscious fanatics and college-orientated snobs. (2) I believe that textbook knowledge is being treated as if it were actually in keeping with current and recent information about the various disciplines. When you consider the rapid growth of knowledge and the great differences involved with the storage and recovery of information, you recognize the problem of hard-covered textbooks. Our students need to know that many concepts once held sacred are now being questioned.

They also need to know that change is not necessarily good or new. By studying both the old and the modern it is possible for teachers to help shape rather than conflict with student thinking. (3) I believe that ethical, moral and esthetic values are the property of all and not of a select few. That every member of our culture can and should learn responsibility to his family and society remains a fundamental obligation of our educational process. (4) I believe that the teaching profession instead of being the recipients of a traditional, textbook educational system are in the position of pioneering a new age in education; an age not of a provincial, walled-in environment but of universal horizons which know the value of the past in its relationship to the present technological and scientific achievements of modern man.

Again, I am not advocating throwing out textbooks because of modern society. Only a fool would remove Homer from our classrooms because that poet wrote of pagan gods; only a pseudo-intellect would remove *Huckleberry Finn* from the library shelves because he thought Sam Clemens was degrading Negroes; and only a slow-learning teacher would think that it was more important to study Shakespeare in the books rather than see *Hamlet* performed by Richard Burton or Christopher Plummer. All I ask is that literature is studied in all its forms: in books, on television and stage, in magazines, journals and motion pictures. I ask that literature be experienced as well as read. Remember Sherlock Holmes constant rebuff to Dr. Watson: "You see my dear Watson, but you do not observe." Let us help the students to get their rights in the schools: the right to learn what is most useful to them; the right to learn without fear of frustration; the right to develop a healthy and useful self-concept; and the right to learn how to use and handle controversial, provocative ideas

Let me suggest one area, which might be beneficial in implementing the aforesaid ideas: motion pictures. Remember this program is in addition to books and not a replacement for current practices. If we want to teach our students the values of science and medicine, why not show films such as *The Story of Louis Pasteur, The Sea Around Us, Madam Curie,* and *Sister Kenny*? If we want to teach about American History, show the motion pictures *Wilson, Abe Lincoln in Illinois, The Grapes of Wrath, Watch on the Rhine, Drums Along *the Mohawk,* and *The Buccaneer.* If we want to teach our students an awareness of contemporary problems and issues, show films like *Rebel Without a Cause, Gentleman's Agreement, Intruder in the Dust, Cry, The Beloved Country, All the King's Men,* and *The Ugly American.* If you feel as I do that it is important to acquaint our students with the pleasures of knowing about foreign lands, exotic places, courageous men and exciting adventures, why not show *Mutiny on the Bounty, Around the World in Eighty Days, El Cid, Tale of Two Cities, Spartacus, Ben Hur,* and *Cyrano de Bergerac*? Some of us feel it is important to show our students how men are influenced in their lives, how it is that in different generations men have different aspirations. In this connection you could show films that discuss the relationship between students and teachers: *Goodbye, Mr. Chips, Good Morning, Miss Dove,* and *Passion For Life;* films that show the relationship of man to man: *The Diary of Anne Frank, The Miracle Worker, The Defiant Ones, The Life of Emile Zola,* and *Exodus;* the relationship between parents and children: *Cheaper by the Dozen, The 400 Blows, I Remember Mama,* and *Please Don't Eat the Daisies;* and the relationship between man and government: *Trial, The Ox-Bow Incident, Sunrise at Campobello, Twelve Angry Men,* and *Mein Kampf.*

If you believe as I do that the good teacher is involved with providing the student with the meaningful experience that will be useful in helping to make sound ethical and social judgments, why not have a unit based on *To Kill a Mockingbird, A Raisin in the Sun, David and Lisa, On the Waterfront, High Noon, Room at the Top,* and *An American Tragedy*?

If you feel that it is impossible to bring these films to your classroom, then take your students to the theatres and have them see current films such as *Tom Jones, Lawrence of Arabia, No Exit, L'Avventura, This Sporting Life, The Servant, Hud,* and *A Tribute to Dylan Thomas.*

You see Ladies and Gentlemen, I am of the school that believes that you cannot teach literature; literature must be experienced. Now some of you will be skeptical. You will say that the students wouldn't be able to understand the concepts; you may argue that it isn't possible to do this within the confines of your school. But I am here to report not only can these things be taught but also they can be taught effectively.

In the fall of 1962 my students contributed money from their allowances so that they could get the type of education that we were both interested in their having. They bought their own books because we felt that if they owned their material the learning situation would be more meaningful. Everyone agreed that books would be read prior to the viewing of any motion picture. The books had to be chosen considering price, accessibility, ease of reading; had to deal with topics the students were interested in, and the story had to have been used in a motion picture which was now available in 16 mm film at a reasonable rental.

That first year we saw *Mister Roberts, Shane, Lost Horizon, Arsenic and Old Lace, Dr. Jekyll and Mr. Hyde, Detective Story, Goodbye, Mr. Chips, The Bad Seed, The Ox-Bow Incident, Nineteen Eighty-Four,* and *Gentleman's Agreement*. By the end of the year, the students were discussing current problems, personal obligations, man's relationships, techniques, point of view, setting, characterization, language, structure, audience, theme, special effects and style. We had arrived at a point in their lives when for the first time that they could remember, they enjoyed English. If you are interested, I refer you to the *English Journal,* March 1964 for a short summary of the program.

The next year 20 teachers and 800 students became involved in the program. This time, students who had never read saw *Light in the Forest, A Raisin in the Sun, The Ox-Bow Incident, Shane, The Citadel, The Portrait of Dorian Gray* [sic],[2] *Beau Geste, All Quiet on the Western Front, Magnificent Obsession, Dr. Jekyll and Mr. Hyde, Cheaper by the Dozen, The Prisoner of Zenda, Huckleberry Finn,* and *Detective Story*.

In an evaluation sheet filled out by the students, teachers found out that 90% of the students said they felt that the program was worthwhile and made for better writing, for better reading, for better listening, and for more enjoyable learning experiences. Then came the next stage in the program. To prove to other members of the faculty that the motivation, transfer of knowledge and the learning experience were valuable, I had the students make their own films.

In addition to the regular problems connected with teaching the slow learner, I had the added problems of technical knowledge and financial support for the making of the movies. The school system did not have any 8mm film, and the department was not willing to finance the venture. The principal suggested calling the Paillard Corporation in New Jersey and asking them for assistance. The company graciously lent us free of charge approximately fifteen hundred dollar's worth of equipment including cameras, tripods, editors, splicers and projectors. I was working with three slow learner groups, and together they were able through individual contributions to raise one hundred fifty-eight dollars and seventy-five cents.

Each group spent approximately four days in discussing an appropriate, original story to film. First, we decided on the type of story we wanted to write, and the various ways we could develop the plot. Each night students would watch television programs and note down interesting techniques. In addition to their homework assignment, they would write a two to three paragraph prose script based on the type of story we decided to film. The following day students read aloud their scripts and various parts were written on the blackboard for class discussion.

In this way we were able to develop creative thinking, literary appreciation, better television viewing habits and useful composition techniques. The latter approach, in particular, was used as early as 1915. When the three stories were completed, they were mimeographed for class distribution. An important point is that we were using different approaches to the same problem of educating the slow learner. He needs to relate what he already knows to new situations. His having to write, to assemble information and to create a film involved his potential and his ability. Developing these areas are most important for the student if he is to achieve success in the school and in society.

Once the stories were distributed, we concentrated on writing a shooting script. Here we incorporated what we knew of various camera shots, making good use of filming techniques employed in evening television programs and in motion pictures. The actual writing took four days. Particularly helpful to an untrained teacher in making a shooting script is Stanley Solomon's doctoral project; particularly Unit XII which concerns film.

Both the writing of a prose and a shooting script involved taking the slow learner at his present level, and by using the mass media as an aid, trying to improve the students' taste and judgments. That this is a primary job of an English teacher cannot be stressed enough. In a recent textbook concerning the teaching of English, the following was noted:

> Listening and viewing are the most popular means of receiving communication in contemporary culture. This recognition neither depreciates the value of reading and the permanence of the printed word, nor ignores the fleeting nature of much that appears in radio, television and motion pictures. Rather it admits that adults devote far more time to those media than they spend with books, magazines and newspapers. High school students alone pass from fourteen to twenty-four hours a week before a television set; junior high, twenty-five to thirty. Since the communication of ideas is a major instructional concern, teachers of English cannot ignore the impact on modern minds of these carriers of the idea and image.

On the ninth day we went about discussing and selecting people to perform various services. Students volunteered to be cameramen, prop men, actors, actresses, set designers, lighting technicians, film runners (purchasing and processing film) and assistant directors. Here the students learned about production in mass communication, particularly about the division of labor and the importance of working together.

During the next week the students *saw* two short movies, *The River* and *The Hunter and the Forest*. Both films used different techniques in filming a story. Mr. Charles Houtenmouser of the Paillard Corporation gave a demonstration on how to use the camera equipment lent to us, and answered questions on making a motion picture. The remaining two days were involved with acting out the shooting script, and having the professional advice of drama coaches who kindly came into the classroom to aid in the project. During these sessions the students learned about the differences between stage and film acting, the advantages and disadvantages of stage and screen production.

The shooting of the film was, at first, done on Sunday. Everything that could go wrong in the filming process went wrong for us. We had double exposures, lighting difficulties, poor ideological and temporal content, bad focusing, faulty equipment, and very bad processing arrangements. Nevertheless, the students were not discouraged. It is to their everlasting credit that they refused to be defeated, and began over again to film their story. The second shootings took place on school days and were concluded in spite of a seasonal blizzard.

The importance for slow learners in learning about films, the use of camera equipment and judgments in producing plays and films lies not in the technical application but rather in the personal and social kinetic activity. Marshall McLuhan makes a similar point to teachers when he writes, "The educational task is not only to provide tools of perception but also to develop judgment and discrimination with ordinary experience." Neil Postman in describing television and its value as a means of studying English communication writes, "…taste and critical judgment are learned habits of mind. As a consequence, Education, as in most things, is the decisive factor." By having students write, view, perform and criticize, the English teacher develops the student's tastes and judgments, not toward mass media specifically but more significantly toward better mental and social judgments and tastes concerning his peers and society.

When the raw film was finally acceptable, we worked on the editing process. Here the students learned much about the role of an editor, and significantly, about the process of obtaining a finished project. A strong argument can be made for the correlation between film editing and composition. Both involve the need for revision, accuracy, precision, and total effect.

As a result of the movie program, the students were written about in the school and local newspaper. They learned about the content of the newspaper article, how much information is included and omitted, and how news photographs are slanted. The films were also shown to approximately three hundred teachers and student teachers at Teachers College, Columbia University and Smith College. A further tribute to their effort was the showing of the films on the NBC program "Education Reports."

It became apparent as each month passed that the instruction for slow learners should begin at their level and that these students should be made to feel a part of the total community. A major part of a comprehensive school's objectives should be to help each child to adjust and to assume his role in society. To do this you need to start with what is familiar to the student and then proceed to the unfamiliar. The slow learner is very familiar with motion pictures and television, not with books and texts. The film-book program and the making of theatrical films is an area where the slow learner can achieve legitimate success; and, as educators know, very few things contribute to an interest in an activity as well as success. Throughout the past two years, the students really proved that the films and books they were studying had value and meaning, and by reading and viewing the materials the learning process was repeated and practiced which insured retention. The instruction provided almost immediate transfer to school and extra-curricular activities, particularly because the material was taught in concrete, socially meaningful situations.

There are many areas that need to be watched in programs such as this, and, competent adequate supervision is a must. One major problem is that there should be professional presentation of the material; specifically, the planned approach to a film unit and not merely the showing of a film to pass class time. Books need to be provided in an accessible manner, and adequate time has to be given in order to read the story prior to the showing of the film. Rooms, projectors, and projectionists have to be scheduled far enough in advance to insure an intelligent and useful experience. Encouragement has to be extended to all teachers involved in the program, and sufficient departmental time has to be allocated to discuss and develop a sequential program that will benefit all concerned. Enthusiasm and concern for the work and the student should be recognized as important prerequisites for participating in the program, and slow learner classes should not be given to individuals who are uninterested in the problems of the slow learner. The department should have a basis for evaluating the work of the student, and should not as is the case in some areas, be a "touch and go" situation.

In conclusion, let me reiterate that mass media presents a challenge to teachers which they cannot neglect. Our students are spending a major proportion of their time in trying to understand current problems and forms of communication. These students need direction and the experience of the educated citizen. Literature, in all its forms, can provide experiences which will be lasting and beneficial.

Notes

[1] Frank Manchel, "The Universal Classroom," Conference on Teaching the Slow Learner. New York: Metropolitan School Study Council (October 31, 1964). Part 3: 1-10.
[2] The correct title is *The Picture of Dorian Gray*.

3. A confused Duff (Ivan Dixon) changes his personal goals after visiting with his father (Julius Harris) and the dying man's common-law wife (Gloria Foster). Michael Roemer, *Nothing But a Man* (1964).

3

Crossroads

We see her as she is. *La Revolution* is not a goddess but a whore. She was never pure, never saintly, never perfect. Passion but no compassion, lust but no love. You want perfection or nothing. Too romantic. *La Revolution* is like a great love affair, but even a great love affair has a terrible enemy: Time.[1]

Jesus Raza (Jack Palance)

Hubble Gardner: "People are more important than their principles."
Katie Morosky Gardner: "People ARE their principles."[2]

The Way We Were

Our individuality is not ours alone.[3]

Amistad

The year 1963 proved to be an eventful time for a young, idealistic teacher. Although the film/book program led me to Columbia University's Teachers College's doctoral program, and the idea had proven popular with New York state teachers, I should have heeded Rudyard Kipling's warning that triumph and disaster are both imposters. That certainly was the case at New Rochelle High School. A new principal, consumed with advanced placement programs, looked down on someone obsessed with both the popular arts and non-regents students. Only five years into my journey, and the winds had shifted dramatically. Not only my status declined once the new administration arrived, but also the non-regents students were returned to the back burner. It was just one more lesson I would learn about the misuse of office and the failure some administrators display when they confuse ego with excellence.

By late November, I had learned another great lesson: education has its own toxic type of "Catch 22." No one ever warned me about how Joseph Heller's satiric concept worked in educational circles. Simply put, you are told by your supervisors that if you do well at your job, you will be rewarded with a chance to try new ideas. So you take your administrators at their word, and go knock your brains out trying to impress them with your talent and your dedication. But, the better you are at doing what they want, the less likely they will give you what you were promised. You become too valuable to move away from their scheme of things. It is too much of a burden for them to find someone to take up your previous responsibilities. Their comfort zone takes priority over their word or their appreciation. Catch 22! Success is your worst enemy. Not once in the past fifty-eight years have I seen that truth violated!

I learned another invaluable lesson that memorable Thanksgiving: never allow yourself to be trapped. The "Objectionables," as Gloria Steinem described the people who block constructive changes to protect their own personal agendas, can only succeed if you stay put, keep your mouth shut, or lose faith in yourself. Administrators mainly win their battles with you when they make you feel helpless or appear to be powerless. Their favorite tactic is stonewalling. "Be patient," they say; "It'll happen, just not now."

Of course, not everyone has the strength or the ability or the temperament to be combative, to be aggressive, or to move away. Even more, few teachers know there is such a thing as a "smell test." Some professionals are like Telemachus, who do what they have to do, or who chose to fight within the system. I have no problem with that decision. They also serve who only stand and wait. But there are others like Odysseus, who elect to seek their fortunes elsewhere rather than be an academic Sisyphus. They can't or won't be bullied. They take risks. I was one of them!

So, "smelling" what was transpiring at NRHS, I activated my employment papers at Columbia University and *quickly* got a job as an assistant professor at Southern Connecticut State College (now University) in New Haven, down the road from you know where.

And so began my decade of discontent. I was about to discover the significant differences between public education and higher education. The former requires you to help students become self-sufficient; the latter expects you to test how self-sufficient they are.

Before we move any further in this narrative, consider for a moment how you perceive college teaching. Choose from any of the following films[4] and see if there is one that matches your ideas about what I might have faced fresh from teaching six years in high school: James W. Horne's *College*,[5] Fred C. Newmeyer's *The Freshman*,[6] John Landis' *National Lampoon's Animal House*,[7] Robert Luketic's *Legally Blonde*,[8] Steve Miner's *Soul Man*,[9] Elliott Nugent's *Mr. Belvedere Goes to College*,[10] Stanley Kramer's *R.P.M.*[11] James Toback's *Harvard Man*,[12] Mike Newell's *Mona Lisa Smiles*,[13] Lamont Johnson's *One on One*,[14] Jeremy Kagan's *The Chosen*,[15] Andrew Bergman's *The Freshman*,[16] Karel Reisz' *The Gambler*,[17] Paul Williams' *The Revolutionary*,[18] Alan J. Pakula's *The Sterile Cuckoo*,[19] Denzel Washington's *The Great Debaters*,[20] Gus Van Sant's *Good Will Hunting*,[21] Arthur Hiller's *Love Story*,[22] Glenn Silber's *The War at Home*,[23] Curtis Hanson's *Wonder Boys*,[24] Andrew Wagner's *Starting Out in the Evening*,[25] Isobel Coixet's *Elegy*,[26] Robert Benton's *The Human Stain*,[27] James Bridges' *The Paper Chase*,[28] Sydney Pollack's *The Way We Were*,[29] Jerry Lewis' *The Nutty Professor*,[30] Spike Lee's *School Daze*,[31] Jeff Kanew's *Revenge of the Nerds*,[32] John Singleton's *Higher Learning*,[33] David Fincher's *The Social Network*,[34] Ron Howard's *A Beautiful Mind*,[35] Lewis Gilbert's *Educating Rita*,[36] and David Mamet's *Oleanna*.[37]

Not one of those worthy movies captures even closely my romantic recollections of those fateful apprentice years in higher education from 1964 to 1967. In a nod to Hemingway and Kael, who inspired me to keep things as simple as possible, let me give you a whiff of what it was like. The college president promised me the moon. If I did well training prospective English teachers; being allowed to teach film courses would be a no-brainer. The department chairperson signed on as well. To this day I believe both men were sincere. But they were also administrators whose agendas differed dramatically from mine.

The opening semester, like the early years at NRHS, proved exciting, challenging, and extremely rewarding. While my literary survey courses seemed on par with what I had done at the high school level, the methods classes were unlike any instruction I had done before. Nevertheless, the students proved receptive and energetic; the subject matter was anything I chose; and the opportunities for growth seemed unlimited. Even better, I travelled around Connecticut supervising student teachers and met one remarkable master teacher after another. The fact I disagreed with particular styles or strategies—e.g., it was hard for me as a Jewish intellectual to interpret every literary hero as a Christ figure—was not a game breaker.

Like writing criticism, I appreciated one has to adapt his teaching to his or her audience. You review movies in the mass media differently from the way you critique them in scholarly journals. In practical terms, that translates into doing what the chair expects you to do! The one downer in the package was sitting every day watching someone else doing what I wanted to do. I found it very hard not to jump up and say, "No, no. That's not right. What are you talking about?" Still, the follow up conferences were fun, and the youngsters turned out to be good listeners with positive attitudes, and they took well to my constructive criticisms.

Added to my joy was the fun of being on a college campus, meeting intellectuals with fascinating insights about anything and everything. For example, my officemate was the unforgettable Walter Tevis. Of course, some of you don't immediately remember he was the author of *The Hustler* and *The Man Who Fell to Earth*. We had a common bond. Each had gone into high school teaching following his college graduation. Each had moved on to college teaching within a short time. Walt was seven years older than I was, so he was further down the path and more experienced: *The Hustler* came out in 1958 (the film in 1961); *The Man Who Fell to Earth* in 1963 (the film in 1976).

Even now, I recall fondly our conversations about the small-time pool hall player who discovers how important character is to achieving success. But what surprised me was how much Walt disliked the film. In his novel, he explained, the pool hall was akin to a cathedral; and Fast Eddie's journey was supposed to be a religious experience. But if you subscribed to Walt's critique, Robert Rossen's screen adaptation missed the book's message and cheapened the tale. I was confident enough to disagree with this gifted author.

(Please tell me you're not surprised.) I praised the cast, loved the production values, and remained totally involved in the narrative. (To this day, Rossen's version of the novel remains one of my favorite films.)

Then came another unforgettable experience with my officemate at SCSC. Walt invited me out to lunch. I remember how excited I was when I called Sheila and said, "I'm having lunch with Walter Tevis!" (See how swift I was at twenty-nine years of age.) We get to the restaurant, and the server takes our luncheon choices. Walt orders a drink at 12:30 in the afternoon; and the waitress turns to me and says, "And you?" And I say, "Whatever Walt is having is good enough for me!" Right? Wrong! My friend had a drinking problem, and I rarely touched the stuff until I was in my mid-thirties. To this day, I do not remember the meal, how I got to my two o'clock American Lit. class, or what I taught that afternoon.

It was the last lunch Walt and I had. He moved on that year to teach creative writing and Milton at Ohio University. Eventually he gave up college teaching and became a full-time writer. He lost his battle with cancer in 1984. He was fifty-six years of age. I remember his kindness and generosity to the new kid on campus with great affection.

Not so SCSC. It's hard to say which literary giant nailed the culture there better than did Jonathan Swift who wrote, "Principally I hate and detest that animal called man; although I heartily love John, Peter, Thomas, and so forth"[38]; or Gore Vidal who believed America is "a country habituated by liars."[39] In fairness, the fault was partially mine. I had unrealistic expectations about teaching in college. I believed to be with a community of scholars was somewhat analogous to being on Mount Olympus or at Camelot. But I had not understood that neither the gods nor the knights in shining armor had ever lived harmoniously together. If only I had read Robert Graves' *Greek Gods and Heroes*[40] earlier, or studied Malory's history of King Arthur more carefully, I would have been prepared for what happens when talented people become resentful, jealous, and indignant.

In essence, I had rattled the English department's cages. College professors are territorial, extremely opinionated, narcissistic, paranoid, and dangerous when aroused. I navigated the waters brilliantly so long as I played by the rules, ignored my colleagues' peculiarities, did my job well, and had a drink with the tenured professors every now and then. But when you disagree with what they are doing, or challenge the rigid curriculum they've erected, or worse, propose something new that appears to threaten their print-oriented life-style, watch out!

Remember, both the president and the chairperson had promised me that I would soon teach film courses. More encouraging, I had already established the mass media as a key variable in my methods classes. Still further, I had already galvanized master teachers around the state to begin incorporating popular culture into their high school curriculums. I had even published a lead article in *Media & Methods*, a new, popular magazine that took on the English establishment.

The article that follows is probably more meaningful to me now than it was then. While it gained some approval in 1964—a low budget movie about African Americans made by a white director at the time blacks argued for "Black Power"'"—my principal focus in using the film was on getting high school teachers to use movies as a tool in the teaching of writing. Up to then, teaching the art of composing was the sole province of the English department; and literary topics, the primary subject matter.

Today, however, I view *Nothing But a Man* as a major reason why I devoted so much of my professional life to black film history. It is also the start of my love for African American female vocalists like Abbey Lincoln, as well as the profound feelings I have for Ivan and Berlie Dixon. (If you are interested why, I encourage you to read *Exits and Entrances*.)

My sojourn at SCSC came to a relatively dead end in November of 1966, when I had a heated discussion about film study with a senior member of the English department. I think what turned the civil debate into a death wish was when I spoke to her, as the Clancy brothers often said, "in a language that the clergy do not know." Afterwards, the chairperson called me into his office and angrily stated, "You will never teach film at this school." Then the president summoned me into his office and asked, "Why didn't you come to me when you were in trouble?" I said to both of them, "I quit!"

Later, I learned an invaluable lesson when I told Sheila what had transpired at school that day. We had two small children, a hefty mortgage, and we needed a new car. Without changing her expression, she sat me down and said, "Honey, first you find a job, then you quit."

By the time my contract ended in June, I already had gotten a plum position at the University of Vermont.

Notes

[1] Richard Brooks, *The Professionals*. USA: Columbia Pictures, 1966.
[2] Robert Redford and Barbra Streisand.
[3] Steven Spielberg, *Amistad*. USA: DreamWorks, 1997.
[4] I want to acknowledge my debt to the film scholar Gerald Perry who compiled a list of 50 top college films for the *Boston Globe*, available at boston.com.
[5] James W. Horne, *College*. USA: United Artists, 1927.
[6] Fred C. Newmeyer, *The Freshman*. USA: The Harold Lloyd Corporation, 1925.
[7] John Landis, *National Lampoon's Animal House*. USA: Universal Pictures, 1978.
[8] Robert Luketic's *Legally Blonde*. USA: MGM, 2001.
[9] Steve Miner, *Soul Man*. USA: New World Productions, 1986.
[10] Elliott Nugent, *Mr. Belvedere Goes to College*. USA: 20th Century-Fox, 1949.
[11] Stanley Kramer. *R.P.M.* USA: Columbia Pictures, 1970.
[12] James Toback, *Harvard Man*. USA: Cowboy Pictures, 2002.
[13] Mike Newell, *Mona Lisa Smiles*. USA: Sony Pictures Entertainment, 2003.
[14] Lamont Johnson, *One on One*. USA: Warner Bros., 1977.
[15] Jeremy Kagan, *The Chosen*. USA: Chosen Film Company, 1982.
[16] Andrew Bergman, *The Freshman*. USA: Tri Star Picture, 1990.
[17] Karel Reisz, *The Gambler*. USA: Paramount Pictures, 1974.
[18] Paul Williams, *The Revolutionary*. Australia: Pressman-Williams Productions, 1970.
[19] Alan J. Pakula, *The Sterile Cuckoo*. USA: Paramount Pictures, 1969.
[20] Denzel Washington, *The Great Debaters*. USA: The Weinstein Company, 2007.
[21] Gus Van Sant, *Good Will Hunting*. USA: Miramax, 1997.
[22] Arthur Hiller, *Love Story*. USA: Paramount Pictures, 1970.

[23] Glenn Silber, *The War at Home*. USA: Catalyst Media, 1979.
[24] Curtis Hanson, *Wonder Boys*. USA: Paramount Pictures, 2000.
[25] Andrew Wagner, *Starting Out in the Evening*. USA: Little Film Company, 2007.
[26] Isobel Coixet, *Elegy*. USA: Lakeshore Entertainment, 2008.
[27] Robert Benton, *The Human Stain*. USA: Miramax, 2003.
[28] James Bridges, *The Paper Chase*. USA: 20th Century-Fox, 1973.
[29] Sydney Pollack, *The Way We Were*. USA: Columbia Pictures, 1973.
[30] Jerry Lewis, *The Nutty Professor*. USA: Paramount Pictures, 1963.
[31] Spike Lee, *School Daze*. USA: 40 Acres and A Mule Filmworks, 1988.
[32] Jeff Kanew, *Revenge of the Nerds*. USA: Twentieth Century-Fox, 1984.
[33] John Singleton, *Higher Learning*. USA: Columbia Pictures, 1995.
[34] David Fincher, *The Social Network*. USA: Columbia Pictures, 2010.
[35] Ron Howard, *A Beautiful Mind*. USA: Universal Pictures, 2001.
[36] Lewis Gilbert, *Educating Rita*. Britain: Columbia Pictures, 1983
[37] David Mamet, *Oleanna*. USA: Samuel Goldwyn Company, 1994.
[38] Jonathan Swift's Letter to Alexander Pope, September 29, 1725.
[39] Nicholas D. Wrathall, *Gore Vidal: The United States of Amnesia*. USA: IFC Films, 2013.
[40] Robert Graves, *Greek Gods and Heroes*. New York: Dell Laurel-Leaf, 1960.

Film Study: "Nothing But a Man."

NOTHING BUT A MAN

CAST

Duff Anderson	Ivan Dixon
Josie	Abbey Lincoln
Lee	Gloria Foster
Will Anderson	Julius Harris
Driver	Martin Priest
Frankie	Leonard Parker
Jocko	Yaphet Kotto
Rev. Dawson	Stanley Greene
Effie Simms	Helen Lounck
Doris	Helene Arrindell
Car Owner	Walter Wilson
Pop	Milton Williams
Riddick	Melvin Stewart

CREDITS

Produced by Robert Young, Michael Roemer, Robert Rubin
Directed by Michael Roemer, Screenplay by Michael Roemer and Robert Young
Photography by Robert Young
Edited by Luke Bennett
Harmonica Music by Wilbur Kirk
Sound by Robert Rubin

> What for centuries raised a man above the beast is not the cudgel but an inward music: the irresistible power of an unarmed truth, the powerful attraction of its example.
>
> *Boris Pasternak*

Experimental approaches to film study are hard to come by, despite the fact that they are sorely needed. Curriculum-oriented programs (*Great Expectations* is coming up in the syllabus; let's get the movie to run along with it), while they serve as excellent camouflage for getting films into the classroom, are only a small part of the picture. They tend to relegate the film to a secondary or supporting role and miss the larger picture of film as the *primary* experience. The see-it-and-react method is fine, so long as it doesn't exist through default; that is, in lieu of an ability to treat film material critically. Teachers who want to work with film yet who, because of their inexpertise, handle it as raw, primitive material without attempting to pre-structure or, for that matter, post-structure it, often resort to this technique.

New approaches (which work off of or use traditional techniques) must be tried; for that is the only way a philosophy and a practice of screen education will develop.

With this in mind, I convinced the principal and chairman of the English Dept. at Cheshire High School (Cheshire, Conn.) to experiment with *Nothing But a Man*. I agreed to supply study guide materials to three experienced English teachers. In turn, the teachers agreed to teach the movie to their 270 juniors in classes ranging from general to honors.

The experiment made possible the evaluation of a number of important objectives. (1) What approaches work best with different abilities; (2) what effects do movies have on the students, the teachers, and the curriculum; (3) how would a movie like *Nothing But a Man* (as an example of an entire genre) sit with students in an all-white suburban school; (4) using film as a base, what ways of extending student interest, broadening their experience and widening their knowledge, could be discovered? I was interested in two further areas: what materials would be most helpful for teachers in preparing film study units and, secondly, how could movies retain their vitality and not be sterilized by the rigors of the curriculum.

The following comments suggest some of our answers.

At our initial meeting, the instructors (Harriet Schilo, Fran McLaughlin, and John Griffin) wanted to know what *Nothing But a Man* was about. I explained that the film portrays—in a highly naturalistic mode—the difficulties that a young Negro, Duff Anderson, encounters in searching for identity and acceptance in a Southern community. The teachers felt that since the role of the Negro in American society had been a major topic in their American Lit. Curriculum, there were many possibilities for classroom correlation (general curriculum tie-ins are, incidentally, usually more fruitful than specific ones). We agreed that each teacher would approach the film differently in order that various approaches could be tested. Mr. Griffin decided that he would present no introduction to the film at all. His students would come to the movie "cold." The others agreed to show a film extract prior to the complete screening. Both approaches worked well. Because the school was using a modular schedule, a double period was set aside for the showing of the film to all the juniors simultaneously. The value here is in seeing the entire film.

Four days before the public screening, the two women teachers (who had decided not to use the "cold" approach) received an eleven-page study guide (prepared for Brandon Films by Dr. Dan Ort[1] and myself) and a film extract. The study guide consisted of credits, parts of the shooting script, synopsis, lesson plan, and suggested activities. The following (together with the credits on the first page) is a sample of that material. It is introduced primarily to suggest the kinds of materials the teacher has to become knowledgeable in before actually teaching a film. Without it, film study becomes a shadow-play.

STUDY GUIDE

Story: As a railroad section hand in Alabama, Duff Anderson enjoys the relative independence and irresponsibility that come with such a job. Yet Duff, unlike his cynical fellow workers, has a capacity for compassion and a dream that he can be accepted as a man. He visits his young son in Birmingham and continues to pay for his support even though he suspects that he may not be the boy's father. Duff also sees his own father in the city. Will, with only one arm and too often drunk, is a wasted man living with his common-law wife, Lee.

Then Duff meets Josie Dawson, the preacher's daughter, at a church festival. As he courts her, he discovers that even in the Negro community, as represented by Rev. Dawson, he is a misfit. With courage and hope, Josie and Duff fall in love and marry, despite Rev. Dawson's objections. Their love promises to sustain them. But their life is not easy. At the sawmill, Duff is accused of trying to organize the Negro workers into a union. Actually he was just encouraging them to stand up to the white man. These cowed workers warn him that he has to act like a "nigger" if he wants to get along. But Duff is too much of a man, and eventually he is fired.

Now marked as a troublemaker, he finds it increasingly difficult to get work. Most of the jobs, like picking cotton and bellhopping, he considers degrading. Finally, with Rev. Dawson's help, he gets a job in a service station. But trouble continues to plague him. Duff is sent out with the wrecker to tow in some white man's wrecked car. The white man, angry because Duff let his car slip off the chain, thinks the Negro is too cocky, too disrespectful.

Later at the station, four white men drive up to demand that Duff apologize to the owner of the wrecked car who is now seated in the back seat. As Duff remains silent, they intensify their efforts to belittle him. He is noticeably angry, but controlled. When they continue to make salacious remarks about his wife, he threatens them. There is an exchange of threats. The filling station owner, bending under the pressure, fires Duff. Returning home Duff takes out his frustration and anger on his wife by physically abusing her.

Jobless, defeated, he leaves his pregnant wife and goes to visit his father. But when old Will Anderson dies, leaving Lee alone and Duff with a wasted life, he realizes his responsibility. He picks up his son and returns with him to Josie and to the only chance he has of becoming accepted as the man he knows he is.

FILM SCRIPT FOR EXTRACT

A gas station at night. Bud Ellis and Duff both approach—Bud from the office. Duff (somewhat behind him) from the garage.

ELLIS: *(to the driver).* Yes?

DRIVER: Like some service from that boy there. *(He indicates Duff.)* Like the way he takes care of us. *(Duff has come up. wiping his hands on a grease rag.)*

ELLIS: *(to Duff).* Okay. (Ellis returns to his office. Duff glances into the car and notices the owner of the car he hauled out of the ditch in the rear seat. A third man is sitting beside him and a fourth is up front with the driver.)

DUFF: *(on his guard, but matter of fact).*

Fill her up?

DRIVER: No, boy. Thirty-eight cents worth of gas. And watch you don't make it thirty-nine. *(All of the men are watching Duff. Duff starts the pump.)* You gonna 'pologize to our friend here'

(Duff says nothing. He watches the pump.)

DRIVER: Didn't hear you say Yessir! *(Duff turns of the pump.)* Don't they say Yessir' where you come from? *(The threat becomes explicit.)* Boy! You hear me?

DUFF: *(coming to the window quietly).*

That'll be thirty-eight cents.

DRIVER: *(enraged).* Dammit nigger! You must think you're white! Who d'ya think you are...the king of Harlem?

SECOND MAN: *(to Duff).* How about this windshield, boy? Like a little service. *(Duff starts cleaning the windshield. His jaw muscles are tense.)*

THIRD MAN: Hell, they're getting too big for their britches.

SECOND MAN: Yeah...His wife's getting the same way...strutting around town like she owns the place. *(With a grin)* ...shakin' that little rear end.

THIRD MAN: It's all that education they're getting.

DRIVER: *(watching Duff tensely).* Real cool ain't he. Just like we ain't here.

DUFF: *(At the window again).* That'll be thirty-eight cents.

DRIVER: You're in a big hurry, boy.

SECOND MAN: *(with a grin).* Yeah...He's trying to get home!

DRIVER: *(To Duff)*. Bet she's pretty hot, huh?
DUFF: *(still quietly, but on the point of losing control)*. Better watch your mouth, man. *(The driver knows that he has Duff close to breaking. He continues with a grin.)*

Both Mrs. Schilo and Mrs. McLaughlin found success in their academic and general classes by discussing filmic technique and its relation to effective communication. The emphasis, for example, was on setting, theme, lighting, photography, music, sound effects and direction. Each class was divided into groups, assigned to look for certain technical aspects and asked to report their reactions following the movie. The film extract plus excerpts from the study guide was used in the classroom the day before the movie was shown.

The assembly period came off well. Here are some typical quotations from short reaction papers written by students in Mr. Griffith's (the "cold" approach) class following the assembly period:

> I found the movie to be quite enjoyably different from what I had expected. Actually, I think that both technically and dramatically it was flawless, mainly because it gave such a clear, "raw" (not coarse, however), and frank picture of the Negro from both points of view, something which I myself had never seen before...

> When I left the room after seeing that movie I felt like I was coming out of a pit. After being accustomed to comfortable middle class suburbia, seeing how Negroes live was tremendously depressing...

> I felt the movie was very good as a whole. I did not find it objectionable, although I was surprised that it was shown to us because normally people are too prejudiced to allow us to see movies where there is any hint that anything may be objectionable...

Now to some specific methods. Mr. Griffin's approach centered mainly on discussing various stereotyped roles and attitudes in the film. During one class period, he very effectively treated the various points of views expressed by the Negro mill workers. In another class session, he discussed the different attitudes of Negro parents. Duff's father, for example, embodies the shiftless individual who believes a man shouldn't get married, should remain free and footloose. When things get rough, you can move on. Reverend Dawson, however, represents the "Uncle Tom" image. Play along with the white man so you can get whatever you want (except. that is, human dignity). Duff stands in the middle, somewhere between responsibility and freedom.

Mrs. McLaughlin taught the movie from the point of view of the home, its definition, and the archetypal character of "the wanderer." She had her students make comparisons between *Nothing But a Man* and previous works studied that year (e.g., 'The Death of the Hired Man" and *My Antonia)*. By referring to specific characters, scenes and actions, the students were able to understand the problems Duff faced. Time was also devoted during the week to class discussions about stereotyping and its relationship not only to film and literature, but also to society and individuals. With her general classes, Mrs. McLaughlin emphasized the importance of making life decisions that are contrary to environment. Having just finished a unit on occupational choices, the students were able to compare Duff with themselves and move towards an understanding of how life choices are made, what problems Duff faced in making his decision, and the relevance of the movie to their own lives.

Mrs. Schilo, proceeding from her pre-viewing assignments, had students write reports, give oral presentations, and discuss the technical qualities of the movie. She also used a rating sheet with her general students to evaluate the quality of the film. Some items that were considered were: social significance, theme, characterization, sound effects and lighting. In addition, each group was asked to write a modified Petrarchan sonnet: one octave presenting one view; the remainder, another. The following example illustrates the advantages and disadvantages of this method:

Her father being a Negro preacher,
He's a man of prominence in the town.
He's willing to be a passive creature
Incapable of putting the white man down.
My husband is so different from my dad,
He'll fight for Negro rights until he dies.
Sorrow and trouble is all he has had,
His hatred for the whites shows in his eyes.
Inwardly I feel my husband is right
But because of my father's impression
I am unable to join in his fight,
As a wife this is my transgression.
My husband will always have my respect
My consolations I hope he'll accept.

In conclusion, let me quote the teachers' evaluations of the units.

Griffin: The racial situation presented in this movie is clearly the source of Duff's dilemma but, as is true in all good works, the lesson Duff learns is relevant and important to all of us. The value in a predominantly white school is not lessened at all by the racial situation. The students are made aware of both the racial problem and also their own worth as humans (i.e., the importance of not sacrificing their own self-respect for the comfort of social stability). I noticed with my low group, a high degree of viewing sophistication. They are very well attuned to film experience, and get a great deal out of it.

McLaughlin: Reactions of the group were unanimously positive in classroom situation. Classes agreed that this film is a good one for inclusion in English curriculum, although students admitted they would not go to see this movie on a Saturday night date. Immediate reactions of students after showing of film—unsolicited personal comments: "great," "so real," "terrific," "Wasn't that just a lot of propaganda for the colored."

Schilo: Slow learners were definitely helped by the film—first, more was covered in a shorter space of time; second, more literary techniques were introduced because viewing was more vivid and faster than reading, and pictures conveyed so much more. For example, tone and mood were explored more through film techniques of light and dark shots, near and far shots, sound and music, etc. Third, the facial expressions at times conveyed more than words.

The value of approaches like these (and, by reflection, of an article like this) is that they are immersed in the materials that surround a film from credits, to script, to actual film. The moral seems to be that teachers must be prepared for the films they want to teach, otherwise the end of the film might well signal the end of student-involvement. The experience of a film must be articulated: to articulate it, teachers must know where the joints and the bones are.

WHERE TO GET IT

Nothing But a Man (*b/w*, 92 minutes)
Rental: Brandon Films, Inc., 221 West 57 St, New York, New York 10019. $5.00 (INFOCARD 88)

Frank Manchel is Associate Professor of English at the University of Vermont. He moonlights heavily, however, in film study. Frank is Book Editor of Film Society Review *and is preparing a book on movies for children for Prentice-Hall (to be published this spring). This issue's* Nothing But a Man *is the first of experimental study guides he is doing for* Media and Methods.

Notes

[1] Dan was a big help and a nice person to work with.

4. The author enjoying himself with friend and former student, Oscar-winning screenwriter/producer David Franzoni.

4.

Don Quixote, Alive and Well

Sometimes it is the people who no one imagines anything of who do the things that no one can imagine.[1]
The Imitation Game

Change is the law of life. And those who look only to the past or the present are certain to miss the future.[2]
President John F. Kennedy

To be a king, and wear a crown, is a thing more glorious to them that see it, than it is pleasing to them that bear it."[3]
Queen Elizabeth I (1533-1603)

Teaching writing remains one of the most gratifying, pleasing, and aggressive activities in my professional journey. Nearly six decades later, my experiences with that difficult academic obligation still echo in my thoughts. Looking back, I find my memories go far beyond the discipline itself and boil over into university politics and my arguments with Objectionables who refused even to consider changing their opinions on the art of teaching composing. The debates also involved multiple disciplines and assorted communities on and off the college campus. Moreover, this nostalgic glance through my rear view mirror illustrates why the teaching of writing brings out the best and the worst in each of us. And for me, it recalls one of the most enigmatic experiences in my career.

To appreciate those first years working on a college campus in the shadow of Vermont's glorious Green Mountains and alongside its beautiful Lake Champlain, I need to explain the circumstances surrounding my initial UVM employment. After the unpredictable events at NRHS and SCSC, I wanted to avoid my previous professional missteps and to safeguard my future aims at Vermont's state university. My last two jobs had delivered four basic academic warnings: doing your job well is no guarantee of upcoming success, there is no peace for nonconformists, even good people sometimes let you down, and always expect surprises.

After ignoring dozens of offers to consider working at campuses across the nation, I decided to accept UVM's job proposal. However, there was just one glitch. The English Department wanted me as an Assistant Professor, which I already was at SCSC. But I was savvy to the game. In those days, the academic pecking order went from starting as an instructor, wait several years, then presumably be promoted every six years to Assistant than to Associate and finally to Full Professor. Given my personality and my conduct, I realized it would only be a matter of time before things could fall apart in the corridors and backrooms of UVM's ivory tower.

Traditionally, the word *chutzpah* is defined as someone who murders his parents and then throws himself on the mercy of the court because he is an orphan. I added a new definition. In December of 1966, I received my doctoral degree, an event that qualifies you for an instructor's job at most respected American institutions. However, my current status at SCSC opened the possibility of promotion by going to a new school. So I called the chairperson, despite Sheila being apoplectic. "You want the job," she ranted. "Why would you jeopardize it?" The prospective chair, stunned by my request, stammered he had given me an Associate's salary, but he had no authority to change my rank. I thanked him for his generosity, but said my perverse personality made it impossible for me to move any other way but up. Twenty-four hours later, I was a UVM Associate Professor of English.

Once again, I found myself in a startling and ironic situation. Living close to my father-in-law's business world, I had been taught that when someone gets a raise, it eventually elevates everyone else's salary because of the need for good morale in the workplace. Thus you become a hero by being promoted. Your colleagues pat you on the back because you are helping raise their salaries by raising your own.

Not so in academia. One person's success is another person's torment. My new colleagues deeply resented my actions and my good fortune. Many were decent, solid, gentle intellectuals who grudgingly played by the rules, made no waves, and waited impatiently their turn to move up the academic ladder. Regrettably, some never made the top rung! Making matters worse in those days, you did not get your own office until you became an associate professor. Thus my new digs proved to be a daily reminder to my disillusioned colleagues of their discouraging circumstances. Years would pass with many of them sharing a small office with a gloomy colleague. It made for much tension with my coworkers for a very long time. Truthfully, I found out none of this until several months after I reached Burlington, Vermont. Just as truthfully, I would not do things any differently today.

What follows sounds irrational but it is nevertheless accurate. In September of 1967, arriving at the English Department in the Old Mill was, for me, like entering the Great Room of the British Royal Academy of 1832, recreated so brilliantly in Mike Leigh's *Mr. Turner*.[4] Everywhere I turned, there were experts, reminiscent of the once nomadic outcasts in François Truffaut's *Fahrenheit 451*,[5] e.g., Milton, Wordsworth, Chaucer, Shakespeare, and Emerson, all prominent people incredibly locked into a traditional, conservative culture. On the floor above in the Political Science department were Hobbes, de Tocqueville, Plato, Mill, and a man who was the shining light in Holocaust scholarship. Outside the Old Mill in other buildings on the campus were intellectuals in every discipline imaginable: the sciences, history, sociology, art, music, theater, psychology, and so on. I would be able to talk with these scholars, work with them, and share their knowledge. But unlike the characters in Ray Bradbury's novel[6] or François Truffaut's film of the same name, these real-life reincarnations were complex celebrities whose inventive and learned natures sometimes made some of them paranoid. They saw "Outsiders" and "Newcomers" as threatening their territorial prerogatives. At such times, driven by such demons, these now altered, forlorn, and frustrated scholars became intolerable and irrational. They became the Objectionables!

The surprising situation I found myself in was not unlike the one Don Quixote, another of my literary heroes, encountered centuries before in Spain's Golden Age. Although I was neither gloomy nor emaciated, I did have my head filled, not with fantasies of chivalry, but with cinematic images of honor and justice and adventure. Equally relevant, UVM, like La Mancha, seemed ideal for inspiring romantic dreams and fighting for humanistic values in a cynical, true-to-life world. (It is not coincidental for this narrative that Cervantes' masterpiece is considered the father of the realistic novel.) I may not have had windmills to tilt at, but I had my share of barriers to break down. Regrettably for my adversaries, they were expecting "the Knight of the Woeful Countenance;" instead, they found Fast Eddie Felson from the rough streets of New York. Lucky for me, I was up against their "B" team.

With many exceptions on the gifted faculty, a small group of colleagues in their own way and for sundry reasons developed a chip on their shoulders toward me. I still stiffen when I remember those times. These talented, hard-working, impressive intellectuals inexplicably thought me arrogant, abrasive, and dangerous (a philistine threating their culture and their terrain). Many of these troublesome coworkers often made these judgments never having met me. They just reacted emotionally to my discipline and to their hatred of popular culture intruding in their print-oriented domain. They fought hard against me, the New York Jewish dissenter, always testing my perceived gullibility by insisting they had the college's best interests in mind. The more we engaged each other, the more I debunked their deception. Their strong egos and fierce competitive spirits looked hateful and spiteful in the light of day, especially when they played their dirty tricks the coward's way. They made their moves in secret meetings, in private offices, and at a long table in the faculty dining room. And, at times, they made me pay for my aggressiveness, more of which in Chapter 6.

At first I believed their resentment related to my unorthodox status, my being an unfriendly Outsider with an EdD Degree instead of a PhD. In retrospect, I realized two other important variables were at work. First, I was not the only target. Several of my friends, also in the Humanities, have come forth during the writing of this chapter to tell me not only were they attacked as well, but also in some instances, the tensions exist to this day. (Since this is my story, they'll have to write their own book.) Secondly, the criticisms against me had historical antecedents and grew out of what Swift so eloquently wrote about in his brilliant essay "Battle of the Books." There the Ancients had always taken arms against the Moderns who opposed traditional views and values, more of which in the next two chapters. I was just one in a long line of mutineers who was on the Objectionables' hit list. What was and is amazing to me is that I was clueless to what we were fighting about. All I wanted to do was teach about film!

One of my academic assignments was teaching expository writing. Before we go another word, let me make some things clear about my skills as a writing expert. Despite sixty years of experience, I still know very little about the art of getting people to express themselves effectively in print. Nor do I know much more today the answers to questions about how best to correct a paper, or whether to emphasize subject matter over mechanics, or what is the proper length of a writing project, or what is the best way to motivate a student to express himself, or even the best number of writing tasks to give in a semester. Imagine what little I knew back then. What I did know was what worked most effectively for me. And I am confident that my gut more than my brains made me successful with my classes.

What does that mean? Well, one example. The early UVM years found me, as usual, getting close with my students. Three individuals in particular who met me each week outside of class for a year to discuss their academic interests were a lovely, imaginative young woman named Bonnie Christensen,[7] who later gained fame as a first class author and illustrator; a brilliant geology student named David H. Franzoni, who became an Oscar-winning screenwriter (see Appendix I); and an industrious youngster, overshadowed by his famous father, named Jason Robards III, who has had a noteworthy career as an actor and screenwriter. I share this information not to brag how good I was, but to prove how little damage I did!

All of this is by way of introducing what happened unexpectedly in the spring of 1968. I was called into the Chair's office and told that a major donor wanted to fund an experimental writing program at UVM. For several months, different faculty had proposed various formats and suggestions, but the demanding patron had rejected each proposal. Would I take a try at putting some ideas together?

What happened is detailed in the two essays that are the focus of this chapter. Known as the La Mancha Project, a name sometimes cynically referred to as the Manchel Project, it involved many generous scholars, exceptional high school teachers, and cooperative business people on and off the UVM campus. In essence, I proposed a model school project where ideas could be tested and reviewed by secondary school teachers around the state.

Reading over the material from nearly forty years past is like visiting, to paraphrase a term from Richard Brooks' *The Professionals*, the "Cemetery of Nameless Men and Women." In recalling the various stages of the La Mancha Project, I remember fondly dozens of ignored teachers who battled mightily against an age-old, uphill problem. That is, since time immemorial influential people have tried to maintain their fragile status by keeping those around them ignorant. We saw this in the days of black bondage, where slaves were refused education less they rise up against their masters; we see it today where women across the globe are denied a basic education. But in 1968, with little compensation and even less recognition, a group of dedicated educators took on the challenge to discover a way to improve the writing skills of the present generation; in essence, to provide the young with the means to live with hope and dignity in the future. (I told you it would sound pretentious.)

The La Mancha Project reminds me that for every negative remark I mentioned earlier about my beginnings at UVM, here is ample proof of just how special and generous many of my colleagues were, far outweighing their momentary lapses on the dark side. The fact is many good-natured, intelligent, trustworthy, and caring teachers did many extraordinary things for people they hardly knew. This is my way of saying I have not forgotten! It is also a reminder of my everlasting gratitude for their help a long time ago.

One scholar deserves special recognition here: the late Professor Donald M. Murray. A man who had a Pulitzer Prize to his credit before he was thirty, an editorial writer for Boston newspapers, and a noted scholar teaching writing at the University of New Hampshire, this remarkable and esteemed colleague had signed on with me to mastermind the project's writing recommendations. If I was the coach, Don was the quarterback. His game plan was smart and simple: "You don't teach anything. You let the students write, you read what they've written with the class, and then you each try to help each of them say what he has to say."[8] His practical suggestions involved teaching the youngsters the importance of seeing and choosing an effective form in which to communicate what was seen. Then you drafted, revised, and revised again until it was time to edit. First, you made it right, and then you made it meaningful. This rare colleague died of heart failure at the age of 82, admired by everyone who knew him. I will forever be in his debt.

For almost three years, our team of specialists worked seamlessly and impressively, based mainly on trust and optimism. As Rocky would say, we had little hope of winning, but we damn well were going to give it our best shot.

Dean Alfred B. Rollins, Jr. introduced the La Mancha Project to the academic community with these words, "Any fresh attack upon an educational problem is an exciting thing. New and vigorous approaches are rare in our bland era. We have accustomed ourselves to the mask of conformity and caution until we have all but forgotten what it is to give our deep enthusiasm to a cause."[9] English Department Chairperson Samuel N. Bogorad offered a cautionary warning about the "sad state "of written English, as well as his belief that "written English could be improved."[10] *The Burlington Free Press* assigned reporter Wally Johnson to do a series on the project and monitor its results.

What happened is covered with a modicum of discretion in two talks presented here. In a newsletter edited by the irreplaceable Professor Littleton "Tiny" Long, we published the anticipated mixed feedback from the participating eight schools. For example, Champlain Valley Union High School wrote, "…students are writing better and they still like to come to class—how much closer to an impossible dream may one dare to go?"[11] North Country Union High School agreed saying, "Basically, I think the La Mancha Project has begun well. I think some doors are opening, some former assumptions are tottering." The writer also made clear, "We have all agreed the La Mancha Project has failed for the lower level student. I have not found this to be as true with the workshop setting. I am not, however, ready to proclaim Murray as the savior of the non-academic student."[12] Hartford High School responded, "Our use of the program may not seem dramatically different or unique on the surface—but the quiet and deep concern for the achievement of better writing habits in each individual student has definitely paid off. We have over thirty folders filled with papers to prove it."[13] Finally, there were the generous comments by South Burlington High School teacher Tim Comolli, one of the guiding spirits of the project: "There have, of course, been failures with the composition based curriculum—we expected that. In proper perspective, however, there have been numerous successful advances. Proof of the success might well be shown in the freshman curriculum for next year, which includes almost the exclusive use of La Mancha techniques as a basis for instruction."[14] In the end, *The Burlington Free Press* stated in its final article on the project, "Not only did the project help the students, it also helped the teachers. There is a greater amount of cooperation than ever before between the university and the schools, and this is an added gain which certainly will aid in furthering this and other projects."[15]

My feeling, these many decades later, is that with all its flaws, missteps, and clashing personalities, The La Mancha Project symbolized what Marshall McLuhan eloquently argued: "…our educational task was not only to provide tools of perception, but also to develop judgment and discrimination with ordinary experiences."[16] Although the program folded before reaching its five-year goal, it left many positive footprints. And while you will no doubt notice how outdated the equipment is, you should also be aware how today's advanced technology can make such a pioneering undertaking easier and more successful. For interested readers who want more information, I suggest reading the July 1970 *La Mancha Newsletter*, where two of my all-time favorite teachers provide an entire 9th Grade syllabus for the La Mancha Program.[17] It is available in the UVM archives.

One last anecdote before we turn to the two reprinted essays. While the La Mancha Program was at its height, I was invited to interview for the chairmanship of New York University's Graduate film program. I did not get the job, but upon my return to the campus the Dean called me into his office. Both my department chair and he were worried that I would soon leave UVM. They felt the NYU offer was a harbinger of things to come. Consequently, to keep me here, I was handed a large raise and given automatic tenure.

Tell me you don't think that was a good sign; that my long quest to teach films was over?

Notes

[1] Morten Tyldum, *The Imitation Game* USA: The Weinstein Company, 2014.
[2] John F. Kennedy, Address in the Assembly Hall at the Paulskirche in Frankfurt. June 25, 1963.
[3] Qtd. in F. Paul Driscoll, "Opera Queen," *Opera News,* March 2016, 4.
[4] Mike Leigh, *Mr. Turner*. Britain: Film4, 2014.
[5] François Truffaut, *Fahrenheit 451*. Britain: J. Arthur Rank, 1966.
[6] Ray Bradbury, *Fahrenheit 451*. New York: Ballantine Books, 1953.
[7] Obituary: Bonnie Christensen, *Burlington Free Press*, January 24, 2015, 6C.
[8] Donald M. Murray, "Give Your Students the Writer's Five experience," *The La Mancha Project: Proceedings of the University of Vermont's First Annual Model School Conference*, eds. Frank Manchel and Tom Devine, Burlington, Vermont: May 31- June 2, 1968. 21.
[9] Dean Alfred B. Rollins, Jr., "Introduction," *The La Mancha Project: Proceedings of the University of Vermont's First Annual Model School Conference*. V.
[10] Samuel N. Bogorad, Introduction," Ibid., VI.
[11] Shirley S. Collins, Champlain Valley Union High School," *The La Mancha Newsletter*, ed. Littleton Long. Vol. 1. May 1969. 3.
[12] Richard Welles, "North Country Union High School," Ibid., 14.
[13] Mrs. Susan Carpenter, "Hartford High School," Ibid., 7.
[14] Timothy Comolli, "South Burlington High School," Ibid., 18.
[15] Wally Johnson, La Mancha Project Is a Hit, According to Students," *The Burlington Free Press*, (Last in a series), September 27, 1969.
[16] Frank Manchel, "The Universal Classroom," in *Conference on Teaching the Slow Learner* (Metropolitan School Study Conference: The English Committee of the Metropolitan School Study Conference, 1964.
[17] Alison M. Dayton and Jean M. Minotti, "Ninth Grade General Program in Mass Communication (Revised Curriculum)," *The La Mancha Newsletter* II: 1 July 1970. 22pp.

Year I

VOLUNTEERS FOR LA MANCHA

My presentation on a philosophy for a model school project is divided into four parts. The first is a working definition of philosophy. The second is concerned with the purposes of the program. The third discusses the type of teacher we need for this work. The fourth deals with the institutions that are connected with this study. To put it another way, I will be dealing with the four questions of *what, why, who* and *where* (in the sense of the situation or environment).

I begin by discussing a relevant meaning of philosophy for this group because we need to create among ourselves what Professor Lewis Leary of Columbia University calls a constellation of discourse rather than a universe of discourse. Before we can hope to communicate effectively with each other, we need to understand each other's way of speaking.

A wag once defined the difference between the philosopher and the theologian by saying that the philosopher goes down into the basement to find a black cat that isn't there—and the theologian finds it.

I prefer to accept the lexical meaning of philosophy, which emphasizes the love of wisdom. To me, this interpretation of philosophy epitomizes a man's search rather than a man's achievements, a dream rather than a reality, a hope rather than a fact.

It is crucial to our common undertaking that we understand the implications of this definition for the task that lies ahead. It means, as Socrates pointed out centuries ago, that we honor wisdom, and not claim to have it. It means that the quest for wisdom is unending; that there is no final answer. And, it means we must have the courage to follow wherever wisdom beckons.

How does one go about finding wisdom, or more precisely for our purposes, of developing an educational philosophy for teaching writing? Here, I was influenced by Professor Philip Phenix at Teachers College, Columbia University. He taught me that philosophy consists of two aspects: (1) analysis and (2) synthesis, the point being that philosophy is not an empirical science, which tells us about things. Rather it is the philosopher's responsibility to try to understand critically what individuals mean in their utterings. What is implicit in their assumptions, pre-suppositions and unstated arguments? Here the philosopher is performing the task of analysis. His next job is to place all experience into some kind of pattern: the job of synthesis, which involves all possible forms of human experience since nothing is foreign to philosophy.

To do this, the philosopher uses the most difficult method known to man: thought. In one way or another, he thinks about what he experiences and tries to establish meanings and relationships.

At this moment you may be thinking, "What does this have to do with a model school writing program?" Let me explain. Writing needs to be an imaginative, all-consuming experience. It is not something that should be done to pass a course. It is not something that begins at 8 a.m. and ends when the class is over. Most important, it is not something that takes place without thinking. The writer needs to reflect on what he wants to write. He needs to develop some method whereby his thoughts can make sense to his audience.

But we, too, need to think about our audience: the students. We need to remember that the youngsters we teach today have as much to learn by studying the problems of the living, as by understanding the lessons of the past.

To put it another way, we need to ask ourselves a number of questions about our present composition programs. For example, are our students really interested in what we are doing? How do we know? Do they respect us enough to be honest in what they write? Should they? Do the members of an academic community in a comprehensive high school or a university recognize their mutual responsibilities to teach writing or is each individual blaming someone else for not doing the job? How much interaction is there between the teacher and the student, the school and the community, the community and the world?

The last question is particularly important for this project. To my way of thinking, we should be working toward a better relationship among widely diverse educational and business groups.

Even more than this, it is my dream that we can bring the young and the old, the bright and the slow, the mighty and the meek to a true ecumenical harmony. If we can agree to set our search on such an impossible dream, then we will truly be in agreement with the best traditions of American education.

II

Let me now move quickly to review how our present quest got started and what are its major goals. I do this because unless we are able to understand what tangible knowledge it is we seek, we will never be able to measure how far we've come.

Near the end of 1967, a private foundation (which chooses to remain anonymous) began negotiations with several professors and administrators at the University of Vermont, myself included, exploring ways in which writing could be improved. Naturally, we recognized the complexity of the problem: the variety of meanings connected with "writing," the variety of schools in the state, the variety of departments involved in writing, the variety of students, and on *ad infinitum*. But we also recognized the fact that methods for improving writing needed to be examined not only because teaching writing is every educator's responsibility, but also because writing is an invaluable skill which every educated person uses throughout his life. We further recognized the need to follow what Northrop Frye calls "...the mysterious law which says no society can flourish, or in the modern world even survive, until it learns never to leave well enough alone." As a result of our initial discussions, it was agreed to design a five-year model secondary school composition program that would involve a number of high schools (ten, so far) and the University of Vermont.

Together the various schools and the University of Vermont have four general purposes: (1) to improve written English utilizing modern theories of learning and technology; (2) to carry on research in the improvement of writing, *e.g.*, methodology, materials and motivation; (3) to coordinate needed writing skills in all departments at the secondary school level (and hopefully at the University); and (4) to disseminate useful materials and findings throughout school systems in Vermont.

These purposes rest on several basic assumptions: (1) the teaching of writing needs to be improved; (2) the teaching of writing can be improved; (3) very few teachers have been prepared to deal with the problem; and (4) present school conditions prohibit effective writing classes.

To this end, the University of Vermont, aided by a sizeable grant from the private foundation, has asked South Burlington High School to act as the model school. It is our hope that what we begin here will help point the way towards solving some of the fundamental problems of technique, interest, and subject matter.

And thus we come to the purposes of our weekend conference. This meeting is to help design a 9th grade composition program for the model school. Assembled here are invited representatives from all the high schools, specialists in the field of composition, members of the business world, and talented educators from several universities. South Burlington High School has agreed to put into practice the theories, suggestions, and materials resulting from this conference.

Following this meeting, and during the summer, seven South Burlington High School teachers, with my help, will write a composition program. It is important to re-emphasize two assumptions of that program: (1) it will be based upon what we discuss here; and (2) it will be for all departments, not English alone.

From September, 1968, until June of 1969, while the 9th grade pilot project is being tested not only at the model school but also throughout the state of Vermont, high school representatives will come to South Burlington once a month to evaluate the program and offer constructive criticism. They will also apprise us of the composition work being done in their individual schools.

In January 1969, we will meet to discuss the progress of the project and to begin planning for the second annual conference so that a 10th grade pilot program can be designed for September 1969.

Hopefully after five years of planning, testing, evaluating, revising, and implementing, we will have the beginnings of an adequate sequential composition curriculum for grades 9-12.

III

At this point, I would like to turn your attention to the type of teacher who should be involved in this impossible journey. Unless we have a person who possesses certain qualities, we will be unable to develop any effective aspect of the program. To me, the following traits are crucial:

1. The first trait is *an ability to live with frustration.* No teacher can exist in this program if he expects to find pleasure or positive results from every method suggested by the conference. The best that he can hope is that each step taken may bring with it a better understanding of the problem, and thus a possible solution. If there is any satisfaction connected with this program, the teacher probably will find it in his students' involvement and growth. Therefore, any tangible rewards should be sought at the conclusion of our work rather than at the beginning.

2. A second basic trait is *a respect for the dignity of all students.* We no longer live in a world that tolerates a few men living well while others are allowed to just live. Nor should we! Similarly, teachers need to understand that all students, in order to have human dignity, need to learn to write, and that *this* program is designed to help every possible student, and not just English majors, college bound.

3. A third basic trait is *a moral awareness of what* is *right and wrong.* In one way or another many teachers have been taught to deny their consciences. They know that much of their methodology is outdated. They know that many of the textbooks used in the schools are inaccurate. They know that it is wrong to deny students the right to disagree. They know that it is wrong for incompetent administrators to retain the power of curriculum decisions. They know that scholarship is an indispensable part of good teaching. They know that schools were meant to meet society's needs and not teachers' egos. They know and yet there are those who do nothing. The teacher in this program needs to feel that what he is doing is honest, based on current research, and worthwhile. He also needs to believe that what he does makes a difference. Scholarship, method, and conscience, rather than vanity, power, and fear should guide his work.

4. A fourth basic trait is *humility.* In the search for truth, a man

needs to recognize his limitations. He needs to know that what he uncovers may be of use only to him and his work. He needs to know that his research may only shed a glimmer of light on the problem. He must be aware above all else that the teacher-learning process is a dialogue. We cannot have in this project the educator who assumes that learning is painless, that the major responsibility for learning rests with the student, that the teacher's knowledge of the subject matter is all-important, and that educational theory is subordinate to content. The teacher in our program needs to reject such nonsense. Instead, he must encourage a critical exchange between students and himself. He must understand that the process will be demanding and trying. He must face the distinct possibility that he may fail in his work, and he must be willing to start again. But the humble teacher knows that unless one is willing to learn himself, he is hardly qualified to teach others.[1]

5. A fifth trait, which is basic for the model schools' teacher, is *an ability to change.* Nothing is more ludicrous than the idea that there can be a great teacher who has nothing worth learning. The educational world is going through a much needed and long overdue revolution. Students, parents, politicians and the lunatic fringe are raising issues, which need to be faced. All of these people have the right to question. All of these citizens have a stake in the educational process. It is true, mass media coverage notwithstanding, that much of what they criticize in us is a result of their past ignorance and meager contributions. We cannot have good schools and good teachers unless we have the help and cooperation of the community. But there are some objections they raise which are valid. Why, for example, should students have to meet day after day at the same time in the same seat discussing the same material in the same way? Why must youngsters always be homogenously grouped in their academic classes? Why must young adults always be graded with letters or numbers? Why is it harder, as Professor Edward Gordon of Yale University points out, for students to get into a school library than any other room in the building? Why do the schools continue to exist in a print-oriented setting while the world has become a mass media society? Why is there hardly a book studied in the English classroom which gives a positive view, for example, of the business world, the professions, or politics?

The teacher in this program recognizes the need for adapting his methods and materials to meet the changing requirements that a true twentieth century education demands. He knows, among other things, that it is more important for his students to write on a variety of subjects than just to write literary analyses for the English teacher; that it is more helpful to understand the influence of motion pictures than the problems of Silas Marner; that it is more relevant to study a nation's shame through modern means of communication than by reading *The Last of the Mohicans* or *Uncle Tom's Cabin*; and it is more vital to the mental health of nations to appreciate the necessity for seeking justice whatever the price than for defending one's limited interests.

6. The sixth and last trait I will deal with here is *a personal commitment*. There are those in teaching who have forgotten how important it is to keep abreast of current research, to maintain standards of excellence in their classrooms, and to pursue better ways of doing their important work. The teacher in this program needs to know that the major responsibility for accomplishing his objectives in his classroom rests with him alone. He must direct himself and he must feel that no matter what others may think or do, success with students will ultimately depend on his ability to devise a method that allows for intellectual curiosity.

IV

We come now to the final part of this paper: the schools. From the outset, I have tried to suggest a model educational community for teachers and students alike. To do this work, therefore, we need a proper atmosphere. If our purposes are to be achieved, then the schools have the responsibility for creating a climate that will allow us to reconstruct a new image of education. The schools must be seen as an oasis where people who thirst for knowledge can come to drink and not be denied. The schools must be seen as a beacon that lights the way to bettering mankind rather than signals a society's mediocrity. The schools must be seen as a leader among sincere but misguided men, rather than a follower of undesirable philistines.

I, therefore, would like to suggest the following seven recommendations as a beginning towards this dream:

Recommendation 1. School systems in this program set-aside time once a month for a composition council (made up of representatives from the various disciplines) to plan, discuss, and evaluate the progress in their schools' composition program.

Recommendation 2. School systems should allocate money so that representatives can be sent to special conferences on writing as well as partake in the evaluation sessions at South Burlington High School.

Recommendation 3. Every effort should be made to help teachers in this program achieve their goals. This applies to scheduling, room assignments, released time, and pilot materials.

Recommendation 4. Each school system should examine the possibility of incorporating more innovative procedures into the program. In particular, school staffs could consider purchasing television-taping materials, movie-making equipment, and tape recorders. They can experiment, for example, with different types of scheduling, teaching, grading, and subject matter.

Recommendation 5. The goals of each school system should act as a measuring instrument for the values of this program. Those aims should be clearly defined so that members of the project can have some guidelines for developing useful materials.

Recommendation 6. School systems should prepare an annual statement regarding the progress of their composition work. Such reports should include constructive suggestions for improvement, as well as a genuine reaction to the project.

Recommendation 7. One person in each school system should be assigned the responsibility for implementing the writing materials. That individual would also have the task of coordinating the school's activities with outside members of the composition project.

In conclusion, I have tried to suggest a composition program based upon humanistic principles rather than on polluted procedures. Perhaps you do not agree with my point of view. Perhaps you feel that it can't be done because of present conditions in the educational world. Perhaps you are right. But we need to try. We need, more than ever, to be true to our youthful dreams, and, to paraphrase the words of a popular song:

The world will be better for this,
That some teachers, scorned and covered with scars,
Still strive, with their last ounce of courage
To reach the unreachable stars.

May 31, 1968

Notes

[1] My discussion of the following traits is indebted to a speech given by Professor Sheila Schwartz at the CEE Boulder Conference in 1968.

5. Members of the La Mancha Project community:
   Top, left to right: Prof. Robert Cochran, Prof. Don Gregg, Prof. Frank Manchel, and Prof. Don Murray.
   Bottom, left to right: Mr. Tom Devine, Ms. Lucille White, Ms. Esther J. Urie, Prof. David Howell, and Prof. Don Murray.

Year II

REVERSING THE PROCESS

Three important facts have emerged from the initial year of the La Mancha Project. First, the incredible inefficiency of the existing educational system. Second, the demonstrated ability of enthusiastic and competent teachers to reform that system. And third, the undeniable necessity to study mass media in the schools.

No one needs to describe to professional teachers the mess in our classrooms. We have lived too long with programs designed to comfort the lazy, to placate the spineless, and to shelter the incompetent. For too long we have excused this educational sham by worshipping the idol of precedent, by deceiving ourselves that tradition was synonymous with truth. Fortunately, this mental mediocrity is coming to an end. We are at last realizing, as Emerson pointed out decades ago, that "Education dwarfs those who conform to its standards."

If the warning buzzer has sounded for the long awaited reforms, it is, in part, because of the dedication and skill of the La Mancha teachers. They have succeeded in spite of insufferable scheduling problems, extremely limited funds, and unbelievably complacent colleagues. If next year, many more ninth grade, college-bound students are involved in writing workshops, inter-disciplinary curricula, and mass media studies, it is because a handful of people, scorned and scarred, are still reaching for the unreachable stars.

Even so, many teachers I meet still question the value of this romantic quest to improve the teaching of writing in the schools. They skeptically ask, "Just what's so new or so good about the La Mancha Project?" I try to explain the value of our three annual state conferences—September, January and April—during which we bring high school teachers and students together to discuss curricular matters; the value of composition workshops at the University of Vermont where *we pay* teachers to study evaluation techniques for use in *their* classrooms; the value of having both a state literary magazine and a state newspaper to publish students' writings; the value of a state newsletter for teachers to improve their own writing skills while at the same time providing an exchange for information about writing; and the value of frequent lesson plans and study guides to stimulate discussion about composition.

"That's fine:" they say, "but what's so new about the teaching of writing? We've been using Professor Don Murray's workshop methods and Dr. James Moffett's sequential approach for years." Maybe so. But when I go into these teachers' classrooms, talk with their students and question how often they write each week, meet in small groups to read each other's papers, get to choose their own topics, discuss the techniques of writing in history and science classes; select their own books, see full-length feature films, and so on *ad infinitum*, their usual responses are "Not very often…rarely… never!"

Maybe what we're doing here in the state of Vermont is not new or refreshing. Maybe the thousands of college freshmen who enter the University of Vermont have forgotten how they were taught to write, or maybe the hundreds of high school classrooms I visit each year are not valid examples of what teachers are doing in today's dehumanized educational environment. Maybe so!

No matter. Our main thrust is not to prove how revolutionary we are. Nor is it to show how meaningful changes can be achieved by moderate, able and determined individuals who choose to remain in the school system rather than escape from it. Instead, the La Mancha Project is concerned with *studying the process of writing, especially the areas of composing and communicating.* Starting with the assumption that the most important ingredient in studying student writing is the student himself, each of us is trying to discover not only how we can be more effective in helping adolescents to express themselves better, but also how we can make the work more enjoyable for everyone.

With such vague and non-behavioral objectives, it is not hard to understand why the program has a number of critical weaknesses. Our communications operation is badly constructed and articulated. Our methods of evaluation leave much to be desired. Schools find it difficult to implement some of our materials. And many English departments are unable to co-ordinate their classes with their counterparts in the physical and social sciences. It would appear to those outside our world that we are indeed madmen hopelessly fighting windmills which, as in another romantic setting the arrogant De Guiche told Cyrano, "may swing round their huge arms and cast you down into the mire."

But this is only *a* possibility. Another possibility suggested by Cyrano is that we might go "up—among the stars." Fortunately, there is reason for optimism in our work. By not deluding the schools or ourselves that there were any ready-made solutions, we have had to re-examine what we have been doing, and we have re-learned some essential propositions about writing in general and program organization in particular. First, it has become clear to all of us that writing is essentially a process of weaving many varied strands into a finished work. It cannot be taught or learned quickly. It cannot be structured the same way with each individual, let alone with each class and school. And no one involved with the process can succeed without patience, skill, and motivation. Still further, the learner benefits more from encouragement than from negative comments. Too often, critics and colleagues forget this. Second, no one writes just for the sake of writing. Hopefully, he has something to say. His subject matter consists of ideas, facts, and opinions, shaped by language and syntax. To a large degree, that subject matter is the basis of a significant academic program and those who administer the schools need to provide a suitable setting, which will improve, not impede, the learning process. Third, the writer needs both imagination and discipline to communicate effectively with his intended audience. He must, in effect, be stimulated by the unlimitable possibilities that are open to him and then helped to discriminate between what he thinks he sees and what he actually sees. Fourth, the teaching of writing requires that we ourselves be willing to learn: learn not only about the writing process but also about the art of teaching. There is no place in our program for those who have already decided that there is nothing new worth discovering.

We have also realized that our work is most effective when the following organizational plan is carefully followed:

1. Teachers from the various disciplines set aside a predetermined time each month for the entire school year to plan, discuss, and evaluate the program.

2. Administrators give the teachers money, time, and respon-

sibility for attending La Mancha conferences and evaluation sessions.

3. High school departments maintain their individuality; otherwise they have nothing of value to offer us except servitude. All that we ask is that our materials and methods be tried, and that the schools inform us of the results coupled with the reasons why.

4. One person in each school, designated as a coordinator, maintains continuous communication both with the staff and the La Mancha director.

5. When the approaches prove successful, the schools implement them in their curricula next year for all students at that grade level and in that program. For example, departments should now be planning a ninth grade college-bound curriculum which includes field trips, in-class reading libraries, motion picture screenings and discussions, class publications, peer-group paper conferences, and inter-disciplinary writing assignments.

In essence, our investigations so far have helped us to discover a great deal about our needs, about our relations with other human beings, and about ourselves. In each instance, we have witnessed the tremendous influence of the mass media not only in our lives but also in our culture. Consequently, the La Mancha Project, in 1969-1970, is turning its attention towards more meaningful ways of using films, books, drama, radio, television, speech, tape recorders, magazines, newspapers, and recordings in the teaching of writing.

Our main concern now is how to relate the teaching of writing to the student's thoughts and experiences, how to encourage adolescents to examine and to understand themselves through writing and working with the mass media. In effect, we are reversing the existing educational system. Instead of prescribing, we are searching: instead of limiting, we are extending; instead of talking, we are acting. To repeat, the essential problem for us is how the student adjusts himself to the world in which he lives. And following the teachings of the distinguished scholar Jean Piaget we are not ashamed of the concept of adjustment. Its meaning denotes stopping and starting, winning and losing, comprehending and gaining knowledge. As Piaget explains it:

Knowledge is not a copy of reality. To know an object, to know an event, is not simply to look at and make a mental copy, or image, of it. To know an object is to act on it. To know is to modify. To transform the object, and to understand the process of this transformation, and as a consequence understand the way the object is constructed. An operation is thus the essence of knowledge; it is an interiorized action, which modifies the object of knowledge.

It is our hope, therefore, that through the study of the process of communication, we will become more knowledgeable about the teaching of writing. Furthermore, we believe that knowledge of the various communication processes will help interested individuals to discover for themselves what they think and feel about the mass media, and why they accept or reject one work of art rather than another.

So much for next year's major theme. Unless we understand *the emphasis on examining the processes of mass media,* we will fail before the school year begins in September. Let me focus now on some other relevant matters for 1969-1970: such concerns as the need for standards, the two new programs to be developed this summer, and the individual school responsibilities.

Basic to any study we conduct is the tacit agreement that we are not going to vulgarize the curriculum. It is one thing to want to teach about mass media and something else to know how. Students, for example, spend thousands of hours watching television, and we need to exercise judgment in deciding what is worthwhile discussing. Watching movies is also a valuable experience as is listening to recordings or reading newspapers, but not when they are used as escapes from the more important job of critical discussions and inquiry. Therefore, we encourage, not discourage, teachers to use discrimination in their selection of classroom materials.

Another difficulty with the teaching of mass media is that many people unwittingly accept the current pop fallacy, "anyone born later in history knows more than his predecessors." It is not our intention to replace the study of the past with the study of the popular and the present. We intend, instead, to combine the best of both worlds because they share a common heritage and thus similar human experiences and difficulties. To put it another way, our study of the mass media rests on the principle that acknowledges both the psychological needs of the young and the logical demands of the material. We do not intend to compromise either our educational principles or our responsibility to provide sound leadership.

As a result, we are preparing two mass media programs for 1969-1970: one for ninth-grade general students at Champlain Valley Union High School; one for tenth-grade college-bound students at South Burlington High School. Both courses will be based on a sound educational foundation, not on an emotional one. CVU's curriculum, for example, will emphasize not only the various kinds of mass media that influence an individual's opinions, attitudes, and judgments, but also how these media function and develop. The overall objective is critical thought.

At the same time, students will be encouraged to explore filmmaking, television production, and newspaper publishing. The SBHS curriculum will also explore these areas; only the emphasis will be more on drama, speech, television, and motion pictures. In each school, including those in the Project that will try these materials in other curricula, the students, across departmental boundaries, will be communicating their feelings, their ideas, and their standards. What they say, how they express it, and what it means for education form the nucleus of this year's La Mancha Project.

Let me illustrate just one way in which we are going about our work for the next year: film study in the schools.

Recognizing that some of the formidable problems connected with screen education—a responsibility that also includes the study of television—are accessibility and availability of equipment and materials not only for instructors but also for individual students, the La Mancha teachers are implementing many of the major findings of the recently concluded Project in Educational Communication of Teachers College, Columbia University, under the able direction of Dr. Louis Forsdale. The TC project, for example, established that an important solution to availability was the 8mm cartridge projector, which allows individuals as well as groups to examine closely and repeatedly particular motion pictures. While the value of close reading has always been a part of any worthwhile academic enterprise, it has not always been possible with movies.

Now, with the 8mm cartridge projectors, films can be carefully and continually scrutinized.

Consequently, the La Mancha Project, in cooperation with several Vermont high schools, is beginning to build a collection of important silent films in cartridges, and five Fairchild Mark IVRV projectors have been ordered for a number of learning centers in the state. Included are films by D. W. Griffith, Charles Chaplin, Douglas Fairbanks, Sr., W. S. Hart, Edwin S. Porter, George Melies, and Mack Sennett. Students and teachers will be able to use these motion pictures both as a source for serious study and for enjoyment.

We are using a number of sources for ordering such films, almost all of which are listed in *8mm Film Directory* (Comprehensive Service Corporation, 250 West 64th Street, New York, 10023).

Since the Fairchild cartridge holds approximately twenty-five minutes of film, it will be most useful for short movies. Full-length features will be serialized, i.e., put into a series of cartridges. Because the Mark IV - RV projector requires no special lighting conditions, skill, or room orientation, students are able to operate the machine after several minutes' instruction. Each cartridge will be labeled and shelved in a special reserve section either in the library or a designated learning center. As we continue in this area, critical commentaries on each film plus relevant books, articles and still-shots will be added to the resource areas.

Students will also make their own films, many of which will be subsidized by the Project. In this connection, we have purchased and made available to the cooperating schools cameras, projectors, and editing equipment. Explicitly and implicitly, the La Mancha Project is trying to provide a film study program that creates opportunities for individual development in such important areas as taste and creativity.

The relation to writing should be clear. By studying films closely, the student has another source for ideas in his written work. By having to organize, develop, and translate his ideas into a finished film or report, he is going through another example of how one must discipline his imagination in order to communicate effectively with an audience. By editing his rough cut of the film, the student is learning the value of re-examining and re-working his raw material. This is not to say that film production and writing are exactly similar. It is to say that they have a lot in common. It is not to say that we are throwing out writing for filming. It is to say that by relating one to the other, the student may see more clearly the differences inherent in each. In short, teaching a person to be sensitive to one art is a beginning in teaching him to be sensitive to all arts.

Finally, there is the problem of each school's responsibility for next year. Here it is mainly a belief in one's ability to accept the challenge of change. The La Mancha teacher needs to acknowledge that somehow his success in the project will depend to a large degree upon the extent of his commitment. He must acknowledge that there is a need to close the shocking gap between the world and the classroom; he must realize that in spite of the present crisis of belief that extends from the sunken earth to the majestic heavens, an effective teacher can make a difference. He must understand that what he does with his students in relation to mass media study has a relevancy not only for writing but also for helping develop a better world. And he must believe that no matter how great the challenge, it must be met.

This then is what the La Mancha Project means for 1969-1970. It will not be any easier than in past years. The world has not changed dramatically and we be but mortal men. Nevertheless, as George Bernard Shaw once said and as Robert Kennedy reminded us anew, "Some men see the world as it is and say why; others dream of things that never were and say why not?"

6. The author with Clarence Muse, The Dean of Black Character Actors during the first half of the Twentieth Century.

5.

From Mediocrity to Excellence

Cinema's historians should celebrate, as audiences always have, not only the obsessed geniuses but also the adaptable ruffians who made many of the most entertaining movies ever to come out of Hollywood.[1]

David Denby

Hollywood is collaboration. There are many rulers in the Hollywood power game. The most important is the collaboration between the director and the producer. Movies are a medium based on consensus. Now in the old days, you dealt with moguls and major studios. Today you have executives and giant corporations instead. But one iron rule remains true: every decision is shaped by the money men's perception of what the audience wants.[2]

Martin Scorsese

Trust yourself.[3]

Ralph Waldo Emerson

I am always amazed by the changing seasons, Nature's wondrous display of birth, death, and rebirth. Or take the images of a harsh winter, where walking in the snow can be cold, dangerous, and painful. Then you watch David Lean's Lara in her winter home, and the snow glistens on the trees and magic is everywhere. In Julie Christie's eyes, there is hope and excitement and beauty. But like the seasons, Lara's fate changes, and Lean adapts Boris Pasternak's novel into a poignant, nostalgic screen drama about obsession and revolution a century ago.[4]

Doctor Zhivago hit the movie houses at about the same time I began writing my doctoral dissertation at Teachers College, Columbia University. A year earlier, 1963, TC had become for me the equivalent of finding King Solomon's mines. Recognized as one of the world's finest teacher training institutions, its impressive English Department helped initiate a new graduate program, and the school boasted of having some of the nation's most important educational trailblazers. Three of them would shape my career ever after: Louis C. Forsdale, Robert A. Bone, and Robert L. Allen.

Before I share my memories of those extraordinary men and introduce this chapter's selection, let me, briefly and in simple words, put my doctoral adventures in a historical context.

For over half a century, the nation's tastemakers had disparaged the mass media in general and American movies in particular. Simultaneously, educators falsely preached refinement and art came only from Europe, whereas our popular indigenous culture was immature, trite; even worse, it corrupted our standards and values. The movies, for the most part, were perceived as anti-intellectual and irresponsible, the medium demonized bankers, wealthy people, and our nation's leaders; while at the same time, films glorified self-made nobodies who irrationally championed morality over self-interest. Thus, the self-appointed and mistaken educational gurus had tried unsuccessfully to make me feel as if my great love was little more than a lowbrow distraction, one that impeded my intellectual growth. The only films they considered artistic were those with subtitles.

But after World War II, the cultural winds shifted. No longer were matters of taste and judgment one-dimensional. Economics provided the major incentive for change. The international film industry, damaged by incalculable chaos, was on the mend. Hollywood, too, had a silver lining. Overseas distribution sources, foreign movie theaters, and once thriving international production centers, now re-emerging, proved a windfall for America's producers and distributors. European artists felt the same about our markets.

Topping the artistic cross-fertilization was the new Italian film movement, known as Neo-Realism. Basically a low budget, on location style showcasing Italy's postwar problems, these heartbreaking movies moved away from escapist themes toward a documentary-like quality and took hold of our collective consciousness. One of the best films was Vittorio De Sica's *Ladri di Biciclette (Bicycle Thieves)*,[5] a realistic tale about a working class man and his son desperately searching for his stolen bike and his only means of earning a living. If the Neo-Realists had any drawbacks, it was that our self-appointed political guardians feared the Italians' subversive leftist ideology. Meanwhile, other countries around the globe produced their own significant film movements.

Hollywood responded first by exporting our quarantined films from World War II. The impact these highly anticipated movies had both on overseas audiences and European filmmakers was electrifying. Then, as the foreigners started sending us their groundbreaking pictures, we opened up Art Houses, where the highly acclaimed movies received a royal reception.

One of the most sweeping events growing out of this period resulted from a film aficionado named Henri Langlois, who had established the legendary Cinematheque Francaise before the war. Not only did this legendary archivist preserve many remarkable films during the late thirties and early forties, but also after 1945, his marvelous film library became a major source for Europeans to learn about film history. Among his most devoted viewers were a group of delinquent college students who spent most of their time watching old and new films instead of going to their scheduled classes. Because economic events made it impossible for them to make their own movies, the cinephiles, as they came to be known, inspired by the great film critic Andre Bazin, created a new magazine, *Cahiers du Cinema*. These radical French reviewers praised films from around the globe, but they insisted the gold standard was Hollywood. Their critical views were branded the Auteur Theory.

This cinematic renaissance produced a wealth of outstanding American film reviewers, none greater than Pauline Kael and Andrew Sarris. Their wondrous battles over the merits of the Auteur Theory, as well as their contrasting critical styles, showed us a new way to see and to talk about movies. Kael did this. Sarris did that. But not until I came to TC did I grasp the enormous influence these wondrous critics exerted on our culture.

The film world I first encountered as a kid had led me to directors like Frank Capra, John Ford, William Wyler, Billy Wilder,

John Huston, Otto Preminger, George Stevens, Alfred Hitchcock, and Howard Hawks. During the post-WWII era the Art Houses exposed me not just to Vittorio De Sica, Federico Fellini, and Michelangelo Antonioni, but also to the likes of Ingmar Bergman, François Truffaut, Akira Kurosawa, Kon Ichikawa, Andrzej Wajda, Roman Polanski, Michael Powell, Joseph Losey, Carol Reed, David Lean, Jean Renoir, Satyajit Ray, Marcel Ophuls, Ismail Merchant, Jan Kadar, and Milos Forman. Add to them the new American artists like Woody Allen, Robert Aldrich, Warren Beatty, John Cassavettes, Mel Brooks, John Frankenheimer, George Roy Hill, Mike Nichols, Sam Peckinpah, Stanley Kubrick, Stanley Kramer, and Orson Welles. Is it any wonder that by 1963, film became the academic community's intellectual coin of the realm? More important, my self-styled education had put me accidentally close to film education's vanguard.

Strangely, these developments had not completely entered my consciousness. I had come to film by necessity, not by intellect. My instinct, not logic, guided me. I watched rather than studied films. For example, I valued Sarris not for his film reviews, but for his constitutional positions published in the *Village Voice*. Still further, I remained clueless why film, now a hot scholarly commodity, remained so controversial to both public and higher education circles. Despite the fact my professors saw many films, talked about them over lunch, and used them as metaphors in their classes, the scholarly bookworms refused to consider admitting the movies to the curriculum.

What was the problem? My journey had benefited considerably from experiences in the darkened theaters. Why did celebrities like Joe McCarthy, Richard Nixon, Ronald Reagan, Cecil B. De Mille, and many of my conservative peers feel so threatened by the mass media? Demonizing these shameless personalities as elitists, snobs, super patriots, right-wingers, or fanatics didn't pass my smell test. Didn't Dalton Trumbo point out that we were all victims during the peaks of the Cold War? So what was going on? (More about the McCarthy era is in Chapter 8.)

Thus we come to 1963, TC, and three professors who played such a central role in my career: Louis C. Forsdale, Robert A. Bone, and Robert L. Allen.

Let's start with the last first. Bob Allen's specialty, linguistics and education, resulted in his pioneering an innovative approach to language study: Sector Analysis. The Iranian-born scholar's grammatical insights intrigued me. And I loved the schematic breakdowns that were at the center of his pioneering method. Ironically, in spring, 1963, Allen agreed to teach Sector Analysis to students at Southern Connecticut State College. He graciously brought me along as his teaching assistant. (Several years later I would teach a similar course to English teachers at Cheshire High School.)

Although Bob Bone did not arrive at TC until 1965, the Yale-educated intellectual brought with him not only excellent teaching techniques, but also an expertise in African American studies. He appeared on the scene much like an academic Alexander the Great. His masterly account of black literature in *The Negro Novel in America*[6] became one of the touchstones in my writings on the black film experience, culminating years later in *The Interviews*, a two-volume set of my conversations with screen veterans on black film history.[7] What made Bob's book so important to me was not only its scholarship, but also the fact it was written by a white man discussing African American issues.

But most influential was Lou Forsdale, who became not only my thesis advisor but also one of the men I most admired in my life. Although in poor health and plagued by personal problems, this amazing man befriended me in a remarkable way. Realizing his ill health made him unpredictable, he had me bring each chapter of my dissertation to his home. He then proceeded to critique it on the spot. I have never witnessed then or since so much integrity and dedication given generously from one person to another. I'd only add that Lou became justly famous for introducing Marshall McLuhan to American students.

All three mentors have passed on, but to me they remain like T.S. Eliot's characterization, men who are dead but very much alive. My admiration for them and what they did for me remains unqualified and unshakable.

What is it that I learned at TC from 1963 to 1966 that relates most to this narrative? The reader might think it would be screen education, or black literature, or possibly language study. Actually, the crown jewel was my study of mass communication history.

You need to remember my growing up independent and mostly self-educated resulted in my taking the mass media for granted. I saw it as rich and diverse and infinitely valuable as a learning tool. At TC, I learned that judging and appreciating media like film and television was much more complex than relying just on instinct and emotion. In our communication classes, I also discovered how information and news and advertising could educate and inspire us.

Just as importantly, I came to appreciate the dangers from the misuse of communication theories in the hands of evil people and authoritarian nations. In places like Germany, Italy, and Russia, wicked men could establish despotic governments that would destabilize the world. A group of academic émigrés, fleeing these fascist countries, came to the United States and founded a controversial movement called the Frankfurt School and taught about mass communications' many possible vices. For decades, impressionable teachers moving through the educational system studied how the mass media might, did, and continued to manipulate, distort, and degrade not only our tastes but also our very lives.

But I also studied how the popular arts and mass communication could be invaluable in keeping us informed, entertained, and in many cases, protected. The intellectual keys were context and public awareness. Thanks to the vigilance of a responsible and aggressive mass media, we could witness how differently mass communication behaved in different societies and unique situations. We observed the complex effects it might have on behavior, attitudes, opinions, and emotions. For example, when it first exploded on the scene in the nineteenth century, pioneered by journalism, and later motion pictures, mass communications challenged the establishment's misuse of power, prestige, and influence.

Suddenly, thanks in large part to mass media, ordinary and uneducated people realized they not only had options, but also they were not alone. The powerful realized almost immediately the forceful social and political revolution as well, and so began a struggle on how best to understand, to control, and to use mass communications. The power brokers' operating theory was the media acted as a hypodermic needle; and we, the audience, were passive, gullible, and directly affected by the media's message.

Absolutely not true! Mass communication scholars made clear there were many variables coming between us and the message—

e.g., age, gender, education, class, and economic status to name but a few. Among the greatest battles over the merits of the mass media took place in educational circles, where reputation and influence are so important. It was from these intellectual disagreements that a cold war between the Objectionables and me emerged. I would urge you to read Frank Rich's important book, *The Greatest Story Ever Sold*,[8] to see how mishandled and dangerous the mass media is in contemporary America. I would urge you just as strongly to watch HBO's brilliant documentary, *Nixon by Nixon*, to see how politicians manipulated the media at the end of the sixties and early seventies.[9]

From NRHS to SCSC to UVM, the issues about my passion for the popular arts remained basically the same. Was I or was I not a danger to traditional education? Would the movie mythmakers threaten our established ideas about how best to prepare our young people to assume their leadership role in the future? Did the cultural elite remain committed exclusively to the past or were they receptive to innovative ideas about life and learning? Most important, what should I do about my beliefs?

So by 1964, when my doctoral studies began in earnest, I found myself wrestling with the dilemma in three subcultures: where I worked, where I studied, and where I saw screen education throughout the nation. As I understood it then, the solution to the popular culture debate depended on scholarship and perseverance. But where was the leadership? What should be my role?

My thesis topic, therefore, focused on film as a new form of literature. Widespread confusion in the schools was evident. Misinformation left teachers eager to go into film study, but just how remained confusing. I would attempt to solve that problem by offering a framework for screen education.

But my proposed unconventional methodology caused a predictable uproar among the TC faculty. Based upon six different ways to study film, the format baffled some scholars who wondered what it had to do with this or any graduate English department. Foremost among the initial doubters was one of my idols, Bob Bone. He even halted my seminar presentation to convene an executive committee meeting to have Lou explain what the hell was going on.

Once that hurdle was passed, I submitted my prospectus to the college review committee, and they too raised serious reservations about the project, taking two years to resolve their skepticism. Meanwhile, the unruffled and brilliant Forsdale had me write the thesis. I finished it at almost the same time the committee approved the project in 1966.

For seven years, I tried to get my doctoral dissertation published, meeting resistance and scorn everywhere it was submitted. Meanwhile, I continued to teach and to write and to train prospective English teachers. There were, however, significant changes. No longer was I a nameless entity, subject to the whims of my grumpy colleagues. I began to publish both articles and books here and abroad (more of which in the next chapter). Particularly important, I was admitted into the Society for Cinema Studies, an exclusive and prestigious group of screen scholars numbering no more than thirty people nationwide. Their mission was to make film study a respected and serious academic discipline. This goal led to their holding a nationwide convention on film at UVM in 1973. Of great historical significance, this was the conference where the first panel ever on women's studies took place.

Then a visionary and supportive publisher named Julien Yoseloff decided to publish my doctoral thesis. In 1973, when *Film Study* appeared, the American Library Association honored it as the best reference book in its field! That same year a new dean was in office, thanks in large measure to the political machinations of the Objectionables. So it was that the elected leader of UVM's College of Arts and Sciences gave me the lowest raise in my career, justifying his actions by telling me to my face that it was a reprimand for getting too much too soon. This was the College's way of demonstrating intellectual leadership.

Notes

[1] David Denby, *Do The Movies Have a Future?* New York: Simon & Schuster, 2012. 198.
[2] Martin Scorsese, *A Personal Journey with Martin Scorsese Through American Movies*, England: British Film Industry, 1995.
[3] Ralph Waldo Emerson, "Self-Reliance: Essay II," *The Collected Works of Ralph Waldo Emerson*, Volume II. Introduced and edited by Joseph Slater.

Cambridge: Harvard University Press, 1979. 28.
[4] David Lean, *Doctor Zhivago*. USA: MGM, 1965.
[5] Vittorio De Sica, *Ladri di Biciclette (Bicycle Thieves)*. Italy: Produzioni De Sica, 1948.
[6] Robert A. Bone, *The Negro Novel in America*, Rev. Ed. New Haven: Yale University Press, 1965.
[7] Frank Manchel, *Every Step a Struggle: Interviews with Seven Who Shaped the African American Image in Movies*. Washington, D.C.: New Academia Publishing, 2007 and *Exits and Entrances: Interviews with Seven Who Reshaped the African American Image in Movies*. Ibid, 2013.
[8] Frank Rich, *The Greatest Story Ever **Sold**: The Decline and Fall of Truth From 9/11 to Katrina*. New York: The Penguin Press, 2006.
[9] Peter W. Kunhardt, *Nixon by Nixon: In His Own Words*. USA: HBO Documentary Films, 2014.

Introduction

> The question of educating the public to a better more critical appreciation of the films is a question of the mental health of nations.
>
> *Bela Balazs,* Theory of Film

This is not a methods book on how to teach about film, though it does offer in each of its eight chapters observations on current practices. Nor is this book an attempt to list definitively the various sources or materials connected with film study, though such a work would be welcome. It is a survey designed to describe six popular approaches to the study of the cinema, along with a practical analysis of selected books, materials and information about motion picture rentals.

It comes at a time when film study programs are rapidly increasing in the schools. In spite of this activity, most institutions still continue to relegate movies to the status of a textbook, an audio-visual aid to stimulate students to learn more about other academic subjects. No doubt A-V films, like textbooks, serve a variety of useful purposes. But there are many films, like books, which are works of art and deserve special consideration. Long ago educators realized such books existed. Now they have grasped that the same is true for the cinema.

While there is considerable interest—particularly among young people—in learning more about movies, few instructors are able to present useful film programs. Not only do lean budgets and poor facilities limit their efforts, but also the instructors themselves often have only limited knowledge about movies. They have not considered the principles of film art, or how these principles stem from the nature of the medium. Therefore, it comes as no surprise that film study in many schools is unsatisfactory, and that teachers need and want help in remedying the situation.

There are a number of groups and individuals trying to provide that help: workshops at national conventions and regional meetings, special summer courses, the efforts of the American Film Institute and sectional organizations, state-subsidized programs and aggressive academic departments. But the average teacher is often bewildered by offers of help. He needs assistance in choosing between the quality and suitability of the programs, the procedures for joining and participating in the activities, and in following up the suggestions made at these meetings. This book tries to help film students find useful sources of information about such film study aids.

There are other problems confronting confused teachers. We live in a cavalier age where irresponsible suggestions are not only available but also popular. Articles and books continue to appear suggesting that anyone can teach about film. No training is necessary; all you need to do is walk into a classroom and get students "involved" with the "relevance" of film and they will have a "meaningful experience." Behind these over-used and ill-defined concepts lie the false assumptions that we have nothing to learn from the past and anything new must be better than what has come before. I do not accept these assumptions. Certainly we can enjoy a film just by seeing it. Yet knowledge of history leads to a deeper appreciation of movies, and an understanding of film aesthetics increases our sense of enjoyment. This book reaffirms what competent teachers have always maintained: that good teaching provides bridges between the past and the present, which are meaningful and enjoyable. Where mediocrity and dullness are, bad teaching is also. Here methods and materials need revision. But we should not confuse change with progress. How to improve our teaching is a complex problem. And the best that can be said about a simple solution to a complex problem was phrased by H. L. Mencken, "It is simple, direct and it is wrong."

In considering change, it is useful to examine where we are. This book is organized so that the six most common approaches to film appreciation can be examined: a representative genre; stereotyping; thematic approach; comparative media; a representative period; and the history of film. None of the approaches has been exhaustively discussed. Appropriate materials (films, books, articles) have been suggested to help film students explore the subject further.

Each film entry, depending upon its context, is listed alphabetically and contains, in addition to its titles, the releasing company (country of origin), the film gauge (16mm, 35mm or 8mm), the year of its initial release, running time in minutes, special information (black and white or color, cinemascope prints, subtitles, etc.), and a special code abbreviation of the American distributor who has the film for rental, lease or sale.

The following is a typical entry:

> *The Prime of Miss Jean Brodie (Fox-16mm: 1969, 116 mins. b/w, sound, R-FNC)*
> *Ronald Neame directed this memorable film about the Edinburgh spinster, Jean Brodie, who shocks her colleagues at a staid school for girls by snubbing the prescribed curriculum and developing her own coterie of "Brodie girls." Maggie Smith is superb as the dogmatic schoolteacher who preaches the virtues of Mussolini and Franco, warps young minds, and ends up alone. Unfortunately, Jay Presson Allen based the screenplay on the stage play, which, in turn, had been adapted from Muriel Spark's novel. The book should have been the original source since it is much stronger.*

After the title comes the country of origin (or studio name when dealing with American films), that it is a 16mm print, first released in 1969, with a running time of 116 minutes, in black and white, with sound, and that it can be (R) rented from Films Incorporated; (S) would indicate that it is for sale; and (L) for lease. Also included is a brief description plus key personalities connected with the film. More often than not useful articles dealing with the movie or its cast will be footnoted on the page. Space and emphasis, however, sometimes require additional footnoting elsewhere and readers should check the index for more possible information.

In preparing the material and selecting the films, I have also used the following criteria:

1. The films had to be available to schools and students.
2. The range of the films had to represent the history of motion pictures, significant genres, and important artists.
3. The films, for the most part, had to demonstrate aesthetic excellence. I have drawn upon the judgment of recognized and re-

spected film critics and film historians as well as my own preferences.

4. The major emphasis is on fiction films: as a result, the majority of movies chosen are well-known theatrical films from different countries.

Books, monographs and screenplays have been, for the most part, annotated in the text proper. These annotations, chiefly critical and descriptive, suggest, in my opinion, the best of the existing materials now available in libraries and bookstores. Each has been read by me, and in most cases my opinions have been checked against book reviews by major scholars in many of the reputable film periodicals. The dates given suggest the best editions to study; the publishers listed are American, whenever possible; and asterisks are used to indicate paperback editions available at the time of this writing. To keep abreast of the new editions, readers should consult *Paperbound Books in Print*. Those who wish to study these works or purchase them should consult Appendix V, which lists major archives, libraries and rare book dealers.

Over the years, I have found it useful to consider the art of film as a systematic ordering of images, which might be said to have its own language, composition and literature. Such metaphorical extensions of traditional terms provide us with the means of approaching a new medium in familiar terms. What I mean by *language*, therefore, is the audio-visual mode of expression which is characteristic of film, and yet shares with other "languages" the traditional properties of being systematic, symbolic, learned, socially employed and consistently evolving under the pressure of cultural change. By *composition*, I refer mainly to the arrangement of filmic properties, such as images and sounds, which create the total film. And *literature* suggests the films, which represent the outstanding achievements of the cinema.

Finally, this book is not meant as a substitute for an individual's need to devise and develop an approach to film teaching, which is right for his students and himself. Only he knows what is best for him. But for too long movies have been ignored as a significant art form and as a valuable mode of expression. My hope is that you will find in the following pages materials and suggestions that will help change this situation. It is intended as a survey, which offers practical advice to students of film.

7. Sylvester Stallone ina publicity photo for Rocky, an inspiring film about an unknown Philadelphia boxer chosen to fight for the Heavyweight Championship of the World.

6.

Where Have All The Heroes Gone?

He marks—not that you won or lost—
But how you played the game.
Henry Grantland Rice

...Life can be
Lost without vision, but not lost by death,
Lost by not caring, willing, going on,
Beyond the ragged edge of fortitude
To something more—something no man has ever seen.[1]
Stephen Vincent Benet

Sport has the power to change the world... It has the power to unite people in a way that little else does. It speaks to youth in a language they understand. Sport can create hope where once there was only despair.[2]
Nelson Mandela

If I thought the teaching gods were having fun at my expense in the first decade of my career, I had no idea the time at New Rochelle High School and Southern Connecticut State College only set the stage for what was to come during my early days educating students at the University of Vermont. So far the Objectionables felt I had bad manners, disparaged the great works, and refused to grovel to authority. Now they probed my publishing performance.

Although most of my writings followed a traditional academic route—book reviews, scholarly essays, conference reports, and published talks—the subject matter, as you might suspect, remained peripheral to the English Department's intellectual interests and expectations. In fact, my interesting but irreverent approach to traditional priorities might well have suggested I seek employment elsewhere. But in the late sixties, publishing, although important in the College Handbook, did not hold much sway in the school's corridors of power.

Three criteria allegedly determined your professional fate in the College of Arts and Sciences: Scholarship, Teaching, and Service. But how you defined the standards and what department you were in was critical. If you were in Department X, scholarship required peer-reviewed publications, rigorous teaching evaluations, and positive external reviews testifying to your talent and professional contributions. Service was expected, but not stressed. Presumably, you were too busy writing and teaching to waste time debating abstract issues in meaningless committees whose conclusions were generally ignored by the administration. But if you were in Department Y, it was Alice Through the Looking Glass. Scholarship was whatever you claimed it was. After all, you had your union card; you didn't need anyone to tell your colleagues you were a learned person. Even more, you could demonstrate your knowledge through your teaching. Your student evaluations more than validated how erudite you were as a professor. That newspeak elevated the importance of Service. Catch 22! Service meant not contributions to the university or your discipline but access to the fourth and unnamed criteria: Collegiality.

Undoubtedly, Collegiality defined you as someone respectful not only of your colleagues' behavior, but also of their abilities. It fostered cooperation and intellectual growth. Seen negatively, close faculty relationships mainly freed you from all professional activities and responsibilities. The former version resulted in hard-working faculty earning promotions, reappointments, and tenure. The latter type produced lethargic individuals who traded on friendship not only to survive but also to wield untold influence in the College.

To be fair, in my initial years I tried to work both sides of the aisle. I was new at the game and felt that reasonable people could be converted to my point of view with time and patience. To be even fairer, the college faculty gave me a wide playing field. They engaged in a wait and see contest. But there was a joker in the deck. What I was publishing most were young adult books for the secondary schools, hardly standard higher education discourses.

What was this about, and what justification did I use to break with past academic practices?

Interestingly, conditions not intentions determined my path. In 1966, while at SCSC, I met and became friendly with an impressive, creative science professor: Dr. A. Harris "Bud" Stone. Later, he would found and head The Graduate Institute. But when we met, in addition to his teaching duties, he consulted for the Connecticut public schools and for Prentice-Hall publishers. His editor, the incredible Jean Reynolds, had Bud not only writing science books for youngsters, but also recruiting possible authors for new areas.

So it happened that Jean and I met and explored mutual interests. I was intrigued with doing a book on film history; she wanted a book on the making of Hollywood movies aimed at nine year olds. We compromised. I would do *Movies and How They Are Made* (1968), if she would let me do two books on film history: *When Pictures Began to Move* (1968) and *When Movies Began to Speak* (1969). All three books appeared in my first two years at UVM. The reviews for the making a movie text only your worst enemy would wish for you. The reviews for the next two books could have been penned by doting mothers. Ironically, it made no difference to administrators at UVM. All that really mattered to my colleagues was that I was publishing!

Here, a brief observation is useful. During the sixties in the College of Arts and Sciences, publications did not appear routinely. Usually, a teacher would write something either when tenure or reappointment or promotion was on the horizon. Then, achieving the desired goal, the professor would lapse back into a comfortable lifestyle until the next academic obstacle appeared. Then, and only then, would the writing process start over again. Almost no one was expected to produce on a regular basis.

Of course, the world was entirely different back then when it came to doing research. Computers had yet to take hold in the humanities. We worked at a different pace, with different expectations. The University, promoted as a research institution, was in fact little more than a teaching institute, where most of the faculty in the College of Arts and Sciences had been recruited for their general skills rather for than for a specific discipline or subject expertise.

Then fate stepped in. Film study was on the rise in the country, but as explained in the last chapter, conditions were chaotic. For example, when I arrived at UVM in 1967, the library had very few film books (not many were being published), and those we had often had their stills sliced from the volume. Thus most of material I used in my doctoral publication had to be purchased by me. And in the public schools, the only books being used were adult film texts, none of which were geared to adolescents. Even further, the vital road to stimulating students' interests was being blocked by school librarians with tight budgets, who were definitely not interested in "wasting" funds on books about the popular arts. Even worse, nowhere in the world had anyone even considered publishing young adult books on the mass media. Where was the audience? Where were the financial rewards? Where was the academic justification for such publication?

Those variables constituted the formidable publishing challenges in 1969: write movie books presumably no one wanted to read or to buy, and then persuade conservative librarians to rethink their purchasing and educational priorities. Even if I overcame those obstacles, how would such an undertaking affect my resume?

In retrospect, given my teaching interests and my academic relationships, the fact that not only did my department but also my institution support my efforts remains to this day testimony to their generosity, their kindness, and their vision. I doubt seriously, knowing what I do now about higher education, that many colleges and universities would have allowed me, let alone encouraged me, to pursue that unconventional route.

My department proved supportive in other ways. Although it honored its promise to let me teach film, the circumstances were not ideal. My first course, *The Black Man in Film*, had to first demonstrate evidence of its academic qualifications, then gain departmental and college approval, before being allowed to be offered as a one-time only, experimental course. Nevertheless, my first students and I had a great experience; and even today, when I meet those "first-nighters," we speak with considerable fondness of the class. It was, after all, on the cutting edge of the social revolution concerning black literature and black writers in the sixties.

With this in mind, let me turn to the story of the Young Adult Book adventure. First at Prentice-Hall and then at Franklin Watts, Jean became my editor and major supporter. I would suggest a topic, and if she approved, I'd go ahead and write a book. My agenda was fivefold: please Jean, impress the librarians, provide texts for secondary school students, popularize research in the field, and grow as a film intellectual.

All the books were geared to film genres. If you recall my early childhood, you'll remember how central formulas were to both the business end of movie making and to audience enjoyment. Simply put, the moviemakers owned theaters across the country that had to be filled with new movies on a weekly basis. Thus, the studios became virtual film factories. They each had their own stable of performers, producers, directors, writers, cinematographers, set designers, sound experts, and publicity people who used various recipes to link the productions to the patrons' desires. Each formula—e.g., westerns, gangster movies, and musicals—had a set of conventions: characters, settings, themes, and styles—which hopefully proved popular with the public. But weekly filmgoers wanted not only predictability, but also novelty. A studio's success depended on skillful production teams cleverly manipulating audience expectations. It became a game. For example, you went to see a western expecting to see certain types of cowboys and villains fighting over the usual social and political injustices, but the great westerns tweaked the action, the stars, the production values, and the stories. What few viewers realized was the way the embedded messages either reinforced or challenged traditional norms.

Not so society's self-appointed censors. A Motion Picture Production Code was set in place to insure what messages the moviemakers were or were not permitted to send out, especially since Jews, outsiders, appeared in control of the movie industry. Examining the battles over film content proved one of the most rewarding experiences in my film career.

Obviously, the movie story is far more complex than that brief overview. Producers, writers, and directors constantly faced censorship issues in the scenes they created, the dialogue they produced, and the stories they told on screen. We still debate today whether such conditions improved the quality of films or blocked creativity. But a whole generation of youngsters growing up in those pre-computer/iPad days never even knew movies as anything other than entertainment. (Of course, that's not true today. Right!)

What I tried to do was raise an audience's consciousness when they were watching genre movies. I tied the narratives to hidden agendas and to unstated cultural schemes. That's the behind-the-scene scoop on my publishing gambit. It was little more than trying to develop bullshit detectors in everyone who read my books.

Staring in 1968, the books began coming out one a year for almost a decade. They proved groundbreaking in screen education, winning not only recognition here and in England, but also they won over the librarians. It was the second time in my life (the first as a child as explained earlier) these irreplaceable, gifted, and treasured group of people proved indispensable to my happiness and to my future. Vanity requires I mention that every time I attended a professional convention, no matter where in the United States, I made it a point to visit a public library and check out the card catalogue to see if the institution had any of my books. Never once in the decade was I ever disappointed.

But there was always a Catch 22! During the 1970 spring semester, my chairperson asked me to take a walk with him around the campus. During the stroll, he informed me it would be best for everyone if I stopped publishing as much as I was. It was embarrassing other members in the department. I tried to explain I meant no harm; I thought that was what professors were supposed to do. That's what Lou Forsdale trained me to do. (Lest you think I was unique, a close friend tells me the same thing happened to him.)

In deciding which of the fourteen Young Adult books to use by way of illustration, I decided on *Great Sports Movies* (1980).[3] Of the many reasons (in addition to it being dedicated to my youngest son), I have been troubled by recent sports scandals involving almost every athletic competition from baseball, basketball, football, and cycling to badminton and World Cup action. Think how many passionate fans have been disillusioned because of stars like Alex Rodriquez, Tiger Woods, Lance Armstrong, Tom Brady, Jerry Sandusky, and O. J. Simpson. Remember, these sports heroes were our children's role models. For me, these tragic figures made me feel my efforts years ago in writing a book like *Great Sports Movies* might be just as relevant for today's readers.

Just as significant to the following selection is a discovery I made doing the research for this chapter. It seems that the year the book appeared, the prestigious *School Library Journal*[4] assigned the review to a Vermont high school teacher. I found his critique extremely well written, perceptive, and just, except for one thing. The reviewer concluded his comments by writing, "Beautifully reproduced movie stills, and an index and a short bibliography round out this good-quality treatment of a subject of fairly limited interest and importance." I respectfully disagree. Sports were, are, and remain vital both to a nation's values and to its behavior.

But by 1980, that awareness was not high on my radar. Nine years earlier, my time had come for promotion to full professor. As was the custom, the senior members of the English department, along with our new Chairperson, convened to debate the issue in private. Their questionable decision was to deny my promotion; but shockingly, it was not based on the criteria required. Immediately after the meeting, the Chair came to my office and told me I had gotten too much too soon. If I would be quiet and not cause a scene, I would be promoted the following year. After he left the office, I crossed the campus and went directly to the Dean's Office. The next day I was moved to the Department of Communication and Theatre.

Thus we turn to my sports story in the 1980s.

Notes

[1] Lincoln Konkle and David Garrett Izzo, *Stephen Vincent Benet: Essays on His Life and Work*. New York: McFarland & Co. Inc., 2002. 226.
[2] Qtd. in Baron Davis and Chad Gordon, *The Drew: No Excuse, Just Produce*. USA: Preybird, 2015.
[3] Frank Manchel, *Great Sports Movies* (New York: Franklin Watts, 1980.)
[4] Richard Luzer, Fair Haven Union High School Media Center, VT. *School Library Journal*. Sept 1 (1980).

Introduction

The sports movie has made great strides over the past eighty years. It has changed from a crude novelty in 1894 to an Academy Award winner like *Rocky* in 1976.

America's interest in sports has also grown along with sports movies themselves. Today, that interest seems boundless. A few examples should make that clear. For example, the world heavyweight championship fight between Muhammad Ali and Leon Spinks on September 15, 1978, brought in the most money from ticket sales in sports history. Over 63,530 fans paid a total of $4,806,675 to see Ali win back his crown for the third time. Major league baseball attendance has gone over the thirty million people a year mark; professional football, ten million; and horse racing (the most popular spectator sport), seventy million.

These record-breaking statistics seem trivial placed alongside television figures. "Last year alone," reported *TV Guide* on August 19, 1978, "the three networks delivered 1175 hours of pitch, pass and putt—a staggering payload of 376 separate events that garnered total-audience figures of nearly five billion." Knowing that over seventy million viewers followed one game of the 1979 World Series and about ninety-five million followed the Super Bowl in 1979 proves something about America's interest in sports. So does the fact that the film, which drew the largest viewing audience for a single night in the 1977-78-television season, was *The Longest Yard*.

What has not changed since 1894 is the running debate on the evils and benefits to be found in American sports. Is character built through athletics? Are we more physically and mentally fit because of sports? Do athletics provide the underprivileged with greater opportunities for success in our society? Are athletes more courageous, more disciplined than non-athletes? Most important, is the quality of American life better because of our great stress on sports?

The American film industry profits from the debate by presenting both sides of the issues. Those who argue that sports improve the quality of American life find many films to illustrate that belief.

Brian's Song (1971) shows how the gridiron fosters "brotherhood." *The Greatest* (1977) demonstrates how hard work, dedication, and sacrifice in the ring made Ali heavyweight champion of the world. *One in a Million: The Ron LeFlore Story* (1978) explains how a juvenile delinquent escaped his ghetto origins and eventually won fame on the baseball diamond. Such movies claim that sports mold the youth of our country into better Americans.

Those who deny such claims can also find sports movies to defend their beliefs. *Slap Shot* (1977) shows how violence, poor sportsmanship, and foul play can result in a hockey championship. *One on One* (1977) reveals the immoral and nonintellectual side of some major college basketball programs. *North Dallas Forty* (1979) exposes the physical and mental pain professional football players endure to satisfy the demands of ruthless coaches and club owners. These movies stress that sports hurt-not help-our society. By placing too great an importance on winning, athletics teach people to lie, cheat, and become brutal.

No matter which side you favor in the debate, one thing is clear: sports movies are clicking at the box office. Their success has started a new Hollywood trend. Never before have so many major films about sports been made at one time. By the end of 1978, the film makers had already released a surfing movie, *Big Wednesday;* a disaster story at a ski lodge, *Avalanche;* a comedy film about a boxing kangaroo, *Matilda;* a fantasy about a football hero, *Heaven Can Wait;* a picture about a high school basketball team guided by a woman, *Coach;* a chronicle about a high school track star coming of age, *Our Winning Season;* and two TV series about former professional athletes becoming high school coaches: *The Waverly Wonders* and *The White Shadow*. Besides these sports movies, we will soon be seeing more films about boxing, basketball, football, jogging, tennis, bicycling, ice skating, pinball, skiing, bowling, wrestling, and karate.

To understand why sports movies are so popular, consider the ingredients in such recent hits as *The Other Side of the Mountain* (1975), *Rocky* (1976), and *Little Mo* (1978). They all contain the standard Hollywood formula: action, glamour, feats of courage and strength, winning and losing, fantasy, and superstars.

Replacing the early seventies' diet of antiheroes are people we identify with and often admire. In *The Other Side of the Mountain,*

Marilyn Hassett portrays the real-life courageous Jill Kinmont, whose 1955 Olympic bid resulted in an accident that left her paralyzed. *Rocky* features Sylvester Stallone as a two-bit boxer who overcomes ignorance and poverty to gain his self-respect. *Little Mo* has Glynnis O'Connor recreating the true story of Maureen Catherine Connolly, whose brilliant tennis career ended with her tragic death from cancer at thirty-four.

Sports movies also give us relief from our day-to-day concerns. Watching these heroic figures perform spectacular feats, we can forget our own problems for a while. Many viewers even become inspired by what they see and try to imitate the stars' heroic behavior.

The importance of sports movies is not new to our society. It stretches back to the 1890s when America was undergoing an industrial revolution. Technology did more than change methods of production and create large industrial centers. It also changed the nation's social climate.

Many immigrants and rural Americans flocked to rapidly growing industrial centers. Everyone was seeking more money and a higher standard of living. Technology had not only reduced the workweek but also increased people's free time. In 1850, for example, the average person after a day's work had little more than two hours to relax. By 1890, the worker's leisure time had almost doubled.

America's interest in athletics also underwent changes. Before the Industrial Revolution, sports were simple, local pleasures. The average person played games to relax and get away from serious matters. Each community had its own favorite sports and set up matches between local heroes, who competed for regional honors and awards. Such contests were usually financed by the well-to-do and staged for their benefit. This was because the rich had the free time and money to spend on sports.

After the Industrial Revolution, the situation changed. The rise of towns and cities resulted in the widespread popularity of organized games. Events no longer remained simply local events. As a result, sports became a more serious matter. Success or failure had an effect on the community's everyday affairs. The birth of the telegraph in 1844, for example, made it possible to focus national attention on a major sporting event. Victories were reported in newly created mass-circulation newspapers. The growing interest in sports made players and fans more competitive. Spectators demanded better planning for the events, more comfortable seating arrangements, refreshments, and information about the athletes. It was clear that the Industrial Revolution had made sports big business.

As a result, sports promoters came into vogue. They did just what the heads of major industries had done: they organized. Teams were formed, leagues set up, and rules imposed. Professionals were hired to play, coach, and run the events. Baseball, for example, had changed by the 1860s from an early nineteenth-century children's bat-and-ball game into a professional sport. By 1892, football established formal rules about "downs" and "yards." That same decade saw professionalism make advances in boxing, tennis, golf, and bowling. The 1890s also introduced new sports to the American public, including basketball and hockey.

The growing importance of sports was closely tied to the national character. Americans had a dream that made them believe that hard work, courage, and determination could make even the lowest among them become "a somebody." What better way, many people argued, to prove someone's worth than by athletic competition. Success in sports now resulted in dollars and fame. The more successful the athlete, the more money and glory could be attained.

Sports were also linked to the nation's social problems. The promise of a better life in the cities had proven false. The rapid rise of industrial centers had produced urban ghettos and rural slums. People found themselves living in poverty and without any common ties to each other. Consider, for example, the differences among the millions of immigrants who tripled the country's population between 1870 and 1890. They had different languages, customs, and religious beliefs. There were also differences in their levels of education, income, and employment. Sports, on the other hand, offered living proof that the American Dream was a reality. Here success seemed to depend on ability alone. Given the chance, anyone could gain personal fame, wealth, and respectability.

Thus victory became more important than the sport itself. This was true not only for the players themselves but also for communities. Being on the winning side had many rewards for the fans. You gained friends among fellow supporters. Victory signaled your district or town as better than that of the defeated opponent.

There was also ethnic pride. Baseball, for example, produced a host of ethnic heroes in the late nineteenth century. Honus Wagner inspired German-Americans. Lipman Pike was a hero to the Jewish community. Boxing champions like John L. Sullivan and "Gentleman Jim" Corbett were the pride of Irish-Americans.

Yet those who examined the growing myth of sports as the true symbol of the American Dream found a terrible defect. The sports world was filled with prejudice. Women and minority groups, particularly black Americans, were kept out of the mainstream. John L. Sullivan, for example, refused to give black boxers a shot at the heavyweight crown. And by the turn of the century, racism was widespread. Black Americans found themselves barred from private clubs, courts, tournaments, and leagues.

It was during this era that movies made their debut. In 1894, they were just one more way to entertain Americans. The first filmmakers weren't interested in anything but making money. And since sports were so popular and profitable, the movie pioneers simply cashed in on an already successful formula. Movies about sports, from auto racing to wrestling, became a fixture during the film industry's early years.

Since then, sports movies have grown and developed both as an art form and as a multimillion-dollar business. At the same time, sports movies have mirrored America's dilemma over athletic competition. *The Bad News Bears* (1976), for example, shows how ragtag little leaguers learn from a booze-sipping coach (played by Walter Matthau) that success on the baseball diamond is character-building. *The Deadliest Season* (1978), on the other hand, tells the tragic story of a professional hockey player (played by Michael Moriarty) who sacrifices his principles for success and becomes a menace on the ice.

This book cannot attempt to give you a complete history of sports movies. But it can remind you of just how sports heroes have thrilled one generation of viewers after another. Mainly, this book is for all of us who love sports movies.

8. Star pitcher Bingo Long (Billy Dee Williams) and his slugging teammate Leon Carter (James Earl Jones) battle their way through the unforgettable days of Negro baseball, in an effort to break the all-white Major league's racial boycott of black players. John Badham, *The Bingo Long Traveling All-Stars & Motor Kings* (1976).

9. Marcel Ophuls, the Oscar-winning French documentary filmmaker who made *The Sorrow and the Pity*, *The Memory of Justice*, and *Hotel Terminus: The Life and Times of Klaus Barbie.*

7.

Dystopia

I think one of the real misfortunes with our American motion pictures has to do with the fact that it's almost entirely a dollars and cents conjecture. I think there is more to a motion picture than its commerce. I think that its ideas are of untold worth.[1]

George Stevens

It is the strangest thing, that the world is not full of books that scoff at the pitiful world, and the useless universe and the vile and contemptible race—books that laugh at the whole paltry scheme and deride it.... Why don't I write such a book? Because I have a family. There is no other reason.[2]

Mark Twain

Much have I learned from my teachers; even more from my colleagues, but most of all from my students.

Rabbi Chanina, The Talmud

Wikipedia: The Free Encyclopedia defines a dystopia as "an imaginary community or society that is undesirable or frightening. It is literally translated as 'not-good place,' an antonym of utopia." With a few caveats, that's an apt description of how I remember UVM's Department of Communications and Theatre. But in 1971, when dramatically exiting the Old Mill, I pictured my new colleagues housed primarily at Pomeroy Hall as a very attractive group. An odd mix of three different disciplines—Theatre, Speech Pathology, and Communications—, the welcoming professors each brought to the table scholarship, collegiality, and boldness. For example, the Communications wing introduced such revolutionary courses as filmmaking, mass media studies, and television history. By doing what they did, they took great risks and faced much derision from their peers. Nevertheless, they exuded confidence with their radical approaches to evaluation, teaching, and research; they truly believed their style and substance put them on the cutting edge in their respected fields. Justification for their confidence was seen in their courses being extremely popular on campus.

I seemed to be the perfect fit to their tangled web. Passionate about film history and criticism, committed to championing the popular arts, and as adventurous as my newfound friends, the émigré from across the campus rounded out the department's mass media curriculum. I, too, was happy. I had finally achieved my decade-long ambition. I was teaching about film history—fulltime!

Almost immediately, UVM discovered it had a cinema program, covering almost every aspect of the medium. With no one to restrain or to compete with me, I became a film generalist who could teach whatever and whenever he wanted. No writing projects, no teacher training classes, and no literary survey courses; just film history and specialized seminars. Using the basics described in the soon-to-be-published *Film Study*, the Communications position was my illusion of the perfect job.

What I missed and how everything fell apart are the subtexts of this chapter and the next. But for now, we will delay discussing the reading selection that follows. Instead, let's start by looking at two seemingly unrelated events that took place almost precisely at the time I began writing this chapter.

In February 2015, at the Berlin International Film Festival, hosting over a 130 nations from around the globe, director, actor, and educator Marcel Ophuls was honored with the Berlinale Camera Award for his lifetime achievements.[3] Born in Frankfurt-am-Main, the son of the great German film director Max Ophuls (*Letter From an Unknown Woman*, *La Ronde*, *The Earrings of Madame De*, and *Lola Montes*), Marcel fled his homeland as a teenager with his family and went into exile first to France and then to America. During the forties, he perfected his interest in the movies, and eventually became an acclaimed documentary filmmaker, gaining fame initially as the genius who made *The Sorrow and the Pity*, a devastating documentary account of French conduct during the Vichy period in World War II; then *A Sense of Loss*, a heart wrenching look at the violent struggle between Catholics and Protestants in Northern Ireland; and afterwards with the Oscar-winning *Hotel Terminus: Klaus Barbie—His Life and Times*, an agonizing examination of the despicable "Butcher of Lyon" who slaughtered thousands of people during the Nazi Occupation of France.[4]

Two months later, another incident occurred that also has bearing on this chapter. PBS' *American Experience* series aired Barak Goodman's chilling documentary *My Lai*.[5] Using actual footage together with authentic interviews, the film assesses the 1968 scandal of an American ground force that butchered 300 Vietnamese civilians in the Quang Noi province. Did Charley Company faithfully follow the orders of their battalion commander and his officers and execute Viet Cong guerillas, or did they become a vengeful mob insanely massacring innocent, unarmed men, women, and children? The yearlong American military cover-up that followed is examined, concluding with the fact that although 30 personnel from private to general were charged with crimes, only one—Lieutenant William Calley—was convicted. All charges against the other 29 individuals were either dropped, or the men were acquitted.

What has this to do with the reprinted interview that follows? Let me again delay my answer in order to pursue some matters equally important to my teaching journey.

In early November 2007, screenwriter and documentary filmmaker Mikko Alanne wrote an exceptional script called *Pinkville*. The title refers to the fact that on American military maps in 1968, the Quang Noi province was depicted in bright, iridescent pink, allegedly suggesting it was an ideal place for killing Viet Cong infiltrators. Alanne's My Lai script, based on sworn testimony taken during various military inquiries, interviews with participants, and surviving documentary evidence, appealed to Vietnam War veteran and Oscar-winning film director Oliver Stone. He took on the job of making the movie and assembled a pre-production team. Especially meaningful to me was the fact that two of my former students—Jon Kilik and Robert B. Richardson[6]—were handling the production and cinematography respectively. But before the controversial project could go into production, the public expressed its disapproval of a new crop of war films, which included *The Green Berets*, *Hell in the Pacific*, and *The Devil's Brigade*. Claiming that the sluggish box-office receipts for these movies indicated that mass audiences weren't interested in any more war films, Stone's skittish backers withdrew their support, and *Pinkville* was shelved. I never believed the "bad box-office receipts" excuse for a moment. It took three more years for Goodman's film to appear, and five more years before it aired on television.

These cursory details highlight two convenient insights into my teaching priorities, starting in 1971. First, as you no doubt recognize, I had made a major sea shift from the days of the Film/Book program at NRHS to film study at UVM. No longer was I so cavalier about "Guilty Pleasures" and "B" movies. While I recognized viewers' needs and choices, and still do, I began stressing the importance of building an educated audience for worthy films. (We won't quibble here as to what "worthy" means and whose definition you accept.) Without a sophisticated audience, in my judgment, good films rarely get attempted, made, seen, and retained. The more I studied movie history, the more evident it was to me that bad movies drive out good ones. Industry leaders, obsessed with profits, repeat hits and ignore profound projects that sell few tickets. For example, I had once upon a time convinced my friend, Vermont's leading film exhibitor, to show Markus Imhoof's *The Boat is Full*, dealing with the Swiss government's treatment of Jewish refugees fleeing Nazi persecution. Merrill Jarvis called me mid-week and said, "The boat may be full, but the theater is empty." It would be a while before he again agreed to my frequent entreaties to run such unpopular films.

The second critical innovation arising out of the move from English to Film was I had rarely discussed movies as commercial products. No recognition had ever been made by me from NRHS on about how industry practices, not aesthetic determinations, control most of what appears on screen. The move from literature to movies changed my perspective. I now began stressing the business end of filmmaking when critiquing a movie. I frequently examined how mass media censorship operates, dismissed the myth that only Hollywood had such pernicious practices, and refused to believe that producers added nothing to the creative process. With my new outlook of movie history, starting with the Hollywood moguls and studio producers to modern times, I realized that not only could bureaucrats limit and stifle film creativity, but also brilliant people like the Weinstein brothers, Kathleen Kennedy, and Jon Kilik could just as well enrich the lives and visions of both artists and audiences.

Pinkville also triggers in my mind three additional recollections relating to film myths and teaching responsibilities: the complexity of screen education, the necessity for having teaching resources, and the many misperceptions about artistic scholarship.

As usual, we start with the last first. A long held myth about films, historical or otherwise, is that they lack accuracy and credibility. They are not only mere entertainment, but also damaging to our collective consciousness. Why take them seriously?

No doubt poorly-made movies do damage to our psyches and to our historical memory, not just because of sloppy filmmakers but also because of budget restrictions and bureaucratic interference. In such instances, the "accuracy critics," as the Harvard-trained film scholar Robert Sklar called them, are invaluable for pointing out omissions, discrepancies, and distortions.

But when a major motion picture director, for example, takes on a historic subject, the primary reason for omissions and distortions is mainly because of artistic license, not incompetence or ignorance. I know first-hand the impeccable research on ancient Rome done by screenwriter David Franzoni in creating his Oscar-winning narrative for *Gladiator*. I know first-hand the incredible research done by both director Martin Scorsese and cinematographer Robert Richardson for *Shutter Island*, when they ransacked countless film libraries to watch an inexhaustible collection of film noir movies to study the genre's visual style. I know first-hand the precision in which producer Jon Kilik researched the locations, cast, and material for *Miral*.

My favorite example relates to *Pinkville* itself. A good friend and I were discussing how inaccurate such a movie could be, considering it would be a theatrical film and not a historical study. So I challenged my well-meaning but patronizing colleague, a highly regarded historian, to provide me with a list of books that professional historians on the My Lai scandal would consider basic resources. I then sent the impressive list to Bob Richardson, asking him which of the books he had used in preparing his pre-production material. Not only had the brilliant cinematographer read all the books on the list, but also he had added some, had the books on hand, in some cases autographed, and had even interviewed some of the authors and personalities involved in the actual investigation of the cover-up.

My point should be obvious. The strength of a movie is not just in its narrative or cast or theme. Serious actors spend months researching their characters, set designers and costume consultants exhaust art collections to find the perfect inspiration for their artwork, and on and on. Historical films, at their best, are superb resources for revisiting the past, and they deserve from the general public a simple awareness of what their film contributions actually mean to a movie's worth.

If you doubt my examples because of their obvious self-serving appearance, take a look at François Truffaut's Oscar-winning 1973 film *Day for Night*, on the detailed collaboration that takes place in the making of a movie. Study Barry Levinson's marvelous but overlooked 1998 *Wag the Dog* to discover how precisely filmmakers create message movies. If you consider such examples too old, spend some time with 2015's Oscar-nominated foreign film, Andrey Zvagintsev's *Leviathan*. Listen to the supplementary material on the DVD, where the director and producer explain why and how they use Philip Glass' music to open their film about the life and times of contemporary Russian people struggling to survive in an unjust society. Discover how precise they are in almost every part of every frame.

My question is really do you ever truly see a movie, especially if you only watch it once? Do you really believe, like the traditional museum visitor, that you can appreciate a painting, let alone a collection, by taking a two-hour walk through the galleries and then never go back? I'm not being an elitist or a snob. Thanks to what I have learned, I could easily retrace my extended journey and watch all the movies I've seen all over again, just from the point of the visuals, or just from the perspective of the screenwriting, or just from the choices a producer has made in his pre-production process alone. That's what it means to surround yourself with extraordinary people like Robert Richardson, David Franzoni, and Jon Kilik. That's the absolute truth. And that is just one reason Chaplin was right in calling each of us amateurs.

One last observation before we leave this area. Have you ever considered how many of today's generation end their public school education never even knowing about the role genocide plays in our society? Thankfully, Montreal's The Foundation for the Compulsory Study of Genocide in Schools has recently addressed the problem. Sensing that alarmingly few Canadian youngsters are aware of mass murders in any era, now or in the past, including "the Holocaust, Armenian genocide, Rwandan genocide and the cultural genocide of First Nations,"[7] the socially conscious organization offered a way to remedy the intellectual neglect. They called for a required course on the subject to be taught in high school in the eleventh grade. Rather than letting the current practice of individual instructors determine what students do or do not learn about genocide, the Foundation wants a mandatory program set up, starting with the basic necessity of knowing just what is meant by genocide. From there, the plan is to educate adolescents as to the roots of mass assassinations and massacres—e.g., "the gradual growth of racial and cultural intolerance" to "the systematic destruction of a racial, ethnic or cultural group"—and then apply that awareness to current crimes against humanity in the Middle East, Africa, North and South America, and Asia.[8] While it may be too late for a number of American politicians currently campaigning for the presidency of the United States, the recommendation has merits for educational institutions everywhere.

Not surprisingly, the plan has its own set of detractors, who feel the subject is too grim or too inappropriate for today's students, especially at that age level. The argument goes that the youngsters get enough horror stories on the news. Why add to their fears in teaching genocide in the schools? Fortunately, an editorial by the *Montreal Gazette* makes a powerful response to the Objectionables. The reason schools bear a responsibility for studying genocide in their classrooms is because "Education is the key to recognizing and preventing discrimination and acts of hate among our youth, and...knowledge of genocide is essential to preventing such acts in the future."[9]

My second recollection in preparing this chapter relates back to my Gutenberg days teaching film at UVM. For most of my educational life, I had taken for granted the books I was required to read would be available and accessible when I needed them. Any research paper I had ever done had the resources either on the library shelf or in local bookstores. But when I started writing *Film Study* at UVM, there were very few film books in the library, let alone movies to view. There were no streaming possibilities, no video-recording devices, no DVRs, or Pay-per-view channels on television. If I was going to study movies, let alone teach about the riches of film history, a library that contained these essential resources had to be built from scratch. The funds to create such a library were not only limited, but also dispersed among the general academic population. Thus, my request for a film history text had to compete with a request from a chemistry or physics or literary professor.

Knowing now what you do about academic priorities and prejudices, how difficult do you think it was first to build a respectable book collection, and later a fine grouping of films? Since there were no videotaping machines, or DVDs, or DVRs for purchase, we had to rent 16mm films of questionable quality and challenging prices. There were times when just one worn out print exhausted a semester's total budget. And then there were the rooms appropriate for showing of films, along with the equipment and personnel to bring the projectors and screen the movies.

I'm not seeking martyrdom when I recall those apoplectic times. No doubt, today's teachers have just as many challenges, but they are somewhat different from mine back then. I just want you to appreciate what establishing a new discipline without money, without widespread endorsement, and under the guise of doubting Thomases was like. I want to make crystal clear it isn't enough for a dedicated teacher just to be smart in his discipline!

Anyone visiting UVM's Bailey Howe library today can easily recognize how splendid the librarians of days gone by were to me and to my quest. These exceptional, underpaid, hard-working, dedicated, and generous colleagues proved just how indispensable they are to the intellectual life not only of a struggling scholar but also to a respectable university. I shall always cherish their amazing help and their extraordinary friendship for more than half a century.

My final recollection has to do with the popular myth that anyone can teach film, or that being part of a mass media discipline, requires little effort and no special talent. Like being a music critic or an art aficionado, the fairytale goes, anyone can teach and critique movies. One opinion is just as good as another. I would argue, respectfully, nothing could be more ludicrous. As the essay in this chapter hints at, the knowledge of other art forms and of multiple disciplines is a prerequisite for even considering criticizing a movie seriously. Just looking at my essays as an English instructor at the high school or college level shows the quantum differences that are required for people training teachers and college professors being expert in a specific discipline.

Let me be very clear on this point. I make no apologies for what I did as a high school teacher, or how I trained teachers to educate teenagers. Each of us grows in his own way and at his own pace. You need those skills and style to be effective in that arena. I am modestly satisfied with the work I did on my way to becoming an educational masochist.

I feel the same way about film scholarship. Knowing how to communicate is as important as knowing what to teach. I would go even further. Knowing how to make what you know accessible to those too young or too ignorant or too complacent to appreciate on a scholarly level is a skill not to be ignored or dismissed. I am sure that Kael and Hemingway would back me up on this point. Try writing Young Adult books about nuclear physics or music composition or Aristotelian philosophy, and see how far you get. Then take at look at *Great Sports Movies* again. Not Pulitzer Prize material, but definitely not easy!

In my less than humble opinion, the emphasis in effective college teaching is on the wealth of knowledge you bring to the classroom. Here the students need to focus on you and not the other way around. That is not to say film scholars are not required to be good teachers. They most definitely are! Good teaching is good teaching no matter what the discipline or the department or the college. And great universities and distinguished faculties realize that basic fact.

Now that I got that off my chest, we're ready for Marcel Ophuls. In 1972, the prolific French director became involved with a highly controversial project called *The Memory of Justice*. At the heart of the film was the assertion there was little difference between the behavior of the Nazis in World War II, and the actions of the French military in the Algerian War, and the performance of U.S. soldiers in Vietnam. The nearly five-hour movie starts with the 1946-1947 Nuremberg war crime trials. Using archival newsreel footage, actual survivors, and defendants in the docket as his evidence, Ophuls then makes a case the Nazis were not the only modern nation to commit atrocities. Interviews with parents of men killed in Vietnam, critics of the three wars, and contrasting interpretations about alleged war crimes are juxtaposed and compared with each other through the prickly footage.

Controversy existed as well with the marketing of the movie. Behind-the-scenes fighting by the producers and the film personalities over the movie's message remained constant. As well, the moviemakers' worries about how to distribute the finished documentary remained tense and relentless. At the same time, the critical support both for the project and for the results was overwhelmingly positive. *The Memory of Justice* opened four years later to rave reviews, but encountered fervent opposition from powerful parts of society. An anticipated Oscar nomination never materialized, and Ophuls fell on hard times. (Interestingly, *The Memory of Justice* is not available in any form on Netflix, while Amazon only sells *Hotel Terminus; The Life and Times of Klaus Barbie* (1988) and *The Sorrow and the Pity* (1969).)

To survive financially, the French artist took to the college lecture tour. It was his speaking engagement at Dartmouth College that brought him to my attention. Now that UVM had a bona fide film program, I got a call from my colleagues at Hanover, New Hampshire, asking if I might bring Ophuls to Burlington and add to his personal finances. He came, he lectured; and afterwards, I brought him back to my house for something to eat and some friendly conversation.

But Marcel was in a bad way. Breaking down, he spoke sadly to Sheila and me about his experiences over the past five years. Sensing the importance of the situation, I asked him if we could put the conversation on tape. Years later, in a reprint of the interview first published in *Literature/Film Quarterly,* the editors of *Conversations with Directors,* stated their opinion that this interview is "perhaps the most memorably devastating account of what happens when a filmmaker loses control over his own work and its reception...."[10]

And why was this incident so relevant to my growing unrest in the Department of Communication and Theatre? For the most part, it illustrated the developing split between my formalist approach to media study, and almost everyone else's more relaxed teaching styles. In retrospect, I feel it also had to do with the emotional baggage each of us picks up on our respected journeys. Because I had always been under the microscope when it came to legitimizing film study, I bent over backwards to establish rigorous standards that might appease my critics. The Communication professors apparently had no such baggage, and felt no such concerns. They downplayed formal examinations, required almost no academic papers, and rarely gave rigorous reading assignments. Looking back now, they may have been ahead of their times.

Over a seven-year period, the Department received two damaging University evaluations of its non-traditional methods. Unruffled, my colleagues decided to stonewall both reports. In fairness, they were not altogether wrong in their reactions. These were the days where such critical analyses were required by regulations but generally ignored by the college in practice. Academics gave lip service to administration oversight. Everyone seemed content just to recognize departmental deficiencies, but no one seriously believed there would be any serious consequences if you just kept doing what you were doing, especially if the departmental courses proved popular with students. Nothing in recent history suggested that the winds were changing.

Try as I might to adapt, it was not a situation that worked well either for my colleagues or for me. Normally, this would have been the moment when I told Sheila we were moving on. But for the first time in my professional life, I was trapped. My wife and I had always agreed we would never move our children once they entered public school. The kids' welfare was paramount. That meant for the next ten years, I had to find a way to survive intellectually and emotionally at UVM.

One thing I know for sure. Everyone tried his or her best to talk things out, and we debated the issues ad nauseam. But Mark Twain was right when he described Man as "a reasoning animal, open to dispute. However, the results are humiliating."[11] What followed only added to my journey's unconventional nature.

Notes

[1] Qtd. by George Stevens in George Stevens, Jr., *George Stevens: A Filmmaker's Journey*. USA: Castles Films, 1984.
[2] Cited from www.twainquotes.com. Mark Twain, Notebook #29, 10 November 1895.
[3] "Marcel Ophuls," *Wikipedia: The Free Encyclopedia*.
[4] Ephraim Katz, "Ophuls, Marcel," *The Film Encyclopedia*, 5th Edition. Revised by Fred Klein & Dean Nolen. New York: HarperCollins, 2005. 1071.
[5] Barak Goodman, *American Experience: My Lai*. USA: WGBH/PBS, 2010.
[6] For more information about my relationship with Bob, see Appendix II.
[7] Caroline Plante, "Make genocide studies part of high school curriculum: petition," *Montreal Gazette* (February 11, 2016): A7.
[8] Ibid.
[9] Editorial, "Our Views: Studying Genocide," *Montreal Gazette* (February 12, 2016): A9.
[10] Elsie M. Walker and David T. Johnson, "Introduction," *Conversations with Directors: An Anthology of Interviews from Literature/Film Quarterly*, Ed. By Elsie M. Walker and David T. Johnson. Lanham: The Scarecrow Press, Inc., 2008. Xiii.
[11] Hal Holbrook, *Mark Twain Tonight in The CBS Television Network Special*. New Jersey: Kultur Video, 1999.

A War Over Justice:
An Interview...with Marcel Ophuls

It's easy to see why Marcel Ophuls is such a controversial filmmaker. He is an artist who refuses to sacrifice principle for profit or popularity. Starting with The Sorrow and the Pity, which, in 1972, established him as one of the world's foremost documentarians, Ophuls began asking unpleasant questions about our society. He wanted to know, for example, what was the truth about the Nazi occupation of France during World War II. While the movie itself angered the French mythmakers, New Republic critic Stanley Kauffmann summed up the superb critical reaction by stating that the film, "looks at the past," makes us "understand a little more of both the sorrow and the pity," warns us to "be careful of feeling superior to others," and, "rather chillingly, leaves the future to us." That same year in A Sense of Loss, Ophuls explored the complex problems in feud-ridden Northern Ireland. Rather than provide easy answers to complex issues, he chose to disturb audiences with his profoundly humanistic images of an apparently hopeless conflict. Ophuls' commitment to objectivity and his refusal to be compromised by unpopular opinions prompted Time's critic Jay Cocks to pronounce him, "the Orwell of the cinema."

Then, in 1976, after four years of personal agony and court battles with his European producers, Ophuls unveiled The Memory of Justice. The title, attributed to Plato's conviction that mortals in a less than perfect world must be governed by the primeval memory of Justice and Virtue, acted as a guide to Ophuls' investigation about the nature of war crimes. Once again the director became embroiled in controversy. Critics, scholars, and the general public have taken strong stands over the people interviewed in the film, the editing techniques, and the various interpretations resulting from worldwide screenings. Within recent months, the film itself has almost disappeared from public view. Paramount Pictures and New Line Cinema, distributors of the 35mm and 16mm prints respectively, appear to have little success in getting the film circulated. The questions surrounding the reception of The Memory of Justice are disturbing.

Thus when Marcel Ophuls visited the University of Vermont during the week of April 11, 1977, I persuaded him to present his side of the story. What follows is an edited transcript of his feelings about the controversy.

Frank Manchel
University of Vermont

MANCHEL: When did the idea for doing *The Memory of Justice* first begin with you?

OPHULS: Well, Frank, for the sake of honesty, I feel I should throw a bucket of cold water on the idea that filmmakers always have pet projects, and that they are in a position to realize these pet projects, and that is what they consecrate their lives to. In fact, what happened is that after having made a film in Northern Ireland [*A Sense of Loss*] and being once again out of work, I was approached by the BBC, who had had a great deal of success with their showing of *The Sorrow and the Pity* in England. They wanted to have another 4-and-a-half-hour movie, more or less along the same lines. And so the logical and natural inclination for all of us in this connection, once the BBC put up the seed money, was to say, "Well, what about the chronological follow up to *The Sorrow and the Pity?*" This essentially meant the first three or four years after the war in Western Europe. That original project I used to characterize by saying, "Society falling back on its rotten feet." Sometimes I wish we could have stuck to that original idea. I still think it was a good project. We would have concentrated on France after the war, General Charles de Gaulle, Pierre Mendes-France, Albert Camus, Jean-Paul Sartre, the liberation, the trials of Pierre Laval and Marshal Philippe Petain, the Labour Party taking over from Winston Churchill in England, the Germans trying to find their way through the ruins, discovering Hemingway, Faulkner, and the beginning of the Cold War. The Nuremberg Trials would have been just one chapter in that original project. And while I was researching for *that* film, I met Telford Taylor. I had read his book called *Nuremberg and Vietnam: An American Tragedy*. I had also found out from a French journalist that there were fifteen hours of footage done by the United States Army Signal Corps during the Nuremburg Trials, which had been used in various documentary films since the war but never with synchronized sound and picture. Then something happened, which I don't want to go into, and I had to go to the BBC and to my sponsors and say, "Well look, I think this film about postwar France is being done by others and maybe we should do something else." In fact, my meeting with Taylor in New York had suggested a new possibility. And I said, "Well, let's do a film about the Nuremberg Trials." My sponsors at the time were more enthusiastic about the new project than I was, and it is only with hindsight that I have come to understand their enthusiasm.

MANCHEL: When you say your sponsors, you're talking about the BBC, Polytel International, a television packaging company, and Visual Programmes Systems Ltd., a British production.

OPHULS: Yes. They came in at different times. First there was the BBC; then the man who was the head of purchase programs at the BBC and who was my well-wishing sponsor at the time got in touch with the subsidiary of Phillips in Hamburg, a very powerful German production company called Polytel. There were a series of contracts signed. All of this is part of my life and it's very dreary for me and for anybody else. Then they involved a private English firm whose principal stockholder is Evelyn Rothschild.

MANCHEL: Is that Visual Programmes Systems Ltd.?

OPHULS: Yes. A man called David Puttnam. Another man called Sanford Lieberson. They make films like Alan Parker's *Bugsy Malone,* Ken Russell's *Mahler,* and Lutz Becker's *Swastika.* I had had earlier contacts with these people because they had asked me to do a fictionalized version of Albert Speer's memoirs, which they had acquired.

MANCHEL: How significant was the connection between the proposed Speer film and the current problems you were facing with the sequel to *The Sorrow and The Pity?*

OPHULS: It is only a sideline and a dead end. I would have to go into the motivations for wanting to make a picture about Speer's memoirs and about our conversations at that time. I think it would take us too far afield. Anyway, my trying to rescue the project, the original project and the seed money and the groceries, was to suddenly come out with an idea that originally was only supposed to be a chapter. The plan was now to expand the chapter into a whole film, including, of course, the implications in the postwar world of the Nuremberg Trials. The idea, with hindsight, met with a suspicious amount of enthusiasm. When I say that the amount of enthusiasm seemed to be suspicious, with hindsight, what I mean is that I should have been bright enough and analytical enough to understand that a commercial alliance between German co-producers and trendy Wardour Street, young English producers who were aiming for the American market, should have made me aware enough politically and sensitive enough politically to understand what these people saw in the Nuremberg Trials. With a hindsight of thirty years, it was to them an opportunity of relativizing history and of appealing to what they assumed German prejudices to be. In other words, the idea of getting off the hook by demonstrating that evil is not confined to the Third Reich. On the one hand, this would be for the German television audience; on the other hand, this would be appealing to radical chic conceptions, or what they assumed to be radical chic conceptions on the American market. To put it another way, those people, because they very sincerely took very adamant positions against the Vietnam War, would have a tendency growing out of their experiences to equate or to compare My Lai to the crimes committed by the Third Reich which led to the Nazi Holocaust. This, I think, was an attempt to cash in on what the Marxist would call an "objective alliance." The idea would be to attempt to cash in on what these people suppose, wrongly I think, to be the positions of the kind of people in America who would go and see documentary films, left of center, and the German television audience of people who would be glad to find out that there is some connection between My Lai and crimes committed by the Germans during World War II. I have to confess quite openly that because of my naiveté or my innocence or my good faith or whatever you want to call it, I did not perceive this from the very beginning. Or perhaps I did not choose to perceive it, because when you have to make a living in any one profession you have a tendency to discard signs that go against your interest, because your immediate interest is in making a film.

MANCHEL: I want to clarify one point. In Jay Cocks's *Time* essay concerning *The Memory of Justice*, when he wrote about the internal struggles over the film's evolution, he stated that "Ophuls set out to explore the contested—some would say outrageous—theory that Nazi genocide and tragedies like My Lai are somehow comparable, an idea that had widespread currency a few years ago.[1] What I want to clarify is whose idea was it to make the film a Nuremberg Vietnam comparison: yours or the various producing groups?

OPHULS: I guess that when I started out researching the original project, the relative, the historical priorities, in my own mind, were perhaps closer to the product, which the producers and co-producers expected of me than finally turned out to be the case. This is one of the interesting things about documentary filmmaking. If you develop techniques of letting reality come to you, then there is the process of change and hopefully a process of growth in yourself. And therefore, you can then shift positions during the process of the filmmaking. That certainly happened in *The Memory of Justice*, and I'm perfectly willing to say that. In that way, the producers, who fired me at one point, do have some semblance of a case. Because in the preliminary discussions, my own positions were perhaps closer to what they hoped the film would be.

MANCHEL: We're talking about events in 1973?

OPHULS: Yes, this was 1973. In the course of filming, I wrote memoranda to them, which stated, as honestly as I could, the shift in my positions.

MANCHEL: For example?

OPHULS: Well, for example, the fact that by the time that I came to America I no longer wished to confront men like McNamara or Westmoreland or Bundy or Rostow with the question, "Are you, sir, a war criminal?" This had a lot to do with a sense of proportions and a sense of humility, which I had acquired by my research and my work concerning Germany and the German connection and the Nazi connection to Nuremberg. It was in fact a shift in emphasis. And since there was that shift in emphasis, I thought my producers should know about it, and I wrote them a memorandum which stated that shift as clearly as I could.

MANCHEL: Can you be more specific about the shift in your attitudes toward Germany's connection to the Nuremberg Trials?

OPHULS: Well, I just mean that the longer I was confronted by the task I had chosen for myself, the more aware I became that I had no right to substitute myself for trial by law. Since this was ostensibly a film about justice and about the difficulty of judgment and about the ways in which society tries to deal with this, it became more and more apparent to me that any individual, including any individual who has the privilege of having access to the mass media, is not entitled to substitute his own subjective judgments for trial by law. The shift in emphasis, therefore, meant that the theme I assigned to myself had to enable me to talk to people who had been convicted of crimes; that I couldn't cross-cut this with people who my own subjective views, my own political priorities, made me assume were potential war criminals; that this kind of cross-cutting would be detrimental, not only to the film, not only to what I was trying to say, but also to political priorities and to historical priorities in general.

MANCHEL: What is the chronology of these events? You began the contract negotiations and the research for the film in 1973. Later in the year you come to America and the shift in emphasis plus the memoranda between you and your producers begins in 1974?

OPHULS: The filming started in November 1973. By spring of the following year, while at Princeton, I began editing the film. Then during the early summer of 1974, I started writing the memoranda. Shortly afterwards, still in the summer of 1974, I returned to London to complete the editing and the film project itself. And then I was fired *from my own film.* To be quite accurate, I wasn't fired from the film. The film was confiscated from me. It was a blatant power squeeze that took place on December 22, 1974, after what is known in the trade as the rough-cut screening.

MANCHEL: Before we go into the film's being confiscated, let's clarify the state of the film before December 22. How much of *The Memory of Justice* was completed?

OPHULS: It was a four-hour, thirty-eight-and-a-half-*minute* film, which was not absolutely identical with the four hour, thirty-eight-and-a-half-minute film which Paramount is now distributing. But for all practical purposes, it was identical. My contract provided for a film of a minimum length of three-and-a-half hours and a maximum length of four-and-a-half hours. It was the BBC who insisted on having the four-and-a-half-hour length. In other words, I was eight-and-half minutes above the length stipulated in my contract. My argument at that time, which went on for days, was that I was asking for the privilege—I was asking to be indulged in my caprice of mixing and dubbing those eight-and-half minutes. Then, if in the judgment of my producers and co-producers, after the film was dubbed and mixed, they found the additional eight-and-half minutes a breach of contract; I would remove the excess footage. I was being a realist. Having a lot of experience in this profession, I was not about to let myself be put into a breach of contract on a matter of length.

MANCHEL: Then in point of fact people are unfair when they typecast you as a person who only makes four-and-half hour films. The length of this film was dictated by the BBC.

OPHULS: Absolutely! The length of *The Memory of Justice* was determined by the BBC. It resulted from the format they had chosen for the subject matter they wanted filmed. I repeat. This was the BBC's initiative, not mine.

MANCHEL: How much footage had you shot prior to the editing stage?

OPHULS: Ninety hours.

MANCHEL: And you then proceeded during the summer and fall of 1974 to cut it down to a four-hour and thirty-eight-and-half minute film. How was the rough-cut organized?

OPHULS: The first part was called, and is still called, "Nuremberg and the Germans." The second part is called "Nuremberg and Other Places." I must confess again that this is cheating. The second part still has an awful lot to do with Nuremberg and the Germans, and only in the very last third of the film do you get to Nuremberg and other places. This is important because it has to do with what my sense of proportions came to be after the end of my inquiry. Let me now pick up that beautiful Christmas of 1974 in London. The Ritz Bar in London. After the rough-cut screening we met there. The representative of the BBC was present and the representative of the German co-producers was present for a while and then had to catch his plane back to Hamburg, and of course, the two hot shots were present.

MANCHEL: The hot shots being...

OPHULS: Sandy Lieberson and David Puttnam. There seems to be some sort of community between Wardour Street and Carnaby Street. They were, let me tell you, anything but leftists; in their professional policies, in their methods of hiring and firing, in their personal views about the role of capitalism in a market society, they were anything but leftists. But they were leftists about their assessment of how they could make money on the American market with that kind of film. Oh yeah....There were three issues discussed at the meeting at the Ritz Bar. The eight-and-half minutes, which they refused to have dubbed and mixed; there was, of course, a lot of discussion about that and a sort of standstill. By that time, I knew pretty thoroughly what the real issues were. I think I knew. I still think I know. One thing we should all understand is that, in political films whenever a conflict arises, people never admit that the conflict is political. Whenever people try to censor a filmmaker, they never admit that what they are talking about are political issues, because this would be extremely primitive and extremely unsophisticated. They always find other issues. They will tell you that your film is boring or unstructured or too long or too this or too that. Because they know that as soon as they admit that they have political priorities, you can then pounce on them. You can make a public issue on it, and then you can rally support to your side. They are not about to do that. All right, so the conversation at the Ritz Bar, which lasted I think two-and-a-half hours, was mostly about those eight-and-half minutes. There were three issues. The first was on the eight-and-half minutes, which I did not refuse to take out of the film but simply asked for the privilege of mixing and dubbing, so that they could make up their own minds. The second issue had to do with frontal, would you believe it, with frontal nudity. The representative of the SSC—the man who had been my original patron, who had put up the seed money—was by that time, for reasons of his own, a hundred percent accomplice. He was later overruled by the hierarchy of the BBC, which finally did telecast my film and made a public commitment to telecast my film or no film.

MANCHEL: This man's name was...

OPHULS: Gunnar Rugheimer. There are rumors that he is about to quit the BBC to become an employee of Polytel Incorporated International. Whatever that means, he's a former agent of MCA. An interesting man, a very clever man, and a man whom I still have a debt to, because he did support me for a long time. And he is a wheeler-dealer and he is a go-getter with all the advantages and disadvantages that that sort of thing has. As to the frontal nudity, Gunnar was saying that the BBC has codes of standard for, you know, prime hour broadcasting and youth and general audiences and that sort of thing, which made it imperative that frontal nudity not be shown during prime telecasting hours. I knew this to be bullshit because I have seen the BBC things and the BBC is much, much less Puritan than, for instance, American commercial networks are. They have shown frontal nudity over and over again when they showed *Hearts and Minds* [1974], for instance, but I wasn't about to quibble at that stage and I said, "Well listen, Gunnar, I'm all in favor of respecting family standards, and if the BBC has certain standards about frontal nudity, I will eliminate frontal nudity for the BBC, but I will do that in the print destined for the BBC. I don't think that you as a representative of the BBC have a right to demand that I cut it in the negative. Because this would indeed be censorship and I understand very well, dear Gunnar, what your problem is. Your problem is that if the film is going to be presented at the New York Film Festival with the sequence that had frontal nudity, and then is to be presented later on at the BBC with that particular sequence censored, you will then be responsible to answer certain questions asked by discerning journalists. But if you have good reasons and good guidelines for the stand that you are taking, then you must be prepared to answer those questions to those journalists."

MANCHEL: Fair enough.

OPHULS: Fair enough. Whereupon my Wardour Street hustler said, "Well that, Marcel, is not the question, because we also request you to cut this in the negative." And then I said, "No." In fact, all of this, of course, is what Truman used to call a red herring, because by that time they were trying to wave a red cloth in front of the bull so that I would charge out of the arena. They had long ago (or short ago) decided, for reasons of their own, that I was not willing to play their game and they, therefore, wanted to have another man to recut the film, and they were waiting for me to walk out. As it turns out, the issue of the frontal nudity was later settled very, very fast because the program controller of BBC (who had refused to arbitrate when the fight was taking place in Wardour Street, where all he had to do was to take a cab at Christmas time to drive five miles down from Television Center—and who later had to fly 5,000 miles to New York to see the print of the film) reversed the decision of the BBC and said, "We'll take the film, the Ophuls film, or nothing, including the frontal nudity." He felt that was a ridiculous pretext. He is a man by the name of Aubrey Singer. So in the end, the BBC did show my film, including the frontal nudity.

MANCHEL: Without any problems?

OPHULS: Without any problems! The third issue had to do with Russians. The German co-producers wanted me to include a dissident Russian in the film, although they were in no way entitled to do this by contract. Their reasons for wanting to have this in the film, I think, are very obvious. They wanted to lull the German television public into the intellectual comfort of being able to compare German extermination camps with Russian Gulag Archipelago. The intention seems so obvious that it doesn't need much editorializing. I was not unwilling to do this, because I do happen to think that Stalinism is one of the atrocities of modern times, and while I question the motives of my German co-producers, I have no great doubts about the iniquities of the Gulag Archipelago. So I did try to get Solzhenitsyn. I did not succeed. For some reasons of his own, which I think are not too difficult to analyze either. At that time, Solzhenitsyn had just come out of Soviet Russia. He had stayed in Germany, and then gone to Zurich. Perhaps Solzhenitsyn, a genius and obviously a very intelligent man, was afraid of being annexed by the kind of political skullduggery that we are talking about and, therefore, was reluctant to be within the framework of a film on the Nuremberg Trials. So he refused. If I had a tape of the Ritz Bar, those people who have hairs on their head, which I don't happen to have, their hairs would stand up straight, because Mr. Gunnar Rugheimer, the representative of the BBC at that particular conference was saying at one point: "Well, Marcel, you didn't get Solzhenitsyn, so why don't you satisfy our German coproducers by going into a white Russian bar and interviewing some gypsy violinist?" I am quoting textually, "Our German co-producers are unhappy because you have not come up with a Russian dissident. So why don't you give them their Russian dissident under any terms?" And I was trying to explain to them that unless it is Solzhenitsyn, or unless it is Sakharov, who happens to live in Moscow and who is unavailable, it did not seem to me to make a great deal of sense.

I also tried to explain to them that Stalinist war crimes and Stalinist crimes against humanity were touched upon in the film, and that as far as my sense of proportion was concerned, this seemed to me to be adequate. I also tried to explain to them that the motives of the German co-producers seemed to me to be so transparent as to be a major turnoff. Furthermore, I had no contractual obligation to do this, because there was nothing in my contract that obligated me to furnish one interview rather than another. Finally, I said, "Well listen, if you are willing to give me another ten minutes over and above the four-and-a-half hours that we already have, then I will try to cash in on the contacts that we have made with Daniel... the Russian dissident in Paris. (A very interesting man who was available in Paris.) But I will not do it to the detriment of the four hours and thirty-eight-and-a-half minutes that I have now, because it seems to me that the four hours and thirty-eight-and-a-half minutes that I have now are more to the point and more pertinent to what I want to say than a Russian dissident whom the German co-producers feel should be in the film." At that point, David Puttnam, who I think is 32 years old, suddenly said, "Listen, Marcel, I'm getting very tired of this. We've been arguing about these things for two-and-a-half hours." And I said, "I've been working on this for two-and-a-half years. I don't mind arguing about it for two-and-a-half hours." He said, "Yes, but I have other things to do. And I'll tell you this right now, our intention is to cut up the film in any way, shape, length, or form that our American clients would judge to be adequate." Whereupon I said very quietly, "David, if you do that you will be in breach of contract." Whereupon David said to me, "Marcel, that may well be, but you'll have to take us to court and by the time that the judgment is given in court, we will have recouped, hopefully, our money." Whereupon I said, "I think this is morally perverted." Whereupon he said, "I don't know how someone who has breached his contract in terms of budget and scheduling has any right to question our morals, because I think that you are morally degenerate."

MANCHEL: This was Christmas time.

OPHULS: This is the 22nd of December. Whereupon I got up and said, "Gentlemen, I think I have seen enough of you," and walked out of the Ritz Bar in London. Twenty-five minutes later they went to the cutting room and told the editors that I had walked out of the film and that they were justified, therefore, in taking custody of the work print. On the very next day, which was the 23rd of December, and a Sunday, it was very difficult to get a British solicitor to give me advice. So even before I could get that advice, I sat down and wrote a letter to them by registered mail pointing out the difference between walking out of a meeting and walking out of a film. And I said that there was no clause in my contract which obligated me to suffer their physical presence. There is no clause in any contract as far as I know between filmmakers and producers, which obligates either party to ever suffer the physical presence of the other party. You can correspond by mail, by lawyers, or by telephone. This is not a breach of contract. They chose to interpret it as such. They chose to interpret it as such not only on legal grounds but also simply on power grounds, because they assumed, quite rightly, that I would not be able to afford to sue them. Okay, so after trying to get out an injunction against them, after trying to rouse the British unions to blackball the work in the lab, unsuccessfully, but with a lot of support from people like Lindsey Anderson, Robert Boles, Stanley Kubrick, I left England and went back to Princeton, which was at that time my only job, and more or less gave up on the whole thing because they were right. I could not afford the services at that time of lawyers and lawsuits. So they proceeded to have the film recut.

MANCHEL: By Lutz Becker.

OPHULS: He was the one who did *Swastika* and *Double-Headed Eagle.* Now the proof of the pie is in the eating, and their denial that they had political motivations in confiscating the film from me is totally ludicrous once you have seen the Becker version, which they took five months to do and which was broadcast on German television. I will try to confine myself to a couple of examples. In the Dresden sequence, I question former Wing Commander Rose about whether he would have accepted to go to Nuremberg if the London charter had been different and had included allied war crimes and if "Bomber" Harris had been in the dock. In the interview with him, Wing Commander Rose, who had just testified to the fact that he, as the Chief of British Air Force Intelligence, had given very, very solid information to the Allied High Command

and to the American and to the British Air Force to the effect that Dresden was not a military target. And, therefore, should not be bombed. The American General Spaatz, who was in charge of strategic bombing, thereupon reacted by saying, 'Well, if the British agree not to bomb Dresden, we will not bomb Dresden." Whereupon Jim Rose, who is now a publisher of Penguin Books, incidentally called up his own chief at headquarters, Air Marshall Saunby, and told about the information that he had from totally reliable German intelligence sources, that the S.S. Panzer divisions were joining the Eastern Front northeast of Prague, a hundred miles from Dresden. "Bomber" Harris' second-in-command said, "Well, that makes no difference to us. We are going to bomb Dresden." Whereupon at the end of the Dresden sequence in *The Memory of Justice,* I ask Wing Commander Rose, "Well, if the London charter had not excluded allied war crimes from the deliberations in Nuremberg would you have accepted to go to Nuremberg and testify about what you knew?" He says, "Yes, of course." And being an Englishman and a decent Englishman, he then immediately adds, "but I would have had to listen to what the defense had to say, because perhaps I did not have the whole picture. But as far as I know, Dresden was a war crime." Then there was a pause and I asked, "And in the twenty-eight years since, have you ever heard of anything that would make you change that assessment?" And he hesitates for a fraction of a second and he says, "No." And then he smiles. All of that was cut from the Becker version. So much for British susceptibilities! What was also cut from the Becker version were things like Albert Speer showing his home movies, including meetings with the economic bosses of the Third Reich (people like Porsche, who designed the Volkswagen) and then remarking quite casually that these people got back into top jobs after the war and took over German industry. That was cut from the film. For reasons of length? Interesting question isn't it? You think it's length?

MANCHEL: No.

OPHULS: No. In the interview with Admiral Karl Doenitz, my question about his having made an anti-Semitic speech and whether he sees any connection between that anti-Semitic speech and the extermination camps has been cut from the Becker version. Do you think this is for reasons of length?

MANCHEL: No.

OPHULS: I'm sorry I'm using you as a patsy. I do not think that it's for reasons of length. But the most flagrant thing, when we talk about the proof of the pie being in the eating, is something that I came across very late when I was waging a lawsuit against the German co-producers and against German television, because they had programmed the Becker version in contradiction to our agreements and had left my name on the film. In a way, I suppose it is flattering that they should have thought that it was in their interest to keep my name on that truncated version. So, there had been an injunction in a German law court two weeks before the thing was supposed to go on the air on German television. Meanwhile, I was seeking evidence for that lawsuit. Very late one night, my assistant Anna Carrigan stumbled across a passage in the transcript of the Becker version, and all of a sudden she said, "Hey, Marcel, here is something on page 3." This was in the very first minutes of the Becker version. "Look at this." I then looked at something which later became known as the Telford Taylor distortion. My own film starts with the montage of the defendants of the Nuremberg Trial.... "Nicht Schuldig...Nicht Schuldig...Nicht Schuldig!"...pleading not guilty, not guilty, not guilty, not guilty. The Becker version, interestingly enough starts with atrocity footage from the Vietnam War. Burning of a village, hutches, napalm bombings. This is then followed by the testimony of Colonel Tony Herbert, which also is included in my film, but only in the very last reels, saying that when he first discovered the atrocities being committed in Vietnam, he thought that these were field incidents, that once he got back to Saigon, he would be able to clear them up. He then proceeded to report them in Saigon and discovered that various Saigon generals were interested in the cover-up and were accomplices to these acts. Then he thought that when he got back to Washington he would be able to clear it up, and he found that once he was back in Washington, it went all the way up to Westmoreland. Herbert finally had to resign from the Army. This is placed in the first 60 seconds of Lutz Becker's film, long before you ever get to see Goring, Hess, and the other defendants in Nuremberg. Before you ever see anything about the Nuremberg Trials. You see how emphasis can change things. And the third segment, within the first three minutes of the film, was a statement by Telford Taylor. He was Chief U.S. Counsel at Nuremberg and led the follow-up trials, and he was the chief assistant to Justice Jackson at the main Nuremberg Trial. And he is made to say in the German version that was put on German television and was seen by millions of Germans—he, chief of the former prosecutors of the Nuremberg Trials—was made to say the following thing, and now I quote, literally: "It would seem to suggest that American forces at Vietnam had been guilty of the same crimes and to the same degree as the Nazis that we had convicted in Nuremberg." Quote, unquote. This is the passage, which Anna Carrigan, very late one night in the editing room in London, had suddenly discovered in the Becker transcript. She called me over and I looked at it. My first reaction was to say, "They must have used an actor," or "They must have used false sync. This is not possible." I mean, if you know Telford Taylor, if you have read his book, and if you know his extremely complex attitude towards his own past, towards his own involvement in Nuremberg and his anti-Vietnam stands, then you know that he could not possibly have said anything of the kind. He, incidentally, is as close as anyone to being my spokesman in the film. It sounds arrogant for me to say that, because Telford Taylor is very much more than my own spokesman; he is Telford Taylor, a great, great man. I thought: "Wait a minute, now, this is not possible." Then I said, "Well, let's look through the transcripts of his original interview," and it took us about an hour and a half to find the passage in the transcript of the original interview. I must tell you that the original interview was five or six or seven hours long, I remember. I finally found that in the earlier reels of the interview with Telford Taylor (those reels were where I was trying to break the ice with him) I had asked a series of questions about the paperback editions of his book, *Nuremberg and Vietnam: An American Tragedy*, because I had discovered quite by accident that the first edition, the first paperback edition, had on its cover an American flag with a swastika superimposed upon it. And that in subsequent editions of the paperback that swastika had been eliminated. Only the American flag was left on the cover. And, since by the time I was doing the interview with Taylor, I had a pretty good idea about what Taylor's political ideas were—I said, "Telford, tell me, why is this? Why is there the swastika on the American flag in the first editions and then it disappears?" I already had a pretty good idea of what the answer would be. Then he said, "Well, I guess a lot of people objected" and so on. Then there are another two pages of transcript where I try to pin him down. He was still quibbling a little, being a lawyer, and finally, I got him into the position where he says, "Yes, well I guess I was the one who was instrumental in getting the editors to remove the swastika from the American flag." This was, of course, the one moment I was waiting for and said, "Why?" My question was "Why?" And the answer was, "Because it did seem to suggest that American forces in Vietnam had been guilty of the same crime and to the same degree as the Nazis that we condemned in Nuremberg and I don't believe that is so." Quote, unquote.

MANCHEL: This was a very fine editing job that they had done.

OPHULS: Isn't it though? The proof of the pie is in the eating. If ever there was any doubt about the difference in political priorities and the difference in political opinion and the difference in political assessment between my original sponsors and me, this example that I just quoted at great length seems to me to be absolute proof that by the time we came to the Ritz Bar, my suspicions were justified, because this is indeed the version that they wanted to put on German television, a version that had the chief American prosecutor making that statement, which was the absolute opposite of what he had originally said. It's like cutting the word, "not" out of a statement. When I discovered that, I telephoned Telford Taylor, and I said, "Telford, I think that the time has come for you to join my injunction in a Hamburg courtroom, because your case is even clearer than mine." And he did. Now, incredibly enough, it took German television and my German co-producers another six months to remove that statement. And there even came a time when my new sponsors, the people who had got me back into control of my own film, called up Telford Taylor one night and said, "General or Professor, this guy Ophuls, he's crazy! In his own interest and the interest in getting his film out, please remove your injunction from that Hamburg courtroom. Because until you remove that injunction from the Hamburg courtroom, the German co-producers will not give way, and therefore, the film will never come out. And therefore, in the interest of the film, in the interest of our investment, please remove your injunction from that Hamburg courtroom." And Telford being the man that he is, and that I expect him to be, said, "I'm sorry, I can't give you any promises and I have to talk to Marcel about the conversation that we just had." He then picked up the phone, called me and told me about it. And I said, "Telford, please don't remove the injunction."

MANCHEL: With the lawsuits in process, you then had the film taken over by Paramount?

OPHULS: Yes. Paramount and Max Palevsky, who is the man I just talked about. He is and has been a friend of mine, and he quite spontaneously and quite voluntarily, when there were the articles in the American press, called me and said, "Marcel, can I help you? How much money will it take to buy these other people out so that you can finish your own film?" And life, being as ambiguous as it is, he is also the man who then called up Telford Taylor one year later to tell him that I was crazy and that he should remove his injunction.

MANCHEL: Nevertheless, the film was then released and was put on the list of many critics' best 10 films of the year in 1976.

OPHULS: Twelve of them.

MANCHEL: Twelve of them. And much to your surprise and many others' when the Academy Award Nominations were announced, *The Memory of Justice* was not even among one of the five documentary films nominated.

OPHULS: We even got a headline in *Variety*. I was off in Switzerland trying to get the first chapter of my book written, and I was so foolishly confident about there being no problem about the nomination that I wasn't even in touch either with Max or with Paramount or with anybody else about it, because I thought that there might be some problems about the Oscar, but there certainly couldn't be any problems about the nomination. So I was off in a remote corner in Switzerland doing some skiing and doing some writing.

MANCHEL: Various circles have speculated about the possible reasons for your film's not being nominated and its subsequent poor distribution and trouble at the box office. You are, of course, aware of those speculations.

OPHULS: You bet I am, Frank. But you are now in the realm of speculation, and we must be careful about what is and is not true.

MANCHEL: Nevertheless, can you comment, agreed that we're in the area of speculation, about what it is that bothers certain people and groups about your attitude toward the Nuremberg Trials?

OPHULS: It is not only ironic, it is traumatic. It's the sort of thing that can land you in the booby hatch and that has landed me in the booby hatch. To devote four years of your life to fighting the sort of thing that I am trying to convey to you, and then find that some supercilious bastards on the pedestal of their own granite self-righteousness will attack the film for equating My Lai with Auschwitz—when I had just gone through four years of hell endangering my own future and that of my family, fighting against that idea. And, therefore, I say that these people are supercilious, self-righteous, insensitive bastards.

Now when you talk about the Academy Award nominations, I'm not talking about the Oscar. I haven't seen *Harlan County U.S.A.* and I certainly haven't any quarrel, not having seen *Off the Edge*, not having seen *Hollywood on Trial*, not having seen *People of the Wind*, and not having seen *Volcano*. I have no quarrel at all with the idea that the majority of the Academy Award members may prefer these films that I have just named to my own film. I mean that's part of show business and that's part of the things that I have to contend with, and I am perfectly willing to play the game. But there does seem to be a discrepancy between a documentary being the only nonfiction film to be on the ten best lists of a majority of the most important American critics, of having received honorable mentions by the New York Film Critics, by the National Board of Film Critics, and not even being one of five films nominated for the Academy Awards. There does seem to be some sort of discrepancy there. And if we bother to talk about it, it has to do with the importance of the film, not only with the importance of the subject matter, but also, quite concretely with the importance that the judgment of one's, quote, "peers," unquote, has for one's own professional future. What happened? I don't know what happened. One thing is certainly detrimental to *The Memory of Justice:* the Academy, which is supposed to be the judgment of one's peers, does not have compulsory attendance to the screenings. I'm perfectly willing to have people vote by their feet at the box office. Again, this is part of the reality of show business. But I'm certainly not willing to accept the judgment of my peers, except on the basis of compulsory attendance. And certainly not when I make a four-and-a-half-hour film and am then forced to compete with one-and-a-half hour films. I'm not willing to admit to the validity of the judgment of out-of-work actors on that basis.

MANCHEL: Let me bring you back to the issue, though, of the criticism leveled against the film.

OPHULS: There is a suspicion you have, Frank, and that I may or may not share, that certain Jewish...Let me start from another angle. *The Sorrow and the Pity* had what I have become accustomed to call "the Jewish Seal of Good Housekeeping." And therefore, part of the commercial American success of *The Sorrow and the Pity*, even though it was also a four-and-a-half-hour movie of "talking heads," was to a very great extent predicated on attendance in New York and other places where live a very large percentage of the Jewish community. However, I think artists have an obligation to react against what they feel are the misunderstandings on which their previous successes have been predicated. It's one of these mysterious obligations that I think we have. And therefore, I quite consciously and openly confronted certain issues in *The Memory of Justice*, which I feel have to do with good conscience on false grounds. Therefore, I courted and eventually obtained the opposition of a certain segment of Jewish opinion in this country, which I would characterize as a neo-conservative segment of Jewish opinion, which one should further try to define as being middle-aged. We don't want to go too far into this point of view because it would take too much time. I understand their motives. I sympathize with some of their motives.

MANCHEL: We both do.

OPHULS: We both do. I feel some solidarity in this realm.

MANCHEL: Again, we both do.

OPHULS: I think that Auschwitz was unique. I think that the Holocaust of World War II, in its proportions, in its premeditation, in its ideology, in the fantastic support that this ideology obtained with the majority of the German people is unique. I agree with that and I agree with the solidarity with Israel, when Israel is in trouble. So I can understand how people, who in their youth had certain radical-liberal ideas, which made them, sympathize with radical-liberal causes, discovered in the process of aging, what the clichés were, what the pitfalls were, what the traps were. They re-examined the causes which they had formally subscribed to and were brought, because of Israel, because of the Holocaust, to revise their positions. But having said that I understand that, I must also add that I think that using the millions of victims of the Holocaust to give you a perpetual rain check on good conscience to take whatever political attitudes you care to choose concerning Nixon, for instance, or concerning the Vietnam War, then I cannot think of anything more indecent or more obscene for a Jew to indulge in.

MANCHEL: Now let's be clear on this so that there can be no misunderstanding. There is an attempt to put *The Memory of Justice* in the same category as Louis Malle's *Lacombe, Lucien,* or Lina Wertmuller's *Seven Beauties.*

OPHULS: Yes. Yes, because these people have chosen certain positions for their own reasons, which, I repeat, I understand: American power is what does, in fact, guarantee the survival of Israel. And therefore, I can understand that some people would come to adopt certain positions on Vietnam which I personally happen to believe that Jews, because of their experience, should not adopt when it comes to trying to assess who is the oppressor and who is the victim. But I can understand how this can come about. But to then use the monument of evil that Auschwitz and the Holocaust represent to vindicate their own options about Vietnam and about Israel, I repeat, in my opinion, is indecent and obscene, and *The Memory of Justice,* in comparison to that kind of attitude is, whatever else it may be, a decent film. I don't know if it is a good film. I don't know that it's a successful film. But I know that in comparison with that attitude, it is, on the purely humane level, a decent film.

MANCHEL: And you agree with Bruno Bettelheim and his criticism of *Seven Beauties?*[2]

OPHULS: Most emphatically.

MANCHEL: Now, two other points which are important to bring up. First is the question that Harold Rosenberg raises in the *New York Review of Books,*[3] when he refers to a book by Bradley F. Smith, entitled *Reaching Judgment at Nuremberg.* (Basic Books, 1976). Rosenberg claims that you make a factual error. You read the Smith book after it came out. What was your analysis of the Smith book, following your review of the book?

OPHULS: Do you think we should go into that? To explain what Bradley Smith says...?

MANCHEL: The point that Harold Rosenberg makes in his "Shadow of the Furies" is that Smith's book argues that Roosevelt and Churchill agreed on the summary execution of Nazi leaders, along with Stalin. You and the film make the statement, or the statement is made in the film, that only Stalin was responsible. Although Rosenberg admits that you didn't have access to the book at the time of your film, is it nevertheless true that your film presents inaccuracies?

OPHULS: Yes. I mean this is the only example of fair play that he displays in his whole article. He does say that I obviously did not have access to the book, because the book was published after the film was made. I thank him for his fairness.

MANCHEL: But since then you have read the book. Is Rosenberg right?

OPHULS: Let me try to explain. After having read the Rosenberg article, I couldn't read the Smith book because I was in Switzerland at that time. But as soon as I returned to Princeton, I got the book and read it. Now, here's the interesting thing as far as I can see. The statement in the film was made by Lord Hartley Shawcross, who was very much closer to sources of power at the time of the Second World War than any professional historian can be, including Bradley F. Smith, both on the basis of his position and the basis of his age. Lord Shawcross was Attorney General of the government at the end of the war and at the time of Potsdam. But the fact is that having read Mr. Smith's book, I find that there is no contradiction between the information that Smith had access to, and the statement that is made by Lord Shawcross in the film. Let me try to explain that as briefly as I can. In wartime, people, including the leaders of states, have a tendency to use the fury and the justified anger vis-a-vis the enemy in a certain way at the beginning of the war and then, as the peace draws closer and closer, that tendency will gradually be amended by various other considerations. This is one of the facts of life, of politics. And what Smith is talking about in his book which Rosenberg, fair play or no fair play, fails to mention, is in connection with the early stages of the war, the Quebec Conference between Roosevelt and Churchill. There is no contradiction, in fact, between my film and the new book whatever—these were all, of course, secret conferences. Bradley Smith, who is a very competent historian, had access to the diaries of a man called Biddle, who was a judge at Nuremberg and a very highly placed man in Roosevelt's brain trust during the war. And of course, all these were secret conferences, but the Quebec Conference between Churchill and Roosevelt, happened rather early in the war. I think 1942, if my memory serves me. And the Yalta Conference, which is what Shawcross talks about in the film, came two years later. So it is quite possible, and psychologically not at all unlikely, that by that time Churchill and Roosevelt had come to have other priorities, because the necessity of creating a just, democratic, peaceful society in the postwar world was at that time high in the order of priorities of sincere and dedicated democrats, which I believe both Churchill and Roosevelt were in their own way. And by that time a totalitarian ideologue and, as we now know, butcher and criminal like Stalin would not have had the same positions in Yalta, that by that time I assumed Roosevelt and Churchill could have adopted. So there is really no real contradiction, and Rosenberg's ingenuous attempt to rally Churchill and Roosevelt to what he thinks should have taken place after the war, namely summary executions, is extremely disingenuous, because it has to do with Biddle's diaries about Churchill's and Roosevelt's rage and commitment and dedication in the beginning of the war, before they actually confronted the necessities and the priorities of what are we going to do with the Nazi leaders after the war.

MANCHEL: Your defense of the film against the critics might lead some people to believe that you don't admit to any errors or misjudgments in the film. In point of fact, didn't Professor Raul Hilberg, author of *The Destruction of the European Jews*, point out to you that you made a serious omission in your questioning of Albert Speer?

OPHULS: Yes. This was—my visit here with you—this was a very unhappy moment for me. After my lecture and during a question and answer period, a middle-aged man who was obviously not a student, whom I therefore, assumed to be a Professor, but who did not identify himself, pointed out in the course of his comments and his question, the existence of a correspondence between Speer and a man called Pole, who was in charge of the construction of the concentration camps and the extermination camps. In the course of that correspondence, Speer apparently pleaded for harder measures and more ruthless measures to get the concentration camp-inmates to aid in the construction of their own camps.

MANCHEL: More primitive conditions.

OPHULS: Yes. Well, more ruthless conditions to get them to do the work. And the fact is that I was not aware of that correspondence, and that in my attempt as a movie-making amateur to do my homework and my research prior to making the film, I did not come across the correspondence, for whatever reason. And it then later turned out that the man who had made that comment during the question and answer period is Professor Raul Hilberg, who has written a very famous book on the Holocaust called *The Destruction of the European Jews*, which I indeed had read, or at least I had thought I had read, during my research. As a matter of fact, if I hadn't read it I would have been extremely remiss, because it is an extremely important book, but I guess I didn't read it thoroughly enough. It's like students preparing for an exam. You read some books, page by page, and chapter for chapter, and some books you read one chapter or two chapters and then you put them aside, read another book, and somehow you get into a process where after having read 30 or 40 books you don't remember which ones you have read page by page, and which ones you have glanced at, and you just take them all back to the library. And the fact is that I missed that particular thing, and this is a major sin of omission, because this is as far as I can ascertain a real down to earth objective fact. Had I been aware of that, it would have been certainly my job, as a journalist and as a filmmaker, to confront Speer in the course of the very long interview I did with him, with that particular piece of evidence and get his reaction to it. Had I done my homework properly and exhaustively, I certainly would have done that. There would have been no reason why I shouldn't have done that, and I certainly would have done that and, therefore, I feel very guilty and very responsible about this, because while there are a great number of journalists who have had and are still having access to Speer, still

I am one of maybe fifty or a hundred. And in not very many years Speer will be dead and I will be dead and Professor Hilberg will be dead and then nobody will have asked Speer that question.

MANCHEL: One final question after four years of hardship and agony, and now this severe critical attack from a certain element in society—where do you go with *The Memory of Justice?* Is it over? Do you walk away from it, or "Fight on?"

OPHULS: My mood shifts from one moment to the other, because it's an albatross hanging around my neck. I have obligations to my own family and to myself and to my own life and also to what I have learned from my father to be the priorities of show business, to go on being creative and productive as long as I possibly can, and *The Memory of Justice* in this time of my life is preventing me from doing that. Therefore, [I] very much wish to get away from it. I don't think I can, I don't think I can.

Notes

[1] Jay Cocks, "A Battle over Justice," *Time* (May 12, 1975), 77.
[2] Bruno Bettelheim, "Reflections: Surviving," *The New Yorker* (August 2, 1976), 31-36, 38-39, 42-52.
[3] Harold Rosenberg, "The Shadow of the Furies," *The New York Review of Books* (January 20, 1977), 47-49. See also Ophuls's and other responses in "The Memory of Justice: An Exchange," *The New York Review of Books* (March 17, 1977), 43-46.

10. A 1993 visit to UVM by famed writer Stephen King and director Mick Garris.

8.

Interpretations

When I listen to poetry and music, then I can live. You see, darling, the rest of the time it's just me. And that's not enough.[1]

Trish (Maureen Lipman)

Progress is impossible without change, and those who cannot change their minds cannot change anything.[2]

George Bernard Shaw

The rules of art are bullshit.[3]

Mick Garris

Someone once asked Mortimer J. Adler, the late and much-admired Columbia University philosopher, "What makes a great book great?" To me, his answer applies equally as well to films as to literature. "Great books [films]," he explained, "are those that contain the best materials on which the human mind can work in order to gain insight, understanding, and wisdom."[4] Adler made clear that each of us, since the dawn of civilization, searches for these "materials" because life's challenges remain universal and perennial. We need help in navigating our individual journeys. Failure is to be expected; not preparing for the possible problems, however, is foolish. Using imaginative resources as potential solutions often make the difference between the life well lived and the life not lived at all.

Particularly telling to me was Adler's admission the search for answers never ends, the solutions never found. That's why we keep studying, keep searching for better results than we have yet obtained. That is not to say there haven't been important ideas located. It is to insist they are not the total package. In other words, we do what we do not only because we have little choice if we want a meaningful life, but also because the arts—popular or classical, high or low, domestic or foreign, accessible or unattainable, spiritual or worldly, book or movie—provide welcome options in the eternal search. Such pursuits illustrate how and where the past imposes itself on the present. That's what I take the Great Conversations chiefly to be about.

And that's approximately where I was in 1976, nineteen years before I wrote the Stephen King essay showcased in this chapter. So why put it here in my chronology? Good question! I could be a wise guy and answer, "Why not? It's my story, and I'll damn well put it anywhere I want." But the truth makes for more interesting and dramatic discoveries.

Let's start mundanely with what was happening in the Department of Communication and Theatre when Milos Forman's *One Flew Over the Cuckoo's Nest* won the Oscar for Best Picture and swept all the major Academy Award categories. By then, I had realized I couldn't escape what I perceived to be UVM's black hole. So I became political and aggressive. Previously in my career, my fights had been about teaching what I wanted. Now I realized that wasn't enough so long as the "wrong" people dominated the status quo. Clearly, the smart thing to me was to boot the Objectionables out of office.

At first glance, the challenge seemed achievable. By the mid- to-late seventies, the Department's two damaging reviews were having a psychological impact on all of us. Both the Theatre and the Speech Pathology wings began making plans to break away and form their own independent divisions, which they soon did.[5] Also, a large group of my peers (unfortunately not large enough) supported my frustration and my uncool behavior. In addition, the chairperson, my primary nemesis, decided to step down.

So the Communication faculty went through the sham of selecting a new leader. I say "sham" because the outcome was never in doubt. Normally, the Dean would have gone for an outside Chair in such difficult circumstances. But no one was wasting any money on this Department. Twice I ran against a member of the opposition, and twice I got defeated. The numbers weren't there. Astonishingly, the winners always expected me to be a good loser and move on. They never understood that a kid from New York's mean streets grows up on the words of the immortal sportswriter Jimmy Cannon: "Show me a good loser, and I'll show you a schmuck."

Being trapped and outmanned in the confrontational Department of Communication was an outrageous state of affairs. What proved especially infuriating was not only my interacting on a daily basis with unpleasant people, but also my rationalizing the stupidity of the situation. Here was a community of scholars, intellectually trained, possessing invaluable information about the human condition, and they persisted, in my opinion, in squandering their time in an irresponsible, petty, and tasteless manner. Fool that I was, I was going head to head in a reasonable manner with the Objectionables. Making matters even more insufferable was the fact that neither the administration nor the faculty at large did anything to resolve the situation. Perfect material for a Stephen King horror story?

On a more intelligent and lofty level, *The Shining* essay, the focus of this chapter, reflects what I was learning about teaching in general and film study in particular.[6] For example, Jean Cocteau, artist and intellectual extraordinaire, once said, "The greatest crime an audience can commit against a work of art is the crime of inattention."[7] That concept had become one of the underpinnings in my teaching. No matter what the class, lecture or discussion, my approach was straightforward. I challenged the students to tell me what the film, the scene, the theme, or the technique was. Then I asked them to prove it. Tell me from where did they get this idea? Show me! Finally, I asked, "So what?" What was the advantage of knowing this? (A major challenge for me always was finding films that merited this scrutiny.)

My subtext, however, was never to get students to agree on a film's meaning or a director's intentions. I was never even certain the artists knew exactly what they had done and why and how. (I was just becoming sensitive to postmodernism film criticism that, as Rodney Ascher reminds me, argued artists rarely knew most of what their films contained.)[8] For example, there is the memorable scene in Cocteau's 1950 *Orphee*, where the poet (Jean Marais) sits in a parked car, turns on the radio, and writes down the words he hears from an unknown source. So much for seeking your muse! On the other hand, there are ludicrous interpretations of a work, as we will discuss later, that need to be discouraged and abandoned.

My style, therefore, was to develop in the students a strong self-confidence so they felt comfortable expressing their opinions, no matter how outrageous, and then defending those half-baked ideas. In a sense, the practice grew out of what Sheila had taught me about childrearing. You bring up your children to have wings and be independent. The worst thing you could do is to make people dependent on you in how they reason and live their lives. I challenged my students to think creatively, but also intelligently and responsibly.

Additionally, and admittedly oversimplified, I came to believe artists, consciously or not, immerse themselves into an intense communication process. For example, if it's a genre film they're making, they master the conventions and then play with the audience's expectations. The more the spectator knows, the richer the viewing experience becomes. You expect this interaction to happen because of past film practices: the directors anticipate what you are expecting; and then they, the artists, manipulate your attitude and your perceptions to enrich your viewing experiences. An ignorant director does not know or understand either the genre or the conventions. An inept audience lacks both the tools and the desire to appreciate a good director's techniques. To the unwise, you watch the movie once and then forget about it. They miss, as Auntie Mame so shrewdly stated, life's feast.

Thus, the best film viewings, as I understand the aesthetic dance, occur when both the artist and the audience are at the top of their game. No matter how often you see the action, hear the dialogue, listen to the music, study the production values, and analyze the screenplay, you learn something new about the artists' purposes, styles, and themes. The filmmaker provides the stimulation, I counter with the academic discipline, and you, the onlooker, walk away better for the involvement. Not a bad definition about what we mean by getting a formal education.

Still further, I came to believe that the greatest films focus both on irony and complexity. That is, if the questions Adler addressed earlier remain forever insoluble, the essential artist, for me, forces us to study a paradoxical situation, analyze our intricate options, and then make tentative but workable choices. What is not readily acknowledged is how much research and preparation an artist performs in creating a complex and complicated work of art. If more viewers recognized the intense effort that goes into the pre-production process, we might have less foolish explanations of what the finished product means. Also, the more empathetic the movie is, the more we benefit from reasonable artistic readings dealing with our values and habits. In this way, we come to recognize how film masterpieces contribute to the Great Conversations.

For example, in Federico Fellini's Oscar-winning *La Strada*,[9] a boorish Zampano (Anthony Quinn) literally buys the poor, ignorant Gelsomina (Giuletta Masina) from her mother. He then uses the naïve woman to service his needs and his desires as he arrogantly wanders the roads entertaining peasants with his crude strong man act. But unlike her tormentor, the simple-minded Gelsomina intuitively understands life's most valuable lessons, evident in the way she relates to a philosophical clown (Richard Basehart). He explains to her even a solitary rock is part of G-d's plan. Tragically, Zampano remains ignorant of the Fool's wisdom, and the sad character ends his days wandering the highways depressed and despondent. Among the many questions about the movie is why *La Strada*, considered one of the most influential films in motion picture history, is so revered? How does Fellini work his magic? What is he trying to tell us about life? Do we agree? What do we take away from the film?

Try another example, Stanley Kubrick's *Paths of Glory*,[10] where a hateful World War I French General (Adolphe Menjou) gives an irresponsible and tragic order to his beleaguered troops to attack a German battalion in nearby trenches. When many of the terrified French soldiers refuse to obey the suicidal directive, the detestable officer decides to make an example of what happens when you refuse to comply with a superior's direct order. The story then follows a courageous Colonel (Kirk Douglas) trying unsuccessfully to prevent the unjust execution of three randomly selected soldiers, falsely accused of cowardice. Both Humphrey Cobb's novel and Kubrick's film focus on the poet Thomas Gray's ironic line, "The paths of glory lead but to the grave."¹¹ What should a person do given these types of irrational choices in wartime and with no political or social justice possible? For that matter, how reasonable is war itself? How are these issues communicated through visuals, costumes, music, dialogue, editing, and set design? What benefits, if any, do we derive from pursuing these academic quests?

Returning one more time to Adler, I suggest to my students several ways you can recognize greatness in a work of art. For instance, does it stand the test of time? Can you watch *La Strada* and *Paths of Glory* over and over again and not be bored? Are they rooted just in the era in which they were made? Are their ideas and themes immediately accessible, or do they require repeated viewings to begin to understand their greatness? Is there only one meaning to a great film? Can a work of art be understood by anything other than serious study? Do these two films make genuine contributions to the Great Conversations?¹²

By 1976, struggling to perfect these ideas, I had reached two inescapable conclusions. First, I alone could not resolve the severe professional problems taking place in the Department of Communication, nor could other teachers here and in the future avoid similar ordeals. Humanity's nature produces in each generation senseless and inexcusable conditions that each of us needs to oppose. Second, unless you are a genius, you could not see, appreciate, or intelligently discuss how a great film, let alone an ordinary one, operates on multiple levels in a single screening. You need to return again and again to explore what you presumably missed in the initial experience. That goes for appreciating any great work or event! Intellectuals know this, and once they find a film or a book or a painting or a subject that captures their imagination, they return to it throughout their lives, always in pursuit of a better understanding both of the work and their grasp of it. Moreover, they also have a responsibility to speak out when foolish or irresponsible ideas are circulated about the work or the intentions of the artist.

Kubrick's *The Shining* touches on all these issues. Clearly, I am not the only person through the decades that has revisited this film masterpiece. Professor Tony Magistrale, who first stimulated my imagination about the movie, has done it repeatedly. So has the brilliant Stephen King who wrote the book that served as the source for the Kubrick movie. So has the prickly director Rodney Ascher who provided us with the imprudent documentary *Room 237*.[13] Such investigators are forever seeking in their actions something they have missed, looking to better understand what they thought they understood about the film, and how they can make better use of their imaginations to reinterpret the narrative. It is important to add, the results are not always useful to our quests. What do I mean by these assertions?

Let's start with the last first. As I began putting together this chapter, I came across Professor Magistrale's notable 2015 article, "Sutured Time: History and Kubrick's *The Shining*."[14] One of the world's leading authorities on the remarkable Stephen King, Tony had not only written articles in the past on *The Shining* in its various permutations, but also had edited an anthology on the book and film. You would have thought he had exhausted the subject. Not so! For this well-known scholar, "*The Shining* seems somehow special. Like Shakespeare in its depth and resonances."[15]

Among the many singular finds my colleague makes in "Sutured Time" are his judgments concerning King's intentions, the director's disagreements with the author, and the movie's possible meanings. For instance, Tony argues the modern master of horror wrote about the demonic forces of the past destroying Jack Torrance. Kubrick, however, went in an entirely different direction, giving us primarily a domestic drama. In the course of Magistrale's invaluable essay, we are told about the possibility of seeing *The Shining* as an adventure in time travel, in which the twenties are contrasted with the eighties, revealing historical patterns we as a culture choose to repress and to deny. He cites the gifted Frederick Jameson's Marxist perspective about the narrative deconstructing the economic gap between the rich and the poor. By the end of Magistrale's article, we find ourselves considering the insightful possibilities that Kubrick's movie makes us conscious of why so many people nostalgically yearn for a more "stable and business less regulated" life, why some people continue to "glamorize" the twenties as a "belle epoch" and not as a decadent age.

For his part, Stephen King who remained apoplectic about the Kubrick film, not only made his own version of his book, a 1997 ABC miniseries of the same name, but also ranted against the Kubrick movie for decades. Then, continuing his interest in the subject matter, King, in 2013, wrote *Doctor Sleep*,[16] a narrative that catches up with Danny Torrance in middle age.

Fortunately for me, I had a chance to "discuss" my unconventional article with the legendary author himself. In early 1993, while making a four-part TV miniseries of his book, *The Stand*,[17] Stephen King, along with Mick Garris, the author's favorite TV director, visited UVM. A distant relative of mine, who was producing the TV series, asked me to put together an audience to preview the production and provide feedback. Worth pointing out, it was the incredible success of this miniseries that led directly to both King and Garris making a TV series on *The Shining* in 1997. All together, the creative duo has collaborated on eight television films.

During the lunch break; as King, Garris, and I were walking across the campus to get something to eat, I explained my revisionist article to the famous author. Amazing as it sounds, King grasped the concept immediately, and he simply said, "It works. No problem."

Finally, there is the notorious Rodney Ascher documentary, *Room 237*. Just when I thought I had enough material to introduce the essay you are about to read, I saw Ascher's controversial movie and found a number of far-fetched interpretations of *The Shining*. It seemed to me as if nothing previously studied had proved so intellectually irresponsible. Let me cite just two examples by way of illustrating my disbelief. The first concerns the typewriter that Jack uses in the film. Citing the speculations of a recognized historian in German studies, Ascher insists Kubrick's movie could be interpreted as a subtext on the Holocaust. Starting with the fact the typewriter is of German make and pointing out the constant references Kubrick makes to the number 42, the undisciplined documentarian concludes the director is ironically setting the narrative back in Europe in 1942, when the Nazis decided on the death camps as the Final Solution to the Jewish problem. To buttress his argument, he cites Raul Hilberg's masterwork, *The Destruction of the European Jews* as evidence of his theory, explaining that the Holocaust scholar in his impeccable research focuses on how bureaucrats used mechanical apparatus to destroy the Jews. Still further, the film narrator turns to Steven Spielberg's *Schindler's List* to demonstrate how lists and typewriters proved indispensable to the Nazi genocide. Even further, Ascher claims that both Hilberg and Kubrick discussed these matters over the phone.

This last assertion I know to be untrue, because when Kubrick first contacted Raul in the early 1990s, long after *The Shining* came out, my colleague called me to find out what I knew about the famous filmmaker. It seemed the director was considering making a Holocaust film and wanted to fly Hilberg to England to discuss the various possibilities. Being busy with other matters, Raul declined the invitation.

Thus the Holocaust interpretation, while imaginative and stimulating, does not pass the credibility test. It lacks both the necessary facts, and also ignores how the production of *The Shining* was researched and constructed.

Another example from *Room 237* proves how often well-intentioned people disagree about the same material. Ascher offers the theory *The Shining* may be about Kubrick insisting the past routinely impinges on the present. If that is true, he argues, then thinking the movie's theme is overly influenced by the past is a mistake. Using Hallorann's discussions with Danny as proof, the documentary filmmaker maintains Kubrick does not want us to get depressed about humanity's past atrocities. Thus, if the filmmaker takes us down the corridors of history metaphorically in the Overlook Hotel, it is because he wants us to realize the past is not real. The horrible events that allegedly took place in the twenties no longer exist except in our minds. We can and should excise them from our consciousness and be free of the past. Then, Ascher concludes, you can view *The Shining* as a positive experience that encourages us to ignore history and to move on.

I, as a Jew and someone who lived through the thirties and forties, like Kubrick himself, find such a belief inexplicable. If anything, I, and I assume Kubrick does as well, subscribe completely to the notion we should never ignore history, and the value of the past is to help us prevent such atrocities from happening in the future. I see us as not being victimized by history, but as being encouraged to become better educated and to develop a greater awareness of our responsibilities and our challenges. At the very least, I find Ascher's assertions weak.

158   *Take Two: A Film Teacher's Unconventional Story*

Finally, before we move to *The Shining* essay, it seems appropriate to end this overview of the mid-1970s at UVM with one last look back on my professional problems. My nemesis, the former Communication Chair, desperately wanted a way out of our professional quagmire. So in late 1976, he brought to my attention that the College had a new Dean, a chemist with impeccable credentials from Harvard and MIT, who had sent out an e-mail to the faculty asking for candidates to fill the job of Associate Dean. "Frank," the ex-Chair said, "why don't you apply for the position?"

Notes

[1] Lewis Gilbert, *Educating Rita*. USA: Columbia Pictures, 1983.
[2] Qtd. from Brainy Quote.com.
[3] Rodney Ascher, "Secrets of *The Shining* Panel Discussion," *Room 237*. DVD. USA: Highland Park Classics, 2012.
[4] Mortimer J. Adler, "What Makes a Great Book Great?" *Great Ideas from the Great Books*. New York: Washington Square Press, Inc., 1961.121-122.
[5] According to Dean Joel Goldberg, the Department of Communication and Theatre divided into three departments—Communication, Communication Sciences and Disorders, and Theatre—on June 17, 1977. E-Mail to the author, 6/15/15.
[6] For an interesting look at how another young person learned about Kubrick's *The Shining*, see David Gilmour, *The Film Club*. New York: Twelve, 2008. 61-63.
[7] Jean Cocteau, "Sunday, the 28th," *Beauty and the Beast: Diary of a Film*. Adapted by George Amberg. Mineola, New York: Dover Publications, 1946. 74.
[8] Rodney Ascher, *Room 237*.
[9] Federico Fellini, *La Strada (The Road)*. Italy: Dino de Laurentiis Distributions, 1954.
[10] Stanley Kubrick, *Paths of Glory*. USA: United Artists, 1957.
[11] Thomas Gray, "Elegy Written in a Country Churchyard," 1751.
[12] Mortimer J. Adler, 120.
[13] Rodney Ascher, *Room 237*.
[14] Tony Magistrale, "Sutured Time: History and Kubrick's *The Shining*," *The Shining: Studies in the Horror Film*. Ed. Daniel Olson. Lakewood, CO: Centipede Press, 2015. 187-202.
[15] E-Mail from Tony Magistrale to the author. June 1, 2015.
[16] Stephen King, *Doctor Sleep: A Novel*. New York: Scribner, 2013.
[17] Mick Garris, *The Stand*. USA: Greengrass Productions, 1994.

What About Jack? Another Perspective on Family Relationships in Stanley Kubrick's "The Shining"[1]

> In the end we all come to be cured of our sentiments. Those whom life does not cure death will. The world is quite ruthless in selecting between dream and reality, even where we will not. Between the wish and the thing, the world lies waiting.
>
> Cormac McCarthy, *All the Pretty Horses*

If anyone in 1980 wanted to see a modem dysfunctional household being demolished by violence, they could watch Stanley Kubrick's *The Shining*, a screen adaptation of Stephen King's 1977 best-selling novel.[2] This horror story of a family in crisis ends with Jack Torrance, an insane husband, first terrorizing his wife and next murdering the man who had come to save their five-year-old son, Danny. Then, calling himself the "Big Bad Wolf," the beastly, limping father madly pursues the boy through the snow-covered maze of the Overlook Hotel. Cleverly, however, Danny retraces his steps, and not only escapes from his ax-wielding father but also succeeds in ending Jack's reign of terror over the Torrance household. The shot most of us remember is that of the deranged, grinning Jack hunched over in the snow, frozen to death.

For more than a decade, the fate of the Torrance family has been blamed on Jack's insanity and the evil forces at the Overlook Hotel. This essay re-examines those sentiments. My hypothesis is that *The Shining's* reception is skewed by a contemporary critical desire to make Jack Torrance, the white, American, middle-class father, the scapegoat for the sins of a patriarchal society. While the surface facts—e.g. Jack's drunken rages, his deranged pursuit of Wendy and Danny with an ax, and the murder of Hallorann—find him guilty as charged, I argue that a closer reading of the evidence produces a different verdict on Jack's behavior, and that there are mitigating circumstances for his diabolical role in the disintegration of his family. I think more attention must be given to his condition prior to the attacks on his relations and murder of the hotel chef. In short, this essay asks why, when so many critics often associate the terms "fantasies," "victimization," and "exploitation" with this film, does Jack get left out in the cold?

In taking this tack, I want to be clear that I am not excusing wife-bashing, child abuse, or homicide. Nor is this exercise part of a backlash against current interpretive criticism revolted by the predicament of women and children in a patriarchal society. My quarrel is not with stated academic judgments, but with the omission of any serious empathy with Jack's predicament. Debates over other issues, like Kubrick's "signature," his revolutionary use of the Steadicam, the chess parallels, the significance of an African American being killed in the film but not in the novel, or the meaning of the "shining," I leave to others. My desire is to do what Anthony Magistrale perceptively claims both Kubrick and King do: offer insights "about the deathless struggle to define what it means to be human," and to contemplate the "psychological terrors" that spare no one when a household breaks apart.[3]

That a revisionist approach is necessary would not surprise Kubrick, who is acutely aware of just how long the public takes to understand and to appreciate his works.[4] None of his twelve films has ever opened to widespread critical and commercial successes.[5] Whether it is his painstaking emphasis on non-narrative techniques, his novel exploration of popular film genres, or his refusal to be pigeonholed, Kubrick remains an enigma to most audiences. Consequently, his works are often misunderstood, with observers berating him for lacking a consistent style, a failure to get his ironic messages across, an obsession with detached narratives, and a mean-spirited attitude about human nature.

These by now predictable charges greeted his 1980 screen adaptation of *The Shining*.[6] James Hala's survey of the movie's reception showed that popular reviewers "loved" it, journals "defended" it, and intellectual magazines "disliked it intensely."[7] Norman Kagan put the case more gently: "A majority of the critics, although they found *The Shining* flawed, said they felt Kubrick must be praised for seeking to move beyond the horror genre."[8]

Equally predictable, *The Shining's* reputation, as with almost all of Kubrick's works, increased upon closer inspection of his techniques. Even during the film's first run, Janet Maslin commented that *"The Shining,* like *Barry Lyndon,* is so richly textured, it improves immeasurably upon second viewing, once an audience moves beyond worrying about a storyline or taking the facts at face value."[9] A decade later, Mark Madigan, comparing the film to Kafka's *The Metamorphosis,* concluded that while both works "envision worlds of futility and disorder, they offer salvation through their superbly crafted, highly ordered depictions of chaos."[10]

This essay probes one constant audience interest about that chaos: how a nuclear family falls apart as symbolized by the fate of the Torrance household. Whereas King's novel is preoccupied with the fears of the five-year-old son, Kubrick's movie centers on the traumas of the father. Both creative labors, however, describe a structural relationship where everyone feels alienated, where their values are shallow, and where an inability to discuss dehumanizes Jack, tyrannizes his family, and leads to his doom.

A quick scan of the critical literature on Kubrick's film readily reveals Jack's status. He is seen either as a well-meaning unemployed Vermont schoolteacher who eventually turns into a monster; or as an unredeemable alcoholic who in rapid order abuses his son, loses his job, and becomes a homicidal maniac. His tenure as an off-season caretaker of an isolated luxurious Colorado hotel not only destroys his self-esteem, but also turns him into a primal beast. Even when critics claim that the tragic events are manipulated by the surrealistic ghosts of the Overlook Hotel, the spectators dole out all their sympathy for Wendy, Danny, and the murdered head chef, Hallorann. In fact, Jack is more often perceived as an appendage of the Overlook Hotel's diabolical forces than as a tragic person dominated by powers greater than himself. About the closest critics come to sensing Jack's dilemma is labeling it either as a "nightmare"[11] or as the allegorical fantasy of "the American Breadwinner."[12]

The surface reasons for these antipathies are revealing and very pertinent to a revisionist approach. First, the Kubrick and King labors are clearly identified as the products of their age. In commenting on the film's origins, P. L. Titterington affirms that *"The Shin-*

ing works primarily through elements that evoke America's past history and its present state of society."[13] Alan Cohen's analysis of the novel is even more specific. He points out that the seventies epitomize the radical shift in our values and behavior because of Watergate, the Vietnam War, a sexual revolution, and the skyrocketing divorce rate.[14] Not surprisingly, film reviewers, socialized by reactions to the book and sensitized to the toll that such events were having on American society and families, dwell on Jack's violent nature and lament the vulnerability of his wife and child. Why waste time scrutinizing the beast within us, when, like the nation itself turning to an optimistic Ronald Reagan, we could find comfort in the illusory salvation of a terrorized mother and son? "The urge," Magistrale wisely points out, "is to see the evil 'out there' in someone or something else (an evil empire) [rather] than to the locus on the self."[15]

A second reason for ignoring Jack's humanity was the consciousness-raising activities of feminists. What we read in the film journals about the victimized Wendy reflects a long overdue awakening to the horrors that far too many desperate wives experience daily. For example, Flo Leibowitz and Lynn Jeffres interpret the tragedy of the Torrance family as an allegorical tale of the problems women face in a male-dominated world: "Jack's sense of self and his relation to others in his often fantasized world shows him to be animated by a patriarchal authoritarianism."[16] Susan White makes a similar point, but in a different context, insisting that Kubrick's view of sex and aggression are simply facilitators of "fantasies about women," and are yet one more example of "the adaptation of the male to the demands of a ritualistic male group."[17] Even in the critiques of the novel, a feminist critic like Patricia Ferreira downgrades Jack's problems to valorize "a contemporary Hester Prynne, [who] possesses the strength and the courage to turn away from her husband and to lead herself and Danny away from the Overlook."[18] Each critique, in its own way, attacks the values of those males who not only abhor feminine characteristics in men but also encourage anti-feminine behavior. This legitimate culturally political perspective often associated with Kubrick's films—*i.e.* he identifies male sexual power with aggression—is not limited to feminist critics.[19]

My position is different. Denouncing unacceptable behavior is not enough. By failing to scrutinize why Jack is seduced by false myths of success and patriarchal authoritarianism, we ignore the appeal of such seductions and focus only on the symptoms. I believe that Kubrick also wants us to study the dark side of Jack's personality and recognize that each of us has the potential to be overcome by our Id. Why else would Kubrick insist that "One of the things that horror stories can do is to show us the archetypes of the unconscious: we can see the dark side without having to confront it directly."[20] This perspective permits us to interpret the narrative symbolically through the signs and subtexts of the fantastic. Thus, the filmmaker's emphasis on associative editing,[21] deep focus, *mise en scene*, and repetition guides the spectator to specific images of a tormented man who needs help, but finds only manipulation and rejection. His dilemma over how to reconcile his dreams with reality must be addressed if the family structure is to improve.

A third reason for neglecting Jack's problems is Kubrick's handling of the horror genre. While some reviewers are quick to dismiss *The Shining* as an artless retelling of familiar material,[22] many observers theorize that Kubrick's first full-blown use of the film formula provides important ideas about the flaws in patriarchal family values.[23] For example, he uses the "haunted-house" convention to symbolize the decadence of the present and the guilt of the past.[24] The frequent shots of photographs and artifacts decorating the hotel's corridors, floors, and rooms add credibility to the diabolical hold that history has on us today.

To that end, Leibowitz and Jeffres argue that "...Kubrick seems to be saying that America has a right to be superstitious, that its ghosts are real, capable of driving men mad, and that the most dangerous ghosts of all are the myths of success ('The American Dream') and of the authoritarian father."[25] Moreover, he uses the Western motif to rethink our myths about the American frontier, seeing it not as a place for opportunity and justice, but as a setting for ruthlessly destroying our dreams. It is not accidental, therefore, that there are frequent allusions in both the book and the film to the exploitation of Native American traditions and ancestral burial grounds. According to Thomas Allen Nelson, Kubrick uses"...both Jack's madness and the Overlook's past [to] express a decidedly masculine ethos, one which not only threatens the structures of normality (man/woman, family) but also the integrity of psycho/sexual duality."[26]

While these reasons for Jack's infamy are presented imaginatively, they are woefully insensitive to the father's crisis. Who in this "sexual allegory" about the decline of the American family is most injured? Who is the one person most traumatized by twisted fantasies about success? When you study the relationship in the film between violence and control, who is the one person conditioned to believe that the best way to end chaos is by "legitimate" force? Still further, who is the one member of the nuclear family destroyed by the ghosts of the past and their insistence on maintaining traditional sex roles?

Obviously, I feel it is Jack Torrance.[27] For that matter, so do the evil forces of the Overlook Hotel. Clearly, they see him as the ideal candidate to manipulate because of his traumatic childhood experiences, his substance abuse, and his feelings of inadequacy as a patriarchal figure. Again, my purpose is not to take away from the pain suffered by Wendy or Danny. Nor is it to excuse Jack's bestiality. Rather, if this film reflects the toll that our culture is taking on the American nuclear family, we need to see why and to ask how we can help all the members of the household.

In the interests of space, let me comment on just two specific elements: the opening scenes of the film (primarily "The Interview" sequence) and the relationship between Jack and his family. Given a start in a new direction, others then can pursue the pattern of Jack's deterioration. My strategy is to observe Kubrick's restructuring of traditional family connections to underscore Jack's frustration and disenchantment with the myths of success, middle-class family values, and marital life.

Consider our introduction to the screen narrative.[28] Before the credits appear, a helicopter shot furnishes us with an omniscient long take of a glacial lake surrounded by towering mountains, as Bartok's music plays on the soundtrack. Then the credits begin. In the background, the expressionistic camera tracks inward and tilts to the right, foreshadowing something both threatening and unnatural. Cutting soon establishes that we are following a small, at first barely perceptible car[29] moving along a tortuous route (Kagan calls it "serpentine roads"[30]), carrying its solitary passenger to a prearranged interview for a job as the off-season caretaker of the isolated Overlook Hotel. Ominous horn music and sounds of animals cue us to the inhuman dangers that lie ahead.

From the outset, Kubrick presents Jack's terrible isolation and impending doom. Whatever illusions he may have about the job or "making it big" have already been predetermined by a hostile universe. As we discover shortly, he and his family have recently moved from Vermont to Colorado in search of a fresh start. But the film permits no escape. Neither Kubrick nor his co-scriptwriter, Diane Johnson, includes any of the novel's biographical information about Jack's abused childhood or his regrettable relationship with the wealthy and irresponsible surrogate father-figure, Al Shockley. In the novel, these details help to explain Jack's drinking problems, his drunken rage that resulted in his accidentally dislocating Danny's shoulder, his being fired from his teaching position, and his troubled marriage. The screen collaborators, however, provide us with few details. It's as if the Reagan-Bush generation were given the chance to draw from their personal experiences so that they can identify individually with a fragmented family struggling to survive economically in an indifferent world. On the surface, Kubrick shows us an apparently normal person seeking peace and quiet in an ideal winter setting for a budding writer. But closer examination reveals the truth of F. Scott Fitzgerald's cynical observation that there are no second acts in America.

"The Interview" sequence concentrates on one major event: Stuart Ullman, the hotel manager, reviewing the caretaker's responsibilities, along with his explanation of the tragic events of 1970. This section is framed by a prologue, showing Jack's arrival at the Overlook Hotel, and an epilogue, when he calls Wendy to say he's got the job, Significantly, Kubrick intersperses this central event with scenes of Wendy and Danny at home discussing the impending news, Danny being frightened in the bathroom, and a doctor's house call to the Torrance apartment.

I view Kubrick's editing as ironic, calling attention to the difference between what is said and what is shown. To me, his associative editing creates two different "interviews," so that we can graphically witness the conflicts in the Torrance family.

Let's examine the sequence from that position. It starts with

Jack entering the large, plush, almost empty hotel and asking the desk clerk (a woman) where Ullman's office is. Once there, he announces himself to the chief executive, who then asks Betty, his secretary, to get the two men some coffee and to ask Bill Watson, a hotel employee, to attend the meeting, Thus, Kubrick's visuals document the shift from the vastness of space seen in the trip and in the lobby to the narrow and confining room in which the interview takes place. He also shows the unequal status of women in this contemporary setting. This is a familiar approach in Westerns, used to contrast the expansive purity of the wilderness with the corrupting, claustrophobic nature of civilization.

In that same generic mode, the entrance to the office has, on one side of the wall, four photographs of the changing seasons at the Overlook Hotel, and on the other side, a Native-American tapestry. Kubrick, through Ullman and the Navaho furnishings of the hotel, will remind us that America's exploitation of American Indians is evident in the sacrilegious building of the hotel on ancestral burial grounds and in using their artifacts for decorative purposes. The objects themselves testify to the presence of the past in the present.

To underline the symbolic import of our plagued heritage, Kubrick steers our attention to the first of several American flags, this one a small model placed prominently on Ullman's desk as he discusses the hotel's checkered history. The advantage of identifying the Overlook with America itself is to have us view the hotel symbolically as a warehouse for the nation's values. Thus, parallels are drawn between the past and the present. Just as we come to appreciate the links between the nineteenth century and post-World War II America, we also come to see Jack's personal history as analogous to his father's. Kubrick punctuates this perspective by associating each time change with acts of violence. It is another reminder that the Torrances are following in the path of previous victims. Titterington cleverly points out that "The theme of America is... pervasively present in the elaborate color scheme of the film, using a red, white, and blue base, the colours of the American flag."[31] That patriotic imagery would have Jack wrapped up in the myths of success as well as seduced by a ritualized male society. His problems then are our problems and not to be ignored. As Leibowitz and Jeffres claim, "Jack is caretaker not only of the hotel but also of the American dream, depicted in the film as empty and haunted."[32] True enough, but that dream also remains formidable and seductive.

Before we get to the Overlook's past, a dissolve to an apartment complex in Boulder redirects our attention to Wendy and Danny. They're seated at the kitchen table having lunch. The *mise en scene* is very telling. The boy is in the background eating, a television is running a violent *Roadrunner* cartoon, and the mother is screen right reading and smoking. Their appearance—e.g. clothes, posture, movement—and the milieu dramatize the dismal existence they lead. As Anthony Macklin tells us, "...Kubrick sees human beings as empty, their values shallow and vacuous....Their basic banality is most evident in their dialogue."[33] The brief conversation between mother and son reveals that in the three months they've been in Colorado, neither the parents nor Danny has made any friends. Eventually, Wendy asks the child what Tony, his imaginary friend, thinks about the possibility of moving to the hotel for the winter. We can't be sure whether she takes Tony seriously or is just placating Danny. But she tells her son that she is sure Tony is looking forward to the new surroundings. Danny says he isn't. Before another dissolve takes us back to Ullman's office, Wendy assures her son that they're "...all going to have a real good time there." This cliché-ridden comment represents the first of her many denials about impending psychological dangers threatening the family.

Thus, Jack's precarious economic situation, his troubled home life, and his "honorable" responsibilities position him to be exploited by corporate interests. The world of big business is narrowing in on him. Lest anyone think such a judgment is a stretch, study Jack's facial expressions as he rationalizes every possible objection to his taking the job. Asked if the physical tasks are too demanding, he smiles awkwardly and says no. Asked if he's worried about cabin fever, being physically isolated from October 30 to May 15 in the snowbound hotel, he tells his male listeners that he craves solitude so that he can work on his proposed book. In this instance, his response seems a bit defensive, as if he is trying to appear more independent and intellectual than he is. Ullman responds approvingly, pointing out that, in contrast, for some people "solitude and isolation" can be treacherous. The theme of corporate exploitation is also apparent in the frequent references later by Lloyd, the bartender, and Delbert Grady, the ex-caretaker, to "the management of the Overlook." Equally telling is Jack's refusal to vacate the hotel to get his son medical help because he has "signed a contract" and has to stand by his legal obligations.

For Kubrick, the focus here and throughout the film on snow and isolation functions metaphorically, reminding us just how "cold" reality and relationships have become in the modem world.[34] For Jack, the interview with Ullman gives him an opportunity for male bonding and to prove his conformity to the stereotypical Western male ethic. He's a tough hombre who cherishes the chance to prove his worth isolated in a remote part of the country. This is how "real" men make it big in the New World. Later in the film, in his conversations with Lloyd and Grady, Jack will again display his desire to fit in with the sex-role socialization of a ritualized male society. He has to prove again to them that he "has the belly" for the task, and that the hotel was not wrong in choosing him rather than Wendy for the "assignment."

The full extent of corporate manipulation becomes apparent when Ullman asks if Jack has been told about the events of 1970, knowing that the executives back in Denver didn't want to scare Jack away. As the manager tells the tragic story of Charles Grady, Kubrick cuts to Watson's study of Jack's reactions. Both hotel agents are watching Jack to see how he reacts to hearing that the former caretaker became crazed during the winter, murdered his family (wife and two daughters) with an ax, and then blew his brains out. Jack listens intently, but says that he's not superstitious. In his mind, he can't afford to be. The code of the West says that a man has to do what a man has to do. And being a "man," he needs to provide for his kin. So he quickly dismisses Ullman's question about how the family will take to the anecdote by saying, "That's quite a story. I understand why the people in Denver left it for you to tell me. And as far as my wife is concerned, I'm sure she'll be absolutely fascinated by it. She's a confirmed ghost story and horror film addict."

A third dissolve takes us back to Danny, who is brushing his teeth in the bathroom. Like Jack, the boy is shown in a claustrophobic setting, also having a conversation about the hotel. Only his talk is with his imaginary friend. This time, Kubrick removes any doubts about the boy's psychic credibility. Not only do we hear foreboding music as Tony warns the boy about the Overlook's bloody past, but he also tells him that Jack will call shortly to say he's got the job. Danny relays this information to Wendy, who is washing dishes in the kitchen while the TV plays silently in the background. The call comes seconds later. While Wendy and Jack exchange perfunctory comments, Kubrick cuts to Danny uttering a silent scream before the screen goes completely black. Unlike his foolish father, the boy fears the sins of the past. On another level, it symbolically reaffirms that the father and son do not relate well to each other. They think, feel, and behave differently. Their alienation evokes strong feelings from ex-servicemen in the audience who, being away from home for long periods, experienced similar problems with children who didn't know or remember their fathers.

In the darkness, we hear a voice asking Danny to lie completely still. The scene then opens to a doctor (Anne Jackson) examining Danny and trying to find out about his imaginary friend. When the boy refuses to discuss him, the physician and Wendy retire to another room. She then questions Wendy about the boy's background and their present circumstances. Wendy's dialogue makes it appear that she is putting the best face on why Jack's drunken behavior one evening five months ago is really not the direct cause for his grabbing the child and dislocating his shoulder—"It's just the sort of thing you do a hundred times with a child…in the park and the street." Moreover, she dutifully assures the doctor that her husband hasn't touched a drop of liquor since and that he has told her to leave him if he does.

Kubrick's *mise en scene*, however, makes it abundantly clear that neither the wife nor the physician accepts what she says as the truth. Nervous and smoking rapidly, Wendy personifies a deeply troubled woman who has genuine concerns for her child's safety and the future of her marriage. To underscore this point, Kubrick has the doctor sitting passively on the couch, listening intently, and offering no encouragement. One might even speculate that the physician is quite familiar with parental denials of child abuse and marital turmoil. Interestingly, given the time frame, she never asks if Jack has gotten any help for his drinking problem, or whether the parents have sought any family counseling. Equally troubling is why she doesn't pursue the point that Danny first discovered Tony after the boy was injured by his father, or the fact that Danny was taken out of his Vermont nursery school because of his psychological problems and never re-enters school once the family gets to Colorado.

That is the way "The Interview" sequence ends. In a logical progression, the film establishes a dysfunctional nuclear family unable to talk effectively with each other. Except for the isolated case of the doctor, women exist as clerks, secretaries, and mothers. None of them is aggressive. They serve coffee, rear children, and don't get involved in making it big. Wendy portrays the suffering wife, homebound, caught in a loveless marriage, and ineptly trying to keep the family together by suppressing any doubts about Jack or Danny's mental health. This is Wendy's seduction by patriarchal authoritarianism. In her mind, that is what a good wife is supposed to do: wash, weep, and wait patiently. Under no conditions is it "proper" for her to take action "against her sea of troubles." Self-control, not anger, is the traditional way. Not until she discards her submissive role and becomes the "contemporary Hester Prynne" will Wendy escape her cultural trap. The tragedy is that she has to flee her marriage, rather than find a way to make it work.

Kubrick's casting of Shelley Duvall as Wendy is vital to the portrayal of the mother's image in the disintegrating nuclear family. Unlike the self-reliant character described in King's novel, she appears neither attractive nor bright. Otherwise, Kubrick explains, the film audience would "wonder why she puts up with Jack for so long." Unlike the Jack of the novel, the film's protagonist is not a loving or kind husband. Whereas King stressed this positive aspect of Jack's personality, Kubrick eliminates it completely. More to the point, he adds, "Shelley seemed to be exactly the kind of woman that would marry Jack and be stuck with him."[35] Her quirky mannerisms and nondescript appearance superbly capture the sense of despair and disappointment that makes Wendy's existence so depressing.

Simultaneously, we see Jack's crisis. No one alleviates his guilt for what has happened. Neither his wife nor his child appears ready to forgive him for his mistakes. The move westward has not improved interpersonal relations, provided more love and security for the family, or made Danny happier. Unlike King's novel, the film never shows the wife or the child being affectionate to the father, nor he to them. It is one more example of Kubrick commenting on the modem American family. Jack is spiritually alone. His patriarchal conditioning tells him to work hard, provide for his family, and repress "feminine" characteristics. Interestingly, Jack is an educated man, whose career allows him ample time to enjoy his family. Yet, he neither plays with his son nor shares any of his wife's interests. Driven by a warped masculine mentality that violently blames women for men's failures, he personifies the symbolic misogynist who finally reverts to an apelike creature.

Nevertheless, it is particularly telling that Wendy never confides to him that Tony may be more than a delusion; that maybe Jack should not take this job because of Danny's fears and the circumstances surrounding Tony's warning before the phone call; that maybe Jack's drinking and behavior are symptoms of problems more deep-rooted than they care to admit, thus requiring professional help. With so much riding on this job and Wendy's passivity, with no one offering Jack any alternatives to the false standards by which "real men" are being judged, Jack has few choices and is easily seduced by corporate interests. He then deludes himself further by thinking that he's a writer and that the off-season job fits perfectly into his plans.

But we are not so naive. We see his predicament, we watch the male interplay in the office between the have's and have not's, we hear the menacing music, and we observe the symbolic settings. Like many anxious and insecure men, out-of-work and deluded by myths of success and a second chance, Jack Torrance is a sad figure more deserving of our pity than our contempt. I am not justifying or condoning what he does. I am arguing that pain clouds judgment, that a too materialistic society celebrates patriarchal authority, and that what happens to Jack is predictable if one chooses to put profit and prestige over personal relationships.

The choice of Jack Nicholson to play this ordinary, unimaginative human being only added to the film's mixed reception. Those who, like King himself,[36] found the star's persona and broad acting style antithetical to Kubrick's ironic story dismissed the decade's most famous anti-hero as dull and miscast. Even Macklin, who recognized that the part of Jack required an actor who effectively combined the ordinary with the absurd, found Nicholson's performance "out of synch."[37] I, on the other hand, find him ideal for the part, especially because we do identify the actor with his previous roles in *Easy Rider, Five Easy Pieces,* and *One Flew Over the Cuckoo's Nest.* Who better to symbolize a generation's sense of an absurd world where it is fashionable to make Faustian pacts? Jack Kroll makes an equally telling point: "Nicholson [is] the most eloquent smiler on the screen....The movies have never shown a more haunted face than this..."[38]

Seen from this perspective, we can appreciate the rich texture of the next scene, which begins the film's second episode, "Closing Day. "Kubrick repeats the tortuous drive back to the Overlook Hotel, this time with an interior shot of the family packed together in the yellow Volkswagen. Jack is sullen, Wendy pensive, and Danny troubled. Why? They should be excited by the upcoming adventure. But something is wrong. On the surface, everyone is anxious and the child is hungry, having refused to eat breakfast before the trip began. The tense silence is broken when Wendy asks if they are traveling the same route that the ill-fated Donner Party took years ago. Jack caustically points out that was farther west—in the Sierras. When Danny asks what the Donner Party was, Jack explains that they were settlers trapped in the snowbound mountains who resorted to cannibalism to stay alive. He tells the boy, "They did what they had to do!" When Wendy tries to end the conversation, fearing how Danny will react to it, the boy says it's okay, "I saw it on TV." Jack maliciously replies, "See, it's okay. He saw it on television." As Keeler observes, "He [Jack] is like so many family men who hunch up in their little trap and bubble with sarcasm because their resentment is acceptable only in that form."[39] The scene ends in stony silence as Kubrick dissolves to a shot of the foreboding Overlook Hotel.

Again, Kubrick's expository scenes examine the dissolution of the nuclear family. The Western motif returns us to the illusion of settlers taking a dangerous journey through unexplored territory. Just as the inexperienced organizers of the original quest, George and Jacob Donner, found frontier conditions more difficult than they imagined, fought among themselves, and squandered precious time, so will the Torrances. And as we will see later, the allusions to Native Americans also will remind us of the parallels between the hotel's shameful history and modern American values.

On the surface, Jack's rudeness to his family reveals their vulnerability. On another level, however, it is symptomatic of his frustration and disillusionment. Together, they symbolize the failure of human communication to solve our problems. TV becomes the scapegoat for the perpetuation of America's fantasies, and no one feels responsible for looking further into the real reasons for their personal crises. Trapped in the small car are three, not two, discouraged and unhappy people grappling with the memories of the past and uneasy about the future.

Once we reorient our focus, we search for ways that Jack's disappointments could have been treated before they led to his dehumanization. What could Wendy and Danny have done to offset his feelings of inadequacy as a breadwinner, writer, husband, and father? Why couldn't the family have shown more love and understanding to each other instead of so much suspicion and disdain? Let me be clear on this point. I do not know if compassion and caring could have compensated for the depth of Jack's frustrations and fury. But then neither does anyone else. It is the road not taken. And as the narrative shows us, the family's failure to try contributes significantly to Jack's embracing the "warmth" of ghosts.

Consider how differently the film's dialogue sounds when we study it from the perspective of a disenchanted husband and parent. Very important is Wendy's wrongly accusing Jack of injuring Danny. Her insensitivity in blaming her distraught husband for the strangle marks on the boy's neck motivates much of the action that follows. From this point on, the two parents became permanently estranged. We see why the disgruntled Jack is attracted to Grady's treatment of his family when they "got out of line." Wendy's terrifying discovery of Jack's manuscript containing only a continuous statement, "All work and no play makes Jack a dull boy," now reminds us how tormented he is by his "masculine" failings. No wonder he sneers at her, "Do you like it?" He blames Wendy for his disappointments. She, and almost everyone else, blames him. In the male bonding scene in the hotel ballroom, Jack rationalizes to Lloyd that part of Jack's problem is that there is "Something wrong with the sperm bank upstairs," and then adds, "Nothing I can't take care of, though." No wonder we are both shocked and amused by the scene of the insane Jack, breaking down his apartment door with an ax and screaming, "Honey, I'm home!" But neither self-pity nor finger-pointing relieves these adults of their responsibilities for each other's support and safety. Finally, I can't help wondering what kind of man Danny will become, having grown up in such a world and being forced to kill his father. Certainly, it was an issue that King raised at the end of the novel, when he has Hallorann counsel Danny to forgo his self-pity and get on with his life.

In conclusion, this essay argues that any concern with the dissolution of the American nuclear family as symbolized by the fate of the Torrance household must empathize with Jack's crisis as well as Wendy and Danny's. To date, that has not been the case, mainly because existing judgments are so intertwined with critical priorities related to the times in which the film was made and released. However, the past decade should have taught us that the horror genre contains marvelous insights about the negative aspects of the American Dream, and that *The Shining* contains much more wisdom about the deterioration of the nuclear family than we first realized. Only when we have wrestled with the negative impact of patriarchal values on both men and women will we move toward a more humane society where families work and live in more harmony than existing cultural myths now permit. I reject assertions that Kubrick is detached, mean-spirited, and obtuse in *The Shining*. If anything, his ironic approach to every member of the Torrance family is one of empathy, sadness, and hope. He tells their story so that we can better understand what it means to be human and to experience vicariously the consequences of neglecting our psychological terrors. When that message is understood, maybe then families won't have to be destroyed in order for some of their members to survive.

Notes

[1] This essay is an outgrowth of a seminar, "The Films of Stanley Kubrick," that I conducted at the University of Vermont during Spring 1993. In addition to thanking my students for their contributions, I also want to thank the following colleagues whose comments helped shape the final form this essay took: Virginia Clark, Littleton Long, Mark Madigan, Anthony Magistrale, Alan Shepherd, and Denise Youngblood.

[2] *The Shining* was produced, co-scripted (with Diane Johnson) and directed by Stanley Kubrick for Warner Bros./Hawk Films at EMI Elstree Studios in Borehamwood, England in 1978. The narrative follows the chilling fate of the Torrance family—Jack, Wendy, and Danny—as they face the horrors of being isolated in an off-season Colorado hotel atop a snowbound mountain. The cast includes Jack Nicholson (Jack Torrance), Shelley Duvall (Wendy Torrance), Danny Lloyd (Danny Torrance), Scatman Crothers (Hallorann), Barry Nelson (Stuart Ullman), Philip Stone (Delbert Grady), and Joe Turkel (Lloyd).

[3] Anthony Magistrale, "Introduction," *The Shining Reader*, Ed. By Anthony Magistrale (Mercer Island, WA: Starmont House, 1990): vii-viii.

[4] For his precise assessment, see John Hofsess, "Kubrick: Critics Be Damned. *Soho News* (May 28. 1980): 60.

[5] Tony Magistrale points out that the same reactions have greeted each of King's novels. Note to the author. June 26. 1993.

[6] For the record, I feel that a film should be judged on its own merits and not as a companion piece to its source. The fact is that books and films are two different media. Comparing the two works often leads to a literary analysis of a cinematic achievement. While it is usual for the public to expect "faithful" adaption of the original work, filmmakers are under no aesthetic obligation to comply with those presumed expectations. Commercial ambitions, however, frequently force artists to compromise their visions. Under appropriate circumstances, examining the strategies a filmmaker uses in adapting a work to the screen proves very rewarding. For a more complete discussion of this complex issue, see Frank Manchel, "Chapter 5 Comparative Literature," *Film Study: An Analytical Bibliography*, Vol. 2. Cranbury: Fairleigh Dickinson University Press, 1990.

[7] James Hala, "Kubrick's *The Shining:* The Specters and the Critics," *"The Shining" Reader*. 203.

[8] Norman Kagan. *The Cinema of Stanley Kubrick, New Expanded Edition*. New York: Continuum. 1993. 212.

[9] Janet Maslin, "Flaws Don't Dim Kubrick's *The Shining*," in *New York Times* (June 8, 1980): Cl.

[10] Mark Madigan, "Orders from the House," *The Shining Reader*, p. 200.
[11] Greg Keeler, "*The Shining*: Ted Kramer Has a Nightmare," *Journal of Popular Film and Television* 8:4 (Winter 1981): 2-8.
[12] Flo Leibowitz and Lynn Jeffres, *"The Shining," Film Quarterly* 34:3 (Spring 1981): 45.
[13] P. L. Titterington, "Kubrick and *The Shining*," *Sight and Sound* 52:2 (Spring 1981): 118.
[14] Alan Cohen, "The Collapse of Family and Language in Stephen King's *The Shining*," *The Shining Reader:* 49.
[15] A Note to the author, June 26, 1993.
[16] Leibowitz and Jeffres, 46.
[17] Susan White, "Male Bonding: Hollywood Orientalism, and the Repression of the Feminine in Kubrick's *Full Metal Jacket*," *Arizona Quarterly* 44:3 (Autumn 1988): 121-122.
[18] Patricia Ferreira, "Jack's Nightmare at the Overlook: The American Dream Inverted," *"The Shining" Reader:* 32.
[19] For some male criticism of Kubrick's sexual politics, see Michael Pursell, *"Full Metal Jacket:* The Unraveling of Patriarchy," *Literature/Film Quarterly* 16:4 (1988): 221; and Claude L. Smith Jr., *"Full Metal Jacket* and the Beast Within," Ibid., 228.
[20] Cited in Jack Kroll, "Stanley Kubrick's Horror Show," *Newsweek* (May 26, 1980): 99.
[21] 1n his impressive study of the filmmaker, Thomas Allen Nelson discusses Kubrick's considerable debt to the editing techniques of the great Soviet filmmakers in the 1920s. See Thomas Allen Nelson, *Inside a Film Artist's Maze.* Bloomington: Indiana University Press, 1982. 12-13.
[22] For comments on Kubrick's use of horror conventions, see Leibowitz and Jeffres, 45.
[23] Nelson, 198.
[24] Titterington, 118.
[25] Leibowitz and Jeffres, 47.
[26] Nelson, 219.
[27] The answer could also be the African American chef, Hallorann. But in the context of this analysis, he is not placed in the nuclear family. His traumas, also ignored by critics, deserve their own essay.
[28] Anyone seeking more complete descriptions of the film should begin by consulting Kagan and Nelson's works.
[29] Closer scrutiny reveals that it is a yellow Volkswagen. I feel it is useful to remind readers that Kubrick is a Jew who grew up in Brooklyn during World War II. He began his filmmaking career in the postwar era and was deeply influenced by the cynical values in *film noir* Hollywood. For many Brooklyn born-and-raised Jews of that generation, a Volkswagen

evokes memories of Nazi Germany. Magistrale also points out "A 'bug' on the face of the enormous universe further suggests Jack's cosmic insignificance." A note to the author, June 26, 1993.

[30] Kagan, 208.
[31] Titterington, 118.
[32] Leibowitz and Jeffres, 46.
[33] Anthony Macklin, "Understanding Kubrick: *The Shining,*" *Journal of Popular Film and Television* 9:2 (Summer 1981): 93.
[34] Titterington, 119.
[35] Michel Ciment, *Kubrick.* New York: Holt, Rinehart and Winston, 1980. 189.
[36] According to King, Nicholson was miscast as Jack Torrance: "People have said to me that Nicholson is crazy from the beginning of the film; there's never any progression. That is not right. The man is sane at the beginning. People impute that craziness to Nicholson because of the other parts he's played. When he smiles you think he's crazy just because of the kind of smile he's got." Cited in Tim Underwood and Chuck Miller, Eds. *Feast of Fear: Conversations with Stephen King* (New York: Carroll and Graf, 1992): 100. Another source claims that the novelist "had reservations about the casting of Jack Nicholson as Jack Torrance, feeling that unless Kubrick stops him, he'll overplay the part, turning Torrance into a 'really gifted writer.'" See William Wilson, "Riding on the Crest of the Horror Craze, "*New York Times Magazine* (May 11, 1980): 63.
[37] Macklin, 94.
[38] Kroll, 96.
[39] Keeler, 7.

11. Geoffrey Holder, *The UnCola Man*. The caption reads: To Frank, With Best Wishes Always, Geoff.

9.

War and Peace

Sometimes, it does seem a shame that Noah and his party didn't miss the boat.[1]
Mark Twain

It was morality that burned the books of the ancient sages, and morality that halted the free inquiry of the Golden Age and substituted for it the credulous imbecility of the Age of Faith. It was a fixed moral code and a fixed theology which robbed the human race of a thousand years by wasting them upon alchemy, heretic-burning, witchcraft and sacerdotalism [the notion that only priests can speak to G-d.].[2]
H. L. Mencken

Life is a journey and it's always most interesting when you are not sure where you are going.[3]
George Stevens

This being a teacher's unconventional story, it may not be surprising to include in my narrative a chapter describing my administrative activities. Just as unusual, considering my enduring distaste for administrators, you might be amused to discover that working in the Dean's Office turned out to be the longest I ever stayed in one job. Stranger still, being Associate Dean of the College of Arts and Sciences for close to twelve years proved to be, at best, a bittersweet experience. But most peculiar is the fact that the administrative position provided me with many of my most fortunate events in my film studies career.

As you recall from the previous chapter, going over "to the enemy" was not my idea. Like many hardened faculty, administrators, to me, represented self-centered, hypocritical, arrogant, and greedy individuals who abused their privileged positions to further their personal ambitions. (The only caveat I would make after spending so much time in their company is that the rare, dedicated official is indispensable to the health and welfare of an institution. Simply stated, however, I can count on two hands the administrators who fit that description.) Still, I went after the job because it seemed the only available escape from the dysfunctional Department of Communication. I knew nothing about the new dean or about running a college, nor did I harbor any ambitions about supervising my colleagues. But given my options at the time, I thought it a sensible solution to my being forced by family priorities to stay at the University of Vermont.

My initial interview with the new Dean proved surprising. Instead of discussing my candidacy for the Associate position, he wanted to talk about my becoming Chair of the Communication Department. I explained that was not in the realm of human possibility. After quickly quashing that proposal, we spoke not about academic matters but about our families, and what he was experiencing in his transition from being Dean at Ohio University to a similar post here at UVM. It soon became clear how similar and dissimilar we were. He was reserved; I was not. He was a scientist; I was a humanist. He was guided in his actions by logic; I lived by instinct. Yet we both were committed to what we did, and we both felt the College needed reshaping in almost every aspect of its organizational structure. And I sensed, correctly, he had the moral courage to make the needed changes. The meeting ended with my having a sense of optimism. He agreed to forget about my being a Chair, and said he would consider me for the Associate's job.

Weeks passed before we met again. Clearly, the Dean had numerous other candidates to interview, and I busied myself with teaching my classes. Then came a call back from his office, and a second meeting was arranged. This time the Dean talked exclusively about what he was looking for in his Associate. Having come in from the outside, he recognized the need to appoint someone familiar with the faculty and the College's problems. He was also looking for a person he could trust. But most importantly, the Dean wanted someone willing to tell him honestly and unflinchingly what he thought about the policies and decisions they would be making together in their day-to-day running of the College.

By the end of May 1977, I was offered the job and immediately accepted. Neither the Dean nor I found the first year of our association easy. He had considerable difficulty adjusting to my personality and my temperament. I had considerable trouble having to filter my views and my actions to an incisive and demanding supervisor. For my entire career, I had said and done what I felt right, never once choosing my words to satisfy anyone other than myself. But I did not speak for the Dean's Office. Dean John G. Jewett did. And he was often unhappy and disturbed by my easygoing and permissive behavior. We argued repeatedly and heatedly. But we both were determined to make the relationship work.

Gradually, we came to respect each other's style. Consequently, I not only stayed with him in the Office for nearly twelve years—the longest serving Deans since the sixties to now—but also we became close friends that remains true to this day. For the record, the greatest compliment I ever received during my administrative career was from a dear colleague who, after I left Office, said no one at UVM knew the Dean and I ever disagreed about anything.

The story of those volatile years administering the College of Arts and Sciences is rightfully Dean Jewett's narrative, and it is his to tell, if he so chooses. Accurately told, it is an account of two uncompromising men who made sweeping changes in nearly every aspect of the College's life, including curriculum, salaries, academic standards, hiring policies, departmental priorities, and minority issues. I will only comment on three tales because they relate to *Film Study: An Analytical Bibliography*, two sections of which are reprinted in this chapter.

A year after John and I began working together, we discovered the College had been losing large sums of money because of prior administrations' dubious handling of evening division classes and summer school projects. I was assigned the job of fixing the problems. Both of the prior difficulties existed mainly because of the chemistry between the Dean's office and the Continuing Education Division (CE). Fortunately for me, a gifted and dedicated young woman named Lynn Ballard now ran CE. She remains in my judgment one of the most able administrators I have ever encountered, and I remember our joint days with great fondness.

In all the time we spent together, I recall only one serious disagreement. It had to do with the faculties' contracts. Simply put, professors proposed evening and summer school courses to us early in the year, Lynn and I then approved the requisite number, and the professors were out of luck if the courses didn't garner the needed enrollment. I could not live with that arrangement. Because I had taught such courses my entire career, I knew the hard work that went into preparing the classes. Just as important was the fact that the people who taught those courses usually needed the money to supplement their inadequate salaries. I, therefore, "persuaded" Lynn to guarantee teachers' wages whether or not the courses went. If they didn't go, professors were to be given administrative duties to justify their salaries. The year I left office, that policy disappeared and has never been reinstated.

Lest the reader be dismayed by my laissez-faire behavior, considering the tens of thousands of dollars the College was loosing with its CE operations, I want you to know that at the end of my first year with Lynn, the College of Arts and Sciences made $75,000. And we never ever went into the red for the remaining years I was there.

Now comes the superb part of the story. At first, John and I were puzzled with what to do with the $75,000 windfall. It was, however, a brief crisis. At the time, scientists in the College had been integrating computers into their work with great results. The Dean decided I should see if these new machines had any value for humanists. The experiment was straightforward. I would contact my *Film Study* publisher, and see if he was interested in a revised edition. If so, he would provide me with a personal computer, and the Dean would give me time to do the update. The $75,000 was kept in reserve, until we had enough evidence for a decision; and then, if the experiment provided positive results, the money would be used to supply computers to the Humanities faculty.

Although it was only a short time before the computers were forthcoming, I did not finish the rewrite until ten years later. Why it took so long is illustrated by the next two anecdotes, and serves as the entre to the chapter's two sections from *Film Study: An Analytical Bibliography*.

By the end of the seventies, Dean Jewett had reviewed the status of the College's 22 departments as part of his overall plan to strengthen the academic climate on campus. One of several glaring problems, as he already had discovered, was the Department of Communication. Since 1970, and following two critical reviews, the department had made only minor progress in addressing its problems. In addition, the search for a new Chair had produced no suitable candidates. Unlike his predecessors, the Dean felt that the troublesome situation had gone on ten years too long. What follows, admittedly, is an oversimplified and subjective account of what happened.

Aware of my contentious relationship with the Communication faculty, Dean Jewett proposed yet another review of the Department. This time, however, in order to avoid a perceived conflict of interest, he wanted the evaluation done by a team of external scholars. The Dean's Office and the Department jointly selected and approved the off campus reviewers. When this third review again proved negative, the Dean decided to propose that the Department be discontinued, the tenured faculty relocated to other departments within the College, and the Department's major programs be phased out over a three-year period, allowing for the already enrolled students to complete their studies in Communication.[4]

I was under strict orders to make no statements about the proposal, except, when asked officially; and then, I was to quote factually from all three departmental reviews. This I did during my public testimony at a College Curriculum Committee hearing and a visit to the Student Council. The Dean alone addressed all other public responses throughout the two-year ordeal.

Regrettably and unwisely, the Department, in defending itself, ignored the reviews and used as its primary defense an ad holmium attack on me, claiming that its troubles were the result of the Associate Dean's opinions and influence. They made this character assassination despite the fact the first review of the program's troubles had begun in 1970, the year before I entered the Department, and continued for three years after I had moved into the Dean's Office. Being skilled in mass communication, the angry faculty waged a passionate attack on me within the College and on the outside with the public and the media. Particularly upsetting to me, the Department convinced many of the Communication students to go along with its strategy. Because of my pledge to the Dean, I was unable to respond to the charges.

Meanwhile, Dean Jewett's proposal worked its way through the University process for eliminating programs. After the College Curriculum Committee accepted the recommendation, it went to the College faculty who approved it with a vote of 77 to 44. From there the proposal moved to the University's Academic Affairs Committee, where out of a group of nearly eighty individuals voting, only six declined to support the Dean. Finally, with the backing of the University President, Vice President Robert G. Arns, on July 31, 1981, wrote a memorandum to the University's Board of Trustees, which began,

> The Discontinuation of the Department of Communication and Establishment of a Program in Communication on August 14, 1981.
>
> RESOLVED, that the Board of Trustees (1) authorizes discontinuation of the Department of Communication effective September 1, 1981, in accordance with the memorandum of July 31, 1981; and (2) authorizes establishment of a Program in Communication effective September 1, 1981, with termination of the Program to coincide with the timely completion of major programs by currently admitted students."[5]

The Board approved the Vice President's recommendation, and it appeared that my nightmare was over. Not so!

Two years had passed since the Dean had made his decision to disband the Communication Department, but there was no resolution as to who was going to chair the Program to transition the existing Communication students. The appointed Search Committee had yet to make a recommendation. Although John and I had had no formal discussions about the matter, we planned to address the Chairperson issue once the Department had been officially discontinued and a Program for the transition formally established. I firmly believed, however, the new chair would either be a prominent scholar from another department in the College, or a visiting external academician appointed for a three-year duration.

Imagine my shock when the Dean told me I should do the job, primarily because of my familiarity with the situation, my loyalty to him, and my expertise in the field. I said, "Absolutely not!" We debated the matter for days. Finally, John asked me to do it as a favor to him. He trusted no one else. We had been friends for four years, and he had done many kind things for me during that period. So I agreed under protest, on one condition. The Search Committee had to recommend me for the chairmanship. After much anguish on their part, I got the recommendation and took the onerous job, adding to my other responsibilities as Associate Dean.

Between 1981 and 1984, while Chairing the Program, I recruited distinguished scholars to teach new courses and to enrich the existing curriculum. I also travelled to the University of Kansas to hire a new debate coach, who for thirty-three years at UVM did a first-rate job. (Forensic Professor Alfred "Tuna" Snider died on December 11th, 2015, admired and respected by his friends and colleagues.[6]) Once the visiting scholars came aboard, the Program proceeded seamlessly in an atmosphere of resentment, distrust, and deceit. I did not have, nor did I expect to find, a single friend in the process, from staff to scholar. But much to my relief, everyone behaved professionally, doing what had to be done in the best interests of the students. In retrospect, I see that difficult period as the Communication faculty's finest moment. Moreover, the experience confirmed a basic rule in administration: you do not have to like or be liked by the people you work with; you just have to be able to work effectively together.

Only once during those troublesome days did I drop my guard. Shortly after becoming Chair, John and I had a particularly unpleasant conversation. I was so upset by what was said, I decided to quit. Enough was enough! Coincidentally, and following the blow up, I had a lunch date with an exceptional colleague, Rev. Daniel P. Daley. A unique human being, Father Dan listened sympathetically as I spelled out all I had gone through only to be treated in such a problematic way. "Where was the justice?" I asked. "How could G-d let this happen?" I questioned. Then this wise clergyman replied, in a manner I will try to recall to you just as I heard it over thirty-seven years ago. "Frank," he said, "when we were in divinity school, we used to debate issues like this on a daily basis. Why does G-d do what he does? It makes no sense. Finally, the answer we settled on was "Shit floats and gold sinks. That's G-d's way!" It made sense to me. So I went back to work, and never again got into a heated argument with John about the Communication Program.

I do not want you to leave thinking that all was doom and drudgery. One of the scholars I brought to the Program was Dr. Worth McDougald, a journalism expert and the head of the prestigious George Foster Peabody Awards. After a few months on campus, he became sympathetic to my situation and respected the way I handled myself. Consequently, he asked me to serve on the Peabody Awards Board. I remained on that remarkable Board for seven years, two of which I served as Chair, and it proved to be one of the most rewarding and enjoyable experiences of my life. The troubled kid from the rough streets of New York hobnobbed with the rich and the famous and the powerful, and loved every glamorous minute of it. I also gained great respect for the contributions to society provided annually, since 1945, by the University of Georgia's Grady School of Journalism. What I learned about the immense positive forces available to our nation by the television and the radio industries from those memorable days in Athens has guided my judgment about the extraordinary gifts of Broadcasting ever since. In addition, I will be forever grateful for Worth's friendship and teachings. I feel the same for the other members of the staff, especially Worth's successor, the late and talented Barry Sherman.

The last anecdote to explain the time it took to produce the massive document that follows concerns the issue of diversity. By the mid-eighties, schools across the United States competed furiously to integrate the educational environment. John addressed the issue relating to women's studies; I took on the job of bringing African Americans to campus.

In admittedly simplified terms, what follows is a brief overview of the events associated with carrying cultural diversity to a conservative New England university. Realizing that the College's resources made it basically non-competitive in securing a full-time African American position, I proposed in 1986, we set up a Minority Residence in Artist Program. In essence, I would select four departments in the College—English, Art, Music, and Theatre—and bring in a notable Black personality for a one-year visiting stint in each area. By paying these individuals higher salaries than usual and offering them advantageous employment arrangements, we would gain two basic advantages: the College would demonstrate to all concerned the enormous benefits of a diverse faculty, and we would have access to key figures who would help us recruit future African American talent. To insure the widest possible support, an Artist in Residence Committee was set up with colleagues highly supportive of the Program.[7]

But the idea was fraught with problems. First was the name of the program itself. Almost everyone I approached for the visiting professorships was offended by being referred to as minorities. It was the La Mancha experience all over again. Clearly, I meant no harm; just as clearly, I should have selected a better title. Secondly, a key issue concerned departmental prerogatives. Does a dean, or any administrator, have the right to recruit faculty for a department? Shouldn't experts in a discipline be the ones to select their own colleagues? Even more, do administrators govern best by a top-down strategy, or is it best to work by consensus?

I took the former approach for two reasons. Since this was a tense situation challenging long-standing outworn practices in the College that had resulted in the noticeable absence of minorities as well as women, I felt the responsibility to put top-down pressure on the faculty to bring about a desired and necessary change. Secondly, having lived through the Communication Department experience and being somewhat "radioactive," I felt the consensus approach would be non-productive for me at this time.

For three years, and fully prepared for the predictable problems, I successfully recruited visiting African American artists, who were then brought to the campus and eventually accepted under some duress by the faculty as visiting professors, with one exception. Although I had been instrumental in the mid-seventies in persuading the distinguished actor and Shakespearian authority Earle Hyman to work in the Theatre Department, his appearance in a scheduled production of *Macbeth* failed to materialize, because of an illness he experienced during the pre-production process. He left UVM and never returned. In addition, the Department also had an African American woman on the faculty. Thus it would appear, they needed no help from me on integrating their Department.

Nevertheless, given my current challenge, I was determined to gain greater diversity for our academic community. I first brought Morgan Freeman to the campus for the visiting Theatre position. The Department and the distinguished actor could not come to an agreement on how he might fit into their program. I next brought the equally gifted Geoffrey Holder to campus. He too proved unsuited to the Department's needs. Let me summarize the situation by printing the letter I sent Mr. Holder following his meeting with the Theatre Department in June of 1986:

> Dear Geoffrey:
> I hope that this letter finds you healthy, happy, and productive. When last we spoke you were in the midst of a dozen exciting projects, any one of which would have kept me busy for years.
>
> Unfortunately for us, those projects make it impossible for our immediate needs to mesh. After thinking through what you would like to do here at the University and what we would like to have done as an Artist-in-Residence, it does not seem sensible to pursue at this time an extended visit by you to the campus.
>
> In fact, the Theatre people have decided to postpone inviting anyone next year. Your visit forced them to reevaluate what was and was not reasonable from an artist of your magnitude.
>
> I can only suggest to you how disappointed I am over this turn of events. For me, the opportunity to spend some time with you has been wonderful. Please send my best to Jacque[8] and say that Sheila and I think of you both often and fondly.
>
> Best regards to you.
> Cordially,
> Frank Manchel
> Associate Dean[9]

When Dean Jewett and I left office in the summer of 1988, the Vice President at first asked me to continue the program and then later relented. The Minority in Residence plan never became operational again.

Hopefully, the previous anecdotes give you a suitable picture of why completing the revised *Film Study: A Resource Guide* took so long. Together with my publishing commitments for the Young Adult book series, doing various stints on television (more in the next Chapter), serving on the Peabody Board, running the Communication program, and the day-to-day decisions on the sweeping changes taking place in the College, the needed time was not readily available. Just as important was how beneficial the research and the writing were to my mental health. By being deeply involved in producing the best possible research tool for film scholars, I was more than able to channel my administrative frustrations into interesting and exciting developments in screen education.

In conclusion, five important observations are worth knowing about the new edition and my years in administration. First, computing software was in its infancy during the eighties. Even though I was given generous support in doing the rewrite, I was never adequately provided with a system for spelling corrections and for indexing. Consequently, the four-volume reference work has many more mistakes then I find acceptable today. Secondly, the completed revision revealed once again how little I knew about film itself. For example, my years in the Dean's Office had distanced me from a new trend in the discipline away from Popular Culture to Cultural Studies. This ignorance on my part limited the audience for my scholarship. Thirdly, unlike in previous chapters, I have retained elements of the exact makeup of the new book. This approach is to show you what scholars have waiting for them as they search the entire work. Fourth, I believe, as Raul Hilberg told me when he looked at the Revised Edition, generations from now, when scholars want to know what film education was like in the first hundred years of its existence, this document would be the work they would consult. Finally, I return to Mencken, whose ideas opened this chapter and whose beliefs represent my views on administration: "The most dangerous man to any government is the man who is able to think things out for himself, without regard to the prevailing superstitions and taboos."[10]

Notes

[1] Hal Holbrook, *Mark Twain Tonight in The CBS Television Network Special*. New Jersey: Kultur Video, 1999.
[2] H. L. Mencken, *The Philosophy of Friedrich Nietzsche*. (1908/1913)
[3] George Stevens, Jr., *George Stevens: A Filmmaker's Journey*. USA: Castle Films, 1984.
[4] The full details of the report presented to the Board of Trustees chronicling the events can be found in Vice President Robert G. Arns' Memorandum of July 31, 1981.
[5] E-Mail from Joel Goldberg to the author, 6/11/15.
[6] Brent Hallenbeck, UVM debate king 'Tuna' Snider dies," *Burlington Free Press* (December 12, 2015).
[7] The Committee consisted of the following people: Al Loving, Bill Schenk, Ed Owre, Jim Chapman, Larry McCrorey, Dolores Sandoval, Jack Clemmons, Bonnie Ryan, Tony Bradley, Virginia Clark, Catherine Donnelly, and Donald Parks.
[8] This is a reference to the famous French screenwriter, Jacques Sigurd, who accompanied Mr. Holder on his visit to UVM in May 1986.
[9] The letter is dated June 4, 1986. It is available in my papers at the University of Vermont library.
[10] H.L. Mencken, *The Smart Set* (December 1919).

I
Preface to the New Edition

> The animals other than man live by appearance and memories, and have but little of collected experience; but the human race lives also by art and reasonings. Now from memory, experience is produced in men; for several memories of the same thing produce finally the capacity for a single experience...And in general it is a sign of the man who knows and of the man who does not know, that the former can teach, and therefore we think art more truly knowledge than experience is; for artists can teach, and men of mere experience cannot.
>
> *Aristotle*, Metaphysics

I do not claim that this new and retitled edition of FILM STUDY: A RESOURCE GUIDE is definitive, nor do I argue that the approaches suggested and discussed are completely reflective of how I think film should be studied in the classroom. Instead FILM STUDY: AN ANALYTICAL BIBLIOGRAPHY should be seen as reflecting a maturing awareness on my part of the significant contributions made by film scholars to the ongoing, ever-changing, complex issues associated with our discipline. The growth in both quantity and quality of film materials and theories since 1973 is extraordinary. One need only scan the indices of my first edition to be struck by the absence of then-unknown and emerging researchers and theorists like Jeanne Thomas Allen, Robert C. Allen, Dudley Andrew, Bruce A. Austin, Tino Balio, David Bordwell, Larry Ceplair, Richard Corliss, David Culbert, Patricia Erens, Steve Englund, Regina K. Fadiman, Lucy Fisher, Tom Gunning, Charles H. Harpole, Larry Hillier, Beverle Houston, Annette Insdorf, Marsha Kinder, Garth S. Jowett, Larry Landrum, Daniel J. Leab, James M. Linton, Timothy J. Lyons, Joan Mellon, James Monaco, Charles Musser, John G. Nachbar, Bill

Nichols, Nicholas Pronay, George Rehrauer, Thomas Schatz, Robert Sklar, Anthony Slide, Thomas Sobchack, Vivian C. Sobchack, Pierre Sorlin, Janet Staiger, Elizabeth Grottle Strebel, Philip Taylor, Kristin Thompson, David Welch, and William F. Van Wert. I mean no disrespect to the many scholar-teachers whom I have neglected to mention here. But the aforementioned individuals come most readily to mind when I think about the revisions that have occurred in this updated work. In 1973, the study of film itself was still considered a controversial subject and was not perceived by many academicians as worthy of a place in the basic curriculum. And we should not forget that film publications were often ignored or dismissed as trivial.

This new edition, therefore, attempts to place these changes in perspective both in the main portion of the text and in the appendixes; there is a concerted effort to show the increasing stature and quality of film study and researchers. This maturity is reflected in the burgeoning resources donated by the film industry to the academic world: e.g., the Warner Bros. collection housed at Princeton University and the University of Southern California; RKO at the University of California in Los Angeles; Disney at the studio in Burbank, California; and United Artists at the University of Wisconsin, Madison. Readers will find additional information about other new library acquisitions in Appendix V. The improvement in film scholarship is also evident in the increasing number of publishers committed to making available scholarly resources for serious students: e. g., Ablex Publishing Corporation, Associated University Presses, Gale Research, Garland Publishing, Greenwood Press, Indiana University Press, Rutgers University Press, the Scarecrow Press, Southern Illinois University Press, and UMI Research Press. Most of all, the growth in film scholarship is reflected in the quality of the publications since 1973. A new generation of scholars has taken upon itself the difficult task of re-examining almost every aspect of film history, theory, and criticism. Because their work, and indeed the issues themselves, are so exciting and because this new edition is concerned with a broad perspective on important research material, I have included in my study as much information on this research as is reasonable. In addition, I have offered more extensive book and film annotations than in the previous edition.

At times, however, my commitment to completeness has resulted in minimal documentation of certain books and articles that I could not obtain through interlibrary loan. In one instance, in Chapter 7, insurmountable problems related to computer access and cost made it financially and technically impossible for me to continue with the annotations for the section on the Contemporary Cinema. Rather than end the chapter with the 1960s, I included the material from the first edition, listed the new publications and information, and provided an overview of American films from the 1970s to the present. Here, as elsewhere, I felt the existence of these works and the references to their value by other scholars justified inclusion in this revision.

This book is based on my conviction that other reference works are unsatisfactory in two specific areas. First, they fail to capture both the flavor and the insights of the material they routinely recommend. Second, teachers and students have to spend hundreds of dollars to own the basic reference works dealing with film resources. This expanded edition of FILM STUDY: AN ANALYTICAL BIBLIOGRAPHY addresses these two problems by building on the comprehensive resource guide methodology begun in 1973. No one will fail to recognize my biases in the evaluations and in the space devoted to specific authors and theories. On the other hand, my respect for and gratitude to the hardworking scholars reviewed in the following pages can never be fully stated.

To underscore the major changes in the study of film since the original 1973 edition, I have expanded considerably the variety of perspectives relating to film production, distribution, exhibition, and reception. For example, Chapter 2 not only points out the nature of film genres, but also examines in detail the historical context in which war films emerged, developed, and changed from decade to decade. The primary intent is to identify the multitude of conventions associated with narrative film formulas and to survey the socio-historic and artistic elements that influenced their use over an eighty-year period. As in the first edition, more attention is given to description than to analysis. The latter has been done voluminously by gifted critics deeply involved in analyzing cinematic narratives. What is missing generally from such worthwhile studies is an awareness of the historical and industrial context in which these film narratives incorporated specific elements into their screen characterizations and themes. Even more to the point, film students often find that the resources available for critical study are poorly defined in scope or too fragmented. Thus Chapter 2 is subdivided into sections (e.g., genres, propaganda, history on film, and history in film). This allows me greater latitude in exploring the relationship between a specific genre, the larger context of the film industry, and American society. Chapter 3, on the other hand, explores the nature of film as a social force in society. Here the primary emphasis is on identifying the variety of attitudes and responses to the film industry's desire to maximize profits and to minimize economic risks. Again, the methodology stresses description more than analysis. Although the subsections treat different issues (e.g., ideology versus entertainment, the pleasure factor, and the multiple role of movies), the intent remains the same: to point out the historical and industrial context in which particular themes and characters originated, developed, and changed from one decade to the next. The chapters taken collectively thus provide an overview on how film history, genres, themes, narratives, characters, theories, and industrial pressures combine to form a very complex mass communication product.

A word about the Indexing in this edition is necessary. Because the amount of material is voluminous and constant cross-references are made throughout the work, I have resorted to seven Indexes. The Article-Title Index and the Article-Author Index contain no surprises. The Book-Author Index and the Book-Title Index, however, include the names of short story writers and playwrights, as well as the titles of short stories and plays out of which movies were made. The Film-Title Index has a listing of the English-language titles and (where appropriate) the foreign titles of the films. The Film-Personality Index contains not only the names of people connected with the film industry—e. g., producers, directors, screenwriters, and stars— but also major influences on these personalities (e. g., novelists and philosophers). With few exceptions, this is the index to use when looking for information on an individual. The Subject Index is a listing of important topics, themes, and events that relate to or affect the history and criticism of film. Whoever wants to get the fullest information on a particular personality, film, or event is advised to consult more than one Index.[1]

Notes

[1] Frank Manchel, "Preface," *Film Study: An Analytical Bibliography*, Volume 1, 26-27.

II

The American Dream and the Hollywood Inquisition

What sobered many writers in 1933 was the fact that the unknown members of the International Alliance of Theatrical Stage Employees (IATSE) had more bargaining power with the film moguls than the celebrated screenwriters, directors, and stars. That fact set in motion the major movement to unionize Hollywood. Over the next thirty years, the radical and turbulent stages that marked the evolution of the Screen Writers Guild (SWG) would rend the film community. What's more, the IATSE would play a crucial role in an episode of film history characterized by the participants as thirty years of "treason," "scoundrel time," "Inquisition," "the time of the toad," witch hunts," and "the plague years." Because the harrowing events significantly affected the image of Hollywood and screenwriters, in addition to being indicative of the persecution experienced by many nameless Americans, the basic elements of that complicated story are worth knowing.[1]

America in the early thirties was beset by a number of problems: e.g. widespread social upheavals, massive unemployment, economic despair, and deep-rooted fears about foreign ideologies destroying American society. Drastic steps were needed to bolster the nation's spirits and defend it from the alleged danger posed by the Communist Party of the United States (CPUSA). Thus Franklin Roosevelt in the first hundred days of his presidency included in his New Deal legislation the National Industrial Recovery Act (NIRA).[2] A controversial attempt to revive the chaotic economy and to stem the growing unemployment, the NIRA gave birth to the National Recovery Administration (NRA), whose primary function was to supervise the establishment of industrial codes between labor and management.[3] The immediate relevance for Hollywood was the NRA' s Section 7A.[4] Theoretically; it gave employees the right to organize and to select their own representatives for collective bargaining. Progressive screenwriters saw an opportunity in this new legislation to counteract the repressive measures long used by the film mandarins twice before—1914-1916 and 1920-1927—screenwriters had attempted to form a strong union but had failed.[5] The second effort had resulted in the creation of the weak Screen Writers Guild.

But even that well-intentioned subsidiary of the Dramatists Guild of America became obsolete when on May 4, 1927, the newly formed Academy of Motion Picture Arts and Sciences (AMPAS) was incorporated. Considered a "company union engineered by Louis B. Mayer and his fellow producers to control studio employees,"[6] the AMPAS on the surface supported technical research, encouraged merit, and shared information. One of its major and most controversial responsibilities was settling film labor disputes.[7] Between 1927 and 1933, the settlements dealing with wage cuts and layoffs invariably favored management.[8] However, when the full force of the Depression and the ensuing economic chaos hit the film industry, studio employees no longer were willing to tolerate the AMPAS's acting as their mediator in labor negotiations.[9]

Among the studios going into receivership by 1933 were RKO, Paramount, and Fox. In fact, on March 8, 1933 (the day President Roosevelt took over the White House), MGM was the only studio able to meet its payroll. As summarized in THE HOLLYWOOD WRITERS' WARS, "Universal suspended all contracts; Fox notified its employees that salaries would not be paid; and Paramount, Warner Bros., Columbia, and RKO, due to meet their payrolls the next day, faced bleak prospects. For the first time since the studios had formed, a general shutdown in the film industry seemed possible."[10]

On March 9, the producers met clandestinely and decided to impose a fifty percent pay cut on any employee earning more than fifty dollars a week; those earning less than fifty dollars received a twenty-five percent cut. The wage cuts were to remain in effect for eight weeks. (What was scandalous was the fact that producers— but not other employees—could recoup their pay cuts through their annual bonuses.) During the next few days, the studio executives held large meetings with staffs and coerced them into accepting "austerity measures" for "the good of the industry." Within a week, employees at MGM, Paramount, Columbia, and Warner Bros. reluctantly accepted pay cuts. Only the IATSE, with its long-term collective bargaining contract, stood firm against the cuts.[11] This led to a one-day shutdown on March 13. Well-informed screenwriters, directors, and stars suspected that the cuts were a ruse to maintain studio profits and producer bonuses. The IATSE won. The big studios revised their emergency measures. Only the top stars, directors, and producers would take pay cuts.

The anger and frustration generated by these March events began an era of social consciousness in Hollywood that would soon turn into political activism and have profound effects not only on the film industry, but also on the nation as well. When the academy attempted to assume its by-now traditional mediating role, the studio employees balked. Screenwriters and performers, in particular, felt compelled to form their own unions.[12]

Fortuitously, a number of Eastern writers had met early in February to consider reviving the Screen Writers Guild. Among the ten charter members were two destined to be part of the Hollywood Ten: Lester Cole and John Howard Lawson.[13] Each had ties to the Dramatists Guild (DG), along with progressives like Samson Raphaelson, Kubec Glasmon, Courtney Terrett, Brian Marlowe, Bertram Block, John Bright,[14] and Edwin Justus Mayer.[15] Other significant screenwriters who soon participated in the February meetings were Louis Weltzenkorn,[16] Samuel Ornitz,[17] and Francis Edward Faragoh.[18] Particular attention in the secret meetings was devoted to discussing the 1919 strategies that the DG had used in getting organized, and the way Broadway producers had been forced during the late 1920s into giving playwrights more equitable salaries, subsidiary rights, and script control. Using the DG model,[19] committed to giving screenwriters more authority over their own work, and incensed by the studios' dirty tricks,[20] the hearty band of screenwriters, led by Lawson, resurrected a now-militant Screen Writers Guild (SWG). By April the membership included nearly two hundred significant Hollywood writers; by September the number had doubled.[21]

The SWG's initial appeal sprang from its concern over economic issues, not political or social causes. Furthermore, the SWG took credit for getting the producers to withdraw their demand for fifty-percent pay cuts. Consequently, conservatives joined with liberals and leftists in recognizing the need to improve the working conditions of all screenwriters. With the academy discredited and the New Deal pro-labor, it looked as if producers were beaten. But only the naive accept perceptions as facts. What few writers recognized was that the NRA Hollywood Code, as administered by Roosevelt appointee Sol Rosenblatt, proved more beneficial to the studios than to the employees. The Labor Code set in place salary scales, anti-studio raiding rules, and talent agency control provisions, which the producers eagerly wanted. In addition, conservative screenwriters had no intention of doing anything to seriously alienate the producers. They saw the battle as an issue between "gentlemen" and not between bosses and laborers.

By the end of 1933, therefore, neither the SWG nor the newly formed Screen Actors Guild (SAG),[22] incorporated in July, anticipated that it would take nearly six years to gain recognition for their local unions, or that a final contract would not be ratified until 1941. Although the two guilds succeeded in getting President Roosevelt in 1933 to eliminate the most objectionable sections of the NRA Hollywood Code, they were unable to benefit from the enforced NRA committee structure designed to negotiate differences between labor and management.

Each of the Hollywood NRA committees—writer-producer, actor-producer—had ten members, five from each side, known as "five-five" committees. Their purpose was to mediate disputes over salaries and working conditions. But the producers never accepted the "five-five" committees as a reasonable approach to collective bargaining. Instead, the studio bosses resorted to massive layoffs, coercion, and studio reorganizations in their counteroffensives against the union organizers.

Negotiations between the warring factions became more intense during the following two years as the progressives initiated moves to amalgamate their local union with a national federation of writers known as the Authors League of America (ALA).[23] The ALA consisted of the Radio Writers Guild, the Authors League, and the DG. (SAG gained considerable strength when it joined the American Federation of Labor in 1935.) The idea of amalgamation incensed Hollywood conservatives, who saw it as an attempt by left-wing Eastern groups to take over the independence of the film community. While this issue was being debated, the SWG and SAG, in May 1935, suffered a damaging blow when the Supreme Court declared the NIRA illegal, on the grounds that the executive branch had assumed legislative powers not guaranteed to it by the Constitution. The New Deal countered two months later with the passage of The National Labor Relations Act. Known as the Wagner Act, the bill, among its many provisions, outlawed company unions and granted employees the right to strike.

However, no one knew if the Supreme Court would rule the new law unconstitutional. Conservative members of the SWG, led by James Kevin McGuinness, John Lee Mahin,[24] Rupert Hughes, Howard Emmett Rogers,[25] Robert Riskin,[26] Herman J. Mankiewicz, and Bess Meredyth[27] now decided to break openly with the militant policies of the progressives. Rather than sit by idly, they joined with the producers to test the validity of the Wagner Act and created in 1936 a company union called the Screen Playwrights (SP). Among the concessions the producers offered to the warring screenwriters, vis-a-vis an immediate SP pact, were standardized contracts, a say in the assignment of screen credits, minimum wages, standardized hiring and firing procedures, and no speculative writing assignments without payment guarantees. The producers were even willing, if formally asked, to let screenwriters know who else was working on scripts-in-process. Of course, ultimate power and control remained in the hands of the producers. Very few members of the writing establishment were fooled by the puppet union, but the wary screenwriters feared that the SWG was too powerless to win its battle. Thus by the summer of 1936, the SWG virtually disappeared and once more the studios seemed in control. But screenwriters like John Howard Lawson, Dudley Nichols, Dorothy Parker, Donald Ogden Stewart, Dashiell Hammett, Lillian Hellman, Maurice Rapf,[28] Budd Schulberg, Lester Cole, Dalton Trumbo, and Ring Lardner, Jr.,[29] refused to quit. However, to survive they had to meet secretly. That need for confidentiality shrouded the surviving members of the SWG in a conspiratorial role.

Complicating the dispute in the mid-to-late thirties was the fact that the issues were no longer solely economic. Political and social ideology now overshadowed questions of script control and screen credits. A national conservative backlash by Republicans and businessmen against the New Deal, organized labor, and interventionists was in full swing. Roosevelt was being accused of turning the country toward socialism, and Red-baiting attacks on progressives, liberals, socialists, and New Dealers reached alarming proportions. Stefan Kanfer tells of the fanatical Mrs. Elizabeth Dilling, who personally published her own blacklist called THE RED NETWORK in 1934. Among her pet radicals were Margaret Bourke-White, Clarence Darrow, John Dewey, Sigmund Freud, Eleanor Roosevelt, and Thornton Wilder.[30]

A year later the militant Communist Party of the United States of America (CPUSA) organized a Popular Front composed of fellow traveling organizations, in order to protect and strengthen the Soviet Union against Nazi Germany. "Stalin had finally decided that Hitler was here to stay," explains Professor Bernard Bellush "and that he needed every support he could get throughout the world, and in the form of popular fronts."[31] Nevertheless, each nation tailored the ideas to its own needs. Popular Fronts existed not as dues-paying, "card-carrying"[32] organizations but as political consciousness-raising confederations to fight against social injustices. In America, for example, many individuals joined not because they were Communists but because they were rabid anti-Fascists. At the time, these social idealists had no idea they were being manipulated by a totalitarian government opposed to the very freedoms the American Anti-Fascists craved. In fact, the CPUSA thrived on misleading well-intentioned social idealists. It selected issues dear to progressives and then deviously used the group's aims to benefit the CPUSA. A case in point was the way the Popular Front in America operated.[33] Its four main objectives, summarized by Ceplair and Englund, were to press the Roosevelt administration in the direction of a world anti-Fascist allegiance, to aid the defenders of democracy and the victims of Fascist aggression, to counter the widely perceived threat of domestic fascism, and to defeat the efforts of conservative big business to thwart the trade union movement and block the passage of social reform measures.[34]

Many of Roosevelt's most ardent film supporters saw the CPUSA as a means of correcting international and domestic problems.[35] They naively assumed that Russia was the only major power combating Hitler, Mussolini, Franco, and the Japanese militarists.

Furthermore, the CPUSA seemed the most effective group in fighting for the rights of studio employees. No one else was as willing to expend time and money for union organizing and contract negotiations. In short, reform groups appeared powerless to fight domestic racism, sexism, and poverty, as well as international fascism, terrorism, and oppression. (Tragically for romantics who joined the CPUSA, hard-nosed patriots in the post-World War II period ignored the real reasons why perplexed Hollywood progressives and over 200,000 other Americans became Communists and fellow-travelers[36] in the thirties and early forties. Equally shameful, many hypocritical members of the CPUSA avoided blaming Stalin for his anti-Semitic policies inside Russia and the mass murders resulting from his ruthless forced collectivization and infamous purge trials.) In the interim, Hollywood's largest progressive labor union, the IATSE, had been infiltrated by racketeers in league with the producers. (Eventually, the union's president, George E. Browne, and his colleague, Willie Bioff, were convicted, along with producer Joseph M. Schenck, of extortion and conspiracy.)[37] To many California progressives, therefore, joining the CPUSA became the "in thing." Once members, they worked hard at trying to control Hollywood by controlling its labor unions.

The result was that studio heads, first and foremost conservative Republicans and businessmen, pilloried dissident employees as "subversives," "fifth columnists," Communists;" and "traitors." Many people who hated the New Deal, organized labor, and interventionists encouraged the stereotype of Hollywood as "a hot bed of left-wing radicals," while anti-Semites labeled the film colony part of an international conspiracy to overthrow the United States government. The dissidents replied to their antagonists by calling them "fascists." Isolationist meetings, anti-Fascist rallies, CPUSA seminars, SWG membership drives, and intra-studio politics thus polarized the members of the film community. Screenwriter Mary McCall joked about the Hollywood political atmosphere in an article for the SCREEN GUILDS' MAGAZINE:

> We're up to our necks in politics and morality just now. Nobody goes to anybody's house any more to sit and talk and have fun. There's a master of ceremonies and a collec-

tion basket, because there are no gatherings now except for Good Causes. We have almost no time to be actors and writers these days. We're committee members and collectors and organizers and audiences for orators.[38]

While, during the period 1935-1939, as Bellush points out, "the social idealism and the anti-fascist struggle behind the Spanish Civil War tended to unify liberals, leftists, and Communists, there developed a sharp divergence during this period over the destructive role of Spanish Communists in subverting and murdering Spanish Trotskyists and left-wing Socialists."[39] Less sophisticated observers tend to gloss over this rift when describing how the Spanish Civil War operated as such a unifying and positive experience for Hollywood progressives.

But on August 23, 1939, the Hitler-Stalin Pact destroyed the Popular Front.[40] It made clear not only Russia's duplicity, but also the CPUSA's domination by the Comintern. For many of the duped social idealists, their good intentions resulted in "personal humiliations, public shame and loss of work."[41] Now friend turned against friend, and families became estranged as shocked, angry, and disillusioned progressives fled the CPUSA and dissociated themselves from the Orwellian rhetoric that justified Stalin's heinous acts, including the unprincipled invasions of Finland and Poland. From then on, as Kanfer, succinctly states, the show business Left became vulnerable to charges of "hypocrisy, self-deceit, and factionalism."[42]

Played out against this background, the Supreme Court's approval of the Wagner Act on April 12, 1937, the successful intervention of the National Labor Relations Board in the screenwriters' war,[43] and its certification of the revitalized SWG on August 10, 1938, brought fleeting joy. Hollywood was a battlefield filled with casualties. And the war was far from finished.[44]

Notes

[1] In addition to the works of Larry Ceplair, Steven Englund, Stefan Kanfer, and Nancy Lynn Schwartz, my account of the screenwriters' war with Hollywood producers is based primarily on the following books: Eric Bentley, ARE YOU NOW OR HAVE YOU EVER BEEN, AND OTHER PLAYS (New York: Harper & Row, 1972); Eric Bentley, ed., THIRTY YEARS OF TREASON: EXCERPTS FROM HEARINGS BEFORE THE HOUSE COMMITTEE ON UN-AMERICAN ACTIVITIES, 1938-1968 (New York: Viking Press, 1971); Alvah Bessie, INQUISITION IN EDEN (New York: Macmillan and Company, 1965); John Cogley, REPORT ON BLACKLISTING: I - MOVIES (New York: The Fund for the Republic, 1956); Lester Cole, HOLLYWOOD RED: THE AUTOBIOGRAPHY OF LESTER COLE (Palo Alto: Ramparts Press, 1981); Bruce Cook, DALTON TRUMBO (New York: Charles Scribner's Sons, 1977); Philip Dunne, TAKE TWO: A LIFE IN MOVIES AND POLITICS, Foreword Anthony Lewis (New York: McGraw-Hill Book Company, 1980); Gordon Kahn, HOLLYWOOD ON TRIAL: THE STORY OF THE 10 WHO WERE INDICTED (New York: Boni and Gaer, 1948; Rpt. New York: Arno Press, 1972); *Lillian Hellman, SCOUNDREL TIME, Introduction Garry Wills (Boston: Little, Brown and Company, 1976); *Howard Koch, AS TIME GOES BY: MEMOIRS OF A WRITER (New York: Harcourt Brace Jovanovich, 1979); DICTIONARY OF LITERARY BIOGRAPHY, Volume 26 of AMERICAN SCREENWRITERS, ed. Robert E. Morsberger et al. (Detroit: Gale Research Company, 1984); Hugh G. Lovell and Taisle Carter, COLLECTIVE BARGAINING IN THE MOTION PICTURE INDUSTRY (Berkeley Institute of Industrial Relations: University of California, 1953); *Victor S. Navasky, NAMING NAMES (New York: Viking Press, 1980); Helen Manfull, ed. ADDITIONAL DIALOGUE: LETTERS OF DALTON TRUMBO, 1942-1962 (New York: M. Evans and Company, 1970); Perry, Louis B., and Richard S. Perry, A HISTORY OF THE LOS ANGELES LABOR MOVEMENT, 1911-41 (Berkeley: University of California Press, 1963); Murray Ross, STARS AND STRIKES: UNIONIZATION OF HOLLYWOOD (New York: Columbia University Press, 1941; Rpt. New York: AMS Press, 1967); Howard Suber, THE ANTI-COMMUNIST BLACKLIST IN THE HOLLYWOOD MOTION PICTURE INDUSTRY (Unpublished Ph.D. dissertation: U.C.L.A., 1968); __, THE 1947 HEARINGS or THE HOUSE COMMITTEE ON UN-AMERICAN ACTIVITIES INTO COMMUNISM IN THE HOLLYWOOD-MOTION PICTURE INDUSTRY (M.A. thesis: U.C.L.A., 1966); *Dalton Trumbo, THE TIME OF THE TOAD: A STUDY OF INQUISITION IN AMERICA AND TWO RELATED

PAMPHLETS (New York: Harper and Row, 1972); and Robert Vaughn, ONLY VICTIMS: A STUDY OF SHOW BUSINESS BLACKLISTING, Foreword Senator George McGovern (New York: G. P. Putnam's Sons, 1972).

[2] President Roosevelt signed the National Industrial Recovery Act on June 16, 1933.

[3] For a discussion of the Marxist approach to analyzing the benefits of the NRA to big business, see *Robert C. Allen and Douglas Gomery, FILM HISTORY: THEORY AND PRACTICE (New York: Alfred A. Knopf, 1985): 134-38.

[4] For a good overview, see Douglas Gomery, "Hollywood, the National Recovery Administration, and the Question of Monopoly Power," JOURNAL OF THE UNIVERSITY FILM ASSOCIATION 31:2 (Spring 1979): 47-52.

[5] Christopher Dudley Wheaton, A HISTORY OF THE SCREEN WRITERS GUILD (1920-1924): THE WRITERS' QUEST FOR A FREELY NEGOTIATED BASIC AGREEMENT (Unpublished Ph.D. dissertation: University of Southern California, 1974): 13-37.

[6] Pierre Norman Sands, A HISTORICAL STUDY OF THE ACADEMY OF MOTION PICTURE ARTS AND SCIENCES (1927-1947) (New York: Arno Press, 1973): 30-44. For a valuable account of how Mayer rigged California's 1934 gubernatorial race, see Greg Mitchell, "How Hollywood Fixed an Election," AMERICAN FILM 14: 2 (November 1988): 26-31.

[7] Five branches—producers, writers, directors, actors, and technicians—represented the major divisions of the film industry in the newly formed AMPAS. Each branch had one member on the Academy Conciliation Committee, which resolved labor-management disputes; the intent of the AMPAS' By-Laws was to prove that in labor negotiations, producers were outnumbered four-to-one. It soon became apparent that there was a way around appearances. Although each group elected its own representatives to its governing bodies, membership to the AMPAS was by invitation only. This insured that the AMPAS would be controlled by a select body. For more information on how the AMPAS operated, see Chapter 3. For information on the labor problems generated by this unusual labor-management system, see Murray Ross, STARS AND STRIKES: UNIONIZATION OF HOLLYWOOD: 27-44; and ___, "Labor Relations in Hollywood," ANNALS OF THE AMERICAN ACADEMY OF POLITICAL AND SOCIAL SCIENCES 254 (November 1947): 58-64.

[8] Sands (p.45) claims that the AMPAS, in the area of labor disputes, functioned successfully between 1927 and 1932. For example, "In a period

of four years the academy settled 344 major actor cases, effected more than 3,600 interviews and minor adjustments, and collected approximately $112,000 for the actors—an average of more than $500 a week. This was a considerable sum for players whose employment is casual and remuneration modest. It is a tribute to the Academy that its interpretations and decisions in actor-producer relations are frequently consulted by the present actors' union—the Screen Actors Guild."

[9] The academy withdrew from all major labor negotiations within the industry by 1937. For more information, see Sands, 202-26.

[10] Schwartz, 9.

[11] For a helpful overview of the film industry's first union, see Cogley, 48-53; and Ross, 3-22.

[12] The Screen Directors Guild was founded in 1936.

[13] The first president of the SWG and the intellectual leader of the Hollywood branch of the American Communist party, Lawson's literary roots were in left-wing theater movements. He came to films in the late twenties and played a major role in Hollywood labor wars over the next twenty years. Lawson was the first "unfriendly witness" to appear at the 1947 HUAC hearings and set the tone for the confrontations between the House committee and those witnesses who refused to answer questions that they felt violated the safeguards of the First Amendment. Following a prison term for a contempt citation, he was blacklisted and never again gained a screen credit. His books on film history and technique—THEORY AND TECHNIQUE OF PLAYWRITING AND SCREENWRITING (1949), FILM IN THE BATTLE OF IDEAS (1958), and FILM: THE CREATIVE PROCESS (1964)—contain many of his ideas on propaganda and responsibility in filmmaking. Among his screen credits are ALGIERS, BLOCKADE (both in 1938), ACTION IN THE NORTH ATLANTIC, and SAHARA (both in 1943).

[14] The former journalist-turned-screenwriter was one of the few radicals who revived the SWG, but never served as an officer or board member for the guild. Budd Schulberg identified Bright as one of the men who recruited him for membership in the American Communist party. (See Bentley, p. 450.) Rather than appear before HUAC, Bright took refuge in Mexico and sold his scripts through black market connections. By the early sixties, he returned to the United States. Among his best-known screenplays are THE PUBLIC ENEMY (1931), SHE DONE HIM WRONG (1933), and SAN QUENTIN (1937). The man who played a major role in developing the Hollywood gangster film died on September 14, 1989. For more information, see C. Gerald Fraser, "John Bright, 81, a Screen Writer," NEW YORK TIMES A (September 16, 1989): 12.

[15] A well-known playwright, respected by his peers, Mayer was known

for his flippant wit and caustic scripts. The clever dramatist had a difficult time adjusting to Hollywood politics in the thirties. He left the SWG when it began arguing for a national federation of writers. Mayer did, however, join many of his progressive friends as a board member of the Anti-Nazi League. Among his screen credits are ROMANCE (1930), DESIRE, TILL WE MEET AGAIN (both in 1936), THE BUCCANEER (1937), MIDNIGHT (1939), TO BE OR NOT TO BE (1942), and A ROYAL SCANDAL (1945).

[16] The ex-playwright and former journalist became a member of the first Board of Directors for the SWG. Despite his desire to see sweeping changes in the way screenwriters were treated, he did not play a conspicuous role in the fifteen-year struggle with the producers. Among his screen credits were BROADCAST OF 1936 (1936) and KING OF THE NEWSBOYS (1938).

[17] A former social worker-turned-screenwriter, Ornitz was one of Hollywood's most respected insiders and a valued member of the SWG's executive board. His successful 1926 novel HAUNCH, PAUNCH AND JOWL caught the attention of Hollywood producers, and in 1928 he left New York and started his screenwriting career. Accused of being a Communist, he testified as an "unfriendly witness" at the 1947 HUAC hearings, was cited for contempt, and served nine months of his one-year prison sentence in 1950. Among his screen credits are THE CASE OF LENA SMITH (1929), LITTLE ORPHAN ANNIE (1932), THE HIT PARADE (1937), and MIRACLE ON MAIN STREET (1939).

[18] A refugee from the left-wing theater, Faragoh served as an executive officer of the SWG in the mid-thirties and was accused of being a Red repeatedly during the HUAC hearings. He never appeared as a witness. Among his screen credits are LITTLE CAESAR (1930) and MY FRIEND FLICKA (1943).

[19] For more information on the specific strategies and relationships, see Cole, 121-28; and Ross, 52-63.

[20] What added to the 1933 crisis was the failure of the studios to adhere to the principles of a writer-producer code of practice established for the industry by the AMPAS on May 1, 1932. Three basic points concerned the issue of layoffs and quitting, the payment by the studios to writers of treatments and continuities, and the problem of screen credits. Five years of negotiations had provided the basis for the code, yet the agreement proved unenforceable. Film historians like Ross indicate blandly (p. 61) "the administration of the code became very lax during the trying years of the depression." More recent chroniclers, however, express no faith in the studios' willingness to honor any agreements unless forced to do so. Ross is right in his assertion that also angering

the writers in 1933 was the intention by the studios, to set up a "central artists' bureau for the centralized purchase and exchange among studios of stories, actors, properties, and other essentials of film production..." This, in effect, would have controlled writers' salaries and maintained permanent cuts.

[21] According to Dore Schary, other leaders in forming the SWG were Philip Dunne, Howard Eastabrook, Ernest Pascal, Dudley Nichols, Wells Root, Oliver H. P. Garrett, and Allen Rivkin. See Dore Schary, HEYDAY: AN AUTOBIOGRAPHY (Boston: Little, Brown and Company, 1979): 66.

[22] Ever since the Actors' Equity Association won its battle against Broadway theater managers in 1919, union organizers worked to find an appropriate representative for screen actors. In the early 1920s, the struggle involved four groups: Actors' Equity Association, the Screen Actors of America, the Motion Picture Players Union, and the Associated Actors and Artists of America. For a good summary of the steps that led to the formation of the Screen Actors Guild, see Ross, 23-47.

[23] The ALA was founded in 1912 to safeguard the economic interests of writers. For more information, see Ross, 48-63.

[24] One of Hecht's boys brought to Paramount, Mahin's screenwriting career lasted for more than thirty years. He helped establish the revived SWG and then opposed it as president of the Screen Playwrights. In 1948, he rejoined the SWG. Among his many distinguished screen credits were RED DUST, SCARFACE (both in 1932), CAPTAINS COURAGEOUS (1937), DR. JEKYLL AND MR. HYDE (1941), SHOW BOAT, QUO VADIS (both in 1951), and HEAVEN KNOWS, MR. ALLISON (1957). In 1958, he joined with screenwriter Martin Racklin to produce their own script, THE HORSE SOLDIERS. Two years later, the Mahin-Racklin Company repeated the collaboration with NORTH TO ALASKA. Mahin received the Writers Guild of America's Laurel Award in 1957.

[25] Among Rogers's better-known screen credits were BILLY THE KID (1941), FOR ME AND MY GAL (1942), and CALLING BULLDOG DRUMMOND (1951).

[26] Among Riskin's most famous screen credits are these earned with director Frank Capra: THE MIRACLE WOMAN (1931), AMERICAN MADNESS (1932), BROADWAY BILL and the Oscar-winning IT HAPPENED ONE NIGHT (both in 1934), MR. DEEDS GOES TO TOWN (1936), LOST HORIZON (1937), YOU CAN'T TAKE IT WITH YOU (1938), and MEET JOHN DOE (1941). His specialty was in delineating how a character lost control of his status and then suddenly won back both respectability and his loved one. He received the Laurel Award

in 1955.

[27] Among Meredyth's many screen credits covering both the silent and sound eras, the best known are WONDER OF WOMEN (1928), UNDER TWO FLAGS (1936), THE MARK OF ZORRO (1940), THAT NIGHT IN RIO (1941), and THE UNSUSPECTED (1947). She was also the wife of the noted Warner Bros. director Michael Curtiz.

[28] Son of MGM's producer Harry Rapf, the lifetime friend of Budd Schulberg played a central role in the Hollywood writers' wars. He symbolized the social idealist manipulated by the CPUSA. He was blacklisted by Hollywood at the start of the fifties and spent many years working in the audiovisual field. In the mid-seventies, he returned to his alma mater, Dartmouth, to head their film studies program. Among his screen credits are WINTER CARNIVAL (1939), SONG OF THE SOUTH (1946), and SO DEAR TO MY HEART (1949).

[29] Son of the famous humorist Ring Lardner, the distinguished screenwriter began his film career as a story editor at Twentieth Century-Fox in 1937. One of his first assignments at writing scripts was an unaccredited contribution that he and his good friend Schulberg made to the 1937 film A STAR IS BORN. That same year, the young writers (including Rapf) drifted into the CPUSA. By the start of World War II, Lardner, Jr., had established himself as an important screenwriter. His first big hit was his Oscar-winning WOMAN OF THE YEAR (1942). Other successes prior to his appearance before HUAC in 1947 were LAURA, TOMORROW THE WORLD (both in1944), CLOAK AND DAGGER (1946), and FOREVER AMBER (1947). Once he became known as a member of the Hollywood Ten, Lardner was blacklisted and served a one-year jail term. During the fifties he wrote under various pseudonyms. His first screen credit under his own name after being blacklisted was for THE CINCINNATI KID (1965). He won his second screenwriting Oscar for M*A*S*H (1970).

[30] Kanfer,15, 16.

[31] Comments in an August 19, 1984 letter to the author.

[32] Presumably, very few Hollywood Communists owned CPUSA cards, mainly because no one ever wanted to be put in the compromising position of having a party card used as evidence of subversive activities. Dalton Trumbo makes a major point about the existence of Communist party registration cards in THE TIME OF THE TOAD. He claimed that investigators at the 1947 HUAC hearings failed to understand "that a registration card is not a membership card, nor a duplicate of one, but merely the alleged office record of an alleged card." He then argues that the United States government established the fact that the CPUSA was dissolved in 1944 and reconstituted in 1945 as the Communist Par-

ty. "Yet the alleged cards introduced into evidence [in 1947] were all 'Communist Party registration cards dated in November or December 1944 to cover the year 1945. They were 'Party Cards' when no Party was in existence." See THE TIME OF THE TOAD, p.29. (Ring Lardner, Jr., made a similar point, quoted in HOLLYWOOD ON TRIAL, pp.202-03.) However, Bruce Cook (p.148) quotes Trumbo as saying he lost his party card when he left his shirt at his mother's house. That was in 1944: "It was not a traumatic moment in my life." Cogley (p.21) also disputed Trumbo's position about party cards. Denying that all the presumed cards were merely registration cards, Cogley explained, "In the case of Adrian Scott and Edward Dmytryk, for instance, 'Communist Political Association' cards were introduced into evidence...The cards [were] clearly marked '1944 Card No...They were not intended to cover the year 1945,' as Trumbo asserted."

[33] For an interesting perspective, see Leonard Quart, "Frank Capra and the Popular Front," CINEASTE 8:1 (Summer 1977): 4-7.

[34] Ceplair and Englund, 99-100.

[35] Ceplair and Englund (pp. 65-128) estimate that no more than three hundred members of the film colony ever belonged to CPUSA during the thirties. Of that figure, screenwriters numbered nearly half. That is, close to thirty percent of working screenwriters, fifteen percent of the SWG, became members of the CPUSA. (Why Ceplair and Englund don't consider these numbers significant is curious.) An impressive twenty-five percent of the Hollywood community joined activist groups during the period from 1935 to 1940.

[36] The figure is attributed to J. Edgar Hoover. See Bentley, p.260. Navasky (p.26) claims, "The party never achieved a membership approaching one percent of the Americanfilm collection."

[37] For useful summaries of the events, see Gertrude Jobes, MOTION PICTURE EMPIRE (Hamden: Archon Books, 1966): 343-56; Cole, 210-16; and Ross, 192-202.

[38] Mary McCall, "My Name Isn't Costello," SCREEN GUILDS' MAGAZINE 3:12 (February 1937): 7.

[39] From an August 19, 1984, letter to the author. Readers interested in further information should see George Orwell, HOMAGE TO CATALINA, Introduction Lionel Trilling (New York: Harcourt Brace Jovanovich, 1980).

[40] Trumbo argues that "New Liberals" make much of the Nazi-Soviet Pact but ignore other agreements during the Popular Front period that affected the August 23, 1939, pact: e.g., the French-Italian agreement and the Anglo-Nazi treaty (both in 1935); the British-Italian accord, the Mu-

nich Pact, the Anglo-Nazi nonaggression pact, and the French-Nazi nonaggression pact (all in 1938). See THE TIME OF THE TOAD: 37-8.
[41] Copley, 45.
[42] Kanfer, 35.
[43] In the summer of 1938, the NLRB presided over an election of who would represent the Hollywood screenwriters in their collective bargaining with the studios. The vote was 267 to 57 in favor of the SWG.
[44] Richard Meryman, MANK: THE WIT, WORLD, AND LIFE OF HERMAN MANKIEWICZ (New York: William Morrow and Company, 1978): 160-1.

12. Industrialist Oscar Schindler (Liam Neeson) confers with a worried Itzhak Stern (Ben Kingsley) about the fate of thousands of imprisoned Jews during the end of World War II. Steven Spielberg, *Schindler's List* (1993). From the core collection of production photographs of the Margaret Herrick Library, Academy of Motion Picture Arts and Sciences.

10.

Hilberg's Dilemma

Raul Hilberg is one of the great scholars of our century. More than anyone else, he has exposed the behavior and thought processes of ordinary people carrying out a genocidal project.[1]

Robert Jay Lifton

To understand something historically is to be aware of its complexity, to have sufficient detachment to see it from multiple perspectives, to accept the ambiguities, including moral ambiguities, of protagonists' motives, and behaviors. Collective memory simplifies; sees events from a single, committed perspective; it is impatient with ambiguities of any kind; reduces events to mythic archetypes. Historical consciousness, by its nature, focuses on the historicity of events—that they took place then and not now, that they grew out of circumstances from those that now obtain. Memory, by contrast, has no sense of passage of time; it denies the 'pastness' of its objects and insists of their continuing presence.[2]

Peter Novick

How did we go from the country of Schiller, Beethoven, and Bismarck in a few hundred years to the country of Goebbels, Goring, Hess, and Hitler? What do you make of it? Probably that Darwin was wrong.[3]

Warner Finck (Mort Sahl)

Thus far, I have been commenting on my previously published work, in an effort to discover why and how I became a teacher, how my teaching priorities evolved, how I discovered my scholarly responsibilities, and how these selected memories reflected my relation to the world around me. While these recollections are unique to me, the act of recalling a previous time and analyzing it is not. Director Martin Scorsese's own self-reflective journey served as an example that influenced me in crafting this Chapter. "Obviously," the celebrated artist reasoned in discussing his memories, "this autobiography is very personal and very subjective. These were the days when movies colored my dreams, shaped my perceptions, and even my life in some cases."[4] Nowhere do his observations prove more relevant to me than in the chapters that follow.

At this stage of the journey, therefore, it seems best to talk candidly, emphasizing what I feel to be the influence of the Popular Arts on complex and complicated matters, thereby minimizing as much as possible any obstacles in explaining myself to the reader. In doing so, I make clear I am no fan of political correctness or of conforming to traditional narratives. This attitude is not because I deny the value of such ideas for scholars or for the public. Unquestionably, there are benefits to be gained from being sensitive and tactful. But they are not always appropriate in situations where honesty is required. Besides, such virtues sometimes hinder the tone of how I prefer to remember the times and the events under review.

I, therefore, begin this fond memory with an unusual January 1994 phone call from Professor Raul Hilberg. Less than a month earlier, famed director Steven Spielberg had released his unforgettable film *Schindler's List*. Based on Austrian novelist Thomas Keneally's *Schindler's Ark*,[5] Steven Zaillian's brilliant screen adaption traced the exploits of a controversial German-Austrian industrialist who had also doubled as a spy for Nazi intelligence (the latter fact is almost totally missing from the screen narrative). The film opens in 1939, when the opportunistic Schindler seized on the chance, during the Third Reich's occupation of Poland, to make millions of dollars by using forced Jewish labor in his recently acquired enamelware factory. The multi-layered chronicle then offers a six-year perspective of the Nazi genocide up to 1945. Against the background of this appalling period in human history, Schindler gradually becomes personally involved with his endangered workers, culminating in an inexplicable decision to sacrifice his wealth in order to save approximately 1,100 Jews from Nazi annihilation.

My colleague explained to me that a well-known scholar from a prominent history journal had asked him to write a review of Spielberg's film. But the noted political scientist had turned the editor down, saying he did not feel qualified for the assignment. He did, however, know just the person to do the job. (His words, not mine.) In short, Hilberg told me to expect a phone call from the journal editor about doing the proposed film review.

To appreciate the two documents—the film article and a later book review— that are the focus of this section, I revisit various people and events from my past to outline how I felt about the Holocaust, the mass media, and my famous colleague in the spring of 1994. To describe what follows as a broad generalization is a vast understatement. As you will learn quickly, I am going to talk about intense and difficult subjects—e.g., justice, responsibility, duty, war crimes, and the nature of evil—that challenged, and continue to challenge, my intellect, my morality, and my teaching commitments. My task here is to make these abstract ideas accessible to you without being pedantic, preachy, sanctimonious, disingenuous, and sentimental. To help get around such difficulties, the reader needs to appreciate what moved Professor Hilberg to choose me to take his journal assignment. Second, you need to understand what I mean by the word "Holocaust," and how the term was perceived then and now. Finally, there are the basic issues of anti-Semitism, America and the Holocaust, and Hollywood; and how they affected my journey and shaped my scholarship.

In refreshing my memories of the mid-thirties to the mid-nineties, I have consulted books, academic articles, newspapers, films, and television documentaries that more often than not emphasized America did not know much about the gathering storm overseas, was isolationist in nature, and was conflicted about the European events that metastasized into The Third Reich's "final solution" to the Jewish problem. Even so, you would be right to express skepticism about what I knew and reasonably remember from my youth seventy-five years ago. My only rejoinder is to recall what Professor

Hilberg said when I asked him what was known about the Holocaust during the years from 1933 to 1945. "Knowledge," he said, "is a matter for the individual. Some people sleepwalk through history, and others pick up the tiniest threads and conclude something is going on."[6] Much of what I found useful in my current inquiry I had already written about long ago, mainly in *Film Study: An Analytical Bibliography*. Thus the narrative that follows moves rapidly, principally because this is a story based on memory more than on history; and the historical research already exists for those who wish to pursue specific topics and themes.

As always, we start with the last first. Surprisingly, I go back to July 22, 1935, the day this American Jew was born. It was in the midst of the Great Depression. Joblessness was widespread. The economy was in shambles. Immigration quotas and policies were under attack by various sections of society. Jews living in this country continued to be perceived as a major and controversial voice in revolutionary social movements. The Communist Party (CPUSA) had duped many innocent Americans into thinking it was an idealistic solution to many of the nation's social evils. In addition, Nazi Germany would introduce its Nuremberg Race Laws two months later (September 15), systematically stripping German Jews of their citizenship and basic rights, while, at the same time, the United States was deeply concerned about Eastern European immigration poisoning our social and economic values. On the front page of *The New York Times*, the key story in the upper left-hand corner had to do with "Catholic Priests Silent on Nazi-Church Dispute, Except in South Germany." The argument referred to the Nazi Party's youth movement and its ambivalent relationships to the Church. Even various Jewish organizations were divided on how best to respond to the horrors abroad and the anti-Semitism at home. And, finally, the year's Oscar-winning picture turned out to be *It Happened One Night*.[7] Each of these topics would worry me in one form or another to the present day.

What would also trouble me in thinking back on those terrible times was the role that President Franklin Delano Roosevelt played in relation to the Jews and to the Holocaust. On one hand, the four-term leader would appear to me one of the greatest presidents in American history. On the other hand, I came to despair over his knowledge of what was happening to European Jews and how he responded to the growing realization of Nazi genocide. Did he ever really deliver on the promises he made to save nearly 6 million Jews? Could he have done more given the circumstances, the resources at hand, and the nation he governed? I do not know the answers to these difficult questions. But I often become stressed about such matters and the predictable result is confusion, anger, and disbelief.

So far, the two authors who seem best at sorting out my unresolved feelings about President Roosevelt are Richard Breitman and Allan J. Lichtman in their prize-winning book *FDR and The Jews*.[8] "For most of his presidency," the investigators write, "Roosevelt did little to aid the imperiled Jews of Germany and Europe," the scholars report. But then the same two men explain, "Still, at times Roosevelt acted decisively to rescue Jews, often withstanding contrary pressures from the American public, Congress, and his own State Department." And as a further caveat, the scholars add, "Oddly enough, he did more for the Jews than any other world figure, even if his efforts seem deficient in retrospect."[9] What to make of these contrary positions remains an ongoing problem for me, and lasts beyond the sheets of this book. I allude to my dilemma early on in the chapter to alert you to a subtext in writing this chapter.

As you may recall from earlier pages, by the time I reached the first grade in 1941, the movies had become a major resource in my basic education. But how does my dysfunctional childhood and the emergence of World War II relate specifically to my being conscious of my Jewish heritage and writing my essay on *Schindler's List*? To answer those questions, I look back to how Hollywood Jews and the movie industry helped influence my underlying political and social consciousness.

Once more, for clarity's sake, I want to stress that what follows is my story, not anyone else's. Moreover, it is not the whole story, just a small section to explain where I was when I returned from the Dean's Office as a tenured full professor in the English Department by the end of the 1980s.

Almost every major film historian understands how Jewish immigrants from Eastern Europe came to America to escape yet another painful chapter in their 2,500 year history suffering from persecution and oppression, and in search of a new home and a better life.[10] Much to their chagrin, the émigrés found the Land of Milk and Honey dominated by an intolerant, white, Anglo-Saxon hierarchy that insisted the unwelcome refugees—e.g., falsely perceived as radical, scheming outsiders—not only assimilate but also accept a marginalized place in the nation's public life.

Again, to avoid any unnecessary confusion in this complicated narrative, I want to make clear that there is not, in my judgment, an immigrant group—e.g., Chinese, Blacks, Japanese, Latinos, Italians, Armenians, Greeks, Muslims, and Irish—without a horror story to tell about their coming to the Promised Land. Nor should we leave out the tragedy of Native Americans. I have no interest in prioritizing which group has the most horrific chronicle. Let me also be clear, I am not attacking the United States. Without reservation, I consider it the greatest nation on earth. But it has its significant and not to be ignored painful flaws. Moreover, we bear the burden of redressing those wrongs so that our country can be all that it wants to be.

As for the turn of the nineteenth century, there is little guesswork in remembering how these insecure, persecuted, and defenseless Jewish exiles were perceived and received as they exited Ellis Island. All through the centuries, when things went wrong, society after society senselessly made the "Rootless Outsiders" the prime scapegoats, justified or not, for any of civilization's problems or calamities. To be accurate, Jews were not, and have never been, the only ethnic and religious group to be victimized by national groups during the history of the civilized world. That said, by the time the hundreds of thousands of Jewish refugees fled Europe for America, they had become the prime focus of anti-Semites throughout the Western Hemisphere.[11] Thus, by 1900, to ensure the undesirable "Greenhorns" remained second-class citizens, the nation's power brokers established educational quotas, closed out opportunities in highly regarded professions like medicine, law, and banking; and made certain the "aliens" lived in restricted areas and under brutal and demoralizing conditions.

The small band of Eastern European Jews who saw the fledgling movie business as their best hope for the future did so knowing the secret to their success rested on what was loosely called a "melting pot" theory, with a specific set of rules. If you want to be accepted, don't fight the establishment. If you want to succeed, hide your ethnic and religious traditions. Make yourself over so as to be like anyone else in the Gentile community. Learn and speak "proper" English. Change your name. And most of all, don't call attention to your origins and to yourself. It was too dangerous. Anti-Semitism, in all its vile and cruel variations, will be ready to destroy you.

This last point was especially important once the first stirrings of the Bolshevik Revolution occurred in 1905. Twelve years later it was in full swing. But by the end of the first decade of the twentieth century, it was commonplace to hear hate speech about "Yids" and "Kikes" who spread "treasonous" communist ideology. Jews were stereotyped as labor organizers, socialists, religious fanatics, and malcontents upsetting the status quo. [By the time I was born, as noted in the previous chapter, communism was both a perceived and a real problem not only for Americans in general, but also for Jews in particular.]

Interestingly, the consistently conservative movie messages in the early days of film were aimed at the working and lower classes primarily. After all, educated and prominent people paid little attention to this insignificant and popular amusement dominated by deceitful foreigners. In retrospect, this misguided attitude seems remarkably foolish, given the fact that three-quarters of the country went to the movies each week. In fact, it was by watching films like *It Happened One Night* that I would develop my unwavering suspicion of the upper classes and instead place my faith in the ordinary person.

In the movies I viewed in my youth, the assimilationist, anti-intellectual, and middle-class message, overtly or not, was implanted in almost every film. Whatever genre I watched, I learned how to dress, how to speak, how to behave, and what to do to be accepted. The fact that I didn't buy totally into the mass media propaganda is interesting. I also picked up on how widespread discrimination, oppression, and suffering frequently resulted, illogically and idiotically, because of stereotyping a person's race, color, and gender. (Film and theater historians would tell me later the same lessons were taught to all turn-of-the century audiences in venues like Burlesque, Vaudeville, and the Yiddish films.)[12] In the much-underappreciated newsreels of the day especially, I gradually became aware of what was happening around me worldwide.

Of course, at six years of age, I did not know why the Jewish moguls kept me ignorant of what was happening to our *Lanzmann* in Poland, Austria, Lithuania, Germany, and the USSR. How was I to know that a former member of film's elite group, the man who had run RKO Pictures in the early thirties, and had recently been appointed ambassador to England, Joseph P. Kennedy, had warned his one-time associates to mind their social and political behavior, lest their anti-Nazi concerns be construed as dragging the nation into an unwanted and unnecessary war? Professor Stephen Whitfield speaks for many film historians when he points out, making anti-Nazi movies ran the danger of being perceived by the moguls as too parochial, too limited in their perspectives, and in particular, drawing attention to themselves.[13] And lest you think Ambassador Kennedy was a lone racist voice, I could hear on the radio bigoted programs by Father Charles Coughlin, or read the Federal government news reports to see what various anti-Semitic lawmakers were ranting about on the floors of Congress, labeling President Roosevelt's New Deal as the "Jew Deal." I could discover the renaissance of the Ku Klux Klan, hear the suspicions raised about the Jews' loyalty to America by our most prominent religious groups, read Reverend G. A. Simons' atrocious publication *The Protocols of the Elders of Zion*, or pick up the bigoted material widely distributed by industrial tycoon Henry Ford.

But despite these dangerous conditions, there were courageous people who made some anti-fascist films by end of the thirties.[14] One rare case was Anatole Litvak's *Confessions of a Nazi Spy*.[15] Looking at the film today exposed how I was manipulated then. Basically, the narrative acted as a spy thriller warning us Nazi Germany was out to destroy our values and our way of life. Built into the espionage narrative, however, is an expose of the German American Bund movement, the brain washing of naïve young people by home grown fascists, and the racist caveats that Germans living in America pose a menace to our national security. Not once is there a mention of what is happening to Jews in Germany. Hitler, we are told, is not threatening one group, but all Americans.

What fascinated me today was how back then almost every part in the film was played by a non-Jew, with one exception: Edward G. Robinson (formally Emanuel Goldenberg, an ex-performer in the Yiddish theater), had the key role of the heroic FBI agent, Ed Renard, who exposed the spy ring. Secondly, the story draws attention to the Nazi invasion of Austria on March 13, 1938. We are told Hitler duped a naive world into thinking he only attacked the small country to protect Austrian citizens from the chaos threatening them. What stunned me was, historically, the man who helped provide the pretext for the Anschluss was Oscar Schindler. He allegedly helped set up the false broadcast that ignited the invasion of Austria.[16] Finally, the film made clear that something terrible was happening back in Berlin to people who went against Nazi leaders. We are never told what; only that it was ugly and barbaric.

If this frightened first grader had any doubts about what was happening to his kinsmen, Charles Chaplin's *The Great Dictator*,[17] released the following year, spelled out the dangers Nazism posed to Jews specifically. The film's Prologue states: "This is a story of a period between two World Wars—an interim in which Insanity cut loose, Liberty took a dive, and Humanity was kicked around somewhat." Scene after scene in the courageous, satirical, political, and contentious movie illustrate how Jews were being humiliated, beaten, and deprived of their liberties **publically** in the mythical country of Tomania (Germany). Chaplin plays dual roles: the confused Jewish barber who, because of injuries suffered in the First World War, is baffled by the barbarism going on around him; and Andenoid Hynkel, the crazed dictator out to conquer the world. The film concludes with Chaplin, posing as Hynkel, having a change of heart and making a plea to the world to rise up and to fight for its freedom. I recall that I was more afraid than amused; while Chaplin would later say that if he truly knew what was going on in Germany, he would never have made the film.[18]

Up to December 7th, 1941, what little emerging political consciousness I had was focused on Europe. But after the bombing of Pearl Harbor that view changed. As for knowing about the start of World War II, I have an unforgettable recollection of waking up on Monday morning, December 8th, intending to go to school, only to find the streets overcrowded with men and women going to enlistment centers to join the fight against the Japanese who had carried out the sneak attack on our naval base near Hawaii. And all through the era, the war bonds, and the patriotic stamps, and the propaganda films, plus what I learned both in public school and in Hebrew school, kept me constantly aware that if my grandparents had not immigrated earlier in the century from Austria, Poland, and Russia to America, neither my sister nor I might be alive.

During the Second World War, however, Hollywood, working closely with the Federal government, reworked its propaganda practices to focus on demonizing the Axis powers. For example, German villains became culture-loving monsters who fanatically followed their Fuhrer and got defeated mainly because of their inflexible mentality. (This emphasis on unquestioning, perverted thinking became a crucial concept in the world's view on how "mindless" the Nazis were. They were just following blindly their Fuhrer's orders.) Japanese villains proved to be the most racist people imaginable, exemplified best in the detestable 1944 film *The Purple Heart*, surprisingly made by the distinguished Lewis Milestone.[19] Of course, the Nazis and the Japanese had their own propaganda factories. But such pictures had little effect on me.

Nonetheless, what I remember most about the war years was how straightforward everything was. We were in a racist struggle to the death against evil nations, resulting in a "we versus them" motion picture strategy. The bad guys committed horrible, unthinkable crimes to purify their would-be ideal fascist world, while we were pictured as ordinary, peace-loving people who forgot our racial differences and joined ranks to preserve our basic freedoms. Except for an occasional newsreel showing what was happening in Europe, the movies kept me focused on the survival of our allies and us, and rarely about what was happening to the Jews. Interestingly, newsreels, the supposedly minor theater fillers, proved to be an important precursor to the future television news programs.

Then, in 1945, when the War ended, new and disturbing Hollywood films began to appear. Over the next decade, the movie studios dramatically transformed their genre conventions to make viewers like me socially conscious about racial problems in our society.[20] One such film was Elia Kazan's Oscar-winning *Gentleman's Agreement*,[21] exposing anti-Semitism not only among Christians, but also among Jews. No doubt, this Jewish racism was related to the division between the German Jews who immigrated here in the late nineteenth century and Eastern European immigration at the turn of the twentieth century. For me, it was mainly a confirmation of what I had been told and had experienced throughout my childhood.

Other intriguing shifts in Hollywood messages involved our European enemies. For example, the Nazis now were juxtaposed with good Germans in movies like *The Desert Fox*, *The Sea Chase*, *The Enemy Below*, and *The Young Lions*. Later I would read Martin Dworkin's fascinating study pointing out the reasons for the change: the new, reopened German markets had become important for Americans, returning veterans were cynical about the War itself, and we needed to make sure our former enemies became our allies in the oncoming Cold War against the Soviet Union.[22]

But I recall strikingly the horror I felt at learning about the death camps and the mass murder of nearly six million Jews. Why hadn't I known about this before then? Why hadn't the newspapers, the radio shows, and the movies alerted me to this enormous tragedy? How could something so massive be such a secret? Why didn't the world's political and religious figures take a stand against the atrocities? What was going to be done to the perpetrators of this carnage?[23] Was it even imaginable that America and England and Russia would look the other way about the Third Reich's atrocities and recruit thousands of Nazi war criminals to work for the CIA, the FBI, and various other agencies?[24] Such thoughts began what I discussed earlier: my questioning the relationship between FDR and the Holocaust.

My Hebrew schoolteachers made similar points about a conspiracy of silence, but they had another agenda. Zionists, who once were relegated to the margins of the American Jewish community, now were prominent and pushing for a Jewish homeland for nearly 300,000 displaced Jewish survivors. Then came the 1946 Nuremberg Trials, where an international tribunal was trying twenty-one Nazi big wigs for crimes against humanity. I was reminded that this was the first time in human history mass murderers would be held accountable for their crimes. I heard about villains like Herman Goring, Albert Speer, Alfred Jodl, Wilhelm Keitel, Rudolf Hess, Franz von Papen, and Julius Streicher. They had done the unthinkable and the unimaginable, but they were insisting they were "only following orders." Curiously, there was nothing about the Jewish tragedy in the four major indictments against them. But I thought it would be a no-brainer these terrible people would all be put to death. But many were not. Some were given prison terms, while others were acquitted.

Fifteen years later in Stanley Kramer's Oscar-winning *Judgment at Nuremberg*,[25] Richard Widmark as the troubled prosecutor Colonel Tad Lawson is told by his superiors to go easy in asking for the death penalty because we needed the German nation as our ally. Widmark replies, "Just tell me, what was the war about?" Burt Lancaster as a disgraced eminent jurist told Spencer Tracy cast as the decent Judge Heywood, "I never meant it to come to this." Tracy replied, "The day you sentenced the first innocent man, it came to this." So how was it a number of these degenerates went free? What is meant by the concept of "justice"? (It is vital that we recall that these same questions about how one not only behaved in World War II, but also how one survived the conflict were being debated or denied in places like Palestine, the Soviet Union, and Germany.)

Complicating matters even more for me were the 1947 House Un-American Activities Committee Hearings intended to root out Communist conspirators in the film industry. I saw in the newsreels, on one hand, the loyal, friendly Americans like the Hollywood moguls, Ronald Reagan (President of the Screen Actors Guild), and movie stars like Gary Cooper and Adolphe Menjou. On the other hand, were the Hollywood Ten: unfriendly, disloyal, shouting screenwriters like Dalton Trumbo,[26] John Howard Lawson, and Ring Lardner, Jr. Although they had made a short 16 mm film, *The Hollywood Ten* (1950),[27] to explain their position, it did not do much to make things any clearer to me.[28] What troubled me most, as I have written elsewhere, was that my new screen idol, Larry Parks, was among the blacklisted.[29] Did anyone really believe he was out to destroy the United States? Was there a hidden agenda to these hearings? Could it be the bad guys were the good guys? Adding further to my confusion in the fifties was when the ever-shifting propaganda battle once again led to prejudiced moviemaking. For example, Elia Kazan's *On the Waterfront*[30] made the case for those who named names; Stanley Kramer's *High Noon*[31] made the argument decent Americans could depend on no one in times of crisis.

Adding still further to the variables that eventually led to my teaching about Jews in the film industry was the fact that in 1948, Orthodox Jews came to my house to plead with my parents to make me study Hebrew as a second language at Midwood High School. Although I did take two semesters, the program was short-lived. This futile attempt was part of the growing support in America for the proposed State of Israel. One of the major rationales being circulated to justify the creation of a Jewish homeland was the world had done nothing to prevent the destruction of the nearly six million Jews in World War II. Now, people had a chance to make amends. (Years later, I discovered there were other reasons, plus people began using the Shoah story as a defense mechanism to prevent any criticism of Israel.)

In those days, however, I remember clearly how we lobbied for the Palestinian Jews, mainly because six weeks after the UN proclaimed Israel a State on May 14th, I was bar mitzvah on June 19th. Without question, the subject of Israel was an everyday topic. The one constant refrain from those times was Rabbi Hillel's message: "If I am not for myself, who will be? If I am only for myself, what am I? If not now, when?"

During the fifties, television began to emerge as a major force in my ethnic education. Not only did Jewish comics dominate the small screen and tutor me about comedy as a valuable defense mechanism against bigots, but also the new art form changed Hollywood's technology. To compete against the revolutionary medium, the film industry turned to large screen productions, especially Biblical epics. Once again, the movies said one thing, but meant another. For example, the jaded moviemakers, more fearful than ever about their fragile economic and social status, also faced the problem of how to build support for the new State of Israel without bringing down on themselves the wrath of the ambivalent Americans. (These were the days when I became an American Jew, not a Jewish American. This was not a parsing of my having dual loyalties. I wanted there to be no doubt that my first allegiance was to the United States and not to Israel.) So the studio heads came up with the idea of turning out historical films using ancient persecutions against Christians as a cinematic metaphor for the oppression of modern day Jews.

A year after I was married and moved to New Rochelle (1958), the first mainstream film about the Nazi genocide came to the silver screen: George Stevens' *The Diary of Anne Frank*.[32] Initially a book, then a Tony-award winning stage drama, and now a screen narrative about a thirteen year-old girl's tragic two years hiding in an Amsterdam attic during the Nazi occupation of Holland, the wrenching screenplay stressed the strength that tough times produce in ordinary individuals, that horrible phases in life and society will pass, and what occurs to us is all part of a greater pattern than we realize. The director and his cinematographer, William C. Melior, who both earlier had actually filmed the survivors at Dachau during the allied liberation of the camp, decided not to include any documentary footage in the film, because they feared it would turn audiences away. It was just too painful to see.

Revisiting the motion picture today produced two memories worth sharing with the reader in the context of this Chapter. First, in the fiftieth anniversary DVD's audio commentary with George Stevens, Jr. and Millie Perkins (then a twenty-year old inexperienced actress who played the adolescent Anne Frank), the now seventy-year old woman remarked that in 1978, nineteen years after the film had been released, she was in a teaching program in Oregon. At the time, NBC showcased a TV mini-series, *Holocaust*. Mainly an overwrought narrative and poorly acted drama that focused on a Jewish family's struggle to survive expulsion and annihilation, the four-part series included many controversially recreated scenes of Nazi atrocities and persecution. During that week when the mini-series was screened, Perkins walked into the teachers' room to find her colleagues visibly upset. They knew she had been in the Stevens' production and asked her was what the mini-series was showing true? Did such things really happen? It couldn't be, they insisted. Perkins explained how astonished she was that "at this time in history" Americans still didn't know much about the Holocaust.[33]

The second anecdote concerns the University of Vermont's 199th Commencement exercises on May 18th, 2003. A new President had chosen the distinguished alumnus Jon Kilik as the Keynote speaker, and I had the honor of introducing my former student. Another important degree recipient was Mrs. Marian von Binsbergen Prichard. This notable Dutch citizen had witnessed the Jewish deportation in

Occupied Holland and had personally saved 150 Jewish children. Moreover, the courageous woman had actually killed a Nazi rather than let him take three youngsters away from her. Following the ceremony, we retired to the President's house for lunch. During the meal, I casually remarked that of the more than 350 films then available on the Holocaust, the only two movies consistently shown in the public schools were *The Diary of Anne Frank* and *Schindler's List*. I hazarded a guess it was because both pictures featured Christians saving Jews. The elderly Mrs. Prichard responded by saying the Frank family and the film had nothing to do with the Holocaust. Kilik agreed. Stunned, I stayed silent for the remainder of the luncheon.

While *The Diary of Anne Frank* won many awards and garnered much critical acclaim, it did not do well at the box-office. Nevertheless, a year later the Austrian-born filmmaker Otto Preminger released *Exodus*.[34] Based on Leon Uris' novel of the same name published the year before, the film gained prominence because among other reasons Dalton Trumbo, a blacklisted writer, wrote the screenplay. (In Israel, however, the citizens showed their disdain for the movie by laughing continuously at much of the screen dialogue.[35])

The film narrative breaks into two parts. The first half is set in 1948, on Cyprus, where a recently widowed Christian nurse (Eva Marie Saint) finds herself drawn to the problems of Jewish Holocaust survivors imprisoned at a British internment camp. Although friendly with the compassionate British commander (Ralph Richardson), she discovers his adjutant (Peter Lawford) hates the Jews and insists no one wants them.[36] This way, the commercially minded filmmakers offend no one. Enter a Hagannah hero, Ari Ben Canaan (Paul Newman), who devises an escape plan that is also designed to raise the world's consciousness about the need for 300,000 survivors to have a Jewish homeland in Palestine. He obtains a boat, the *Exodus*, manages to smuggle over 600 Jewish refuges aboard, and organizes a hunger strike when the British refuse to let the ship go to Palestine. Eventually, the British capitulate. The second half of the film follows the Zionists in Palestine as the United Nations is getting set to vote on turning the British mandate into the State of Israel. Although much screen time focuses on the refugees' problems with the Arabs, various Jewish factions, Zionist aims, and the seeds of the coming war should the United Nations decide in favor of the Jewish immigrants, almost as much time is devoted to two love stories: Paul Newman and Eva Marie Saint, and Sal Mineo and Jill Haworth (both playing Jewish survivors of the death camps).

In revisiting the popular but flawed film, I realized how much the action-packed story provided me with the opportunity back then to sort out my feelings about the birth of the State of Israel. To illustrate what Hilberg meant by "tiny threads," let me cite three examples from the film. The first begins with two of the very few Jewish actors in the film: Lee J. Cobb (born Leo Jacob to an Ashkenazy Jewish New York family) and David Opatovsky (born David Opatoshu, also in New York City and the son of a Yiddish author). In *Exodus*, the men are cast as estranged brothers; Cobb believes in the peaceful approach to Jewish statehood taken by the Hagannah, while Opatovsky plays the leader of the terrorist Jewish Irgun.[37] When Newman visits with the Irgun leader, he tries to get his uncle to explain why he does what he does. Opatovsky justifies his actions by saying the world only responds to terror and violence, and the group he heads is merely a "midwife" who brings free nations into being. He goes on to say Justice is an "abstraction devoid of reality"; to talk of Justice "in connection with Jews in the same breath is an absurdity"; in addition, the Arabs have Justice on their side every bit as much as the Jews; and finally, no one can deny that the Jews have not had their share of suffering the past decade. "Let the next injustice," he concludes, "work against someone else for a change." This focusing on the abstract notion of Justice would become a major theme throughout future feature films and documentaries on the Holocaust. It is also one I struggle with each time I dig more deeply into these historical events.

The second "tiny thread" occurs when a very troubled Sal Mineo (Dov Landau) asks to join the Irgun. In a brilliant, slowly drawn out interrogation, the scene begins with the youngster lying about his death camp experiences to an Irgun interrogator. Then the older, knowledgeable Opatovsky takes over the questioning. He gets the tormented youth to admit what he did at Auschwitz in order to survive. While the filmmakers felt squeamish about showing actual footage, we do learn through the questions about the selection method, the gas chambers, how the victims had the responsibility to manage the death process, to clean up afterwards, and also the horrors of being a Sonderkommando. No subject matter would prove more acrimonious to Jews in all of film history than the contentious behavior of Jews in concentration camps, and the debatable cooperation of Jewish leaders with the Nazis in occupied countries.[38]

The final "tiny thread" relates to Arabs friendly to the Jews, but who are murdered by the followers of Mohammad Amin al-Husayni, the Grand Mufti of Jerusalem, the Palestinian leader of Muslims opposed to the creation of Israel. We are told that the Grand Mufti takes his orders directly from former members of the Nazi Party, who in essence are carrying out Hitler's insane belief that the Fuhrer's glorious defeat would inspire others to follow his vision and give rise to a restored Reich. Once again, the theme of blind obedience to a demented philosophy becomes part of Holocaust genre conventions.

One last recollection to illustrate how the rise of my Jewish film consciousness relates to the capture and trial of Adolf Eichmann.[39] (Here I am especially indebted to two films in clarifying my recollections: ABC News' *The Trial of Adolf Eichmann*[40] and Margarethe von Trotta's *Hannah Arendt*.[41]) Briefly, just as the 1946 Nuremberg Trials were set to begin, SS-Obersturmbannfuher Adolf Eichmann considered one of the most wanted Nazi war criminals and on the Nuremberg tribunal's defendant list, secretly obtained a Red Cross passport provided with help from the Vatican and escaped, via the "rat line," to Argentina.[42] Nearly fourteen years passed before David Ben-Gurion, President of Israel, discovered Eichmann's whereabouts and ordered the Mossad to kidnap him and to bring the morally bankrupt Nazi sadist back to Israel to stand trial for his war crimes against the Jews. Once the UN Security Council resolved the legitimacy of the kidnapping issue, the trial began in April 1961. For the first time in history, television broadcasted the proceedings of a criminal trial.

What I may have sensed but did not know was how and why the trial proceeded as it did. A major part of Israel's early years rested on not acknowledging what precisely had happened during the Holocaust. Whether out of a misguided shame for what concentration camp Jews did to survive, or the survivors themselves feeling guilty for having lived where others died, or because it was too painful to talk about, much of the Holocaust history was absent from the nation's and the world's consciousness.[43] President David Ben-Gurion felt the Eichmann trial would and could change this mindset. He felt both the Israelis and the world's population should know what the Nazis did, how it affected the victims, what was meant by Bureau 6, and just what was intended by "The Final Solution."

Another priority was to establish the concept called the "Law of Conspiracy." Since there were few survivors that could directly link Eichmann to the death of millions of Jews, the Israeli court needed to demonstrate that anyone who participates in a scheme to murder people is himself "representative of all."[44] Of course, everyone argued about whether a Nazi criminal could get justice in a Jewish court. Eichmann, protected from harm in a glass cage, said, "I admit my participation freely and without pressure. After all, I was the one who transported the Jews to the Camps. What is there to admit? I carried out my orders."[45]

Like everyone else, I waited and watched to see how the three judges and the prosecutors proceeded from there. Using witnesses and documents to discuss concepts of removal and extinction to showing actual footage of the death camps, the trial moved painfully through a process that focused not so much on the prisoner but on people and material that demonstrated conclusively the facts to ignorant and uncertain viewers who previously didn't know or want to know about the Holocaust. At the same time, we watched an unrepentant Eichmann boast about his inspired organization skills in transporting millions of Jews to their death. The demented bureaucrat argued he had no interest in where the trains went or what happened to the occupants. He was just trying to be the best bureau manager in The Third Reich. He wanted us to appreciate how creative he had been. These trains bound for Auschwitz, as Primo Levi would explain elsewhere, "heavily laden with human beings went in each day, and all that came out was the ashes of their bodies, their hair; the gold of their teeth."[46]

How one perceived Ben-Gurion's plan depended on one's personal history. No one could deny, however, the proceeding raised issues about Jewish behavior between 1933 and 1945. Other subjects prominently presented dealt with denials about the Holocaust, what it was and how it operated, what role the Jews paid in their own destruction, and what happened on January 20th, 1942 at the Wannsee Conference (more later). In particular, the trial proceedings gave precise descriptions of what the death camps were actually like. All this was to be explained in the context of establishing a legal process for this and future war crime proceedings. Interestingly, some observers questioned whether Eichmann became almost an excuse for a trial, and not a criminal in the dock.

Covering the courtroom events for *The New Yorker* magazine was a distinguished Jewish philosopher and Holocaust survivor, Professor Hannah Arendt. Simply stated, and much to the consternation of people around the world, she described Eichmann not as an anti-Semite, not as a vicious member of the despised SS, and not as a traditional satanic monster. Instead, the former Zionist argued that in Eichmann, the world was presented with a new phenomenon: a nobody, a mediocre, insignificant bureaucrat, who merely followed orders. Arendt insisted many people like him simply stopped thinking about matters of morality or conscience once they gave their allegiance to the fascist state and its leader. They believed they were doing their duty. Therefore, if you followed Arendt's divisive logic, the destruction of the European Jews occurred not because of monsters, but because ordinary people became monsters. She called her theory "the banality of evil." (By coincidence, her thinking on this issue bore a striking resemblance to ideas in a new work, *The Destruction of the European Jews*,[47] published in 1961, by a Viennese-born scholar named Raul Hilberg. Adding to suspicions of plagiarism, Arendt's first of five articles for the *New Yorker* did not appear until February 16, 1963.[48])

But just as sensational and unnerving in the journalist's reporting was her second theory. Arendt argued that the courtroom evidence showed the Jewish leadership was complicit in the death of Europe's Jews. That second theory became key in the world's reaction to the scholar's legacy. "The whole truth," explains the fictional Hannah Arendt (Barbara Sukowa) in the riveting Von Trotta film, "is if the Jewish people had been unorganized and leaderless, there would have been plenty of misery, but the total number of victims would hardly have been between 4½ and 6 million people."[49]

Thus by the time Eichmann was sentenced on December 15th, 1961 and later hanged on June 1st, 1962, you might have hoped these prickly issues would have been clarified, that people everywhere would have better understood the Holocaust. But for me it was never clear, it would never be clear, and when it came time to focus on my doctoral thesis, I consciously had difficulty making any notable mention of the Jew in film.

One other "tiny thread," however, carries us to the question of how I would forever address this dark period in history. In the film *Hannah Arendt*, a lifelong friend turns against her when the *New Yorker* articles appear, saying, "You behave like a superior German intellect who looks down on us, and you accuse us of being accomplices in the Shoah."[50] She has no idea why he feels that way.[51]

This brings me to my second concern in these introductory comments. We need to remember that at the time I was discussing the destruction of the European Jews, the word "Holocaust" was not in common parlance. Although the world knew of the existence of the death camps by the end of the forties, the term did not become fashionable until some time in the fifties, when the word gained widespread currency among everyday Americans. Many Jewish intellectuals, however, referred to the Nazi mass murders of the Jews during the time of The Third Reich as the Shoah, the Hebrew word for "catastrophe," "destruction," or "calamity."

When I consulted my expert colleague on such matters, Dr. Richard Sugarman, he told me the etymology of the word goes back to the ancient Greek translation of Hebrew and the practice of burnt offerings. Mentioned in "Leviticus," he explained, "The offering was given for transgressions by individual Israelites."[52] When I later talked to Professor Hilberg about the "Holocaust," he also expressed a dislike for the word, as did Claude Lanzmann. Both men found it far too encompassing of mass murders to gypsies and other genocides. Still further, the awarding-winning historian Peter Novick listed numerous ways in which the word had been misunderstood and misused in society. And I have already discussed in the Marcel Ophuls chapter the problems the concept had for him and his film *The Memory of Justice*. It is for such reasons that I decided to include my book review of a text written by the eminent Jewish historian Lawrence Baron. His important work on

Holocaust films illustrates my problems with the word and where I stand today.

Also, I need to point out I still don't think the word "Holocaust" is understood, nor have the issues raised in the Eichmann trial ever been resolved satisfactorily. My reasons for feeling that way stem in part from an incident at the screen premiere of Julian Schnabel's exceptional film *The Diving Bell and the Butterfly*[53] on November 30th, 2007 in New York City. Jon Kilik produced the movie and graciously invited Sheila and me to attend opening night. Afterwards we had dinner at a private party, where Jon seated us with the major figures tied to the film: the cinematographer (Janusz Kaminski), the screenwriter (Ronald Harwood), and the associate producer (Kathleen Kennedy).

As the reader probably knows, both Kaminski and Kennedy worked on *Schindler's List*, while Harwood won an Oscar for his screenplay on *The Pianist*. You would assume correctly that they were well informed in Holocaust studies, since they researched the subject for their respective film productions. Astonishingly, in 2007, they knew who Arendt was, but they did not know about Hilberg. Just as startling, when I brought up Raul's theory that there was little the Jews could do to escape their fate during the Holocaust, Kaminski, a gentleman and very bright man, disagreed and left the table rather than provoke an argument.

Finally, there is the question of studying the Holocaust. What do we hope to learn from the past? I remember Raul's take on that thorny issue. He did not believe that history repeats itself. "Of course, anything can happen," he explained. "I don't believe in carbon copies, so I don't think it would be wise to look for exact repetition. But within the context of something in a different society and a different time, this kind of process can emerge and replicate itself."[54]

And so I now turn to my professional relationship with the great scholar. You note I do not say personal. Raul and I met frequently over a twenty-year period to discuss many, many things not only about films and the Holocaust, but also about administrative practices and behavior at the University of Vermont. He had arrived on campus in 1957, more than a decade before I did. He sought me out; I did not approach him. In those early days, Raul loved movies and welcomed a chance to discuss them with a film historian. If you want to know which films in particular we discussed, I suggest you get Dr. Baron's magnificent work, *The Modern Jewish Experience in World Cinema*.[55] Whatever movies Raul and I debated are to be found there. What is not apparent is how much he disliked French director Alain Resnais' documentary film *Night and Fog*, and why he despised Italian director Lina Wertmuller's satirical *Seven Beauties*.

Also worth mentioning is we both believed that talking about such catastrophes should never be to the exclusion of other calamities. It was an issue we both felt strongly about, and it was one that Lawrence Joffe mentioned in his obituary of the great historian: "Hilberg believed the Holocaust should not be seen in isolation, either from other wartime events or from other acts of genocide. Returning through the American Deep South in the 1940s, he was shocked to see separate benches for blacks and whites. 'Don't tell me that what happened [in Europe] can't happen some place else….'"[56]

Before going any further, a word about my remarkable companion's personality is necessary. No one I ever met was a superior raconteur, or could anyone gain greater command of a room better than the ex-soldier who served in the 71st Infantry Division, which liberated the Gunskirchen concentration camp in 1945. Whenever Raul held court, people listened, especially when it was at a college faculty meeting. No one I ever met impressed me more with his intellect than did the Brooklyn College graduate student who would later be considered the Father of Holocaust Studies.[57] His restraint, his sly smile, and his encyclopedic knowledge were spellbinding. But there was another side to him. He could suddenly become a cantankerous, unpredictable, and unfiltered human being who appeared "off the wall." His temper got him into all sorts of trouble; and later, when I became Associate Dean, many people often turned to me to settle him down or to defuse a sensitive situation he had created. In fact, almost always, when I would meet his wife, Gwendolyn (she was for a while, an administrative assistant in the Economics Department), I would jokingly say, "Gwen, how do you live with him? You're a saint, a saint!"

That said, I remember him with great fondness. For over a decade, 1967 to 1978, he lived, according to my recollections, a paradoxical life. Outside the University, he had already become one of the most important and influential men in his field. But on campus, except for the admiration of those few colleagues who knew the value of his research, Raul existed as a respected professor teaching about a footnote in World War II studies. His classes were small and rarely talked about. I also remember clearly how much sadistic pleasure he took in telling me what a stupid move I had made in going to the Communication Department, that the academic ship was going to sink, and no matter how good I was, unless I got away, I would go down with the ship.

Then in 1978, with the telecasting of NBC's "Holocaust," everything changed. The Shoah became a major field of academic study, Raul's classes mushroomed, and his reputation in Vermont soared. Really, for the first time, I realized just whom I was friendly with. At the same time, television began a concerted effort to bring the Holocaust to the public's mind and attention. Starting in the late seventies, the small screen became the mass media's dominant spokesperson for Holocaust film projects.

Now I sought Raul out. What we talked about was what anyone who wanted to understand the Shoah could read about in his published works. Our discussions took place in our respective offices and over lunch in the faculty dining room. He explained in detail how bureaucratic obsessions were at the heart of the Nazi mass murders (see his 1985 second edition of *The Destruction of the European Jews*), he talked about the behavior of the various groups during the years from 1933 to 1945 (see *Perpetrators Victims Bystanders: The Jewish Catastrophe 1933-1945*),[58] he wrestled with the behavior of the thorny issue of Jewish leadership in the dark days (see his collaborative work with his departmental friend, Dr. Stanislaw Staron, *The Warsaw Diary of Adam Czerniakow: Prelude to Doom*),[59] and we had conversations over the years of what he thought of some of his fellow Holocaust scholars (see *The Politics of Memory: The Journey of a Holocaust Historian*.)[60]

One of our most fruitful discussions for me involved director Heinz Schirk's film *The Wannsee Conference*, a fictionalized account of fourteen prominent Nazi officials meeting on January 20, 1942, to plan and to agree on "the Final Solution," the annihilation of the

European Jews. Presumably based on notes recorded at the actual meeting, the 90-minute narrative portrays vain, ambitious, jealous, and unconscionable officials coming to a relatively quick decision about the annoying Jewish problem. In what may be Hilberg's only written "film review," he discussed his reservations about seeing a staged movie about SS and ministerial officials convening in a luxurious building in the Wannsee section of Berlin. He quickly pointed out the secretarial notes supposedly serving as the authentic source for the screenplay never existed. What little was known about the meeting was a summary document prepared by one of the conference participants, Adolf Eichmann; hardly a suitable source for a movie script. According to Eichmann, he never uttered one word at the meeting. After bashing motion pictures that purportedly deal factually with historical events, Raul gave examples of what the filmmaker missed and misconstrued, at one point referring to the artist as an "amateur." He concluded his remarks by writing, "The makers of *The Wannsee Conference* did not cling to the structure and chronology of the historical record. They made a hybrid film. Yet they approached the subject seriously and left a fascinating experiment." It was a valuable history lesson, but hardly an example of effective film criticism.[61]

Some of the most meaningful meetings Raul and I had appeared on television. By the mid-eighties, I had become fast friends with one of Vermont's most beloved and respected broadcasters, Jack Barry.[62] When the skilled broadcaster went on vacation I sometimes acted as a substitute host on his local PBS show, *Vermont Reports*. Twice, I had Raul on as a guest. While I have a tape of the second program, the first one is lost. All attempts to locate the show dates or professional copies have been in vain. But one story he told me on camera is forever embedded in my consciousness. It is also my favorite memory of the man.

As best as I can remember, Raul told of receiving an unexpected phone call sometime in the late sixties from a total stranger, claiming to have just come across *The Destruction of the European Jews*. Explaining that he too was a writer and very much interested in using the Holocaust in his forthcoming book, the stranger in New York asked if it were possible to fly to Burlington, Vermont to discuss historical matters with Raul. Come ahead, Raul said. The two men, both great walkers, spent three days talking and discussing the Holocaust. Finally, the stranger asked point blank if Raul would read and react to a manuscript he had written. Hilberg readily agreed. The man, as you might have guessed, was Herman Wouk; and the work was *The Winds of War*. Raul also copyedited the Holocaust sections in *War and Remembrance*. After telling me how much time and effort he put into the projects, I was curious as to how much money he had charged Wouk. "Nothing," Raul replied. "I did it because it was my responsibility."

The only story I ever told Raul that came light years in range of his anecdote had to do with the 1985 Peabody Award ceremonies. That year, President Ronald Reagan, on a planned diplomatic trip to Germany, had agreed to join West German Chancellor Helmut Kohl and visit the Bitburg Military Cemetery, where nearly fifty Waffen SS officers were buried. According to the President's problematic understanding of the past, the Nazis buried at Bitburg were just as much "victims," as those millions murdered by the Nazis in the concentration camps.[63] A major controversy erupted in the United States, and Holocaust survivor Elie Wiesel even made a trip to the White House to plead with the President to please not make this terrible gesture. All to no avail! At the Peabody ceremony in New York that year, two of the people being given awards were former Israeli UN Ambassador Abba Eban, and veteran broadcaster Bill Moyers. Before the actual ceremony, I met briefly with the ambassador and praised his extraordinary TV series *Heritage: Civilization and the Jews*. When we finished talking, he put his hand on my shoulder, and kindly remarked, "You're a very smart young man." But it was Moyers who had the final word. In accepting his Peabody Award, he said, "Abba Eban has shown us how to honor history, and President Reagan has shown us how to dishonor it." One of the reasons I suspect Raul liked the story so much was because he would later appear in an episode on Moyers' PBS series, *Facing Evil*.

But nothing cemented our relationship more than did the 1992 Festschrift ceremony at UVM, where many distinguished scholars came to honor Raul for his enormous contributions to the field. Among the invited dignities was Claude Lanzmann, the director of the brilliant and unique film *Shoah*. He was the only man I ever saw Hilberg praise unqualifiedly. As Raul told me, Lanzmann was "one of the very few heavyweights he had ever met." The two came together at a scholarly conference in 1975, where Lanzmann asked Raul to be part of his forthcoming movie *Shoah*. Having agreed and become a major figure in the extraordinary film, the two intellectuals became closely knit friends. Since I was given the privilege of introducing the director before he spoke, Lanzmann and I spent some time together. It was not an altogether pleasant experience since Claude was a brilliant but difficult man to deal with, and we disagreed about whether fiction films should be made about the Shoah. He did tell me about his new project, a movie dealing with the Israeli defense forces. After the three-day event ended, Hilberg published his book, *Perpetrators Victims Bystanders* and gave me a copy. The inscription read: "To Frank Manchel. You know what I have invested in this book because you understand how writing is hard. Please accept this volume as a sign of our association and friendship. Raul Hilberg."

So it was when the question of my doing a film review on *Schindler's List* arose, Raul felt safe in recommending me for the assignment. We did not speak again on the matter, and I had no contact with him while I wrote the essay. When it came out, Hilberg called me, and said, he considered it the "finest Holocaust film article ever written." Do I have to tell you what that meant to me? Then six months later, Raul called again. He had been spending some time with Claude Lanzmann. His friend's film on the Israeli defense forces, *Tsahal*,[64] had been released and was doing very badly at the box-office. Furthermore, Claude had another child and desperately needed money. In the meantime, *Schindler's List* was a worldwide sensation. Not only was Lanzmann jealous because of the money issue, but also he was extremely angry. He was frustrated that Raul would have anything to do with fictional movies about the Shoah. He considered such films an obscenity and a disservice to what happened to the 6 million Jewish victims. In short, Raul quietly told me, he could no longer support what I was doing with fictional works about the Shoah out of respect for his friend. I always felt that although Raoul told me what he was doing, I believed that he was not convinced Claude was right.[65]

We rarely talked after that. Raul kept busy with various speeches, projects, and ceremonial events. And within a year I contracted Non-Hodgkin's lymphoma, which affected all my future professional activities. The legendary scholar died of cancer in 2007.

In summing up, I want to make clear that what may be just another chapter on academic publications is very meaningful to me. As to the Shoah and its status in the world today, the issues remain just as volatile as ever. Meanwhile, film and television companies routinely produce movies about the destruction of the European Jews that an apathetic public dismisses or ignores as merely entertainment or narratives too painful to watch. For example, the film industry recently released *The Monuments Men, Ida, Hannah Arendt, Labyrinth of Lies, Son of Saul, Woman in Gold,* and *Vita Activa: The Spirit of Hannah Arendt.* Claude Lanzmann has produced an important movie about the Jewish leadership council in Theresienstadt in *The Last of the Just.*

Educators persist in thinking of the Holocaust as an intellectual pursuit restricted to abstract studies, refusing to build meaningful film and TV libraries housing important and empathetic feature films and documentaries making the subject available and accessible to the general population. In addition, some Jewish organizations question the way the Vatican is treating Pope Pius XII's legacy from World War II, scholars are still bitterly debating the relationship between FDR and the Jews,[66] we are still reading about what happened in the key twenty-seven SS camps in new accounts by distinguished historians,[67] and the *New York Times* periodically reports about the mass Jewish exodus now occurring in Europe.[68]

And, you may ask, what about Hilberg? How do you feel about him today? Let me answer with a recent news story. *The New York Times* reported on July 15, 2015, a German court had convicted a 94-year-old ex-SS soldier formally stationed at Auschwitz-Birkenau of being complicit in the mass murder of 300,000 Hungarian Jews. At his sentencing, Oskar Groning, appearing frail but mentally alert, offered an apology for his actions but did not deny his responsibility. The evil of the Holocaust, he told the court, was too great to entitle him to a pardon from anyone other than God. For his wartime crimes, he received a four-year sentence. The reason it took 70 years for justice to be administered, explained reporter Alison Smale, is the country's legal system made prosecuting former

SS followers and camp guards problematic unless prosecutors had direct evidence linking the individual to the murders. The problem lessened when John Demjanjuk, a Ukrainian soldier who served at the Sobibor killing camp, had received the death sentence in a Munich court in 2011.[69] Ironically, Demjanjuk died before his appeals were exhausted. It may be the same situation for Groning.[70] In various media reports, one gets the feeling many people object to hounding these old men who had transgressed in their youth. It was so long ago, the rationale goes, and they are different men today.

Professor Hilberg would have said no. As he once explained to me, anyone who is going to go on trial for Shoah war crimes is going to be old. The further we get from the mass murders of World War II, the older they're going to be. (Raul had been involved in a number of such cases here and in Canada.) "All I can say," he told me, "if one is not to ignore the presence of such individuals in society, one must do something. And if this society happens to be one that has law enforcement, then the only way in which to do something, other than to interview them as Lanzmann did [in *Shoah*] is to put them on trial. And in many cases, putting them on trial is the only way to interview them, to force them to say something."[71]

Teaching about the Shoah remains for many of my peers and for me an extremely difficult and unavoidable responsibility, because of the complex issues surrounding not only the tragic fate of the European Jews but also its relevance to the untold horrors experienced by the world at large. The leaders of great nations made difficult and controversial decisions about the horrendous period from 1933 to 1945 that still are not yet fully understood by generations then and now. We must debate those choices and determine their merit. Unless we probe why people did what they did in those unforgettable days, we run the risk of repeating the mistakes and suffering similar consequences in the future. Simply put, to avoid examining the past is not only to allow injustice the opportunity for rebirth, but also to dishonor those whose sacrifices and courage we need to remember.

Notes

[1] Qtd. on cover, Raul Hilberg, *Perpetrators, Victims, Bystanders: The Jewish Catastrophe 1933-1945*. New York: HarperCollins Publishers, 1992.
[2] Peter Novick, "Introduction," *The Holocaust in American Life*. Boston: Houghton Mifflin Company, 1999. 4.
[3] Marvin J. Chomsky, *Inside The Third Reich*. USA: The History Channel, 1982.
[4] Martin Scorsese, *A Personal Journey with Martin Scorsese Through American Movies*. England: British Film Industry, 1995; USA, 1996.
[5] Thomas Keneally, *Schindler's Ark*. Austria: Hodder and Stoughton, 1982.
[6] Frank Manchel, "Interview with Raul Hilberg," *Vermont Reports*. Vermont Public Television, June 1985.
[7] I was to learn that a similar comment was made about *It Happened One Night* in Simcha Jacobovici and Stuart Samuels, *Hollywoodism: Jews, Movies and the American Dream*. USA: Associated Productions, 1997. For the record, the film was made in 1934, but received its Oscar at the 1935 ceremonies.
[8] Richard Breitman and Allan J. Lichtman, *FDR and The Jews*. Cambridge: The Belknap Press of Harvard University Press, 2013.
[9] Ibid., Loc 65-66.
[10] For some useful films on the matter, see David Grubin, *The Jewish Americans*. USA: David Grubin Productions, 2008; David Eistein and Russ Karel, *Almonds and Raisin: The History of the Yiddish Cinema*. USA: Brook Productions, 1984; Alan Rosenthal, *Heritage: Civilization and the Jews*. USA: Thirteen/WNET New York, 1984; Ben Loeterman, *1913: Seeds of Conflict*. USA: Ben Loeterman Productions, Inc., 2014; and Simon Schama, *The Story of the Jews*. England: Baltic Film Services, 2013.
[11] Breitman and Lichtman, Loc 121.
[12] Irving Howe makes similar points in his wonderful book, *World of Our Fathers*, paying particular tribute to Abraham Kahan, the influential editor of the Yiddish paper *The Forward*. Kahan is praised as well in the TV series *The Jewish Americans*.
[13] Qtd., *Hollywoodism: Jews, Movies and the American Dream*.
[14] See Frank Manchel, *Film Study: An Analytical Bibliography*, Vol. 1. Rutherford: Associated University Press, 1990. 252-287.
[15] Anatole Litvak, *Confessions of a Nazi Spy*. USA: Warner Bros, 1939.
[16] Jon Blair, *Schindler: The Real Story*. England: Thames Television, 1994.
[17] Charles Chaplin, *The Great Dictator*. USA: United Artists, 1940.
[18] Notes on the jacket of the CBS Fox Video Laserdisc of Chaplin: *Legacy of Laughter—The Great Dictator*, 1993.
[19] Lewis Milestone, *The Purple Heart*. USA: Twentieth Century-Fox, 1944.

[20] Manchel, *Film Study*, Vol. 1, 567-569.
[21] Elia Kazan, *Gentleman's Agreement*. USA: Twentieth Century-Fox, 1947.
[22] Martin Dworkin, "Clean German and Dirty Politics," *Film Comment* 3:1 (Winter 1965): 37.
[23] Interestingly, the dilemma of what was known and not known about the Shoah has become an important topic in recent international films like Giulio Ricciarell's *Labyrinth of Lies* (Germany: Naked Eye Filmproduktion, 2014) — dealing with the question of denial in postwar-Germany; and Gaylen Ross' *Killing Kasztner: The Jew Who Dealt With Nazis* (France: GRFilms Inc., 2008) — dealing with Israeli society and Shoah survivors after WWII.
[24] Eric Lichtblau, *The Nazis Next Door: How America Became A Safe Haven For Hitler's Men*. Boston: Houghton Mifflin Harcourt, 2014; and Richard Rashke, *Useful Enemies: John Demjanjuk and America's Open Door Policy for Nazi War Criminals*. New York: Delphinium Books, 2013.
[25] Stanley Kramer, *Judgment at Nuremberg*. USA: United Artists, 1961.
[26] Invaluable to the uninformed and to those among us with bad memories on this subject is Jay Roach's *Trumbo*. USA: Groundswell Productions, 2015.
[27] Available on Stanley Kubrick's *Spartacus* DVD.
[28] For more details, see *Manchel, Film Study: An Analytical Bibliography*, Vol. 2, 1077-1108.
[29] Frank Manchel, *Exits and Entrances: Interviews with Seven Who Reshaped African American Images in Movies*. Washington, D.C.: New Academia Publishers, 2013. 50-55.
[30] Elia Kazan, *On the Waterfront*. USA: Columbia Pictures, 1954.
[31] Stanley Kramer, *High Noon*. USA: United Artists, 1952.
[32] George Stevens, *The Diary of Anne Frank*. USA: Twentieth Century-Fox, 1959.
[33] 50th Anniversary Edition DVD of *The Diary of Anne Frank*.
[34] Otto Preminger. *Exodus*. USA: United Artists, 1960.
[35] A fact told to me by historian Mark A. Stoler, July 14, 2015.
[36] Worth remembering in this context is that General George S. Patton, the U.S. officer overseeing the Displaced Persons' camps, not only had "utter contempt" for the surviving Jews under his command, but also wrote in his diary, he found the Jews "lower than animals." Eric Lichtblau, *The Nazis Next Door: How America Became A Safe Haven For Hitler's Men*. Boston: Houghton Mifflin Harcourt, 2014. 5.
[37] Some readers have speculated that Lee J. Cobb represents David Ben-Gurion, and David Opatovsky, Menachem Begin.
[38] To witness how far we have come since *The Diary of Anne Frank* and *Exodus*, I urge the reader to see László Nemes' Oscar-winning foreign

film *Son of Saul*. Hungary: Laokoon Film Arts, 2015. Starting with a definition of who the Sonderkommando were and what were their duties at Auschweitz, the filmmakers focus on a specific inmate attempting to give a single victim a proper Jewish burial. We also see how the Sonderkommando resisted their captors and produced the only armed revolt at the camp in October 1944. Especially brilliant is how the atrocities at the death "factory" are detailed but never shown in focus, always keeping the camera blurry in reconstructing specific events and behavior.

[39] This infamous Italian escape route, managed by the Vatican, was considered by the U.S. State Department, "the largest single organization in the illegal movement of emigrants," and [the Agency] concluded that church leaders had helped 'former Nazis and former Fascists' to flee Europe for South America and elsewhere 'so long as they were anti-Communists.'" *Lichtblau*, 9.

[40] ABC Production, *The Trial of Adolf Eichmann*, with David Brinkley narrating. USA: ABC News, 1997.

[41] Margarethe von Trotta, *Hannah Arendt*. Belgium: Heimatfilm, 2012.

[42] Well worth reading in this connection is Laurie Gwen Shapiro, "My Lower East Side Neighbor Caught Adolf Eichmann," *Forward*.Com (April 28, 2016): 1-15.

[43] Important to understand, there was an earlier trial prior to the Eichmann case that suggested the post-war Holocaust problem in Israel. The events concerned a Hungarian Jew named Rudolph Kasztner, who in 1944, negotiated with Eichmann to free thousands of Jews from being deported to Auschwitz. The details, the controversy, and the relationship to the Eichmann trial are powerfully recalled in Gaylen Ross' *Killing Kasztner: The Jew Who Dealt with Nazis*. France: GR Films Inc., 2009.

[44] Qtd. in *The Trial of Adolf Eichmann*.

[45] Ibid.

[46] Roger Cohen, "The Cruelty and the Depravity: A historian depicts the concentration camps where many of the Holocaust's millions died," *New York Times Book Review* (July 12, 2015): 12.

[47] Raul Hilberg, *The Destruction of the European Jews*. London: W H. Allen, 1961.

[48] For more on this issue, see Nathaniel Popper, "A Conscious Pariah," *The Nation* (April 19, 2010).

[49] Qtd. in *Hannah Arendt*. Belgium: Heimatfilm, 2012.

[50] Ibid.

[51] Another screen version of Hannah Arendt's depiction of Eichmann is Ada Ushpiz, *Vita Activa: The Spirit of Hannah Arendt*. USA: Zeitgeist Films, 2016.

[52] E-mail from Professor Richard Sugarman to the author. July 1, 2015.
[53] Julian Schnabel, *The Diving Bell and the Butterfly*. France: Pathe, 2007.
[54] Frank Manchel, "Hilberg Interview," *Vermont Reports* II.
[55] Lawrence Baron, *The Modern Jewish Experience in World Cinema*. Waltham: Brandeis, 2011.
[56] Lawrence Joffe, "Raul Hilberg: Historian prepared to risk his career to expose the Holocaust," *The Guardian* (September 19, 2007). Internet. 3 pp.
[57] Lawrence Joffe, "Raul Hilberg: Historian prepared to risk his career to expose the Holocaust," *The Guardian* (September 19, 2007). Internet. 3 pp.
[58] Raul Hilberg, *Perpetrators Victims Bystanders: The Jewish Catastrophe 1933-1945*. New York: HarperCollins, 1992.
[59] Raul Hilberg, *The Warsaw Diary of Adam Czerniakow: Prelude to Doom*. New York: Stein & Day, 1978.
[60] Raul Hilberg, *The Politics of Memory: The Journey of a Holocaust Historian*. Chicago: Ivan R. Dee, 2001.
[61] Raul Hilberg "Is It History Or Is It Drama?" *New York Times* (December 11, 1987): H34, 42.
[62] For useful information on this exceptional man, see Doug Bassett, "Jack Barry, R.I.P.," Internet, (May 6, 1997) and an Associated Press article written by Christopher Graff.
[63] Eric Lichtblau, *The Nazis Next Door: How America Became a Safe Haven For Hitler's Men*. Boston: Houghton Mifflin Harcourt, 2014. 184-185.
[64] Claude Lanzmann, *Tashal*. Germany: Bavaria Film, 1944.
[65] An interesting postscript to Lanzmann's views on Holocaust fiction films is found in a recent HBO documentary nominated for the 2016 Academy Award (Short Subject), *Claude Lanzmann: Spectres of the Shoah* by Adam Benzine. Not only does it refresh our memories of the legendary filmmaker's extraordinary motion picture, but also Lanzmann pays tribute to key people—e.g. Jean Paul Sartre (1905-1980) and Simone De Beauvoir (1908-1986)—who helped him over the twelve years in making the movie. Raul Hilberg is never mentioned nor is there even a clip of him in the 40-minute documentary. One point more. In an interview about the movie, conducted by an unnamed *Hollywood Reporter*, Lanzmann has lavish praise for *Son of Saul* director László Nemes' fictional film using brilliant documentary techiques to recreate the sense of what it was like being a Sonderkommando at Auschwitz. See "'Shoah' Filmmaker Claude Lanzmann Talks Spielberg, 'Son of Saul,'" *Hollywood Reporter.com* (May 5, 2016): 1-4.
[66] For a list of relevant scholarly books, see Joshua Shapiro, "FDR and the Holocaust," Published online, April 25, 2014.

[67] Nikolaus Wachsmann, *KL: A History of the Nazi Concentration Camps*. New York: Farrar, Straus & Giroux, 2015.
[68] The Opinion Page, "The Great Jewish Exodus," *The New York Times* (February 21, 2015).
[69] Alison Smale, "Oscar Groning, Ex-SS Soldier at Auschwitz, Gets Four Year-Sentence," *The New York Times,* July 15, 2015. Internet, 4 pp. See also Lawrence Douglas, *The Right Wrong Man*. New Jersey: Princeton University Press, 2016; and Liel Leibovitz, "The Nazi Who Lived in Ohio," *The Wall Street Journal* (February 18, 2016): C6.
[70] For more on scrubbing Nazi records clean in the post-WWII world, see Eric Lichtblau, *The Nazis Next Door: How America Became A Safe Haven For Hitler's Men*. Boston: Houghton Mifflin Harcourt, 2014; and Richard Rashke, *Useful Enemies: John Demjanjuk and America's Open Door Policy for Nazi War Criminals*. New York: Delphinium Books, 2013.
[71] Frank Manchel, "Hilberg Interview," *Vermont Reports* II.

Review Article

A Reel Witness: Steven Spielberg's Representation of the Holocaust in *Schindler's List*[1]

Frank Manchel
University of Vermont

This essay explores why Steven Spielberg's *Schindler's List* is significant for American cinema, for movies about the Holocaust, and for the artist himself. Two primary concerns guide its search: (1) to review the relationship between film history's "prince of profit" and his account of the Holocaust and (2) to emphasize how moving pictures might offer us something not possible in academic historical studies. The thesis is that the movie and the filmmaker are inextricably intertwined and that an understanding of that bond is useful not only for appreciating the film but also for reducing misconceptions about depicting the Holocaust in a commercial medium.

My goal is to suggest to readers that movies do not function in a vacuum, that their ability to entertain and to educate is tied to uncertain market conditions, daily censorship battles, prevailing industry practices, and powerful financial considerations. The more one understands these aspects of the film's background, the more one appreciates Spielberg's challenges and accomplishments. Thus, a subtext of this exercise is that mainstream theatrical films are both a business and an art, that historical and biographical movies make use of the past to comment on the present, that the mass media mediate between us and the events they depict, and that audiences often mistake that mediation for reality.[2]

The reader should also know at the outset that the tone of this essay differs markedly from that of many film studies. Rather than denigrating pragmatic moviemakers for bowing to commercial realities, I want to explore how artists like Spielberg employ their box-office clout to express their personal visions to a mass audience. As William D. Romanowski aptly stated, "Film has long been realized as a powerful transmitter of culture because it transmits beliefs, values and knowledge; serves as a cultural memory; and offers social criticism. Consequently, the cinema remains a continual battleground in the cultural conflicts in America."[3]

Although released only in December 1993, *Schindler's List* has already become for the present generation the most important source of historical information affecting popular perceptions of the Holocaust. According to one trade publication, the film's global popularity, four months after release, had already netted its makers $170 million, an unheard-of sum for a movie about the Holocaust.[4] While some groups heap honors on those connected with the movie, other circles condemn its perspective and motives.

Such reactions make it clear that *Schindler's List* is not just a movie. It has become part of an ongoing worldwide cultural war that for decades has been debating both the nature and causes of the Holocaust and the advisability of having artists interpret the events surrounding the Nazi genocide. My observations on Spielberg and his work, therefore, are meant to provide a perspective on their place in this important cultural conflict.

A word on methodology. Rather than confining itself to a straightforward review of the movie, this essay examines Spielberg's treatment of the Holocaust in the light of his prior cinematic career."[5] The plan is to position the film in its historical and cultural context and then to speculate on why it took so long for the book to be adapted to the screen. I will focus on three major areas: the subject matter and its visual presentation; the challenges that filming the Holocaust presents; and Spielberg's interpretation of this uniquely monstrous event. Because I assume that artists stimulate our imagination and scholar's discipline it, the essay is divided into two major sections reflecting these divisions.

Stimulating the Imagination

At the end of World War II, Holocaust survivor Leopold Pfefferberg became obsessed with the idea of persuading some gifted individual to tell the inexplicable story of Oskar Schindler, an apparently amoral German-Austrian businessman who nonetheless saved the lives of 1,100 Jews. Finally, in 1980, a chance meeting with Australian writer Thomas Keneally resulted in the publication two years later of the novelist's critically acclaimed book, *Schindler's List* (in Europe, *Schindler's Ark*).

Based on more than fifty interviews with the *Schindlerjuden* (Jews saved by Schindler), it recounts the spellbinding story of the lustful Catholic industrialist and Nazi spy who came to occupied Poland in 1939 to exploit the persecution of the Jewish population. Using all the wiles of a master con artist, this enigmatic entrepreneur took over a confiscated enamelware factory and manufactured pots and pans for the Nazi war effort. Rather than pay wages to Polish workers, Schindler used Jewish slave labor. Eventually, he convinced the authorities that his workers should be quartered on his factory grounds. Using his talent for scheming, bribing, and black marketeering, he not only amassed a sizable fortune but also endeared himself to the Nazi bureaucracy. Then, for reasons never explained, this most unlikely of heroes underwent a transformation and recklessly risked his life and literally gave away his wealth to protect his Jewish laborers. As the Nazi war effort began to fall apart in the waning months of 1944 and word came that all surviving Jews were being deported to Auschwitz, Schindler persuaded the authorities to transport his factory and its "essential workers" to his hometown of Brunnlitz in Czechoslovakia and there convert the plant into a munitions factory. A list of 1,100 Jewish names, "Schindler's List," was prepared. To get on the list was to escape extermination in the gas chambers. Shortly after the announcement of Germany's May 7, 1945, surrender reached Brunnlitz, Schindler, now a presumed Nazi war criminal, fled. In the years that followed, his marriage and business ventures failed. But his courageous actions during World War II earned him the gratitude of the Jewish survivors. In 1956, a carob tree was planted in his honor on the Avenue of the Righteous near the Yad Vashem Museum in Israel. When he died in Frankfurt in October 1974, virtually ignored by the German people, Schindler's body was transported to Israel and buried in the Catholic cemetery of Jerusalem.

Recognizing the stirring dramatic possibilities of the story and inspired by its heroic tale, Music Corporation of America (MCA) president Sidney Sheinberg immediately purchased the screen rights to Keneally's book. The powerful CEO believed that it was the perfect vehicle for his protégé, Steven Spielberg. More than ten years would elapse, however, before Hollywood's box-office king began shooting the film. Why? Clearly, it was not a matter of financing. Unlike other producers who wanted to put Schindler's story on the screen, Spielberg did not have to worry about either financing or distribution.⁶ After all, as Richard Schickel observes, "Since no filmmaker has a track record like his, none had his power to encourage both a studio and the young mass audience to take a risk on a movie the subject of which is inherently repellent, not to say terrifying."⁷

Ironically, film is a medium where the more successful you are commercially, the less acceptable you are to the critical community. Not surprisingly, for years Sheinberg was one of the few people, including the director himself, who thought Spielberg capable of making a movie about the Holocaust. In 1982, the thirty-five-year-old phenomenon was markedly different from other Hollywood wunderkind types like George Lucas, Francis Ford Coppola, and Martin Scorsese, who had studied film in college. Spielberg basically learned what he knew from watching movies and making them. His more educated peers might frequent the art houses, appreciate the great subtitled masterpieces, and aspire to Andrew Sarris's pantheon of cinematic masters, but he preferred the world of B movies: the serials, westerns, science-fiction films, action-thrillers, and war movies.⁸

A few years' work in television during the late sixties and early seventies had landed Spielberg his first theatrical feature, *The Sugarland Express* (1974). Although the public paid scant attention to the film, one critic, Pauline Kael, identified the strengths and weaknesses that would define Spielberg's work up to *Schindler's List.* Characterizing his first feature as "commercial and shallow and impersonal," the *New Yorker* critic also praised the director's ability to make the mundane entertaining. She then went on to write: "The director...is twenty-six; I can't tell if he has any mind, or even a strong personality, but then a lot of good moviemakers have got by without being profound. He isn't saying anything special...but he has a knack for bringing out young actors, and a sense of composition and movement that almost any director might envy."⁹ Within six years, Kael would blame Spielberg, as well as his friend Lucas, for representing everything that was wrong with modem American cinema, especially the industry's emphasis on marketing rather than on creating a movie.[10]

By 1982, most critics echoed her influential judgments, with one major change: no one doubted that Spielberg's films were extremely distinctive. His brilliant cinematic technique had made him the most popular and commercially successful director in film history. Thanks to works like *Jaws* (1975), *Close Encounters of the Third Kind* (1977), *Raiders of the Lost Ark* (1981), and *E. T.: The Extra-Terrestrial* (1982), Spielberg had become the modern Walt Disney. Like his presumed model, he delighted in making movies aimed at entertaining the child in each of us. The phenomenal successes of *Indiana Jones and the Last Crusade* (1989) and *Jurassic Park* (1993) give him the current distinction of having made four of the ten top-grossing movies in film history.[11]

Judging *Schindler's List* from this perspective, one can easily recognize the work of a master film technician in love with the classical Hollywood tradition. Audiences are given not only what they know about the Holocaust from past films but also a format with which they are comfortable. We have a central figure, Oskar Schindler (played superbly by Liam Neeson), who faces a series of obstacles that occur in a specific way during a specific period and are resolved by the film's conclusion. Through a spectacular reconstruction of historical events—for example, the rounding up of the Polish Jews by the conquering Nazi forces in 1939, the establishment of the Podgorze Ghetto in March 1941, the construction the following year of the Plaszow Forced Labor Camp, the destruction of the ghetto in 1943, the dehumanization of helpless people terrorized by merciless guards, the exhuming and burning of ten thousand Jewish bodies in 1944, and the horrors of arriving at Auschwitz—Spielberg and his ingenious collaborators visually "document" Raul Hilberg's unforgettable explanation of how the Nazis adapted centuries of anti-Semitism to the three stages of their Final Solution to the Jewish problem: "The missionaries of Christianity had said in effect: You have no right to live among us as Jews. The secular rulers that followed had proclaimed: You have no right to live among us. The German Nazis at last decreed: You have no right to live."[12]

For more than three hours the moving picture creatively reconstructs details of what only the survivors can remember. No films of the atrocities at Plaszow exist, and, as Janet Maslin reminds us, the only surviving photographic record is a set of stills produced by Raimund Titsch, an Austrian Catholic factory supervisor who ran a uniform plant inside the Plaszow Forced Labor Camp.[13] Thus, for countless viewers, Spielberg's staged recreation of the humiliation, torture, and murder of millions and millions of Jews becomes "proof" that the Holocaust occurred. Using actual locations in Poland to heighten the movie's claim to verisimilitude, the filmmaker parades thousands of extras before us to illustrate a mass exodus from the suburbs to the city, from the city to the ghetto, from the ghetto to the labor camp, from the labor camp to the extermination center.

In classical Hollywood style, the story of the millions is demonstrated by the fortunes of the few. We see how, in the early years, individuals plead hopelessly for help from the *Judenrat*—a council of twenty-four elected Jews given modest authority by the Nazis—who supervised and administered the conqueror's law. We watch in disbelief the displacement on March 20, 1941, of a rich Jewish family from its comfortable home and follow them as they join other refugees in the street on a forced march to a sixteen-square-block Krakow ghetto. The sound of Polish onlookers yelling "Goodbye Jews" is chillingly presented. Equally memorable are the images dramatizing the atrocities committed in the ghetto, the forced labor camp, and finally Auschwitz.

The narrative dictates the action, the pace, and the imagery. This is a story of a culture that disappeared in six horrifying years, and how the efforts of one man made a difference to the few survivors. Our emotions are powerfully evoked from the beginning as the opening shots, in color, focus on a Jewish family welcoming the Sabbath and then proceed to quick dissolves eliminating first the parents, then the one remaining child, to the single flickering candle and finally to a wisp of smoke that imaginatively transports us back to the black-and-white era of 1939, with the smoke rising from a locomotive carrying Jews to the Krakow railway station. We see a single clerk set up his typewriter, ink pad, pens, and table to register the dozens of Jews forced out of their neighboring communities and into the urban trap created by the Nazi warlords. In rapid order, a corps of clerks is registering the confused and bewildered Jews at the rate of ten thousand per week. In true Hollywood tradition, Spielberg synthesizes the process by which Hitler's minions meticulously constructed their death lists. Later in the film, Schindler and Itzhak Stern (magnificently portrayed by Ben Kingsley), his Jewish accountant, will repeat the process by compiling another list, but this time one of "essential workers," a list of life; theirs consisted of 1,100 names, constructed hurriedly over a few days in a poorly lit private room.

Relying on the classic Hollywood technique of interpreting history through the actions of centrally motivated characters, Spielberg contrasts the fate of Poland's 3.3 million Jews with the fortunes of Schindler. The effect is fascinating. The camera introduces us to Schindler, the avaricious Nazi opportunist, by showing us not who he is but what he is: a man preoccupied with a decadent lifestyle. All we are allowed to see initially are his preparations for dining out. Still keeping his actual identity hidden from us, the film shifts to a raucous nightclub scene, where the playboy/opportunist systematically curries favor with the top Nazi brass. Slowly, Spielberg acquaints us with the film's major protagonist. First we see him physically: suave, stylishly dressed, amazingly confident, and incredibly presumptuous. Not until several people wonder aloud about the identity of this ebullient host are we told, "That is Oskar Schindler!"

Only in hindsight can we appreciate the reason for the detailed way in which the camera records Schindler's hypnotic style—bribing head waiters, ordering the best food and wine, spending money freely, ignoring anti-Semitic jokes, and having his picture taken with his honored guests. Throughout the movie, Spielberg repeatedly shows the successful results of Schindler's charming behavior; and each new time we witness the outcome of his charismatic ways, the rewards he receives take on greater significance. What is at first only an episode showing how a master manipulator gets valuable war contracts and weasels his way into owning an impounded enamelware plant eventually becomes a major motif in the film, educating us to the fact that it was these unique talents that saved over a thousand Jews from annihilation. As for Spielberg's reason for teasing us in the opening scenes with the secret of who this flamboyant man is, clearly the director is foreshadowing the fact that the reason for Schindler's heroic metamorphosis will forever be an enigma.

Besides its scenes of nudity, terrifying violence, outstanding performances by the film's three major actors, and spectacular cinematography—all ingredients that appeal to mass audiences—the film contains a macabre sense of humor. Initially, one is uncertain how to react. Then one is grateful for the momentary relief in tension. Consider the first exchange between Schindler and Stern. The former is trying to convince the accountant to become his bookkeeper. The latter points out that most people have more urgent problems at this time. Schindler replies incredulously, "Like what?" He then explains his scheme to acquire the enamelware factory. Stern listens in bewilderment and then says, "Let me get this straight. The Jews put up the money, and I do the work. What do you do?" Another scene shows the black market operating in the church during a mass. We see Leopold Pfefferberg (effectively portrayed by Jonathan Sagalle) complaining to his sources that recent merchandise he has bought from them and sold to the Germans was defective. They laugh at him and say that it is not their problem. He answers that he will give their names to the Nazis, and they quickly realize, "Now it's their problem."

As the fate of the Jews becomes more perilous, this humor is given greater scope and visual power. Consider the scene when Stern is put on the wrong list and placed on a deportation train. Schindler goes to the station and demands that a clerk remove Stern's name from the list and free him. The clerk refuses, and the unruffled Schindler tries an authoritarian bluff. He demands to know the clerk's name. The stakes escalate when a young German officer also insists that nothing can be done. At that point, Schindler assures both adversaries that they will be in the front lines within a week. Cut to the three men walking down the station, yelling "Stern! Stern!

And once again in classical Hollywood style, we are given one of the screen's most unforgettable villains, Amon Goeth (memorably played by Ralph Fiennes), who epitomizes for the audience the horrors of the entire Nazi war machine. While the top brass routinely take bribes and individual soldiers only follow orders, Goeth is a psychopath who appears to murder indiscriminately. He is first seen killing an educated Jewish woman overseeing the construction of the Plaszow Forced Labor Camp, not because she is wrong in her opinion (he acknowledges that she is right) but because she criticizes Nazi incompetence. Later, we see him standing on the balcony of his home at the base of a hill overlooking the camp, watching the morning roll call and then casually, apparently randomly, shooting Jews for target practice. In the end, Spielberg shows an unrepentant Goeth executed by the Poles for crimes against humanity.

If one studies the general reception of *Schindler's List,* it is obvious not only that Spielberg's image has been transformed in the public's mind but also that the film's subject matter has affected our society. *New York Times* critic Janet Maslin echoed the sentiments of most of her peers when she declared, "Mr. Spielberg has made sure that neither he nor the Holocaust will ever be thought of the same way again."[14] Emilie Schindler, the eighty-six-year-old ex-wife of the film's hero, announced the official reaction of many Holocaust survivors from Buenos Aires, "That film is pure truth. It shows some ugly things, but when you realize it's the truth, it's more powerful. The truth was even worse than the film."[15]

Schindler's List also stimulated other interpretations. "Citing everything from the Hebron massacre, in which a Jewish extremist killed Muslim worshipers," explained reporter Bernard Weinraub, "to the assertion that the movie is 'propaganda with the purpose of asking sympathy' to the traditional Muslim abhorrence of nudity and sex in movies, various Islamic governments have given the film a cold, if not hostile, reception."[16] Art Spiegelman, the author of *Maus: A Survivor's Tale,* insists that the movie is not really about the Jews or the Holocaust: "It's a movie about Clinton. It's about the benign aspects of capitalism—capitalism with a human face.... Capitalism can give us a health care program, and it can give us a Schindler."[17] And to make matters even more curious, President Clinton—mired in the enormous dilemma of how to get the American public to support military action in Bosnia to stop two years of "ethnic cleansing"—urged everyone to view Spielberg's film.

Whatever interpretation one gives to *Schindler's List,* it is undeniable that the public has reacted strongly to Spielberg's supposed documentation of the Holocaust. Worldwide audiences applaud its seeming authenticity, they marvel at his visual virtuosity, they honor his storytelling genius, and they are inspired by his humanity. But these were all strengths that he displayed in 1982. For more than a decade, serious students of the cinema have known about Spielberg's artistry in creating worlds others cannot imagine and making them visually unforgettable. His emphasis has always been on the emotional rather than on the intellectual. He enjoys making the epic event personal. Why should anyone be upset with such a virtuous production?

Disciplining the Imagination

To understand why there has been a significant backlash to *Schindler's List*, we need to return again to the years between 1982 and 1993. If box-office clout and cinematic talent were not the problems in delaying the screen adaptation, what were the difficulties? Clues to what worried Spielberg surface in his recent statements to the press. For example, after receiving the Directors Guild Award on March 15, 1994, he commented that, "When I first read this book, I said, 'there are a lot of directors in this world who are much better than me to make this picture.' I did not *see* it when I committed to direct it in 1982. I didn't see it because I wasn't ready to see it...I didn't want to see it." On another occasion, he said, "I've never given up the ghost of my childhood....I've been hanging on to that. I really feel I stopped developing emotionally when I was 19."[18] To one reporter, the genre director talked about how making the film made him feel "liberated for the first time in my career."[19] To another reporter, Spielberg explained that the film's length and black-and-white monochrome photography are the result of his commitment to remaining "true to the spirit of documentaries and stills from the period."[20] Other interviews reinforce his litany of self-doubts about his need to grow up, to reject his strictly Hollywood orientation, and to deal, on the screen, more truthfully with life. They also dwell on his "born-again Jewishness," how "I was so ashamed of being a Jew and now I'm filled with pride."[21] In talking about his Arizona childhood, he frequently admits that "I was always attempting to assimilate into popular culture."[22]

In reporting these quotations, my intention is not to suggest that they necessarily represent Spielberg's true feelings. Who knows what agendas he had in mind to promote his picture, to change his image, or to curry favor with different award-granting organizations? Spielberg's comments, therefore, can be seen as a shrewd businessman's public relations strategy. He knew that to make his Holocaust film attractive to hesitant mass audiences it had to be a hit at the box office, and that required a special type of marketing approach guaranteed to produce major awards and public approval. One can see such an approach in the filmmaker's concluding remarks in his interview with the German news magazine *Der Spiegel*, where he stated, "If the German reaction to my film should be shame, then it is important to me that the viewers understand, that shame also motivated me to this film. Namely, the shame of having been ashamed to be a Jew."[23]

More to the point, Spielberg's comments suggest that in 1982 the Hollywood oriented director realized the immense problem of making a Holocaust film, as well as his professional and intellectual limitations. He also may have suspected that the time needed to do justice to the subject matter might best be handled on television rather than in the movie theater. He would not have been alone in that opinion. After all, the Holocaust had become an effective moral catharsis for American viewers after the Vietnam War. Between 1978 and 1989, no less than six major network miniseries dramatized the monstrous events: *Holocaust* (1978), *Playing for Time* (1980), *The Wall* (1982), *Wallenberg: A Hero's Story* (1985), *Escape from Sobibor* (1987), and *War and Remembrance* (1988-89). The reception of those uneven but often gripping projects would make almost anyone realize that professional artistry is no substitute for comprehending the subject matter. Nevertheless, Spielberg understood that film's rare ability to delude viewers into believing that they are experiencing reality carried with it tremendous responsibilities.

To be fair, problems related to treatment and reception were not unique to Spielberg. They are part of the cultural wars. They are part of the tools that scholars use to discipline our imaginations. For example, the issue of whether the Holocaust is an appropriate subject for the arts started when Auschwitz was liberated. Those who have studied the work of such Holocaust scholars as Primo

Levi, Elie Wiesel, Theodor W. Adorno, and George Steiner know far better than I their arguments that silence is preferable to almost any fictional reconstruction. For such people, it is incomprehensible that there is an art in reconstructing atrocities, beauty in authenticating horrors, and a profit in dramatizing human misery. These are not, of course, idle or irrelevant arguments. Those who raise them are drawing an aesthetic line not just for Spielberg but also for anyone who makes a film about the Holocaust, and most especially for American movies and television features where entertainment is the primary goal.

That having been said, it is also important to appreciate that artists seek to create a world of illusions to provide experiences that enable us to better understand ourselves and the human situation. They force us to examine the unexamined, to imagine the unimaginable. Even mawkish and melodramatic works like the groundbreaking *Holocaust* force the public to rethink its attitudes toward the role of the media, the meaning of the event, and the responsibility of individuals in our society.

Imagine the questions that Spielberg probably considered. His entire career had been devoted to making sentimental movies with optimistic endings, always reassuring his audiences that they can triumph over their fears if they have the courage and the will to do so. Is that an appropriate approach for interpreting the death of six million Jews? His box-office appeal rested, in large part, on his ability to manipulate people's emotions through the recycling and revitalization of film clichés and stereotypes. Does one bear witness to the past by using trite and trivial imagery? If the film industry demands stars more than statistics, fun more than fact, is film a suitable vehicle for examining the essence of evil? Does it make sense to mix entertainment and education? And what about ratings and box-office grosses? As the history of show business demonstrates conclusively, those who work regularly are those who have the attention of the public. Does one's drive for popularity require misrepresentation? If so, is the danger of factual distortion more disturbing in film because the work is accessible and acceptable to more people? And are factual distortions about the Holocaust insignificant? If the argument is that film will become the visual witness of the past for future generations, what can we do to insure that audiences observe the difference between perception and reality? How can we ensure that they understand that the representation is not the event itself? And what if exposure to a representation misleads the spectator into believing that, having experienced the event itself, there is no need to examine it any further?

I suggest that Spielberg's approach to these types of questions in *Schindler's List* is related to his shame about being Jewish, his orientation to filmmaking, and his exposure to films that he had seen about the Holocaust. I further contend that the film's reception is also related to legacies associated with class, age, race, education, and status. Moreover, the cultural and historical context in which film is received assures us that one cannot control the public's reaction or the use it will find for the movie. If it is true, as Walter Lippmann argued decades ago, that first we define and then we see, it is important to understand that it is only in the last fifteen years that public education has begun to elevate the story of the destruction of the European Jews from the status of a footnote in twentieth-century history to a serious place in the curriculum. No one should be surprised, therefore, that different groups not only see *Schindler's List* differently but also battle each other over its relevance to the past, the present, and the future.

For Spielberg's generation and those who came earlier, television and the movies were their primary classrooms on racism and the Holocaust. This is not the place to review the complex and controversial combination of world events, domestic crises, the nature of acculturation, and the difficulties in attaining basic human rights that affected the policies and practices of the Jewish film moguls who ruled Hollywood. Suffice it to say that American films for the first half of this century struggled to make Jews acceptable to the Gentile world and therefore changed from decade to decade to keep pace with the minority's desire for economic, social, and political freedoms. During Spielberg's personal and professional formative years, the screen image of Jews underwent radical changes. Freedom from studio domination and from a conservative Motion Picture Production Code allowed filmmakers to reexamine their conservative attitudes toward ethnicity and to stress diversity rather than conformity. The new emphasis on cultural pluralism produced a range of Jewish characterizations with multifaceted personalities. Not all of the images were positive, and many people began to talk openly about screen anti-Semitism and vulgarity. In considering how he was going to present the image of Jews, Spielberg no doubt was influenced by the debates over whether negative ethnic characterizations contribute to or undermine racial bigotry.[24]

Another legacy of American film and television history that influenced Spielberg's sense of Jewishness was the Holocaust productions themselves. Most informed viewers realize that the majority of popular productions stress how catastrophic World War II was for people other than the Jews, that victimization was not limited to one race, and that performances are prized more highly than are honest scripts. Scholars would find it difficult to locate a single American film or television miniseries on this monstrous subject that was not accused by at least one noted commentator of being too melodramatic, simplistic, and trivial. But we need to put such glib positions in perspective. European films also have shortcomings, which rarely get mentioned. Raul Hilberg, for example, is one of the few intellectuals who has dared to criticize *Night and Fog* "as an erroneous and dangerous presentation of the facts....[Because] in it the gas chambers appeared to be destined for Belgian, French or Dutch prisoners, without...the Jews...being mentioned once."[25]

This essay is not the place to debate the biases of critics. Let me just say in vastly oversimplified terms that conventional wisdom castigates America's film approach to the Jewish catastrophe on four specific grounds: (1) we place too much emphasis on emotional rather than informational issues; (2) we dishonor history by emphasizing the sensational rather than the factual; (3) we underestimate the intelligence of our audiences by oversimplifying complex material; and, worst of all, (4) we sin against the victims of the Holocaust by universalizing the Jewish experience.[26] Only the European filmmakers seem acceptable to a certain class of scholars, mainly because their theatrical works and documentaries are perceived to take great intellectual risks, stress original interpretations, explore complex moral positions, and deal sensitively with the pain associated with the memories of the past.

Sensitive to these issues and haunted by *Schindler's List*, Spielberg began a new cinematic journey after 1982. As Kathleen Kennedy, the former production head of Spielberg's company, stated in

1994, "I have known him for fifteen years...and he has spent twelve years talking about it."[27] During that period, he tried to break out of his "Peter Pan" mode by making serious films like *The Color Purple* (1985) and *Empire of the Sun* (1987), although with very mixed results. Particularly significant were his comments in 1983, when he told the *New York Times* that he was troubled about "doing a movie [*The Color Purple*] about Black people for the first time in my career" and that he feared he'd be "accused of not having the sensibility to do character studies."[28] His forays into World War II had started earlier with *1941* (1979) and *Raiders of the Lost Ark* (1981), and they continued not only with the remainder of the Indiana Jones trilogy (1984, 1989) but also with *Empire of the Sun*. One need only study his treatment of the Germans and the Japanese to see how Spielberg's maturity was tied to his choice of scriptwriter and cinematographer. For that matter, you could gauge how far his sensitivity to Jewish pride had come from his productions of *An American Tail* (1986) and *An American Tail: Fievel Goes West* (1991), two animated cartoons starring Jewish immigrant mice. His intellectual shortcomings in these efforts contrast enormously with the substantive progress he demonstrates in *Schindler's List*.

The question of what approach to take to Keneally's novel, however, was paramount. To help decide, Spielberg (and later his collaborators) studied movies about the Holocaust. Surely he examined films like *The Shop on Main Street* (1965), *Wallenberg: A Hero's Story* (1985), and *Shoah* (1986), all of which include Christians who risked their lives for the benefit of Jewish victims. Clearly he benefitted from the 1955 documentary *Night and Fog*, where Alain Resnais contrasted the past, using black-and-white photography, with the present, using color film, and made a point of showing how the Nazis made use of everything that the Jews owned or wore or had. Obviously, Spielberg must have studied *The Sorrow and the Pity* (1970) and *Shoah* to grasp the importance of displaying hatred and anti-Semitism rather than merely describing it. And certainly he was aware that impolitic casting (Vanessa Redgrave in *Playing for Time*) and inappropriate analogies (comparing the Vietnam war to the Holocaust in *The Memory of Justice*) had created storms of controversy in the past.[29] He may even have discussed the problems of interpreting social issues with William Styron, the author of *The Confessions of Nat Turner* and *Sophie's Choice*.

And how could Spielberg have ignored the fact that the Europeans were the only ones ever to win Oscars for films about the Holocaust? Up to 1990, for example, only four American movies treating the horror had ever been nominated: *The Diary of Anne Frank* (1959), *Judgment at Nuremberg* (1961), *Ship of Fools* (1965), and *Cabaret* (1972). None of them won. In contrast, ever since the foreign film category was introduced in the late 1950s, seven European features about the Holocaust had been entered—*The Shop on Main Street* (1965), *The Garden of the Finzi-Continis* (1971), *The Tin Drum* (1979), *The Boat is Full* (1981), *The Assault* (1986), *Au Revoir les Enfants* (1987), and *The Nasty Girl* (1990)—and only three times (1981, 1987, and 1990) did one of them fail to receive an Oscar. The Academy of Motion Picture Arts and Sciences has even given an Oscar to the French documentary *Hotel Terminus: Klaus Barbie* (1988). For a man who by 1983 had been nominated three times for best director yet had failed to receive the honor, the European successes must have meant something to Spielberg. What was just as evident was that the American films did well at the box office, while their award-winning counterparts were rarely seen outside intellectual circles.

My contention is that this ingenious filmmaker designed a self-study program to discover what distinguished filmmakers like Alain Resnais (*Night and Fog*), Marcel Ophuls (*The Sorrow and the Pity, The Memory of Justice,* and *Hotel Terminus: Klaus Barbie*), Claude Lanzmann (*Shoah*), George Stevens (*The Diary of Anne Frank*), Stanley Kramer (*Judgment at Nuremberg*), Sidney Lumet (*The Pawnbroker*), and Alan Pakula (*Sophie's Choice*) had accomplished.[30] His purpose presumably was to find a way to merge the documentary approach of Europe with the box-office appeal of Hollywood.

In essence, then, Spielberg the businessman and Spielberg the artist knew that getting his movie across to the public and having that film's message have a significant impact on society depended on approaching the project in a specific way. The film had to account for the attitudes of Holocaust survivors toward the subject matter. The screenplay must incorporate Hollywood's tradition of making an epic story personal. Spielberg would have to distance himself from his commercial interests and convince the public that the film was made out of commitment beyond personal gain. Moreover, the sheer number of Holocaust films on television and on the big screen required his approaching the by-now "familiar" material with a "new look." The manner in which he depicted the events would also provide the opportunity to improve his stature in film history. Finally, Spielberg had to find the right time to release the movie—not just the season of the year but also the moment when society could appreciate its relevance to the present.

His conclusions can be seen in *Schindler's List*. For our purposes, let me indicate five specific areas: (1) the re-creation of sensitive historical incidents, (2) the black-and-white cinematography, (3) the issue of how one survived the Holocaust, (4) the characterizations of Schindler and Goeth, and (5) the ending of the film.

Nowhere is there a greater danger of misunderstanding or misusing *Schindler's List* than in the area of re-created historical incidents. With all due respect to the film's imaginative depictions of the destruction of the ghetto, the selection scenes in the labor camp, and the shower incident at Auschwitz, they are dramatizations, even though a large portion of the public assumes that what they see are the actual events. It is not, as some critics have suggested, just a question of fidelity to detail, or even of the filmmaker's humility in the face of such adversity. Even as far back as Plato's *Republic*, responsible critics realized that art was imitation and several steps removed from reality. If we understand the power of the medium to shape cultural and historical values, then we must curb our enthusiasm for an extraordinary piece of filmmaking and discipline our imaginations to the difference between fact and fiction. While I might put it less harshly than commentators like Frank Rich, Leon Wieseltier, or Philip Gourevitch, *Schindler's List* is not an antidote to the 1993 Roper Organization poll, which indicated that nearly 25 percent of all Americans doubt that the Nazis murdered six million Jews,[31] nor can brilliantly re-created scenes of misery and cruelty be used to disprove Holocaust revisionism. But because such scenes have the ability to affect people's values and attitudes, we assume that the most such attempts at authenticity can do is connect us to the event and stimulate our intellectual curiosity about the reality of the past and the possibilities for the future. In such instances, it is not, as Wieseltier suggests, Hollywood's honor that is at stake but education's. It is we, not filmmakers, who are responsible for teaching visual literacy to the public, so that they can recognize the distinctions between perception and reality.

Turning to the issue of the black-and-white cinematography, one clearly sees the lessons that Spielberg learned from European film culture. The quasi-documentary style, making masterly use of German Expressionist lighting, offers striking allusions to the perils of living in Nazi-occupied Poland from 1939 to 1945. Working with his great Polish cinematographer, the director uses his hand-held cameras to show not tell us how human beings could be degraded, humiliated, and dehumanized. The cinematic world that we are given offers unforgettable images of Nazi soldiers who enjoy killing helpless people, horrifying reminders of the lengths to which the Germans went to get gold from their victims, and the painful choices that the hunted had to make in their struggle to survive. Rarely in film history have we witnessed details of a road being built with the gravestones from a Jewish cemetery, or of children innocently singing as they are driven off to their deaths.

But black-and-white cinematography and the avoidance of Hollywood crane and dolly shots do not translate into documentary footage. No pictures, "documentary" or otherwise, can capture the misery, fear, illness, and suffering that occurred; and it is foolish to assert, as some viewers do, that *Schindler's List* can replace the true witnesses of the Holocaust. When Spielberg defends himself by arguing that he did not make a movie about the Holocaust but only "one story from the Holocaust," he misses the point.[32]

One major lesson that Spielberg did not learn from artists like Resnais, Ophuls, and Lanzmann is humility in the presence of complexity. The fast-paced shooting and the audacious voyeurism of the Hollywood production place far more emphasis on the emotions than on the intellect, on the art rather than on the event. That is not to say, however, that one style is better than the other. Stirring emotions is one powerful way to get millions of uninvolved and uninterested audiences into examining a complex issue. Spielberg's way is not the Europeans' way, and the two should not be confused.

Much thornier than these aesthetic concerns are the intellectual issues raised by *Schindler's List*. Consider the question of how the film presents the question of survival. Spielberg demonstrates the conventional wisdom that survival depended on chance, that there was nothing anyone could do to outlast the Nazis' barbarism. One sees scenes of hiding places being discovered, of accidental encounters with murdering soldiers on snow-covered streets, of random shootings among prisoners when one of their peers escapes from a work detail. But the film also shows that there were things people could do to improve their own and others' chances. The rabbi who at first survives because Goeth's gun refuses to work is immediately transferred to Schindler's factory by Stern. The daughter who dresses up to gain entrance to Schindler's office does save her parents from death. The quick-thinking child who identifies the dead man as the thief who stole the chicken is rewarded by Schindler, who gets him transferred to the factory. And most important, Goeth does not kill prisoners randomly from his balcony. He shoots only those who are resting. Once the other prisoners begin running, the shooting stops. Even the shooting of the boy whom he twice "pardoned" is the result of an individual not performing his job according to Goeth's twisted standards.

Again, let me make it plain that I am not endorsing Spielberg's interpretation of why people survived the Holocaust. How could I? What do any of us know about the totality of that monstrous experience? J. Hoberman is quite right in arguing, "In the Holocaust, Jews were not saved. Were not snatched from the jaws of Auschwitz. The showers didn't sprout water."[33] That is true. But it is also true that some people did survive. With hundreds of movies being made about the absence of choices, what is wrong with skillfully created films examining another perspective? What I am arguing is that the director, the screenwriter, and the cinematographer offer convincing arguments that many of the 1,100 *Schindlerjuden* survived because of individual initiative. Considering that many Holocaust historians take the opposite point of view about how one survived the Holocaust, it is a bold and courageous interpretation to make in a Hollywood movie.

But that daring stance is overshadowed by the brilliance of the film's approach to Oskar Schindler and Amon Goeth. In many ways the film's treatment of these two men appears to be modeled on Plato's discussion of the differences between the virtuous man and the tyrant; and the comparison seems designed to demonstrate Plato's concept that when the state goes bad, salvation can be found in those individuals who put morality above self-interest.[34] Or, as Plato would argue, virtue is its own reward whatever the consequences. We are also told in the *Republic* that the difference between the good man and the tyrant is razor thin. Thus, what distinguishes the virtuous man from the tyrant is often very difficult to discern — as the comparison of Schindler and Goeth demonstrates.

How one becomes virtuous is developed in the film through the use of editing and irony. Consider first a handful of parallels between Schindler and Goeth. Neither one acts virtuously when we first meet them. Schindler goes to the *Judenrat* to get Stern's help in running his business; Goeth arrives at the construction site of the forced labor camp to establish his authority. Both Schindler and Goeth use Jewish slave labor to operate their "businesses." Just as Schindler interviews ten Jewish women for a secretary's job, focusing on their physical beauty rather than on their professional skills, so Goeth "interviews" a line of Jewish prisoners for a maid's position, selecting the one least qualified for domestic work. Following the massacre in the ghetto, Schindler reflects on the tragedy by looking down from his upstairs office on the empty factory floor below, while Goeth looks down from his balcony on the morning roll call. When Schindler first meets Goeth, their initial conversations are about clothes, money, and business pressures. In short, both are consumed with material pleasures, and both eventually are perceived to be "mad" by those closest to them.

Their differences are not as obvious as one might suspect. In fact, there is a crucial scene where Schindler defends Goeth to Stern, arguing that you have to understand the commandant's position: "He has a lot to worry about." It's the war that's making Goeth behave as he does. (Earlier, the industrialist had explained to his wife that the war is the reason for his success.) Schindler argues that Goeth is really not such a bad fellow and that the two of them have a lot in common: womanizing, drinking, a love of the "good life." It is at that point that Stern reminds Schindler and us that the chief difference between the two men is that Goeth is a killer. Spielberg then intercuts Goeth's random shooting of twenty-five laborers in a returning work group. The point is again brought home in a drunken balcony scene, where Schindler lectures Goeth about the importance of temperance, power, and justice. He tells him the parable about the emperor who had the ability to execute but preferred to pardon. Goeth tries to apply this principle but is unable to do so. Schindler can. And near the end of the film, after we have been shown countless examples of Schindler's ability to bribe officials successfully, we see Goeth trying to imitate his friend to get him out of jail and failing miserably. Lest anyone forget the comparison, Spielberg lets Schindler bribe the commandant of Auschwitz to free the three hundred imprisoned Jewish women. Of particular importance is the fact that the film omits the novel's references to how much Schindler hated the Nazis. That omission intensifies the parallels between the industrialist and the commandant.

The difference between the virtuous man and the tyrant becomes clear when one realizes the loyalty that Schindler feels for "his family" (the *Schindlerjuden*) and that Goeth feels for money. In a telling scene, the two men bargain for the fate of 1,100 "essential workers" while visually a window post divides the pair. Schindler gives away all that he owns in order to save his workers; Goeth takes all he can get but complains that he just does not understand the scam Schindler is playing on him. And lest anyone miss the message, there is the ring-giving scene outside the factory, where Stern explains that the caption on the ring is taken from the *Talmud*: "Whoever saves one life saves the world entire." The final touch is to show that both men died with all their material goods taken from them. Nothing mattered in the end except virtue.

Throughout the film, Spielberg and his technical crew reinforce this Platonic idea by the use of chiaroscuro lighting, reminding us of the *Republic's* explanation that light allows one to see knowledge and wisdom but that these forces can be eclipsed by darkness, filth, and duplicity. Thus, Schindler's triumph lies not only in seeing the error of his ways but also in doing something about it.

Crediting Spielberg with such a quantum leap in intellectual content is a double-edged sword. On the one hand, it acknowledges the substantive merits of the luminous script and rejects the idea that either Spielberg or Hollywood is limited to merely manipulative, emotional exercises. On the other hand, it illustrates once again how the uniqueness of the Holocaust is universalized. Clearly, one can see why the filmmaker is so intent on showing his movie to children, and why state governors are eager to use it as a means of combatting racial intolerance. At the same time, it obscures the fact that the Holocaust is a specific event in history, not a generalized horror.

My last concern is with the final scenes of the film. Schindler gathers his factory workers, persuades the Nazi soldiers to disperse, explains why as a "war criminal" he has to flee, and then breaks down over the realization that he could have saved more Jews if he had sold his Nazi pin (worn prominently throughout the film) and expensive car. Most reviewers comment negatively about the melodramatic nature of the scene and its overly sentimental presentation. Others attack it for its downright dishonesty, pointing out that Schindler was too scared about his fate to say anything, that the car was lined with money for a safe getaway, and that he fled not only with his wife but also with his mistress. Equally important, Steven Zaillian admitted that including the ring-giving ceremony—an incident not described in Keneally's novel—was done precisely to remind the audience "that although Schindler saved some 1,200 people, 6 million more died during the Holocaust."[35] Here one must decide how much dramatic license we are willing to give the artist, whether one wants the work to be faithful to the world of illusions or to the world of reality, and whether factual truth is an aesthetic requirement for art.

A similar point can be made about the final scene, where the players and their true-life counterparts file past Schindler's grave on Mount Zion. Many people believe that this is a striking reminder of what the Holocaust was about, as a printed screen statement tells us that only four thousand of the 3.3 million Polish Jews survived but that there are six thousand survivors and descendants of the *Schindlerjuden*. I believe that statement is necessary at the end of the film because emotionally audiences are mourning Schindler, not the Jewish victims. At the same time, I am certain that there are those viewers who see the statistics as yet another reminder about Schindler, not the Jews. Thus, no matter whether one is uplifted by Schindler's heroism or saddened by his death, once again a film about the Holocaust has used the Holocaust as a backdrop to a powerful historical drama.

Schindler's List illustrates many important ideas not only about Spielberg but also about the problems associated with depicting the Holocaust in the mass media. First, its images remind us of previous movies about the Jewish catastrophe. A careful study of this film reveals the artist's debt to other works, as well as his many new contributions to the subject matter. Second, the questions raised about the movie's authenticity and historical relevance serve as meaningful reminders about the cultural debate surrounding aesthetic works about the Holocaust. The discussion reminds us anew, as Professor Garth Jowett discovered decades ago, that there is a difference between history *on* film and history *in* film. The former refers to historical dramas like *Schindler's List* that try to re-create the past. As historical records of the subject matter, they fail to measure up to the criteria used in judging historical evidence. History in film, however, refers to the medium's relation to society: how it reflects and affects people in a particular place, time, and period in history.[36] Here, Spielberg's work provides invaluable documentation on the attitudes and values of society in 1994. Third, an analysis of why the movie is so popular worldwide reveals that many of the cinematic techniques used in *Schindler's List* can be traced back to the director's skill in his earlier works. It is a mistake to assume that this movie is not based on decades of training and expertise. Fourth, the accolades bestowed on Spielberg and his film, while richly deserved, also tell us about the critics and *their* maturity in finally recognizing a very talented filmmaker. Fifth, the critical reception of the film reinforces the notion that there is no way that artists can control how an audience interprets and uses their motion pictures.

Once we understand that movies do not appear in a vacuum and that their ability to entertain and to educate is tied to industry practices and to audience expectations, we recognize that movies can be, and often are, misunderstood and misused by the public. *Schindler's List* demonstrates that art is not about factual truth but about experience and that experiences are provided by artists who use the legacies of the past to interpret the present. Recognizing that each experience is different, we should realize that one film need not compete with or replace other works on the Holocaust. In this case, *Schindler's List* takes its place as one of the great achievements in the history of motion pictures, for it teaches us that momentous experiences must always be critically examined as both history and art.

Notes

[1] This work has benefited from the comments of the following colleagues at the University of Vermont: Virginia Clark and Littleton Long, English department; Jan Feldman and Alan Wertheimer, Political Science department; Dennis Mahoney, German and Russian department; and Denise Youngblood, History department. In addition, I owe a debt of gratitude to Martha Day for her generous help in securing research materials.

[2] For a more complete discussion of these assumptions, see Frank Manchel, *Film Study: An Analytical Bibliography*, 4 vols. Rutherford, N.J.: Fairleigh Dickinson University Press, 1990.

[3] William D. Romanowski, "Oliver Stone's JFK: Commercial Filmmaking, Cultural History, and Conflict," *Journal of Popular Film and Television* 21, no. 2 (Summer 1993): 63. [*The Journal of Modem History* 67 (March 1995): 83-IOOl © 1995 by The University of Chicago. 0022-2801/95/6701-000401.00 All rights reserved.]

[4] James Ulmer , "In Transit: Schindler Dodges Unkindest of Cuts," *Hollywood Reporter* (April 8-10, 1994): 18.

[5] My focus on the director as an auteur, the primary author of the movie, is not meant to slight the collaborative process of filmmaking. Nothing could be more obvious than the fact that this film demonstrates Spielberg's dependence on the combined efforts of people like screenwriter Steven Zaillian, cinematographer Janusz Kaminski, and editor Michael Kahn.

[6] In 1983, Thames's Television produced a fine documentary on Schindler's life. Jon Blair was the writer, producer, and director. *Variety* reports that producer Arthur Brauner, himself a Holocaust survivor, struggled ten years to get backing for *An Angel in Hell* (a film about Schindler) but was never able to raise the necessary funding (see Michael Williams, "Spielberg Adds DGA to 'List': Helmer Wins Friends on Euro Tour," *Variety* (March 7, 1994): 36.

[7] Richard Schickel, "Heart of Darkness: Ghosts in Their Millions Haunt Steven Spielberg's Powerful *Schindler's List*," *Time* (December 13, 1993): 75.

[8] In fact, at one point Spielberg thought of turning *Schindler's List* over to Scorsese.

[9] Pauline Kael, "Sugarlands and Badlands," in her *Reeling* (Boston, 1976): 300.

[10] Pauline Kael, "Whipped," in her *Taking It All In* (New York, 1984): 207-14.

[11] As of April 1994, *Jurassic Park* is in first place; *E. T.: The Extra-Terrestrial*, second; *Indiana Jones and the Last Crusade*, fifth; and *Jaws*, eighth.

12. Raul Hilberg, *The Destruction of the European Jews* (Chicago, 1967): 3-4.
13. Janet Maslin, "Imagining the Holocaust to Remember It," *New York Times* (December 15, 1993): C19.
14. Ibid.
15. "Schindler's Wife 'Lists' Stake," *Daily Variety* (February 10,1994): 23. I write "official" because John Gross reported that Emilie Schindler gave a bitter interview about her ex-husband just before the film was released (see John Gross, "Hollywood and the Holocaust." *New York Review of Books* (February 3, 1994): 15). In "Schindler's Wife 'Lists' Stakes," we are told that she is currently negotiating for a percentage of the picture.
16. Bernard Weinraub, "Islamic Nations Move to Keep Out *Schindler's List*," *New York Times* (April 7, 1994): CI5.
17. Reported in *"Schindler's List:* Myth, Movie, and Memory," *Village Voice* (March 29, 1994): 30.
18. *The Economist* in Spielberg List [online], December 25, 1993; available from NEXIS Library, NEWS File: CURNWS.
19. Schickel (n. 5 above): 76.
20. Andrew Nagorski, "Spielberg's Risk: The Director Takes a Chance with a Holocaust Drama Shot in Black and White," *Newsweek* (May 24, 1993): 60.
21. John N. Richardson, "Steven's Choice," *Premiere* 7, no. 5 (January 1994): 72.
22. *Atlanta Journal and Constitution* in Spielberg's Crusade [online], December 12, 1993, sec. NI; available from NEXIS Library, NEWS File: CURNWS.
23. "Die Ganze Wahrheit Schwarz auf Weiss" (The whole truth in black and white), *Der Spiegel* (February 21, 1994): 186. Translated for me by Dennis Mahoney.
24. For a discussion on books, films, and articles dealing with the history of Jews in film, see Manchel, *Film Study* (n. 1 above), 1:818-51.
25. Sylvaine Pasquier, "Raul Hilberg: Un Acte Majeur" (Raul Hilberg: A major act), *L'Express* (February 24, 1994): 92. Translated for me by Dennis Mahoney and Eileen Riley.
26. For useful material on these issues, see Ilan Avisar, *Screening the Holocaust: Cinema's Image of the Unimaginable* (Bloomington, Ind., 1988); and Annette Insdorf, *Indelible Shadows: Film and the Holocaust*, 2d ed. (New York, 1989).
27. Jacques Buob, "L'honneur de Herr Schindler" (The honor of Mister Schindler), *L'Express* (February 24, 1994): 90. Translated for me by Stephanie Giry.
28. Cited in Pauline Kael, *Hooked* (New York, 1989): 81.

[29] See Frank Manchel, "A War over Justice: An Interview with Marcel Ophuls," *Literature/Film Quarterly* 6, no. I (Winter 1978): 26-47.
[30] Other possible filmmakers who may have influenced *Schindler's List*, mentioned by reviewers, include Andrzej Munk, Aleksander Ford, Andrzej Wajda, D. W. Griffith, Orson Welles, and David Lean.
[31] Frank Rich, "Extras in the Shadow," *New York Times* [online], January 2, 1994, sec. 4, 9; available from NEXIS Library, NEWS File: CURNWS. Leon Wiesel, "Washington Diarist: Close Encounters of the Nazi Kind," *New Republic* (January 24, 1994): 42. Philip Gourevitch, "A Dissent on *Schindler's List*," *Commentary* (February 1994): 49-52.
[32] Martin A. Grove, "Hollywood Report: *Schindler* Global Hit; *Maverick* Sneaks Well," *Hollywood Reporter* (April 6, 1994): 8.
[33] J. Hoberman, "Parting Glances," *Village Voice* (January 11, 1994): 49.
[34] I can't help noting in Spielberg's marketing strategy for *Schindler's List* the extent to which he portrays himself as the virtuous man, stating that profits from the film will be turned over to Holocaust charities and that his intention is to benefit those who do not know, not those who do. Remember, Plato argued that disassociating oneself from the benefits of one's art, understanding its nature, and understanding one's audience were signs of virtue.
[35] "Backstage at the Oscars," *Variety* (March 22, 1994): 35.
[36] For more on this important subject, see Frank Manchel, *Film Study: An Analytical Bibliography*, Vol. 1. Rutherford, N.J.: Fairleigh Dickinson University Press, 1990. 252-279.

BOOK REVIEW

Projecting the Holocaust into the Present: The Changing Focus of Contemporary Holocaust Cinema

Lawrence Baron. Lanham: Rowman and Littlefield, 2005. 307 pp. $29.95 paper. $85.90 cloth.

Introducing the Holocaust through fiction films to new generations presents a formidable challenge. Not only does a scholar have to grasp the horrors that occurred during the Nazi era, but also an author needs considerable judgment in how best to represent this unprecedented human tragedy, while not trivializing the memory of the event itself.

The noted cultural and intellectual historian Dr. Lawrence Baron, the director of the Lipinsky Institute for Judaic Studies at San Diego, confidently accepts this formidable challenge. He understands completely how fiction films have emerged as the major guardians of mainstream Holocaust memory. Twelve years of teaching cinema courses on twentieth-century Jewish history, plus his extensive academic film research, provides the history professor with the self-assurance to take on the task. He views "the Third Reich as a 'racial state' [...that victimized] any group [...that] supposedly posed a biological, cultural, political, or social threat to the Aryan race."

To illustrate how between 1933 and 1945 the Nazis used "discrimination, incarceration, liquidation or sterilization," Baron employs a film genre approach that highlights commercial, feature-length movies from 1945 to the present that have proved popular both with audiences and critics. His criteria for choosing a specific theme or genre rests heavily on several variables: an ability to update past studies of Holocaust films (concentrating mainly on 1990s productions), the chance to contextualize a specific country's history through mainstream movies (e.g., Poland then and now), and the opportunity to examine the reception of the films as well as their directors' intentions (misunderstood or misguided). Also important is the author's determination to shed insights on the postwar world of the Holocaust in areas like displacement, immigration, and punishment meted out to war criminals.

Anyone looking for an awareness of the controversies in Holocaust film study should benefit from Baron's disagreements with his predecessors and peers. His ideas on the scope of the Holocaust are broader; his revisionist analyses of movies like George Stevens's 1958 *The Diary of Anne Frank* and the 1978 miniseries *Holocaust* go against the grain of current taste; his views on Hollywood films are much more sympathetic than those of scholars like Annette Insdorf and Ilan Avisar; and he may possess the greatest acceptance of Holocaust film comedies on record.

Eight data-packed chapters offer selected examples of what took place during the Holocaust to Jews, homosexuals, lesbians, gypsies, communists, the mentally ill, and other perceived enemies of the Nazi regime. For example, the section representing the major villains, their atrocities, as well as the heroic battles against such monstrous actions, focuses on biographical films: *The Empty Mirror, Korczak, Triumph of the Spirit,* and *Europa, Europa.* Baron routinely begins with an overview of the specific genre, followed by a look at the above-mentioned films, offering plot summaries, character descriptions, production credits, and quotes from critics. He concludes with his blunt judgments on the films themselves. Other chapters concentrate on censured sexual relationships, Holocaust films for children, remembrances of the historic events, humor in Holocaust films, and production trends in the present century.

But no work of this magnitude presented in such admittedly cramped space can escape criticism or avoid lapses. For what Baron has set out to do, he does admirably.

I am, however, less comfortable with his strategy. Genre study, by its nature, excludes quality in favor of quantity. That is the case in this book. It would seem better to approach the memory of the Holocaust without distorting or trivializing it, using what scholar Raul Hilberg skillfully summarized in his 1992 book on the "the Final Solution," *Perpetrators, Victims, Bystanders: The Jewish Catastrophe* 1933-1945. Such categories might avoid the need to focus on films like *American History X* and *X-Men* to show breadth, while excluding important comments about current films like *Divided We Fall* and *Rosenstrasse,* and earlier movies like *Ship of Fools, Voyage of the*

Damned, Marathon Man, The Spy Who Came in from the Cold, The Man in the Glass Booth, and *Music Box.* A different strategy might also allow for valuable time to consider the relationship between films like *Playing for Time, Schindler's List, The Harmonists, Swing Kids,* and *The Pianist,* and the role of music in the Third Reich. In this instance, Baron has the chance to analyze *Taking Sides,* but chooses not to, for reasons unknown. Then there is the role of the Christian Church, as well as the recent change in Popes as they pertain to the Holocaust, that certainly merits attention in an introductory book. And given this opportunity with *Amen,* the author chooses not to engage a meaningful topic. Finally, how does he justify the omission of Oscar winning director Marcel Ophuls in his narrative based on critical and commercial excellence?

Having pointed out the strengths and weaknesses of this praiseworthy effort, I wish to recommend this book without reservation to anyone even remotely interested in the subject. For me, it serves as a reality check in my memory, and delineates what "bearing witness" means. To the reader, it may provide invaluable insights on what can be done to explain the inexplicable.

Frank Manchel
University of Vermont

13. Lawyer Ann Talbot (Jessica Lange) has the painful task of defending her Hungarian-American immigrant father Mike Laszlo (Armin Mueller-Stahl) against charges that he is a Nazi war criminal. Costa-Gavras, *Music Box* (1989). From the core collection production photographs of the Margaret Herrick Library, Academy of Motion Picture Arts and Sciences.

11. History Redux

Great artists reveal slowly. You need to keep coming back to them like a painter you keep coming back to in a gallery.[1]
Richard Schickel

Masterpieces are not created as stones but as bottomless wells that forever surprise, astonish, inspire, excite, and elevate us.[2]
John Gennari

I don't believe any painter can use a mural or an easel painting to give you a precise and sophisticated analysis of the complexities of human politics. That is not the role of art. But art, on the other hand, can inform, can enflame, it can propagandize, it can make people think....[3]
Rick Tejada-Fares

On April 3, 1997, the Graduate College notified me I had been selected as the 1997-1998 University Scholar in the Humanities, "the highest honor the University of Vermont awards to its faculty in recognition of contributions to research and scholarship."[4] Remarkably, it came almost thirty years to the day I began lobbying in Burlington for Film to be recognized as one of the great art forms of the twentieth century. Along with my award went the responsibility to deliver a public lecture at the following year's annual University-wide Seminar Series. After much thought, I chose as my subject the recently released film, *Amistad*. I entitled the talk, "So Who Are You Going to Believe? A Reconsideration of *Amistad*." On the flyer circulated around campus, there was the following abstract: "*Amistad* is one of the memorable film mysteries of 1997. Steven Spielberg's epic movie had everything that normally would have made for an award-winning picture: a great story about the only kidnapped Africans who rebelled against slave traders, won their freedom back in American courts, and returned to their homeland; a fine cast; an ingenious script; wonderful production values; splendid cinematography; and a timely message linking the past to the present. Instead of being a hit, it proved a box-office disappointment. What went wrong?"

That April 2, 1998 talk is the focus of this Chapter. Reexamining those times and wrestling with what to say about why that film was selected, what troubled me professionally in the mid-to-late nineties, and why my teaching style necessitated changing, proved, for me, not only stimulating but also surprising. "Stimulating" because I can now recall objectively how my having contracted cancer was affecting both my life and my work. "Surprising" because unlike previous Chapters, this introductory section refused to follow a conventional narrative route.

Let's first get the Cancer issue out of the way. In late November of 1995, Sheila and I discovered "we" had Intermediate Non-Hodgkin's Lymphoma. Almost immediately, the decision was made "our" sickness would be dealt with confidentially, because we consider it a private problem. Also, the illness would not be allowed to disrupt our children's lives. To keep them endlessly abreast of treatments and developments, we felt, would have them constantly worried and preoccupied with "our" state of health at the cost of paying attention to their everyday way of life. If and when the time came for the family to be informed of dire circumstances, we would do so. Until then, the disease's progress remained between Sheila and me. Contrary to what many people close to us suspected, given the circumstances, I was extremely glad that the Cancer had attacked me rather than my wife or my children. It would have been far more upsetting to me if things had been otherwise. Lastly, Sheila and I approached the days ahead with curiosity and optimism rather than doom and gloom.

Two weeks after receiving the diagnosis, we happened to be shopping in Burlington's Barnes & Noble Bookstore. While Sheila went in pursuit of some books, I strolled over to the medical reference section and looked up what Intermediate Non-Hodgkin's Lymphoma was, and what I could expect in the coming days. The information unnerved me. So when I went later that week to the oncologist and asked how much time I had left. He looked at me and said, "Listen carefully. Don't you ever again research your illness like that! What you read are national statistics. Each case is unique. Your cancer has little to do with that material." Now, twenty-one years later, I still follow the good doctor's advice.

While I am more than holding my own against the disease in my personal life, the illness has had extensive effects on my teaching career. It not only sapped my strength but also dramatically affected my concentration and my work habits. Teaching became extremely more difficult, due in large part to the new problems connected with doing research and my dwindling attention span. So I adapted. I gradually moved away from lecturing to a Socratic approach in my classrooms. In addition, the English Department generously gave me a teaching assistant to make the large lecture classes manageable. This chain of events allowed me more time before I eventually had to give up my career and go on permanent disability.

As to the years under review and how best to explain them to the reader, I remember several academic issues bothering me, along with some inventive glitches: the difficult preparation for the University Scholar speech, unresolved questions from the *Schindler's List* chapter, the treatment of historical films, and how my declining health raised questions about my teaching methodology.

In addition, this Chapter contains two subtexts. One nuance concerns my firm belief smart answers don't come from film masterpieces alone. Quite frequently, so-called "B" movies rejected in one period resurface as important film discoveries in another era. The second subtext is how to use ingenious films to help judge the moral force of our governments. As you will see reaffirmed in this section, our political institutions may be necessary, but they regularly have corrupt individuals within them who cheapen our values and shame our nation. This subtext is another way of asserting the Plato reference from the previous chapter: when governments go bad, we need to turn to virtuous individuals who put morality above self-interest. So one of the issues considered in the pages ahead, is it possible for our institutions, or any ruling group, to routinely behave morally? If not, what can we do about it?

As always, let's start with the last topic first: the question of teaching.[5] Ever since the mid-fifties, when starting my serious study of literature, I had always been enthralled, first, with understanding the multiple types of analysis open to me; and then, secondly, with how best to pursue and to explain my choices. If I was going to be a good teacher, what essential tools did I need? If I was going to be a responsible teacher, should I teach my students what the community expected them to understand or what I felt my novices needed? Should I follow traditional critical guidelines in my discipline or should I seek out more up-to-date methods and ideas appropriate to the current student population? Not surprisingly, these abstract concerns took many forms, went through constant revisions, and only intensified in complexity when I turned to film education.

Now nearing the end of the twentieth century, with my Cancer making significant inroads into my well being, my teaching behavior required obvious reconsideration. Time seemed more precious, and my strength more limited. I needed to narrow my classroom priorities if I was going to continue to be effective with my students. Should I still take a formalist approach? Maybe I should focus on the students' reception of a particular film. Should I concentrate on what the artist presumably intended? Is it even possible to determine an artist's real intentions? Would it be more efficient to view films as works of art, or more economical to see films primarily as a social force? Which were the most important variables in critiquing a movie: the characters and the themes, or the production values and the style? Should I base my class time on the controversial "Auteur theory"[6] alone? Does the auteur change from film to film? What other analytical skills should I discuss besides just the Auteur theory? Do you have enough time to teach everything? Should I judge a film's worth more on its critical reception or on its commercial success? Shouldn't I perform analyses differently if I am speaking on TV, in the classroom, or at a public lecture? If so, what are the differences? Should I dramatically cut back on my outside classroom commitments? Do I argue for an unequivocal standard, or do I offer a variety of critical approaches, allowing my students to decide which method they find meaningful for them? Do I remain non-committal or do I push my critical preferences? Is there a best way to understand what a film means, how it was created, or what makes it timeless? What is my role as a teacher? Do I educate the community to works it misses or ignores or misunderstands? Or do I stimulate the public's awareness of a movie currently being watched and discussed? Should the films I critique in the classroom be mostly mainstream movies, or should they be treatises too difficult for popular consumption? Should they be historical or contemporary? Most important of all, how much teaching or public speaking should I do, given my current health? I could go on, but these questions should suffice for what was going on in "my little gray cells" as I addressed the changes taking place in my teaching in the mid-to-late nineties.

But it wasn't enough just to re-evaluate crucial methodologies. I felt the need to re-examine my perspectives on previous scholarly interpretations and evaluations. Consequently, I spent time re-reading the great critics from Plato, Aristotle, and Horace up to Northrop Frye, I. A. Richards, Alfred Kazin, Lionel Trilling, and Cleanth Brooks. It was very frustrating. I kept vacillating from clarity to confusion when it came to deciding on which ideas I found most useful. Whomever I read at the time took over my thoughts. Then came the reconsideration of my film gurus, mostly American movie critics, from John Simon, Pauline Kael, Andrew Sarris, Stanley Kauffmann, and Dwight Macdonald, to overseas theorists such as Andre Bazin, Rudolf Arnheim, and Siegfried Kracauer. Each of these major critics had strengths in one area or another, but no one pointed me where best to spend my now limited energies in film study: e.g., theory, directors, producers, industrial patterns, economics, film content, performers, technology, film masterpieces, genres, national schools, feminist ideology, popular culture, or film criticism. In the end, it came down to a matter of trial and error. Last, but certainly crucial, were my publishing and speaking priorities. It made no sense to know your discipline if you couldn't communicate effectively what you learned to others. And my relating what I knew to my classes became more of a problem with each new semester.

Despite these obviously important instructional issues, they remained secondary to my health and to my mental state. Without my strength or my concentration working well, what was the point? Only Sheila's influence and support made solving these issues practical and possible. These were the days when I also momentarily doubted what I had learned from my literary heroes: Shakespeare, Swift, Cervantes, Twain, Rostand, Shaw, Hawthorne, and Maugham. Was the world really as bad as they thought it was?

Interestingly, illness altered my longstanding negative perspectives on humanity. While I still viewed the world as a living horror for most people, I now championed an alternative existence filled with many individuals to admire. It also became abundantly clear I no longer was in tune with film studies' changing national priorities. Popular culture was being replaced by cultural studies. Teachers were distancing themselves from the public more than ever before. Pauline Kael's worst fears had gone beyond her wildest nightmares.

As I muddled my way through the mid-to-late nineties, I often found myself distracted by abstract academic debates concerning the screen image of intellectuals, identity schemes, chaos theory, international migration, ethnography, reception studies, the end of an era, and the culture of celebrity. This constant chatter was taking place on the H-Net List for Scholarly Studies and Uses of Media website. On that stimulating link, my favorite topic involved the treatment of historical films.

Ever since 1973, when the first edition of *Film Study* appeared, one consistent area that fascinated me was why both the public and historians didn't respect historical films as important historical documents. Why was it so difficult for educated people to recognize this particular movie genre functioned as a genuine and important source of historical evidence? I had been aware of the genre's insights about the past and the present since I had entered public school nearly forty years earlier. By the eighties, I had readily embraced film scholar Kenneth R. M. Short's sensible academic assumption: "The historian must be prepared...to adopt the hypothesis that feature-length movies, despite being almost exclusively fictitious in nature, have the ability to reflect historical realities in a useful, if not unique manner."[7]

Other intellectuals had built on that argument. Why was there no breakthrough with the academic community at large? Thankfully, the perceptive film historian Marc Ferro summarized the progressive thinking on the issue: "Grasping film in relation to history requires more than just better chronicles of the works or better descriptions of how the various genres evolved. It must look at the historical function of film, at its relationship with the societies that produce it and consume it, at the social process involved in the making of these works, as cinema as a source of history."[8] In fairness, few people even appreciate the relationship between movies and our national consciousness. Thus it is not surprising they don't understand the damage that poor historical films cause to our collective memories. "We have an obligation," historian Warren Goldstein effectively argued, "to say what we know, to support what's correct, and to criticize what's wrong or misleading."[9] The reader may remember, these thoughts had attracted my attention in previous chapters in discussing such films as *Gentleman's Agreement*, *Confessions of a Nazi Spy*, *The Great Dictator*, *The Diary of Anne Frank*, *Nothing But a Man*, *The Memory of Justice*, *Exodus*, and *Schindler's List*.[10]

That ongoing curiosity takes us to my second concern at the end of the twentieth century: the treatment of historical films by historians and the public. Since we have neither the time nor the space to consider sufficiently the many stimulating opinions provided on this subject, I simply want to mention how historians viewed the genre in the past, and, in many cases, still do. I also want to suggest how I believe historical films should be received. For convenience's sake, I will focus on the 1996 publication of Professor Robert Brent Toplin's *History by Hollywood: The Use and Abuse of the American Past*.[11]

Aware that academics remained disgruntled with how movies interpret the past; and reminding us paradoxically these same scholars spend their energies "analyzing films for the insights into the changing interests of past generations," Professor Toplin proposed a new intellectual direction: we should study more closely what we see displayed on the silver screen.[12] That is, we should research the attitudes artists use in conveying their cinematic ideas to their audiences: how the films connect to the existing interpretations of the events under review; and how trustworthy the artists are in examining historical evidence. Moreover, it made sense to discover the filmmakers' motivations in creating their historical films in the first place. In essence, scholars should directly address the matters troubling historians.[13] At the same time, Professor Toplin pointed out university teachers ought to offer both praise and criticism in their analyses. Since no historical film is made without external and internal problems, we should concern ourselves with an artist's choices; as well as gauge his trustworthiness in offering his interpretations. Still further, researchers would do well to be more sensitive both to market conditions and to the cultural climate at the time the film was released. Movies are not created in a vacuum.

In the end, however, Professor Toplin reiterated the challenges he faced: historical films get poor ratings because intellectuals do not believe artists respect historical truths, the film narratives place an overemphasis on personal relationships rather than on historical accuracy, and profit-minded producers pander to the public's thirst for sex and scandal rather than the audience's need for truth or accuracy. As a result, he reluctantly admitted, many scholars simply did not believe intellectualizing historical films is worth their valuable time.

While such conclusions are reasonable for film as a whole, they falter when dealing with individual movies. That being said, what always intrigued me was showing the differences between the sloppy and the superb? Professor Toplin suggested studying a film's pre-production process and then contextualizing the movie with regard to its critical and commercial receptions. Ask what are the circumstances that produced these results?

Dr. Robert Sklar, in his review of Professor Toplin's book, took issue with his respected colleague's position. Such an approach, the aggressive academician argued, put too much emphasis on a movie's prosaic aspects and not nearly enough on its aesthetics, especially the visual evidence provided through style, imagery, production values, and sound. What Toplin did, Professor Sklar opined, was to set up film historians as a band of "accuracy" policemen, assigned primarily to exposing a film's omissions, distortions, and misapplications."[14] We had more important work to do, the perceptive critic argued, than just pointing out a movie's superficial characteristics.

The debate did not end there. Professor Steven Mintz next weighed in, reminding us although Sklar's review was stimulating; it appeared similar to Professor Leger Grindon's 1994 book, *Shadows on the Past*.[15] Professor Sklar's contribution, Mintz stated, is that he sees the historical film as "a distinct genre...which has its own formulas, conventions, rules, and discourse, and which exists in dialogue with academic history and also public consciousness and memory, and which also serves contemporary political functions."[16]

My reflective overview brings us to the third and recent concern in this introduction: the unresolved questions surrounding *Schindler's List*. "Unresolved," I feel, because in looking back at what I have written, two points seem grossly understated. For example, I ended the last Chapter giving the impression that prosecuting former National Socialists who entered this country illegally was a rare occurrence. That is a gross understatement. While various scholars have documented what happened to former Nazis brought to America during this shameful period in American history, I found Eric Lichtblau's Pulitzer Prize-winning study, *The Nazis Next Door: How America Became a Safe Haven for Hitler's Men* an especially disturbing and eye-opening examination of this particular American disgrace.[17] That national blot requires much more attention than I have given it so far.

Although my primary focus in this Chapter is on the *Amistad* talk, I cannot comfortably get to the Spielberg film until I at least alert the reader to certain issues still bothering me about America and the Shoah. For example, almost six months before the end of World War II, the United States government, now seeing the Soviet Union, not the Third Reich, as our greatest danger, started a systematic, secret campaign to locate high-level Nazis wherever they could be found—in detention camps, on the battlefields, and in various occupied countries—and then to enlist them as unique assets in fighting the Cold War. We ignored what the monsters had done, scrubbed clean their atrocious resumes, and covered up their vicious role in the Shoah; we even played down the accountability of some individuals in the murder of millions and millions of

Europeans, not just six million Jews alone. We justified our indecent behavior by insisting America was in a life-and-death struggle against the Soviet Union; and by far, our best defense against the barbaric Reds was the unprincipled talents of pre-eminent Nazis. These "butchers" allegedly possessed unique skills when it came to exposing and to destroying many of the present-day Communist threats both at home and abroad. We even made it a political contest, not only in how we could surpass the Soviets in locating and obtaining more Nazis than they could; but also in how attractive a "package" we could put together to entice the Nazis to our side.

Many Americans knew very little about the clandestine and unconscionable recruitment. Those that did, often believed it was only a handful of Nazi scientists we squirreled into the United States. But it wasn't. We brought in war criminals from many areas by the thousands! Knowledge about the disturbing program reached the highest levels. Not only did one President after another buy into "Operation Paperclip," but also whitewashing Nazis eventually became a public brainwashing program in the media and in political circles. The twisted thinking maintained difficult times made for difficult decisions. And when the government's dirty secret started to see the light of day after the Eichmann trial, a large segment of the American population turned the immoral debate into a patriotic justification. The past was the past. We needed to look to the future. "Our" Nazis made it possible for us to win the Cold War, as well as to win the space race. The argument often was as simple as that! Of course, it didn't help the apologists' cause to discover only a very few of the Nazis met our expectations. The crucial point was we won the Cold War.

My second unresolved and misleading difficulty concerns the sprinkling of Holocaust films mentioned at the end of the last Chapter. I realize my moral outrage has little weight beyond this page. I grasp the fact no one is going to rush out to immediately watch these suggested movies on Nazi genocide. Nonetheless, I believe there are historical films that can do the job that I cannot. Such films have both the strength and the art to draw the public to the subject and learn about the Shoah. Remember, I have already made that case repeatedly: motion pictures possess great empathetic power. Yet, as previously discussed, most historical films rarely gain public acceptance, much less scholarly interest, or even survive the period of their initial release. So to ease my conscience, as well as to illustrate the value of historical films and bind this discussion to the *Amistad* speech, let me discuss briefly one movie I find exquisite in recalling just one small part of America's appalling partnership with the Devil: Costa-Gavras' unjustly overlooked *Music Box*.[18]

Let's proceed in four simple steps: the pre-production process, the narrative, the film's critical and popular receptions, and my interpretation of the movie.

In the mid-1980s, Joe Eszterhas was one of Hollywood's most commercially successful screenwriters.[19] Born in Hungary in late November 1944, he always carried with him horrific memories of his earliest years being raised in an occupied country: bombings, widespread chaos, and hardships in one refugee camp after another. In early 1945, for example, the Eszterhas family found itself imprisoned in Mauthausen, one of the more than twenty-seven Nazi death camps. But what proved most disturbing later on in the middle-aged writer's persist nightmares, according to his autobiography *Hollywood's Animal*,[20] were the shocking stories and images of the Communists and their ruthless treatment of Hungarians who had collaborated with the Nazis during their occupation of Hungry. When Eszterhas had difficulty remembering precisely what had happened, his father willingly provided him with vivid details about Soviet anti-Semitism, brutalities, and murders.[21]

By the mid-1950s, the Eszterhas family had immigrated to America. Joe studied hard, graduated from Ohio State University, and he became a reporter for a Cleveland newspaper. Eventually, he left journalism, tried his luck as a novelist, and eventually became a screenwriter.[22] Considered a working-class artist who thrived on shock value, Eszterhas authored such popular movie narratives as Adrian Lyne's *Flashdance* (1983), Richard Marquand's *Jagged Edge* (1985), and Costa-Gavras' *Betrayed* (1988).

After the release of *Betrayed*, the filmmaking team of producer Irwin Winkler, director Costa-Gavras, and screenwriter Joe Eszterhas decided to do another political thriller, one closer to home than the courtroom whodunit they had just done about the FBI uncovering white supremacy in Chicago. Ironically, as the writer thought about his next script, he turned to his current obsession with the complicated trial of John Demjanjuk, a retired American steelworker residing in Cleveland, Ohio, accused of being a Nazi guard who in "reality" was the notorious "Ivan the Terrible," the monster who had murdered hundreds of thousands of prisoners at Poland's infamous Treblinka death camp.

Similar to Eszterhas, the suspected Ukrainian war criminal had been in a death camp, come to the United States in the early fifties, and eventually settled in Ohio. But unlike the popular screenwriter, Demjanjuk admitted being a former Nazi war prisoner who then became a Nazi prison guard and served at the Sobibor and Majdanek death camps. He insisted, however, he had never been to Treblinka. Deported to Israel in 1986, he was tried and convicted of crimes against humanity, in large measure because of the testimony of nearly a dozen elderly Holocaust survivors. In 1988, a Jerusalem court sentenced him to hang for his war crimes. [After *Music Box* was released, Eszterhas would learn Demjanjuk's case was appealed to the Israeli Supreme Court, where to everyone's shock, the survivors' accusations were proven false. While Demjanjuk was indeed a Nazi war criminal, he was not "Ivan the Terrible." His citizenship was restored; he resumed his Ohio retirement, and foolishly expected his ordeal was over. It wasn't. As noted in the previous chapter, Demjanjuk was eventually convicted of Nazi war crimes in a Munich court, but died before he could be executed.][23]

Demjanjuk's troubles resonated with Eszterhas. What would it be like, the scarred writer wondered, to be the innocent child of a Nazi war criminal? As historian Eric Lichtblau would later document, a question like this one was very common for the times: "Overwhelmingly, the children—many of them first-generation Americans and products of the war themselves—believed in their fathers and their innocence, even in the face of overwhelming evidence. It was simply too painful to do otherwise....Every child was convinced his father was one of the innocents."[24] But Eszterhas just happened to be the first artist to dramatize the trauma on screen. Using his troubled memories, his father's shocking stories, and his vivid imagination, the inspired screenwriter created a fictional courtroom drama stirred by current events.

Titled *Music Box* (1989),[25] the narrative concerns the ethical struggle of Ann Talbot (Jessica Lange), a first-generation Hungarian-American lawyer. Devoted to her family, the highly regarded Chicago attorney is shocked when she learns her elderly father, Mike Laszlo (Armin Mueller-Stahl), is being accused of World War II atrocities in Hungary. Believing the terrible allegation to be an obvious misunderstanding, she takes on her victimized parent's defense. But the United States government has no misgivings about whether they have the right man. They institute deportation proceedings against Laszlo, contending he is in reality a Nazi war criminal who lied on his naturalization papers. Thankfully, for Ann, she is not alone in criticizing the devastating charges. Her younger, tough-talking brother (Michael Rooker) tells her to go after the Justice department lawyer, Jack Burke (Frederic Forrest), and emasculate him. Equally outraged is her ex-father-in-law, an eminent corporate attorney (Donald Moffat), who promises to help Ann with whatever she needs. He even turns over his corporate offices to the idealistic advocate. A major subplot in the narrative involves the effect the trial will have on Ann's young eleven-year-old son (Lukas Haas). Not only do both his grandparents dote on him, but also the boy idolizes Laszlo.

Most of the movie focuses on the courtroom battles to establish Laszlo's guilt or innocence. In one cross-examination after another, Ann cleverly distracts attention to the various witnesses' credibility, thereby creating reasonable doubt about the validity of their testimony. The witnesses' range from a forensics expert who identifies the father as a member of the Arrow Cross, the notorious Hungarian death squad, to people who presumably not only suffered war crimes at Laszlo's hands, but also worked with him. Eventually, the daughter's skills prove effective, and she wins the case; only to discover by accident her father is indeed the monster he is accused of being. To protect her son as well as to see justice done, the ethical Ann courageously breaks with her father and provides Burke with the evidence he needs to deport Laszlo back to Hungry.

A quick search suggests Eszterhas may not be entirely accurate in saying the movie got good critical reviews but did poorly at the box-office. Roger Ebert, for example, found the film much too pat and lacking "heart." Arguing the filmmakers used their moral righteousness to misrepresent themselves as serious artists, Ebert dismisses *Music Box* as much too predictable.[26] Paul Chutkow's perspective for the *New York Times*, first draws attention to Eszterhas' background, making clear the screenwriter was not Jewish, before labeling the movie both a Hungarian's perception of the Holocaust as well as a political thriller. The cultural critic then quotes the screenwriter as saying the undertaking was for him "personally purgative, cathartic writing," while stating Costa-Gavras' aim was in "showing the destiny of the father becoming the destiny of the daughter, and she has to live it."[27] Reviewing the film for the same paper, Caryn James dismissed the project as having "an overblown script" and "simplistic direction." She concluded her damning analysis by saying "*Music Box* finally tells us nothing about wronged innocence or monstrous evil."[28] The most important supporter of the film may have been the Nobel Laureate and Shoah survivor Eli Wiesel.[29]

From my outlook, a quarter-of-a-century later, and having the benefit of Eric Lichtblau's detailed description of how America became a safe haven for thousands of Nazi war criminals, *Music Box* offers rich historical evidence on a national scandal. Time and space again permit only two examples. First, to me, the Costa-Gavras thriller illustrates how film aesthetics delivers useful reminders on what the Justice Department faced in prosecuting Nazi war criminals illegally living in the United States during the eighties. For example, we discover how effectively these sadistic WWII villains had concealed their true identity once they became naturalized Americans.

The movie opens at a Hungarian dance where we meet a closely-knit ethnic family, with special attention given to Laszlo's professed love for his grandson. Here is a person with considerable community and racial support. Once we learn the "patriotic" old man is being accused of unspeakable war crimes, the filmmakers show us the facade the ex-Nazi has taken to mask his true identity: "I hate nobody," Laszlo says. "I work at a steel factory. I raise my kids. My boy, my girl. My boy was an American soldier. He fought in Vietnam. My girl, I'm proud. She's an American lawyer. You laugh at me, you son-of-a-bitch." Seen from the present, it is a textbook on the emotional and human camouflage used by real-life, transplanted ex-Nazis to gain acceptance in America and disguise their past.

In presenting the Office of Special Investigation's case, Prosecutor Jack Burke often has trouble getting evidence about Laszlo's past. Costa-Gavras frequently has crucial information appearing miraculously, at the last moment, or surprisingly provided by unknown sources. We see how vast a protective network Laszlo has here and overseas. Using Professor Hilberg's concept of "tiniest threads," one recognizes how the film suggests the difficulties Nazi hunters had in identifying war criminals living illegally in the United States, convincing the government to prosecute them, justifying the trials to the general public, and then obtaining documents from embarrassed intelligence agencies who are understandably reluctant to inform on the ex-Nazis who may have worked for them. At the same time, Ann Talbot's courtroom tactics serve as a Dummies' Guide to obfuscating the truth. Every time new evidence is presented against her father, she brings in "buzz" words like "Jews" and "Communists" to bank on the viewer relating in his own doubts or prejudices to question the validity of the testimony: Maybe there are other reasons why these prosecution witnesses' say what they say. Seen from this point of view, it shouldn't require much effort to realize how the film reflects the age in which it was made.

The second crucial perspective concerns the characterizations. Consider Armin Mueller-Stahl's controversial stoical performance. Assuming the role of a moral, devout human being, the thoroughly corrupt man constantly exclaims, "I didn't do any of this. That's not me. I'm a good American." While Ebert may complain about the actor's steely presence providing no explanation of why Laszlo did what he did, I question whether anyone knows why ordinary people became monsters by the millions during the Shoah. And when Laszlo tells his trusting daughter how he often goes to his dead wife's grave for spiritual advice, we can only imagine what other unsuspecting children experienced in having disguised war criminals as parents. And whenever Ann begins to doubt her father, we see how quick he is to lie about his past. Adding to the dialogue are the visuals. At times, when Ann seeks answers, a background lamp is on; when Laszlo responds, the same lamp is off. When Ann talks, her face is half in darkness; when her father speaks, his face is in shadows.

Then there is Donald Moffat's oddly overlooked performance

as an anti-Semitic corporate attorney, who tells his grandson the Holocaust never happened. He makes light of the trial, saying it will probably take years to resolve. He tells Ann he was in the OSS and later the CIA. Here, the dialogue makes a direct reference to the role of intelligence agencies in recruiting ex-Nazis to come to America. Moffat even brags to his ex-daughter-in-law he shared drinks with high-level Nazis. "None of those men were monsters. They were all salt of the earth types." Especially important is the scene at the end where Laszlo is declared innocent; and Moffat, in the background, conducts a news conference, during which he summarizes various reasons for not bringing ex-Nazi war criminals to trial, while also casting aspersions on Justice Department lawyers like Burke who, Moffat claims, are mislead by liberals and communist sympathizers. "The trouble with those young clowns," the slimy corporate attorney says, "they're so full of Glasnost and burning Hilton hotels over there." Again, *Music Box* takes us through the eighties; and shows us how difficult it was for dedicated government attorneys to deport ex-Nazis and the shocking effects such proceedings had on the criminals' unsuspecting families.

My favorite moments in the movie, however, come from Jessica Lange's inspired and universally praised performance. Rarely up to the late eighties had there been in motion picture history a more positive film portrait of an intelligent, beautiful, and independent woman succeeding so superbly in society. Ann Talbot divorced her husband rather than buy into his questionable upper-class values. She pursues a highly successful career, while at the same time being a dutiful, single mom. Principled, and a loving daughter, she risks everything to protect her father, only to be deceived along the way by both her ex-father-in-law as well as Laszlo. But it is when she confronts her unmasked father, Lange gives a performance for the ages: "It was you, Papa; you killed them....You killed that boy in front of his father. You threw those bodies in the Danube. I went to see that place. The son was seven years old....You shot him in the head. You shot them all in the head....Why did you do those things?" In those extraordinary moments, Lange's astonishing acting personifies the pain thousands of first-generation Americans must have felt when they discovered the truth of their parents' terrible legacy in the Shoah. The horrifying questions she asks might well represent the terrible questions asked by thousands of children both in America and abroad from that generation.

But my fascination with *Music Box* does not end with its release in 1989. Not only did the film appear at the precise moment the Office of Special Investigations was gaining public acceptance, but also other government lawyers were preparing war crime charges against Eszterhas' eighty-three-year-old father. In the shattered screenwriter's memoir, he details the pain he suffered in learning Istvan Eszterhas' horrific past. Almost identical to the fictional Laszlo, the retired journalist at first denied any involvement in war crimes. Then, as Sharon Waxman reported, "His son wanted to believe him. But when confronted with the evidence, neither the father nor the son could deny it any longer.[30] In the 1930s Istvan Eszterhas wrote 'Nemzet Politika' ('National Policy'), a book in which he called Jews parasites."[31] To Joe Eszterhas, Lichtblau explained, "the book read like a Hungarian version of *Mein Kampf.*"[32] The scholar concluded, "*Music Box* was supposed to be a made-up story, but the Hollywood screenwriter's own life had come to imitate his art in haunting ways, and the guilt and shame of his father's role with the Nazis were passed from one generation to the next.... Eszterhas felt that his father's hidden past had left him with a moral burden of his own. 'It's the responsibility of the son to do penance:' Eszterhas said, 'to correct what the father has done.'"[33]

Thus, for me, *Music Box* remains an engrossing thriller, which also raises vital questions about the Shoah resulting from "pure Aryan ideology and genocidal rage."[34] It requires us to question the morality and ethics of the United States government in these war crime cases.[35] Especially effective is the way the screenplay reminds us how governments sometimes are very supple when it comes to interpreting our laws and to applying our morality. On a much larger scale, the narrative challenges us to confront a national policy based on the political philosophy that the means justifies the ends.

And so we arrive at the question of why *Amistad* was selected for my University Scholar speech. First, I loved the film and wanted to spend time studying it. Second, it encompassed many of the ethical concerns preoccupying me in the mid-nineties. Third, I was intrigued by our government's flexible conduct in the "Amistad affair." Fourth, Spielberg and his colleagues were not being treated well by historians and the public. But there was still one more reason, not admitted at the time.

David Franzoni, the remarkable young man, the reader recalls, who had been one of my first UVM students, was given a breakthrough opportunity as the film's screenwriter. But everything seemed stacked against him. His amazing script seemed not to please the film's director, so Steven Zaillian, *Schindler's List*'s acclaimed screenwriter, was brought in to help on the narrative. Then Zaillian petitioned the Screen Writers Guild for equal writing credits. It didn't help my frustration that he lost. It seemed as if David was getting more headaches than he deserved. And then came the charges of plagiarism,[36] which also got dismissed. Finally, in all the marketing material associated with the movie, the media focused on the director, the producer, and the actors; never the screenwriter. I felt I wanted to address those professional and artistic slights publically. The Amistad speech seemed the best way to do it.

I want to make clear David and I have never talked about theses issues then or now. What follows is my interpretation alone of the film and the circumstances surrounding it. I'm not even sure my former student and friend will be pleased in my resurrecting the troubled film's legacy. But I hope he will appreciate my motives.

In summing up, let me leave the reader with two observations. First, as I write these words, an unusual coincidence is taking place in Burlington, Vermont. The Office of Special Investigations is preparing to retry a war-crimes suspect accused of falsifying his naturalization application. While his crimes originate out of the Bosnian War, not the Shoah, the facts surrounding the case echo back to what I have discussed throughout this introduction.[37] Second, I want to underscore how this chapter has helped me deal with my negative worldview of how nations have behaved badly since time immemorial. That is, I imagine that in the future many young people will encounter government corruption, cruelty, and extremism in their battles to reform society. When that happens, you can be sure the powerbrokers will push back. The reformers may feel their fights appear futile; they may assume the world will not change.

My hope is that this chapter will suggest another possibility. Moreover, I take great comfort, however, in being an American-

Jew. I remain optimistic despite studying how our country has handled its many blemishes since the days of slavery, the disgraceful treatment of Native Americans, to its racist immigration policies, our colonial behavior in Panama and the Philippines, and to the thousands of ex-Nazis it brought to our shores. What gives me hope is what made the distinguished historian Stephen E. Ambrose optimistic: America is the only nation so far that has the courage to remedy its mistakes. "We've made the world a better place and we will continue to do so. Our American spirit comes from the Founding Fathers..."[38] The painful truth, regrettably, is so much pain and suffering and death must take place before things are made right. All that said, I still believe, as Swift wrote centuries ago, "I cannot but conclude the bulk of your natives to be the most pernicious race of little odious vermin that nature ever suffered to crawl upon the surface of the earth."[39]

Notes

[1] Richard Schickel, *Gary Cooper: American Life, American Legend*. USA: Turner Network Television, 1991. 60 mins.

[2] John Gennari, *Blowin' Hot and Cool: Jazz and Its Critics*. Chicago and London: The University of Chicago Press, 2006. 196.

[3] Rick Tejada-Fares, "Rivera in America," in *American Masters*, ed. Susan Lacy. USA: Eagle Rock Entertainment, 2006.

[4] Dean Delcie R. Durham's letter to the author, April 3, 1997.

[5] Helpful in organizing my thoughts was an article in *The New York Times Book Review* (January 2, 2011), "Why Criticism Matters," 9-11.

[6] Simply stated, the "Auteur theory" places a director's personal vision as the primary force in a film's production.

[7] Kenneth R. M. Short, "Introduction," *Feature Films as History*, ed. Kenneth R. M. Short. Knoxville: University of Tennessee Press, 1981. 31.

[8] Marc Ferro, "Film as an Agent, Product and Source of History," *Journal of Contemporary History*: 18:3 (July 1983): 358.

[9] Warren Goldstein, "Bad History Is Bad for a Culture," *The Chronicle of Higher Education* (April 10, 1998): A64.

[10] For more information, see Frank Manchel, *Film Study: An Analytical Bibliography*, Vol. 1. Rutherford, N.J.: Fairleigh Dickinson University Press, 1990: 252-365.

[11] Robert Brent Toplin, *History by Hollywood: The Use and Abuse of the American Past*. Champaign: University of Illinois Press, 1996.

¹² Ibid., viii.

¹³ Ibid., xii.

¹⁴ Robert Sklar, "Historical Films: Scofflaws and the Historian-Cop," *Reviews in American History* 25:2 (June 1997): 346-350.

¹⁵ Leger Grindon, *Shadows on the Past*. Philadelphia: Temple University, 1994.

¹⁶ Steven Mintz, U. Houston, H-NET List for Scholarly Studies and Uses of Media (Tue. Feb. 17, 1998).

¹⁷ Eric Lichtblau, *The Nazis Next Door: How America Became a Safe Haven For Hitler's Men*. Boston: Houghton Mifflin Harcourt, 2014.

¹⁸ Another post-Shoah film dealing with the new lives that the Nazis created for themselves in America that could have been discussed in this section if not for space limitations is Atom Egoyan's *Remember* (2015). A Canadian-German co-production, screenwriter Benjamin August's dramatic thriller tells the story of an elderly man (Christopher Plummer), suffering from dementia and terribly repressed memories, who goes on a mission to kill the Nazi officer who murdered his parents at Auschwitz. Among the many questions the movie raises are how does one bring justice to past war crimes, how does one explain to the young about an evil so unimaginable that even presented with the evidence individuals still deny it happened, and how did such human depravity come about? An added bonus of the Blu-Ray DVD is a valuable visual essay entitled "A Tapestry of Evil: Remembering the Past" talking about the networks that helped Nazis escape capture and punishment.

¹⁹ David Thomson, *The New Biographical Dictionary of Film*, Expanded and Updated. New York: Alfred Knopf, 2004. 278.

²⁰ Joe Eszterhas, *Hollywood Animal: A Memoir*. New York: Vantage Books, 1994.

²¹ Ibid.

²² Ephraim Katz, *The Film Encyclopedia*, 5th Edition. Revised by Fred Klein & Ronald Dean Nolen. New York: HarperCollins, 2005. 443.

²³ Lawrence Douglas, *The Right Wrong Man*. New Jersey: Princeton University Press, 2016; Richard Rashke, *Useful Enemies: John Demjanjuk and America's Open Door Policy for Nazi War Criminals*. New York: Delphinium Books, 2013; and Liel Leibovitz, "The Nazi Who Lived in Ohio," *The Wall Street Journal* (February 18, 2016): C6.

²⁴ Eric Lichtblau, 138.

²⁵ Costa-Gavras, *Music Box*. USA: Tri-Star Pictures, 1989.

²⁶ Roger Ebert, "Music Box," *Roger Ebert.Com/reviews/music-box-1990*.

²⁷ Paul Chutkow, "From the 'Music Box' Emerges the Nazi Demon," *The New York Times* (December 24, 1989).

²⁸ Caryn James, "'Music Box' on Innocence, Evil and the Holocaust," *The New York Times* (December 25, 1989): 49.

[29] Eszterhas, 482. Elie Wiesel, Nobel Laureate and long-time witness of the Shoah died July 2, 2016. He was 87.
[30] An extremely effective documentary going into considerable detail about the pain of children whose fathers were complicit in the Shoah is David Evan's *My Nazi Legacy*. Released in 2016 on PBS' Independent Lens (Season 17, Episode 15), the 90 minute film presents the painful memories of Nikas Frank and Horst von Wachler, whose fathers were major mass murderers accounting for hundreds of thousands of deaths in the Third Reich's "Final Solution of the Jewish Problem." What makes this film so unusual is that the two sons interpret their fathers' behavior so differently: Frank is revolted by what his dad did; Wachler refuses to admit his father did anything wrong.
[31] Sharon Waxman, "In a Screenwriter's Art, Echoes of His Father's Secret," *New York Times* (March 18, 2004).
[32] Lichtblau, 151.
[33] Ibid., 151.
[34] Ibid., 143.
[35] Ibid., 147.
[36] Bernard Weinraub, "Spielberg Faces Charges of Plagiarism," *The New York Times* (November 13, 1997); Frank Rich, "Who Stole History?" Ibid. (December 13, 1997); and Todd Williams, "Troubled Waters," *Premiere* (January 1998): 53-56.
[37] Elizabeth Murray, "Court targets 2016 for war-crimes retrial," *Burlington Free Press* (August 18, 205): 4A. At nearly the same time in Germany, the Associate Press reported two more alleged ex-Nazis—Reinold Hanning (age 94) and Hubert Zafke (age 95)—were scheduled to go on trail for murder. See "Germany: Ex-Auschwitz SS Guard, 94, Goes on Trial," *Montreal Gazette* (February 11, 2016): NP4.
[38] Stephen E. Ambrose, *To America: Personal Reflections of an Historian*. New York: Simon & Schuster, 2002. 250.
[39] Jonathan Swift, *Gulliver's Travels*. Edited with Notes & Commentary by Arthur E. Case. New York: The Roland Press Company, 1938. 135.

"So Who Are You Going to Believe: A Reconsideration of 'Amistad'?"

Frank Manchel
Memorial Lounge, Waterman
University Scholar
April 2, 1998[1]

Let me open this talk with an anecdote. Thirty-five years ago, I had a debilitating illness. I had been in a car accident and suffered severe whiplash. Fortunately, I also had a wonderful doctor, Dr. Hans Freundlich, who in those days, used to treat me in my home. (Remember those physicians who used to come to the house?) And Hans told me a story. It had to do with the fact he was a German Jew, and he had fled his homeland during the Holocaust.

But years before he escaped, he had once taken a course with Albert Einstein at the Berlin Academy of Sciences. And in those days in Germany, some of you may remember, when you walked into a professor's classroom, you walked in with a black book, and he signed you in. And then when you left the last day of class, he signed you out. So it was on the last day of that class Albert Einstein signed Hans' book and said, "Hans, I want to thank you for the great honor that you have paid me."

And Hans looked at him and said, "Herr Professor, you've won the Nobel Prize. You're one of the most famous men in the world. It's an honor to be in your class."

"No, Hans," he said. "You took this course as an elective, and that's a very great honor, and I want you to know that I appreciate it."

Well, I wanted to tell you that story because I don't think I've had a chance to go around to everyone individually and thank you for being here. And my wife said that I could only use the story if I promised to say I do not consider myself equal to Albert Einstein. I just wanted to thank you all for coming to this talk.

Well, I guess there's no delaying this any further.[2]

In William Faulkner's 1950 Nobel Prize Acceptance Speech for Literature, he said, "I believe that the human spirit will prevail forever. It is our privilege to help it endure by lifting people's hearts, by reminding them of courage, and honor, and hope, and pride, and compassion, and pity, and sacrifice; which have been the glory of their past."[3] I believe that Faulkner's statement could just as well be about films. In fact, I would argue that by appealing to our emotions, more than to our intellect, movies make our moral abstractions come alive.

In a recent book on historical films, the scholarly author discusses the genre's importance to our national consciousness.[4] His views are especially true of recent films, where the past is used to inspire the present. Borrowing a page from my colleague's important work, he refers to historical reconstructions like *Glory*, *Hester Street*, *The Return of Martin Guerre*, *Gallipoli*, and *Schindler's List*, and insists they are more than just costumed adventures. They are perceptive, human dramas. They encourage us to find out more about who and what we are, where we came from, and how we differ from each other. They provide us with remarkable opportunities to transcend time and place. No wonder then, that ever since films began, whether in Europe, America, or Asia, movies have used the past to entertain, to educate, and to elevate audiences.[5]

But historical films also create conflicts. They are after all industrial products created for profits. So it is natural to ask whether commercialism has compromised their aesthetic integrity? Whose point of view are we getting? What kind of historical settings are we seeing? How accurate are these settings? Nowhere have the debates about historical accuracy been as controversial as those surrounding Hollywood films. To paraphrase my perceptive colleague again, "Serious people get angry about the answers provided in *Gone with the Wind's* mint julep approach to the ante-bellum south."[6]

To understand what upsets the public, experience suggests we examine the accuracy of movies depicting "demagogues" such as William Randolph Hearst and Huey Long, as in *Citizen Kane* and *All the King's Men*. We should scrutinize the ideology of filmmakers who employ "simplistic left-wing perspectives in presenting screen heroes" like John Reed in *Reds*, and Ron Kovic in *Born on the Fourth of July*. And what about those directors who whitewash history, failing "to recognize the contributions of minorities in American life," as in Alan Parker's *Mississippi Burning*; and distort "the historical record to advance their own agenda," evidenced by Oliver Stone's *JFK*? No one disputes that such films exert a powerful influence on our society.[7]

The debate is over the danger that imaginary characters and invented dialogue present to our collective consciousness. How can we deal rationally with the present, the critics ask, if the public is misinformed and misled? And why do people seem to excuse certain inaccuracies and not others by insisting that there is no one interpretation of history. There are even some in our midst who prefer to experience the past, not as it was, but as they think it ought to have been. There was no way, for example, director James Cameron was going to risk two hundred million dollars making *Titanic*, and not have beautiful stars and a fictional story to sugarcoat the historical events. So what happened? The public made *Titanic* one of the biggest box-office hits in motion picture history. There was little interest in how accurate the film actually was. Not surprisingly, many intellectuals fear the hold such questionable historical films have on our imagination.

One reason I chose to discuss *Amistad* today is because it shows the other side of the Hollywood debate; the one I've spent my academic life defending. Here is a wonderful example, as Janet Maslin of *The New York Times* points out, of the power of Hollywood at its best: "It's the ability," she says, "to make a seventy-five million dollar holiday movie about a shameful chapter in American history, simply because one thinks that's the right thing to do."[8] Another reason to consider *Amistad* is that it challenges the conventional wisdom over how historical movies are made; the politics of their critics, and the difficulty that worthwhile films have in finding an appreciative audience.

But there is still another reason, equally important, that recommends the study of *Amistad*. It's an intriguing movie mystery. People are wondering what went wrong with Steven Spielberg's latest film epic. It is everything that makes for a box-office hit: a great story about the only Africans enslaved by whites who rebelled and sailed back as free men to their homeland; a fine cast, an ingenious script, wonderful production values, splendid cinematography; and a timely message linking the past to the present. What's more, the people who made this movie wanted to make a contribution to our national heritage. Spielberg did the film, he explained, as a legacy for his children: "I wanted them and the public" he said, "to realize the horror of slavery, the brutality of the slave traders. I wanted them to understand why it was necessary to fight the Civil War."[9] Screenwriter David Franzoni was equally passionate. "Right from the start," he said, "there was a sense on *Amistad* that we were doing something that could change the world, or at the very start at least, make some serious ripples."

Yet when the ten best lists appeared at the end of the year and the film societies doled out their honors, *Amistad* was nowhere to be found. The Golden Globes gave it four nominations but no awards. Next were the Oscars, with *Amistad* again getting four nominations, and again the film coming up empty handed. As for the box-office results, the unbelievable happened. A Steven Spielberg film, almost always a predictable commercial hit, fell from the top ten moneymaker lists just seven weeks after it opened, meeting with mixed reviews and doing mediocre business. And when the movie finally made it to Burlington, just before Martin Luther King's birthday, one month after it had been released, the public didn't even know *Amistad* was in town, let alone where it was playing.[10] For the first time in my thirty-one years in Vermont, I witnessed a major movie open without any studio advertising in the local media.

A number of my valued, socially conscious friends don't see any mystery. They just wrote the film off as a bad movie. Moreover, one of my most respected colleagues summed *Amistad* up by claiming, "It may be the worst film that Spielberg ever made."

Now, this is going to surprise you. I have a different opinion. I believe *Amistad* is a remarkable movie. Its strength lies with its imagery and its imagination. The creative team that made *Amistad* rejected the conventional approaches in recreating the past; and instead, gave us a story with a unique opportunity to approach current struggles over affirmative action, cultural diversity, and changing racial demographics.[11]

Those are the reasons for the talk; now let me give you the strategy. First, I want to cover the pre-production history of *Amistad*. Second, I want to suggest a way to view the production itself. And finally, I want to discuss the film's critical reception.

The genesis of the film started in the late 1970's when performer, director, and producer, Debbie Allen, read two volumes of essays, *Amistad One* and *Two*, published in 1970,[12] where she learned the details about the neglected 1839 insurrection. For those of you who aren't familiar with the details of *The Amistad Affair*, and I suspect there are a lot of people here who have not seen the film yet, let me present the history in an over simplified form.[13]

In 1839, Portuguese slave traders pirated thousands of West Africans from the British Colony of what is now Sierra Leone. One man in particular, by the name of Sengbe Pieh, later to be called Joseph Cinque by his captors, a twenty-six-year-old rice farmer, and a father of three small children, was ambushed near his Mende village by several African tribesmen. Shackled and marched from the interior to the west coast of Africa, to a slave fortress on the Isle of Lomboko, one of fifty such slave fortresses at the time. Here, Sengbe was sold to a slave trader named Pedro Blanco. Eight weeks later, Sengbe and seven hundred other captured Africans, were put aboard a Portuguese vessel, the *Tecora*, bound for Havana, then a Spanish colony. Illegally enslaved, chained, and brutally treated, Sengbe somehow survived the two-month barbaric journey known as The Middle Passage.

The irony was that Britain had outlawed the slave trade, but not slavery, in 1807; the United States in 1808; and Spain in 1817. Yet the European slave trade continued illegally because it was so lucrative. It was also incredibly monstrous. One historian conjectures, "That between ten and fifteen percent of the slaves, estimated at thirteen million, who left Africa over a four-hundred-year period, died along the route of The Middle Passage." Another source claims that only a third of the enslaved Africans survived their first three years in the New World.

When the *Tecora* reached Cuba, its crew unloaded the human cargo at night because slave trading, you remember, was illegal. It was legal in Cuba, but not outside of Cuba. However, once on shore the kidnapped Africans were fed, rested, lathered, and shaved, to mask the telling effects of The Middle Passage. After about two weeks, they were taken to barracoons, slave markets, where they now could be bought and sold. Finally, corrupt Cuban officials issued false papers, declaring the kidnapped Africans had been born on Spanish soil, therefore making it all legal.

On June 28, 1839, two Spanish slave traders named Pedro Montez and Jose Ruiz herded forty-nine adults and four children on to the Spanish schooner *Amistad*. The ship left Havana, bound for a sugar plantation on the eastern part of the island. On the fourth night out, the chained Africans, led by Sengbe, managed to free themselves and rebel. They killed the captain and almost every member of the crew, and they took possession of the vessel. Only the two Spanish slave traders were kept alive, because Sengbe believed they alone could navigate the *Amistad* back to Africa. But the Spaniards deceived the Africans, sailing east during the daytime and then northwest at night. Soon there were stories up and down the eastern seaboard of a ghost ship manned by cannibals heading towards the United States.

After two months of this zigzag voyage, the ship reached Montauk Point off Long Island Sound. By then, only forty-three of the fifty-three blacks, the original ex-slaves, remained alive. The others had starved, perished in the mutiny, or died because of the thirst, which drove them to drink medicine that was in the hold below. At Montauk Point, the U.S. Navy patrol boat, *The Washington*, captured the *Amistad*.[14]

The *Washington* brought the battered slave ship and its sick and starving passengers to Connecticut, where the Africans were imprisoned in a New Haven jail, and forced to undergo several trials for piracy, murder, and possible extradition to Cuba. Only if they could prove they had been abducted against their will, could the *Amistads* go free.

Throughout their nearly three-year ordeal, the Africans lived in subhuman conditions, terrified every day that they were going to be killed. Sengbe, recognized as their leader, spent most of the first year in chains, and was quartered in a separate cell. Within weeks of their capture, three more Africans died from the diseases contracted on the *Amistad*. Two extradition trials became a cause célèbre for the abolitionists. Almost immediately upon hearing about the Africans' capture, the anti-slavery society established an *Amistad Committee*, spearheaded by two wealthy and devout New York merchants named Lewis and Arthur Tappan, who soon acquired the legal skills of three lawyers, including Roger Sherman Baldwin, another abolitionist and later Governor of Connecticut. The fate of the Africans hinged on the relevance of U.S./Spanish treaties, maritime laws, personal property claims, and the natural laws of civilization. Both Queen Victoria of England and Queen Isabella of Spain became embroiled in the legal maneuverings.

Meanwhile, there was an ongoing search for someone who spoke Mende. This was for two reasons. First, it would enable the Africans to tell their side of the story; and second, it would allow the abolitionists to Christianize the Africans. Finally, the defense team located James Covey, an ex-slave who spoke Mende, and who had been raised by missionaries, and was now a seaman aboard a British war ship anchored in New York City. Covey obtained leave to act as an interpreter for the defense team. But the defense teams' problems increased considerably when President Martin Van Buren insisted that the Africans be returned to Cuba, regardless of the merits of their case, because he was convinced that a victory for the Africans would hurt his 1840 re-election bid, and also lead the nation further towards Civil War.

There were at the time more than two-and-half-million slaves in the United States, and slaves continued to be smuggled into the country until 1862. Consequently, Van Buren, also known as 'The Little Magician,' initiated an executive conspiracy with John Forsyth, his Secretary of State, to see that every decision in the Africans' favor was appealed. [The following information might make you feel good: Van Buren lost his re-election bid between the time the case was being tried in the lower courts, and the time it was headed towards the United States Supreme Court.]

Although John Quincy Adams, former President of the United States and now a Congressman from Massachusetts, showed an early interest in the proceedings, he only agreed to take an active role in the case when it was headed for the Supreme Court. Adams, nicknamed "Old Man Eloquent," was reluctant to take the case because he was seventy-three years old, burdened by his work as a Congressman, and it had been more than thirty years since he had argued before the Court.[15] Moreover, Adams had his problems with the Supreme Court of 1841. He had appointed no sitting justice, while President Andrew Jackson had appointed five; and President Martin Van Buren, two. Furthermore, five of the nine Justices were from slave states.[16]

On February 22, 1841, the litigation came before the United States Supreme Court, in what some historians call "The Trial of the Presidents." The arguments continued for four days. One justice from a slave state was ill and did not hear the case, thus the bench was divided when "Old Man Eloquent" began his delivery. He spoke on the first day for four-and-one half-hours. [My speech is not that long]. In his forceful and sarcastic address, Adams attacked the administrations' shameful role as Spain's agent. "We had offered," he said, "not justice to these poor, unfortunate, helpless, and defenseless Africans, but sympathy to their oppressors. Sympathy with the white, antipathy for the black." Before he could resume his arguments the next day, an Associate Justice from Virginia died. Now the court was tipped in Adams' favor.[17] After a week of mourning, "Old Man Eloquence" resumed his arguments on March 1, and here he spoke for another four hours, before he rested his case for the defense. The decision was rendered eight days later, six to one in favor of the Africans.[18] The Court denied the restitution claims of the Spanish government, but it remained silent on the institution of slavery. Once and for all, however, they declared the Africans free men. Meanwhile, a British warship destroyed the slave force at Lomboko.

Everyone of the surviving thirty-five *Amistads*; four more were now dead from disease and one by presumed suicide; decided that they wanted to return to their homeland, but President John Tyler, who became president after President William Henry Harrison's death, refused to provide a ship to take the *Amistads* home, and they became the wards of the New England Missionaries. In order to raise money for their return voyage, the Africans created a traveling program putting on dances and dramatizations. It is generally believed that the missionaries were reluctant to send the *Amistads* home until they had been properly Christianized.

Finally, on November 27, 1841, the *Amistads* and five missionaries sailed out of New York Harbor aboard the *Gentlemen*. Two months later, they arrived in Sierra Leone. Although the American Missionary Association met with little success on the windward coast, it did become the source of hundreds of African American schools and colleges in the United States. As for Sengbe, he never saw his family or friends again. His village had been destroyed either by tribal warfare or the population taken into slavery. Not much else is known about him except that he died in 1879, thirty-seven years after he returned to Africa.

Now it should not be difficult to imagine the appeal that *La Amistad* and *The Amistad Affair* had for Debbie Allen. She saw not only its relevance to contemporary divisive racial problems, but also it provided her the opportunity for revising Hollywood's negative legacy on African Americans. For nearly fifty years, movies reflected the derogatory stereotypes inherited from the stage and plantation literature of fat mammies and docile Uncle Toms, of tragic mulattos and dancing clowns, and of savage and brutal bucks. Not many people here today remember that there was once a time in American movies when Africans were placed strategically within a film, so that their image could be cut out by the exhibitor if the image was too offensive to an audience. A film about *The Amistad Affair* would allow the public and experts to gauge just how far the American film industry had grown since its earliest depictions of slavery, from the various versions of *Uncle Tom's Cabin* beginning in 1903, to *The Birth of a Nation* in 1915, to *Gone With the Wind* in 1939, and *Song of the South* in 1946. *Amistad* would show a different picture of slavery.

More to the point, for an African American like Debbie Allen, in all of film history, there were no more than a handful of films about the slave trade itself, beginning with the 1937 film *Slave Ship*. The plot, adapted to the screen by no less a writer than William Faulkner, featured a slave ship captain trying to get out of the slave trading business, because of his love for his new bride. The first slave ship film I remember watching was the 1959 film, *Tamango*. This problematic French film had the light-skinned Dorothy Dandridge playing the refined mulatto mistress of a white captain of a slave ship bound for Cuba. Gradually, she develops a racial consciousness and becomes part of the African's conspiracy to mutiny. You should note that both *Slave Ship* and *Tamango* focused on romantic conventions, much the way *Titanic* in its fictional elements, focused on a love affair involving class warfare.

The next two movies were revisionist films coming out of the civil rights movement. The 1969 film *Slaves*, and the 1970 film *Mandingo*. As one writer noted about these films, "Finally, black audiences could experience the catharsis of seeing a slave rise up against the white power structure." But even these films exploited confrontation between the races, and seemed simply to trade one stereotype for another. In the place of the child like fool, we had the noble savage, who threatened to sexually conquer the white master's woman.

"It's as if," as one author explained, "Hollywood has two essential themes. Slaves were either passive clowns, to be treated like children; or they were insurrectionists to be feared for their physical and sexual power." In essence, the industry always seemed to be saying, "Blacks can be patronized, ignored or feared, but never, never be empowered." Again, Allen hoped to change that point of view with *Amistad*.

And there was yet another significant problem with historical films dealing with blacks and whites. From mainstream movies like *Intruder in the Dust*, and *To Kill a Mockingbird*, to recent works like *Mississippi Burning* and *The Ghosts of Mississippi*; there was the overriding perception that "repressed" African Americans required the guidance and assistance of whites to achieve liberation from racist tyranny.[19] These were just a few of the concerns facing Allen and her thirteen-year struggle, going from studio to studio to studio to get *Amistad* made. She described her ordeal as "heart wrenching." Allen remembers that there was no one shy about rejecting the film. "This is, it's not really an important story," they'd say. "Nobody's interested in some revolt on a slave ship."

One of the smartest things she did, however, was to option Harvard historian William Owens' novel, *Black Mutiny*, written in 1953. For a paltry two hundred and fifty dollars, she would, as we will see, save her project ten million dollars. It is significant that Allen realized the necessity to option a book on *The Amistad Affair* even though the story was recounted in a number of historical documents. The fact that author Alex Haley had recently been sued for plagiarism on *Roots* may have had an impact on her thinking. She knew, as film insiders well know, that plagiarism suits are as popular in Hollywood as cows are in Vermont. For that matter, Spielberg has been sued on almost every film he has ever made, receiving over a hundred and twenty lawsuits for *ET* alone.

The turning point came in 1994, when Debbie Allen saw

Schindler's List, and decided that Steven Spielberg was the man to do *Amistad*. Although Spielberg had heard of *The Amistad Affair* from several sources, he was reluctant to do this particular historical drama, mainly because of his experiences making *The Color Purple;*[20] and the fact he felt there would be intense negative reaction to a white man doing an African American film. Debbie Allen's passionate appeal in her argument was we were *way* beyond those times; I want you to remember that line; we were *way* beyond those times, convinced Spielberg that maybe, maybe, he was wrong.

By the end of 1994, Spielberg agreed to produce and to direct *Amistad* if two major problems could be solved: one, locating an actor who could make Sengbe in his words "overwhelmingly believable;" and two, finding the right screenwriter. He found the performer Djimon Hounsou, an out-of-work actor and model from Africa, who was living and working in Paris. Finding the screenwriter was equally fortuitous. In 1995, the possibility of David Franzoni writing *Amistad* surfaced at DreamWorks, Spielberg's new studio. At the time, Franzoni was pitching another historical screenplay, this one about Montezuma and Cortez, or as David says, "A story about two of the biggest bastards that ever lived." To move our story along, Franzoni got the assignment.[21] Both he and cinematographer, Janusz Kaminski, talked about the need for a rush job that had to be done on *Amistad*. Spielberg was fitting *Amistad* in between his last film, *The Lost World*, and his next project, *Saving Private Ryan*.

Now what about Franzoni's slant on the story?[22] The crucial element for the screenwriter was the relationship between Sengbe and John Quincy Adams. For Franzoni, the driving force in Adams' life was to keep his father's work, the creation of America, alive; and slavery was a despicable stain on that work. But Adams, in 1839, was in an impossible position. The way Franzoni explains it, the House of Representatives had created the gag rule, which was an instantaneous tabling of any issues concerning slavery. In other words, Adams was gagged over his opposition to slavery. Moreover, abolitionists were considered so fringe that Adams' association with them as former president might help shove the country towards Civil War. Thus the dilemma: Sengbe and the Africans needed to be free, and to free them Adams needed to argue before the Supreme Court. So Franzoni wrote the screenplay from this perspective, and he gave it to Spielberg.[23] But Spielberg was unsure of Franzoni. Remember Franzoni and Allen are the only two key outsiders on *Amistad*. Everyone else, the cinematographer, the set designer, the costumer, editor and musical director; they're all from *Schindler's List*. To assure himself of the script's merit, Spielberg gave the first draft to Steven Zaillian, his Oscar-winning screenwriter from *Schindler's List*.

Both Zaillian and Spielberg wanted *Amistad* to avoid some of the criticism leveled against *Schindler's List*. For example, the filmmakers were criticized for their allegedly sensationalized representation of the Holocaust, particularly the images of the women in the shower scene at Auschwitz. Thus when Spielberg depicts the wholesale rape of African women during The Middle Passage, he does it in a long shot and with a traveling camera. We also have to rely on our imagination to understand the anguish and the pain that motivates an African mother to kill her infant child and to commit suicide in shark infested waters, rather than endure any more suffering. In addition, the scene showing hundreds of enslaved naked Africans, chained together, never becomes sensationalized.

Then an incident occurs that would eventually contribute to the film's future problems. Although Spielberg had asked Franzoni to do seven rewrites over a yearlong period, Zaillian decided that he wanted to share credit with Franzoni on the script. The issue went to the Writers Guild Arbitration Board, who awarded Franzoni the sole credit, but in their report they insisted that Franzoni gave them the impression he had read Barbara Chase-Riboud's book. Although, and I quote from the report, "Although Mr. Franzoni never said at the hearing that he had read *Echo of Lions*."[24]

Now to the actual film. Having assumed responsibility for the film's historical credibility, Debbie Allen hired Mende expert, Dr. Arthur Abraham, from Sierra Leone, as a major consultant on issues of language. Other noted consultants were John Hope Franklin, Lerone Bennett, Jr., Howard Jones, and Henry Louis Gates, Jr.

Shooting began on February 18, 1997, and took approximately forty-eight days to be completed. Rather than beginning with the capture of Sengbe, now called Cinque, in Mendeland, Spielberg opens the film on a dark stormy night, when Cinque shackled on board the *Amistad*, leads a mutiny and murders all but two of the crew of the Spanish slave ship. In this way, Spielberg plays on white obsessions, fears, anxieties, and stereotypes, of a savage black man threatening to rise up and destroy Euro-Americans. Who is he? What is his story? From this point, through costumes, set design, music, lighting, composition, casting, editing, camera work, sound effects, make up, performance, and dialogue; all those elements on which movies should be judged and are not; we find out the worth of *Amistad*.

Spielberg reveals how the world discovered the truth about these kidnapped Africans, and the duplicity of the American and Spanish governments. Early on, we have a magnificent scene when the terrified Africans deceived by the Spanish slave traders, stare in amazement as an American vessel hosting a lavish dinner party passes them in the night. It emphasizes the point that it's as if the Africans and Americans come from two alien worlds. Another memorable scene has the black abolitionist, Theodore Joadson, going through a nightmarish experience on the *Amistad*, reminding us how differently an ex-slave feels about the case from a white lawyer. Still another marvelous scene has Cinque responding to the news that after winning two trials, the case has to be tried yet a third time before the United States Supreme Court. Ripping off his American clothes and throwing them into a roaring fire he asks, "What kind of place is this, where you almost mean what you say, where laws almost work? How can you live like this?" Still another unforgettable moment occurs when Adams recounts the African story before the Supreme Court. "And the proof is" Adams says, "the length to which a man will go to regain his freedom once taken. He will break loose his chains. He will decimate his enemies. He will try and try and try against all odds, against all prejudices, to get home."

And nothing, nothing in the film, matches the emotional impact when Cinque recounts his story, and we see the kidnapping, the barbaric behavior of the whites, and the cruelty of The Middle Passage. *New York Magazine*'s David Denby is eloquent in describing his reactions: "Spielberg" he says, "stages these scenes with a power that perhaps he alone in film history is capable of."[25]

For those of you who don't believe that the movies can stimulate the imagination because they show you what to think, there are episodes throughout the film that make you think and think again about the reasons why people did what they did. As Professor Glenda Dickerson says, when talking about the hardships of women during The Middle Passage: "What I think about as a woman," she said, "what I think about as a woman is the humiliation of it. I think about those women to whom cleanliness was an integral part of their being. To be subjected to the filth and the dirt, to have to lie in their own feces, to have to live among blood and vomit."

Never do we see a Cinque who is not sympathetic, courageous, and dignified.[26] What's more, careful attention is paid through sight and sound to remind us always of the Africans' longing for their homeland, their respect for their native traditions, their love for their families, and their indomitable spirit.

Cinematographer Kaminski, influenced by the paintings of Goya, with their dark and gloomy images, shoots the Africans in darkness. First, he says, in the nightmarish conditions of the slave ships and then in the damp dirty confines of the Connecticut jail. And almost always, he keeps the heroic Cinque visually separate from his peers. Rarely during the film are we ever free from hearing the sound of chains rattling or seeing the physical hardships of the prisoners. Kaminski noted that throughout the film Spielberg avoided the elaborate camera moves that had become one of his trademarks, opting instead for a proscenium-like film. "There are only three dolly moves in the entire film," Kaminski says. "We wanted to keep things very realistic, and big camera movements can sometimes distract from reality."

Clearly, the filmmakers took liberties with the historical record. After all, the events cover nearly three years. And there are fictional characters like the black abolitionists and the tormented Judge Bertram Coglin. Even so, argues *Newsweek*, "*Amistad* stays more true to the facts than most big budget historical dramas, and it manages to simultaneously echo modern day frustrations over the justice system and put a positive spin on the use of legal technicalities to advance larger causes."[27]

What is unique about *Amistad* in relation to history, and to previous movies about slavery, is that *Amistad* gives us the experience that makes the past painfully accessible. This is not to say it is a perfect movie. What work of art is? There are problems with performances and characterizations and incidents. Nevertheless, *Amistad* demonstrates why movies should be judged as movies, and how history can come alive through the conventions of film.

As *Amistad* was being edited, several events occurred that would influence its eventual reception by the critics and the public. On October 16, 1997, novelist Barbara Chase-Riboud, filed her ten-million-dollar suit to stop the release of *Amistad*, and created what *Variety* described, "A media frenzy." She charged the filmmakers with misappropriating dialogue, plot and characters from her historical novel, *Echo of Lions*. One of Chase-Riboud's major assertions was that she had created the notion of a black abolitionist for the *Amistad* defense team. She had created him.[28] By DreamWorks using the fictional black abolitionist Joadson, played by Morgan Freeman, Franzoni and Spielberg, Chase-Riboud claimed, infringed on her rights. Professor Howard Suber, an expert witness for the defense responded, "It would have been untenable for the filmmakers to have made *Amistad* for a modern audience without including at least one strong black male who worked on behalf of the African's freedom, especially since they showed Cinque captured by blacks. Besides, the film was aimed at African Americans as well as whites. In addition, there were a number of black abolitionists at the time. Each could have been the model for Joadson."

In a turnabout, DreamWorks sued Chase-Ribaud for plagiarizing *Black Mutiny*, written thirty-five years before her book, and cited eighty-eight questionable similarities. While admitting that *Black Mutiny* was consulted during the writing of *Echo of Lions*, Chase-Riboud denied using it as a basis for her book. DreamWorks won the first round. On December 8, 1997, two days before *Amistad* was set to open, U.S. District Court Judge Audrey Collins ruled that there is little likelihood Chase-Riboud's suit could prove its claims. But Chase-Riboud had gained the high ground in the public's eye. She was proving that in Hollywood, perception is often more powerful than truth.

In the months that followed, race became a central issue in the critical debate over the source of *Amistad*. Typical of the problem was the exchange by DreamWorks's attorney Bert Fields, who admonished Chase-Riboud for not embracing the film; and of Chase-

Riboud's lawyer, Pierce O'Donnell, who lashed back, "I don't know where a white male gets the nerve, the gall, to tell a black woman writer that she should be happy that Steven Spielberg resurrected the Amistad." It was under this storm that the film opened in New York and Los Angeles on December 10, 1997. It then went into limited release two days later.

Now we turn from the external factors affecting the film's reception to the reception itself. By the end of 1997, *The Los Angeles Times* was reporting the film was doing respectable business. Fifty percent from African American audiences, according to DreamWorks, but that the movie was not living up to the public's expectations. The main complaints were about "The film's veracity, and about Spielberg, indeed any white man as the director." Particular attention was paid to how the black community responded to the film. In Los Angeles, an African American periodical insisted that not only were black audiences not impressed with the movie, but they were, "Intensely negative, though not always in public." *The New York Amsterdam News*, however, proclaimed the film, "A towering [film] of saga heroism and courage, masterfully staged, choked with emotion, and filled with high drama." Stanley Crouch summed up the opinion of many African Americans when he said, "What we need are people who recognize that integrated teams have always been instrumental in the advancement of the country, from abolishing slavery to ending segregation. Blacks never did it alone."

On December 18, a second plagiarism suit was filed against Spielberg. This time as executive producer of the 1996 blockbuster hit, *Twister*.[29] Thus when everyone was handing out honors for the best film of the year, or considering nominations for major awards, Spielberg, his tainted film, and those associated with him, were in the pariah class.

Let me now turn to four major problems the film faced in addition to bad publicity. First, the film fails by being compared to *Schindler's List*. DreamWorks' greatest mistake, in my opinion, was in marketing *Amistad* as being similar to *Schindler's List*, especially in emphasizing how each film dealt with the same agonizing issues. The public mistakenly believed that Spielberg would do for the African experience what he had done for the Jewish Holocaust. But Spielberg long before had decided that *Amistad* would be about

American history, not just African history, and the courtroom was an essential part of that. Audiences never adjusted to the film they saw. They wanted something else because they felt they had been promised something else. And their disappointment gave the film bad word of mouth. The critics also joined in the attacks in the way that the studio publicists misrepresented the film. For example, *Washington Post* writer Courtland Milloy stated, "Spielberg and *Schindler's List* brought to life the existential terror of The Holocaust, and in a very dramatic form stayed focused on what the horrors of that situation were. In *Amistad*, the focus is on white lawyers." Not even a reviewer with the impact of *The Boston Globe's* Jay Carr could influence the public's negative reaction to the film. "Don't let anyone tell you," the critic said, "*Amistad* is just a dry history film. It's permeated by a thrilling level of conviction and commitment."[30]

Second problem: is it right a white man should produce and direct a film mainly about the black experience? Here it did no good to remind people that being Jewish did not help Spielberg with the critics of *Schindler's List*, or being black did not help Spike Lee with those who attacked *Malcolm X*. The feeling among certain segments of the population was that African Americans had to be, "In control of their own stories, just like their own destinies." As one black critic said: "I'm not saying that Spielberg isn't capable of making a decent film about blacks. What I'm saying is that blacks should be given the first chance at their own story." A West African periodical put the issue more strongly: "So whose story is *Amistad* anyway? If the truth be told, it is universal. And as such, it is as much the white man's story as it is ours, for it was Caucasian arrogance and savagery that made the story possible. It was the white man's moral turpitude that provided the glue for the drama of the insurrection. For the sake of profit, white people deliberately mistook other human beings for beasts of burden. But these beasts of burden spoke when Cinque unleashed the rebellion, and taught the world the lesson and the fundamentals of freedom."

And of course there were the charges that Franzoni feared; that *Amistad* was going to be criticized as just one more story of righteous whites riding to the rescue of imperiled blacks. But Spielberg also had his defenders. "Despite its flaws," wrote one sympathetic reviewer, "*Amistad* is a bold step forward compared to many of the slave stories made popular in years past." And *Time's* critic Richard Schickel made the important point, "In our own age, with democracy travestied by ethnic and interest group politicking, the most instructive thing about *Amistad* may lie in its demonstration that a broad principle, shrewdly advanced, can find ways to assert itself amidst factional clamor."[31]

As for me, I believe that it takes money and talent and courage and power to make movies. In an ideal world there would be enough for minority artists and women directors to make these issues irrelevant, but given where we are, I think *Amistad* was damn lucky to have both Debbie Allen and Steven Spielberg shepherding the project.

The third problem: how accurate is *Amistad*? As I've said earlier, the film does take poetic license with a number of characters and incidents. But I believe that there is something inherently troublesome in being part of what Robert Sklar describes as "The accuracy police, the historians; whose primary job it is to identify a film's fabrications, inaccuracies, manipulations, and distortions."[32] Like Sklar and a number of other film historians, I believe in keeping our attention focused more on a film's stylistic and aesthetic elements and less on its plot summaries.

Let me be very clear on this point because I don't want to be misunderstood. I believe that historical accuracy is very important. I have to. Some of my closest friends are historians. But I also believe the best historical films present the past through creative film techniques that do justice to historical accuracy. But for those who think that that may be begging the issue, I refer you to Howard Jones, the recognized authority on *Amistad*. In his judgment, films always have fabrications, but he has no quarrel with such liberties; in his words: "So long as they do not change the essential truths of the story." What about the accuracy of *Amistad*? Jones says it passes his criteria. It shows among other things, the uniqueness of blacks being kidnapped in Africa, brought to America, tried by American justice, freed, and returned to Africa. It demonstrates the manner in which blacks and whites cooperated with each other to achieve freedom. It portrays Sengbe as a noble human being who did not seek leadership, but embraced it heroically once it was forced upon him. It illustrates the greed and cruelty that encouraged slavery even after it had been outlawed. It reminds us of how the Founding Fathers never resolved the conflict between freedom and slavery. It illustrates how Americans tried to resolve that conflict within the law rather than outside it. It demonstrates the importance of effective communication in resolving our racial differences, and it shows us that politics can create as many problems as it solves. In Jones words, "The fabricated parts of this movie do not change the basic thrust of the truth."

Finally we turn to the plagiarism suits themselves. On February 9, 1998, the day before the Oscar nominations, DreamWorks and director Steven Spielberg won their case against Barbara Chase-Riboud. It was Spielberg's second plagiarism victory in two weeks. In the prior case, a St. Louis Federal Court had ruled against the Missouri screenwriter who had sued Spielberg. Now, after all the attacks that Chase-Riboud had made upon the character of Spielberg and David Franzoni, of having in her words, "brazenly stolen" her ideas to create *Amistad*, she issued the following public statement: "After my lawyers had a chance to review the DreamWorks files and other documents and evidence, my lawyers and I concluded that neither Steven Spielberg nor DreamWorks did anything improper. I think *Amistad* is a splendid piece of work, and I applaud Mr. Spielberg for having the courage to make it."

In summary, I believe that *Amistad* never received the recognition it deserves, and that there's plenty of blame to go around for why that happened. As I've tried to demonstrate, I admire this film because it raises our consciousness about our past, and offers us hope for the future. And because it reminds us how far we've come and how much further we have to go. Thank you for your patience.

Notes

[1] Two important points regarding this essay. First, I thought it was lost. No copies could be found. Then Ms. Shelley Barbour, a former student and a friend, discovered a tape made by her father of the talk. She then proceeded to transcribe it superbly. For that I owe her a great debt of gratitude. But it is still a speech, and it needed tweaking from time to time to appear in its present form. I have also had considerable difficulty in locating the sources of some of the quotations.

² Key works relied upon for this presentation includes William A. Owens, *Black Mutiny: The Revolt on the Schooner Amistad*. New York: Plume Book, 1953; Mary Cable, *Black Odyssey: The Case of the Slave Ship Amistad*. New York: Penguin Books, 1971; Howard Jones, *Mutiny on the Amistad: The Saga of a Slave Revolt, and Its Impact on American Abolition, Law, Diplomacy*. Revised Edition. New York: Oxford University Press, 1987; and Iyunolu Osagie, "Historical Memory and a New National Consciousness: The Amistad Revolt Revisited in Sierra Leone," *Massachusetts Review* 38 (Spring 1997): 63-83.

³ http://www.nobelprize.org/nobel_prizes/literature/laureates/1949/faulkner-speech.html

⁴ Robert Brent Toplin, *History By Hollywood: The Use and Abuse of the American Past*. Champaign: University of Illinois Press, 1996.

⁵ Ibid.

⁶ Ibid.

⁷ Ibid.

⁸ Janet Maslin, "Pain of Captivity Made Starkly Real," *New York Times* (December 10, 1997).

⁹ Joseph C. Terry, "Amistad," *Oprah*. USA: Harpo Studios, December 1997; David Ansen and Allison Samuels, "Amistad," *Newsweek* 130:23 (December 8, 1997): 60; and Claudia Puig and Andy Seiler, "In Hollywood, ideas are worth fighting for; Amistad suit just one of many disputes," *USA Today* (December 9, 1997): 1A.

¹⁰ I spoke with the Assistant Manager at the Merrill's Nickelodeon Theater in Burlington, Vermont, on January 23, 1997, about the film. He said the deal with the Hoyts Theatre chain and DreamWorks was no advertising. Because *Amistad* was doing poorly across the country, they would spend no more money on marketing. The reason he gave for the film's poor reception included subject matter, violence, and too much "thinking" involved.

¹¹ Two important films used by me in preparing this talk were by director Christien Harty Schaefer: "Ship of Slaves: The Middle Passage," The History Channel. US: DreamWorks, 1989; and "The Making of Amistad," Supplementary Materials, *Amistad* DVD, 1999.

¹² *Amistad*. New York: Random House, 1970.

¹³ Invaluable in this section is Armond White, "Against the Hollywood Grain," *Film Comment* 34:2 (Mar/Apr 1998): 34-42.

¹⁴ Interestingly, UVM Professor Don Grinde, has information that three or four of the *Amistads* as they were now called, went ashore for preserves, and, rather than going back to the ship, escaped to the Shinnecock Indian Reservation, the oldest Indian territory in America, about 1700.

¹⁵ Theo Lippman, Jr., "Trial was longer in movie, *Amistad*," *Baltimore Sun Journal* (December 18, 1997): 2A.

16 Eric McKitrick, "JQA: For the Defense," New York Review (April 23, 1998): 53-58.
17 Bruce Fein, "As the Amistad edict evolved," Commentary (December 31, 1997): A15.
18 Lippman, Jr., 2A.
19 Eric Gutierrez "News Analysis: The Politics of Filmmaking," New York Times (December 25, 1997): F62.
20 White, Pp.36, 42.
21 Puig, .1A.
22 Robert J. Elisberg, "E-Mail Interview with David Franzoni," WGA 1997. 4 Pp.
23 Eller, D1.
24 The following material helped in my discussion of the plagiarism charges against Spielberg: United States District Court: Barbara Chase-Riboud, Plaintiff, Vs. DREAMWORKS, INC., et al, Defendants: CASE NO: CV 97-7619 ABC (Jgx); Barbara Chase-Riboud, Echoes of Lions. New York: William Morrow, 1989; William A. Owens, Black Mutiny; Frank Rich, "Who Stole History?" New York Times (December 13, 1997): A15; Todd Williams, "Troubled History," Premiere (January 1998): 54-56; and Claudia Eller and James Bates, Company Town: Despite 'Serious Questions' Judge To Let 'Amistad' Open," Los Angeles Times (December 9, 1997): D1.
25 David Denby, "Cry Freedom," New York (December 15, 1997): 1-4.
26 William Wells Brown, "Joseph Cinque," The Black Man: His Antecedents, His Genius, And His Achievements. Boston: James Redpath, 1863. Kraus Reprint Company, 1969. 124-128.
27 David Ansen and Allison Samuels, "The Long Shadow of Slavery," Newsweek 41: 23 (December 8, 1997): 60.
28 Puig, 1A.
29 Robert W. Welkos, "Company Town: Another Author Challenges Spielberg," Los Angeles Times (December 18, 1997): D6.
30 Jay Carr, "Bold And Brutal 'Amistad' A Powerful And Compelling Work," Boston Globe (December 26, 1997).
31 Richard Schickel, "Amistad," Time 150:25 (December 15, 1997): 108.
32 Robert Sklar, "Historical Films: Scofflaws and the Historian-Cop," Reviews in American History 25:2 (June 1997): 346-350.

14. Tom Jeffords (James Stewart) tries to convince the great Chihuicachui warrior Cochise (Jeff Chandler) to make peace with white settlers. Delmer Daves, *Broken Arrow* (1950).

12. Now That the Buffalo's Gone

[A] Cardinal rule: the American filmmaker has always been interested in creating fiction rather than reality. For better or worse, the Hollywood director is an entertainer; he is in the business of telling stories. He is therefore saddled with conventions and stereotypes, formulas and clichés, and all these inventions were updated in great genres. This was the very foundation of the studio system. Audiences loved genre pictures, and the old masters never seemed reluctant to provide them.[1]

Martin Scorsese

We are a ferocious animal. We humans are a terrible animal. Here in Europe, in Africa, in South America, everywhere .... We are extremely violent. Our history is a history of wars. It's an endless story, a story of repression, a tale of madness.[2]

Sebastião Salgado

Without love, without a cause we are nothing. We stay because we believe. We leave because we are disillusioned. We come back because we are lost. We die because we are committed.[3]

Jesus Raza (Jack Palance)

If ever a chapter concerning my teaching career clarifies my passion for screen education, it is this one on the Western film genre and its destructive images of Native Americans. My reasons are straightforward. Starting in my youth, movies performed a major role in defining who I was, how I acted, and what I understood about my nation's history. Those were the days when orthodox filmmakers persuaded me life was simple and uncomplicated. People were right or wrong, good or bad. My problems could be solved, justice would triumph in the end, and the best things in life were free. No Hollywood formula proved more supportive of those naïve attitudes than the stirring stories about cowboys and Indians, the Saturday matinee horse operas, and the epic melodramas about settling and winning the American West.

Every time I think about those early years, I recall how my dear mother was keeping me occupied and out of trouble, before I even started watching movies at the age of four, by buying me David Cory's *Little Indian* series.[4] Long before I read James Fenimore Cooper's classic *Leatherstocking Tales* and followed Natty Bumppo with his Indian friend Chingachgook on their pathfinding adventures, I was filling my head with romances describing the simple but amazing childhood of the imaginary Red Feather. In each of the several volumes I read about this "noble savage," who remained untainted by "civilization" and embodied humanity's most desired virtues. I was absorbed by how he learned to trap and to fish, to find religion, to grow into a brave manhood, and eventually to marry the beautiful Star Maiden. Of course, I don't remember any specific details, only that I devoured the stories and couldn't wait for the next book to arrive.

Deepening my fascination with the make-believe west were the movies and the radio shows (later television adaptations) that continually captivated me with their gripping exploits: the likes of O. Henry's The Cisco Kid (Warner Baxter) and Lopez (Cesar Romero); Stephen Slesinger and Fred Harman's Red Ryder (Don 'Red' Barry) and his youthful Indian partner, Little Beaver (Robert Blake); Zane Grey's masked Texas lawman known as The Lone Ranger (Robert Livingston) and his faithful Indian companion, Tonto (Victor Daniels); Clarence E. Mulford's fictional hero Hopalong Cassidy (William Boyd) and his sidekick, Windy (George "Gabby" Hayes); Roy Rogers (Leonard Franklin Slye), billed as the "King of the Cowboys," and his several partners; and Gene Autry (Orvon Grover Autry), "the singing cowboy." In the decades to follow some of the actors would change in these classic roles, but never the energizing escapades. Making my life even sweeter in those thrilling days of yesteryear were the double features and the "B" westerns at the local movie theaters.

The late thirties and mid-forties were also the time of famous directors, who were seen as "experts" on the American West: Cecile B. DeMille, Henry Hathaway, Michael Curtiz, Raoul Walsh, King Vidor, and John Ford. From them I discovered an awe-inspiring image of the western frontier, one encompassing many nations, religions, and agendas. While there might be a handful of fictional visionaries and noble savages, the "real" western towns were populated with prostitutes, drunkards, gamblers, shady lawyers, corrupt politicians, and crooked saloon owners. Powerful landowners, who callously controlled politics in town, appointed dishonest sheriffs to manage local revolts. I was inspired, however, by the honest folks who somehow managed to find a reluctant hero like Owen Wister's Wyoming ranch hand known simply as the Virginian (Joel McCrea) to help the timid citizens overthrow the villains and bring law and order to their chaotic community.

Now and then, in my impressionable imagination, vicariously riding the Overland stagecoach to Lordsburg, New Mexico, I encountered society's social outcasts—e.g., an ex-Confederate soldier and gambler, a fallen woman with a heart of gold, a well-meaning alcoholic doctor, and a fearless fugitive from justice—and found them more admirable than the "respectable people" who marginalized them. I learned that bank thieves and train robbers like the murderous Frank and Jesse James who once rode with the notorious William Quantrill's Confederate guerrillas were more victims than desperadoes. And I became intrigued with the conflicting accounts surrounding New Mexico's Lincoln County Wars, where John Simpson Chisum, a God-fearing, hardworking cattle baron who helped move beef northwards with Charles Goodnight and Oliver Loving, was fighting corrupt businessmen such as James Doolan and Laurence Murphy. The soon-to-be–deceased rancher managed, however, to find a defender in a mixed-up youngster named William H. Bonny (Billy the Kid), who was friends with Sherriff Pat Garrett, who eventually killed the Kid for reasons I never fully understood. Curiously appearing in these absorbing tales, somewhere in the background were humiliated Mexicans, Blacks, Chinese, and Native Americans, all consigned to minor roles and inserted periodically into shameful situations. If nothing else, these original films encouraged in me not only counter culture values, but also they made a good case for cultural diversity.

So it was these colorful, rousing stories, filled with violence and action and adventure awakened my love for American history. But they also made me intellectually lazy. It never occurred to me to question our conventional wisdom about how we conquered a continent and forged a new nation. I had no reason to think historical films might be only half-true, let alone harmful. Thus, these unassuming movies and many others like them familiarized me with the mythologized breadth and scope of the American West: brave man and vicious renegades, trappers and mountain men, the U.S. cavalry and raiding Indian warriors, courageous pioneers and ill-fated wagon trains, pony express riders and stagecoach drivers, cattlemen and sheepherders, corrupt Indian agents and dishonest politicians, lonely settlements and isolated military outposts, boom towns and gold rushes, as well as idealistic immigrants, overzealous missionaries, morally bankrupt fortune hunters, and greedy magnates; all moving westward across the North American continent, all in search of a new start, a quick buck, a personal empire; all struggling against an iconic landscape as treacherous as it was magnificent. I reveled in watching those fast-moving cinematic tales showing how we survived during the French and Indian War, won our independence from the British, explored the wilderness west of the Mississippi, defeated the Mexicans, clashed with our brothers in the Civil War, built the Transcontinental Railroad, wiped out the Hole-in-the Wall gang, subdued the Native American tribes of the Great Plains, and finally annexed the great Northwest.

In hindsight, I'm intrigued by what I did and did not discover about Native Americans from the westerns of my youth.[5] By the time I was in high school, for example, Hollywood, never my teachers, had made me familiar with the names of various tribes—e.g., Pueblo, Sioux, Seminole, Cherokee, Kiowa, Iroquois, Comanche, Nez Perce, Arapahoe, Cheyenne, Muscogee, Chickasaw, Navajo, Mohican, Algonquin, Shawnee, Choctaw, Huron, Creek, Seneca, Shoshone, and Apache—, but I didn't have a clue what part of the country they lived in, what wars they fought against Euro-Americans, just how long some of the struggles had been going on, and what their "real" gripe was with the white settlers and the military, other than everyone was fighting fiercely for control over vast, unoccupied lands and for their cultural, economic, and political survival. Nothing wrong in that I thought. Everyone was motivated by what he believed in. I matter-of-factly assumed most of these nomadic warrior tribes were "primitive" and needed to be brought willingly or not into the New World's growth and civilization; next I believed the Native Americas represented serious obstacles to our manifest destiny. And on rare occasions, I saw these uncivilized people as tragic victims of broken promises, lawless settlers, a racist military, and dishonest bureaucrats.

My views changed with each new epic drama released by the moviemakers. The mythmaking films also reminded me, however, that there were honest diplomats who meant what they promised to the peace-seeking Native Americans, but circumstances, greed, ambition, political reality, and human nature—e.g., land grants, gold rushes, religious fervor, obeying orders, and partisan compromises—made peace treaties meaningless. And as I matured, I became revolted by what I saw in revisionist films showing what was happening to Native Americans on their mandated reservations because of government incompetence, shady agents, and thoughtless troopers: disease, starvation, physical and cultural abuse, depression, and widespread poverty. More often than not, sensitive screenwriters reminded me of the massacres at Sand Creek, the Washita River, the Little Big Horn, Mountain Meadows, and Wounded Knee; as well as the tragic consequences resulting from the ill-fated commands of General George Armstrong Custer, Captain William J. Fetterman, and Lt. George Bascom.

Eventually, I came to know the names of some of America's most famous chiefs and the besieged women who humanized the Native American villages, all crusading personalities who battled against white injustice for hundreds of years but especially in the nineteenth century —e.g., Red Cloud, Black Hawk, Hiawatha, Sacagawea, Quanah Parker, Pocahontas, Tecumseh, Pontiac, Osceola, Black Elk, Black Kettle, Geronimo, Cochise, Tarza, Victorio, Sitting Bull, King Philip, Looking Glass, Lean Elk, Chief Joseph, Crazy

Horse, Spotted Elk, and Wovaka—, but I couldn't remember many of the specific battles they fought in, which they won, and how they lived or died.

At one time in my life, I actually thought the only U.S. military outfit warring against the Sioux was the Seventh Cavalry, and I never realized there were actually ten units on the frontier, made up mostly of ex-Confederate soldiers, Union officers, Irish and German immigrants, and fugitives from justice. The many westerns I watched growing up also kept me briefed about false Indian prophets, the inexperienced but brave West Point lieutenants, and ignorant senior military leaders who sadly knew next to nothing about Native American customs, values, and behavior.

Hundreds and hundreds of these escapist accounts also filled my head with cherished ideas about the American Dream: we were a new nation imbued with precious ideals about life, liberty, and the pursuit of happiness; we were all created equal; we were a country governed by just laws, and this land was the land of the free and the home of the brave. Sure, there were racist and sexist glitches in the stories, but we were also human; we made mistakes. Whatever evils we had in our society came from the degenerate actions of perverted individuals and not the system itself.

While attending my Brooklyn public schools, where I studied our whitewashed past, I was told by my hard-working parents not to question my teachers: "They know best." Consequently, I learned American history by painstakingly memorizing mimeographed lists, dates, and facts. But in the darkened theaters, on my own, I felt I actually experienced many of America's most important and scandalous events. The empathetic moving pictures made history come to life for me long before there was a *Night at the Museum* franchise. I hunted and trapped with Kit Carson, Daniel Boone, Jim Bridger, James "Jim" Bowie, and Davy Crockett; witnessed, alongside the legendary William F. "Buffalo Bill" Cody, the mighty buffalo herds thunder across the Great Plains, long before our coast-to-coast political leaders instituted an infamous national policy to slaughter the legendary animals; and I drove the Texas cattle herds along the Chisholm Trail. I was there when stoired buffalo hunters, Indian fighters, gunslingers, gamblers, and lawmen like Wyatt Earp, Doc Holiday, Bat Masterson, and Wild Bill Hickok brought law and order to Wichita, Laramie, Julesburg, Deadwood, Dodge, and Abilene.

Simply stated, I came away from my elementary school days in the mid-thirties to mid-forties believing education didn't have to be dull. With all its weaknesses and mistakes, Hollywood could make learning easy and fun; make us believe working hard insured success; true justice was blind to race, color, and gender; and the ends often justified the means!

But in the words of an old Irish song, "I've met some folks who say that I'm a dreamer, /and I've no doubt there's truth in what they say...But dreams don't last—Though dreams are not forgotten—And soon I'm back to reality...."[6] As I grew into adolescence, the film industry underwent dramatic upheavals (more of which in future chapters). After World War II, filmmakers insisted Hollywood discard its out-of-date conventions to take much-needed moral stands on discrimination in America. Hardly a week went by when some new film like Elia Kazan's *Gentleman's Agreement* (1947; anti-Semitism against Jewish-Americans), or Alfred L. Werker's *Lost Boundaries* (1949; racism against African Americans); or John Sturges' *Bad Day at Black Rock* (1955; bigotry towards Japanese-Americans) didn't challenge what I believed true about American history and the traditional myths of the pre-war films.

The Westerns were just as much a target for the revisionists as the urban dramas. So it was revolutionary to me as I entered high school to see a progressive movie like Delmer Daves' *Broken Arrow* (1950) depict indigenous American people as misunderstood and mistreated by white settlers and the military.[7] Over the decade, I saw my naïve ideas on Native Americans fine-tuned by such wide-ranging films as George Sherman's *Battle of Apache Pass* (1951), William Castle's *Conquest of Cochise* (1953), John Farrow's *Hondo* (1953), Budd Boetticher's *Seminole* (1953), Charles Marquis Warren's *Arrowhead* (1953), Robert Aldrich's *Apache* (1954), Douglas Sirk's *Tarza, Son of Cochise* (1954), Robert D. Webb's *White Feather* (1955), John Ford's *The Searchers* (1956), Richard Brooks' *The Last Hunt* (1956), and Ray Nazarro's *Apache Territory* (1958). But as scholars remind me, these movies may have increased my perspective but their superficial approach to the issues left the conservative film industry and many false myths about the past still center-stage. The closest the movies ever got me to contemporary Indian issues, as my colleagues document, was Michael Curtiz's *Jim Thorpe-All American* (1951).[8]

I cannot stress enough how these "social problem" films[9] affected me. They made an even greater impact when the filmmakers put the nation's political differences into the mix. In my 1971 young adult book, *Cameras West*, where I offered an overview of the ties between Hollywood and American history, I recalled how both liberal artists and I lost our innocence because of films like Fred Zinnemann's *High Noon* (1952) and Howard Hawks' *Rio Bravo* (1959). The former not only reevaluated the traditional images of frontier people but also covertly acted out screenwriter Carl Forman's problems with the House Un-American Activities Committee and the public's unwillingness to come to his aid. Making the story even more dramatic for me was the fact Gary Cooper, who had appeared as a friendly witness before HUAC, now starred as a disillusioned sheriff opposed to the Committee's values. *Rio Bravo* gave me director Hawks' views on why *High Noon* was "a foolish picture," and the movie had the iconic John Wayne point out a more positive view of American behavior.[10]

By the time I entered college in 1953, I had become deeply disturbed by the serious flaws preserved and prolonged in traditional movie myths about United States history. I had moved away from my childish beliefs and realized many ethnic Americans are sometimes not only treated unequally and unfairly, but also that this pattern had been established by our traditional politics. Our Presidents told terrible lies and did awful things. Might often triumphed over right. Not all laws were good. Working hard and following the rules did not insure success. Telling the truth wasn't always smart.

Most important, therefore, challenging my teachers was anything but imprudent or inappropriate. Just the opposite was true. Unless we opposed the misguided educators and their false facts, we would not only remain ignorant about our past but also carry the lies forward. (I have a lot more issues with public education, but these examples should suffice.)

So I began thinking more seriously about the Hollywood products I had consumed uncritically; I started examining more closely the messages and motives of the profit-driven movie business [and later the television industry's lucrative philosophies]. I took more notice of what was said and what was missing from the silver screen's accounts of America's westward movement. I began to probe the emotional and intellectual injury, initiated intentionally or accidentally, that these terribly dishonest adventures did to me by creating a false sense of reality concerning our checkered history. I now became apprehensive that what I took away from the entertainment world was not what I thought I had taken away.

But I also found out something equally troubling: these distorted chronicles about American history and their embedded ethnic stereotypes had their roots in our nation's long-standing popular literature and dramas, in our history books and journals, and in our music and magazines. I sadly came to the conclusion we learned these falsehoods not from bigots, glutons, and extremists but from the very people we trusted most: parents, clergy, friends, entertainers, and educators.

Appropriately, many of these alarming, deluded, and hateful assumptions about outsiders, nations, and cultural values now became a major focus of my academic pursuits. In the transformation I re-evaluated these widespread and enduring out-of-date myths about our manifest destiny. I realized the "truth" was often tied to a white, male, elitist storyteller's perspective; I examined how unethical political leaders—e.g., Presidents Martin Van Buren, Andrew Jackson, and James K. Polk—used prevailing prejudices for their personal ambitions. Gradually, I also became fascinated with the "Real" American West and the rich legacy of nomadic North American Indian tribes.

As the movie industry evolved and grew more pervasive in the second half of the twentieth century, I watched in disbelief as the insupportable myths about our nation and its culture become even more prevalent than before in theaters and on television channels. Despite new research and an aroused intellectual community, the trusting public still remained apathetic and ignorant about the potential harm of these flawed media messages. I could not fathom how facts never bothered the misguided opinion makers. Now a film legacy of more than three-quarters-of-a-century became, for many viewers, nostalgic memories of "the good old days" when it didn't matter, for example, whether Native Americans were noble savages, vicious human beings, tragic reminders of our nation's social injustice, or vanquished impediments to America's progress. It didn't even matter if the Native Americans played themselves on screen. Who cared?

The ill-informed public continued to believe the so-called inconsequential movies were all part of our cultural amusements, harmless audio-visual dramas emotionally satisfying to watch and then easy to dispose of in intellectual trashcans. No harm done! It didn't matter that Native American leaders had railed against the cinematic and literary perversions of their resplendent heritage; it didn't matter that reliable information about the West became more readily available due to the Internet and social media; and it didn't matter that new documentaries and feature films appeared offering alternatives to the stereotypes of the past. Audiences justified their conduct by claiming such options were boring; public school teachers found them not worth their time and too old-fashioned for their texting students; overprotective parents insisted socially conscious teachers shy away from controversial issues and focus on just providing the essential, approved traditional curriculum. So most of the business people in the mass media moved on, insisting the subject provided them with no commercial benefits and offered no emotional appeal to a modern materialistic and technological society.

Probably one of the most disturbing realizations was that as a nation we had become woefully ignorant of our own history. Few people understood how dangerous being ill-informed was to our survival as a country. For example, *Newsweek* not long ago reported the negative effects of our historical illiteracy, and how it made effective governing difficult. "The problem is ignorance, not stupidity," Yale political scientist professor Jacob Hacker explained. "We suffer from a lack of information rather than a lack of ability. Whether that's a treatable affliction or a terminal illness remains to be seen. But now's the time to start searching for a cure."[11] It has also interested me what Wilcomb E. Washington, the former executive of the Smithsonian Institution, said about Gore Vidal's perspective in his *Screening History*: "…the history we believe we 'know' is the history presented in film. Vidal would prefer an earlier era when the novel conveyed the reality of the past, but he recognizes that this era cannot be recovered by either historians or novelists in a time when the public prefers to see—rather than read about—the past."[12] While I might find fault with Vidal's faith in literature and history books, I embrace his negative perspective on the influence of film in our society.

So, back in the days when I first decided to become an educational gadfly, I chose to war against the mental mess we were in. It was obvious the mass media was not mere entertainment.[13] I saw film and television, powerful forces for harm, just as capable of doing good. To me, these much discounted, trivialized, escapist products could just as easily function as dynamic weapons for helping us act intelligently and humanely in the modern world. Significant material could be found not only in what Dr. Garth Jowett pointed out long ago, the history on film, but also in the history in film. The former refers to historical motion pictures that attempt either to recreate or to preserve the memories of crucial events that changed our minds about the frontier and Native Americans, like the Battle of the Little Bighorn—e.g. Raoul Walsh's *They Died With Their Boots On* (1941),[14] Sidney Salkow's *Sitting Bull* (1954),[15] Joseph H. Lewis' *7th Cavalry*, (1956)[16] Arthur Penn's *Little Big Man* (1970),[17] as well as television films such as Norman Foster and Sam Wanamaker's *The Legend of Custer* (1968),[18] and Mike Robe's *Son of the Morning Star* (1991).[19] Such films directed our attention to the historical events.

History in film, however, discloses how the movies interact with society: how they reveal and move people in a particular time, place, and period of history. For example, what do these aforementioned films tell us about the changing attitudes toward Chief Sitting Bull, War Chief Crazy Horse, and Gen. George Armstrong Custer? How have we changed in our understanding of the 1867 Ft. Laramie Treaty, the Cheyenne nation's sacred Black Hills, the illegal stampede for gold in the protected Native American territory, and the "final solution" to the Indian problem set forth by Generals Philip H. Sheridan and William Tecumseh Sherman? How do we judge through the years the behavior of the men who carried out Sheridan's orders: Generals George Crook and Nelson A. Miles, Major Marcus Reno and Captain Frederick Benteen?

Just as vital to our national debate are differing perspectives about the widely accepted accounts of the massacres of Native

Americans. Were they actually carnages, or were they pitched battles between warring groups? As I wrote a quarter of a century ago, "History on film is justifiably scorned for its lack of insights, historical inaccuracies, and cheapening of national cultures, while history in film is gaining long overdue recognition for the historical value of its symbolic content and the conceptual framework imbedded in film characterizations, dialogue, settings, plots, props, sound effects, and themes."[20]

A major addition to these concerns occurred in 1973, when I got to meet and to interview such legendary individuals as actor Woody Strode and director John Ford.[21] Although I had seen Ford's ground-breaking *Sergeant Rutledge*,[22] the story of a dedicated black trooper (Strode) being unfairly court-martialed for raping and murdering a white woman, before killing her father didn't make a big impression on me. But talking to these two exceptional filmmakers completely turned me around. Now for the first time, I began thinking seriously about the tales of the legendary Buffalo soldiers, the Army's famous African American 9th and 10th Cavalry troops, shaped and posted at Fort Leavenworth and Fort Davis in the mid-1860s. It didn't hurt that the renowned battles of this overlooked western regiment dovetailed seamlessly with my other mushrooming academic interests about Hollywood and our collective consciousness.

Now, more than ever, I hoped once we grasped how film artists operate and affect mass audiences, the problem of audience neglect would be resolved. I thought the combined efforts of filmmakers like Sam Peckinpah, Robert Altman, Robert Redford, Kevin Costner, Michael Mann, and Clint Eastwood and their progressive westerns, as well as the brilliant documentary filmmaker Ken Burns and his stunning programs on the Civil War and the West, might change the way sleeping movie audiences related to movies and television. I expected independent films on current Native American issues like those exposed in Jonathan Wacks' *Powwow Highway* (1989), Lee Tamahori's *Once We Were Warriors* (1994), Chris Eyre's *Smoke Signals* (1998) and Zacharias Kunuk's *Atanarjuat: The Fast Runner* (2001) might prove more appealing to intellectually curious viewers.

I am embarrassed to admit that I actually believed if you just demonstrate to scholars, teachers, parents, politicians, the clergy, and the public in general that watching such allegorical movies carefully and considering what messages they were sending would convince onlookers not only to spend more time analyzing their movie-going experiences, but also the socially conscious productions would create a demand for more informed and entertaining films on the subject. Root out the propaganda, expose the distortions, and latch on to the affirmative. The means of how to do this would soon be taught in our classrooms. State Boards of Education would realize we could not operate competently as a society without discussing mass entertainment's inappropriate ideas about our past. It was too important to ignore, considering popular culture's massive influence on our mental health.

I was encouraged, moreover, by the shifts taking place in education and television.[23] For a while at the end of the twentieth century, I heard of teachers putting more films in their syllabi, offering multi-media courses like the ones I had advocated back in 1961 at New Rochelle High School with the film-book program, and in 1969 with the La Mancha Project at UVM. I grew excited over the efforts of television stations like The History Channel, the Arts and Entertainment network, and PBS to offer films, programs, and "talking heads" discussing historical issues and events. I welcomed enthusiastically the fact academic organizations were devoting panels and programs on the relationship between film and history. And nothing pleased me more than the attraction the subject had to many of my colleagues in the developing discipline of television and film studies.

"But dreams don't last—Though dreams are not forgotten—And soon I'm back to reality...."[24] I realized there were major obstacles to many of these welcomed endeavors: the programs often lacked the support of budget-minded school administrators, job-oriented students, and anti-mass media parents. Just as crucial was the failure of educational institutions to develop a much-needed audience for such activities. Going back over these issues now, I see how far we have come, but how very much further we need to go. With all due respect to director Martin Scorsese, whom I deeply admire, I see Hollywood filmmakers as much more than mere entertainers and storytellers; and the conventions, stereotypes, formulas and clichés they employ, to me, matter a great deal to the health and welfare of our collective consciousness. The rest, as you know, is the meat and potatoes of my academic journey.

Thus my focus in the pages that follow is on an article I wrote in the mid-nineties first for a film journal, then delivered as a paper at a national convention, before the piece eventually found its way as a chapter in a noted scholarly anthology.[25] This modest essay concerns the 1950 Hollywood western, Delmer Daves' *Broken Arrow*, and illustrates why this problematic film, rarely seen or remembered today (except perhaps by intellectuals, my students, and moviegoers having grown up in the immediate Post-World War II period) remained an indispensable artifact in my film classes over several decades. The article also reminds me of how I taught film criticism, how I matured slowly over the years, and of the critical genre itself and how it rode roughshod over conventional historical treatises.

Today the Indian haters may have mostly disappeared and contemporary audiences may have more progressive fables and fantasies about our past, but as you can tell from this intense introduction, I have my misgivings about what is still unknown about our history and about how far we have come in Native American-U.S. government relations. For example, director Oliver Stone strikes a responsive chord with me when he explains (and here I paraphrase), "When I was growing up in New York City, I thought I received a good education…not getting any better education than I did. I want more for my children and for the world in which I live: the tyranny of now, what is being neglected; history does have a meaning, many questions are not answered; [they] raise many problems, [it's] alright to debunk if not done with malice; [and I am] conscious of forgotten or overlooked heroes…A man isn't old until regrets take the place of his dreams."[26]

And there are the thoughts of author and book reviewer Jane Smiley in her 2015 critique of William T. Vollman's novels about Native Americans and the European's invasion and conquest of the West. She observes that when the novelist discusses Gen. Oliver Otis Howard's efforts to move the Nez Perce to a new reservation, "the issues of betrayal Vollmann raises have not gone away [and] is demonstrated by the fact that Congress recently voted to hand over Apache holy lands in Arizona to a copper-mining company."[27]

Is it any wonder then I still respond emotionally to the lyrics of the Canadian singer Buffy Sainte-Marie, when she cries over how Native Americans have "been mistreated and wronged," how treaties were signed and "broken again and again." Finally, I remain deeply saddened when she laments about the foolish notion, "Oh it's all in the past you can say/But it's still going on here today…It's here and it's now…/Now that the buffalo's gone.[28]

Notes

[1] Martin Scorsese, *A Personal Journey with Martin Scorsese Through American Movies*. England: British Film Industry, 1995; USA, 1996.
[2] Wim Wenders and Juliano Ribeiro Salgado, *The Salt of the Earth*. France: Decia Films, 2014.
[3] Richard Brooks, *The Professionals*. USA: Columbia Pictures, 1966.
[4] David Cory's stories started in 1934 and were published by Grosset and Dunlap. I believe I read at least four, if not more, of the ten books.
[5] Extremely helpful in shaping my comments about Native Americans are the 1991 TV program *The Great Indian Wars: 1540-1890*, a 5-part documentary series written by Marlene Carabello; and the TV documentary *Reel Injun* by Neil Diamond et. Al. Canada: Rezolution Pictures, 2010.
[6] "The Lake of Innisfree," Lyrics by Dick Farley.
[7] I have refreshed my memory by reading Michael Hilger, *Native Americans in the Movies: Portraits from Silent Films to the Present*. London: Rowman & Littlefield Publishing Group, 2016; Frank Manchel, *Cameras West*. Englewood Cliffs, N.J.: Prentice-Hall, 1971; George N. Fenin and William K. Everson, *The Western from Silents to the Seventies*. New York: Grossman, 1973; Raymond William Stedman *Shadows of the Indian*. Norman: University of Oklahoma Press, 1982; Will Wright, *Six Guns and Society*. Berkeley: University of California Press, 1975; Thomas Schatz, *Hollywood Genres*. Philadelphia: Temple University Press, 1981; Peter C. Rollins and John E. O'Connor, Eds. *Hollywood's Indian: The Portrayal of the Native American in Film, Expanded Edition*. Lexington: The University of Kentucky, 2003; Elizabeth Weatherford, senior author of "Native Americans on Film and Video," *The Native American Almanac: A Portrait of Native Americans Today*; Michael T. Marsden and Jack Nachbar, "The Indian in the Movies, "Wilcomb E. Washburn, ed. *History of Indian-White Relations*, Vol. 4. Washington: Smithsonian Institution. 1988; Duane Champagne, ed., "Chapter 13: Media," *The Native North American Almanac: A Reference Work on Native Americans in the*

United States and Canada. Detroit: Gale research Inc., 1994; and Jim Kitses, *Horizons West*. Bloomington: Indiana University Press, 1969.

[8] Peter Roffman and Jim Purdy. "Preface," *The Hollywood Social Problem Film: Madness, Despair, and Politics from the Depression to the Fifties*. Bloomington: Indiana University Press, 1981. 252-253.

[9] Social problem movies, as one study described them, were movies "with a point of view and a sense of social commitment; a genuine liberal concern, a need to say something significant about social and artistic achievement marshaling the resources of film to provide vivid commentary on the times." See Roffman and Purdy. "Preface," *The Hollywood Social Problem Film*, vii

[10] Frank Manchel, *Cameras West*. 126-130.

[11] James Fishkin quote in Andrew Romano, "How Ignorant Are Americans?" *Newsweek*, March 20, 2011.

[12] Wilcomb E. Washburn, "Forward," *Hollywood's Indian: The Portrayal of the Native American in Film, Expanded Edition*. XI.

[13] Frank Manchel, *Film Study: An Analytical Bibliography*, Vol. 1. 252-279.

[14] Raoul Walsh, *They Died With Their Boots On*. USA: Warner Bros., 1941.

[15] Sidney Salkow, *Sitting Bull*. USA: United Artists, 1954.

[16] Joseph H. Lewis, *7th Cavalry*. USA: Columbia Pictures Corporation, 1956.

[17] Arthur Penn, *Little Big Man*. USA: National General Pictures, 1970.

[18] Norman Foster and Sam Wanamaker, *The Legend of Custer*. USA: Twentieth Century-Fox Film Corporation, 1968.

[19] Mike Robe, *Son of the Morning Star*. USA: Preston Stephen Fischer Company, 1991.

[20] Manchel, *Film Study*, 254.

[21] Frank Manchel, "The Man Who Made the Stars Shine Brighter," *Every Step a Struggle: Interviews with Seven Who Shaped the African American Image in Movies*." Washington: New Academia Publishing, 2007. 355-441.

[22] John Ford, *Sergeant Rutledge*. USA: Warner Bros., 1960.

[23] Robert Brent Toplin, "Film and History: The State of the Union," *Perspectives* 37:4 (April 1999): 1, 8-9.

[24] "The Lake of Innisfree," Lyrics by Dick Farley.

[25] Peter C. Rollins and John E. O'Connor, Eds. *Hollywood's Indian*: Ix-xi.

[26] Oliver Stone, *Untold History of the United States*. USA: Ixtian Productions, 2012.

[27] Jane Smiley, "The Bluecoats Are Coming: William T. Vollmann's novel looks to the 1870s as westward expansion ignites the Nez Perce War," *New York Times Book Review* (August 2, 2015): 11.

[28] Buffy Sainte-Marie, "Now That the Buffalo's Gone." Lyrics Published by Lyrics ©Kobalt Music Publishing Ltd., Universal Music Publishing Group.

Cultural Confusion: A Look Back at Delmar Daves' *Broken Arrow* (1950)[1]

For many people, Hollywood's depiction of Native Americans in the Western film provides a moral gauge not only for the history of our nation but also for the film industry.[2] Nowhere is this more evident than in movies about the taming of the wilderness, where our modern mythmakers recount the fate of Native Americans, lumped all together, who stood in the way of Manifest Destiny.

Central to any revisionist approach is an awareness that the conflicts between Euro-Americans and Native Americans over the settling of the West began during the days of Columbus and not in the 1800s. For more than four hundred years, the two vastly different cultures engaged in a violent conflict that was predicated on radically different perceptions of the earth both wanted. As Haffner and Lusitania's television series *The Real West* points out, Native Americans never conceived of land in terms of ownership. They viewed it as "part of their family." Euro-Americans, on the other hand, "saw the continent as empty; by their perception, there were no cities or towns, no fences—the Indians were just another obstacle to be overcome in obtaining the land." This immense cultural disjuncture between whites and Indians established a formidable conceptual chasm that exists to the present.

Film scholars take different approaches to the theme of Native Americans in film. Their initial historical research highlighted how Hollywood typed, distorted, stereotyped, misrepresented, and patronized the American Indian. Often obscured were the roots of the conceptual conflict between the two cultures. Almost never did anyone raise the issue of why whites insisted on viewing the West as a wilderness that needed taming, or why it was to the white man's advantage to depict Native Americans as romanticized opponents who fiercely fought against our mass migration westward.[3]

At the end of the 1960s, a new generation of scholars avoided value judgments on the positive or negative depiction of American Indians and downplayed the film industry's historical, cultural, and political distortions. Their approach was to scrutinize the filmmakers responsible for the production of the formulaic conventions that embody the ethics and immorality of mainstream America (Aleiss, "Hollywood's Ideal," 54). Fair enough, but such scholarship sometimes minimizes the possibilities that integration, assimilation, and brotherhood were Euro-American ideas that euphemistically relieved whites of making legitimate concessions to Native American desires, rights, and values.

This essay examines one film, *Broken Arrow* (1950), to illustrate the critical differences between perception and reality. It explores the relationship between movies and society in a historical context. One useful way to make the comparison is suggested by Pierre Sorlin.[4] He identifies four criteria in selecting a film for historical analysis: "the originality of the film, its relationship to current events, its favorable reception by the public and the fact of its being produced and distributed during a time of crisis."[5] That is, by taking a commercial film that meets his criteria, one can recognize how it may serve to influence public opinion at a particular period in history and gauge how it holds up over time.

Few Westerns illustrate Sorlin's prerequisites more completely than Twentieth Century-Fox's production *Broken Arrow*.[6] Made in 1949 and released a year later, it came during crises both in America and in Hollywood. As the nation struggled with the problems of the Cold War, the resurgence of the Red Scare, urban blight, and social injustice, the film industry reeled from the breakup of the studio system, the advent of television, costly labor strikes, divisive blacklisting practices, and the "invasion" of foreign films into America's movie theaters. Hollywood resorted to many new approaches to break out of its box-office slump, including ones that would not antagonize audiences confused by conflicting demands for cultural diversity (Native Americans should be recognized for their ethnic heritage) versus assimilation (African Americans should be integrated into white society).

The relationship of *Broken Arrow* to these issues, especially in its groundbreaking efforts to promote tolerance and racial equality, is discussed in the major commentaries on the film. It is worth noting that when the film appeared, almost a quarter of all Hollywood movies made up to that time had been Westerns,[7] and that the film *Broken Arrow* was one of the first movie Westerns to be adapted into a television series.[8] By the start of the 1960s, at least twenty Western shows were shown each week in prime time on television.[9]

Knowing about *Broken Arrow*'s popularity with audiences and critics permits us to turn to the issues of content and reception. One important caveat is needed. I do not find historical inaccuracies irrelevant in films, especially ones that claim to be true accounts of events or personalities. Although we need to understand that some errors are less pertinent than others, what could be more foolish than to ignore how the creators of *Patton, Malcolm X, JFK,* or *Schindler's List* treated the accepted accounts of the events depicted in their biographical interpretations? If such works are influencing our national memories—and I think they are—then we need to appreciate what perspective is being presented and why.

Consider the book-film issue in *Broken Arrow*. Elliot Arnold's 1947 novel *Blood Brother* covers the years from 1855, when Euro-Americans settled in Arizona, to 1874, the year Cochise died.[10] The issue, for me, is not that the filmmakers—studio head Darryl F. Zanuck, producer Julian Blaustein, director Delmer Daves, and screenwriter Michael Blankfort—omitted half the novel and focused basically on the relationship between Tom Jeffords and Cochise. What is important is how that relationship is treated and what historical inaccuracies do to the film's approach.

Far more vital for this essay is the fact that the filmmakers and their marketing experts made a concerted effort to depict accurately the life-styles of the Apaches and the thinking of Euro-Americans during the post Civil War era in the Arizona. Our concern, therefore, is with what this film tells us about the Chiricahua Apache culture. How does Daves treat Cochise, Geronimo, Euro-American settlers, the prospects for peace between the two cultures, and the role of the U.S. government and the military during the Indian Wars?

Because other commentators have pointed to the movie's many flaws—for example, Native Americans speaking English, a romanticized culture, and whites taking Indian roles—this essay explores several key scenes dealing with Indian/white relations and the issue of peace between the Chiricahua Apache and the U.S. government. The intent is to compare what the film states and shows with omitted historical realities.

Broken Arrow begins with a long take of a parched Arizona landscape; the voice-over narrator, Tom Jeffords (James Stewart), tells us:

> This is the story of the land, of the people who lived on it in the year 1870, and of a man whose name was Cochise. He was an Indian, leader of the Chiricahua Apache tribe. I was involved in the story, and what I have to tell happened exactly as you will see it. The only change will be that when the Apaches speak, they will speak in our language. What took place is part of the history of Arizona. And it began for me here, where you see me riding. Since getting out of the Union army, I've been prospecting for gold off and on. One day I got a message that a new colonel had come to Tucson and wanted to see me.

Let's stop to consider both image and narration. The focus on the "land" is perfect: the history of White/Native American relations is tied to land ownership. But two interesting omissions result from the choice of the date, 1870. First, it allows the filmmakers to skip over the inconvenient fact that the Chiricahua Apaches had been fighting for more than sixty years with Spaniards, Mexicans, and Euro-Americans.[11] Equally important, this introduction makes Jeffords's traveling alone, at this point in American history, somewhat artificial, mainly because government policies encouraging the slaughter of the buffalo, allowing unlawful prospectors to mine for gold and silver on Indian reservations, and giving away "free" land to white settlers had started the nation's greatest westward migration. Second, in claiming that Cochise was "the" leader of the Chiricahua Apaches, *Broken Arrow* suggests that the tribal government functions in much the same way the U.S. government operates. One leader speaks for the entire group. Cochise could not and did not. A council representing each of the tribes in the nation had to decide what the collected tribes would do.[12]

In suggesting the reason Jeffords has come to Arizona—"prospecting for gold"—we are given very important information about the motivations of the whites. It is crucial to how we see the film to realize that Jeffords does not mention that he is prospecting in the "off limits" area of the lower Salt and Middle Gila river basins belonging to the Chiricahua Apaches, that there have been a number of frontier gold strikes since 1849, or that a treaty had been signed in 1867, tricking Native Americans on the Southern Plains into relinquishing important buffalo grazing lands and coming under the protection of the U.S. government.[13] It was largely due to the failure of Washington to honor its treaty obligations and to protect the "new" territorial rights of the Indians that the scope and the intensity of the Apache Wars increased.

It is also not trivial that Jeffords mentions that a "new colonel" had arrived in Tucson. The comments raise important questions about the military's intentions, and why Tucson, the territorial center then attracting hordes of prospectors and located along the route of the newly completed transcontinental railroad, is selected for the film's major white settlement.[14]

We should not overlook the fact that it is at this stage in American Indian warfare that General Philip Sheridan, commander of the military forces in the West, issued his infamous comment, "The only good Indian I ever saw was a dead one." As for Tucson, it is not enough that this was the setting in the novel, or that this is where Jeffords worked. Just who is opposing the Chiricahua Apaches?

Jeffords's voice-over narration tells us, "The story started when I saw some buzzards circling in the sky. Buzzard is a smart bird. Something...or somebody was getting ready to die. I figured it was a hurt deer, or a rabbit, or a snake. Not a rabbit, not a deer. His kind was more dangerous than a snake. He was an Apache. For ten years we'd been in a savage war with his people, a bloody no-give, no-take war." Compare that statement with the acts of omission already noted, and you can see the Euro-American perspective being developed. By arguing that the hostilities are only a decade old, and that neither side is more reprehensible than the other, Daves's narrative confuses and obscures the major issues between the two cultures.

As the film story begins, we learn that the Apache is a fourteen-year-old Chiricahua boy who is on his "novice time," the period when adolescents go on treks alone to learn how to survive and how to become men. The importance of this idea is that it establishes the Apaches as a warrior nation. Jeffords gives the boy some water, and though the youngster tried to kill him and is wounded in the struggle, the white man stays to tend to the youngster's wounds. Days later, when they are about to part as friends, Jeffords learns that the Apache's family must be worried about him, their only surviving child, his brother and sister having been killed at Big Creek. A voice-over narration tells us that Jeffords is stunned by the news that Indian mothers cry for their children. "Whites," he tells us, "had always considered Apaches like wild animals."

At this point, a band of five Apache warriors find the missing youth. Though they want to kill Jeffords, they do not because the boy intercedes for him. The voice-over narrator tells us that he learned something else that day, that Apaches were men of honor. The plot now moves into one of the major themes of the movie: the parallel misconceptions that white and Indians have about each other. For example, Daves stresses that the boy's father is upset that his son has become a "tame Apache." (In a later scene, a white father will justify his hatred of the Apaches because of the death of his wife and the near-killing of his son.) The Indians are curious that Jeffords did not kill the boy, inasmuch as white men pay money for Indian scalps, and say, "It is the way of all whites." Jeffords replies that it is not his way. He explains that he is not like other white men; he does not kill for scalps, and neither do the Apaches.

Again, it is interesting what the film states about the Indian Wars. The scalp issue is an extraordinary reference, inasmuch as it reminds us not only that during much of the eighteenth and early nineteenth century, the Mexican government encouraged people to scalp Indians, but also that the intense hatred that Cochise and Geronimo had for Mexicans could be traced back to an 1850 Mexican raid on an Apache village, where Geronimo's mother, wife, and three children were killed and scalped."

The most outrageous distortion, however, occurs when Jeffords explains to the Apaches that he is looking for gold and silver. Daves has the Indians puzzled about the white man's words. They do not understand about gold and silver. Keep in mind that this is 1870, and for more than twenty years the U.S. government had been following a deceptive policy, making treaties with Native Americans to clear the way for further westward migration and protecting prospectors who had illegally established claims on Indian lands. At the core of much of the trouble between the whites and the Indians was the way in which they understood the significance of treaties. As Hyatt and Terkin's television program *Time Machine: Savagery and the American Indian* observes, Native Americans initially were willing to sign treaties and share: "Their understanding of what they were signing was different from the Euro-Americans. They felt the agreements were about sharing an open landscape; the Euro-Americans thought of it as owning continually and fixing boundaries of property." But as the land became more lucrative to the goals of new administrations, Euro-Americans "used treaties as short-term devices that could be altered or ignored. Indians, on the other hand, were appalled at the speed with which treaties were torn up and new negotiations required." The cultural confusion created by Daves's perspective so early in the movie is the result of the filmmakers' failure to establish that the war between whites and Indians is a war in which the former are concerned with material acquisitions and the latter are fighting for their very survival.

The remainder of the film reinforces the approach taken in these opening moments of the movie. From time to time, we are given tidbits about the Chiricahua Apache culture, but rarely any crucial information about the essential meaning of the struggle between the two cultures. In almost every instance where the reasons for the hatred and distrust between Indians and whites are raised, the explanations are simplistic, misleading, and meaningless. Equally disturbing are the images of the Indians and whites themselves.

There are many examples of cultural confusion in *Broken Arrow*. A case in point is Jeffords's first encounter with whites and his defense of Chiricahua Apaches. Aligned against him is a fictitious Col. Bernall (played by Raymond Bramley), who has just been given the command of Fort Grant, with orders to clean out Cochise and his Apaches from the Pinaleno Mountains area. Like the screen Jeffords, he knows nothing about Indian culture or warfare, and, as will soon become apparent, he is really inept at his job.

The dialog, again, is useful for suggesting the film's cultural confusion. On the one hand, most of the men stationed on the frontier were ill equipped to deal with the Indian problem, but it is false to suggest that the military benefited mainly from the help of white scouts like Jeffords. It was not until the recruitment and use of Indian scouts, approved by Congress in 1866, that men like Sherman, Sheridan, and Custer were able to undertake successful campaigns against the Plains Indians and especially against Geronimo. The irony of *Broken Arrow* is that it takes place in 1870, the year that Indian scouts began depending on their military status for economic and social survival (primarily because the buffalo were being annihilated). The reservations had become death traps; this was their last "legal" chance to practice their warrior lifestyles.[15]

Another disturbing bit of dialog takes place during Jeffords' initial defense of Cochise against the hatred of the whites. He reminds his antagonists that Cochise did not start this war: "A snooty little lieutenant fresh out of the East started it. He flew a flag of truce, which Cochise honored. And then he hanged Cochise's brother and five others under the flag." The reference to an 1861 incident with an inexperienced, young Lt. George Bascom is fascinating. Not only does it omit the fact that Cochise hanged hostages in a futile attempt to free his family and that no one is sure which hangings took place first, but also director Daves conveniently overlooks the fact that Cochise had been at war with Euro-Americans soon after the government annexed all the land from the Rio Grande to the Pacific Ocean following the Mexican-American War.

Audiences learn a lot about *Broken Arrow's* understanding of history and the Chiricahua Apaches while witnessing Jeffords' experiences in Cochise's camp. Instead of seeing a weak, hungry, and ravaged tribe, viewers see an idyllic setting, where many strong, healthy Native Americans live peacefully and comfortably with their families. Instead of a tired and weary Cochise, eager for peace because he understands that the whites are too numerous and too strong for his people to overcome, audiences see the Noble Savage, all wise and all knowing.

When the two men first talk in Cochise's *wickiup*, Jeffords convinces Cochise that there is a distinction between the U.S. Mail and military dispatches. This is another major distortion in the film. Although it is true that the screen Jeffords believes what he is saying, we need to remember that much of the government duplicity against the Indians was based not on military dispatches but on the news sent back East by prospectors, settlers, pioneers, buffalo hunters, and railroad men complaining about the Indians' obstructing progress and murdering whites. Public opinion generated by civilians and propagandists, not the military, decided the nature and course of the Indian Wars.

We turn now to the actual peace negotiations themselves. The central figure is Gen. Oliver O. Howard, who, we are told in *Broken Arrow,* has been sent by President Grant to negotiate a peace with Cochise. The reason for Gen. Howard's peace mission, never explained in the film, is that on April 30, 1871, five hundred peaceful Aravaipa Apaches, who had settled near Camp Grant for the protection promised by the U. S. government, were massacred by vigilantes and enemy Indian scouts. Their boasting of the killing created such revulsion among Easterners that a new government policy was instituted to protect Grant's political image (*How the West was Lost*).[16]

Knowing that, notice how the dialog between Howard and Jeffords produces a different reaction from the liberal intentions of the filmmakers. Howard tells Cochise's friend that President Grant wants peace. Jeffords replies, "To be changed later." "No," is the answer. "Any treaty I make will stand. I have President Grant's absolute word on that." Jeffords asks what Howard means by a "fair" peace. Howard replies, "Suppose you tell me." To which Jeffords says, "Equality. The Apaches are a free people. They have a right to stay free on their own land." (Clearly, this was not the only issue. It was a question of land and culture, both of which were, and would be decimated by the treaty and reservation life.) But there is more. Howard responds, somewhat irritated, "You mean the whole Southwest?" (Why not? It's their land!) Cochise's friend never raises that issue. Instead, he says, "No. Even Cochise wouldn't ask for that now. (The operative word is "now.") He's a realist about that. But a clear territory that's Apache. Ruled by Apaches. No soldiers on it. That's what I mean." Howard agrees in principle, and Jeffords goes out to set up a meeting between them and Cochise.[17]

Finally, *Broken Arrow* comes to the actual peace treaty itself. Because Cochise cannot decide this matter by himself, he convenes the leaders of the Apache nation.[18] They deliberate for four days in private; then Howard and Jeffords are brought before them to answer questions. Just three inquiries are raised: (1) Can the Apaches still war against the Mexicans? The answer is no. (2) What if the "Chief of the Whites" dies—will the treaty still be kept? The answer: "His word is a bond on the chief who follows him." (3) What will happen if white men break the treaty, enter the restricted territory, and kill Apaches? The answer is that the military will take care of things.

The final affront is that the primary troublemaker at the peace council is Geronimo, shown as Cochise's contemporary and chief antagonist when in reality the relationship was one of deference and respect. The trouble begins when the white men leave, and Geronimo, yet unnamed, addresses the peace council: "I trust none of it." He points out that in the short time they have been discussing peace they have lost the right to raid Mexico,[19] and their territory has grown smaller.

The insult to history is compounded when Cochise agrees to try the peace, while Geronimo and a handful of supporters are forced to leave the territory. Then, the prescient Indian warrior announces to the gathering that, from now on, he will be known by his Mexican name, "Geronimo." Keep in mind that this was the name he adopted in 1850, twenty years earlier, when he took revenge for the massacre of his family. For the remainder of *Broken Arrow,* one of the greatest Apache leaders is shown as a renegade who refuses to accept peace for foolish reasons, when in fact he honored Cochise's word and lived on the reservation until Cochise died on June 8, 1874.

Moreover, the film ends with no mention that Jeffords became the only Indian agent for Cochise's tribe and that the conditions on the "Chiricahua" reservation were deplorable: lack of food and supplies, widespread disease, malnutrition, and constant humiliation. In the end, Washington betrayed the Apaches, and there was nothing that Jeffords or Howard could do to stop the racist policies of conquest.

Many film historians who have discussed *Broken Arrow* point to its groundbreaking role in Hollywood's treatment of the American Indian. This essay suggests that there is yet another perspective. *Broken Arrow* did more than reflect the mood of the times. It portrayed Indian/white relations in the Old West not as they were, but as Euro-Americans wanted them to be. The film's treatment of the Chiricahua Apache culture minimizes the importance of land to their lives; ignores the diseases, devastation, and disruption brought by Euro-Americans to Native American society; and legitimates the treaty signed between Cochise and the U.S. government. Its characterization of the relationship between Cochise and Jeffords grossly distorts the experiences of both men, misrepresents their motives for peace, and callously ignores the consequences of their tragic treaty,

White men do not come off much better. Whatever the misconceptions that Euro-Americans had of the American continent and its inhabitants, the pioneers and settlers who trekked westward took serious risks, fought against great hardships, and showed enormous courage in pursuing Manifest Destiny. They were probably too possessed by their dreams of wealth and rebirth to be charitable or reasonable when it came to the grievances of Native Americans. But to present them as primarily weak, revengeful, and simple-minded is absurd. In a metaphor about a "wilderness" filled with so much hatred, hostility, loneliness, and death, why does anyone want to stay, let alone die to own it?

The image of the military is also disturbing. They were not simply of two types: incompetent troopers or Bible-thumping good Samaritans. The men who rode against the Chiricahua Apaches were tough, no-nonsense combatants who enforced Sheridan's policy of "total war," which resulted in the destruction of the enemy's property and the annihilation of his family. They achieved their mission by crushing Native Americans with ruthless methods and uncompromising strategies. Although there might have been naive or idealistic officers who deluded themselves that their civilian leaders could be trusted, few military men of the West ever advocated a policy other than violence as a solution to the Indian problem.

If *Broken Arrow* is remembered by many as a well-intentioned film, it may be because they are willing to say that in 1950 people did not know any better, that this was a significant step forward compared to what had come earlier. Reasonable people will have no difficulty in accepting Angela Maria Aleiss's position that the film reflects the controversial policies of "termination" that Congress pursued in the 1950s, which effectively jettisoned any federal responsibility for Indian lands, treaties, and individuals. But there is a need to go beyond recognizing the policy to commenting on its consequences. One need only read Vine Deloria's *Custer Died for your Sins* to see how calamitous the termination policies were for both Native Americans and Washington. By distorting and misrepresenting the reasons for the cultural clash between the two parties, *Broken Arrow* sowed more seeds of distrust against the film industry and further undermined our trust in our institutions.

Furthermore, as film historians, we make a serious error when we discount the importance of historical inaccuracies in films purporting to the truth about the past. Movies are not just escapism, and when they offer simplistic, emotional solutions to complex problems, they muddy not only the problem but also create cultural confusion. From this perspective, there is an ironic truth in Twentieth Century-Fox's extolling *Broken Arrow* as an accurate rendition of "the American traditions of justice, tolerance, and dignity for all men."

Notes

[1] This article first appeared in *Film & History*, Vol. XXIII, Nos. 1-4 (1993): 58-69.

[2] I am grateful to the valuable reactions to an earlier draft of this paper by Nick Danigelis, Littleton Long, and Denise Youngblood of the University of Vermont. In addition, I owe a debt of gratitude to Martha Day for her generous help securing research materials.

[3] For a good introduction to George Washington's designs on Native American property, see Reginald Horsman, "American Indian Policy in the Old Northwest, 1783-1812." *The William and Mary Quarterly* Vol. 18, No. 1 (Jan 1961): 35-53.

[4] Frank Manchel, *Film Study: An Analytical Bibliography*. Vol. 1. 276.

[5] Ibid., 276.

[6] Julian Blaustein produced *Broken Arrow* for Twentieth Century-Fox in 1949. It premiered on July 17, 1950. Directed by Delmer Daves, the story is set in the Arizona territory in 1870. The plot, narrated by Tom Jeffords, an ex-Union officer whose admiration for the Chiricahua Apaches alienates him from his white associates in Tucson, follows his attempts to mediate between Cochise and the U.S. government and bring about an honorable peace. His efforts also lead to Jeffords' falling in love and marrying an Indian woman. The film stars James Stewart

as Tom Jeffords, Jeff Chandler as Cochise, Debra Paget as Sonseeahray, Will Geer as Slade, Basil Ruysdael as General Howard, Arthur Hunnicutt as Milt, Raymond Bramley as Colonel Bernall, Jay Silverheels as Geronimo, and Billy Wilkerson as Juan. Michael Blankfort bases his screenplay on Elliot Arnold's novel *Blood Brother*. Ernest Palmer is the cinematographer. Made in Technicolor, the film runs ninety-three minutes.

[7] Howard Suber, in his commentary on the laserdisc version of *High Noon* (Voyager Special edition).

[8] The series ran on ABC television from September 23, 1958, to September 20, 1960. John Lupton played Tom Jeffords; Michael Ansara played Cochise. Particularly significant is the fact that Jeffords is an Indian agent working with Cochise to keep the peace. In the film version, we never learn that he has become an Indian agent. For more information, see Terrace 94.

[9] *The Real West*. In the show's 1994 opening monolog, Jack Perkins points out that there were twenty Westerns aired in prime time every week in the early 1960s.

[10] For the most detailed analysis of the novel, see Angela Maria Aleiss *Hollywood's Ideal of Postwar Assimilation* and *From Adversaries to Allies*.

[11] *The Real West*. Those readers who would like to know more about the historical sources used in *The Real West*, should consult the writings of the series major consultants, including Paul Andrew Hutton (University of New Mexico) and Brian W. Dippie (University of Victoria, British Columbia).

[12] The filmmakers overlooked that the Apaches were not a tribe but a nation, with many bands living in areas from Oklahoma to New Mexico and Arizona to northern Mexico. For more information, see *How the West Was Lost*.

[13] By 1867, the U.S. government had created the Department of the Missouri-Southern Plains. It had also signed the Medicine Lodge Treaties of 1867, which allegedly were fashioned to bring a peaceful solution to the Indian Wars. On the surface, the treaty was hailed as a humane effort: Indians got a safe reservation in Oklahoma, and they were protected by the military. In practice, the deceitful pact compelled the Indians to leave their buffalo grounds and live under white rule. Moreover, the U.S. government abandoned its responsibilities within a year. Almost none of the supplies promised to the Indians ever reached the reservation. Gen. Philip H. Sheridan, who commanded the bulk of the western frontier during the timeframe of *Broken Arrow*, balked at any attempts to air reasonable Indian protests about broken promises. Thus the Cheyenne, Arapaho, Comanche, and Kiowa, who had once again

put their trust in a white man's treaty, were disillusioned. Sheridan, on the other hand, never put any faith in Indian treaties. Like his commanding officer, William Tecumseh Sherman, he insisted on a policy of "total war" against Native Americans. To help him implement such a policy, he secured the services of his Civil War friend, George Armstrong Custer. Together, these three military officers—Sherman, Sheridan, and Custer—would search for any excuse to attack the Indians. For more information, see *General Sheridan & the Indians*.

[14] Talks about forging a transcontinental railroad began as a result of the Mexican War and the land annexations of 1848 and later years. Actual construction began in 1862, and the railroad was competed on May 10, 1869. It ran through the Arizona territory. Every company that participated in the construction of the railroad received a square plot of ten acres of "public land" for every mile of track laid. In 1864, Congress doubled the land grant. To encourage business for the railroad, the companies sold their land cheaply. Moreover, railroad crews slaughtered the buffalo herds for meat. For more information, see *The Real West*.

[15] For more information, see *Indians and the Army*. It is useful to reflect on reservation life. According to one source, "reservations were like prisons." Traditional culture was destroyed; disease, despair, and poverty were widespread. Native Americans had lost their autonomy. Moreover, "A new culture was imposed by missionaries, Indian agents, and teachers." See *The Final Clash-Wounded Knee*.

[16] *How the West Was Lost*.

[17] The irony of this discussion is that the reservation proved devastating for the Apaches, and that later Gen. Howard, who lived to see Washington break its promises, not only follows orders but is also the officer assigned to pursue the Nez Perce and capture Chief Looking Glass and Chief Joseph. This is the same Chief Joseph who said, "No man's business to divide [the land]; only the one who created it has the right to dispose of it. The government treaties are based on hollow words." For more information, see *The Real West*.

[18] The event took place at Dragoon Mountains in November 1872.

[19] The fact is that the Apaches continued their Mexican forays. Cochise and his people never had signed a peace treaty with Mexico. Although he kept his word, Cochise never interfered with other Apaches who continued the raids. For more information, see Edwin R. Sweeney, *Cochise: Chiricahua Chief*, 366.

Works Cited

Aleiss, Angela Maria. "From Adversaries to Allies: The American Indian in American Films, 1930-1950." Ph. D. Dissertation, Columbia University, 1991.

___. "Hollywood's Ideal of Postwar Assimilation: Indian/White Attitudes in *Broken Arrow*." MFA Thesis, Columbia University, 1985.

Deloria, Vine, Jr. *Custer Died for Your Sins*. New York: Avon Books, 1969. Horsman, Reginald. "American Indian Policy in the Old Northwest, 1783-1812," in *Promises to Keep: A Portrayal of Nonwhites in the United States,* ed. Bruce A. Glasrud and Alan M. Smith, 97-112. Chicago: Rand McNally, 1972.

How the West Was Lost. Discovery Channel documentary series, 1993.

Manchel, Frank. *Film Study: An Analytical Bibliography,* Vol. 1. Rutherford, N.J.: Fairleigh Dickinson University Press, 1990.

The Real West. Arts & Entertainment Network documentary series, 1993.

Sweeney, Edwin R. *Cochise: Chiricahua Chief.* Norman: University of Oklahoma Press, 1991.

Terrace, Vincent. *Fifty Years of Television: A Guide to Series and Plots, 1937-1988*. Cranbury, N.J.: Cornwall Books, 1991.

Time Machine. Arts & Entertainment Network documentary series, 1991-1992.

15. Author Emile Zola (Paul Muni) and his dear friend, artist Paul Cezanne (Vladimir Sokoloff) remember their past history together. William Dieterle, *The Life of Emile Zola* (1937). From the core collection production photographs of the Margaret Herrick Library, Academy of Motion Picture Arts and Sciences.

13.

Nickel Psychology

The educational task is not only to provide tools of perception, but also to develop judgment and discrimination with ordinary experiences.[1]

Marshall McLuhan

There is a history in all men's lives.[2]

William Shakespeare.

The purpose of civilization and growth is to reach out and empathize a little bit with other people. And for me, the movies are like a machine that generates empathy. It lets you understand a little more about different hopes, aspirations, dreams, and fears. It helps you to understand with people who are sharing this dream with you.[3]

Roger Ebert

Early in February 1999, I received a very surprising but extremely pleasant phone call from Dr. James H. Overfield, a UVM history Professor I knew and liked but had little contact with during my past thirty years on campus. Unbeknownst to me, Jim, a specialist in late medieval German intellectual and social history, headed the local Chapter of Phi Alpha Theta (ΦΑΘ), an organization as unfamiliar to me then as I suspect it is to lay readers now. My colleague was calling to say I had been selected as the honored speaker for the year's Chapter ceremonies at the University.

Although flattered by the professional respect, especially coming from someone like Jim, I had no idea of what the distinction meant, why I had been chosen, or who my audience would be. My cordial colleague explained Phi Alpha Theta was a national honor society for undergraduate and graduate students and professors of history, involving more than 300,000 members spread among 860 local Chapters in the United States. The organization was established more than three-quarters-of-a-century ago by a visionary University of Arkansas academician who believed what was needed in American higher education was a society of scholars dedicated to the study of history. So on March 17, 1921, Professor Nels Cleven saw his dream come true, and the society came into being. Seventy-eight years later, the UVM chapter had decided to identify a teacher who for decades had been battling intellectuals to recognize film as an important historical source for historians and college students.

After expressing gratitude for the award and happily agreeing to deliver a talk in April, I probed Jim as to whom my audience would be. He said they would be a very heterogeneous group: colleagues, students, parents, staff, librarians, and friends of the History Department. "What do you think I should say to them?" I asked. "After all, this was really not my usual constituency." Jim casually responded, "Whatever you want." In the past, he explained, the honorees had come from various walks of life and had delivered matter-of-fact comments about their lives, their interests, and their thoughts on history. In other words, you're on your own. Make it simple, but explicit; entertaining but educational; take as much time as you like, but not too long. And whatever else you do, don't make it appear as if we chose the wrong person to speak.

Understandably unsettled by that mystifying advice, I went to two of my closest colleagues at the University, who just happened to also be in the History Department and were going to introduce me at the ceremony, and sought their advice. They assured me whatever I said would be well received. I had no reason to be anxious, they laughed. "Do what you always do: be abrasive, confrontational, and self-serving." Now I was half-heartedly convinced the History Department was secretly getting back at me for my questioning their traditional views and practices.

Left to my increasing self-doubts, I began to think about the Hollywood myths this diverse audience might be harboring. What did they really know about film history, other than what they had been exposed to in watching movies in theaters and on TV? What did they expect from me, except that I might predictably lecture on history in film versus history on film. More to the point, what did they really want to know about that academic subject? They were coming to honor the society's new inductees, and they probably could care less about an ex-Dean and belligerent English Professor crusading for film legitimacy in academia. Besides, many in the audience were lay people who undoubtedly were puzzled why movies were even accorded academic status.

Almost immediately I dismissed the idea I would lecture professional historians on how their discipline was changing, and why they had to change with it. Even I was not that arrogant, particularly since they just had been so kind to me. So I began thinking about explaining the bond between Hollywood and literature. That is, "the relationship between Hollywood and literature takes us out of the realm of theoretical conjecture and into history." I remembered a film scholar back then who saw the film colony as a noteworthy social marvel, "an important and influential force in the imaginations and moral lives of its inhabitants, a symbol rather than a setting."[4] Here might be a chance to connect the audience's experiences with a popular literary genre known as "Hollywood Fiction," a novelistic formula defined by film expert Carolyn Penelope See as "an extended work of fiction set in Hollywood which includes at least one major character or several minor ones working in show business, or any novel of the American film industry on location so long as the action of the book focuses on motion-picture making and the lives of the motion-picture people."[5]

From there, I could entertain my listeners with my knowledge of authors like Horace McCoy, James M. Cain, John Dos Passos, Raymond Chandler, Budd Schulberg, John O'Hara, Nathanael West, Evelyn Waugh, Ben Hecht, Wright Morris, Norman Mailer, Christopher Isherwood, Gavin Lambert, Joan Didion, and Gore Vidal. I could also get the crowd to think about the genre's conventions popularized by studio publicity departments in romanticized fan magazines: images of great wealth, unbelievable mansions containing luxurious swimming pools and employing lots of servants, splendid parties attended by gorgeous and sexually-liberated personalities, magnificent cars, designer clothes, and incredible indulgences. I could pander to the audience's fantasies about the New Eden that represented the epitome of what was commonly called the American Dream. I could also tease my audience with the Cinderella stories about ordinary people who overnight were discovered by the filmmakers and turned into famous movie stars, thus personifying America's basic myth that we lived in the land of limitless opportunities, where anyone could be anything he or she imagined.[6]

If the name-dropping or my critiquing of the undying American myth didn't impress them, I could quickly shift to the many movies that mythologized the movie colony and express my opinions on films like *A Star is Born* (1937, 1954, 1976), *Sunset Boulevard* (1960), *The Player* (1992), *Singin' in the Rain* (1952), *The Bad and the Beautiful* (1952), *S.O.B.* (1981), *Sullivan's Travels* (1941), *Get Shorty* (1995), *The Day of the Locust* (1975), and *Silent Movie* (1976). For the movie aficionados in the audience, I could even throw in *Day for Night/Lu Nui americaime* (1973), *Contempt/Le Mepris* (1963), *The Cameraman* (1928), and *The Carpetbaggers* (1964).

But, as the date for the event drew closer, I thought why be so pretentious. Be modest, tone it down; and talk about an author closely identified with film, literature, and the public's fantasies: F. Scott Fitzgerald. After all, no writer more carefully shaped the nation's false perceptions on the ties between Hollywood and the public; or more effectively attacked the country's cockeyed ideas about the Dream Factory.

Selecting an American novelist identified with history was not difficult. I had written about Fitzgerald in some detail.[7] Surely, many of the people in the audience, ranging in age and intellect, as they must, would have read at least one of this powerful writer's books that had been adapted into film: three versions of *The Great Gatsby* (1926, 1949, 1974);[8] *This Side of Paradise* (1991),[9] *The Beautiful and the Damned* (1922),[10] *Tender is the Night* (1962), and *The Love of the Last Tycoon* (1976). For the Q & A session, I could throw in Budd Schulberg's *The Disenchanted*[11] or Sheila Graham's *Beloved Infidel*.[12]

With just two weeks before the talk, I came up with what I thought would be a great idea. Less than a month before my address to UVM's Phi Alpha Theta Chapter, a major movie controversy had caught the public's interest. The famous but controversial stage and film director Elia Kazan had been given an honorary Oscar by the Motion Picture Academy at their 71st annual event. Many protestors reminded us that while the 89-year-old-artist who had given us such landmark films as *Gentleman's Agreement* (1947), *Pinky* (1949), *A Streetcar Named Desire* (1951), *On the Waterfront* (1954), and *East of Eden* (1955); he had also aided HUAC by testifying before the Committee in 1952 and naming names, thereby contributing to the corrosive power of blacklisting in the motion picture industry.[13]

Why not, I reasoned, use Kazan's *The Last Tycoon* (1976), a screen adaptation of Fitzgerald's unfinished novel about Hollywood, as the focus of the talk? The thinly veiled narrative depicted the fabled struggle between Irving Thalberg and Louis B. Mayer, the rise of the Screen Writers Guild, the industry's fears about Communism taking over the movie business, and the conflict between Wall Street and Hollywood and where the true power rested in the film-making world. Not only could I illustrate what Hollywood fiction looked like, but also the movie had an all-star cast: Robert De Niro (Monroe Stahr/Thalberg), Robert Mitchum (Pat Brady/Mayer), Jack Nicholson (Brimmer/the Red-baiting union organizer), Ray Milland (Fleishacker/the NY Lawyer), plus Tony Curtis and Jeanne Moreau symbolizing just what Hollywood stars were really like back in the thirties. And if that wasn't enough to impress my audience, I would point out the script was penned by no less a literary giant than Harold Pinter.

I intended to begin the speech with a clip from the film, the one not only demonstrating the contempt notable writers had for the movies, but also illustrating the magic of filmmaking. Studio head Monroe Stahr (De Niro) is sitting in his plush office when Boxley (Donald Pleasence), the eminent British author recently hired by Stahr, bursts into the room, accompanied by two studio screenwriters assigned to work with the novice. Stahr is surprised by the visit and asks what's wrong.

"I can't go on," the famous novelist complains.

"Why?" asks the studio boss?

"You've stuck me with two hacks. I can't write…They louse up everything I write."

"Why don't you just write it yourself?" Stahr asks.

"I have," explains Boxley. "I sent you some."

Monroe responds: "That was just talk; you'll lose the audience."

Bewildered, Boxley complains, "You people don't read!" The author points out the actors were dueling when the conversation occurred.

Stahr asks the novelist if he would put such dialogue in his books.

"Of course, I wouldn't!" he responds.

Now the producer shifts gears and asks the writer if he ever goes to the movies.

"Rarely," Boxey responds.

They agree most movies deal in rubbish. Then Stahr poses a hypothetical situation. "Suppose you are in your office. You've been fighting duels all day. You are exhausted. This is you. A girl comes in [furtively]. She doesn't see you. She takes off her gloves. She opens her purse and dumps it [the contents] on the desk. You watch her…She has two dimes, a matchbox, and a nickel. She leaves the nickel on the desk, but puts the two dimes back in her purse. She takes her gloves—they are black—and puts them in the fireplace. Lights a match. Suddenly the phone rings. [She picks it up and listens] "I have never owned a pair of black gloves in my life," she says. Hangs up. Kneels by the fireplace. Lights another match. Suddenly you notice you are not the only person in the room watching every move the girl makes.

Monroe smiles and sits down. Boxley, on the edge of his seat, asks, "What happens?"

"I don't know," replied Stahr. "I was just making pictures."

"What was the nickel for?" asks the dumbfounded author.

The producer turns to one of the two studio regulars: "Jane, what was the nickel for?"

She responds, "The nickel was for the movies."

Before I could get my act together, the Phi Alpha Theta speech was upon me. And so I did what most teachers do, I improvised!

Notes

[1] Frank Manchel, "The Universal Classroom," in *Conference on Teaching the Slow Learner* (Metropolitan School Study Conference: The English Committee of the Metropolitan School Study Conference, 1964.
[2] William Shakespeare, *Henry IV, Part II*, Act III, Scene 1, line 80. *Shakespeare: Major Plays and the Sonnets*, ed. G. B. Harrison. New York: Harcourt, Brace and Company, 1948. 395.
[3] Steve James, *Life Itself*. USA: Magnolia Pictures, 2014.
[4] Frank Manchel, "Hollywood and Literature," *Film Study: An Analytical Bibliography*, Vol. 2, 1040.
[5] Ibid., 1041-1042.
[6] Ibid., 1054.
[7] "The Hollywood Fiction of and by Fitzgerald, 1108-1144.
[8] Two later versions appeared in 2000, and 2013.
[9] Another version appeared in 1999, directed by Jonas Mekas.
[10] Another version appeared in 2010, directed by Wayne Blair.
[11] Benoit Jacquot, *The Disenchanted/La désenchantée*. France: Centre National de la Cinematograpie, 1990.
[12] Henry King, *Beloved Infidel*. USA: Twentieth Century-Fox, 1959.
[13] For a similar interpretation, see David Gilmour, *The Film Club*. New York: Twelve, 2008. 28-30.

My Mother Didn't Raise Her Son to be a Fool[1]
Phi Alpha Theta Ceremony Speech
April 9, 1999

My mother didn't raise me to be a fool. So I have no intention of explaining history to a group of distinguished historians and history undergraduates. And my mother would have told me if she were alive today that if this audience hasn't learned from Professor Denise Youngblood, your distinguished resident scholar in film, about the relationship that exists between film and history, then there is nothing I can say to you that will help.

However, what I will attempt during these brief remarks is to relate some personal stories and to comment on several events in the last half of the twentieth century. For example, back in the spring of 1953, when I was a freshman at Ohio State University studying to be a sadist, I took a course with an elderly geography professor who was about to retire. I remember nothing about what he taught us, except that he had just come back from visiting with Albert Schweitzer in Africa and hated the Nobel Prize winner, because my professor thought that Schweitzer exploited the Africans. Sometime during the lecture a jet plane zoomed over the Columbus campus. And I remember the professor turning to us with tears running down his face and saying:

> "When I was born, the transcontinental railroad had just been completed; there were no electric lights or cars or telephones or radios or television or movies. Now your generation is talking about going to the moon." He then moved toward the door, stopped and turned, and said, "The future—it's all yours if you only know what to do with it."

In this place and at this time, I'd like to share with you some memories that hopefully pay tribute to the past. There is a tendency in our travels through life to forget sometimes the efforts of those who came before us, the lessons they tried to teach, and the sacrifices they made on our behalf. It isn't that we are disrespectful. It's just that we get so wrapped in the ways of the world that we forget our debts. There is also a tendency in every age to cover up the mistakes and misdeeds of individuals and nations. Some do it because of ignorance, others because of cowardice, and still others because of shame. As Jean Renoir once said in his great film *The Rules of the Game*, "The tragedy of life is that everyone has a reason." For me, two of the great advantages of history are that it makes us remember; and that it forces people to be accountable for their actions.

Like many of my friends, who went into teaching nearly a half-century ago, I did so with a boy's heart and a young man's dreams about making a contribution to our times. In simple but honest words, my dream was to try to make people see that movies were more than just escapism and entertainment; that they were indeed the greatest art form of the twentieth century. I am still a work in process.

What may surprise you is that one thing I've learned these many years is the more I studied the more I realized how little I knew. Believe it or not, that attitude is often a major difference between the students I've been privileged to teach and myself. They know all there is to know in the world, and I know the rest.

There is a wonderful anecdote attributed to Mark Twain, in which he recalls working as a reporter and receiving a letter from a 17-year-old undergraduate. Among the things the student told the American genius was that he was just starting college, and that his parents were immigrants and quite illiterate. Four years later, Samuel Clemens received a second letter from the student who was just about to graduate from college, and the youngster explained to Twain, "It is amazing how much my parents had learned in the last four years."

Another detail I've discovered by vacationing all these many years in academia is that very few people ever view the world the same way. Consider the mass media as a case in point. And here I equate film and TV as one, as the moving image. Despite all the research and all the evidence praising the contributions of film and television's roles in our society, a vast majority of the world still makes the media the scapegoat for many of society's problems. I never understood why that was so. Maybe it is just too easy to think more plainly about our roles and our responsibilities and our actions.

Let me be clear on this point. I know about the ways the media manipulates us and how it often distorts the truth. Take, for example, the recent ABC telecast on the Oscars. A protest had been organized to demonstrate opposition to the Motion Picture Academy bestowing a Lifetime Achievement Award to Elia Kazan. If you watched the camerawork during the presentation, you would have thought the protest failed. Only a few people were shown not standing, or applauding. Most of the camera shots, 85% according to one source, focused on the standing ovation accorded Kazan. Only by reading the accounts in the press could one discover that the protest was a success. Liz Smith in *Newsday* reported that most of the audience did not applaud; film critic Roger Ebert told us that only 40% of the people in attendance applauded and stood for Kazan; *Daily Variety*'s noted columnist Army Archard thought the figure was closer to 20% as regards those who honored Kazan, while the *Los Angeles Times* pegged the number of people not standing at 75%.

So I do know something about the evils of broadcasting. But I also know something about what it does right. The issue I have with the medium's critics is that they dwell only on the negative. It's much like Sherlock Holmes used to say, "You see my Dear Watson, but you do not observe." In teaching I've always thought it was better to spend my time explaining about the best in broadcast history, rather than railing against its negative effects in our society. For me, television is a marvelous tool for human knowledge and inspiration. If one were to study seriously the history of the medium, we could easily learn about its many contributions in this century.

What's fascinating is that even many of those who work in the industry don't always know how they contribute to humanity's betterment. For example, Nichelle Nichols, who played Lt. Uhura in the original *Star Trek*, tells the story about attending an important fund-raising dinner for the NAACP. One of her biggest fans she discovered that night was Dr. Martin Luther King, Jr. In their conversation together, she told Dr. King that she intended to leave the show, and he argued strenuously for Nichols not to do that.

"You cannot...and you must not," he stated firmly. "Don't you realize how important your presence, your character is?" he went on. "Don't you realize this gift that... [Gene Roddenberry] has given the world? Men and women of all races going forth in peaceful exploration, living as equals....Don't you see? This is not a Black role, and this is not a female role. You have the first non-stereotypical role on television, male or female." Dr. King continued to argue, saying, "You have created a character of dignity and grace and beauty and intelligence...For the first time the world sees us as we should be seen, as equals, as intelligent people—as we should be."[2]

Again, let's be clear on this point. I'm not claiming that TV is good or bad; I'm claiming that TV offers choices, and that we have the responsibility, not just the artists and the industry, to make the best use of the medium for the world around us and for ourselves.

In many respects, I have always found it useful to personalize history, to remember where I started, and to measure how far I have come. Let me tell you a story. When I came to Vermont in 1967, the naysayers against mass entertainment were so powerful in Burlington that when the film industry switched from a production code to a ratings system, the *Burlington Free Press* refused to accept advertisements for X-rated films playing in town. As far as the local paper was concerned, you've seen one X-film; you've seen them all. So in 1969, when John Schlesinger's *Midnight Cowboy* was showing, all the publication said was that the film was at the Flynn. Even when *Midnight Cowboy* won the Academy Award, changes in perception about so-called X-films and R-films came slowly. No one discriminated between good and bad films. People today still think simplistically about movies having two stars, thumbs up or down, or being R-rated. But what do they actually know about the films themselves?

But that's not my main point. In Burlington in the late sixties and early seventies, when all over America there was a black revolution going on in general and in movies especially, you couldn't see African American films in our local theaters. It wasn't just that we were racially intolerant; it wasn't even that we were frightened what trouble black films—with their alternative lifestyles and language—could cause if the young and the impressionable, or the old and the intractable, saw them. It was, we were told, because hardly anyone went to these films. The rationale given by theater owners was that they didn't want to lose money showing bad box-office movies.

They had the same problems with films about the Holocaust. I once convinced my dear friend Merrill Jarvis to show the extraordinary movie, Marcus Imhoof's *The Boat Is Full* (1981). It describes the anti-Semitism in Switzerland that resulted in desperate Jews who fled Nazi Germany being turned back to Hitler's troops. Three days after the film opened in Burlington, Jarvis called to tell me that the boat might be full, but that the theater was empty.

And it wasn't just African American and Holocaust films. Our society had no tolerance for cultural differences. We, the educators, built no audiences to support artists who dared to be different, who wanted us to expand our horizons; there were no courses about African American literature and the Holocaust in most of our schools. In effect, we were using worn-out nineteenth century tools in the twentieth century to teach young people how to succeed in the twenty-first century.

Again, let's have no misunderstanding. I have no quarrel with the great books or the significant lessons of the past. But greatness and relevance are not limited just to the past, and we must make room in our lives and in our society for new ideas and important achievements. I don't know how many times in my career I've quoted Stephen Vincent Benet's memorable lines to illustrate that point, but it's worth quoting them for this audience:

All the people of this little town—
Rise up, rise up—the loves you have are not enough
Something is loose to shake this sullen world and with it
you must change.[3]

But that still isn't the main point I want to make about society's negative misperceptions about the media. In the late sixties, when I began my serious study of African American movies; the only way that I could see these controversial films was by going to New York. So off I went; in fact, my entire family went with me. I remember in 1972, taking Steven, my eleven-year-old son, to see Jim Brown, the great football player turned movie actor, starring in Jack Starrett's

Slaughter. While the black press was praising the rise of black action heroes, the white media was denouncing Brown for his violent and vicious behavior as an ex-Green Beret who dared to defend his community against the all-white crime syndicate. The press was doing this while the film industry and historians were praising famous film gangsters like James Cagney, Humphrey Bogart and Edward G. Robinson for their contributions to American culture.

But that still isn't the main point that I want to make about the media's role in society. Imagine this. Steven and I are the only Caucasians in a picture palace on Broadway, and there are 2,000 African Americans responding to Jim Brown's violent deeds by screaming, "Kill the honkies." All of a sudden, I hear my son screaming, "Kill the honkies." I shushed him, and told him just to watch the movie. Another time, I remember taking Gary, my youngest son, to see a horror film, which showed heads being cut off and bouncing all over the screen. Gary's reaction was to yell out, "Slick." And because I was well known in the theaters, I yelled out, "No Gary, it's not slick."

That's my small but significant point about the media. I know first hand about the negative reactions that movies can cause. But I used those same experiences to educate my children, much as King Arthur did in the musical *Camelot*, to explain that violence is not synonymous with strength or being a man; that compassion and sensitivity are not signs of weakness.

The movies are an ideal classroom for learning about life and values. What thrills me these days is that my precious daughter-in-law Sharon is using the same methods to teach my grandchildren. In the movies, age does not separate the teacher from the student, nor does education or class or wealth or geography. The greatness of film as an art is that it is so democratic. For more than forty years, I've argued that we should use the media to examine the world as it is and then bring about the changes that intelligence and survival dictate.

Right now I'm teaching a course on the Films of John Huston. The students tell me their peers often ask them, "What did Huston ever do that he deserves a class?" Parents sometimes harass their children by saying, "Did I send you to college to watch movies? Why don't you study something that will give you a good living?"

For starters, hardly a week goes by without there being a John Huston film screened on TV. This past Easter Sunday, they showed his film *The Bible*. Tomorrow night, *The Maltese Falcon* (1941) is on. And many people have seen a number of Huston's other memorable movies: for example, *Key Largo* (1948), *The Asphalt Jungle* (1950), *The Red Badge of Courage* (1951), *Moulin Rouge* (1953), *The Misfits* (1960), *Heaven Knows, Mr. Allison* (1957), *The Night of the Iguana* (1964), *Fat City* (1972), *Reflections in a Golden Eye* (1967), *Wise Blood* (1979), *The Life and Times of Judge Roy Bean* (1972), *The Treasure of the Sierra Madre* (1948), *The African Queen* (1951), *The Man Who Would Be King* (1975), *Prizzi's Honor* (1985), or *The Dead* (1987).

Now there are still many people who think of John Huston as merely a delightful personality, a good storyteller, and a popular filmmaker. But there are others, like my students and me, who view him as one of the most significant artists of this century. Consider, for example, *The Misfits*, his 1960 film based upon Arthur Miller's extraordinary script. The movie has one of the most outstanding casts in the second half of this century: Clark Gable, Marilyn Monroe, Eli Wallach, Montgomery Clift, and Thelma Ritter. One could spend a semester just going over the ill-fated histories of these stars and the lessons their sad lives could teach us about our society and ourselves. One could also explore the brilliant cinematic techniques Huston used to tell a story of suffering and death and change in their world. But in this instance, the importance of *The Misfits* may be in reminding us of many of Huston's themes used throughout his fifty-year career: the courage it requires of people who are confused and alone yet refuse to be beaten, who seek to rebuild their lives after tragedies strike; the quest for a home that has been lost or never found; the ability to trust in oneself despite what others may think of you and the mistakes you've made; the importance of love in healing your pain, and the realization that your quest is often greater than attaining the goal you seek. In *The Misfits* and in other Huston works, life is all about the need to come to terms with impermanence. Nothing is forever, he argues, not even death. Moreover, each of us will face failure and disappointment and tragedies in our lives. There is no way to escape them. The test of who and what we are, he argues, is how we how we deal with these human realities. Find something and someone, Huston points out in movie after movie, to sustain you through the hard times. Huston's legacy, like that of Stanley Kubrick, Akira Kurosawa, Charlie Chaplin, Orson Welles, Federico Fellini, and dozens and dozens of great film artists are all there to help us, if, as my old geography teacher says, we only know what to do with them.

On another related matter, I know that there are those here who assume that when you talk about history and the movies, the assumption is that scholars are supposed to function as the accuracy police. We're supposed to point out factual errors, expose the lies in the story and the flaws in the characters. Such an assumption I believe is often wrong. The way I see our ties is that the historians examine the intellectual details of the past, while the filmmakers explore the experiences of the past.

Let me give you a couple of examples from among thousands of films I've experienced in a half-century of study. I have an extraordinary TA this year, who pictures himself as a "snooty" medievalist. He was explaining to me that he never fully understood the Holocaust although he had studied it in his course work. Something, he said, was missing. But once he viewed *Sophie's Choice* and saw Meryl Streep forced to choose which of her children would live or die at Auschwitz, he began to realize what the Holocaust was about.

Another favorite reaction concerns my sister and the first run of Francis Ford Coppola's *The Godfather*. Rose went to see the film in Brooklyn Heights, and that day in 1972, the movie theater was packed; that is all except for one seat in front of her. Five minutes before Sonny (James Caan) goes to beat up Carlo (Gianni Russo), his brother-in-law, for slapping his sister Connie (Talia Shire) around, a woman came into the audience and took the empty seat. Then for five minutes, as Sonny pounded Carlo, this woman laughed hysterically. After the visual beating, she left the theater and did not return. When the movie was over, my sister happened to see the manager in the lobby and told him the story. He said it was an everyday occurrence. The woman was the ex-wife of the actor playing Carlo, and she had a deal with the theater owner to reserve that seat for her during the run of the film. It was so funny to him that he didn't even charge her for the five minutes she appeared at every showing for weeks on end.

My point here is to remind my audience that there are many

types of films that serve many different purposes. And we should never presume to think that all people perceive movies the same way in our society or in our classrooms; nor should they. Movies play many roles in our culture, and the film industry should be encouraged to stay that way.

For me, there have always been three questions I ask of any film I study: What does it say? How can I prove it? And so what? Just as history at it highest moments must obey the dictates of its discipline to avoid judging the actions of its subjects, so I presume in the final analysis to avoid detachment and instead to weigh the ethical and moral choices films offer me. I want to know whether or not I am a better person because of the experience of seeing this film. And I want to understand why that is so. It may make me a poor historian, but I feel better about what I do and why I do it.

Again, I don't want my words misunderstood. I know that generalizing from anecdotes is not credible research in scholarly circles. I know it isn't logical to presume that my experiences or goals should necessarily be the same for all people. But I also know from experiencing *Man of La Mancha* that logic is sometimes the enemy of truth.

That's the point many in the public don't grasp about this year's Academy Awards. Movies aren't divorced from politics and philosophy and art! How can mature people still think that films are only about art and money? After all that we've seen, from *The Birth of a Nation* to *Life is Beautiful*, how can mature people still think that movies are only meaningless entertainment? Don't audiences realize, as one of my colleagues wisely pointed out, that movies affect national agendas, stir up public debates, and shape cultural values? That what we watch also influences our memories and stimulates our dreams? Don't we yet realize that by identifying with specific characters and stars and genres that we help shape who and what we are?

Let me focus on just two issues at this year's Academy Awards: the best foreign film and the lifetime achievement award to Elia Kazan. I'm not saying that Roberto Benigni isn't a talented artist, or that *Life Is Beautiful* isn't a technically well-crafted movie. I'm not arguing the film doesn't have an uplifting message. Nor am I denying that the film moved many people to tears, or that the writer-director-star didn't go into the project with the best intentions. Clearly, Benigni is no Leni Riefenstahl. But good intentions are not the same as substance.

What film historians like me are saying is *Life Is Beautiful* grossly distorts one of the major lessons of the Holocaust: there was very little optimism to be found in the death camps, and people could do almost nothing to save themselves from the Nazi genocide. Understand me clearly. I am not a detractor about comedies dealing with the Holocaust; there are those who think it sacrilegious to profit by the suffering of nearly six million murdered Jews. That person is not me. I am not opposed to a Holocaust film because it is a comedy. I admire enormously Charlie Chaplin's *The Great Dictator* and Ernst Lubitsch's *To Be Or Not To Be,* both film comedies courageously made at the times Jews were actually being slaughtered by the Nazis. But neither film had the chutzpah to make jokes in the midst of the death camps themselves. These films respected history because they remained faithful to the essence, to the spirit, to the horror of the event. But films like Lina Wertmuller's *Seven Beauties* and Roberto Benigni's *Life Is Beautiful* make a travesty of history because they distort and trivialize the past. To state it somewhat differently, people like Chaplin teach us how to honor history; Benigni teaches us how to dishonor history.

I do not expect you to agree with many or any of my prejudices. But in the brief time we've spent together I wanted you to know that a man of many years still teaches with a boy's heart; I wanted to suggest that for me history has always been something that makes us aware of who and what we are; it stimulates us to think and to dream of things that never have been and ask why not.

With your permission, I'd like to end my reminiscences with a special nod to my generous colleagues with whom I've spent so many unforgettable hours. I want to thank you not so much for this honor, but for the many kindnesses for all these years. Rather than become maudlin at this point in our lives, let me simply recall a scene from a 1937 Warner Bros. movie, William Dieterle's *The Life of Emile Zola.* Two elderly French artists, long-time friends, are having dinner, the naturalistic author Emile Zola (Paul Muni) and the post-impressionist painter Paul Cézanne (Vladimir Sokoloff). At one point, the painter turns to the novelist and says that he is leaving Paris. "What's wrong?" asks the novelist. The painter reminds Zola that they have come a long way since they starved together in an attic. Cézanne explains to the muckraking author that he knows the temptations that ambition can bring and that such temptations must be avoided at all costs. The great artist then turns to leave, hoping that he hasn't offended Zola by stating the truth. The famous novelist, with tears in his eyes, pleads with Cézanne to stay, but the painter says no. Then in one last try, Zola asks Cézanne if he will at least write. And Cézanne answers, "No, but I will remember."

16. Studio head Monroe Stahr (Robert De Niro) decides to remove director Red Ridingwood (Dana Andrews) to rescue a failing film. Elia Kazan, *The Last Tycoon* (1976). From the core collection production photographs of the Margaret Herrick Library, Academy of Motion Picture Arts and Sciences.

Notes

[1] The title is paraphrased from a comment in John Ford's *Rio Grande*. USA: Republic Pictures, 1950.
[2] Nichelle Nichols, *Beyond Uhura: Star Trek and Other Memories*. New York: G. P. Putnam's Sons, 1994. 164–65; and Abby Ohlheiser, "How Martin Luther King Jr. Convinced 'Star Trek's Lt. Uhura to stay on the show," *The Washington Post* (July 31, 2012).
[3] Lincoln Konkle and David Garrett Izzo, *Stephen Vincent Benet: Essays on His Life and Work*. New York: McFarland & Co. Inc., 2002. 226.

17. An elderly Don Vito Corleone (Marlon Brando) advises his youngest son, Michael (Al Pacino) how to run the family business. Frances Ford Coppola, *The Godfather* (1972). From the core collection production photographs of the Margaret Herrick Library, Academy of Motion Picture Arts and Sciences.

14.

Far from the Lonely Crowd

A fellow who doesn't take risks is despicable.[1]
Henri Langlois

Though your own self remained hidden from the sight of all; Yet, your own eye could perceive the world unveiled.[2]
Dr. Sir Mohammad Iqbal

The advice of the elders to young men is very apt to be as unreal as a list of the hundred best books.[3]
Associate Justice Oliver Wendell Holmes, Jr.

Sometime during 1998, two of my colleagues pitched an idea to their publisher: let's put together an anthology for Freshmen and Sophomores that introduces and integrates the various disciplines taught in a contemporary English Department—e.g., literature, cultural studies, creative writing, and mass media. I was asked to contribute the film section, while another associate was assigned the television segment. The focus of each essay was on how to initiate neophytes to your discipline. Not only was the project supposed to aid most Arts and Sciences undergraduates in fulfilling their two-year General Education requirements in the humanities, but also the anthology would provide hopefully a snapshot of a Modern English Department.

At that precise moment in my career, the proposed assignment contained an ironic twist. After nearly forty years of experience studying, writing, and teaching about film, a new and ardent generation of teachers (neither surprisingly nor unique) saw me as behind the educational times as well as a major obstacle to adjusting film study so it could fit seamlessly into the profession's shift away from Popular Culture to Cultural Studies. What was so ironic was that it had taken me so long to get to this stage; and now that I had finally reached my goal, my younger peers were suggesting the train had already left the station.

You can't blame me if I was somewhat crestfallen. On the one hand, my colleagues and I didn't seem that far apart. Each of our teaching methods examined how "culture" first starts, then functions, and finally shapes our personal lives and human relations. On the other hand, our significant differences centered on methodology. I emphasized concrete techniques, while my colleagues stressed abstracts theories. This simplistic explanation may not be the best statement of our disagreement, but it is a fair idea of how I felt. Furthermore, the notion that young and developing experts knew more than tested and experienced intellectuals has always made me smile. That's because I was once just like them. It's also because I remember the wonderful Man Ray's delicious remark, "There is no progress in art, any more than there is progress in making love. There are simply different ways of doing it."[4]

To my biased mindset, this back and forth debate about knowledge and who possesses it at any given time remains a recurring dilemma existing in almost all aspects of civilization. For example, the brilliant and irascible Jonathan Swift in his 1704 satire "The Battle of the Books," the recognized model for such self-serving struggles, ridiculed the various factions that routinely claim modern ideas should supplant traditional wisdom. Such debates, frequently resulted, for me, in each narcissistic speaker trying to prove who is the smartest person in the room. I always viewed such intellectual competition as silly and a waste of time. In the great author's ingenious parody, the Ancients' texts, repositories of reason and common sense, battled the Moderns' works that are opposed to traditional views and values. Such struggles, in Swift's world, always saw the Moderns bested by the Ancients. Of course, my position changed with age. For the record, my all-time hero in such futile historical fights is the immortal Giuseppe Verdi, a penetrating, confident genius who never found it necessary to seek favor either with the public or with his critics.

In reflecting back on those tiresome times and the unproductive pressures they produced, I sensed now would be a perfect opportunity to make sure that the reader and I are in sync with each other. We've been moving along at a fairly fast pace. That is, from Chapter 1 to now, we have covered nearly sixty-five years! In the process, I fear you might be lulled into the reasonable mistake my unconventional journey was little more than a collection of uneven essays on assorted topics that could easily be cherry-picked. You might even mistakenly assume it didn't pay to read the previously published material. All that really mattered was focusing on my reflections of the past. Or as the late Sir Francis Bacon might quip: "Some essays to be tasted, some swallowed, and some to be chewed and digested." Just as maddening to me is the idea you found this very personal story had no closely integrated structure, that one chapter did not follow from another. Of course, a reader may decide whatever he or she likes. But tasting and chewing were not and are not my intentions in sharing my thoughts with you.

If my misgivings have merit and you fall into that unconvinced category, I willingly concede the fault is mine, not yours. However, the only sensible way to remedy the problem, for me, is to look back at where we have been and to reiterate more clearly my intentions; and how, despite my many limitations as a writer and an intellectual, my specific aims have been organized and offered throughout this relaxed but heartfelt narrative in a logical way. Much the way Thelonius Monk structured his music!

Even before warning you about my doubtful gifts as a teacher, I set out an initial page of quotations, meant in my mind, to make available to the reader an important framework for the chapters that followed. The citations are not a random mixture of opinions, nor are they presented as a pretentious list to strengthen my pseudo-intellectual interests. If you take the time and grant me some reasonable leeway, you can see in hindsight how each reference reflects the basic ideas I discuss in describing my unconventional journey. Above all, they are the genes embedded in my genetic evolution as a teacher. The thoughts, the authors, and the group itself function as living material for how I developed and how I function. They represent, as T.S. Eliot, once said, "Those who are dead, yet living."

Moving to Chapter 1, the narrative outlines how the child is the father of the man. Besides emphasizing that my teaching career is deeply rooted in my past, I stress I never considered myself, now and then, as anything other than an "amateur." But within that statement, there is a subtext that may not have been evident, or that I should have made clearer to the reader. That is, within each anecdote describing what I meant by the concept of being a novice, there is a tacit remark on how I applied that admission to the world of teaching. For example, when I talk about how enjoyable and important movies were to a dysfunctional kid growing up on the Lower East Side and the streets of Flatbush prior to the start of World War II, I am underscoring the necessity for a teacher, in order to be effective, both to know his students and their needs, as well as to recognize how film genres operated in the "Golden Age of Hollywood." I am also suggesting, because of my idols like Pauline Kael, Ernest Hemingway, and other historical heroes, the indispensable necessity in making what you know clearly accessible to your students. In other words, communicate rather than pontificate. When I emphasize the time spent in movie theaters watching films over and over again, I am reminding the reader that no one really sees a movie until he has watched it several times. What separated me from my peers, probably more than anything else, were multiple viewings that made me conscious of movie formulas and conventions.

Let me be very clear on this point. The benefit of those enchanting experiences in the dark was not that I had earth-shattering emotional experiences, or that I understood all that I saw, but that those empathetic incidents nurtured in me powerful feelings about human relationships and behavior: rebelliousness, independence, and a distrust for authority, almost all directed against despotism, corruption, and repression. When I tire you with movie titles signifying the range of themes and genres I saw in those formative years, I am stating straight out that a major difference between film and literature is that the former is a visual and oral tradition, while the latter is a print-oriented practice. When I describe my awful elementary school experiences, I am arguing that the way you measure a good teacher versus a poor one is not based on degrees, rank, publications, student evaluations, or titles; rather, a good teacher is someone open to new ideas, takes risks, cares more about his students than his status, and seeks to increase rather than defend his understanding of his discipline. Good teachers take chances; bad ones are complacent and smug. Probably the most important subtext in Chapter 1, to me, is how my street-smart mother kept me occupied with books and movies in a non-threatening environment. Intuitively, this wise woman understood one learns best when one wants to learn and is free to do so!

In Chapter 2, "Paradoxes," covering my years at New Rochelle High School and the unpredictable experiment with the film/book program, I explain how my love for literature and my rebellious background subconsciously directed me to the needs of marginalized students. I saw in them parts of myself; so consequently, I drew upon my life experiences as essential tools for teaching and for learning. But two major subtexts in that enjoyable memory were the necessity for a suitable teaching environment and an appropriate laboratory for learning. If my initial supportive administrators had not stimulated me to experiment and to explore, I would never be where I am today. I cannot stress enough how much I believe this position. In training tomorrow's teachers, I believe not enough is made of where one teaches; the emphasis is far too often on getting a job, being part of the team, and making no waves. Moreover, not enough in teaching and in life is made of the importance of failure and rejection as necessary tools for growth and improvement. Let me put the argument another way. There is not a chapter in this unconventional story that does not address those issues of success and failure. In fact, a major goal in this narrative is to assert in the strongest terms possible that mavericks can not only survive but also succeed.

Another sensitive subtext is what makes an effective teacher. I honestly believe that great educators, like legendary athletes and artists, are born, not made. You either have it or you don't. No matter how hard you study, or how many hours you work, or how committed you are to doing well, if you are not blessed, you will rarely rise above the level of being competent and adequate. The great teachers are, as others have observed, G-d's miracles to the human race. We lesser beings can tweak and refine and assist in the true scholars' contributions to our civilization. But that is basically all we can do! Edna Ferber used to describe this intellectual landscape as the domain of the emeralds and the wheat.⁵ In her judgment and mine, both are needed to make the world go round. Nevertheless, we are not all equal!

Another slightly less but still very important subtext is a teacher's relationship with his colleagues. Rather than give you a narcissistic account of what I mean, let me recall a scene from Steven Spielberg's *Amistad*. Ex-President John Quincy Adams (Anthony Hopkins) is now serving as a Massachusetts Congressman. When the audience first sees him at the Capital building, the great man is meeting an abolitionist named Theodore Joadson (Morgan Freeman). Joadson is trying to get the distinguished public servant to take on an exceedingly controversial case involving a falsely imprisoned African, but Adams refuses. He tells Joadson he's not interested; at which time, the abolitionist gives a very erudite explanation of why Adams should change his mind. The legislator looks at the speaker and says, "You're quite the scholar, Mr. Joadson, aren't you? Quite the historian." Adams pauses for a moment and then continues, "Let me tell you something about that quality, if I might. Without an accompanying mastery of at least one–tenth of its measure of grace, such erudition is worthless, sir. Now you take it from one who knows."

I will not test your patience by going through one chapter after another, trying to rationalize the links among the quotations, the various subtexts, and my goals for this book. That point has now been made. Nor will I draw your attention to the many discrepancies in my well-intentioned conclusions, nor will I dwell on my many disappointments with people or institutions. Moreover, I have no interest in defending myself once more against my critics, or of reminding you how optimistic I remain because of the arts and my friends and loved ones. These personal issues are more interesting to me than I think they are to the reader.

But I would like to emphasize for the sake of clarity some key narrative threads. First, you should be aware of a theme stated at the outset and embedded in in every commentary: without "humility," there is little possibility of personal growth. Far too many people I know still fail to recognize this trait in our times together. Unless you realize how trivial are the facts you know, you have little reason to strive to learn more. Each essay you have hopefully read illustrates that belief. These recollections also serve as reminders of how easy it is for an educator to be misunderstood and to be stereotyped as a hopeless romantic or a "show boater." Once you learn to ignore what you cannot control, your life becomes more manageable but not necessarily easier.

Secondly, I cannot emphasize enough how each chapter, as I indicated from the beginning, supports Cyrano's practical cautions about what you face in teaching as well as in your life: "Dishonesty, Compromise, Prejudice, Ignorance, and Corruption."[6] They are life's constant companions. Let me be very clear on this subtext. I am a teacher. Like T.S. Eliot's Prufrock, "I am not Prince Hamlet, nor was [I] meant to be."[7] All that is in my power to control are my attitude and my behavior. It is not an earth-shattering discovery that everyone faces an uphill battle in teaching, in human relations, and in life. In each chapter you read, therefore, the subtext remains that my secret for success was staying focused on the prize. (Of course, it didn't hurt I had Sheila in my corner!)

And third, a major thread in every chapter is my unshakable conviction about the imperfect world we live in. It is probably for that reason I emphasize the importance of history in and on film. Although I believe an effective teacher should be able to argue both sides of an issue in the subject matter that he presents to his audience, as you discover in numerous chapters in this book, I remain convinced you need to confront, to challenge, and to understand who is saying what to whom and for what reason. One of the worst mistakes in my profession may be the unwillingness to speak out against injustices. To me, silence should not be an option.

Another issue troubling me is the academician's commitment to the concept of detachment. By that I mean the notion scholars should be open-minded and non-judgmental when communicating with their students in the classroom. In theory, the idea seems splendid. Many humanists and their multiple disciplines pride themselves on their intellectual impartiality in teaching their disciplines. They do not see themselves as refereeing history and evaluating events, but in reporting the content accurately and even-handedly. While I admire their discipline and their goals, I nevertheless find their idealistic beliefs often falling short of their objectives. One reason is that the world in which we presumably discover facts is tied to our individual perceptions. What we see many others may not see. Another difficulty is that our perceptions do not exist in a vacuum. Once we appreciate how we are influenced by a host of variables, it should be easy to see how subjective our judgments are. Moreover, most of us, being human and flawed, from time to time give into our biases and our egos, while ignoring the dangers and misrepresentations that result from unbridled passion. Being human does not worry me. But being tied to an unrealistic attachment to objectivity might unnecessarily result in a possible disconnect with our students.

Based upon my experience, we first define, as Walter Lippmann said decades ago, and then we see. That simple fact has profound ramifications for what we teach, why, and how. I just wish we would spend more time with our students sharing our educated opinions about the merits of what we study. Why do we think, for example, we have so many incidences of human depravity in our history of civilization? If we risked offering our opinions more frequently, I believe there might well be better understanding about what it is that needs changing and improving in our times and in our lives. Consequently, my heart is almost always with those souls who defy the conventional curriculum and the traditional means of communication that inform society. It is because of the aforementioned reasons, I continually return to Swift and his profound declaration spelled out centuries before I was born that resonates so much with me today: "I have ever hated all nations, professions, and communities, and all my love is toward individuals...."[8]

That outburst brings me to another subtext that is hopefully evident in each chapter's footnotes: the gratitude and respect I have for so many wonderful people who helped me in my career. Those unsung individuals are my major caveat to Dean Swift's admittedly harsh verdict. To restate, what I wrote earlier: I have always been optimistic about things getting better. I learned that from the Hollywood dream factory. Life has shown me that in each generation there are pioneering individuals who through their imagination and influence make a significant contribution to fighting "man's inhumanity to man."

What has troubled me, however, has been the price they, and

the world, pay for their success. For example, I know that Hitler was defeated and the Third Reich destroyed. But it cost the lives of 50 million people! My unconventional journey, therefore, reveals hopefully a passionate individual sharing his experiences in the expectation he will provide his students with fresh and significant opportunities to enrich their lives.

Some, like Roger Ebert believed that the purpose of knowledge is for a better tomorrow.[9] Jascha Heifetz felt a teacher "passes on traditions."[10] And Ben Zoma says, "Who is wise? He who learns from every person."[11] For me, the recurring subtexts in this book relate to the belief that knowledge is best used when it both honors those who came before us and inspires each of us to be all we can be.

Now, having gotten that off my chest, I return to this departmental anthology. The intended television essay never materialized; and as a result, my film comments were not included in the book. The publisher felt that a single essay on film was too much of an imbalance in the text. Nevertheless, the essay had been written. Having spent considerable time on what I felt were worthwhile suggestions for beginning film students, I sent it off for publication. Looking at the essay now, I'm almost satisfied by what I wrote nearly sixteen years ago.

Let me leave this sprawling chapter with this cinematic metaphor from Christopher Nolan's impressive science-fiction film *Interstellar*.[12] At an undisclosed time in the future, two men are sitting on the front porch ruminating about life today and in the past. The younger man, Cooper (Matthew McConaughey), observes wistfully: "Explorers, pioneers, not caretakers. We used to look up at our place in the stars. Now you just look down at our place in the dirt."

Notes

[1] Jacques Richard, *Henri Langlois: The Phantom of the Cinematheque*. France: Les Films Elementaires, 2004.
[2] Qtd. in Ann Donnelly and Elizabeth Woledge, *Shakespeare: Work, Life and Times*. London: Jigsaw Design and Publishing, 2012. 15.
[3] Oliver Wendell Holmes, Jr., "The Path of the Law," *Harvard Law Review* (1897): 10.
[4] Man Ray, *Source/Notes: To Be Continued, Unnoticed*. 1948. Izquotes.com.

[5] Edna Ferber, *So Big*. New York: Doubleday, 1924.
[6] Edmond Rostand, *Cyrano de Bergerac*. Translated by John Murrell. 1897. Loc 4114-45.
[7] T. S. Eliot, "The Love Song of J. Alfred Prufrock," *The Complete Poems and Plays 1909-1950*. New York: Harcourt, Brave and Company, 1950. 7.
[8] Jonathan Swift, *The Correspondence of Jonathan Swift*. 1725.
[9] Qtd. in Steve James, *Life Itself*. USA: Magnolia Films, 2014.
[10] Peter Rosen, *God's Fiddler: Jascha Heifetz*. USA: Kultur International Films 2011.
[11] Pirke Avos, *Ethics of the Fathers*. Chapter Four, Section 1.
[12] Christopher Nolan, *Interstellar*. USA: Paramount Pictures, 2014.

What Does It Mean, Mr. Holmes?

An Approach to Film Study[1]

It can be difficult to introduce film analysis to students in a beginning English course not primarily oriented around film. Students taking such a class probably have never looked at movies in a serious way. They may be compared to fans at a ball game who sit behind a post and miss the action. Time is limited, funds are scarce, and equipment is minimal. The challenge, therefore, is how to sensitize such students both to the medium of film and to how that awareness relates to the field of English studies.

What follows is a way to introduce film study to novices, which I have found effective. The focus will be on Hollywood theatrical movies. The reasons are straightforward. Paramount in English studies is the art of storytelling. I believe that American filmmakers collectively are the world's best cinematic storytellers. Their knowledge of craft and their state of the art resources remain their greatest strengths. Other reasons include the fact that for nearly a century Hollywood's theatrical films have remained the dominant movie experiences of people worldwide, while Hollywood's commercial and cultural strengths have established it as the yardstick by which films are created and judged everywhere. That is not to say the American film industry is the only industry of merit. Nor is it to claim that American fiction films are the only movies made in the motion picture industry, that American theatrical movies are made exclusively in Southern California, or that Hollywood's standards of excellence exist unchallenged. Clearly, no such conclusions are true. But by using history as our tutor, it seems reasonable to assert that in the twentieth century there were only two types of feature fiction films: American movies and those films that offered an alternative to them.

If we are to begin a serious study of movies, it makes sense to start with the art form most people know and enjoy: the Hollywood film. What are the aesthetics of motion pictures? How can we increase the emotional and intellectual pleasure of watching films without creating linguistic and ideological obstacles to the experience of movies? At the same time, how can we see movies as more than mindless escapism?

HYPOTHESES

Like everyone else who professes to know something about film criticism, I bring to the task a number of assumptions. Acquainting you with those ideas provides a key to understanding as to why I take the pragmatic position I do about film study.

Let us start with my basic assumption that *no single critical theory in history is indispensable for analyzing film art*. What exactly does that mean? It does not mean that cinematic conjectures (or those speculative beliefs borrowed from literary theory) are useless. Far from it. Speculations resulting from systematic hypotheses about what a film means often offer insights. The critical debate is over the value of such insights. That is, do they tell us why one story is stronger, more appealing, than stories in other movies? I think not.

My refusal to endorse any one film theory reveals my critical biases. I contend that the critical awareness gained from such diverse areas as linguistics, anthropology, psychology, the new historicism, feminism, the *auteur* approach, sociology, formalism, reception theory, or Marxist economics remains highly suspect. Judgments based on their canons **do not and never have** enabled us to understand and to appreciate significantly why one film is better than another, and why we feel the way we do about the movies we experience. In fact, film theory routinely reveals more about the critic than the work criticized. As Stuart Kaminsky so aptly states: "That judgments will continue to be made is obvious; that they reflect anything beyond the acquired taste of an individual or culture segment is doubtful; that they can be substantiated with any kind of detachment is alchemical" (43).

Like other relativist critics, I make no claim to originality. My point is simply that my judgments result from my experiences and the experiences of people who produce movies. They are not based on *theoretical* positions.

At the very least, my pragmatic approach tries to demystify the process of film analysis. It illustrates at the outset why you do not need a special film vocabulary or a course in film criticism to start to examine film seriously. Obviously, it helps to know what we mean by a "frame," a "cut," a "shot," and a "moving camera." But I assume you know that. What you mostly need is imagination and an inquiring mind. What is invaluable, Dudley Andrew explains, is recognition that "films are both cultural objects to be mastered and experiences that continually master us. We must learn to experience, to remove ourselves from experience, to understand experience, and then to re-experience in what amounts to a perpetual internal revolution" (43-44). In other words, *we examine critically why we feel as we do about the movies we view.*

I also assume that you might misunderstand what is meant by "film." How many times have you seen people getting into arguments because of misperceptions and misunderstandings? That is, before we can argue about whether a film means this or that, we have to agree it is a film. Before we disagree as to whether we "read" or "experience" a film, we need to agree about what we are studying. In essence, we need to begin by recognizing that Hollywood is more a concept than a reality, that subtitled films are not synonymous with art, and—perhaps most important—that movies are different from literature.

Scholars like Thomas Sobchack and Vivian C. Sobchack explain that "Film" is not just a description of "a particular material and medium of communication that has certain specific properties governed by certain physical laws." These theorists point out that film "is also the term we use to describe both a single work and an entire body of works produced through this material and in this medium." However, these authors emphasize that "Film" is more than the material and a medium. Film is also the use of this material and medium "to produce particular communicative texts that formulate particular fields of symbolic meaning and effects, and meet particular sets of criteria that give them particular value." Not surprisingly, the Sobchacks avow, "...*film* can be perceived as variously associated with the communication of information, with personal expression as art, with the argumentative power of rhetoric, and, of course, with the undemanding pleasure of entertainment" (3).

Equally important is the Sobchacks' insistence that the term "film" also describes "a commercial product made in the context of American capitalism" (4). That is, movies are both a business and an art. What we see and hear in film results in large part from the economic demands of an industry that produces films. The plots, characters, situations, imagery, and themes result from marketing research refined and standardized by filmmakers over the past century. That is, economics dramatically affects film technique and content. People who make theatrical films routinely put profit over purpose.

Almost from the birth of moving pictures, filmmakers became preoccupied with minimizing financial risk and maximizing profits. This desire led them to the advantages of formula filmmaking, which relies on using tried and tested material repeatedly. The more expensive a film is to produce, the more conservative are the producers who make movies. Consequently, it is no accident that the public, today more than ever before, is routinely offered remakes, spin-offs, and sequels to previous hit movies. Effective film publicity draws the audience's attention to the formulaic similarities between a current release and previous hits, between the prior roles of the stars and this new characterization. That is why, as John Cawelti detailed decades ago, we have film "formulas" (as opposed to the literary term "genres") such as Westerns, science fiction films, gangster movies, and family melodramas (27-28, 33).

This point about most mass-produced theatrical movies being standardized products cannot be overemphasized. The people who create films play on the expectations of the public, while the public selects films that *promise* them the repetition of a previously enjoyable experience. Nevertheless, an artist cannot simply repeat a formula's conventions. The public demands novelty as well. Thus, an essential ingredient of a successful commercial and critical product is whether the filmmaker has adequately updated the conventions of the formula, without ignoring the conventional expectations of the audience.

The commercial nature of motion pictures and the prominence of film formulas are two of the major differences in the academy's approach to film and literature. Let me be very clear on this point. It is not that film and literature do not share many similarities. They clearly do. Elsewhere I explain in detail what those similarities and differences include (Manchel). Many existing essays in this significant journal demonstrate what benefits film accrues from literary theory. Moreover, as my colleagues show, film is not the only art form that is tied to commercial pressures. A number of literary critics explore the commercial constraints, similar to the problems experienced by filmmakers, placed on literary works throughout history.

What I am stressing for film study, however, is *the recognition of what makes film a film,* and not another literary form. For example, literary genres stress originality; film formulas, stereotypes. Literary works create essentially with words; films, with sights and sounds. Writers tell us; filmmakers show us. If we examine how a writer writes a narrative, then we should explore how a filmmaker produces a cinematic narrative.

What do I mean by a cinematic analysis? Certainly, film, as does any narrative art form, uses a pattern to structure its ideas. That configuration customarily draws on familiar literary ingredients like story, plot, character, setting, point of view, and style. Again, the issue is *how they are used uniquely in film,* not if they are literary concepts.

Because movies exude verisimilitude, audiences often assume that what they see is real, that it is true. A crucial first step is to disabuse viewers of that notion. For example, cinematographer Vladimir Nilsen states emphatically, "A photograph is by no means a complete and whole reflection of reality: the photographic picture represents only one or another selection from the sum of physical attributes of the object photographed" (qtd. in Giannetti, 1). Stanley Donen, the director of films like *On the Town* (1951), *Singin' in the Rain* (1952), and *Charade* (1963), insists, "Cinema lies 24 frames a second. I mean that everything is planned, written, rehearsed, staged and put down into very specific spots. That doesn't reek of truth. It reeks of planning and forcing [people, things] into situations. Making it go. That is not truth" (Donen).

My approach is to foreground an awareness of cinematic techniques. In class, focus your discussion about film by asking how the craftsperson makes his or her ideas cinematically known to the spectator. What do we see and hear at the start of a movie? Why?

Because that is where we get our initial cues about the film's theme and purpose. Artists, Donen points out, want to "State...[their] case as soon as possible in a movie." Mike Nichols, director of movies like *Who's Afraid of Virginia Woolf?* (1966), *The Graduate* (1967), and *Silkwood* (1986), argues that the opening of a movie is where we identify an artist's style: "Style is beginning something that will make everything happening later necessary and inevitable" (Nichols).

This classroom exercise reveals the collaborative nature of film, the roles played not just by people in front of the camera and the director, but also by lighting technicians, cinematographers, editors, costume designers, casting experts, art decorators, and screenwriters. For example, the *mise en scene* (how the shot is handled) focuses your attention on how sets, costumes, lighting, and movement of the camera and actors set the stage for what follows in the narrative. This inquiry is standard operating procedure for Sidney Lumet, director of films like *Twelve Angry Men* (1957), *The Pawnbroker* (1965), and *Serpico* (1973). In his words, you always ask, "What is the *mise en scene* trying to achieve?" (Lumet). And we have not yet discussed cinematography, editing, sound, and performance. According to Lumet, the way in which you tell a story and what story you tell is "influenced by the scale of the screen."

How important is casting? According to Michael Caine, who has appeared in more than a hundred films, "the art of direction is casting" (Caine). Many of cinema's greatest directors—John Ford, Alfred Hitchcock, John Huston, Jean Renoir, François Truffaut, and Woody Allen—provided very little direction to their casts once the movie began. The assumption has always been that if you hire the right actors, they provide the behavior and the emotions called for in the characters.

How do you enter such an analysis? You ask questions like, "Why this shot? Why that camera angle? What is the motivation for this behavior?" David Bordwell and Kristin Thompson prove very useful in this scenario. In their introduction to the art of film, they put particular emphasis on five principles of film form: function, similarity and repetition, difference and variation, development, and unity/disunity (78-85). To oversimplify their notion, Bordwell and Thompson believe, as do many film critics, that twentieth-century audiences have been socialized to a Classical Hollywood narrative.

The effects of this socialization remain in place to this very day. That is, in most Hollywood movies, psychologically motivated characters need to resolve a specific problem. By means of causality, the characters' actions, occurring through time and space, eventually reach closure. Filmmakers identify the movie's essential issues, characters, and motifs through the multiple functions they perform in the film. Through repetition and differentiation of a situation, for instance, we became aware of the development in the narrative. The assumption is that everything in the well-made film contributes to its resolution. Time refers to real time as well as film time, to a story's chronology and the duration of the plot; space, the settings of a narrative and a frame's visual composition. Usually, everything remains subordinate to telling the story. Susan Sarandon, probably unwittingly, takes the same approach in creating her characterizations: "If it's not something new about the character or new about the plot, I'd rather cut it" (Sarandon).

These principles can provide you with tools to discover why sights, sounds, situations, motifs, and characters occur in the film and how they relate to the structure and meaning of the movie. That is, what sights and sounds are used in *The Wizard of Oz* (Victor Fleming, 1939) to represent Kansas during the Depression? Why? What visual compositions in the opening of *A Place in the Sun* (George Stevens, 1951), the screen adaptation of Theodore Dreiser's *An American Tragedy*, are crucial to understanding the movie's theme? Why? What is important about the physical settings in *Paths of Glory* (Stanley Kubrick, 1957)? How do you know? As Norman Jewison, the director of films like *In the Heat of the Night* (1967), *Moonstruck* (1987), and *The Hurricane* (1999) exclaims, "Every picture must have a point" (Jewison). The same can be said for every shot, camera angle, and sound.

Thus, we come to the problematic issue of "reading a film." I have no problem with that approach for literature. Literature is, for the most part, a narrative form. My feeling, however, is that no matter how important the narrative is, there is much more to watching a movie than following its narrative. Like Bordwell and Thompson, I think you need to see how literary qualities and cinematic techniques interact. My interest is in how the artist has communicated his/her feelings about the meaning of the story, how a particular scene contributes to a narrative's progress, why a character is behaving in a certain way, why the director selected this particular lens in this particular scene, why the camera is moving in this fashion, why the action is lit with these particular lights, and why music is present one moment and then absent the next? To put it in Bordwell and Thompson's language, "To understand form in any art, we must be familiar with the medium which that art utilizes" (168).

Let us be clear on this issue. Using techniques associated with "reading a text" have merit for film study. It would be silly to argue otherwise. Nevertheless, to start with those methods at an introductory level in film is to become bogged down in literary rather than cinematic analysis.

Having alerted you to my biases, let us turn to the approach itself. We do this while gently reminding you of Sherlock Holmes's admonition to his longtime friend, "You see, my dear Watson, but you do not observe."

TESTING THE APPROACH

How do we experience a film? Begin by selecting a moving picture that demonstrates the assumptions already made. Two *movies — The Searchers* (John Ford, 1956) and *The Godfather* (Francis Ford Coppola, 1972) — work well for non-film classes I have guest taught recently in the English Department at the University of Vermont. They are also highly regarded movies, familiar to many students, and easily accessible. The pre-class strategy involves two easy tasks: an awareness of the formula in question, and a *recent* viewing of the movie.

For example, *The Searchers* is a Western. Students I meet find no difficulty in generalizing about what is meant by a "Western." That is a central technique. I am not interested here with the accuracy of their formulaic classification. What I am after is what the group *expects* from a Western. Remember that one of my assumptions is that filmmakers make movies that play upon audience expectations. John Sturges, for example, who directed *Gunfight at the OK Corral* (1957), *The Magnificent Seven* (1961), and *Joe Kidd* (1972), believes,

"It's a Western because of the story form, because of the traditional and conventional aspects of a western story: isolation, one man up against it; he's got to resolve it by violence, no one can help him. It's good versus evil; it's a morality tale" (qtd. in *American Cinema: The Western*).

My students often believe that Westerns focus on conflicts between civilization and the wilderness, between settlers and townspeople, between outlaws and heroes, between Euro Americans and Native Americans, between the West and the East, and between the Old World and the New World. In fact, these morality plays explore the American character, its ideas about justice, gender relationships and racial equality. Later, hopefully, the complexities of film formulas, the subtleties of individual classifications, and the cultural role played by a formula-based industry in our society will become apparent to the intellectually curious.

A major consideration is that director Ford shaped many of the Western's conventions up to the start of World War II. But when he returned from active military service in the postwar period, Ford had a different attitude about American history. That is the only major cue I will provide you before you see the film.

Do not wait to watch the film in class. Either put it on reserve in your Media Center two weeks before you begin your discussion, or you can rent the movie from a local video store.

A word of caution is in order. Not all films have one version. For example, it makes a difference if you see the original theater releases of films like *The Wild Bunch* (Sam Peckinpah, 1969), *Star Wars* (George Lucas, 1977), *Close Encounters of the Third Kind* (Steven Spielberg, 1977), *Once Upon a Time in America* (Sergio Leone, 1984) and *Blade Runner* (Ridley Scott, 1982). All of these films were recut and rereleased, in each instance significantly altering the cinematic experience. Here is not the place to dwell on various problems one may discover with existing prints of movies shown on television, rented at video stores or purchased from the Internet. Suffice it to say that you must know what print you are using, and everyone in the class should be exposed to the same print to be discussed before coming to class.

I also need to stress how important it is to see the film as close to the class as possible. Without the events and characters being fresh in your mind, it is difficult to make the jump from the start of the film and the cues provided by the director/editor to later scenes and behavior in the movie.

Now to the approach itself. What I suggest we do is scrutinize almost every choice the filmmakers have made in constructing their cinematic narrative. Pretend that you are one of the collaborators, and you know what you want to do in the film. In a way, this is a story conference, and everyone is sharing ideas as to how to proceed with the construction of the plot. The point is to raise your consciousness about the medium of film. Once you grasp how one communicates information through film, the awareness leads quickly and valuably into an educated and expansive discussion of what the film is about.

I will not provide specific strategies here. My essay deals with suggestions for introducing the art of the film, not with a detailed film analysis. The idea is to read this essay and then apply the method to a specific film. I will, however, give several examples of what I mean about a pragmatic film analysis for a non-film class. Let us begin with *The Searchers*.

At the start of the session, you should reach a consensus about what a Western entails and what the film narrative involves. The conventions we have already mentioned. The story itself focuses on an epic Western adventure by two Texans, who search over six years for a young girl kidnapped by Comanches, in the aftermath of the American Civil War. The main characters we meet at the start of the film include Ethan Edwards (John Wayne), Martin Pawley (Jeffrey Hunter), Capt. Rev. Samuel Clayton (Ward Bond), Chief Scar (Henry Brandon), Martha Edwards (Dorothy Jordan), Aaron Edwards (Walter Coy), Lucy Edwards (Pippa Scott), and Debbie Edwards, as a little girl (Lana Wood).

Now start the film. As soon as the title appears, pause the film. A question I might begin with is, "What does the title, *The Searchers*, mean? Are the searchers looking only for Debbie, or are they interested also in answers to their character and their values? Do you think the title raises questions about what the formula itself represents in the contemporary world? Why? Why not?"

After a brief discussion, play the film through the title song by Stan Jones." Pause the film and ask, "How do the words of the song set the mood, introduce the film's theme?"

After a few minutes, play the film through the first few moments until you see Ethan. Pause and ask, "Who in the film sees him first? Why does director Ford present the events this way? How is Martha's vision visually framed? What was she doing before she 'felt' Ethan's presence? What functions does Ford have in mind when he presents each member of the Edwards family in a specific order? How has the setting contributed to the questions raised by Ethan's relatives?"

Play a few more moments of the film, up to the point, where everyone enters the house, and pause the film. "When does the music change in these opening moments? Why? How are Lucy and Debbie differentiated from the others? Does Ford want us to believe that everyone in the Edwards household is happy to see Ethan? If not, why does Ethan pose a threat to the family? How do you know that he does? What are the questions that the Edwards ask Ethan? Are his answers truthful? What does he have to hide? How do we know that he is hiding something?"

Play the film up to the point that Martin arrives home for dinner, and pause. "How does Ford visually link Martin to Ethan? What is unusual about Ethan's reactions to Martin? Martin's to Ethan? What functions does Ethan's military coat play in the opening scenes?"

In the time remaining, pursue the relationship between your classroom ideas, suggested by the answers to the aforementioned questions, and the rest of the film. For example, "When do Ethan's actions with Debbie reoccur later in the film? Why? How does Ethan's meeting with Chief Scar near the end of the film call into question Ethan's remarks about his relationship to Martin? Why does Ford end *The Searchers* with a shot reminiscent of the beginning of the film? How does everything in the film relate to the idea of family relationships?"

Take advantage of the conventions of the film's formula. What conventions does Ford use at the start of the film? In what way does he alter the perception of the hero? How does Wayne's stature contribute to a revisionist look of the Western? My goal is to get you to observe the way Ford and his collaborators construct the film, the way they cue the audience into motifs, themes, character relationships, and stylistic flourishes. If you wish to pursue these issues after the session, begin your research with Peter Lehman's splendid essay on *The Searchers*.

If you do not like Westerns, try the experiment with gangster films. *The Godfather* works wonderfully with my students.

You know the drill. A word of caution. Be careful in selecting the movie by name alone.

When I asked our film librarian recently to place *The Godfather* on reserve, she mistakenly set aside *The Godfather Saga* (Francis Ford Coppola 1981). The latter film is a brilliant restructuring of the three *Godfather* movies, only in chronological order of the events and not the release dates of the actual films. My point is that you need to check the film on reserve, not just request it. The class might begin with an introduction to movies as both a business and an art. In this way, you discover something about the medium of film and how it relates to the art of storytelling.

Quickly, we identify the film formula as the gangster film. What does that mean to the class? The most frequently mentioned responses relate to class warfare, the focus on ethnicity, the centrality of the American dream perverted; the importance of fate and time; the inevitability of the gangster's destruction; the preoccupation with success and power; the tragedy of the protagonist; the sense of paranoia and betrayal among friends, family, and business associates; the isolation of the protagonist; and the pervasive use of irony.

Rarely will you find a student who has not seen the unfolding fate of the Corleone family several times. The main characters we meet at the start of the film include Don Vito Corleone (Marlon Brando), Michael Corleone (Al Pacino), Kay Adams (Diane Keaton), Tom Hagen (Robert Duvall), Clemenza (Richard S. Castellano), Santino "Sonny" Corleone (James Caan), Connie Corleone Rizzi (Talia Shire), Tessio (Abe Vigoda), Fredo Corleone (John Cazale), Mama Corleone (Morgana King), Luca Brasi (Lenny Montana), and Bonasera (Salvatore Corsitto).

Now start the movie. As soon as the title appears, pause the film. A question I might begin with is, "What does the logo of a hand pulling the strings signify? Is there any irony intended? Why?" After a few minutes restart the film, run through the credits to the darkness and the sound of Bonasera speaking, and pause. "What mood has the music set? Why begin the film in darkness?

Why do we first hear Bonasera rather than see him? How is sound used to advance the narrative and foreshadow the future? What is Bonasera's profession? How many conventions of the gangster film can you identify just by the statement Bonasera is making? Start the film and go through Bonasera's plea but stop before you see the Don's face. "How many links has director Coppola made between the funeral director and the Don? To whom is Bonasera speaking? Are you sure?"

Because the film is so well known you can move quickly from the recognition that the first two petitioners for the Don's help are Old World parents concerned with the welfare of their children to the Don's self-delusion that he can protect his own children. "How many children does the Don have? How are we shown their characters, their status, and their fates before the end of the wedding? What is the time frame of the film? How does the family portrait set Michael off from his siblings, while at the same time linking him to his father's status? How many important functions can you identify in Michael's wearing of a Marine uniform at the wedding? What important character traits of Michael are revealed by his relationship with Kay during the wedding festivities? How does director Coppola reveal the ironic situations of both the Don and Michael? How important is the casting of the roles? How valuable are the settings to the story?"

Again, we each may have our own interpretations to these questions. You may even have different sights and sounds you want to explore than those suggested above. That is not the purpose of the session. Its value lies in recognizing that movies show their stories, not tell them.

Whichever film you use, the trick is to focus on the way the filmmakers have made concrete choices to construct the film narrative. Why this rather than that? Move slowly rather than quickly. Pay attention to details before jumping to general conclusions. The most useful techniques, my dear Watson, are to observe, to listen, and to reflect on your experience.

Notes

[1] Frank Manchel, "What Does It Mean, Mr. Holmes? An Approach to Film Study," *LFQ* Volume 31:1 (2003): 69-76.

Works Cited

Andrew, Dudley. "An Open Approach to Film Study and the Situation at Iowa." *Film Study in the Undergraduate Curriculum.* Ed. Barry Keith Grant. New York: MLA, 1983.
Bordwell, David, and Kristin Thompson. *Film Art: An Introduction.* 5th Ed. New York: McGraw, 1997.
Caine, Michael. Interview with James Lipton. *Inside the Actor's Studio.* Bravo. Film and Arts Network, New York. 1997.
Cawelti, John. *The Six-Gun Mystique.* Bowling Green: Bowling Green UP, 1970.
Donen, Stanley. Interview with James Lipton. *Inside the Actor's Studio.* Bravo. Film and Arts Network, New York. 1998.
Giannetti, Louis. *Understanding Movies.* 7th ed. Englewood Cliffs: Prentice-Hall, 1996.
Jewison, Norman. Interview with James Lipton. *Inside the Actor's Studio.* Bravo. Film and Arts Network, New York. 1997.
Kaminsky, Stuart. *American Film Genres.* 2nd ed. Chicago: Nelson-Hall, 1985.
Lehman, Peter. "Texas 1868/America 1956: *The Searchers.* "*Close Viewings: An Anthology of New Film Criticism.* Ed. Peter Lehman. Tallahassee: Florida State UP, 1990. 387-415.
Lumet, Sydney. Interview with James Lipton. *Inside the Actor's Studio.* Bravo. Film and Arts Network, New York. 1995.
Manchel, Frank. *Film Study: An Analytical Bibliography.* 4 vols. Rutherford: Fairleigh Dickinson UP, 1990-91.
Nichols, Mike. Interview with James Lipton. *Inside the Actor's Studio.* Bravo. Film and Arts Network, New York. 1997.
Sarandon, Susan. Interview with James Lipton. *Inside the Actor's Studio.* Bravo. Film and Arts Network, New York. 1998.
Sobchack, Thomas, and Vivian C. Sobchack. *An Introduction to Film.* 2nd ed. Boston: Little, 1987.
"The Western." *American Cinema.* Exec. Prod. Lawrence Pitkethly. New York Center for Visual History. PBS. KCET, Los Angeles. 30 Jan. 1994.

18. The forgotten star Calvero (Charles Chaplin) and his partner (Buster Keaton) do one last turn together before they end their careers. Charles Chaplin, *Limelight* (1952). From the core collection production photographs of the Margaret Herrick Library, Academy of Motion Picture Arts and Sciences.

15.

Laugh and Learn

To write history, one has to empathize.[1]
Niall Ferguson

Any struggle worth having takes place across generations.[2]
Ta-Nehisi Coates

No matter how smart and well-educated you get, you can be deceived.[3]
James "The Amazing" Randi

Imagine how shocking and awful it was to learn in December 1999 that my teaching days would soon be over. Forty-two years had passed so quickly, and there was so much yet to be done. But I had no choice. Not only had cancer crippled my concentration and sapped my strength, but also the future looked bleak, and it demanded my full attention. Forced to end my career and go on disability starting in June 2001, I needed to turn my efforts to solving the health crisis, so Sheila and I could then live out our dreams in our beloved state of Vermont.

But like Don Michael Corleone and Captain Nathan Brittles before me, my retirement plans proved a bit premature. In March of 2000, Associate Dean Donna Kuizenga sent a letter notifying me I had been given the Dean's Lecture Award. Established in 1991, this gracious gesture by the College of Arts and Sciences initiated a tradition of recognizing and honoring those colleagues, who in the judgment of the Arts and Sciences community, had "consistently demonstrated the ability to translate their professional knowledge and skill into exciting classroom experiences for their students; faculty who [had met] the challenge of being both excellent teachers and highly respected professionals in their own discipline."

I must admit my receiving the Award at this stage in my career was a bit problematic. Although flattered by the act; it did seem a little late in coming. And in my more thoughtful moments, I truly believed this honor, in my case, wasn't any more than the proverbial gold watch for having stayed around so long.

Let's not kid each other. For more than thirty-three years I had been a royal pain-in-the-butt to administrators, colleagues, and staff, challenging the rules, shifting jobs at the University, being a blunt Associate Dean, an unpopular chairperson, and refusing to play the obligatory collegial game. Not only had I made more than my share of mistakes, but also I had consistently refused to be a team player. Chairpersons knew I couldn't conform, and colleagues realized I never turned a blind eye to academic misconduct. From my earliest days in Burlington, I had insisted I had come to UVM not to impugn whatever sacrosanct curriculum was in place, but rather to expand what socially significant subjects should be studied.

Change rarely sat well with my peers; and because we really didn't understand each other, I frequently found myself described by troublesome colleagues as abrasive and insubordinate. Neither label was entirely fair or accurate. More to the point, many of the reforms I helped initiate did not originate with me. They grew out of a situation in which the university experienced a need to change intolerable conditions. As Bob Dylan would sing, "The times they are a changin'." I just adjusted more easily than others around me.

Nonetheless, my iconoclastic behavior resulted in harsh consequences, especially when it came to my interpersonal relations. People who misperceived my intentions often became angry, jealous, and outright unpleasant. Yet, I learned to live with the pushback from my exasperated colleagues.

While I had truly tried to move on from my past robust battles with the Objectionables, I sensed that they had not forgotten or forgiven my criticisms of their exclusively print-oriented practices. Now we were tangling over issues like equal opportunity, political correctness, and cultural diversity. And while the new generation of talented scholars appeared bent on making their academic ideas more complex than clear, I still persisted in making my beliefs more candid than complicated. Adding even more to my intentional isolation from the conventional college community, I understandably had spent my time mostly with my family and with my students. Finally, except for a handful of exceptional friends, there probably wasn't anyone on campus who had even read, let alone accepted, my radical notions about the mass media being central to the mental health of nations. In short, if I had wanted to win academic awards, I had certainly taken an unconventional approach.

Thus, I harbored no illusions about why the College of Arts and Sciences had chosen this moment to accept me as a distinguished scholar. Now that I was finally ending my UVM calling, I thought, they were more than willing to show both their genuine sympathy for my situation and their unbridled enthusiasm for my imminent departure.

These disconcerting suspicions about the College honor prejudiced my attitude as I began preparing the required address for the May 2000 ceremony. My initial idea was to give the scholars and students one last reminder of whom they were losing. Maybe in their excitement to see me depart, they had forgotten what the last four decades had been like with me around. I may not have reached the heights in my profession, but I felt I had made a small contribution to my discipline and to my institution.

I wanted to remind the perceived audience what I had tried to do with my time in academia. They would expect me to talk about my love for film. Instead, I would describe my passion for literature. They would expect me to reminisce about my controversial years lobbying for film study at UVM. I would remind them I came to my professional life as an English teacher. They would expect me to share what film had taught me and how I saw the medium functioning in society. I would tell them about vital books from my errant youth, and how these literary works had been the seminal forces in my lifelong journey. They would expect me to be mellow and sad at this startling stage in my story. I would "give 'em hell" about this imperfect world, and let them know "it ain't over till it's over."

With my roguish juices invigorated and the cancer temporarily pushed aside, I began writing a make believe speech that recalled the initial scene in Richard Thorpe's 1939 screen adaptation of Mark Twain's *The Adventures of Huckleberry Finn*.[4] Opening in a rural classroom, a priggish teacher is seen taking attendance. Once she discovers that Huck, the hopeless truant (Mickey Rooney), is again absent, she says to the class: "Children, I want Huckleberry to serve as example to you. I want you to realize how he has wasted his time....We mustn't get angry with him. We should feel sorry for him. He must be a very unhappy boy."

I would then turn smugly to my captive audience and remind them of how much I identified with Huck. We were anything but unhappy, and we had never wasted our time. I would wonder aloud if many of my listeners even had read the famous but sometimes banned book, although it had once been a required reading assignment for nearly two-thirds of the children across the nation. I would remind them what Hemingway had said about the novel the very year I was born in 1935: "All modern American literature comes from one book by Mark Twain called *Huckleberry Finn*." Then I would chime in how the novel had never known a moment's peace since it appeared in 1885. I would describe how it had been condemned and censored down through the century.[5] I would add sanctimoniously I knew something about what it was like being criticized and being disliked.

"Why do you suppose Mark Twain's story was so attacked?" I would coyly ask. To help them answer the question, I would summarize what the book was about and explain why Twain's immortal protagonist had such a grip on my imagination. From there I would single out Huck's ethical dilemma starting in Chapter XVI of the satirical masterpiece; when Jim, the runaway slave, and the uneducated boy get close to Cairo, Illinois; a free state. Up to that moment, the young maverick who hated school and lived by his own moral lights had never realized how offensive his friendship was with a fugitive slave. "It hadn't ever come home to me before," Huck told himself, "what this thing was I was doing." He had aided Miss Watson's "nigger" escaping his rightful owner and done nothing to stop it. Here was a woman who had been so good to him, and this was what she got from Huck for her troubles. Even worse, Jim, once he got his freedom, was going to come back and steal his children away; "Children that belonged to another man" Huck didn't even know, "and who had done the boy no harm."

Huck's problem focused on why he felt he couldn't betray Jim, who despite his "inferior race," was the boy's friend. They had been through a lot together; Jim, who seemed "white" inside, had saved Huck's life; and what's more, Jim trusted him. As the conflicted boy's journey progressed down the river, he struggled with his great, inescapable moral dilemma. All the good people, the right people, believed it was only "natural" a slave should be returned to his legal owner. These wise folks had been properly educated to follow the rules and to obey the laws. The boy knew right well that if he had had a proper Sunday school learning, he would have realized what he was doing would send him straight to the fiery furnace.

But the more Huck was around these decent, G-d fearing people, the more he saw how cruel they were. To him, doing right or wrong really didn't matter because "a person's conscience ain't got no sense." In addition, Tom Sawyer, his boyhood friend, who "was respectable and had been brought up properly," had no qualms about shaming his family by helping a slave get free. So in the end, Huck follows his "perverted" conscience rather than society's "virtues," and Jim goes free.[6] Those unforgettable passages describing civilization grew even more meaningful to me once I saw Hal Holbrook dramatize them in his unforgettable one-man show, *Mark Twain Tonight*.

From this pious disclosure, I would remind my by-now attentive audience what President John Quincy Adams had told abolitionist Theodore Joadson in *Amistad*: a teacher needs more than information to succeed. He needs grace. I would add, he also needs style and confidence. Of course, a distinguished dramatist and filmmaker like David Mamet would ridicule such advice as showboating, pretentious, and egotistical in *Oleanna*.[7] But being popular and clever is not the same as being right and credible. There are many interpretations as to what makes for a good teacher.

Often, I would explain to my listeners, when the media described me in print, the press painted me as a left-wing critic of traditional studies. So what? Remember that I had long since believed, as Emerson argued, "What I must do is all that concerns me, not what the people will think." Looking back at what worked for me, I would insist (shamelessly and somewhat tongue in cheek) that I always pictured myself a mixture of Mr. Chips (Robert Donat)[8] and Professor Charles W. Kingsfield, Jr. (John Houseman).[9] Then I would slip in an introduction to one of my favorite literary role models: Cyrano de Bergerac. No doubt, the startled audience would react skeptically to my illogical suggestion; and I'd get a chance to talk about another written work that molded my career.

I'd begin by faking humility and confessing how often in my public persona I had modeled myself, as theatrically as I could, on the way the heroic Cyrano had behaved at the Hotel de Bourgogne in Act One of Edmond Rostand's unforgettable seventeenth-century French comedy. A friend of the fiery literary protagonist, the gifted poet with the horrid nose and a beautiful soul, wonders if Cyrano will appear at the theater's production of Balthazar Baro's *La Clorise* that evening. "Why do you ask?" says his companion. Because, explains the friend, the actor Montfleury is scheduled to perform; and Cyrano has forbidden the fellow to appear on any stage for a month. Again, the confidant asks, "Why?" Because, comes the reply, the insolent actor has had the audacity to fancy himself as a suitor for Cyrano's great but unstated love, the beautiful Roxanne.

After some tense moments, Montfleury timidly makes his entrance before the footlights and begins to act, much to the amusement of the audience who is waiting to see, one, if Cyrano will show; and two, what the fiery celebrity will do. Suddenly, our hero appears, shouting, "Prince of Phonies, purge the stage of your presence!" The startled actor desperately scours the theater hall for help. Again, Cyrano tells him to leave, but now the audience is foolishly taking up the actor's cause. Nevertheless, terrified, Montfleury departs; and the poet-warrior turns his wrath towards members of the angry audience. He not only brazenly castigates them, but also heaps scorn on the playwright and his drama.

When an aristocrat attempts to befriend the disgraced actor, Cyrano turns the folly into a disposition on himself and his nose, proclaiming, "A great nose is the banner of a great man, a generous heart, a towering spirit, an expansive soul—such as I unmistakably am...." Dispatching one adversary, he does the same to another challenger before dismissing the entire theater audience.

The distraught theater manager asks who is to pay the performers, and Cyrano flippantly throws a bag of money on stage. The poet's friend is baffled by the act. "You can't afford this behavior." "True," Cyrano replies, "Ah, but what style!"[10]

Then humbly I'd turn to the by-now enthralled gathering and sadly admit I had failed in my career either to be a Cyrano or even a Mr. Chips. But like Rocky, I had given it my best shot; and, at times, I felt I had come close to my ambition to be more than ordinary. After the thunderous laughter had subsided, I would again turn somber. I would insist that from the likes of Huck and Cyrano, I had wanted to become an authentic teacher, one with strong beliefs, and one who trusted himself. I had had an idealistic vision of what I wanted to do in my teaching; and I had remained confident that things that never were, were possible.

Whichever way you go, I would stress, make sure, as Twain and Rostand had brilliantly displayed in their great works, you use humor to emphasize your opinions. And if some well-meaning person advises you falsely that sarcasm is counter-productive, tell him that Mencken taught you, "The final test of truth is ridicule. Very few dogmas have ever faced it and survived."[11]

Moreover, I would add that when you confront your grumbling, unenthusiastic future students, you should focus on what they are learning rather than on what you are teaching. The moment belongs to them, not to you. You should not insist they be obedient, but rather that they take risks. Teach them when they walk alone, to be defiant and unafraid of the dark. Your tone should be practical but also stirring; you should remember to arm them with important ideas along with your bombastic rhetoric; and your ambition should always be to make them suspicious of those who demand respect and submission. In the end, you must persuade your students of the richness in following the teacher who follows a dream, not so that they can become your disciples but so they can soar off on their own. To illustrate my pitiable impersonation of Polonius, I would turn one last time to literature: George Bernard Shaw's *Saint Joan*.

I would concentrate on the opening scene in the dramatist's brilliant twentieth-century British play. Set in the year 1429 A.D. at the castle of Vancouleurs, the drama starts with a very unhappy

Robert de Baudricourt, captain of the castle, arguing with one of his stewards over the hens not laying eggs or the cows not giving milk. In his defense, the servant insists a prayerful teenage maid is standing outside the castle gates and has bewitched almost everyone in the fortress. Dismissing such excuses as ludicrous, the angry captain replies, "I'm not frightened of any eighteen-year-old country girl!" "No sir," the steward answers, "we're frightened of you, but she puts courage into us."

To resolve the argument, Robert has Joan brought before him. Showing his anger, he demands to know what she wants. The Maid tells him that the Lord has brought her to the castle to get a horse and amour and some soldiers, and then Robert is to send her to the Dauphin to raise the siege of Orleans, crown Charles king at Rheims Cathedral, and drive the English from France. Baudricourt is stunned. He turns to Poulengey, his best friend and advisor, and tells him not only is Joan mad and anything but a witch, but also he's wise to his friend's shameful intentions toward the Maid. Polly replies, he'd "as soon think of the Virgin Mary in that way, as of Joan."

They argue back and forth about the absurdity of the situation, the impossibility of miracles in the modern age, and even the likelihood that an uneducated, lowly commoner like Joan is a servant of G-d. Finally, Polly turns to his exasperated friend, confessing he believes her. With that, Robert exclaims, "You are as mad as she is." To which Polly answers, "We want a few mad people now. See where the sane ones have landed us!" In the end, Joan gets her wishes, and the scene concludes with the chickens laying eggs and the cows giving milk.[12]

Then I would receive the much-merited cheers of the audience, and my teaching career would end positively, with me getting the last laugh. But I couldn't do it! I couldn't allow myself to be smug and sarcastic and skeptical in the final days of my career. At the last moment, I faltered. I knew in my gut that the books I had cited came first to me not from library shelves but from screen adaptations shown in third-run movies theaters frequented in my childhood. Only after watching these literary works on screen did I read the original material. I knew whatever battles I had fought on campus were as much my fault as my foes. Besides, my family had gathered for the event. I wanted them to be proud of the way I laid down the torch. Even if no one else showed up, at least my loved ones would realize I had behaved appropriately. Even if this celebratory occasion turned out to be as bogus as I anticipated, I would not be party to destroying the fantasy.

So I scrapped the self-mocking address and decided instead to write a more conventional talk. I once more spoke of my high school years; and how that amazing time had transitioned me from the threatening streets of New York to Vermont's magnificent Green Mountains. I would not make more of my rollercoaster career than it merited. That more wide-ranging speech follows. My last thoughts before entering Memorial Lounge at the Waterman Building on UVM's campus on May 2nd were I hope I could carry off this make-believe event with dignity.

What can I say? The Amazing Randi was absolutely right: "No matter how smart and well-educated you get, you can be deceived." In that splendid chamber at that wonderful moment was a standing room only gathering of colleagues and students and friends who had come to say one last goodbye. Their generosity and graciousness humbled me and banished completely my anxieties. No one ever felt as ignorant about himself or what he knew about life than I did that day. I cannot explain why what happened that afternoon happened, but I have never doubted it was genuine. Nor will I embarrass myself with repeating what my colleagues and students said. I can, however, state categorically that I never forgot how much the ceremony meant to me then, or how much it means to me now.

The best part, however, may have occurred when I finished my conciliatory talk. No one yelled from the audience, "Encore!" For just a moment, I believed I had got it right.

Notes

[1] Episode S24 213, *The Charlie Rose Show*, (October 14, 2015).
[2] "Conversation with Gwen Ifell," *PBS News Hour* (October 14, 2015).
[3] Julius Weinstein and Tyler Measom, *An Honest Liar*. USA: Left Turn Films, 2014.
[4] Richard Thorpe, *The Adventures of Huckleberry Finn*. USA: MGM, 1939.

[5] David L. Ulin, "Celebrating the genius of 'Huckleberry Finn,'" *Los Angeles Times* (November 14, 2010).
[6] Mark Twain, *Huckleberry Finn*. Milano: Radici, 2014. Kindle edition.
[7] David Mamet, *Oleanna*. USA: Samuel Goldwyn Company, 1994.
[8] Sam Wood, *Goodbye, Mr. Chips*. USA: MGM, 1939.
[9] James Bridges, *The Paper Chase*. USA: Twentieth Century-Fox, 1973.
[10] Edmond Rostand, *Cyrano De Bergerac*. A New Prose Translation by John Murrell. Canada: Talonbooks, 1995. Kindle edition.
[11] H. L. Mencken, "On Truth" in *Damn! A Book of Calumny* (1918): 53.
[12] George Bernard Shaw, *Saint Joan: A Chronicle Play in Six Scenes and an Epilogue*. Definitive Text. New York: Penguin Books, 1951.

Sink or Swim: Hollywood after World War II[1]

By Frank Manchel
May 2, 2000

In the early days of 1946, Hollywood towered over the international movie industry. Its box-office figures were the highest in its history. Movies had become not only a national obsession, but also an insatiable passion for world audiences. In addition, Hollywood's lucrative foreign markets were reopening. Theater owners everywhere clamored for American movies. Hollywood considered itself invulnerable. Then, suddenly, the American system fell apart and it seemed as if Hollywood was doomed.

What happened and why is the subject of this lecture.

Before we can understand Hollywood's nightmare years from 1946 to 1958, we need to know something about the film capital itself, and what the Hollywood system was.

We can start by realizing, in simplified terms, that during the formative years of the American film industry it was controlled by a handful of refugees, most of them from Eastern Europe and all of them Jewish.[2] They had fled the persecution and terrors of Poland, Germany and Russia to seek their fortunes in America. When they arrived, these foreigners encountered a culture determined to make them second-class citizens in the land of opportunity. All of these immigrants and their sons set out to prove that they were 110% Americans. They became the breadwinners in their poverty-ridden families, determined to succeed by any means possible. Their ambition knew no limits. With no formal education, by their street wisdom alone, they carved out a niche for themselves mainly in New York's garment industry, and soon moved into the exhibition side of the new moving picture business.

Contrary to myth, the immigrant Eastern Europeans and their sons did not drive out the early founders of the movies. Most of the pioneers who worked in motion pictures lacked common sense and soon went kaput, destroyed by their inability to maneuver in the marketplace. The immigrant Jews, however, knew how to please the public. How else could they and generations of Jews have survived centuries of anti-Semitism?

By the 1920s, these refugees from the pogroms of Eastern Europe acquired vast theater holdings nationwide. To keep those theater chains operating at full capacity 52 weeks a year, they set up a number of colossal film corporations and proceeded to turn out formula films based on hit movies of the past. In the best traditions of a supply and demand economy, the daring mavericks established a factory-system with tight schedules, requiring a vast array of talents, all under long-term contracts to the studios.

One secret to success was to never deviate from tight Hollywood production schedules. Another technique was to insure that the movies stressed middle-class values and that the stories allowed you to identify with the characters regardless of their race, creed or nationality. And contrary to myth, the movie moguls never opposed artistic movies; they only opposed films that failed at the box-office.

To protect their fabulous investment, the movie moguls set up a vertical integration system, whereby they not only produced movies but also distributed them to their theater chains countrywide. The backbone of the system was ingenious. You did not need to own many of the 18,000 theaters in the US; you only needed to control 70% of the showcase theaters in America's largest metropolitan areas and 60% of them in the smaller cities. Five corporations divided the nation into territories. Each urban area was then sub-divided into first-, second- and third-run theaters. The first-run houses premiered the new movies. It was the secret to Hollywood's power, for here, where the public's thirst for novelty was satisfied, stars were born and box-office hits launched.

To protect these first-run theaters [often called picture palaces], the majors set up clearances whereby a certain time had to pass before the new films could be shown in lesser theaters.

The key, always, was novelty. Any independent producer could make a film, but no one could get a picture widely distributed unless he had permission of the majors.

In addition, because the majors could not produce all the movies necessary to fill their theaters, they openly encouraged the creation of minor studios—corporations that did not own theaters but made movies according to Hollywood's rules. The majors even looked favorably on a corporation formed by nonconformists like Charlie Chaplin, Mary Pickford, Douglas Fairbanks, and D.W. Griffith. It was called United Artists, and became a place where other rebels like Samuel Goldwyn and David O. Selznick eventually released their movies.

To protect their monopoly from government meddling and foreign competition, the moguls established an organization for controlling film producers and distributors. That organization set up an internal censorship office, which insured that the corporations' films, made mostly by foreigners and outsiders, would be acceptable to a non-Jewish society. To demonstrate their sincerity, the movie moguls made certain that the head of the organization was always a non-Jew. They even tolerated the first head of the censorship office being a spiteful anti-Semite.

[Show overhead of Hollywood Industry in 1946:]

THE STUDIO SYSTEM

THE MAJORS
Paramount
Metro-Goldwyn-Mayer (Loew's Inc.)
Warner Bros.
Radio-Keith-Orpheum
Twentieth Century-Fox

THE MINORS
Universal—B films
Columbia—B films

United Artists—Prestigious independents]

"The grand irony of all of Hollywood," as Neal Gabler points out, "is that Americans come to define themselves by the shadow America that was created by Eastern European Jewish immigrants who weren't admitted to the precincts of Real America."[3] That is the positive side. On the negative side, creative talent bristled at the strict rules and regulations. They wanted freedom to develop their skills, but the studios demanded obedience. The nation's exhibitors resented having to rent movies they did not see beforehand or even like. Again, Hollywood ignored anyone's needs but its own.

Educators, theologians, parents and government leaders worried endlessly about the influence of the movies on the lives of the young, the impressionable, and the irresponsible. With so many of the film formulas dealing with subversive approaches to traditional authority, conservatives wanted to control this highly manipulative, controversial medium.

Not surprisingly, the Eastern European immigrants, who suffered from tremendous inferiority complexes, never found favor in the halls of the mighty and powerful. More to the point, they dreaded dealing with intellectuals and clever people. Nevertheless, they tried to gain respectability by bringing the very artists they hated to California. Contrary to myth, Hollywood was not always hostile to foreign talent. In fact, some of the film capital's finest movies were made by such émigrés as Charlie Chaplin, Alfred Hitchcock, Michael Curtiz, Billy Wilder, William Wyler, Otto Preminger, Mack Sennett, Ernst Lubitsch, Fritz Lang, Josef von Sternberg, and Friedrich Murnau.[4]

It is true, however, that many foreign artists and literary giants proved incapable of adjusting to Hollywood's rigid system. They never understood or bought into the film capital's methods. Often ignored by Hollywood's critics, however, is that the essential critics, the audiences, the paying customers, rarely accepted even the few films the Hollywood misfits made here or abroad.

To alibi for their failure and for the fact that Hollywood's stars mainly came from the ranks of the untrained and unsophisticated, the famous artists dismissed the now powerful peasants. Elitist bashing of the world's most democratic art form became a crusade carried on by many intellectuals and politicians. As the Great Depression increased and war clouds gathered abroad, reactionary forces in both New York and California took advantage of America's racist and sexist fears and anxieties. They demonized the progressive causes promoted by the left-wing activists from Broadway and the political refugees from Europe; and substituted instead a narrow nationalism.

However, the moguls could not ignore widespread American xenophobia and ignorance, especially when militant isolationists became overly suspicious about all these radical foreigners working on the West Coast. Moreover, the Great Depression nearly bankrupted the movie industry. To survive, the movie moguls were forced to share their power with the moneymen of Wall Street, who were even more cynical of artists and their liberal values than were the non-intellectual immigrants. The moguls especially hated the attempts by their employees to unionize the industry. Nowhere was the anger more malicious than that directed at the men and women who established the Writers Guild, Hollywood's most progressive union. In addition, as more and more European political refugees fled Nazi persecution and sought sanctuary in Hollywood, right-wingers intensified their harassment of the film industry.[5]

The political and cultural division between the movie bosses, their workers, and conservative forces reached epic proportions during the 1930s. The battles for unionization, the support of radical political candidates, the backing of the New Deal, the growing demand for films against the Nazis, and the hue and cry by the progressives to attack America's isolationist policies only intensified the problems Hollywood faced with right-wingers and conservatives in the years before World War II.

Still the American film industry held off attempts by the anti-Trust division of the government to break Hollywood's monopoly. Another government threat came from the House of Representatives Committee on Un-American Activities, created in 1938. Dominated at the outset by Southern Democrats, HUAC had something for everyone to despise: it was violently against the New Deal, it was extremely isolationist in practice, and its hatred of anyone not 100% white protestant made other white supremacist groups look like wimps. However, in 1939, HUAC was no match for Hollywood, and the movie moguls' successfully squelched HUAC's attempt to paint the film industry as a communist front. In addition, the Eastern European immigrants and their sons withstood the attempt by the US Senate to brand Hollywood as a den of traitors.

Once America went to war at the end of 1941, these battles were put aside for the duration. Between 1942 and 1945, it seemed as if we were one America fighting a common enemy. Therefore, when the war ended, Hollywood was at the top of its form. Things looked even better for the filmmakers when the overseas markets reopened, and Hollywood calculated its potential foreign grosses. The five majors and the three minors, along with the lowly Disney studio—had every reason to assume that they were indestructible.

In hindsight, you wonder why there was not more concern in Hollywood once the war was won. After all, the issues of unionization were not over. The battles with the government had not disappeared, only been put on hold. Moreover, the public mood toward movies changed after the war. People had their minds on other things. How could the movie moguls have been so myopic?[6]

True, overseas, national cinemas struggled to rebuild their war-torn industries; but they were not powerless to defend themselves. These national cinemas knew they could never compete with Hollywood if they did not protect their economic and cultural resources. Thus, they set up quotas for how many American films could be shown a year on the foreign screens; they established tariffs restricting how much box-office revenue could be returned to America. Didn't anyone see this as a potential crisis?

What about the famous directors and performers who wanted more creative freedom? The documentary techniques developed in combat and the horrors the veterans witnessed at the front lines made them determined to change the content and style of post-war Hollywood movies, away from romantic melodramas to a more socially conscious industry. Why didn't Hollywood see that as a serious problem to its rigid system?

Why did Hollywood think it could ignore the pessimism, the desperation, and the disillusionment that grew out of the emerging Cold War and the fear of atomic annihilation?

Equally important, how could anyone ignore the red-baiting, the anti-Semitism, the renewed racism against returning black veterans, and the paranoia in post-war American life? Women, in particular, found themselves in the center of a storm about social priorities: just where did they belong: in the marketplace alongside the men, or in a patriarchal world where they remained subordinate to men?

Whatever illusions Hollywood may have harbored in the days immediately following the Allied victory, they soon began to disappear by the end of 1946. Let's start with the public itself. Men and women who had suffered countless hardships for three and a half years found themselves eager to resume their lives. Consumerism became the passion of the day. The baby boom began in earnest and new attitudes about leisure time took shape in the form of miniature golf and bowling. People wanted cars and a nicer environment to raise families, and so a mass migration, begun at the turn of the century, from the urban areas to the suburbs rapidly increased.

This shift in demographics and social mores radically affected the status of indoor movie theaters. Going to a movie in the suburbs became too expensive and inconvenient. Hollywood recognized the problem and slowly adjusted to the changing times. They created drive-in theaters, so families could go together and avoid baby-sitting costs. In 1948, there were 820 drive-ins; a decade later, the number had grown to over 4,000. The problem was that drive-ins only operated in the evenings. Suburbia found a more satisfying solution in the 1960s, with the creation of multiplex theaters in shopping centers.

Meanwhile, as the postwar issues gained momentum in 1946, the effect on the box office and the first-run theaters became readily apparent. Hollywood's receipts were off by nearly 8%. By 1948, 18,000 movie houses in the US were in trouble. A decade later, one third of them were gone. Europe's tariffs and quotas only added to Hollywood's growing financial instability. Downsizing quickly became the order of the day in Hollywood, and with the layoffs came a reduction not only in the number of films made, but also in the types of films produced.

The start of the Cold War plus the impact of the wartime documentaries transformed Hollywood movies. Middle-class values no longer squared with the state of the world's thinking. Now we saw the rise of a strong socially conscious cinema. We had just fought a war against prejudice and intolerance. What about fighting the injustices and bigotry at home?

The neo-realistic movement in Italy encouraged these rebellious artists to make their movies on location, rather than on studio lots; to focus on everyday people with pressing social problems, shown not with technical splendor but with ordinary language and behavior. In the years between 1946 and 1951, we saw such memorable films as *The Best Years of Our Lives, The Treasure of the Sierra Madre, Crossfire, Gentleman's Agreement, Letter from an Unknown Woman, All the King's Men, Lost Boundaries, Home of the Brave, Pinky, Intruder in the Dust, Sunset Boulevard, All About Eve, Broken Arrow,* and *No Way Out,* the last one introducing a young actor named Sidney Poitier.

And as the box-office receipts dwindled, the studios' hold on its talent loosened even more. It became harder to do business as usual, to keep the formulas safe and apolitical. Nowhere was the paranoia and insecurity of the times more apparent than in an increasingly popular film style known as film noir.

> [Show clip from *American Cinema: Film Noir*,[7] illustrating how German expressionistic lighting and camera techniques revealed America's anxieties over corruption and despair in post-war Hollywood movies.]

True, the source of this movement was the hard-boiled detective fiction of the twenties, but it had not been allowed to flourish until the waning days of WWII. Now the nation's hypocrisy and domestic class warfare made film noir enormously popular with audiences worldwide. What had started out as an economic ploy by the studios turned into a political and social weapon for rebellious artists. It became almost impossible to watch film noir narratives and not believe that America was in danger from numerous conspirators' intent on destroying our basic freedoms.

The reactionaries watched these film noir conspiracies in dismay. More to the point, they saw in the times an opportunity not only to settle long standing scores with liberals and progressives, but also a chance to further their ambitions. What better place for political opportunists to gain maximum visibility than in Hollywood? And what better ally for the Hollywood reactionaries than the recently revived HUAC, now controlled by second-rate Republican politicians?

Under the guise of weeding out communists, HUAC burst back on the American scene. In October 1947, the House un-American Activities Committee resumed its attack on Hollywood.[8]

[Show clip from *Legacy of the Blacklist*, capturing celebrities at the 1947 HUAC Hearings.]

Would it surprise you to know that the first ten individuals singled out for punishment consisted of seven screenwriters, two directors and one producer, and all but a couple were Jewish?

Now there are those who insist that the battle was about safeguarding America from subversives, that all Hollywood conservatives did was demonstrate their patriotism.

Neither Mark Stoler nor I believe that for one moment. As my dear friend Professor Mark Stoler states, "It is clear that there were communist spies and committed anti-Communists during the early years of the Cold War. But most of the spies had already been caught by the time Joe McCarthy began his rampage (he never caught a single spy), and many if not most of the politicians leading the anticommunist crusade (especially those on HUAC) saw it as a way to attack New Deal Liberalism...." In other words, it was a witch-hunt, and as Lillian Hellman astutely observed, a time for scoundrels.

What those plague years were like for Hollywood have been described in films like *The Way We Were*, *The Front*, *The Manchurian Candidate*, and *Guilty by Suspicion*. In essence, a blacklist was instituted by the American film industry and hundreds of lives, careers, and friendships were shattered for decades. Some careers never were resumed. Moreover, there were people who died tragically because of the pressures. It was, as some historians have characterized it, "a time of forced loyalty oaths, star chambers, and stool pigeons."

Each of us from those days remembers one victim more than he or she remembers another. For me, it was Chaplin. The reactionaries in Washington didn't have the courage to exile him directly from America; but in 1952, when Chaplin was sailing on the *Queen Elizabeth* taking him to London for the premiere of his flawed masterpiece, *Limelight*, the U.S. attorney general cabled him that he could not return to the land of the free, where he had lived for the past forty years.

I do not intend to whitewash the progressives. Clearly, Chaplin was no saint, the Hollywood Ten could sling mud with the best of their accusers, and many left-wingers had a convenient lapse of memory when it came to the atrocities committed by the communists around the world.

Nevertheless, we need to understand that this shameful moment in American film history was not so much about people panicking during the Cold War. It was about conservative and reactionary forces using the Communist scare to finally, after many decades, gain control of the motion picture industry. We need to focus on the fact that this tragic period was not so much about innocent people being imprisoned, driven out of Hollywood, and being denied recognition for the films they made, mainly because they refused to cooperate with HUAC. It is about courageous mavericks that taught Hollywood and the world important lessons about freedom and responsibility. As Victor Navasky points out, "By resisting the demand that they confess, recant, inform, sign loyalty oaths, they were the latest in a long line of men and women down through the centuries who have been pressured by church and state to declare their allegiance to God and king (or, in the seventeenth century, official science, which held that the earth is at the center of the universe). Most of those who refused to bow to such pressures did so as a matter of conscience."[9]

But by 1948, blacklisting, the move to the suburbs, the rebellion in foreign markets, and the dwindling control of the studio system were not the only problems Hollywood faced. After years of struggling, the anti-Trust division won its battle against the majors, and the United States Supreme Court declared in the 1948 Paramount Decision that Hollywood's monolithic studio system had to end. The studios had to divorce themselves from exhibition.

In theory, things looked good for the nation's exhibitors. A free market now existed and no one got preferential treatment. But serious problems arose. Small theater owners could not see all the new films. They did not know what pictures to book, and by the end of the fifties, many movie houses went out of business.

The times were just as bad for the majors. Without the theaters in their fold, the studios could not count on box-office receipts to underwrite the cost of producing films and keeping so many people under contract. No longer could they afford their large studio lots or control the work of artists. Now for the first time in decades, the creative talent of the fabulous Hollywood studios found themselves in a competitive jungle with no publicity departments to help publicize their work.

By the end of the 1940s, Hollywood had only two choices: adapt or disappear. As one historian summarized the situation, Hollywood's "once monolithic studio structure splintered into dozens of small companies and individual units." Interestingly, the real winners were the minor studios. They had no theaters to jettison. Thus, Columbia, Universal, and United Artists became the place where creative people formed their own small production units. The most important of these new independent companies was Burt Lancaster's Hecht-Hill-Lancaster Company.

The movie moguls, who thought they could not be beaten, who used revenge as a method of staying in power, found themselves falling out of power. Blacklisting had stripped them of much of their intellectual resources. They proved themselves incapable of understanding the paranoia generated by film noir. In addition, the Paramount decision had robbed them of financial security. Before 1945, for example, 80% of Hollywood productions made money, thanks to the studio system. With the monopoly apparently destroyed, only 10% of the films released in 1950 made their money back.

As if these problems were not enough, the myopic movie moguls had made one more major miscalculation. In 1946, there were only 6,000 TV sets in American homes, and Hollywood thought the new communications technology was a passing fad. Five years later, as one observer noted, a "1000 new sets were being installed [in American homes] every twenty-four hours."

Again, the movie moguls reacted foolishly. They saw TV as their enemy, not as another major market. In 1952, Hollywood promised film audiences things they could not see on TV: widescreen movies in glorious color.

[Show clip from *American Cinema*: "Film in the Television Age,"[10] illustrating various attempts by the film industry to compete with TV programs, ending with the release of Twentieth Century-Fox's 1953 Cinemascope production, *The Robe*.]

By the end of the decade, the freshness of color and widescreens dwindled considerably, and it was over for the moguls. In their place were independent production units working with Universal, Columbia, and United Artists to salvage what they could of the Hollywood system. Art houses gave us inspirational foreign films. It was here we discovered the likes of Ingmar Bergman, Jean Cocteau, Federico Fellini, Satyajit Ray, and Akira Kurosawa.

At the same time, the chaos brought out the best in Hollywood's creative talent. The great stars and directors of the past did some of their best work in this era of fear and distrust. The widescreens and color cinematography also reshaped the content of science fiction movies, Westerns, family melodramas, gangster films, and Hollywood musicals.

To beat the out-of-control costs of independent productions, the new Hollywood started making movies overseas. They became known as blockbuster films, international productions, or "runaway" movies.

In theory, the idea made sense. Hollywood could produce the movies with its overseas revenue held in escrow, attract global audiences, and maximize interest in widescreen productions. These were the days of *The African Queen, Love is a Many-Splendored Thing, An Affair to Remember, From Here to Eternity, The Bridge on the River Kwai, Paths of Glory*, biblical spectacles, and fabulous musicals like *A Star is Born* and *Gigi*. Even TV became an ally by the end of the fifties. Not only did it provide the training grounds for brilliant new talent, but it also expanded the lifeblood of old movies as well as new releases.

However, the biggest boon for Hollywood came not from its own ranks but from a group of French movie nuts. Rather than go to school in the post-WWII period, these die-hard filmgoers watched movies day and night in a marvelous museum called the *Cinematheque Francaise*. When they were not allowed to make their own films, they helped create a new film magazine, *Cahiers Du Cinema*. And from the pages of that militant journal, came an idea called the Auteur theory. In essence, it said that artists could not be contained by any rules or regulations, that if you watched their films you could see their personal visions in every movie they made. In addition, no one, these French critics argued, made finer or more profound movies than the auteurs of Hollywood.[11]

Who were these auteurs? How did the mavericks fare over the next few decades? What were the great contributions of the Hollywood legends to world cinema? To get those answers, you need to sign up for a course in the fall called The Contemporary Cinema. As Dean Joan Smith will tell you, this is a business, not a non-profit operation.

This much I will tell you—the moguls, with all their mistakes, still outsmarted everyone. True, the minors became the majors and the majors dropped down in status. Nevertheless, control of the world film industry remained in the hands of the major distributors. Only they had the money and networks to distribute films nationwide. Films today, more than ever, rely on the old formulas.

And thankfully, on April 16, 1972, the Motion Picture Academy awarded Charlie Chaplin an Honorary Oscar. Here for just a minute, we can relive that memorable moment.

[Clip from *Oscars Greatest Moments*,[12] showing Charlie Chaplin receiving his Honorary Oscar.]

Let me conclude this lecture by reminding you of the words of a blacklisted writer, Michael Wilson, who never received in his lifetime his Oscar for co-writing *The Bridge on the River Kwai*. Mike received the Writers Guild' Laurel Award in 1976, and he said in his acceptance speech the following, which I have slightly altered:

> I don't want to dwell on the past. But for a few moments to speak of the future, and I address my remaining remarks particularly to you, younger men and women who have perhaps not yet established yourselves in... [our profession] at the time of the great witch hunt. I feel that unless you remember this dark epoch and understand it, you may be doomed to replay it. Not with the same cast of characters, of course, or on the same issues.
>
> But I see a day, perhaps coming in your lifetime if not in mine, when a new crisis of belief will grip this republic. When diversity of opinion will be labeled disloyalty, and when extraordinary pressures will be put on writers in the mass media [and educators] to conform to administration policy on the key issues of the time, whatever they may be.

If this gloomy scenario should come to pass, I trust that you younger men and women will shelter the mavericks and the dissenters in your ranks and protect their right to work. The Guild [and the universities] will have the use and the need of rebels if it is to survive as a union of free writers [and teachers]. This nation will have need of them if it is to survive as an open society.[13]

Notes

[1] I want to thank Ms. Shelley Barbour for transcribing this talk from a video recording of the event.

[2] This section is based upon Chapter 3, "The Jew in American Film," Frank Manchel, *Film Study: An Analytical Study*, Vol. 1. Rutherford: Associated University Presses, 1990. 818-851.

[3] Neal Gabler, *An Empire of Their Own: How The Jews Invented Hollywood.* New York: Crown Publishers, 1988.): 7.

[4] John Baxter, *The Hollywood Exiles*. New York: Taplinger Publishing Company, 1976; and John Russell Taylor, *Strangers in Paradise: The Hollywood Émigrés'. 1933-1950.* London: Faber and Faber, 1983.

[5] See Chapter 9, "War and Peace."

[6] Manchel, "Hollywood in the Postwar Years," *Film Study*, Vol. 3. 1944-1989.

[7] Jeffrey Schon, *American Cinema*: "Film Noir." Episode 7. USA: A New York Center for Visual History Production, 1995. Narrated by Richard Widmark.

[8] Manchel, "The American Dream and The Hollywood Inquisition," Ibid., Vol. 2. 1079-1108.

[9] Victor Navasky, "Honor the Blacklistees," *The Nation*. April 3, 2000.

[10] Alain Klarer, *American Cinema*: "Film in the Television Age." Episode 6. USA: A New York Center for Visual History Production, 1995. Narrated by Cliff Robertson.

[11] Manchel, "Film Criticism and Theory," *Film Study*, Vol. 1. 28-30.

[12] Jeff Margolis, *Oscars Greatest Moments*. USA: Columbia TriStar Home Video, 1992.

[13] Judy Chaikin, *Legacy of the Hollywood Blacklist*. 60 mins. USA: One Step Productions, 1987.

19. My 2002 meeting with Spike Lee when he visited the University of Vermont. From left to right, the author, Spike Lee, Jon Kilik, and Sheila Manchel.

16.

My Zip Code[1]

> Certainty generally is an illusion, and repose is not the destiny of man.[2]
> *Associate Justice Oliver Wendell Holmes, Jr.*

> I don't know if mankind has learnt anything from all these horrors [Holocaust, wars, etc.] …Crimes are repeated. Criminals remain unpunished, and the indifference of the world remains. It remains, and it persists.[3]
> *Belgrade Rabbi (Predraj Ejdus)*

> I see nothing to be gained by arguing over the essence of the Media or the inviolability of individual art works, nor by allowing theorists to settle things with *a priori* arguments.[4]
> *Dudley Andrew*

If you had asked me in 2004, after nine years of battling cancer, whether I would ever write or lecture about the media, the humanities, and education again, I probably would have said, with more bravado than common sense, "Why not?" Except for not knowing when or where the opportunities might arise, the thought of not contributing intellectually to my profession and the public remained an anathema to me. Life is, after all, unpredictable; and as you now know after *devouring* previous chapters, very little in my teaching career had occurred as I had planned.

Despite the obvious obstacles in my path, I never lost hope. I strongly believed I could still do something useful for others. It just wouldn't be as easy and as extensive as before. Just because I no longer had a bully pulpit at the University to rationalize my opinions on the vital importance of America's "National Theater," it did not mean I had to be silent. Just because current scholarly journals and editors favored scholarly essays about Cultural Studies rather than Popular Culture, it did not mean there were no alternative outlets to mainstream publications. Just because I was mainly housebound and becoming travel deprived did not mean my listening, viewing, and writing passions disappeared.

Let me be clear on this point. At this stage in my life and ever since, I felt very blessed because of my unconventional journey. Feeling as I did about the flawed world we lived in, I had nonetheless met so many magnificent people who had helped me move from the uncertain streets of New York to a privileged and respected position at an exceptional university. The dream I pursued of finding a community of scholars who would share my professional passions had been realized. While pundits had often said you would be lucky to make one true colleague in a lifetime, I had more than I imagined possible. Also, for over forty years, I had had the utter joy of teaching young, caring, and bright students about values and ideas dear to my heart. Thankfully, the Objectionables I bumped against along the way had provided me with incalculable opportunities to learn and to grow in my profession and in my life. Even cancer had proven a stroke of luck, striking me and not my family. Most importantly, I had the best of all possible worlds: a decent resume and an incredible wife and exceptional children and wonderful grandchildren. When I took the time to think seriously about my situation, what could I possibly complain about?

Something else worth understanding is how hard it had been for me to teach about film, alongside all the pressures surrounding a job and a family. Rarely expressed to the lay public is the difficulty in finding sufficient time to reflect on what you say rather than to just react to your audience's needs. For example, not a day passed in my career when I didn't wonder about my use of simplifications versus particulars in explaining myself to my students. It was one thing to delude myself into thinking I was a modern day Don Quixote who continuously held forth about the mass media's importance to the mental health of nations, as well as what was terribly wrong with our culture.

But it was another thing in the privacy of my mind to convince myself that I was not behaving in a non-productive, reckless manner. Were the lessons learned from the popular arts really as valuable and helpful to others as they had been for me? For decades, since I first sat in a darkened movie theater, I had become determined to question what kind of world I lived in. Were we actually a nation of laws, and were we all truly created equal? As a result, I had long been suspicious about the spotlessness of institutions, politicians, and authority figures. In all those years, I had relied more on instinct than on logic in shaping my values. My persistent doubts resulted not so much from examination as from experience. Now with so much time on my hands, I could retrace my steps by delving into the great books and finding out how intellectual history had approached these very same abstract thoughts. I could do what I had always preached. I could study the past in depth and learn its lessons.

I recognize why you might think that my professed idealism was neither sound nor sensible. Not only was illness a somber obstacle, but also was this the time to get involved with such serious material? For example, when I went on disability in 2000, a well-meaning colleague had given me a list of five books to read while I was sitting in numerous doctors' waiting rooms to get examined or lying about in hospital beds recovering from treatments. This goodhearted scholar of Southern literature didn't realize it, but each of his recommended selections contained an account of a cancer victim who had died.

Comforting material wasn't any easier to find in the film world. Most of the movies up to 2004 almost always featured terminally ill lymphoma patients. And in exceptionally well-done films, I often saw myself in several unfavorable dilemmas. For instance, in writer-director Denys Arcand's *The Barbarian Invasions*,[5] I could be forgiven for my sins, be reunited with my friends, and be surrounded by my loved ones as I bravely had a "good death" by committing euthanasia. Or there was James L. Brooks' *Terms of Endearment*,[6] reminding me that cancer was not just my problem. It affects everyone who cares about me. Then if I wanted to vent my anger over my illness, there was Steven Soderbergh's *Erin Brockovich*,[7] recalling how a disreputable energy corporation's pollution of our water supply and its subsequent cover-up caused Non-Hodgkin's Lymphoma in a number of unsuspecting lives. Who had caused mine? Last, but definitely not all-inclusive, I could empathize with a hardworking mom who learns she has two months to live in Isobel Coixet's *My Life Without Me*.[8] The doomed heroine hides her illness from her husband and kids, and then she sets out to indulge her hidden sexual frustrations. I couldn't imagine doing such a reckless thing. If Sheila found out, my time on earth would have been much shorter than any physician predicted!

Maybe you can appreciate why I felt blessed, but not what made me so optimistic in what was obviously an extremely difficult situation. One reason had to do with a brilliant man I had never met: Professor B. F. Skinner. Back in 1982, the venerated father of behavioral psychology delivered an inspiring convention address on how to deal with the aging problem.[9] Nearing 80-years of age, the Harvard scientist grasped that there were many things in his life that were important for his emotional well-being, but that they might be denied him in the years ahead because of ill-health or old age. While he suggested various approaches to solving the problem, what struck me most was his insistence on generating a thought-provoking home environment. Find a way, he maintained, to make the things that are meaningful to you available and accessible later in life. I took that message to mean, in my case, books, music, television, and movies. So Sheila and I literally began to build several libraries in our home in preparation for the unexpected and the unknown. Thus, when our crisis struck, we were prepared. Contrary to what our family and friends feared in the challenging life change we now experienced, we truly weathered the storm as if we were figuratively on vacation. Every room in our home had books or CDs or DVDs or a television set or a sound system. Rather than grousing about being shut in, we seized on the chance to read and to listen and to watch works of art we had never had time for when we were working. Now scheduling leisure time was not a problem. All that was required of me was the will to live.

Another reason why I was so positive came about in the most undesirable of circumstances. During one very protracted hospital stay, I found myself unable to read or to see movies or to watch TV. I just couldn't concentrate. But music proved magical. I could listen through the use of earphones connected to one or another hand device to the vast range of classical music, folk songs, Broadway show tunes, Irish ballads, and the American songbook. (Jazz comes into play in the next chapter.) Not only was the music therapeutic, but also it stimulated in me a later desire to learn about the composers, the compositions, and the ages they reflected. Listening to the artists perform miracles took my mind almost completely away from my annoying medical problems. And it made me dramatically aware of how much I had ignored the role of music in my study of motion pictures. Terrific! Here was another thing to research and to write about when, not if, things got better.

A third reason for my up-beat attitude in 2004 occurred when I found myself going through my hoarded university odds and ends. In the process of rummaging through my files, I came across a series of academic e-mails on the *H-Film List for Scholarly Study and Uses of Media* website about the topic of "profundity," an area that I had frequently glossed over in my progress as a teacher. Dudley Andrew's quotation that opens this chapter—about setting suitable priorities in your profession—gives you one reason why I became fascinated with the task of better understanding why I taught the films I did. My unshakable enthusiasm for Pauline Kael's critical views and her intense dislike for highbrows theorizing about how art is created is one good place to start. A larger resource, however, is the nature of criticism itself.

Ever since my days as an English major at Ohio State studying to be a sadist, I had taken for granted that I knew what made a great book, a film masterpiece, and a true work of art. (I still do, but for different reasons which I will share with you shortly.) Adding to my growing educated instincts were my stirring literary studies about the basic critical theories of legendary intellectuals like Matthew Arnold, F.O. Mathieson, I.A. Richards, Robert Warsaw, Dwight MacDonald, Edmund Wilson, and Van Wyk Brooks. However, given my iconoclastic history, it should not surprise you that I never thought all the answers came from books.

Even more to the point, the possible answers to moral, ethical, and everyday problems, to me, are anything but binary; they are varied and substantial. While I found literary analyses useful, they never seemed the only valuable, let alone obligatory method to experiencing meaningfully a work of art. Moreover, as I struggled in the halls of academia, I rediscovered the fact that whatever method worked with my audience in one class of students was not necessarily useful for another generation of neophytes.

Let me be clear on this point. I never doubted the value in studying, what Dean Swift labeled, the Ancients. It was then and is now inconceivable to me we could have any chance for an optimistic future without having examined and learned the lessons of the past. They help considerably in teaching us to do the right thing in our lives. The academic dilemma for me had to do with persuading my Modern students, who needed current, relevant reasons, to begin to comprehend what it was I was professing. While moral and ethical issues persist throughout the history of civilization, the way of confronting them requires constant review. For example, even though I came to insist movies were an art unto itself that needed to be studied and to be understood, I still found myself practicing heavy doses of literary analysis in discussing them with film students. Like almost all of the critics I covered in my four intense volumes of *Film Study*, my analytical concern was primarily with characters, narratives, dialogue, and themes. But because film is so vast a subject, as critic David Denby wisely suggests— it involves learning about history, languages, music, art, literature, photography, opera, dance, and theater[10]—, I always needed to remain vigilant of my biases in teaching about the audio-visual medium to a new generation. For example, while many of my colleagues over the past couple of decades persisted in talking about films as a theoretical abstraction, I have always insisted on placing the movies in an industrial and economic context.

Not all was peaches and cream in my approach to the popular arts. I had made one primary error all through my career: I believed all I had to do was say it and explain it, and the world would then follow. The practice, loosely known as a hypodermic effect, is absolutely false. Time does not permit me to list the countless variables involved in effective communication and learning, but Manchel just saying a thing is true isn't one of them!

So it was with more than passing interest that I reconsidered what my erudite colleagues felt about certain films being designated "profound works." As best as I can recall, the discussion began when Brown University Professor Michael Frank raised the question about whether film scholars could break free from their literary biases and discover a more suitable approach to exploring the media's merits. The Ivy League scholar felt the habit grew out of century old traditions. In the past, our forbearers insisted on our studying what they unquestionably deemed "profound" literary works. Today, he argued, movies might function on an even more multifaceted level than literature. If this blasphemy were true, was it possible we could identify specific difficult films that matched the depth of literary works by Shakespeare, Dante, and Dostoevsky? As Professor Frank (I must confess I enjoyed writing this) explained, "To be clear, the issue is not if the cinematic medium calls attention to its artistic virtues, but rather do they offer comparable insights about larger human frames of reference?" So he challenged his colleagues to identify narrative films functioning "in rich and complex ways with the most compelling questions that shape our lives, movies that as a result will reward thoughtful and sensitive scrutiny." And to make the formidable task even more noteworthy, he asked the scholars to justify their claims.[11]

The responses were promising as well as entertaining. For example, Dr. Stefan Cieply reacted by quoting critic Dwight MacDonald's irreverent film category of the "good bad film": "movies we know should be good for us, yet fail to excite any emotion other than boredom—*Marty* and *On the Beach*." [For the record, I always liked these films.] In the view of this recognized mass media expert, "profundity" probably related to particular films highlighting big issues. With disdain, he singled Spielberg out as a disapproving example of this mistaken exercise.[12] [Again, I respectfully disagreed. As you know from a previous chapter, I consider Spielberg a giant in film history.]

Texas A&M University Professor Brian Hilton stated that some critics consider "insight" rather than "timelessness "as a prerequisite for labeling a work "profound." He felt that "insight into what is, of course, is another precarious question." If one wishes to look at how artistic awareness operates in the political issues of the mid-nineties, he recommended such films as *Munich*, *Good Night and Good Luck*, and *The Bourne Ultimatum* to fit the bill. Or take another example: war. Here one might select "profound" films like

Black Hawk Down and *The Thin Red Line*. And the Lone Star scholar added, "If one is looking for more fundamental messages related to man and society...consider *Schindler's List*...."[13]

Before Professor Hinton's response had even been read by many of his peers, Dr. James Calvin Paasche e-mailed the website that saying what is profound to one may not be profound to others. He suggested those who maintain "profound" films are equal to great literary works should take a deep breath and pause before they speak too quickly. In his academic experience, the skeptical educator found he had encountered significant difficulty identifying "many films that manage to be subtle while making profound statements about questions of family, community, nation, and the world in the age of the transnational."[14] Here was another ingredient to add to the simmering profundity pot: delicacy.

Not to be ignored, the formidable Professor Gene Stavis proposed his colleagues might best begin their arguments with a dictionary definition as to what is meant by such an imprecise concept as "profound." Like other contributors, this serious student of film opined "profundity" might be nothing more than what is in the eyes of the beholder. We'd be better off, Dr. Stavis cleverly suggested, if we applied the concept comparatively: "[We] could rate something profound or superficial and trivial." It was, he argued, somewhat like combatting "fundamental traditional arguments about film itself qualifying as a legitimate art." Not surprisingly, however, and much to my delight," he recalled a time in our lives where "snobbish" scholars once dismissed film as trivial. "But in an era in which the best and the brightest and, yes, the most profound," he wrote, "have embraced film and found significant depth in it, it seems to me impossible to defend [snobbishness] at this late date." Nonetheless, he argued like Professor Raul Hilberg had discussed in an earlier chapter, film's status is somewhat stained by its popularity. That is, equating profundity with a mass audience product is heretofore unheard of in an intellectual world.[15]

Much as I would like to continue in this nostalgic vein, I do not have either the space or the time to include the many other valuable contributions to the debate about what constitutes alleged film "profundity." Suffice to say, some witty colleagues also weighed in on the potential weakness in using the difficulty of understanding a film's message as a criteria for anointing a film as profound. Another scholar dismissed such pursuits as the sins of our literary youth, when we were brainwashed to think in terms of masterpieces. Some colleagues even suggested profundity might arise in the interaction between the viewer and the work, rather than in the work itself.[16] And still other contemporaries argued that while they could not explain why certain movies were profound, they recognized one when they saw it.

This summary finally brings me to the essay that is the subject of this chapter. After leaving the university world, I had donated my film book library to Burlington College, a private liberal arts school providing educational opportunities to nontraditional students. Over the years I had become close with the college librarian who worked tirelessly to keep the book collection safe and current. In the spring of 2004, she asked me as a favor to deliver an address to the Vermont Library Association.

A brief aside is in order here. Ever since I was a young truant escaping from dull, strict conventional classrooms, public librarians had become my great muses. No matter what library I strayed into throughout my formative years, many nameless, matchless women had watched over me and guided me towards the best and most appropriate books to read. When I grew to maturity and began publishing, I wrote for librarians and not for the public. These unseen guardians of countless treasures were my targets, because it was they who would bring me to wider audiences. And today, in everything I have written, it has been dedicated librarians who have helped with the research and the material to clarify what I communicated to the world at large. In my eyes, these exceptional, underpaid, and unappreciated individuals have no peers!

So when my friend Jessica Allard asked me to deliver a speech, I readily agreed. Too readily I soon realized. It had been nearly five years since I had written anything, let alone attempted to give a public address. Not only was I rusty, but also my strength was limited. As you will realize when you read the talk that follows, it was like starting all over again with lobbying for the film/book program at New Rochelle High School and motivating the teachers in the La Mancha Project at the University of Vermont.

Finally, I promised I would tell you why I still (arrogantly) believe I can recognize a great book, a film masterpiece, and a true work of art. Simply put, it is because of my extensive artistic experiences, educational background, and highly developed instincts. Before you dismiss that outrageous and unfiltered assertion, let me remind you I am not alone in thinking such undemocratic thoughts. Associate Justice Oliver Wendell Holmes, Jr. asserted, "The life of the law has not been logic; it has been experience....The law embodies the story of a nation's development through many centuries, and it cannot be dealt with as if it contained only the axioms and corollaries of a book of mathematics."[17] I would insist the same is true for the Arts and the way they can be seen and appreciated. And the distinguished writer, documentarian, and philanthropist Hannah Rothschild, also observed that a "good eye" is based on "instinct, knowledge, and experience.'[18]

Notes

[1] Jon Meacham introduced me to the term.
[2] Oliver Wendell Holmes, Jr., *The Common Law* (1881), 10.
[3] Goraan Paskaljevic, *When Day Breaks*. Serbia: Nova Film, 2012.
[4] Qtd. in James Griffith, *Adaptations as Imitations: Films From Novels*. Newark, Delaware: University of Delaware Press, 1997. 73-74.
[5] Denys Arcand, *The Barbarian Invasions*. France: Pyramide Productions, 2003.
[6] James L. Brooks, *Terms of Endearment*. USA: Paramount Pictures, 1983.
[7] Steven Soderbergh, *Erin Brockovich*. USA: Universal Pictures, 2000.
[8] Isobel Coixet, *My Life Without Me*. Netherlands: El Deseo, 2003.
[9] B. F. Skinner, "Skinner Tells His Strategies for Handling Old Age," *The New York Times* (August 24, 1982): C1.
[10] David Denby, "*Do The Movies Have a Future?* New York: Simon & Schuster, 2012. 291.
[11] E-Mail from Dr. Michael Frank at Bentley University. *H-Film List for Scholarly Study and Uses of Media* (November 16, 2007).
[12] E-Mail from Dr. Stefan Cieply at Wayne State University. Ibid., November 17, 2007.
[13] E-Mail from Dr. Brian Hilton at Texas A&M University. Ibid.
[14] E-Mail from Dr. James Calvin Paasche at Indiana University. Ibid.
[15] E-Mail from Dr. Gene Stavis, School of Visual Arts –NYC. Ibid.
[16] E-Mail from Dr. Ken Nolley at English Willamette University. Ibid. November 20, 2007.

[17] Associate Justice Oliver Wendell Holmes, Jr., *The Common Law*. Boston: Little, Brown and Company, 1881, 1
[18] Hannah Rothschild on *The Charlie Rose Show*, S24 EP 229, Nov. 12. 2015.

Joining the Great Conversation

May 25, 2004

In 1952, the Encyclopedia Britannica published *The Syntopican*, a revised collection of the great books of the western world. The collection's introductory volume was entitled *The Great Conversation: The Substance of A Liberal Education*. In the Preface, the collection's editor-in-chief, Robert Maynard Hutchins, made clear the purpose of collecting fifty-two masterpieces of western civilization. It was assumed, he asserted, that educated people knew the worth of the great books of the ages. Such works were revered, he argued, not only because they had endured but also because they contained brilliant ideas and possible answers to the problems that historically preoccupy human beings in such areas as religion, philosophy, science, politics, morality, education, economics, love and death, art and beauty, and social concerns—in essence, humanity's ongoing relationship to the world it inhabits.

Hutchins pointed out, however, that the choices in the collection were not, and could not, be permanent. How could they be? We live in a changing world, he explained, and thus venerated works must always be tested against new ideas and new discoveries as humanity evolves. Consequently, the choice of works studied always changes from era to era. In Hutchins' words, "...this process of change will continue as long as 'men' [quotes mine] can think and write. It is the task of every generation, the noted scholar reasoned, to reassess the tradition in which it lives; to discard what it cannot use, and bring into context with the distant and intermediate past, the most recent contributions to the Great Conversation.[1]

I will assert this morning that there is a strong bond between Hutchins' reasoning and mine. In many respects, the justification for one Great Conversation could stand as well as a rationale for another Great Conversation, one that argues for the inclusion in a basic liberal education the study of extraordinary films like *Citizen*

Kane, *The Grapes of Wrath, Grand Illusion, The Rules of the Game, Lawrence of Arabia, La Strada, Ikiru, 2001: A Space Odyssey, Paths of Glory, Dr. Strangelove Or: How I Learned to Stop Worrying and Love the Bomb, Schindler's List, The Seventh Seal, Jules and Jim, Do The Right Thing,* and *The Seven Samurai.*

Let me start with the issue of relevance. Between 1952 and now, we have witnessed many revolutionary changes in the world, as well as changes that demonstrate the severe limitations in Hutchins' problematic emphasis on western civilization: gender and ethnic preferences, the traditional view of families, and national priorities. These groundbreaking alterations have affected the Great Conversations not only in the humanities, history and science, but also in the arts and government. This morning, we meet to consider the changes in relation to our forms of communication.

It is now nearly two hundred years after the birth of mass communication, a half-century after we have moved from a print-oriented society to a media age; and, yet, there is no sense of urgency among many educators about preserving and studying the momentous contributions of motion pictures, television, and radio in our daily lives. The American Film Institute has produced lists of our most popular films, stars, and heroes. For more than sixteen years, The National Registry of The Library of Congress has selected twenty-five films annually to honor as national treasures. What more needs to be done to convince influential educators to house their own collections in our schools and universities?

It also seems incontrovertible that many nations venerate the outstanding stars and memorable stories of the international film community. My generation was nurtured on the likes of Chaplin, Keaton, Cooper, Bogart, Cagney, Stewart, Hepburn, Colbert, Gable, Tracy, Garland, Hope, Crosby, Crawford, Stanwyck, Fonda, Astaire, Kelly, Sinatra, and Davis. I don't even have to mention their first names. Film critic and author Molly Haskell put it well: "People talk about movies being a reflection of society, and that is partly true. I think they show not so much how we actually were, but what our fantasies were, what our myths about ourselves were."[2] In other words, educators need to study the stuff that dreams are made of.

If movies are so entwined with our myths and our dreams, our past and our future, why is it that movies are marginalized and trivialized in institutions dedicated to making the world better than we found it? If the goal of impressive works is, as Hutchins observes, "to help us to live better now,"[3] how is it possible to ignore the cinema's role in humanizing the mental health of nations? Why is it, as we begin our journey through the twenty-first century, we still insist mainly on print literacy and woefully ignore visual literacy?

Let there be no misunderstanding of my position. I revere the Great Conversation; I appreciate and admire imposing literary works and scientific treatises created by beautiful minds from every corner of the globe since the beginning of recorded time. Moreover, I think it is sheer lunacy to downgrade the study of the classics in our classrooms and in our homes. On the one hand, we cannot do great things if we do not educate ourselves to great ideas. On the other hand, we must never assume that life's momentous lessons are found only in schools. In fact, I have always lived by George Bernard Shaw's view that you "should never allow school to interfere with your education."

I do not have the time or the desire this morning to lecture you on the value of popular culture in our age. You know, better than I do, how to scan the Internet and how to find out about the pervasiveness and influence of movies, TV, and radio in the lives of people around the world. You are not the lay public. You recognize the life-shattering changes being brought about by computers and electronic technology, and where and how movies are part of those revolutionary changes. You are professional librarians. I do not have to explain to this elite audience why we have collections; why we preserve our creative treasures and safeguard them for the young, the uninitiated, and those yet unborn. In truth, our collections are safe houses for the imagination of our muses. You are not naïve about the problems that changes bring—e.g., the painful debates about adequate space, budgets, and content; the political obstacles to creating and to preserving collections. Like you, I recognize how much easier our lives would be, if only we did not have to think and to revise and to rewrite the lessons of the past for the issues of today. But the fact is that we do have to change if we are not only to survive, but also to shine. The lay public may be content with the bottom line. We cannot and must not be complacent about the process in dealing with the issues of our times.

This morning I wish to stir your imagination about the importance of film collections. I want to dwell on one of the great blessings of the mass media in general and movies in particular: The opportunity to make us think independently about alternative points of view. Regardless of age, status, education or geography, every member of a film audience—watching in the theaters, on the TV screens, in airplanes and hospitals and automobiles—, has the ability to see the world in transition and in conflict. Film audiences do not just see the conflicts. They are drawn into the issues and feel strongly about the questions and participants because movies first and foremost are about emotions

I remember my freshman year in a Brooklyn high school, when my history book had only a paragraph about Sambo and the nature of slavery. What did I know, living in a white ghetto, about the difficulties of African Americans in our nation? But thanks to local movie theaters, I saw films like *Lost Boundaries*, *Pinky*, *Intruder in the Dust*, and *Home of the Brave*. In my sophomore year, I saw Sidney Poitier's debut in *No Way Out* and later his roles in *Cry, The Beloved Country* and *The Harlem Globetrotters*. I have never been the same since. What are our young people learning today, not from the classrooms, but from the movie theaters about aids, war, the plight of the homeless, the nature of government, and the gay community?

And despite what you have heard and read, we do not each see things the same way. Some people then and now consider these movies trite and simplistic. Clearly, I do not!

Another good reason to study movies is to expose us to their role in understanding national crises. Consider *Osama*, an Afghan film that has been honored at major film festivals around the world, and won this year's Golden Globe for Best Foreign Language Film. Based on true stories of life under the Taliban as seen through the eyes of a child, the film was shown in three Afghan movie theaters in Kabul. According to the director, the people loved seeing "their own story...their own faces in this sharp mirror." In addition, President George W. Bush, after watching *Osama*, told the nation's governors at their annual conference "You ought to see the film...When you hear talk about being a liberator, that movie will bring home what it means to be liberated from the clutches of barbarism."[4] Following up on his comments, the State Department, in cooperation with MGM, sent copies of the film to our troops in Iraq and Afghanistan.[5] It seems reasonable to me that a movie so timely and honored ought to be seen and discussed in our schools.

Another timely example of the importance of visual literacy appeared in last Sunday's 'Magazine section' of *The New York Times*. Susan Sontag, in her essay 'Regarding the Torture of Others," argued that photographs of the torture in Abu Ghraib prison captured the attention of President Bush and his administration in a way they had not understood for several months. Sontag concluded, "Up until then, there had been only words, which are easy to cover up in our age of digital self-production and self-determination, and so much easier to forget."[6] How many times do we need to be told that a picture is worth a thousand words?

But recalcitrant educators will say, if you ask them about a film like *Osama*, they didn't have the time to see it, they didn't know it was around, they can't afford to make room in their crowded curricula for movies, and it's only a movie—no big deal. Imagine what a difference it would be if *Osama* were added to local libraries and collections? Not only would this low-budget film be available and accessible, but also the filmmakers would be encouraged to tell more of their stories, and I believe the world would be a better place for feeling so strongly about a crisis which has cost, and continues to cost, so many lives and involve so many people.

Movies have always been relevant. John Carpenter, a noted film director, observed the cinematic similarities between his childhood and today: "It's all about us, it's about people. We're all affected by our culture; undercurrents of culture affect us. We're affected by the conflicts in the world, by the conflicts within us. We're affected by everything. And you see it in the movies. We want to go to the movies and see who we are. That's what we did in the fifties, and that's what we do today."[7] To make the point more dramatically, keep in mind that in 2003, according to the Motion Picture Association of America (MPAA), American movies, on the average, cost nearly $64 million dollars to make, and another $39 million dollars to advertise, for a total cost of $102.8 million dollars.[8] It is astonishing to see how much filmmakers will spend to satisfy the public's desires. My point is that filmmakers focus on making movies big to win wide audiences. We need to focus on making such movies transparent and understanding their relevance to the human condition. It is not that *Troy* cost $175 million dollars to make; it is what we got for $175 million dollars.

The MPAA also released two other fascinating statistics. First, although the movies are aimed mainly at the 13-29 age categories, the MPAA reported there has been a 20% increase in the movie-going habits of people in the 50-59 categories. Second, American movies make 51% of their nearly $10 billion dollar box-revenues from abroad.[9] Add to that, the fact that DVD and Video sales have surpassed box-office revenues

My point is that it matters what movies—e.g., documentaries, narrative films, and made-for-TV movies—say about us and our values and our times. Think just about Ken Burns' memorable TV documentaries like *The Civil War, The West, Baseball,* as well as the cadre of directors who gave us *Eyes on the Prize*. We, as educators, need to use this universal language to better our lives and those of others.

Let me cite just two illustrations. Six days from now, in Washington, D.C., we will formally dedicate the memorial to World War Two. At the same time, Turner Classic Movies intends to air thirty-eight hours of war films. If the advance information is correct, there will not be a single film devoted primarily to the contributions of women and minorities in war. To an incalculable number of viewers under fifty years of age, WWII is ancient history. How can they fully appreciate what went on during that horrendous period? They weren't alive at the time.

Seeing theatrical films from the period would help transport them back in time, not to the reality of the era, but to the spirit of the age. From my perspective, it would be extremely useful to screen a TV documentary entitled *Oscar Presents: The War Movies and John Wayne* in conjunction with the WWII Memorial dedication. I believe the program was made in the mid-1970s. Wayne begins his narration with the words, "Today these [movies] bring back memories for a lot of us and also let our children know what it was like to be living then." Over the next three hours, you see clips from some of the 1700 movies made between 1941 and 1945: e.g., *Since You Went Away, Casablanca, Sergeant York, Bataan, Thirty Seconds Over Tokyo,* and *Air Force*.

What struck me in particular were the clips of Mickey Rooney in the extremely popular pre-war Andy Hardy series. Wayne points out that here were "all the myths we wanted to believe about the American Dream: a neat and prosperous world in which parents knew best, and all problems could be solved, and even a boy's fantasies about girls could be rated G." Louise Fletcher, the distinguished actress, added, then and now, we "look to the movies for reassurance and inspiration."

Mixed in with the films made during wartime were movies about WWII made after 1945: e.g., *The Best Years of Our Lives, From Here to Eternity, The Caine Mutiny, The Longest Day, Mister Roberts, Tora, Tora, Tora,* and *Patton*. As the documentary came to a close, Wayne reminded us that movies were an "indelible portrait of the best of what we were…[They] illuminate our heritage and enrich our lives."

Imagine how much we could learn by comparing these movies made during wartime and those films made afterwards? Think of our role in the Great Conversation, tackling issues of religion, philosophy, politics, morality, social concerns, and death, if we challenged the images of the past with other films about war like *All Quiet on the Western Front, The Big Parade, Paths of Glory, Saving Private Ryan, Dr. Strangelove, Catch 22, M*A*S*H, Hair, Born on the Fourth of July, Garden of Stones, Apocalypse Now, Platoon,* and *Three Kings*?

If educators want to discuss traditions that need to be discarded, what better place to begin with than the ideas about the glory of combat and the importance of obedience to authority?

Let me give you yet another perspective, one that is perhaps more personal to me. Earlier this month, Turner Classic Movies aired a documentary, entitled *Gary Cooper: American Life, American Legend*. Clint Eastwood, the anthology's narrator, began by explaining that Coop, whose career spanned more than thirty-five years and included ninety-five movies, was once the greatest of all movie stars. Eastwood then added, "In those days, we saw in his face, the face of all America…In telling Coop's story, we're telling more than the story of a man. We're also telling something about all of us who shared in this century with him: what we loved, what we laughed at, admired, feared, and sometimes where we went wrong."

Recall what Hutchins said about the purpose of the Great Conversation, "to help us live better now"; and reflect on what we could add to the discussion by analyzing films like *Mr. Deeds Goes to Town, Mr. Smith Goes to Washington, Meet John Doe, Sergeant York, The Pride of the Yankees, For Whom the Bell Tolls, The Fountainhead, High Noon, Friendly Persuasion,* and *The Court Martial of Billy Mitchell.* Not all of these are film masterpieces, but they afford us the opportunity to examine their content and construction so that we can develop taste and good judgment. Certainly we could use these films as starting points to talk about the place of religion in war, McCarthyism in America, and, as Eastwood quips, "passivity in the face of evil."

Again, my argument is that movies have an enormous impact on our lives and contribute substantially to who and what we are. Moreover, this enormous influence has been with us for over a century. We need collections of film masterpieces to study how movies can both inspire and educate us to who we are and where we came from.

To explain why, let me focus almost exclusively on narrative films. Let me do so simply.

Before movies appeared, community leaders had the power and the desire to control how their narrow world functioned and behaved. Children were taught to memorize and to obey their teachers in local schools. Citizens were discouraged from challenging authority, and being different was frowned upon. Conformity, not independence, was the order of the day.

But movies from outside our towns, states, and nations invaded these inner sanctums. The roles of parents, the nature of government, the lessons of the past, the values of the present, the dreams of the future, and the very essence of being became problematic on the silver screen. We went to the movies and found alternative points of view. That's why so many people for so many years tried to censor movies.

It's going on right now with Michael Moore's *Fahrenheit 9/11* and its controversial look at the relationship between the Bush family and Saudi royalty. In case you didn't hear, the film just won the Palm d'Or, the Cannes Film Festival's highest award for merit, and one rarely given to a documentary film. Earlier this year, censorship issues surrounded Mel Gibson's anti-Semitic film, *The Passion of the Christ*. Censorship happened last year with CBS and the made-for-TV film *The Reagans*.

My point is that serious people worry about what happens in movies and the effects films have on society. In short, movies are and always have been subversive. It is not just what they say and show. It's also the acts of omissions, the unspoken assumptions, the missing alternatives, and the suppressed information. Movies through their characters, sets, themes, dialogue and cinematography, force us to rethink who and what we are, what it is we believe and why, and how our past brought us to where we are in the world today.

And that is a good thing, not a bad thing. We need to challenge the status quo, not just to be ornery, but to be clear on how the system works. If we are right in our position, the movies can reinforce it. Remember Hutchins' idea that the purpose of great works "is to help us to live better." If we have something to be ashamed of in our past—i.e., our ethnic and gender biases— or in our present relationships—i.e., our ethnic and gender biases— we need to confront our demons and vanquish them so we can move on, so we can live better.

That is one of America's greatest virtues: the willingness to admit our errors and do something about them. In many ways, movies monitor our national consciousness. Think of the influence on our understanding of American heritage that the following films have had: *The Patriot, The Alamo, Gettysburg, JFK, Nixon,* and *Thirteen Days*. Such films dramatically alter our collective consciousness.

Filmmakers make their millions by reminding us of their role. Two examples should suffice. Remember what John Quincy Adams says in *Amistad*, one of the most misunderstood films in recent times, "We are who we were." Remember what the youthful emperor finally learns in *The Last Samurai*, "We cannot forget who we are and where we come from."

A wonderful way to view movies historically is to examine their reflections on the American family. Thanks to a fine 1996 TV documentary, entitled *Homeward Bound*, we get a superb collection of film clips from the 1930s to the end of the twentieth century.

Director Linda Schaffer starts with the classic film *The Grapes of Wrath* to show that even in the Great Depression struggling families stayed together and had hope for the future. The same was true during World War II. After the war, Schaffer demonstrates, the optimism seemed to become reality in films like *A Tree Grows in Brooklyn*, *Father of the Bride*, and *Young at Heart*. Baby booms, the mass production of automobiles, and the mass media gave us the suburbs and a feel good feeling about ourselves. But things started taking a turn for the worse for families in the mid-1950s. Evidenced in movies like *Rebel Without a Cause* and *East of Eden*, Schaffer illustrates the rise of generational conflicts, and presents one of the greatest icons of the times, James Dean. By the end of the decade, Hollywood finally began looking at black families and their problems in *A Raisin in the Sun*.[10] Within a decade we had *Guess Who's Coming to Dinner*? As Schaffer shows, we were challenged to put our money where our liberal mouths were. The sixties stressed rebellion in the family, and one of the all-time favorite examples was *The Graduate*. In effect, Schaffer demonstrates, revolution carries with it consequence for us all. By the seventies and early eighties, families were falling apart as shown in movies like *A Married Woman*, *Alice Doesn't Live Here Any More*, *Kramer vs. Kramer*, and *Ordinary People*. With the breakup of the family came new identities for women and new roles for men.

There is more, of course, but you can do some research on your own. Ask yourselves what recent movies like *Monster*, *Thirteen*, and *Elephant* tell us about modern families and single parents. In brief, what medium of communication today deals more frequently and more openly with the issues of family than do the movies, TV, and the radio?

Yes, you will say, but what is the worth of what the movies say? Look how Hollywood distorts history, see what it does to great books, and watch how the medium glorifies violence and gratuitous sex.

I do not defend the movies for the pandering it does for profit. Neither should you be an apologist for the trash that exists in publishing, art, and music. None of us here can cast the first stone. But remember, we are discussing the Great Conversations of our age. What I am arguing concerns the wonderful works in film that need to be preserved and shared to help make our lives better. Peter Biskind, author, and journalist, put it another way: "The people regard movies as value free and apolitical and just escapism; and I think that is a huge mistake. Movies, by their very nature, carry values and carry political ideas and ideas of all sorts. And the fact that you don't think about it, and they just kind of wash over you, and you just take movies for granted, means that they are all the more effective. You need to understand that you're just not looking at a kind of inchoate series of sensations and images, but that you are looking at ideas and emotions which are embedded in actors and images."[11]

I don't want to leave without answering the general charge that movies mistreat history. It is an assertion that is only half-true. One of the best explanations of the complexity has been given by Professor Garth Jowett, who years ago explained the difference between history ON film and history IN film: History on film occurs in three ways: 1) films that attempt to recreate the past —e.g., *Master and Commander: The Far Side of the World,* and *The Last Samurai*; 2) films that try to preserve the memories of important events—e.g., *The Alamo, Troy,* and *Gangs of New York*; and 3) films about well-known personalities—e.g., *Patton, MacArthur,* and *The Passion of the Christ*. Films that try to exploit history deserve criticism. As more of these biopics and docudramas are being made today than ever before, we must become more skeptical not only of what they say but also of why they are being made. History IN film, however, involves the medium's relationship to society: how it reflects and affects the people in a particular time, place and period of history. In other words, they use the past to comment on today. For example, what does the divisive and exploitive movie, *The Passion of the Christ* tell us about the values, attitudes, and ideas that director Mel Gibson communicated concerning the role of Jews in the crucifixion of Jesus, the role of Pontius Pilate, and King Herod? Does the film's message improve the human condition?

On the one hand, History on film is justifiably scorned for its lack of insights, historical inaccuracies, and cheapening of national cultures. On the other hand, History in film is highly regarded for the humanistic value of its symbolic content and the conceptual framework imbedded in film characterizations, dialogue, settings, plots, props, sound effects and themes.[12]

Let me end my presentation on a thoroughly optimistic note. Today, more than ever we have a chance to build great film collections because of the DVD revolution. Almost anything of merit in the history of film is, or soon will be, available for purchase or rental. Our young people are deeply involved in a film culture, and many of you in the audience represent the most intellectually informed librarians in a hundred years. You must get together to persuade those who govern your educational lives that movies have a major role to play in the Great Conversation. As even the archconservative Charlton Heston acknowledged, "Movies may be only the shadows of reality. Yet they share with us a great and simple secret. That in their midst men see themselves. That often there is more truth in the dream than the facts. It is the dream that brought us here. It's the dream that keeps us moving."[13]

Notes

[1] Preface, X1.
[2] Qtd. *Hidden Values*
[3] Preface xii.
[4] Susan Crabtree, "Afghan pic reels in D.C. pols," *Variety* (March 1-7, 2004): 3.
[5] Ibid.
[6] Susan Sontag, "Regarding the Torture of Others," *The New York Times*, 'Magazine section', May 23, 2004. 24.
[7] Qtd. in *Hidden Values*.
[8] Carl DiOrio, "Valenti Valedictory View an Eye-Opener," *Variety* (March 29-April 4, 2004): 16.
[9] Ibid.
[10] According to *Encore*, "Lorraine Hansberry's timeless play, *A Raisin in the Sun* has been transformed into a smashingly successful musical, *Raisin*, which recalls the Black Experience circa 1959. The soul of this Black statement remains intact, and it comes alive in the hands of a superlative cast." See Lenworth Gunther, "Black Stereotypes," *Encore* 2, no. 7 (1973): 39.
[11] Qtd. *Hidden Values*.
[12] *Film Study, Vol. 1. 1*, 254.
[13] Qtd. in *America at The Movies*.

20. Professor H. Lawrence McCrorey, a distinguished professor of Psychology, and a great champion for social justice and cultural diversity.

17.

Different Agendas

A great deal of oral history, I think, ventures into mythology. Mythology is a certain way of conveying knowledge, keeping tradition in tact. Sometimes it's more accurate in its way than certain kinds of history. This is where beliefs begin to inflect the narratives.[1]

Prof. Richard Macksey

Your book [*Every Step a Struggle*] was painful to read in some respects. It is a piece of history that will be forgotten because no one will take the time to read works such as yours. The anger, the indignities, the situations described in your interviews must have been difficult for you to hear, and I'm sure the memories of those encounters and the flood of emotions that accompanied them are still with you. Thank you so much for chronicling a period of our unfortunate history that needs to be remembered.[2]

Dr. Claude Nichols

A simple thank you for *Exits and Entrances* is just not sufficient. I truly enjoyed it. For most of my adult life, I have been involved in the arts (mostly in theater, prior to marriage and through Ivan [Dixon], theater, television and film). Reading *Exits and Entrances* was like going back through the years. I was aware of the times and knew most of the people you interviewed, both personally and their contributions. Ivan would have been proud to have been included in the book. I sincerely hope that there are others today with such aspirations and perceptions and with the courage to make a difference.[3]

Mrs. Berlie Ray Dixon

By the spring of 2006, I was a relatively relaxed, content, and carefree retired film teacher, believing that whatever contributions I had made to my profession were in the past and long since surpassed. Why? Sheila and the children were doing well, medical treatments were progressing better than any of us had expected, and my rare colleagues, Dr. Peter C. Rollins and Professor Denise J. Youngblood, had surprised me with a very gracious "eulogy" published in the Spring issue of *Film & History*.[4] (As we say in show business, my father would have loved it; my mother would have believed it.) Although the world once again appeared to be falling apart, and I was as deeply disturbed about social and political events as ever, I nevertheless felt at peace in my Vermont sanctuary in the Forest.

Then out of nowhere, Denise decided it's enough with my loafing about, listening to music, reading the great books, and watching my favorite movies. She had a major project for me, one she insisted could no longer be ignored or delayed. While putting together her flattering essay, the noted historian had reread my unpublished interviews with film celebrities conducted in the early seventies. Not only had these unique discussions linked the cinematic past to the modern world, but also the experiences themselves had profoundly affected almost everything I would teach and write about from the seventies on.

Now was the time, she argued, to share this rare material with a scholarly audience. Although we had talked decades before of my writing a book about these idiosyncratic documents, so many distractions in my life had occurred over the years that my private discussions dealing with screen veterans and race relations in the American film industry got filed away and were lying forgotten in the UVM archives. But the perceptive historian saw something in those buried transcripts that I had forgotten. They contained a unique record not only of an appalling time in our culture, but also they were substantial historical documents on individual responsibility available nowhere else in our country's collected consciousness. In addition, they contained a striking social and political reality that merited widespread examination. As Denise explained elsewhere, "I don't like to see great primary sources languish."[5]

My friend demanded, not asked, that I get off the couch and publish those rare and remarkable conversations. To be honest, she seemed to me a bit hyperactive and insensitive. After all, I was seventy-one years old. Not only was I living with the debilitating side effects that come from over a decade of chemotherapy, but also I had forgotten what serious research involves. Furthermore, I had not kept up with a gifted generation of outstanding scholars who had opened up vast new areas of investigation in black studies, and my intellectual proclivities appeared alien to contemporary audiences. And let's not forget the difficulty of being a Caucasian, American-Jewish professor living in the whitest state in the Union publishing his unsolicited, unconventional, and contentious ideas on the black film legacy. There's more! No longer at the University, where was I supposed to get the essential help that comes with doing scholarly research: materials, money, and professional feedback? In desperation and seeking a more reasonable supporter, I went to Sheila, hoping she would understand my circumstances and get Denise off my back. "This is crazy. I just don't have the strength to do it." Her answer: "Suck it up!"

Thus began a stressful journey back through a revolutionary time originating centuries ago in slavery, then to the greatest conflict fought on American soil, followed by two world wars, intermingled by the birth and growth of the movies, and up through the continuing struggle to make America, as Ruby Dee would say, be all it could be. The last time I had taken on such a formidable challenge was in the eighties when I inexplicably wrote a four-volume bibliography on screen education. At least then, I had the extensive resources that come with being an associate dean. But whatever Sheila wants, Sheila gets!

Maybe now is the opportune time to remind some of my readers just how the interviews began, and what it was I tried to do in the hectic days of what later became known in film circles as "The Blaxploitation Era." When I began researching African American movies in the mid-sixties, I freely acknowledge that I lacked wide experience in the subject matter, did not fathom what I was after, and was not conscious of the shameful problems, feelings, and issues I would encounter. I had no specific scholarly approach in mind; and I did not appreciate the complexity of language, race, identity, gender, and class in analyzing my research findings. (I could just as reliably say the same is true of myself today.) To put it bluntly, I was not exactly a rocket scientist about what I was doing. It was probably the greatest reach of my academic journey.

Gradually, I became acutely aware that studying black films at the end of the sixties provided me with unique opportunities to examine crucial subjects concerning African American liberty, domestic civil rights dissents, the need for sweeping reforms in public education, the rejection of Colonialism around the globe, the Vietnam War, and the fight for artistic freedom. Keep in mind these were the days when Black Nationalism boldly and defiantly confronted America's racist, conservative status quo. It was a period when blacks broke away from whites, when marginalized groups were being abused and killed by national and local law enforcement agencies established to safeguard the rights of all the people, when Americans everywhere felt confused and alienated, and when scholars started rethinking the role of the mass media in our society.

Because of these cultural crises, I enthusiastically welcomed the chance to use the study of film and television to make the past clear and helpful to the present in the hope of producing a better tomorrow. If you think this statement too naïve and hyperbolic; remember, I was of a generation that was going to make the world better than we found it. Thus studying the boom in black films opened a window that allowed me to blend my research seamlessly into my teaching about the popular arts.[6]

After a number of false starts, described in *Every Step a Struggle: Interviews with Seven Who Shaped the African American Image in Movies*[7] (hereafter *Every Step a Struggle*) and *Exits and Entrances: Interviews with Seven Who Reshaped the African American Image in Movies*[8] (hereafter *Exits and Entrances*), I decided to visit artists, white and black, who were actively involved in creating, continuing, and then revolutionizing the historical African American film image. Why entertainers and not social data and intellectuals? The rhetorical question allows me to address a misperception not yet tackled in my unconventional story.

For over a century, Hollywood stars who became the backbone of the motion picture industry have bewitched the public. To dwell on these modern-day demi-gods is often to be considered naïve and star struck, emotionally immature and possessed by a child-like innocence. But being the careful and shielding reader you are, you know that movie stars have never been a focus of my life's work. Nevertheless, I have always thought of these incomparable players much like Hamlet did when he greeted them in Act II of Shakespeare's immortal tragedy: "See the players well bestowed," he told his servants. "Treat them with honor and dignity."

My inclusive interviews could not have turned out as consequential as they did if I had done otherwise. Not only have I frequently singled out in my career those matchless performers who have mastered their craft with indiscernible skills, but also I have heeded the Danish prince's advice to treat such virtuosos with respect and appreciation. But unlike Hamlet, I show my esteem for actors not because of what they will say of me when I have gone, but because of what they do for me while I live. Let me be clear on this point. To paraphrase social historian Paul von Blum, "I don't believe film artists can give us a precise and sophisticated analysis of the complexities of human politic. That is not the role of film. But film, on the other hand, can inform, can enflame, can propagandize and can make people think." I also believe, to paraphrase Diego Rivera, that "all films are propaganda... [and that] films are essential for human life....Thus they do not become the property of the few."[9] Still further, I believe like Marlon Brando, the greatest thespian among his contemporaries: "Actors make a contribution to people's lives, giving us a gift you can't buy; something they can imbue with power and beauty and magnificence, something beyond themselves, and we need that."[10]

With those caveats in mind, I'll attempt to retrace my career-changing adventure. At the outset of the project, I had three Aces in my hand. First, my student projectionist in those fledgling film classes was Jason Robards, Jr. His father, one of the great stage and screen actors of his generation, agreed to help me if I made my way to Hollywood. Second, I had the honor of introducing the legendary Lillian Gish at a public lecture, when she visited the University in 1971. She promised to help me if I came to New York. And third, the University awarded me a modest grant to do the research.

The details of my extraordinary experiences gathering seventeen interviews are told tolerably well in the two aforementioned books, collectively called *The Interviews*. Since the publications are readily available, there is no necessity to repeat the details of my adventure here. What would be useful, however, are the names of the exceptional people I met and who changed my calling in so many powerful ways. In no particular order, they were Lorenzo Tucker, Lillian Gish, King Vidor, Clarence Muse, Woody Strode, Charles Edward Gordone, Frederick Douglass O'Neal, Mae Mercer, Brock Peters, William Marshall, Ivan Dixon, Ruby Dee, Jim Brown, Roscoe Lee Browne, James Whitmore, Cicely Tyson, and James Earl Jones. What made these random meetings so significant for me and, I hope, as well for generations yet unborn was the wide-ranging nature of their content, revealing both what each of us thought about racial matters at a critical time in our nation's checkered history and in our individual lives, but also the fact the expressed beliefs were unfiltered, authentic, and penetrating. With each passing year, the expressed views of these gifted people become even more vital links to the passion and creativity of a bygone group of artists that confronted racial issues in the chaotic period following World War II and climaxed at the end of the Blaxploitation era.

Why? What makes their impromptu conduct so valuable for us today? What relevance do the performers' candid remarks about the civil rights movement, movie history, fellow actors, individual struggles, personal ambitions, political alliances, and human rights have for us today? Read the interviews and decide for yourself!

But for now, appreciate the fact these newly published documents put a human face on a complicated and complex period of American culture. Should you choose to read *The Interviews* don't expect any answers to our perennial problems about human confrontation and social injustice. There is no consensus on any one revolting area, because no consensus was sought. Nor will you find either my confidants or me apologists for many black actors who played the lazy, slow-witted, comic characters in the formative and shameful days of motion picture history. However, the reader will learn why those infuriating roles arose, why they were so popular with the public, and why some of these actors, still working in the early seventies, would no longer do what they did back then. You will have, however, a seismic chance to witness change in motion.

Perhaps most noteworthy, *The Interviews* provided me with a forum whereby I might confront the indifferent public with the knowledge that what was done, what was accepted, and what was continued for over a century in American movies was mainly because of what we learned from our literature and our parents and our teachers and our institutions. In other words, these two books are about examining the unexamined legacy of our national heritage and our individual responsibility. To paraphrase the Nobel Prize-winning philosopher Bertrand Russell, "We weren't born stupid; we were born ignorant; society made us stupid."[11]

Again, to avoid any misunderstanding, the difference between these deceptively disarming but important talks and the biographies and profiles written by prominent intellectuals far above my grade level are profound. My conversations, with few exceptions, took place in less than a day and are almost devoid of any preparation other than a lifetime experience of seeing and studying movies. The scholars who have written contemporary massive biographies on such towering individuals as Albert Einstein, George Washington, Lyndon Johnson, George H. Bush, and Henry Kissinger spent years gathering information, and had extensive access to mountains of research. Their intellectual influence on others in this world far outweighs any shabby effect my paltry efforts have produced. In that sense, my interviews come off as mere footnotes in the history of important biographical publications. But when it comes to recording what was actually said and felt at a specific time in our nation's history, and the innumerable insights these unguarded words shed on our weak grasp of film history, the interviews stand aside for no one.

And that's a problem for some people. Two of the remarkable individuals interviewed—Cicely Tyson and James Earl Jones—denied me permission to publish their discussions. Let me hasten to say, that is not only their right but also their actions are not unusual. Furthermore, both players were extremely gracious in their denials, and wished me well in my road to publication. But our relationships had changed since we met in the early seventies. Ms. Tyson then was on the verge of a breakthrough performance in *Sounder* and had visited me at my hotel at the behest of Jason Robards. James Earl Jones, still basking in his fabulous Broadway success in *The Great White Hope*, granted me an interview thanks to the efforts of Ms. Lillian Gish and their joint agent. Now, when

I requested permission to publish those seventies' interviews, the legendary actors were unapproachable and guarded by handlers.

A word about these suppressed interviews. First, there is no smoking gun. Should those atypical documents ever be published once we pass on, readers will find fascinating comments and observations on a multitude of issues; but nothing damaging about the remarkable personalities themselves. Whether the artists agree is another matter. Second, the problem, I think, and I am certain the two actors will disagree, is that my freewheeling interviews are critical and unorthodox. We discuss the ups and downs of their careers in the entertainment world. In that sense, my approach proved disquieting. Celebrities like to dwell on the positive aspects of their journey and ignore the bumps in the road. While it is commonplace for interviewers to pander to an actor's vanity (pick up any newspaper piece on a performer quizzed by an ingratiating reporter; or watch any TV interview featuring an exchange between a fawning host and a distinguished actor to see my point), I find such puff exercises entertaining but hardly worth revisiting. Third, and most important, these artists would probably never again say what they said to me back then. That's what makes the interviews invaluable historical resources. That's also what makes these documents disconcerting to anyone who understandably wants to control his or her personal narrative.

These professionals have their rights, and I have mine. This observation is made without anger or ill will. It is necessary, however, that we make our prerogatives clear. For those of you who have read *The Interviews*, you are aware that a scholarly introductory essay placing the discussion in a biographical context preceded each exchange. Because negotiations with the representatives of Ms. Tyson and Mr. Jones took considerable time, *Exits and Entrances* had only a month or so to go before going to press. When the artists' gatekeepers finally decided to deny me permission to publish the requested respective conversations, my introductory materials to the interviews were already on paper. Because of the importance of these artists to film history and because the research about their contributions to race relations is done, I have decided to publish the introductory essays as one last example not only of my admiration for these legendary performers, but also of the mission I undertook back in the early seventies. They demonstrate one final time a key moment in my unconventional journey.

But there is one more important reason worth explaining my decision to publish the forthcoming essays. In a book like *Take Two: A Film Teacher's Unconventional Story*, where I am trying to provide an overview of my professional interests and pursuits, I sense that my past research might be useful to a new generation. The social, political, and economic issues that empowered the sixties' civil rights movement discussed in my previous writings—e.g., the divisive class struggle between white and black America, the racial barriers that impeded African Americans in their rightful pursuit of their share of the American dream, the lack of fair and equal education in our nation's schools, the systematic breakdown of the black family, the lack of job opportunities for young Africa-American men and women, the disproportionate number of black males in our country's broken criminal justice system, the disastrous relationship between law enforcement agencies and black communities, and the distressing lack of equality for people of color—all are alive and well in 2016. For example, *The New York Times* in its collection of essays by Henry Louis Gates, Jr., Abbey Ellin, Patricia Leigh Brown, and John Eligon spell out the recurring challenges facing a new generation of African Americans.[12] Ta-Nehisi Coates eloquently reminds us that not only does this nation have the largest incarcerated population throughout the world, but also we have sadly ignored what our disgraceful and discredited policies have done to black families.[13] And the gifted author, Michelle Alexander in detailing present social injustices against African Americans, recalls the familiar saying, "The more things change, the more they remain they same." In her significant book *The New Jim Crow*, she covers a multitude of racial horrors and explains, "The arguments and rationalizations that have been trotted out in support of racial exclusion and discrimination in its various forms have changed and evolved, but the outcome has remained relatively the same."[14] Thus by my talking about two major actors of a bygone age, I hope to refresh in the reader's mind my thoughts about crucial problems I discussed but sadly remain unresolved in my career.

Normally, I would conclude this introduction here; and you would turn to the material that is the focus of the chapter. But two exceptional events occurred during the writing of *The Interviews* that deserve comment. One experience revealed how we never know what will happen in a scholarly journey between when you start and when you finish. And two, what happened in preparing this section forever altered how I feel about *The Interviews*.

The first event concerns a book written by a University of Vermont professor I had not yet met, but now consider both the man and his work absolute gems: *Blowin' Hot and Cold: Jazz and Its Critics*.[15] I discovered this eloquent study in the interim between my two anthologies. Written by Dr. John Gennari, his prize-winning text makes a powerful case not only for why jazz critics should not be ignored, but also why the music itself is so extraordinary and important. Moreover, the compelling cultural historian describes both the relationships between art and racial conflicts, as well as how significant the music is to our souls.

I had never thought about Jazz that way. Of course, growing up in the second half of the twentieth century, I was familiar with the likes of Louis Armstrong, Ella Fitzgerald, Charlie Parker, John Coltrane, Paul Robeson, Josh White, Fats Waller, Cab Calloway, and Duke Ellington. But familiar is not the same as passionate. Moreover, in my teenage years, the conventional notion about film music was that it works best when it remains unnoticed. So foolishly, I saw no reason to study the artists who performed or wrote film music. But being overlooked is not the same as being irrelevant. Thanks to Professor Gennari's rewarding research, I now viewed the relationship between Jazz and black film history in a revolutionary light. That welcome change is dramatically apparent from what I say in *Every Step a Struggle* compared to what I write about in *Exits and Entrances*.

But there is much more to my story than that. Remember the period from 1935 to 1950, according to film musicologist Mark Evans, was the "Golden Age of Film Music." These were the days of Bernard Herrmann, John Barry, Alfred Newman, Victor Young, Miklos Rozsa, and Dimitri Tiomkin.[16] I embraced them all. It was a brilliant era for discovering America's songbook and its composers, including Jerome Kern, Irving Berlin, George Gershwin, Richard Rodgers, Cole Porter, and Harold Arlen—; they created the nation's most popular songs. Think of the melodies, tunes, and scores added to that list in your generation. And that doesn't include, for me, the enduring presence of Classical music in film history.

My point, however, is that from the moment I began reading *Blowin' Hot and Cold*, I have been studying a magnificent American-born art form, learning about its genres, listening to haunting artists I never knew existed, and buying Jazz recordings by the dozens. Not a day goes by now when I don't listen to Coltrane or Davis or Simone[17] or Parker, or Holiday, or Young or...To put it another way, by reading *The Interviews* you too might discover invaluable sources of inspiration by which you can navigate this nasty world.

The second event was even more personal and momentous for me. *Every Step a Struggle* was published in February 2007. Later that month, February 25th to be precise, *The Burlington Free Press* ran a very nice story on the book and the seven artists I had interviewed. Early the following morning, I received a surprising phone call from Dr. H. Larry McCrorey, a highly regarded academic physician and University administrator. Now most of my readers probably don't know this extraordinary human being also spent his life teaching about racial awareness, pointing out the the necessity for a multicultural educational environment, and confronting courageously the evils of racism.

Simply stated, no one I ever met served as a better role model for championing human rights than did this special UVM medical professor. Therefore, I can't begin to describe what his phone call that February morning meant to me, or how effusive he was about the book. Even I, a world-class self-promoter, am too embarrassed to list all the superlatives Larry showered on me. I will say this much; it was probably one of the most cherished conversations I've had in my life. We had worked with each other on various academic problems over the past forty years, but there were no personal bonds between us before that moment. We lived in different universes.

In essence, Larry had gotten his copy of the book, and had bought another one for his granddaughter, Ellington. He wanted me to autograph it for her. Could I have breakfast with him the next day? So on February 27 at about 9 AM we met; and the conversation started with him thanking me again for writing *Every Step a Struggle*, and wondering why we hadn't gotten together sooner.

We talked about how he had come to UVM in 1966, and that I had arrived a year later. Then we got to discuss the University and the various social, political and intellectual challenges we had faced, and still faced. And the conversation just kept going on without a pause for two and a half hours. Extraordinary as the exchange was, there was no way to cover all the things we wanted to share with each other; and so we agreed that because we had so much to say about politics, race, culture, history, UVM, administration, teaching, and Vermont that for the foreseeable future we would meet once a month for breakfast.

Then out of nowhere, a woman, a well-dressed white woman, came over to us—Sheila calls her "the Phantom Lady"—and said that she had been sitting at a table next to ours, and had become so engrossed in our conversation that she had missed her eleven o'clock appointment just so she could hear everything. She wanted to know what day we were going to meet again so she could hear more about our lives and interests.

The truth is we never saw her again, but for the next two and half years Larry and I met on and off to talk about individual responsibility, victims and criminals, and the revolting state of affairs in the world. Many of the themes consciously or unconsciously would later appear in *Exits and Entrances*. For example, I was just starting to study black music; and Larry entertained me with stories about the musicians he knew, how much he loved Jazz and the Blues, and the importance of the art form to African American history and the nation itself. I talked about my intentions to use both *Every Step a Struggle* and the new book to survey the black film experience from 1900 to the early 1980s, when the black boom ended.

I explained how *Exits and Entrances* would continue the questioning narrative begun in the first book. It would be about the artists who rejected the status quo, and how they had the courage to change conditions for black people in American films. It would describe the risks they took, and eventually how society slowly began to change. It would be an attack on conformity, and an explanation of how success requires self-determination and self-reliance. It would emphasize that movies do more than entertain us. They also educate us, and in the best of them, they inspire us.

Larry expressed great empathy about how difficult it must

have been for people like Ruby Dee, Jim Brown, Ivan Dixon, Cicely Tyson, James Whitmore, and Brock Peters to reform movies. You didn't have to be a Ph. D. student to see the relevance of the black film experience to how difficult it had been for us to deal with racial and cultural issues at the University and in the state. After a short time, we agreed that movies act as a laboratory for showing audiences how to live and to work in a complex and complicated world. In essence, those observations also made their way into *Exits and Entrances*, making the text much more than an anthology of interviews with screen celebrities. The second half of *The Interviews* also provides recollections about politics, race, American history, UVM, Vermont, the entertainment world, and my personal journey over the past forty-four years in teaching.

Among the many things that were crucial to me in those memorable meetings with Larry was the fact that all through my insecure years with black studies I had experienced a terrible anxiety with being a white man writing about black issues. I knew good intentions were not enough; and that passion was no substitute for knowledge. Larry was helpful here. When I told him about my anxieties, he laughed at me. "How could you be apprehensive," he said, "if I insist that my granddaughter must read your work? Doesn't that tell you something?"

Another concern was the audience for *Exits and Entrances*. Who was going to read it, especially in the whitest state in the union? With all that's going on in the world, with all the problems people face in their everyday lives, who really cares about fourteen people who aren't household names? In this area, Larry didn't preach; he demonstrated by his actions. For example, when Sheila and I went to hear him perform in a downtown Burlington restaurant, Sheila, Larry's significant other, and I were the only three non-musicians in the room. But that never mattered to Larry. He would just take out his saxophone, and he and the group played with as much passion as if they were performing at Carnegie Hall to a standing room only crowd. Another time, the dear man went to Australia to teach a black studies class with only seven students. He taught me you make your contribution wherever you can. The moral was that writing is not about numbers. What matters most is the chance to share your views, and, hopefully, influence anyone you can. That lesson is drummed home again and again in the fourteen interviews.

The last time we met, Larry, now a failing cancer victim, was in a wheel chair; and everyone in his inner group—his daughter, granddaughter, significant other, and a close friend—was there. It was in a local cafe. By then we had long since agreed that the three most important things about the future book was that it not be mainly about victims and stereotyping, but rather about courageous people whose many achievements function as inspirations for others, so readers would not think change was impossible, and they would not believe being a rebel ended your career. Of course, change creates controversy. Of course, you pay a price for going against the establishment. But it also teaches you courage. It illustrates what Ralph Waldo Emerson once said; "None of us will ever accomplish anything excellent or commanding except when he listens to this whisper which is heard by him alone."[18]

A second point was that education was the main element to changing the bigotry, ignorance, and hatred in the world. We agreed no matter what ugliness existed, most people were basically good; and that by getting them to think, to understand, and to re-evaluate their misperceptions, we could get them to behave more positively; and with that transformation, change the world as well. The final thing we agreed on was that no matter what the obstacles were, the book had to be completed and had to be published.

Let me be very clear on this point. In my time with Larry, neither *The Interviews* nor I were the center of our talks. In fact, the best part was gossiping about the University. Nevertheless, our conversations lead to unintended consequences. That's why I believe *Every Step a Struggle* and *Exits and Entrances* are so valuable. Not so much much because they reveal what it was like to live in that politically difficult times, but because *The Interviews* are filled with surprises about films, people, events, politics, race, and music.

Larry died in August of 2009, and I regret deeply he did not get a chance to see the new book in print.

Finally, after all the personal reasons and scholarly justifications in this introductory essay, I truly feel what is most satisfying intellectually and emotionally about having written these two books results from what was said in the two opening reactions offered in the quotation section. Or more sentimentally, my joy from *The Interviews* comes because of the reported response of Matthew

Greene, a freshman I have never met attending Northeastern University in Boston. My lifelong friend, Gary Greene, told me his eighteen-year-old grandson found in *Every Step a Struggle* a connection between his issues and mine. "This is how I feel," the young man purportedly said to his grandfather. (He is now reading *Exits and Entrances*.)[19] I believe these brief words are among the greatest rewards a teacher can get in his life.

Notes

[1] The quote is from Ms. Mame Warren's June 24th, 1999 interview with Prof. Richard Macksey, who founded the Johns Hopkins Humanities Center. The quote is included as well in *Johns Hopkins: Knowledge for the World*, ed. Ms. Mame Warren. Baltimore: John Hopkins University Press, 2000.
[2] E-Mail to author, October 12, 2013.
[3] E-Mail to the author, January 20, 2014.
[4] Denise J. Youngblood, "The Master of the Movies: A Tribute to Frank Manchel," *Film & History: An Interdisciplinary Journal of Film and Television Studies* 36:2 (Spring 2006): 21-24.
[5] Thomas Weaver, "Voices from the past," *Vermont Quarterly* (April 14, 2014): 2.
[6] Ironically, today's generation has a similar opportunity. Because of the highly controversial 88th Academy Awards ceremony where minority artists and works were conspicuously missing from the movies honored, Hollywood has given the green light to more than a number of films focusing on African-American issues. In addition, independent and non-traditional organizations are producing movies about current and past incidents involving inspiring black figures and slave insurrections. A good place to begin considering research options is in Michael Cieply and Brooks Barnes, "Oscars Less White? There's No Shortage of Black Fims in 2016," *New York Times.Com* (May10, 2016): 1-5.
[7] Frank Manchel, *Every Step a Struggle: Interviews with Seven Who Shaped the African American Image in Movies*. Washington, D.C.: New Academia Publishing, 2007.
[8] Frank Manchel. *Exits and Entrances: Interviews with Seven Who Reshaped the African American Image in Movies*. Washington, D.C.: New Academia Publishing, 2013.
[9] *Diego Rivera: Rivera in America*. American Masters, Season 3, Episode 5. USA: Eagle Rock Entertainment. (August 1988).

[10] Stevan Riley, *Listen to Marlon*. USA: Passion Pictures, 2015.
[11] Bertrand Russell, *A History of Western Philosophy*. London: George Allen & Unwin LTD, 1945.
[12] "Voices Rise," *The New York Time Educational Life* (February 7, 2016): 10-20.
[13] Ta-Nehisi Coates, "The Black Family in the Age of Mass Incarceration," *The Atlantic*. Vol. 316, No. 3 (October 2015): 60-80, 82-84.
[14] Michelle Alexander, "Introduction," *The New Jim Crow: Mass Incarceration in the Age of Colorblindness*. New York: The New Press, 2012. Loc.228.
[15] John Gennari, *Blowin' Hot and Cold: Jazz and Its Critics*. Chicago: The University of Chicago Press, 2006.
[16] Anyone wishing to see the riches in discovering the links between Jazz and the disgraceful conditions confronting African American artists in the sixties should examine the life and music of Nina Simone. A brief but important essay to read on that topic is Brent Staples, "To Hollywood, Blackness Is Just a Special Effect," *Editorial Observer, New York Times* (March 20, 2016):10.
[17] Qtd. in Frank Manchel, *Film Study: An Analytical Bibliography*, Vol. 1. Rutherford: Associated University Presses, 1990. 402-403.
[18] Based on a selection from Brainy Quote.
[19] An E-Mail from Gary Greene to Frank Manchel. March 25, 2015.

21. Cicely Tyson as the unforgettable Rebecca who struggles to protect her sharecropping family in the Deep South. Martin Ritt, *Sounder* (1972). From the core collection production photographs of the Margaret Herrick Library, Academy of Motion Picture Arts and Sciences.

Center Stage

Having heard all this, you may choose to look the other way…but you can never say again that you did not know.[1]
William Wilberforce

No matter how big a nation is, it is no stronger than the weakest people, and as long as you keep a person down, some part of you has to be down there to hold him down, so it means you cannot soar as you might otherwise.[2]
Marian Anderson

For over a half century, Hollywood films have dealt with… complex and often contradictory ways. Marked by outrage, indifference, compassion and ignorance, the need to understand and the desire to forget.
Gene Hackman

For over fifty years, Cicely Tyson has created a gallery of resilient black heroines unparalleled in film and television history. What remains remarkable is not only her achievement but also the way in which she did it. This Civil Rights activist and Emmy-Award winning actress possesses all the gifts of her most notable predecessors like Ethel Waters, Lena Horne, and Dorothy Dandridge: beauty, voice, presence, and talent. But rather than take a traditional show business route previously "reserved" for African American women, this inspiring entertainer carved her own trail through a perilous white-male dominated-regulated system. In so doing, she neglected typical ethnic stepping-stones like singing and dancing; and focused instead on her intellect, passion, talent, and purpose in order to shine on screens large and small not as a traditional black performer, but as a much-admired dramatic artist.

Even that was not enough. "I could not afford the luxury of just being an actress," Tyson explained. "There were a number of issues that I wanted to address, and I used my career as my platform."[3] The obstacles she faced in upholding her moral principles prevented her from having a filmography accorded major dramatic stars like Ellen Burstyn, Faye Dunaway, Sissy Spacek, and Susan Sarandon. There were, however, more important considerations. Eloquently stated by the distinguished scholar Bernice Johnson Reagan, the battles fought by civil rights activists like Cicely Tyson demonstrated "culture to be not luxury, not leisure, not entertainment, but the lifeblood of a community."[4] And in the final analysis, by choosing quality over quantity, purpose over profit, Cicely Tyson established herself as an illustrious performer in film, stage, and television's celebrated ranks.

While her movies rarely won the commercial or critical success identified with her stage and television work, Tyson's acting genius enabled her to share with us vicariously the African American experience. With each passing year, her family-oriented movies depicted an astonishing visual chronicle of black history from the shores of Africa to slavery to the Civil War and Reconstruction right up to the present. In such roles as the mother of Kunta Kinte, a 110-year-old ex-slave, abolitionist Harriet Ross Tubman, school innovator Marva Collins, the mother of Rosa Parks, and Coretta Scott King, Tyson's efforts bore witness to a rich black heritage. For reasons like these, her distinguished epic triumph has earned the actress many honors, including Emmys, drama awards, The Spingarn Medal, the highest recognition of the National Association for the Advancement of Colored People; and in 2015, The Kennedy Center Honor for her lifetime contributions to American culture. Such acknowledgments underscore why no one in American entertainment surpasses her in reshaping the screen image of black womanhood.

In the process, Tyson avoided the fate of previous black women who became famous in show business. That is, from the days of Josephine Baker and Nina Mae McKinney through the troubled careers of Fredi Washington, Hattie McDaniel, Ethel Waters, Lena

Horne, and Dorothy Dandridge, an informed public presumed that when the curtain came down on these remarkable performers we would find them bitter and disillusioned.[5] That has not been true for Cicely Tyson. She has passed the test of time, and like Cyrano, did so with, an "unsullied plume."

Let me be clear on this point. In no way do I mean to slight the contributions of earlier black performers. Without question, nearly every African American actress who followed in their fabled footsteps benefitted from their sacrifices and their achievements. Thus author James Gavin, for example, is justified when he writes, "There's no telling how much longer it might have taken for black women to get even a fraction of their due onscreen had it not been for [Lena] Horne."[6] But Tyson, standing on the shoulders of stars like Horne, took the roles of black actresses to a new level. While she too had her challenges, the resolute performer nonetheless schooled this and future generations in how to bring about change and yet not become embittered by the experience. No matter what the blows, she kept her nobility and individuality constant.

Tyson made no Blaxploitation films to express her outrage over deplorable racist conditions past and present. That was in part because she refused to add to the seventies' "'prime beef image' of black women who bed men without establishing any involvement whatever."[7] And as she explained to *People* magazine, she "would rather be unemployed than act in exploitation films like *Shaft* and *Super Fly*." Moreover, she added, "The lesser of two evils for me is to wait, rather than do something that isn't right."[8] She also consciously distanced herself from traditional black female stereotypes as well as from the new distortions emerging from the contemporary black action movies. Tyson was more than an activist debunking labels whose time had past. Her aim was to replace the negative with the positive. She accomplished her goals not by ignoring what was, *Ms.* magazine reported, but by aggressively challenging "the two major stereotypes of the black woman in film and drama: the roly-poly, desexed black mammy and the 'high yaller' femme fatale."[9]

While the world at large embraces the trailblazing artist, some cultural circles appear reluctant to give the noted actress her due. It's an intriguing dilemma. Because much of today's scholarship covers the Civil Rights era and focuses on the rise of modern black movies and Blaxploitation films, Cicely Tyson's crossover work rarely gets addressed in current scholarly books and college classrooms. I suspect that oversight also has more to do with the middle-class, conservative ideology embedded in many of the star's films rather than with her undeniable acting skills or many screen contributions. Moreover, the intellectual slight may be that in our pessimistic age, liberals justly angered over widespread social injustice and racial inequality, pride themselves on their ongoing struggles for oppressed people rather than concerning themselves with African American uplift.

Regrettably, these same well-intentioned liberals sometimes forget that conservatives, as Jonathan Haidt reminds us, likewise have worthy values based upon moral foundations just as powerful as those ideals progressives champion: loyalty, authority, and sanctity.[10] Even further, Tyson's films appeal more to black middle class families than to counter-culture groups. That is, her dramas often portray the black bourgeoisie as a well rounded, visible, productive, and an important force in American society and history.[11] This truth does not appeal to the ardent broad-minded scholars who are devoted less to aspirational goals and more to solving everyday racial injustices to the poor and the disenfranchised.

Thankfully, Professor Ruth Feldstein's passionate feminist study of the women involved in the Civil Rights movements adds to our awareness of the vast contributions that Cicely Tyson made to helping others climb the ladder of opportunity, success and freedom. Along with stirring portraits of iconic figures like Lena Horne, Nina Simone, Abbey Lincoln, and Diahann Carroll, the insightful intellectual points out how Tyson's films, although anchored in the past, inspired her peers to "resist ongoing segregation and prejudice, years after passage of civil rights legislation, and the deaths, jailing, or exile of visible leaders; why family mattered to black activism, and what kinds of African American families were—and were not—healthy; and what constituted 'authentic' and politically meaningful African American culture."[12]

In examining Cicely Tyson's laudable quest, we find that it dramatically accentuates the belief, to paraphrase Wordsworth, that the child is the mother of the woman. Born in East Harlem, New

York, to humble parents who sought the American dream, she grew up never imagining her life would be in the arts. Her father, William Tyson, a painter and carpenter, and Theodosia, his wife, emigrated from the island of Nevis in the West Indies to America, determined to provide rich opportunities for their future family: two girls and a boy. But it was not to be. When Cicely was born on December 16, 1924, she entered a household that barely existed above the poverty line.

What is fascinating about Tyson's childhood is how little we know about her formative years growing up poor. That is because as a teenager, according to one source, "she internalized everything, and never really was able to talk until she went into the theater. Certain things she says are personal and should be kept private."[13] As a result, the actress has remained an unusually secretive person. For example, the public appreciates that her mother, a deeply religious and domineering woman, worked mainly as a housekeeper, while still maintaining her Victorian values. When it came to bringing up her young family, the protective parent insisted on her offspring not mingling with other youngsters in their unsafe neighborhood. Whatever free time the children had, they were meant to spend it in church-related activities: singing in the choir, attending Sunday school, and playing musical instruments. Socializing with the opposite sex was discouraged as was wasting one's time on immoral activities like watching movies. Not surprisingly, given the traditionalist nature of the Tyson household, the youngster appears to have had few friends, and it wasn't until her senior year in high school that she began dating.[14]

When Cicely was eleven years old, her parents divorced; and her mother, who now gained sole custody of the three children, understandably became even stricter. The divorce, along with the absence of her father, hit the young girl hard. From various sources, we learn, however, she loved both her parents. As the family income shrank, the single parent now supported her children by going on welfare. Food, clothing, and basic comforts became even scarcer than before. During these difficult years, the teenager tried to get odd jobs to help the family survive. About the only pleasure she seemed to have outside of her church activities and schooling was to go off from time to time and crisscross New York City on the subways and buses.[15]

Now you might assume, having read the biographies of artists like Waters, Horne and Dandridge, that Tyson over time would have talked about those difficult years, shared with us whom she turned to for inspiration, what she got from her solo trips around Manhattan, provided some insights about how she survived isolated in a tough neighborhood, or even opened up about what her relationship was with her siblings. We also might have gleaned what plans Theodosia had for her rebellious daughter, or perhaps what Cicely herself hoped to become when she became a woman. But we get none of that. No mention is ever made of the arts or the museums or the libraries in her world, except to say the one or two movies she did see as a child left her underwhelmed. Never do we hear about books, music, or history. Never do we discover what kind of public school education she had. Never is a particular friend mentioned or a favorite teacher discussed. We don't even learn whether she was the youngest or the oldest or the middle child in the family.

What is clear, however, is that the future actor developed a strong sense of independence, defiance, and self-determination. Each trait she latter attributed to her mother's upbringing. These were characteristics that remained with Tyson throughout her life. As a mature woman, she compared her comportment to the actions associated with Harriet Ross Tubman: rebelliousness and self-sufficiency.[16] Even so, because the performer's life was so influenced by her mother's religious values, it is extraordinary she turned out as she did both professionally and personally.

What interests me about her poverty-stricken childhood is that Tyson basically remained untouched by racism. As she told me in 1972, the woman did not experience the painful nature of bigotry until she got her first credited film role at age twenty-two. In that sense, we fellow New Yorkers shared in this respect a similar and meaningful background.

I too found much of my lifelong traits outside my home, exploring my narrow world by sometimes riding alone the trolleys, the subway, and buses throughout Brooklyn and Manhattan. Growing up in Flatbush, I also experienced little of racism until I came to Vermont in 1967. It was during the first few months of living in a South Burlington neighborhood that I learned certain children were told not to play with my two young sons because they were

Jewish. Ten years later, when Dean John G. Jewett appointed me Associate Dean of the College of Arts and Sciences, my Conservative rabbi Max Wall told me that I was the first Jew in the history of UVM ever to rise above the administrative ranks of chairperson.

Obviously, Tyson and I are quite different, but here we are both *the same and different*. My purpose in bringing this detail to your attention, as I do often in *The Interviews*, is to reinforce a point, that Professor Emily Bernard dwells on in her work: the riddle of describing the African American experience. That is, you cannot discuss "racial sameness" without recognizing "racial difference."[17] What occurs frequently, at least for me, is that in my discussions I became aware of how much these celebrities and I shared common experiences yet experienced them differently.

One gets the impression that by the time Tyson was eighteen, she was determined to make something special of her life. Where or when the future Civil Rights activist decided black history would be an integral part of that journey is anyone's guess. After graduating from New York's Charles Evans Hughes High School, she found a secretarial job at the American Red Cross. But very quickly, the beautiful, restless and outspoken Tyson declared to everyone in her office, she had no intention of living such a boring and unglamorous existence. So the young rebel got a job as a model. Working for the Barbara Watson Modeling School, Tyson, who always remained fastidious about her appearance, quickly drew the attention of the taste setters in the clothing industry. Soon she appeared on the covers of every important white and black fashion periodical on the newsstands. But still the young woman remained unfulfilled. "I felt like a machine," she told an interviewer for *Time* magazine.[18]

Then came a major turning point in her life. While attending a business meeting with *Ebony*'s fashion editor Freda DeKnight, Tyson's beauty attracted the attention of Evelyn Davis, a black character actress, waiting in the editor's outer office. What followed, as Tyson always tells interviewers, is "When I walked by, [Davis] took one look at me and said, 'Lord, what a face!' She said I'd be perfect for a movie then in production called *The Spectrum*. It was about the problems between light-skinned and dark-skinned blacks. I auditioned for the part and I got it. Actually, the film was never released because the money ran out—but here I am."[19]

The event probably took place in the mid-fifties, because we know that going into show business caused a fierce argument between the young woman and her mother, resulting in the daughter being forced to leave the house. It would be two years before the parent and her offspring reconciled. They remained close ever afterwards. Meanwhile, the budding actress devoted herself to learning her trade by studying at one acting school after another. As her training progressed, Tyson set her sights on breaking into film and drama.

Her early screen ventures foreshadowed much of the star's future career. For example, it is highly unusual that a beginner would have much to say about what role she might have in a movie. Novices take whatever they can get, just to gain some experience. Not Tyson! Right from the start, even in uncredited roles, she was going to be very specific about what she would and would not do in her profession. Of three beginning films normally[20] listed in her filmography—Sidney Lumet's *Twelve Angry Men* (1957),[21] Robert Wise's *Odds Against Tomorrow*,[22] and Daniel Mann's *The Last Angry Man*[23] (both in 1959)—all put the issue of racism front and center. Just as significant, each movie featured major actors. Still further, all of these films were based on literary sources. For the next fifty years, those brands would be identified with almost every significant Tyson venture.

By 1959, the resiliant poor girl from the streets of East Harlem was about to burst forth on the show business world. In addition to the roles she had landed in the Lumet, Wise, and Mann movies, she appeared in her drama teacher Vinnette Carroll's Off-Broadway revival of the play, *The Dark of the Moon*; a Broadway variety show called *Talent '59*; and understudied for Eartha Kitt in the role of Jolly Rivers.[24] When stage parts proved unable to pay the rent, the hard-working actress looked to television, starting with Bande Marshall's adaptation of *Brown Girl, Brown Stones*, a TV narrative about Barbadian émigrés trying to survive in Brooklyn. Parts in fashionable series like *Naked City* and *The Nurses* soon followed; and the actor became sought after for notable roles on Sunday morning melodramas. In one striking TV performance on *Camera Three*'s *Between Yesterday and Today*, the actress, as she told me, decided to cut her hair for artistic reasons related to the script, a move that would later have major significance for black women across America.[25]

Tyson's rise was part of a tidal wave reshaping the black experience at the end of the fifties. One major area being changed was Jazz. Famous musical expert Michael Ullman viewed 1959 as "an *annus mirabili* in modern jazz...It was a year of controversy and innovation."[26] Jazz scholar John Szwed went even further, writing, "up to this point [jazz] had been on what seemed to be a stable evolutionary path, following its own logic, its own distinct aesthetic. People might not have been able to say exactly what jazz was, but they could usually distinguish it from classical and popular music." By 1959, the celebrated jazz critic explains, "the mainstream of jazz was flowing nicely: Louis Armstrong recorded with Duke Ellington, affirming the wholeness of the tradition. Dave Brubeck had just made *Time Out,* an album of compositions with unusual meters (for jazz, at least)...Cannonball Adderley recorded *The Cannonball Adderley Quintet in San Francisco* that year, which became one of the most popular albums of soul jazz, a revitalization of black folk elements and rhythm patterns that were beginning to be called funk. Charles Mingus recorded *Mingus Ah Urn,* which showed how such folk and soul elements could be used not just for popular amusement, but also in compositions of great seriousness and emotional power. Many other musicians at this time were busy recording jazz versions of Broadway and private-eye TV show scores."[27]

A revival of Black Nationalism[28] growing out of Dr. Martin Luther King's earlier bus boycott also developed by the end of the fifties. Reformers like Stokely Carmichael and Malcolm X had begun being noticed. The Congress of Racial Equality considered entering the South with buses loaded with Freedom Riders, while other militant groups talked about voter registration drives for black southerners.[29] Within two years, the activists had matured to the point where the murder of Congolese Prime Minister Patrice Lumumba resulted in a band of black nationalists temporarily taking hold of the United Nations building, while outside the building dozens of African American supporters staged an angry, violent street demonstration. Years later historian Peniel E. Joseph claimed it was this UN protest that signaled that Black Power formally arrived on America's political radar screen.[30]

Taking part in this changing black experience was a new generation of black artists from the fifties set to reform mainstream

American entertainment in the decades to follow. Some like Sidney Poitier, Ruby Dee, Ivan Dixon, and Diana Sands appeared in Lorraine Hansberry's widely acclaimed Broadway drama *A Raisin in the Sun* (1959), directed by Lloyd Richards. Two years later, the play was made into a film, directed by Daniel Petrie and with only one major casting change from the Broadway production: Lou Gossett Jr. replacing Ivan Dixon.[31] That same year saw Jean Genet's highly provocative stage play *The Blacks: A Clown Show* (hereafter *The Blacks*), cast with one of the most celebrated repertory groups in black theatrical history: James Earl Jones, Roscoe Lee Browne, Maya Angelou, Lou Gossett, Jr., Charles Edward Gordone, Godfrey Cambridge, Raymond St. Jacques, and Cicely Tyson. During the drama's successful Off-Broadway three-year run other future stars also emerged like Billy Dee Williams, Abbey Lincoln, Esther Rolle, and Janet MacLachlan.[32]

The Blacks, directed by Gene Frankel, premiered on May 4, 1961, with its all-black cast, and according to James Earl Jones, was "not so much as an experiment in technique as an experiment in haranguing the consciousness of both the audience and us."[33] The controversial drama proved especially significant for Tyson. Starring in the original cast as the prostitute Virtue, Cicely played what she considered a comic role in an absurdist drama about a black man sentenced to death for betraying his people. Her performance won the young actress the important Vernon Rice Award in 1962.

An intriguing aside to Tyson's experiences with *The Blacks* was that the men in the play achieved success faster than did the women. No one, of course, has the answer why. And for those who think they do, I remind them, as one intellect explained, "For every complex question, there is a simple answer. It is simple, it is direct, and it is wrong." Nevertheless, the actor did state her views on the topic. "A famous theatrical producer then affiliated with Lincoln Center told me," explained the actress to a *Ms.* Interviewer, "that when you put a black woman on stage, the audience's mind immediately thinks of sex."[34] Obviously, that image did not translate well into an appreciation of an actress' acting skills.

Tyson's recognition as a gifted dramatic actress increased in 1963 when she appeared with James Earl Jones and George C. Scott in the highly regarded but challenging CBS television series, *East*

Side, West Side. Designed by David Susskind's company, Talent Associates, as a groundbreaking production that exposed the tragic conditions in Northern black ghettoes, the provocative series was yet one more vivid illustration of how far not only mainstream entertainment had come since the end of WWII, but also why the mass media could not be dismissed as irrelevant entertainment. One prominent critic at the time described the show as "undoubtedly the boldest, bravest and most original new series now on your screen this new season."[35]

What especially caught the attention of American black women was Tyson's beauty and hairstyle. While she played a supporting role as Jane Foster, Scott's secretary in the New York City welfare office, Cicely held center stage when it came to creating a national fashion craze. Black hairdressers became some of her greatest fans. African American women began to model their looks after those of Tyson's. According to *New York Times* observer Ellen Holly, "Tyson has always been a lovely actress, easily capable of enameled glamour when it is called for. But here...she passes all of her easy beauty by to give us, at long last, some sense of the profound beauty of millions of black women."[36]

That being said, the network and its advertisers found *East Side, West Side*'s unrelenting attacks on Northern urban racism so disturbing that CBS canceled the series in April 1964 after twenty-six episodes.[37] And despite all the current DVD re-releases of TV shows from the fifties and sixties, not once has there been any indication that this highly significant series will ever find the light of day again.

Two years later, Cicely Tyson's life and career took two important turns, and at approximately the same time. Both had to do with the immortal jazz musician Miles Davis. While many critics have superbly described his life and genius, it makes sense to briefly indicate what Davis meant both to jazz history and to Tyson herself.

The portrait is somewhat marred by contrasting judgments of the man and his music.[38] Isabel Wilkerson helps put the artist in perspective: "Over time, the Migration would transform American music as we know it. The three most influential figures in jazz were all children of the Great Migration. Miles Davis was born in Alton, Illinois, after his family migrated from Arkansas. Thelonious Monk migrated with his family from North Carolina when he was five. John Coltrane left High Point, North Carolina, for Philadelphia in 1943, when he was sixteen."[39] Stanley Crouch renders another major assessment of Davis from today's point of view: "The contemporary Miles Davis, when one hears his music or watches him perform, deserves the description that Nietzsche gave of Wagner, 'the greatest example of self-violation in the history of art.' Davis made much fine music for the first half of his professional life, and represented for many the uncompromising Afro-American artist contemptuous of Uncle Tom, but he has fallen from grace—and been celebrated for it." The distinguished critic adds to this harsh assessment: "Beyond the terrible performances and the terrible recordings, Davis has also become the most remarkable licker of monied boots in the music business, willing now to pimp himself as he once pimped women when he was a drug addict."[40]

Ian Carr provides still another take, albeit a more professional assessment, stressing Charlie Parker's influence on Davis, and calling it "incalculable."[41] That is, both men demanded to be taken as serious musicians, not just as black entertainers. Both individuals were tragic figures who rose and fell because of their demonic desires for women and drugs. Miles was the more sensitive and intelligent of the two, yet both artists, as Carr explains, remained throughout their lives determined "to inhabit the frontiers of experience" and both were "magnificently heroic and magnificently foolhardy."[42] Finally, Crouch, speaks for many people who knew Davis well, saying that his conduct towards women was "disgusting."[43]

One person who disagreed strongly with the criticisms about the man, his music, and his behavior was Cicely Tyson. The two had not yet formally met by 1966, but they were well aware of each other. She knew and loved his music. He appreciated both her stage acting and her TV performances in *East Side, West Side*. When they finally made contact, according to Szwed, Davis was yet at another low point in his life. Twice divorced, an uncontrollable womanizer, a recovering drug addict, and grieving over the death of his mother, Miles hardly seemed poised for a romance with a strong woman brought up with strict moral scruples. Nevertheless, the two took to each other.[44] Friends forecast the celebrated couple would never make a go of it. But for the next three years, they proved inseparable. Tyson later recalled that "it was a beautiful period in my life because I loved him and I knew he loved me...." The thing she found most appealing in the moody jazz figure "was that he is an extremely sensitive human being, a beautiful, sensitive man."[45]

The irony of Tyson's memory is the period from 1965 to 1971 was a troubling one for her professionally. Not much had come her way since the CBS cancellation. Now because of coincidence or because art was trying to draw on real life, she got her first credited screen role, appearing alongside Sammy Davis Jr., Louis Armstrong, Frank Sinatra Jr., Peter Lawford, and Ossie Davis in Leo Penn's *A Man Called Adam* (1966).[46] The original screenplay by Lester Pine and Tina Rome focused on Adam, a great jazz trumpeter (played by Sammy Davis but bearing a strong resemblance to Miles Davis) who is brilliant in front of an audience, but is violently self-destructive away from the bandstand. Tyson plays Claudia, a loving, compassionate civil rights activist who tries to save the angry, addicted musician from his demons. Surprisingly, the movie foreshadowed what was yet to occur between Cicely and Miles over the next three years and beyond.

Before I comment on Tyson's official film debut, let me raise a major point critics have been debating when it comes to the popular arts: the question of whether there is more to film criticism than aesthetics. I raise it now because of its relevance to unorthodox black films made throughout the early decades of film history. Much has been made of their lack of traditional production values and audiences accessibility.

Clearly, here is not the place to resolve the issue. Suffice to say that I believe films are more than art; they are also, as discussed earlier, invaluable educational tools and crucial historical records. Readers should also appreciate the fact that the popular arts do not exist exclusively for intellectuals or critics. Different audiences have different standards and different needs. *New York Times* critic Brent Staples put the case in the context of the era, saying "The black-related films of the 1960s and early 1970s required new aesthetics requiring we see and hear films differently from the past. The emphasis was on distinguishing the real from the ersatz, the authentic geniuses from the hack imitators...People asked were the filmmakers competent and 'responsible'."⁴⁷ And Pauline Kael suggested when dealing with certain movies we need to focus not so much "with the formal aesthetics of a particular piece of popular culture but with everything to do with how popular culture works in a society."⁴⁸ My point is the times they were a changing, and we in the intellectual community needed to decide if we were going to change with them.

In many respects, *A Man Called Adam* is both a film of its time and a film that challenges our critical sensibilities. My initial reaction to what I considered an unwatchable movie was that the acting was amateurish, the direction pedestrian, and the script silly and unconvincing. Except for Tyson, I wouldn't have rehired any of the performers. I also considered the musical score commendable (but you know what my musical judgment amounts to). Neither Armstrong's biographer or *Time* magazine appear to disagree with me. They also could not find much to praise about the movie. As Terry Teachout observed, A *Man Called Adam was* "overwrought and overcooked, a steamy melodrama that *Time* described with curt exactitude as 'a specialty act salted with social protest.'"⁴⁹ Not unexpectedly, the film was dead on arrival at the box office.

But as I studied what made the movie so appealing to my socially oriented colleagues, my critical views changed. I came to believe that Tyson gave a splendid performance as a freedom rider emerging from jail and inadvertently finding herself emotionally involved with a tragic jazz genius. (In many respects her screen personality strikingly reflected the Cicely Tyson I met in 1972.) The script now got kudos for including several fascinating bits of business about manager-agent-artist relationships, offering conflicting views about the civil rights movement then prevalent in the black community, and broadening the era's interpretation of racism as it existed not just in the South but also in the North as well.⁵⁰ Also found noteworthy was Armstrong's role as Claudia's elderly grandfather, the legendary trumpeter "Sweet Daddy" Ferguson. Although a minor character in the movie, his appearance is significant because it is the great musician's last screen appearance (except for a cameo role in Gene Kelly's *Hello Dolly* in 1969), and the part does allow him a few turns on the bandstand.

Film historian Mark Reid adds another positive value, pointing out that the film's importance is tied to its being "a forerunner of the black action film that emphasized a black ghetto environment and a certain type of heroic protagonist."[51] Jazz historian Krin Gabbard argued that the movie helped in "establishing the centrality and sameness of white observers alongside the marginality and otherness of the black jazz artist."[52] He also praised Benny Carter's musical score for its authenticity.[53] Professor Christopher Sieving viewed *A Man Called Adam* as a major attempt by mainstream filmmakers to reflect the growing influence of the Black Power movement. In his words, "The top-level positions occupied by African Americans on *A Man Called Adam* ensured a relatively frank handling of issues related to the integrationist-black power split within black communities."[54] Finally, the IMDB database commented, "This film, made in 1966, was a bold attempt at addressing the contemporary conflicts of race and identity as it affected an African American jazz musician during the turbulent civil rights era." So much for film aesthetics!

I have one more point to address before leaving *A Man Called Adam*. In 1966, being timely, as one colleague reminded me, also meant taking great risks.[55] The country was extremely polarized. On one side were black leaders in favor of integration and non-violence, who strongly objected to the growing influence of the black power movement: Dr. Martin Luther King, Bayard Rustin, Whitney Young, and Roy Wilkins, who, as Sieving pointed out, "equated Black Power to 'a reverse Mississippi, a reverse Hitler, a reverse Ku Klux Klan.'"[56] On the opposite side were the followers of Malcolm X,[57] Stokely Carmichael, and Louis Farrakhan.

But for me, racial politics in 1966 held a different memory. With the formal arrival of black power that year, whites, especially Jews, felt under attack from militant black activists. That antagonistic feeling resulted in large measure because American Jews had worked closely with blacks in a "spirit of openness and trust" since the start of the twentieth century. Now that relationship came under attack from black nationalists. The effects of anti-white and anti-Semitic campaigns launched for whatever presumed justification by African American spokespeople like Malcolm, Carmichael and Farrakhan did not have the public I knew waiting to see the latest black film at special midnight screenings. The fact that such demagoguery concerned itself with establishing who was the greater victim, focused on current ethnic concerns such as police brutality toward blacks instead of common causes that had united Jews and African Americans over time.

The popular prejudices also refused to acknowledge that the Shoah had even occurred, unquestionably produced, as Deborah Kaufman and Alan Snitow reported, in "ignorant attacks on the so-called 'Jewish controlled media'" and put the blame for racism on Hollywood stereotyping. Jews were accused of being the most racist group hurting blacks. Whites were attacked not because they gained privileges by virtue of their merits, but solely because of the fact of their skin color.[58] As Kaufman and Snitow concluded, "The complexity of the issues no doubt drove white audiences away from supporting black causes, let alone black-themed films."[59]

That is the social and political context Tyson found herself in after completing *A Man Called Adam*. In quick succession, the actress accepted roles first in *The Comedians* and then in *The Heart is a Lonely Hunter*. But it took three more long, difficult years before she achieved fame as a result of starring in Martin Ritt's *Sounder* (1972).

Based upon Graham Greene's novel of the same name, Peter Glenville's screen adaptation *The Comedians*[60] assembled a superb interracial cast that included Elizabeth Taylor, Richard Burton, Alec Guinness, Lillian Gish, Paul Ford, and Peter Ustinov alongside James Earl Jones, Roscoe Lee Browne, Gloria Foster, Raymond St. Jacques, and Cicely Tyson. Greene's screenplay, set in "Papa Doc" Duvalier's declining days in Haiti, told the story of a disillusioned white hotel owner named Brown (Burton) who, surrounded by inequality and injustice, experiences a political rebirth. Although poorly received by the press and public in 1967, this unappreciated movie, even with its trite dialogue, provides some nostalgic moments watching important black actors maturing. Unfortunately, Tyson's brief stint as a beautiful but brainless prostitute does not add to any memorable insights into her career, except that it indicates she may have been typecast following her role in *The Blacks*.

In 1968, however, her featured role as Portia in Robert Ellis Miller's *The Heart is a Lonely Hunter*[61] demonstrated both the range and skill of an actress whose roller coaster film career never saw her screen potential fully realized. Adapted from Carson McCullers' first novel of the same name, Thomas C. Ryan's screenplay follows the emotional anguish of John Singer (Alan Arkin), a deaf-mute whose misery and isolation make him particularly sympathetic to people also deeply troubled. The problem is that they fail to communicate with each other. Among those isolated, sad individuals seeking Singer's compassion are Mick (Sondra Locke), a young girl whose hopes are sorely limited by her surroundings; Antonapoulos (Chuck McCann), Singer's mentally-ill friend; Blout (Stanley Keach), an alcoholic drifter; Dr. Copeland (Percy Rodrigues), a dying physician estranged from his daughter; and Portia (Tyson), a rebellious daughter who damns her father's submissive values.

Although there is much to criticize in this overly sentimental movie, with its sometimes-embarrassing dialogue and hackneyed situations, I find the acting by Arkin and Tyson unusual and unexpected. "Unusual" in the sense that their actions, so often stereotyped in lesser films, here seem believable and powerful. "Unexpected" in that no one anticipated that such screen novices could perform their parts so effortlessly and seamlessly. What also caught my attention was the criticism in 1968 by a *New York Times* reviewer who objected to the fact that Portia spoke too intelligently for a southern black woman.[62] The Academy Awards that year reacted more positively, nominating Arkin for his second Oscar (the first being for *The Russians are Coming, The Russians are Coming* two years earlier; in 2006, he won an Oscar for Best Supporting Actor in *Little Miss Sunshine*) and Sondra Locke, in her screen debut, for Best Supporting Actress. As for Tyson, the part of Portia probably typecast her for the rest of her career as the epitome of the strong, black woman.

From a historical perspective, what also proves noteworthy about *The Heart is a Lonely Hunter* is that the generational battle between Portia and her father was one of several such fights being dramatized in important black-themed movies in the mid-to-late sixties: e.g., *Nothing But a Man* (1964) and *Guess Who's Coming to Dinner* (1967). In each instance, we see modern types of black parents being portrayed as out-of-touch and living so-called "Uncle Tom" existences.

Now may be a good time to comment on this anti-middle class black bias by some contemporary intellectuals. Society might take a second look at what Albert Murray defends as an "enduring U.S. tradition of self-control, wisdom, courage, and commitment to human freedom and individual fulfillment, which few other native traditions, in this country or elsewhere can equal and none excel...." Especially relevant for our narrative is the fact that, as the Dean of African American literature points out "For a long time the tradition has...been represented by the educational, inspirational, and political role of the Southern Negro doctor."[63]

Following *The Heart is a Lonely Hunter*, Tyson's life and career fell on hard times. Her relationship with Miles became too difficult to continue. Even though one senses his love for her—he put her on the jacket cover of his 1967 album *Sorcerer*—, the brief romance ended. Adding to her troubles, she made no movies for the next three years.

Meanwhile, the resilient actress found work with small theatrical groups and on television. Her most noteworthy appearance was as a regular on the soap opera *Guiding Light*, the first such continuous black role in television history. Informed readers looking closely at these years would assume things should have been different for Tyson, if not in film at least on the small screen. According to the versatile media historian Donald Bogle, "By the end of the 1960s, African American images had clearly changed...African American actors and actresses had ushered in protagonists whose tensions and troubles were directly related to their status in American society. Other African American actors had created characters that were capable of functioning in—and contributing to—mainstream life in America. Throughout the era, the performances of actors like Cicely Tyson, Ivan Dixon, Bill Cosby,[64] Diahann Carroll, Lloyd Haynes, Denise Nicholas, and Clarence Williams III had made the African American character seem less of the Other."[65]

But Tyson was nowhere to be found on the big screen as we moved into the seventies. There are all sorts of excuses why, none of which adequately explains her absence from American movies. One theory is that there were no good scripts or films by or for blacks planned. Another theory speculates, given the black power fever, Tyson's then views made her persona non grata to the current filmmakers. And finally, there is the belief that even if offered work then being made, she would have turned it down because she found much of what was being done "demeaning."[66]

Whatever the reason, and despite Tyson's stunning appearance and talent—a striking visual presence that totally went against the grain of Hollywood's definition of beauty—the up-and-coming star remained invisible to mainstream movie audiences for several years. Then, to quote a line from the musical *Camelot*, for one brief shining moment between 1972 and 1974, things changed.

First appeared Martin Ritt's glorious screen adaptation *Sounder* (1972). Based upon William H. Armstrong's prize-winning young adult novel, Leone Elder III's superb screenplay set during the early days of the Great Depression dealt with a hard working black sharecropper, his wife, and their three children as they struggle to survive in unbearable conditions. Desperate, Nathan Lee Morgan (Paul Winfield) one night steals some food to feed his famished family, is then captured the next day, and sentenced to prison for an unspecified time. To keep their land and protect their children, Rebecca (Tyson) and her oldest son David Lee (Kevin Hooks) assume responsibility for Nathan's tasks until his eventual return. Sounder is the name of their dog. (ABC's *Wonderful World of Disney* remade the film in 2003, directed by Kevin Hooks, starring Carl Lumbly and Suzanna Douglas, and featuring Winfield as the black teacher who befriends David Lee.)

Cicely Tyson's Rebecca electrified the critics. *Ms.* pointed out that moviegoers witnessed through this performance "a typical black mother and wife: hardworking, resilient, vigilant, and above all, sensitive. Rebecca functions basically as a follower and sustainer, taking the lead only when conditions (in this case, the imprisonment of her husband) demand that she does so. The role is historically accurate because the black family, no less than the white, is patriarchal, with or without the father present."[67] Norma Manatu writes, "Such a universal portrayal gives audiences a rare glimpse into black women's interior lives, images which, in my mind, attempt to represent black women as believable human beings. That this film offered audiences a breadth and depth of the human emotions of black women clearly attests to the filmmakers' ability to represent black women in humane terms."[68] And Pauline Kael asked, "Who would have believed that an inspirational movie about black strength and pride—and one based on a prize-winning children's book, by a white author, that takes its name from a symbolic coon hound—could transcend its cautious, mealy genre to become the first movie about the black experience in America which can stir people of all colors."[69]

Once *Sounder* opened across the nation, Tyson took to the road to promote her new film. In describing her experiences, she gave the definitive reason why she decided to devote the rest of her life to educating Americans about the black experience. It came about during a Q & A session when someone challenged the possibility that African Americans could have a marriage similar to the one Nathan and Rebecca had in the movie. This question and others like it led Tyson to the decision that she had to make a choice. "I decided I could not afford just being an actress. I had some very definite statements to make. It was my way of picketing."[70]

Despite the many honors accorded both the production and the actor, the film itself had an unusual reception. First, as she explained to *Ebony* "There are those movie-goers who are more attuned to swashbuckling black dudes and chicks wheeling and dealing in dope-infested ghettos as they smash 'the man,' [and] have become scornful of *Sounder* and its Southern sharecropper setting of 30 years ago. They feel film critics liked the movie 'because it re-positioned blacks in a slave-like atmosphere.'"[71] And second, Harvard psychiatrist Alvin F. Poussaint lamented "*Sounder*, Sidney Poitier's *A Warm December*[72] and other movies that depict positive and healthy images receive little attention from black moviegoers, and become lost in the deluge of Blaxploitation films." The reason why, he concluded, is because "the American public, and particularly the black sector that supports the new films [Blaxploitation movies]. As long as they are profitable, however, these films will be made and shown."[73]

Right on the heels of her great triumph in *Sounder* came another remarkable performance, this time as a 110-year-old former slave in the CBS Special "The Autobiography of Miss Jane Pittman" (1974), directed by John Korty, and for which the actress won her first Emmy as Best Actress in a Special. Adapted from Ernest Gaines' novel of the same name, Tracy Keenan Wynn's teleplay traced the courage of an exceptional black woman from the final days of slavery to the civil rights movement in the early sixties. "Throughout," observed Bogle, who spoke for many viewers, "the character Jane

Pittman tells the story, moving the viewer with her insights, humor, and, eventually, her wisdom. When first seen, Jane is a girl who watches the Union soldiers arrive victorious in the South. Afterward, as she lives, works, marries, and loses a husband, she is a witness to the great historical events and social changes of the twentieth century."[74] The most stunning moment in the TV film occurs when the elderly woman defiantly drinks from a white-only water fountain.

Just as with *Sounder*, the critical acclaim proved spectacular. Pauline Kael again led the pack trumpeting Tyson's work, writing that the drama was "quite possibly the finest movie ever made for American television." She added that "through knowing Jane Pittman you feel closer to a recognition of the black experience in this country...."[75] TV historian J. Fred MacDonald declared that although the fountain drinking scene was a minuscule moment, "the power Tyson brought to the role made Jane Pittman's act a symbol of racial victory over Jim Crow laws and chronic prejudices."[76] Other critics compared her to Ethel Waters as one of the greatest actresses of her generation. When the Emmys were distributed, *The Autobiography of Miss Jane Pittman* won nine, including two for Tyson.

Thus by the mid-seventies, Tyson stood at the top of her profession and proved extremely popular with mainstream America. But equally as satisfying for the star, was the feeling, as one commentator put it, "I think people like those in *Sounder* and *Jane Pittman*, people who have been through those kinds of years, are the foundation upon which we are standing today."[77]

Not unexpected was an awareness that for every action there is a reaction. There were the usual critical gripes about acting, narrative, and interpretations. But the one credible observation came from Jim Brown who believed, "In the 1970s, those [racial] barriers went right back up. America regressed, Hollywood did the same. Hollywood opened its doors to blacks in the 1960s, pulled in the money, slammed them back shut. If you wanted to see a black woman in a major role, it was Cicely Tyson or nothing. Cicely is a fine artist, but I got Cicely Tysoned out. The industry is replete with talented, attractive black actresses. To represent an entire race with one woman is ludicrous."[78]

In the decades that followed, the superb dramatic actress busied herself with projects that further clarified the black experience. Since Hollywood did not seem in a rush to employ her, she turned to television. She took such notable roles as the mother of Kunta Kinte in the ABC miniseries adaptation *Roots* (1977), from Alex Haley's family history; played Coretta Scott King, the wife of the martyred civil rights leader, in the NBC docudrama *King* (1978); re-enacted the heroic life of Harriet Ross Tubman, the ex-slave who became a legendary abolitionist, in NBC's miniseries *A Woman Called Moses* (1978); starred as the sacrificing Chicago schoolteacher in the CBS drama *The Marva Collins Story* (1981); appeared as an ex-slave descended from African royalty (for which she won another Emmy) in CBS' distinguished miniseries *Oldest Living Confederate Tells All* (1994); performed as Melissa Gilbert, the crusading civil rights New Orleans lawyer in NBC's *Sweet Justice* (1994); revisited Alex Haley's historical journey as the tender but tough matriarch in CBS' *Mama Flora's Story* (1998); insisted we not become resigned to racial injustice as Tante Lou in HBO's *A Lesson Before Dying* (1999); and acted as Leona Edwards McCauley, the mother of the civil rights heroine in CBS' *The Rosa Parks Story* (2002). And this list only touches on her astounding television work.

Her film work since *Sounder* is less meritorious. Among her movies considered enjoyable are Krishna Shah's *The River Niger* (1976), Ralph Nelson's *A Hero Ain't Nothing but a Sandwich* (1978), Oz Scott's *Bustin' Loose* (1981), and Wayne Wang's *Because of Winn-Dixie* (2001).

My favorite post-eighties Tyson movie, however, is a marvelous overlooked work directed by Bill Duke, *Hoodlum*, about the Harlem numbers war in the 1930s (1997).[79] Screenwriter Chris Brancato takes many of the clichés from Hollywood's great gangster films and adapts them to the black experience during the Great Depression. The impressive period piece tracks ex-con Bumpy Johnson (Laurence Fishburne) as he defends the interests of black-rackets queen Stephanie St. Clair (Cicely Tyson) against the vicious encroachment of Dutch Schultz (Tim Roth). Lucky Luciano (Andy Garcia), Schultz's impatient boss who has in his pocket the corrupt but crusading New York special prosecutor Thomas E. Dewey (William Atherton), grows angrier and angrier with Dutch's actions.

While the facts get lost, the imagery and repartee are delightful. There are few scenes in gangster movies as charming as the one showing the Queen and Bumpy, after surviving an attack on their lives, sitting on a couch in her home listening to a recording of Verdi's *Macbeth*. Watching Tyson play a tough but peace-loving mob boss is priceless.

And what of her emotions and personal life during the ongoing struggles in her profession? First came her on and off romance with Miles Davis, in worse condition emotionally and physically than she had found him in the mid-sixties. One source described the trumpeter's situation this way: "Having survived a serious car accident, using far too many drugs, suffering from bleeding ulcers and crumbling hips, plus burnt out from too much touring, Davis abandoned his music completely. For the next five years, he went through a 'dark and silent' period."[80] Nonetheless Tyson took him back. Like *Show Boat*'s Julie singing "Can't help loving that man of mine," she not only saved his life and took over the management of his career, but she also married him in 1981. For eight difficult years, she put up with his depression, drugs, womanizing, and various illnesses, never wavering in her love or commitment.

Finally, in January of 1988, Tyson filed for divorce. What may have hurt her the worst were not his recent affections for another woman, but his embarrassing behavior toward her at a White House dinner honoring Ray Charles. According to biographer John Szwed, Davis became terribly agitated when he discovered that few African Americans were at the party. Matters got worse "when a Washington matron asked him what he had done to be invited, he snapped, "Well, I've changed music five or six times…What have you done of any importance other than be white?" Miles whispered to Cicely, "Let's get out of here as soon as this shit is over. You can handle this shit, I can't." That incident basically ended their relationship and the marriage.[81]

Off-screen and outside her personal problems, Tyson proved just as formidable and inspiring in her outreach activities. She used her celebrity status to help various charities, fought for numerous causes, lectured at many colleges, and assisted the government with goodwill tours. Among her most documented public service has been her tireless work with disadvantaged black youth both at the Dance Theater of Harlem in New York and at the Cicely Tyson School of Performing and Fine Arts in East Orange, New Jersey.

Every now and then one discovers the hurt this remarkable woman has experienced over the years as a result of her refusal to deviate from her principles. The saddest remark, at least for me, occurred in 1983, when Tyson agreed to be the first black actress to play the role of the English spinster Miss Moffat in a Broadway revival of Emlyn Williams' *The Corn is Green*. Ironically, as she prepared for her part as the stubborn teacher who by utter will power converts a clever young coalminer into a future Oxford intellectual, Tyson confessed to reporter Leslie Bennett that despite the fame surrounding her career, she had spent much of her life searching for a job. "The subject," Bennett reported, "is a source of great pain to her."[82] Unfortunately, the pain increased when the revival received terrible notices, closed after only two weeks, and the actress found herself suing the producers for breaking her contract, and a planned TV production got aborted. The good news was that two years later the courts awarded her three-quarters of a million dollars in upholding her claim.[83]

In describing Cicely Tyson's life and career as I have, I am not ignorant of the work yet to be done with the screen image of black women or naïve about the uneven quality of the performer's considerable artistic body of work. Like any major star that needs to keep acting to perfect her craft, she sometimes takes clunkers in order to keep fresh for the good films to come. Like any creative person, she battles and stumbles, but no more than any other artist of her stature. If you have any doubts, check out the films of stars like Elizabeth Taylor, Jane Fonda, Meryl Streep, Natalie Portman, and Kate Winslett. But no matter. This mesmerizing, heroic black performer, who remained unshakable in a white-controlled industry—and I haven't even mentioned the many ugly old-boys' networks she encountered in her career—not only epitomizes the best of black womanhood, but also embodies the gold standard for American actresses. She's not going anywhere!

Of the seventeen people I interviewed (counting Roscoe Lee Browne), Cicely Tyson was the only one who came to me. She appeared at my hotel room late in the afternoon, stunning me with her poise and beauty. Remember, I had not prepared for her visit, and in truth had only seen her in *The Heart is a Lonely Hunter*. Neither one of us knew much about the other, nor was there any reason for her to trust me or to respond honestly to my questions. At this moment in time, America was trying to extricate itself from the Vietnam War; Richard M. Nixon was on his way to his Watergate disaster; and black-white relations were less than perfect. But neither Tyson nor I concerned ourselves with that. From start to finish, this remarkable woman treated me not only as an equal, but also as someone she liked. Me, I have adored her ever since!

When I saw the star live on screen at the 2012 Academy Awards, she was a bit fragile, but still beautiful and jubilant over the treatment accorded Tate Taylor's *The Help* (2011),[84] which ironically cast her as an abused African American maid. Impressively, she was still making crossover films tied to the black experience, and she still spoke out for positive screen images of African American women. Thankfully, the excellent performer had the last word, when she gave a stunning performance as the aging Carrie Watts in the 2013 Broadway revival of Horton Foote's *Trip to Bountiful*. *New York Times* Drama critic Ben Brantley felt as if the play functioned as "a code name for the fountain of youth" in expressing his admiration for Cicely Tyson.[85]

Later, I got to see Michael Wilson's abridged TV version of the play,[86] with Tyson (Mrs. Watts) recreating her moving and tender portrayal of an aging woman determined against all the odds to visit her childhood home one last time. It affected me much more than I had anticipated. Watching again this legendary actress on screen respond to her disillusioned son (Blair Underwood) and his bickering wife (Vanessa Williams) reminded me more than a little of her performances in *The Heart is a Lonely Hunter* and *The Autobiography of Miss Jane Pittman*. Seeing the sickly but determined Mrs. Watts confess about her long lost love to her young traveling companion (Keke Palmer) brought back memories of her years with Miles Davis. And I must admit, when Mrs. Watts finally achieves her overpowering dream and returns to Bountiful, the thoughts she shares with us seemed so appropriate to this essay and to my momentary experience with Cicely Tyson over forty-three years ago. Neither Mrs. Watts nor I can recapture what it meant to me to have had that remarkable young actress educate me on her long journey to the making of *Sounder*. The interview may have been shelved, but I could never forget what it gave me. In a way, it was like the words of the beautiful hymn, *Blessed Assurance*, sung throughout the teleplay: "This is my story, this is my song."

So much had changed since Cicely Tyson hawked papers as a poor nine-year old on the streets in East Harlem (an image that experts like Kael and Bogle used in their recollections of her). What will never change was how much she has accomplished and what we owe her. A glimpse of just what Tyson has done for American culture was reiterated when she was honored at the 2015 Kennedy Center Honors.

I thought at first to conclude this profile with Sinatra's words from "My Way," but chose instead to recall the Henry David Thoreau quote cited from one of her first films, *The Last Angry Man*: "Why should we be in such haste to succeed in such desperate enterprises? If a man does not keep pace with his companion, perhaps it is because he hears a different drummer. Let him step to the music which he hears, however measured or far off."

Notes

[1] Michael Apted, *Amazing Grace*. Britain: Bristol Bay Productions, 2007.

[2] Jan Schmidt-Garre and Marieke Schroeder, *Aida's Brothers & Sisters: Black Voices in Opera and Concert*. 85 mins. Germany: Pars Media 2009.

[3] Unknown, *IBE 2011 Living Legend Award Winner—Cicely Tyson*. USA: Indiana Black Expo Youth Video Institute, 2011.

[4] Brian Ward, *Just My Soul Responding: Rhythm and Blues, Black Consciousness, and Race Relations*. Berkeley: University of California Press. 316-322; and Ruth Feldstein, *How It Feels to Be Free: Black Women Entertainers and the Civil Rights Movement*. New York: Oxford University Press, 2013. 5.

[5] James Gavin, *Stormy Weather: The Life of Lena Horne*. New York: Atria Books, 2009). Biography, 329-30.

[6] *Stormy Weather*, 4-5.

[7] B.J. Mason, "The New Films: Culture or Con Game?," *Ebony* 28, no. 2 (1972): 64.

[8] Joan Goldworthy and Sara Pendergast, "Cicely Tyson," in *Contemporary Black Biography*. Gale Cengage Learning, 1992-. 3.

[9] Yvonne, "Cicely Tyson," *Ms.* (1974): 46.

[10] Jonathan Haidt, *The Righteous Mind*. New York: Pantheon Books, 2012. 285-86.
[11] Well worth reading in this connection is Ta-Nehisi Coates, "The Black Family in the Age of Mass Incarceration," *The Atlantic* Vol. 316, No. 3 (October 2015): 60-80, 82-84.
[12] Feldstein, 145.
[13] Lynn Norment, "Ebony Interview: Cicely Tyson," *Ebony* 36, no. 4 (1981): 12
[14] Louie Robinson, "Cicely Tyson: A Very Unlikely Movie Star," *Ebony* 29, no. 7 (1974): 35.
[15] Charles L. Sanders, "Cicely Tyson: She Can Smile Again after a Three-Year Ordeal," ibid. (1979): 30.
[16] Ibid., 34.
[17] Emily Bernard, *Carl Van Vechten & the Harlem Renaissance: A Portrait in Black & White*. New Haven and London: Yale University Press, 2012. 3.
[18] Robinson, "Cicely Tyson: A Very Unlikely Movie Star," 2.
[19] Ibid., 35.
[20] Although *Twelve Angry Men* is listed in her filmography, there is some doubt if she actually appeared on screen in the film version. The only black woman appears in an overhead establishing shot in the lobby of the courthouse. I have been unable to determine if it is Cicely Tyson. She may have been filmed, but her part cut out prior to the film's release
[21] Sidney Lumet, *Twelve Angry Men*. USA: United Artists, 1957.
[22] Robert Wise, *Odds against Tomorrow*. USA: United Artists, 1959.
[23] Daniel Mann, *The Last Angry Man*. USA: Columbia Pictures, 1959.
[24] Goldworthy and Pendergast, "Cicely Tyson," 2.
[25] Robinson, "Cicely Tyson: A Very Unlikely Movie Star," 38.
[26] Michael Ullman, "The Jazz Column," *Fanfare* 33, no. 2 (2009): 394-95.
[27] John Szwed, *So What: The Life of Miles Davis*. New York: Simon & Schuster Paperbacks, 2004. Biography, 169.
[28] Peniel E. Joseph, *Dark Days, Bright Nights: From Black Power to Barack Obama*. New York: Basic Civitas Group, 2010. 58.
[29] James Earl Jones and Penelope Niven, *James Earl Jones: Voices and Silences*, 1st ed. New York: Charles Scribner's Sons, 1993; repr., 2002. Memoir, 115-18.
[30] Joseph, *Dark Days, Bright Nights: From Black Power to Barack Obama*, 58-9.
[31] Daniel Petrie, *A Raisin in the Sun*. USA: Columbia Pictures, 1961.
[32] Robinson, "Cicely Tyson: A Very Unlikely Movie Star," 38.
[33] Jones and Niven, *James Earl Jones: Voices and Silences*, 115.
[34] Yvonne, "Cicely Tyson," 78.
[35] J. Fred MacDonald, *Blacks and White TV: Afro-Americans in Television since 1948*. Chicago: Nelson-Hall Publishers, 1983. 104-05.

36 Goldworthy and Pendergast, "Cicely Tyson," 3.
37 MacDonald, *Blacks and White TV: Afro-Americans in Television since 1948*, 106.
38 A recent controversial example depicting the great musician is Don Cheadle, *Miles Ahead*. USA: Bifrost Pictures, 2015.
39 Isabel Isabel Wilkerson, *The Warmth of Other Suns: The Epic Story of America's Great Migration*. New York: Random House, 2010. History, 529.
40 Stanley Crouch, *The All-American Skin Game, or the Decoy of Race*. New York: Vintage Books, 1995. 166.
41 Ian Carr, *Miles Davis, the Definitive Biography*. Emeryville, CA: Thunder's Mouth Press, 1999. 41.
42 Carr, 41-3.
43 Stanley Crouch, *Considering Genius: Writings on Jazz*. New York: Basic Civitas Books, 2006. 255.
44 Szwed, *So What*, 257-58.
45 Robinson, "Cicely Tyson: A Very Unlikely Movie Star," 38.
46 Leo Penn, *A Man Called Adam*. USA: Embassy Pictures, 1966.
47 Brent Staples, "Black Characters in Search of Reality," *New York Times*, February 12 2012, 10.
48 Pauline Kael, "The Current Cinema: Cicely Tyson Goes to the Fountain," *The New Yorker*, 49, no. 49 (1974): 73.
49 Terry Teachout, *Pops: A Life of Louis Armstrong*. Boston: Houghton Mifflin Harcourt, 2009. Biography, 352.
50 Krin Gabbard, *Jammin' at the Margins: Jazz and the American Cinema*. Chicago: The University of Chicago Press, 1996. 89-91.
51 Mark A. Reid, *Redefining Black Film*. Berkeley: University of California Press, 1993. 72.
52 Gabbard, *Jammin' at the Margins: Jazz and the American Cinema*, 89.
53 Ibid., 93.
54 Christopher Sieving, *Soul Searching: Black-Themed Cinema from the March on Washington to the Rise of Blaxploitation*. Middleton, Connecticut: Wesleyan University Press, 2011. 90.
55 Harold T. Shapiro, *A Larger Sense of Purpose: Higher Education and Society*. Princeton, N.J.: Princeton University Press, 2005. 8.
56 Sieving, *Soul Searching: Black-Themed Cinema from the March on Washington to the Rise of Blaxploitation*, 91-2.
57 A new and challenging book on the famous black leader relevant to this discussion is by Randy Roberts and Johnny Smith, *Blood Brothers: The Fatal Friendship Between Muhammad Ali and Malcolm X*. New York: Basic Books, 2016.
58 Deborah Kaufman and Alan Snitow, "Blacks and Jews," in *American Documentary, Inc.*, ed. Marc Weiss. USA: Snitow-Kaufman Productions,

1997.
[59] Ibid.
[60] Peter Glenville, *The Comedians*. England: MGM, 1967.
[61] Robert Ellis Miller, *The Heart Is a Lonely Hunter*. USA: Seven Arts/Warner Bros., 1968.
[62] Renata Adler, "'The Heart Is a Lonely Hunter': Alan Arkin Starred in McCullers Story Dean Martin Western is at Local Houses," *New York Times*, August 1 1968.
[63] Albert Murray, *The Omni-Americans: Some Alternatives to the Folklore of White Supremacy*. New York: De Capo Press, 1970. Anthology, 114.
[64] There is no way I can convey to the reader my dismay and distress about the reports of the actor's infamous behavior with women unknown either to me or much of my generation until recent news account appeared.
[65] Donald Bogle, *Blacks in American Films and Television: An Encyclopedia*. New York: Garland Publishing, Inc., 1988. 170-71.
[66] Yvonne, "Cicely Tyson," 47.
[67] Ibid., 78.
[68] Norma Manatu, *African American Women and Sexuality in the Cinema*, Paperback ed. Jefferson: McFarland & Company, 2003. 201.
[69] Robinson, "Cicely Tyson: A Very Unlikely Movie Star," 38-9.
[70] Lynn Norment, "Ebony Interview: Cicely Tyson," ibid.36, no. 4 (1981): 124.
[71] Louie Robinson, "Cicely Tyson: A Very Unlikely Movie Star," ibid.29, no. 7 (1974): 38-9.
[72] Sidney Poitier, *A Warm December*. USA: First Artists, 1973.
[73] Alvin F. Poussaint, "Blaxploitation Movies: Cheap Thrills That Degrade Blacks," *Psychology Today* 7, no. 9 (1974): 98.
[74] Bogle, *Blacks in American Films and Television: An Encyclopedia*, 235.
[75] Kael, "The Current Cinema: Cicely Tyson Goes to the Fountain," 74.
[76] MacDonald, *Blacks and White TV: Afro-Americans in Television since 1948*, 168-69.
[77] Robinson, "Cicely Tyson: A Very Unlikely Movie Star," 38, 40.
[78] Jim Brown and Steve Delsohn, *Out of Bounds*, Paperback ed. New York: Zebra Books, 1990. 230.
[79] Bill Duke, *Hoodlum*. United Artists, 1997.
[80] Mike Dibb, *The Miles Davis Story*. USA: Channel Four Television Corporation, 2001.
[81] Szwed, *So What*, 374.
[82] Leslie Bennett, "How Cicely Tyson Got to Teach in Wales," *New York Times*, August 22 1983, 14.
[83] "How Cicely Tyson Got to Teach in Wales," *New York Times*, August 22 1983, 14.

84 Tate Taylor, *The Help*. USA: DreamWorks, SKG, 2011.
85 Ben Brantley, "Home Is Where the Years Disappear: 'The Trip to Bountiful' at the Stephen Sondheim Theater," *New York Times*, April 24, 2013.
86 Michael Wilson, *A Trip to Bountiful*. TV Movie. USA: Ostar Productions. 2014

22. James Earl Jones as President Douglas Dilman in the midst of a tense news conference. Joseph Sargent, *The Man* (1972).

A Signature Style

Whether they like it or not, whether they admit it or not, black actors owe a tremendous amount of allegiance to their people in terms of upholding a positive black image—and no black actor on this earth can deny that responsibility.[1]
Walter Burrell

Of all art, film perhaps gives the greatest illusion of authenticity, of truth. A motion picture takes a viewer inside where real people are supposed to be doing real things. We assume there is a certain verisimilitude, an authenticity. But there is always some degree of manipulation and distortion.[2]
Annette Insdorf

No facts are to me sacred; none are profane; I simply experiment, an endless seeker, with no pat on my back.[3]
Ralph Waldo Emerson

How do you presume to teach others about black films when there is no agreement among your peers that such a genre even exists, you yourself remain uncertain about the central racial issues, and you fear that your well-intentioned efforts might do more harm than good towards resolving the problems you are researching? That's a sample of what crossed my mind in the late 1960s. Looking back at this stage in my journey, after examining all the conflicting information I collected on black film history, I am still not confident about what useful contributions I made to understanding racism in my apprentice years from the late fifties to the early seventies.

Ever since the start of the twentieth century, Hollywood's immense vertical integration system had systematically stereotyped African Americans with demeaning images that left the nation not only ignorant about black people but also their significant contributions to our society. But after World War II, the film industry fell into disarray and searched for a way out of its economic doldrums. The demographic shift from the urban neighborhoods to suburban communities forced the moviemakers to dramatically revise the content of their moving pictures. Coinciding with the industrial upheaval came the Civil Rights movement. Now, refusing to any longer to be mistreated, misunderstood, and excluded from their inalienable rights recorded in the U.S. Constitution, an aroused African American population started a human rights revolution that was taking place not only in the streets but also on the silver screen.

Inspired by the explosive changes occurring in our culture and welcoming the groundbreaking images in the mass media, I hoped to contribute to the battle for human dignity. But cultural confusion existed everywhere. Not only were many of the aging performers who pioneered black film images coming under vicious attack from a new generation marching to a different drummer, but also the insurgents disagreed among themselves as to which was the best path to pursue. Was racial separation a good idea or not? Did our traditional institutions truly safeguard the rights of everyone? What were America's true social, political, and economic values? Was a political uprising the only realistic option open to marginalized people? Could it be possible our founding fathers' great Democratic experiment was a failure? How many more civil rights leaders and politicians had to be murdered before blacks armed themselves and violently fought back?

The fact that this revolting national state of affairs was not a new phenomenon but had been around for more than a century only further divided the country. What was our moral and political responsibility to reforming this political reality? As for Hollywood, did giving blacks more control of their own films produce positives results? Was it true, as the revolutionary black artists insisted, white filmmakers using African American talent only advanced white objectives and profits? On a national scale, would America be able to come to terms with its Race problem or did we need a civil war to bring about positive results?

I decided to do what little I could to help the cultural revolution; and in the process, discover how I might use feature films to educate my students to doing the right thing and contribute constructively towards solving the great racial dilemma of our day. Please believe me when I describe these romantic and naïve feelings from the sixties. Such beliefs were commonplace among many of my peers. While we saw the situation as depressing, we also convinced ourselves we were making a difference.

In the seventeen conversations described in *The Interviews*, I never foresaw how much valuable material about the black film legacy existed in our mutual experiences. Nor did I imagine that total strangers, daily waging war against discrimination and oppression just to earn a screen credit, would so generously share their personal and painful feelings with me. Yet they did. And as a result, I can never thank them enough

Innocently armed mainly with passion and optimism, I rashly set out with an inexpensive recorder and cheap audiotapes into a strange new world to meet and to talk to battle-scarred screen celebrities, most of whom I did not know I was going to meet until a day before I met them. What took place proved unnerving from the day I began. For example, Leroy Bowser's angry responses to my well-intentioned but simplistic questions startled me, as did the street-smart Jim Brown's unexpected cross-examination about the depth of my racial consciousness.

Although I never had a peaceful moment throughout the three-year adventure, I gained considerable strength and insights thanks to the thoughtfulness not only of people like the great Jim Brown but also because of riveting personalities like Lorenzo and Julia Tucker, King Vidor, Lillian Gish, James Whitmore, Pearl Bowser, Charles Edward Gordone, Clarence and Ena Muse, Woody Strode and Luuialuanna "Mama" Kalaelola, Cicely Tyson, Ivan Dixon, Mae Mercer, Brock Peters, William Marshall, Roscoe Lee Browne, Frederick Douglass O'Neal, Ossie Davis, and Ruby Dee. Their honesty and sincerity in talking with me more than made up for the many doubts and fears I harbored about my mission failing.

When the dust settled, the only "disappointing" discussion was with James Earl Jones. Let me be very clear on this point. My flawed meeting with the great theatrical titan went badly for me, not for the noted actor. I had unrealistic expectations about our get-together; he did not. He was no stranger to confrontations. I foolishly thought I wasn't either. That said, the interview itself remains for me a priceless experience, and I very much view the resulting repressed document as an important historical resource. Additionally, I have met few more impressive individuals than the resilient and talented Jones. And whatever disagreements there were between us about aesthetics, personal, and moral responsibilities, as well as the best way to bring about significant racial changes in a less than perfect society, the opinions were presented in a civil manner. Without question, he is, as Professor Raul Hilberg would have said, a heavyweight.

But no one misjudged my actions or objectives as seriously as did this defensive star with the booming voice. And no one set himself up for failure more than I did.

What follows is a pragmatic essay published three years later than was originally intended. The reason is straightforward. My earlier, unpublished interview with Jones had been transcribed and put into manuscript form by the middle of 2012, six months before *Exits and Entrances* was ready to go to press. Meanwhile, the well-known actor was on tour in Australia with the equally famous Angela Lansbury in a road company of *Driving Miss Daisy*. After weeks of negotiations with his extremely patient go-between, I was told Jones not only had no recollection of either meeting me or of doing the interview (even though I had recently sent it to him for review and for approval). More to the point of contention: Jones felt strongly he would never say the things today that were stated back in our July 1972 New York conversation. So why print them now, he asked?

Let me again be clear. I do not believe his negative decision was made quickly or easily. I sense no ill will on his part directed either against the proposed book or me. I certainly have no malice toward him. I further believe that even if he had known the scholarly collection would eventually be honored by *USA Today* as one of the best works on the performing arts in 2015, it would not have made a difference to him. He did not want this unpublished interview as part of his legacy.

That said, I reluctantly realized his decision was definitive. Despite having done considerable work both on the intended introduction to the 1972 interview and the conversation itself, I abandoned that section of the manuscript and moved on. *Exits and Entrances* appeared in 2013.

But three years have passed; and as I have explained in my opening remarks, I have decided to release a revised introduction, now merely a profile, on this remarkable artist, one that respects his privacy and makes no reference to or use of the "offending" material in the suppressed discussion. At the same time, I hope the reader appreciates how useful Jones' life and his career were to helping me better understand many of the racial problems black artists faced throughout much of the twentieth century.

Few entertainers' careers more significantly and confidently challenged America's show business' blemishes than did that of Jones' work. While he never presented himself as a civil rights' activist, he was a major part of a principled generation, starting in post-World War II America, that relentlessly attacked through their extraordinary gifts outworn attitudes about ethnicity, identity, society, and the performing arts. As well, he was one of those inspired actors who frequently questioned what personal responsibility they as performers had toward their art, their audiences, and their race. As Jones and his peers fearlessly shed their personal demons and diligently pursued their ambitions, taboos were shattered and memorable works of art resulted. Generations yet unborn will benefit from standing on their shoulders.

Yet in the process, individuals were hurt, careers cut short, and dreams deferred like a raisin in the sun. Moreover, not all African American artists tackled the race issue in the same way. Some spoke out forcefully and passionately; others remained stoical and relied on their artistic gifts to bring about much needed change. But let there be no misunderstanding on this vital point. All these courageous performers believed that social injustice could no longer continue as before.

Few of these luminaries, however, were more misread by the public or so unfairly attacked by their peers than this exceptional, intelligent, and strong-minded personality. Like many of the extraordinary veterans in *The Interviews*, James Earl Jones came from a broken home, had his artistic roots in the classical theater, skillfully navigated his way through the turmoil of the civil rights movement, and emerged in the second half of the twentieth century a complicated and complex figure standing tall in the annals of the stage, screen, and television. What's more, he made his way to the top in a circuitous route along an untraveled and contentious road.

In 1993, Jones co-authored with researcher Penelope Niven his autobiography, *James Earl Jones: Voices and Silences*.[4] Anyone seeking unique insights about this peerless individual should start with that valuable book. J.K. Sweeney began his review of the impressive work with the words, "It is possible that a few individuals may exist who are unaware of a significantly talented human being named James Earl Jones. It is also likely that such persons live under rocks at the bottom of the garden and only emerge on February 29 for a brief period at twilight."[5]

That said; let me respectfully offer my take on the artist's career from the perspective of how it addressed my needs as a film teacher during the second half of the twentieth century. Remember, those of us who live in the classroom see movies differently from those who make their living in the film world. Our differences will soon become readily apparent. But at the outset, for anyone seeking a complete discussion of the actor's considerable contributions to the performing arts, I recommend using the Internet. In the pages that follow, you will find only a snapshot of what accomplishments captured my attention, my admiration, and my regrets over the past forty-five years.

Born on January 17, 1931 in Arkabutla, Mississippi to Ruth (Connolly) and Robert Earl Jones, the resourceful and resilient child was blessed with a love of nature, a thirst for diversity, and a desire for a normal family life. But his domestic dreams were shattered before he reached his first birthday. America during the Great Depression did not make it easy for young people to stay married, especially those vulnerable African Americans dwelling in the Deep South; let alone did the times assist such traditional unions in bringing up a child.

After his parents divorced and left for parts unknown, Jones spent his childhood watched over by his maternal grandparents, John Henry and Maggie Connolly, who soon joined the Great Migration northward in search of better lives for their children and themselves, and settled eventually on a Michigan homestead.[6] Years later, with professional help, the now mature Jones came to terms with the emotional fallout from his problematic parents.[7] But for him, his "true" mom and dad would always be his grandparents. In his words, "To be raised on a farm throughout the Depression and the war, through all those years into my adult life, gave me what balance and harmony I possess."[8]

Examining the journeys of artists like James Earl Jones and Jim Brown[9] growing up in their rural roots [like probing what happened to Cicely Tyson and Woody Strode[10] in their urban youth] gave me a clearer grasp of their early encounters with racism. Rather than finding them deeply troubled or in constant conflict, I discovered ordinary children routinely concerned with the everyday, difficult problems of childhood; so very unlike black youngsters of today who cannot avoid being terrorized by the constant presence of prejudice, violence, and ignorance.[11] That is, the young Mississippi farm boy might recall being upset by having to visit his dentist in a different car than his white classmates,[12] or feeling uncomfortable entering a white Michigan church and being the only black person in the congregation.[13] But his pragmatic grandparents always put such unpleasant things in proper perspective. Their invaluable teachings taught him to never let other people determine his actions.[14]

In hindsight, Jones' developing years foreshadowed very little of what he encountered professionally and racially as an adult. If he had one notable problem left over from childhood, it was that by the time he was six, he began stuttering and remained mainly "mute" until he reached his mid-teens. It would take almost eight years before a dedicated English teacher (Donald Crouch) helped resolve the difficulty by getting him to practice using his deep basso voice as a debater and a public speaker.[15] Although today a major star renowned for his magnificent speaking voice, he still retains traces of his childhood affliction.

Sorting through James Earl Jones' high school and college years, I discovered several parallels between us. He may have grown up in Dublin, Michigan, but I was born in Detroit. Although my parents never divorced, my father was a travelling salesman and thus I, too, had an absent parent often in my childhood. Although not a loner like Jones, I was an outsider; and I masked my feelings of isolation by being an extrovert and a frequent truant. Neither one of us followed our religions diligently. I, too, benefitted from an English teacher's sympathetic intervention, only mine was in Brooklyn's Midwood High School [more of this in the next chapter]; Jones met his benefactor at Brethren's Kaleva Norman Dickson High School. While an undergraduate, he sold his old college books to buy new ones; I sold my University football tickets to buy textbooks. Like Jones, I came to distrust political affiliations and their hidden agendas. Like Jones, I too believed that the performing arts could contribute to solving a number of society's issues as well as my own emotional difficulties. He sought his answers mainly in the theater; I found mine primarily in the movies.[16] Another irony is that we were both Big Ten alumni. James Earl Jones entered the University of Michigan in 1949; I became a Buckeye in 1953 [the year he left college to enlist in the army.] We rarely had time off in our undergraduate days, since we both worked several jobs to stay afloat. I even washed dishes at one point to pay for my room and board. He planned to become a doctor; I intended to be a lawyer. He switched to drama; I turned to teaching. His ROTC training landed him several years in the military; I declined being in ROTC and instead served six months in the army, followed by five-and-a-half years in the National Guard.

But after our college days, our paths diverged significantly. My choices you know. I took the more secure route; Jones, the riskier road. In 1952, while on leave from the Rangers, he reunited with his biological father, Robert Earl, an ex-boxer turned actor; and at the time suffering the injustice that resulted from being a progressive thinker during the heyday of the House Un-American Activities Committee and the despicable rantings of Senator Joseph McCarthy.[17] The two struggling performers became good friends, but Jones always made clear they could never have been considered father and son. That opportunity had long since passed. Simply put, two major events occurred during that transitional period in the young man's life that mapped his future: he began training seriously for a career in acting, and Robert Earl's left-wing associations brought Jones in contact with one of the twentieth century's iconic figures: Paul Robeson.[18]

While Jones' professional activities remain paramount in this essay, the acclaimed actor's writing gaps about the Blacklisting era remain frustrating to me. Let me explain. Having just returned from watching Jay Roach's stirring *Trumbo*,[19] my memory was refreshed by how much of black film history is missing from the standard retelling of the McCarthy years. For decades, a whole generation of African Americans who lost their jobs and whose careers collapsed are routinely buried in sweeping statements both in the history books and in the Roach film describing thousands of people victimized during the American Witch-hunts. If you should see the aforementioned biopic of the Hollywood Ten's most famous member, you will be astounded by the "whiteness" of the film. Except for a scene showing the jailed Dalton Trumbo (Bryan Cranston) working with a black inmate (Virgil Brooks), there is almost no African American face in any of the street scenes, hearing rooms, cafes, nightclubs, or on studio lots in the entire 124-minute movie.

Of course, there are many ways to explain or to decry this fact; and the biopic is not without its discerning critics. Here is not the place to debate the evidence. I would merely suggest to you the film works well as a metaphor for African American film history in the first sixty years of the twentieth century. The reason you don't read about black directors, screenwriters, production people, producers, film executives, and cinematographers being blacklisted is because there were few such workers in the mainstream movie industry and in the ranks of the theatrical world! If not for Alexandra Iles' 1998 unheralded documentary *Scandalize My Name: Stories from the Blacklist*,[20] our collective consciousness would be even more ignorant about what happened to actors like Paul Robeson, Frederick Douglass O'Neal, Brock Peters, Ossie Davis, Canada Lee, and Robert Earl Jones during the days of the Red Menace.

James Earl Jones' autobiography, therefore, proves upsetting to me for what it tells us and does not tell us about the author's progressive father and his peers. That is, the actor explains how Robert Earl Jones refused to involve his son in his politics, fearing that it might jeopardize the young man's future. And there the material on blacklisting mostly disappears. We're given countless stories of how the two men worked hard together to find their place on the American stage; the acting classes they attended, the menial jobs they took to survive. You sense the respect that each came to feel for the other starting in the fifties.

But interestingly, Jones does not demonstrate much indignation over what was happening to progressives in the fifties, nor does he attempt to put the fate of his father in the perspective of other black actors throughout the history of American entertainment. In this area he is neither an animated historian nor a fiery campaigner. However, Jones has a reason for his actions. That is not the way he chose to confront racism and bigotry then or now. "I didn't set out to be an influence on anyone," he argues. "I don't believe in role models."[21]

By the end of the fifties and on through the mid-sixties, Jones began making his mark on audiences and critics in a variety of stage productions, most notably in classical plays directed by Joseph Papp in his innovative New York Shakespeare Festival providing free summer productions in Central Park. The youthful performer received his best reviews in *Othello* and *The Emperor Jones* (both in 1964). Not surprisingly, Jones, returned several times to the Moor's problems and spends considerable time in his autobiography describing different ways to perform the part. He also gained attention for his work off Broadway in Jean Genet's absurdist drama, *The Blacks*. Here was a chance for the taciturn actor to express his feelings about finding himself in a situation devoid of meaning in a meaningless universe. At the same time, he gained critical recognition for his groundbreaking work in the noteworthy CBS television series, *East Side, West Side* (both of these events previously mentioned in the Tyson essay), while making his screen debut as bombardier Lieutenant Lothar "Jimmy" Zogg in Stanley Kubrick's brilliant 1963 satire *Dr. Strangelove: or, How I Learned to Stop Worrying and Love the Bomb*.[22] (In what would eventually become standing operating procedure for the demanding Jones, he found fault with the way Kubrick directed him in his role.) Then relatively little else came the performer's way for several years.

In the turmoil of the civil rights movement, where powerful, conflicting voices cried out for African American liberties, the buzzword was often "authenticity." Activists insisted that people be genuine and not susceptible to social and political forces. To be otherwise was seen as demeaning and outdated. I frequently discuss the term's importance to various personalities as well as to other political and social pressures placed on actors during these violent times in the entertainment world in *The Interviews*. Unlike almost all of the people I had interviewed, however, James Earl Jones' self-possessed and rational approaches toward acceptability as a person rather than as an ethnic icon distanced him from from other African American personalities I met on my travels.

His subtle beliefs, however, surfaced in various well-liked television shows, and in Peter Glenville's problematic film *The Comedians*.[23] It was during the making of this screen adaptation of Graham Greene's novel about people trapped in Haiti during the dreaded days of "Papa Doc" Duvalier's reign of terror that the now-accomplished actor got word of a new, remarkable play written by Howard Sackler and soon to go into production. He immediately decided to go after the lead role.[24]

Contrary to what many of Jones' supporters believed, he did not have an easy time. Although director Edwin Sherin originally wanted Yaphet Kotto for the lead, he reluctantly turned to Jones when his first choice proved unavailable. I say "reluctantly" because in those days the actor came across as shy and retiring offstage. But the inventive and determined performer persisted, trained, shaved his head, and won Sherin over.[25] The rest, as the cliché' goes, is history.

The Great White Hope brilliantly told the legendary story of the late, great boxing hero Jack Johnson (in the stage play, the fictional Jack Jefferson) and his tragic fate after he defeated the Canadian fighter Tommy Burns in 1908 and became the world's first black heavyweight champion. Proud and defiant, Jefferson's flaunting of the nation's long held racial taboos so enrages the country that a frantic search begins for a "great white hope" to defeat the colorful black boxer. On July 4th, 1910, in what was billed as "the fight of the century," the overpowering black giant from Galveston, Texas, decisively defeats the ex-heavyweight champ Frank Brady (in reality, James J. Jeffries) who had come out of retirement for the match; and the new champ becomes the acknowledged world titleholder.

A son of ex-slaves, Jefferson's love for fast cars and wild women results in his having constant confrontations with federal authorities. One such encounter, however, changed the boxer's life forever. Because of allegedly violating what is known as The White Slave Traffic law or The Mann Act, the black champ is arrested.

In essence, the frame-up claimed the champ transported his white girlfriend, soon to be his wife, across state lines for immoral purposes. To escape his upcoming, biased trial, the beleaguered athlete flees the United States and lives with his devoted wife a troubled European exile. Persecuted by the American government, eventually broke and demoralized, Jack Johnson agrees to a secret deal where he agrees to lose his title in a fixed Cuban fight with a white boxer, The Kid (Jess Willard), to serve an abbreviated prison term in America, and then to withdraw from public life. The explosive play concludes with the bruised and cynical ex-champion fading into history.

Almost everyone connected with the amazing Broadway production was showered with sundry awards and honors. James Earl Jones became an overnight sensation. Then came the many debates about what message Sackler intended with his liberal narrative, the hue and cry from certain members of the black community about the play's debatable African American depictions, how Jones interpreted his explosive role, Jane Alexander's courage performing romantically in those days on stage with an African American actor, the obvious similarities with Muhammad Ali's life; and finally, Martin Ritt's 1970 screen adaptation of *The Great White Hope*.[26]

Despite the extensive acclaim bestowed on the powerful film, including Oscar nominations for Jones and Alexander, who reprised their stage roles in the movie, serious problems arose. Not only did the star object strongly to Hollywood's Martin Ritt replacing Broadway's Edwin Sherin as the movie's director, but also Jones intellectually and emotionally resented nearly every change in the story and the screen characterizations, even though Sackler was credited with writing the screenplay. Jones never forgave the studio and never embraced the movie. In addition, the film's critical reception has remained mixed down through the years.[27] It is also worth noting the Sackler drama proved important in the stage lives of other actors, including Brock Peters[28] and Richard Roundtree.

For me, not having seen the drama on Broadway, watching this film was like discovering incalculable riches. Why? Because I saw in Ritt's *The Great White Hope* many things that held immediate interest to me but were not necessarily important for Jones. He was a theatrical purist; I was an idealistic teacher who believed there was more to art than just aesthetics. Predictably, I noted not everyone saw the play during its original Broadway run. Surely it was better to have such great acting on screen, available to millions of viewers throughout the ages, rather than have it exist only briefly in the privileged memories of thousands of ecstatic theatergoers.

Let me put my thoughts in perspective. Imagine what this unusual movie meant to those academic individuals like me studying or learning about black film history at the end of the sixties. Remember just how few important films by and about blacks were available since the turn of the century! Try to appreciate why the movie found a place in key studies on the boxing film genre, like Leger Grindon's *Knockout: The Boxer and Boxing in American Cinema* (ironically published by the University of Mississippi Press); and in my young adult study *Great Sports Movies*.

And let's not forget the value I saw in reviewing boxing history to learn what it tells us about white male supremacy and the worth black Americans attached to the sport in terms of gaining information about their survival and sacrifice. As the esteemed social critic Gerald Early explained, "Throughout its history, boxing represented upward mobility for poor males, if they were lucky enough to become champions and make money. [Moreover,] ... prizefighting has symbolized black male revolt from the earliest days of integrated competition in the sport. Whites were always uneasy about blacks beating whites in the ring. And blacks attached far more significance to it than it deserved."[29] Thus, Ritt's movie, to me, proved rich with scholarly research possibilities.

Consider also how Ritt's *The Great White Hope* interpreted the nation's longstanding divisive attitude towards miscegenation as compared to what had previously been presented in the popular movies released during the post-World War II era. Here I am thinking about such films as *Bad Day at Black Rock*,[30] *Broken Arrow*,[31] *King of the Khyber Rifles*,[32] *The Searchers*,[33] *Island in the Sun*,[34] *Kings Go Forth*,[35] *The World, The Flesh, and The Devil*,[36] *The Unforgiven*,[37] *Sergeant Rutledge*,[38] and *One Potato, Two Potato*.[39] How had the discussion changed with the arrival of Ritt's film? And what ideas did Dr. Susan Courtney's pioneering study *Hollywood Fantasies of Miscegenation: Spectacular Narratives of Gender and Race, 1903-1967* provide? How much had changed and how far had we come as a nation?

Each work in its own way validated how I felt about film's importance in our culture.

Too esoteric, the reader might say. Not relevant to the actor's biography you might argue. What about the doors the play opened in my research on racial supremacy, including my interview with Brock Peters; or watching documentaries like William Cayton's Oscar-nominated *Jack Johnson*,[40] or Ken Burns' stunning *Unforgivable Blackness: The Rise and Fall of Jack Johnson*;[41] or Miles Davis' extraordinary musical collection, *The Complete Jack Johnson Sessions*?[42] And, of course, there was the black champion's own point of view in his autobiography *Jack Johnson—In the Ring—and Out*. "My life, almost from its very start, has been filled with tragedy and romance, failure and success, poverty and wealth, misery and happiness," he wrote in 1927. "All these conflicting conditions that have crowded in upon me and plunged me into struggles with warring forces have made me somewhat of a unique character in the world today." He said he hoped his life story would be interesting of itself, but that it might "also shed some light on the life of our times."[43] I feel the same way about the book you are reading.

Now would also be a good time to remind readers about the Biopic genre's significance not only to the black film experience but also how beloved the genre is to Hollywood filmmakers throughout movie history. For reasons too complex to explain here, filmmakers have since the industry's earliest days used the formula not only to tutor us about our past heroes and our national values, but also to get us to espouse those ideals in our daily lives. In other words, empathizing with many different types of heroes helps one, so the theory goes, to behave better in life when confronted with similar social injustices. You notice I make no claim for accuracy or truth. I mean only to suggest how biopics often set the agenda for much of what we discuss in our culture.

No film scholar has explained the process better than Professor George F. Custen. In his major study *Bio/Pics: How Hollywood Constructed Public History*, the perceptive film analyst investigated how moviemakers used the formula's conventions to help shape our cultural debates about our times and our ideals.[44] Crucial to the recurring cinematic practice is to pit the film hero's ambitions and beliefs against society's traditions and practices.[45] Using imaginative situations and pointed dialogue, the slanted narratives allow us to follow the moral debate unfold from multiple perspectives. Obviously, a study of biopics also reveals plentiful details about how artists manipulate the genre to express their counterculture points of view. Few films better illustrate how the conventions evolved over the century than does Ritt's *The Great White Hope*.

More timely, however, is the fact that biopics on film and television screens are more prevalent now than ever before in our culture's history. Just in the last two years, for example, we have been provided provocative movies about Stephen Hawking, Dr. Martin Luther King Jr., President Lyndon B. Johnson, Dalton Trumbo, Mother Teresa, Alan Turing, Jackie Robinson, Nelson Mandela, James Donovan, Jesse Owens, Chris Kyle, Dr. Bennett Omalu, Miles Davis, Walt Disney, and J.M.W. Turner. In short, biopics remain a powerful force in teaching us about the price one pays for going against the status quo. For reasons like these, I never felt we could leave our National Treasure to aestheticians and intellectuals alone.

Starting with my first interview with Lorenzo Tucker, I felt the need to demonstrate how important Jack Johnson was to black film history and why. After all, early newsreels showing his devastating victories over inferior white opponents so infuriated the country that Congress passed laws refusing the inflammatory pictures free movement across the United States.[46]

Finally, as anyone who has read my Jim Brown interview realizes, I see Muhammad Ali's extraordinary career as a pivotal moment in black film history. It was a period in our nation's heritage when radical political positions exerted extreme pressures on African Americans to stand up and be counted. While I have commented on how Cassius Clay became transformed into Muhammad Ali in the aforementioned interview,[47] it seems sensible to remind the reader how Ali's allegiance to the Nation of Islam, a combative, anti-white Islam organization, created considerable problems for his friends and those socially-minded people who defended what he represented to the society. Just as today's fears over radical Muslims divides the world, it did so then. Thus Ritt's *The Great White Hope* exists as a timely reminder to study and to learn from past film productions on the subject.

Briefly then, this is why I embrace the unfairly dismissed movie;

or just the fact why I thoroughly enjoyed the socially-minded production as exciting entertainment! That said, I willingly acknowledge Jones' priorities were with aesthetics, his personal loyalties, and his own performance. He had little interest in seeing the work as a social studies lesson. No problem. His choice. But why must it be either or? Why can't the film contribute to the Great Conversation as well as be a subject for artistic discussion?

On one central issue, however, Jones and I were and are in complete agreement: the nature of authorship. In Sackler's drama, there is a moment when the black champion is praised for his racial achievements. And Jefferson replies," Man, Ah ain't runnin' for Congress! Ah ain't fightin' for no race, ain't redeemin' nobody! My momma tole me Mr. Lincoln done that—ain't that why you shot him?"[48]

It's not what the character says that resonates with me, but the fact that the dialogue was written by a white man. Jones feels the same. In his words, "Just as there is no one voice to speak for white people or Oriental people or Hispanic people, there is no one voice to speak for black people. There are many voices. Howard Sackler, a white man, spoke eloquently through his play about the experience of one black man, but the themes and questions evoked in the play reverberate far beyond that one life."[49]

Returning to Jones' professional progress, his next role had him portraying America's first black president, in what I view as another very significant but unfairly scorned television drama, Joseph Sargent's *The Man*.[50] Based on a novel by Irving Wallace, Rod Serling's screenplay, except for a ludicrous opening, is quite powerful: Due to the collapse of a building in which they were attending a meeting, the U.S. President and the Speaker of the House are killed. Because of the Vice-President's age and recent stroke, Douglass Dilman (James Earl Jones), Senate President pro tempore, becomes America's first black occupant of the White House. The moderate New England scholar and now widower who went quietly into government service suddenly finds himself immersed in revolutionary racial politics. Within a short time in the Oval office, he has to decide not only how to deal with party bigots, disloyal Congressional aides, and his militant daughter (Janet MacLachlan), but also he must adjudicate a highly sensational international case involving an African American man accused of assassinating a white South African politician.

There is no room in this chapter to adequately debate the film's merits, especially the quality of the dialogue, the acting, and the circumstances surrounding the making of this *ABC Movie of the Week*. Back then, critics had a field day nitpicking the movie's perceived banalities. Even so, Jones remains justifiably proud of this unique drama coming as it did in the midst of the Blaxploitation era, calling it an "eloquent film." I completely agree! And in hindsight, the movie looks even more attractive to me as a historical resource. What is regrettable, as so often happens with movies and TV shows I find historically valuable, is that *The Man* is not currently available for viewing.

But *The Man*'s status for me goes beyond its being a notable example of a black President's rejection of violence as a political weapon. It has value as an entrée to an import film genre: Political thrillers in general and movies about African Americans becoming President in particular. For film scholar John W. Matviko, editor of a stimulating collection of articles on the subject, *The American President in Popular Culture*,[51] a movie like *The Man* raises the issue of how films socialize a nation's voting habits and may even have influenced the election of President Barak Obama. Although that's a leap even for me, I certainly share his feeling that "One of the functions of popular culture is that it introduces ideas that are a just a little bit on the edge of what we traditionally find acceptable, so that after a while, it becomes acceptable."

Now we come to my first physical contact with the formidable James Earl Jones. Remember as I describe what follows, that these were the days when black activists put every African American on notice that they needed to make their politics known. You were either for Dr. King's non-violent approach, or you followed the militancy of Malcolm X and Stokely Carmichael. No middle ground was acceptable. Jones was no different from anyone else in that debate. He had to choose.

If one researches the powerful artist's state of mind in those days, especially as explained in his autobiography, you learn what was going on in his head. His 1968 marriage to Julienne Marie (the actress who played Desdemona opposite his Othello in 1964) was coming to an end. The artistic community was in political and social disarray because of militant manifestos and Blaxploitation films. No matter what you said, you got challenged and attacked. Jones described the times as "racial insanity."[52] But as stated earlier, the resolute artist had long since decided no one was going to control his fate but himself.

Recall as well, I was heading west primarily to interview the highly visible performer for my research project. I had no other firm appointments. Not only was my time limited and my funds meager, but also I had yet to contact Clarence Muse, Jason Robards and to discover who else was available to interview. I had no other agenda. I took no sides on individual black responsibility either in the arts or in society, because I didn't know enough to take sides. Like the distinguished actor, I was a moderate until someone radicalized me.

James Earl Jones was the first person I called when arriving in LA. We spoke briefly on the phone, but what he said proved not only one of the most upsetting moments I have ever had in my professional life, but also one of the most prized pieces of historical information put into *The Interviews*. For starters, he told me in a troubled voice he could not see me. Maybe we could catch up later next year, the actor explained, but right now his life was in turmoil. There were just too many unanswered questions in his mind for him to find the time to talk to me. He was conflicted over whether he should first be a black actor and then a white actor; or the other way around. Equally devastating was the issue of whether it was right to be married to a white woman, let alone be married at all.

I was stunned. I felt badly about his problems, but I felt worse for myself. What was I to do, here alone in Los Angeles and nothing yet cemented? You might think I'm overstating how despondent I was, but the reader has only to examine my interview with Charles Edward Gordone to see how upset I became before the trip was over.[53]

For really the first time in starting the black film research project, I asked myself what the hell I was doing. Why am I here in LA? Who gives a crap about what I say about blacks or Negroes or colored people, or African Americans? Almost no one I talked to in my inner circle either in Vermont or in New York City cared a tinker's damn about African American movies or what I was currently doing with my time. The split between Jews and blacks was also deeply upsetting personally to the people I loved and to me. If I wanted to plunge into the civil rights controversy, why not explore it from the perspective of the Jewish side? Jones didn't care a hoot about my needs; why the so-and-so should I care about his? Besides, my first two interviews with the Tuckers and the Bowsers back in New York had raised so much racial confusion in my mind, I wasn't even sure how to address black people. If not for the extremely generous Gordone and his love for the spirit in each of us, this project may well have died a sudden death.

James Earl Jones and I eventually did meet in July of 1972, and we talked about a variety of issues. But neither he nor I had fully recovered from those disturbing December-January days back in Los Angeles. I never will regret meeting him; Jones doesn't even recall any of our contacts. In many respects, he treated me no differently than he treated Stanley Kubrick and Martin Ritt and would later respond to others like Lloyd Richards and August Wilson. He does not appear to be a mean man, or an unreasonable individual. As I have come to see him, he is a private person who stands by his principles and is not bashful about telling you what he thinks about his work or your assertions. He does this because he thinks he is right, he assumes what he is stating is important; and he has no qualms about letting you know when he feels your views are misinformed.

In the years since James Earl Jones and I have talked, he has continued to contribute mightily to our cultural heritage in the theater, in feature films, and on the small screen. Among my all-time favorite movies of his are *The Great White Hope, The Man, Claudine, The Bingo Long Traveling All-Stars and Motor Kings, Matewan,* and *Field of Dreams.* Like almost anyone breathing, his magical voice has thrilled me in such roles as King Mufasa in *The Lion King,* and as Darth Vader in the *Star Wars* films. And I don't mean to exclude the brilliance of his several outings as Othello, or his magnificent performance in August Wilson's *Fences.*

But what remains most memorable about the actor in our post-interview period was his connection to a controversial project that eventually resulted in giving me important life lessons on how to handle racial controversy and political censorship. The story began in 1976 when James Earl Jones first found himself, in what the popular Peter Graves described, "at the epicenter of one of the most intense dramas ever to rock the American theater."[54] The fracas centered on Paul Robeson, a famous football player, a great singer, and a renowned human rights activist.

Back when I was born and through the forties, the African American renaissance hero was one of the world's most admired and acknowledged civil rights activists; but in the fifties and sixties the United States Justice Department blacklisted him; and he became almost invisible to global audiences. The hardships he experienced were cruel and incalculable. (I write about this matter in the William Marshall interview.[55])

However, soon after Paul Robeson died on January 23, 1976; an NBC television producer interested in mounting a TV program on the great activist's life contacted James Earl Jones. Although the plan came to naught, the prospective screenwriter Phillip Hayes Dean refused to give up writing a play about Robeson's career. A year later, Jones was again contacted for another proposed Robeson project, this time by show business personalities in possession of Dean's now completed script. Intense negotiations followed before the actor agreed to do what would become a one-man play about this larger-than-life African American legend.

Not surprisingly, given the times and the egos involved, serious problems emerged about how the passionate progressive should be portrayed, by whom, and what facts should be included as well as excluded in any work on the great man's career and life. Countless people were consulted as to their views. One voice prominently involved but firmly opposed to the proposed production was Robeson's son, Paul Jr. No discussions with any of the parties proved especially productive. Not even the fact that the key people—director, actor, and dramatist—were all African Americans affected the arguments.

After numerous out-of-town trial performances, countless rewrites, and major personnel changes, the flawed *Paul Robeson* reached Broadway at the Lunt-Fontanne Theatre on January 19, 1978. After a stormy run, the one-man show turned off the house lights a little more than a month later on February 26. During that time, Jones, performing as the great humanist, appeared on a mainly barren stage, with relatively few props, and only a pianist for company; and he began acting out the story of a brilliant human being whose monumental career had been aborted because of American political injustice. The larger-than-life character sang, told jokes, and spoke out for civil liberties. (Fortunately, a television adaption of the play exists for getting an idea of what the play was like on stage.)[56] While an impressive audience sat watching the opening night performance, outside noises almost drowned out the actor's words on stage.

From the very early days of the public performances, in every city and at every presentation, Paul Robeson's son had organized protestors to attack the play. Ad hoc statements appeared in the local newspapers, informing the public how inaccurate and inappropriate the drama was; and how the great activist's reputation was being demeaned. While the lead actor and the discontented son met constantly in and out of the theater, nothing was ever resolved. Jones battled not only a weak script, but also a very unhappy critic. Not until the last performance did the fearless artist ever step to the footlights and defend his actions.

The complete details surrounding the historic controversy are available not only in James Earl Jones' autobiography but also in the memoirs of Paul Robeson Jr. and of Ossie Davis. In addition, the disgruntled son would help produce an invaluable documentary film, *Paul Robeson: Here I Stand*, demonstrating not only what he felt was missing from Dean's play, but also what Paul Jr. wanted remembered about his father.[57] In particular, we were reminded that not only did famous celebrities like Josh White, the brilliant folksinger, and Jackie Robinson, the great baseball star, reluctantly testify against Robeson during his HUAC public lynching, but also in 1958, the US Supreme Court struck down the Justice Department's illegal actions.[58]

Looking back to those haunting times, what meant so much to me was not only what I learned about how artists, scholars, and families exercised their rights and responsibilities, but also the way those courageous actions are reported on today. Ironically, I am writing about this in the context of being prevented from publishing my interview with James Earl Jones. Nevertheless, the courage and candor with which the actor describes in detail this unforgettable incident in his career reflects on how much restraint and propriety I used earlier in describing my five-year ordeal disbanding the University of Vermont's Department of Communication.

But more to the point under discussion. Let there be no misunderstanding. No matter how you feel or react to social and political crises, I believe it is indispensable to history that we study the lives and careers of artists who met the great issues of their times. Both Paul Robeson and James Earl Jones are for me such profiles in courage. Moreover, the vital lesson to learn from these men is that it takes courage, strength, and commitment to do the task properly.

In concluding this chapter in my unconventional story, I want to tip once again my hat to the actor's distinctive moral qualities in maintaining his principled behavior towards fighting social injustice, especially during the heyday of the civil rights era and the troubling years that followed. Many of the African American roles he played during his career, explained the performer, "were written around a basic conflict: the character's problems with the white world...." Not only were these parts unsatisfying to him but also he knew that life itself was more interesting. In the end, James Earl

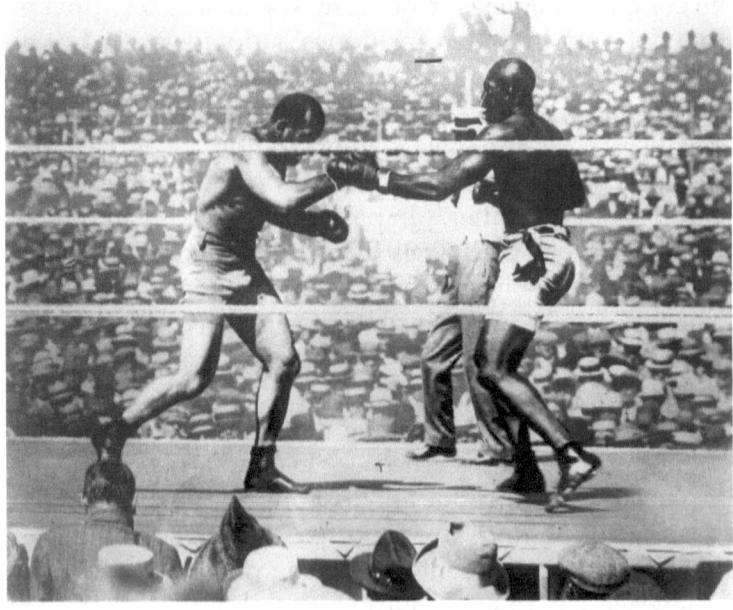

23. Heavyweight Boxing Champion Jack Johnson and former Heavyweight James L. Jeffries in 1910.

Jones made clear to audiences around the world that his mission "was to be an artist and make whatever 'statement' I had through my work...."[59] If his intention all along was to give us meaningful experiences about life and art, the man who has won almost every imaginable honor in his profession has done a damn good job!

Notes

[1] George Flemyng, "The Split," USA: MGM, 1968.
[2] David Anker, "Imaginary Witness: Hollywood and the Holocaust," USA: Shadow Distribution, 2004.
[3] Ralph Waldo Emerson, "Circles: Essay X," *The Collected Works of Ralph Waldo Emerson*, Volume II. Introduced and edited by Joseph Slater. Cambridge: Harvard University Press, 1979. 188.
[4] James Earl Jones and Penelope Niven, *James Earl Jones: Voices and Silences*. 1st ed. New York: New York: Charles Scribner's Sons, 1993. With a New Epilogue. New York: Limelight Editions, 2002.
[5] J. K. Sweeney, ed. *Book Review of James Earl Jones: Voices and Silences*, Magill Book Reviews (2009).
[6] Ephraim Katz, "James Earl Jones," *The Film Encyclopedia*, 5th Edition. Revised by Fred Klein & Dean Nolen. New York: HarperCollins, 2005.
[7] Jones and Niven, *James Earl Jones: Voices and Silences*, 212.
[8] Ibid, 212-13.
[9] Frank Manchel, "Heart and Soul: Jim Brown," *Exits and Entrances: Interviews with Seven Who Reshaped African American Images in Movies*. Washington, D.C.: New Academia Publishing, 2013. 193-254.
[10] Frank Manchel. "The Man Who Made the Stars Shine Brighter: Woody Strode," *Every Step a Struggle: Interviews with Seven Who Shaped the African American Image in Movies*. Washington, D.C.: New Academia Publishing, 2007. 355-411.
[11] Ta-Nehisi Coates, "The Black Family in the Age of Mass Incarceration," *The Atlantic* (October 2015): 60-80,84.
[12] Jan Schmidt-Garre and Marieke Schroeder, "Aida's Brothers & Sisters: Black Voices in Opera and Concert." Germany: Pars Media 2009.
[13] Alan J. Weiss, "James Earl Jones," *Biography*. USA: Alan J. Weiss Productions, 1995.
[14] Jones and Niven, *James Earl Jones: Voices and Silences*, 360-61,63-64.
[15] Ibid., 76.
[16] Elysa Gardner, "'Driving Miss Daisy' Down Memory Lane with a Ghost," *USA Today*, Oct. 22 2010, 1-2.

17 Some memorable examples of Robert Earl Jones' films work can be found in Larry Peerce's *One Potato, Two Potato* (1964), George Roy Hill's *The Sting* (1973), and Francis Ford Coppola's *The Cotton Club* (1984). The noted actor died on September 19, 2006.
18 Jones and Niven, *James Earl Jones: Voices and Silences*, 121-23.
19 Jay Roach, *Trumbo*. USA: Groundswell Productions, 2015.
20 Alexandra Iles, *Scandalize My Name: Stories From the Blacklist*. USA: Unapix Home Entertainment, 1998.
21 Vincent Canby, "Milestones Can Be Millstones: They Call Me Mr. Tibbs," *New York Times*, July 19 1970, 5.
22 Stanley Kubrick, *Dr. Strangelove: or, How I Learned to Stop Worrying and Love the Bomb*. USA: Columbia Pictures, 1963.
23 Peter Glenville, *The Comedians*. USA: MGM, 1967.
24 James Earl Jones, *Voices and Silences*, 158, 189.
25 Alan J. Weiss, "James Earl Jones," *Biography*.
26 Martin Ritt, *The Great White Hope*. USA: Twentieth Century-Fox, 1970.
27 James Earl Jones, *Voices and Silences*, 209-211.
28 Frank Manchel, "The Lamplighter: Brock Peters," *Exit and Entrances*. 130-190.
29 Gerald Early, *This Is Where I Came In: Black America in the 1960s*, Abraham Lincoln Lecture Series. Lincoln: University of Nebraska Press, 2003. 27-8.
30 John Sturges, *Bad Day at Black Rock*. USA: MGM, 1955.
31 Delmer Daves, *Broken Arrow*. USA: 1950. Twentieth Century-Fox, 1950.
32 Henry King, *King of the Khyber Rifles*. USA: Twentieth Century-Fox, 1953.
33 John Ford, *The Searchers*. USA: Warner Bros., 1956.
34 Robert Rossen, *Island in the Sun*. USA: Twentieth Century-Fox, 1957.
35 Delmer Daves, *Kings Go Forth*. USA: MGM, 1958.
36 Ranald MacDougall, *The World, the Flesh, and the Devil*. USA: MGM/Har-Bel/Sol C. Siegel, 1959.
37 John Huston, *The Unforgiven*. USA: MGM, 1960.
38 John Ford, *Sergeant Rutledge*. USA: Warner Bros., 1960.
39 Larry Peerce, *One Potato, Two Potato*. USA: Bawalco Picture Company, 1964.
40 William Cayton, *Jack Johnson*. USA: Big Fights, 1970.
41 Ken Burns, *Unforgivable Blackness: The Rise and Fall of Jack Johnson*. 3 Episodes. USA: WET, 2004-04.
42 Miles Davis, *The Complete Jack Johnson Sessions*. USA: Sony Music Entertainment, Inc., 1971.
43 Jack Johnson, *Jack Johnson—In the Ring—and Out*. Chicago: National Sports Publishing Company, 1927.
44 Well worth consulting in this area is another fine book: Dennis Bingham,

Whose Lives Are They Anyway?: The Biopic as Contemporary Film Genre. New Brunswick, N.J.: Rutgers University Press, 2010.

[45] George F. Custen, *Bio/Pics: How Hollywood Constructed Public History.* New Brunswick, N.J.: Rutgers University Press, 1992. 30.

[46] Frank Manchel, "Heroes and Villains: Lorenzo Tucker," *Every Step a Struggle.* 79.

[47] Frank Manchel, "Heart and Soul: Jim Brown," *Exits and Entrances,* 209-210.

[48] Jack Jefferson, in Howard Sackler, *The Great White Hope. A Play.* New York: The Dial Press, 1968.

[49] George F. Custen, *Bio/Pics: How Hollywood Constructed Public History.* New Brunswick, N.J.: Rutgers University Press, 1992. 72.

[50] Joseph Sargent, *The Man.* USA: ABC Circle Films, 1972.

[51] John W. Matviko, ed., *The American President in Popular Culture.* Westport, Connecticut: Greenwood Press, 2005.

[52] James Earl Jones and Penelope Niven, *Voices and Silences with a New Epilogue.* New York: Limelight Editions, 2002. 379.

[53] Charles Edward Gordon Interview. Frank Manchel, *Every Step a Struggle.*

[54] Alan J. Weiss, "James Earl Jones," *Biography.*

[55] Frank Manchel, "With an Unsullied Plume: William Marshall," *Exits and Entrances.* 372-427.

[56] Don Gregory, *James Earl Jones as Paul Robeson.* USA: Kultur. 200?

[57] St. Claire Bourne, *Paul Robeson: Here I Stand. USA: American Masters,* 1999. I strongly recommend viewing the important documentary to see what people like Paul Robeson, Jr. and Ossie Davis had in mind. Among the many useful insights from the film are excerpts from Robeson's films, speeches and concerts. One in particular comes from his speech at Basque Refugee Children's Concert at Albert Hall in England in 1937. His closing remarks highlighted the shift in his political life: 'The artist must take sides; he must elect to fight for freedom or for slavery. I have made my choice."

[58] Fortunately for today's interested audiences, there is footage and discussion of the events relating to the great athlete's appearance before HUAC available in Ken Burns' 4-hour PBS documentary film, *Jackie Robinson,* released initially on April 15, 2016. The impressive movie is available on DVD.

[59] Eleanor Blau, "James Earl Jones: How Does an Actor Make his 'Statement' as an Artist," *The New York Times,* October 10, 1980. C23.

24. Trying to find a way to make the 2007 controversial war film, *Pinkville*. From left to right, Cinematographer Robert B. Richardson, Director Oliver Stone, and Producer Jon Kilik.

18.

Looking Backwards, Gratefully

…No attempt was ever made before the movies began to please young and old, men and women, rich and poor, learned and ignorant, well-bred and vulgar, urban and provincial, cleric and peasant, by the same means. Everything that is strong and everything that is weak in the moving pictures must have its source in this same attempt at being universal—its wealth in money, its poverty in taste, its splendid achievements, and its disastrous failures.[1]

Gilbert Seldes

It requires wisdom to understand wisdom: the music is nothing if the audience is deaf.[2]

Walter Lippmann

I believe in history. I believe history is continuous. It doesn't begin or end with Pearl Harbor Day or on 9/11. You have to learn from the past.[3]

Ambassador Richard Holbrooke

What could be a more appropriate way to end my unconventional film teacher's story than to hark back to the time I said goodbye publically to my professional career? It occurred thirteen years ago, when my esteemed colleague, the late and whimsical Dr. Peter C. Rollins, asked me to deliver my farewell address to the discipline we both loved and dedicated our lives to serving. "Don't be pompous or esoteric," he counseled. "Have fun with the presentation," he advised, "but also remind today's scholars of who we were and how far we had come since we first dreamed of things that never were." The venue would be The University of Kansas; the occasion, the annual convention of the Literature/Film Association. I would deliver one of the scheduled major addresses. Not only did the invitation come as a flattering surprise (something Peter reveled in doing), but also I felt I could not turn it down.

My first thoughts were to anchor the talk in the context of what it meant to be a film teacher, and what the thirty or so university scholars meeting in Montreal at the end of the sixties had in mind when they discussed the future of a young organization called the Society for Cinema Studies. Those were the days when film organizations were exclusive, and getting a "membership card" required a strong resume and two mandatory academic references. It was, as they say, no walk in the park. What always fascinated me about those long ago visionary gatekeepers was their contradictory behavior. On the one hand, they took film study very seriously. On the other hand, they did not take themselves so solemnly. I remember those trailblazers, their warmth and humor, and the stirring times we shared together with great affection and considerable pleasure.

Of course, we were all unusual, each pursuing a distinctive aspect of our discipline in different ways with mixed results. We wrote books, established journals, held academic conferences, debated scholarly perspectives, and lobbied passionately for film study to become a significant part of the intellectual curriculum. Looking back, I don't recall one of those dedicated teachers failing to help make our discipline a major source of knowledge and a lifelong passion for the thousands of ambitious film scholars who followed us.

I considered explaining to my probable audience just what it was I thought teaching about motion pictures involved. What had I learned, and what was worth sharing with this and future generations? Taking to heart Peter's advice, I had no desire to moralize about some divine calling I presumably possessed to solve mankind's problems. My original plan was to simply say that teaching has always meant two basic things to me: (1) identifying the wisdom of the past so that I could carry those insights over to the present in order that my students could benefit from that knowledge in the future; and (2), insuring to the best of my abilities that what I taught provided meaningful and memorable experiences to those individuals who were considerate enough to trust me with their minds and their ambitions.

To put it even more high sounding, I would be their mediator, their intermediary, between the ancients and the moderns. In our precious but limited time together we would discuss the value of intellectual curiosity, search for important ideas to help them overcome life's problems, and discover the many treasures to be found from scholarly investigation. I never looked for disciples nor did I expect protectors. Teaching, to me, was about using one's imagination rather than learning to regurgitate names, dates, and places. Thus, it should come as no surprise, I have always believed that being in the classroom was a privilege and an honor that should be taken very seriously.

Easier said than done. I cannot speak for the other pioneers who gave rise to film education in America. They had their own worthy agendas arising from many multifaceted experiences. All I hoped to do with my nostalgic remarks was to identify what I assumed to be my most meaningful moments in the history of the popular arts, while at the same time rationalize why I spent a lifetime studying the mass media. But I also wanted to make clear the need for suitable preparation. Before one can teach others, I hoped to remind my listeners, one must first learn for himself. You do that, as Rudyard Kipling explains, "by filling the unforgiving minute with sixty seconds' worth of distance run."[4]

My sources for obtaining this professed knowledge were not always conventional ones. As you know, my heroes are not professional politicians or seasoned administrators misleading the public about what a great world this is, and how they would make it even better. My idols tell a different story. They provide information about what mistakes our ancestors have made and the cost it took and is still taking for society to correct the damage done. These historical and literary giants used their wisdom to persuade me that the best way to move forward is not to repeat the mistakes of the past. Stated differently, these intellectual mentors not only made me see the benefits of being a social critic but also the advantages of pursuing an unconventional life.

My challenge at the convention, therefore, was what to say

about a journey that included being born in the midst of the Great Depression, having a dysfunctional childhood, and then moving forward through World War II, the Cold War, the Nuclear Age, the conflicts in Israel, Korea, Palestine, Vietnam, Afghanistan, Iraq, Lybia, and Syria; as well as discovering throughout the centuries about man's inhumanity to man. The thoughtful world I traveled through was so riddled with horrors, tragedies, and profanities that I could not do justice in one oration to describing its obscenities. However, I did want to suggest to others, that the mass media helped me make sense of what I experienced. That fact had to be part of the message I conveyed to my colleagues.

All that being absolutely true, the speech needed balance. I love life and feel blessed by being with my wife and family; I am proud of my flawed country because of its courage to confront its mistakes and to try to change for the better, and I am passionate about my extraordinary profession. Obviously, that last point was important to include in my speech. I wanted to credit the mass media with making me appreciate many of the things I hold dear. What's more, I take Auntie Mame at her word: "Life's a banquet and most poor bastards are starving to death."[5] Try explaining that monumental inconsistency to any sane person who can't understand the riches the popular arts provide. I have been doing that dog and pony act for over sixty years. And because of what I have read and studied and learned, I have also been one traumatized human being.

Happily, I don't have to dredge up all the excuses that I have used over the decades to justify what I discussed in my final speech to my profession. You know already the value and the trust I place in music, movies, television, literature, sports, opera, and culture in general. What I needed to sort out was how to make those stream of consciousness ramblings coherent to a large audience.

Just the other day I came across a book review of Matt Ridley's timely work *The Evolution of Everything: How New Ideas Emerge*.[6] In this recent publication, the author inadvertently puts my feelings and arguments into a larger perspective. A British journalist and a fine science fiction writer, Mr. Ridley offers considerable evidence of how the worst of times can also be the best of times. He valiantly insists that mankind's many virtues and talents can frequently result in major scientific, social, and economic breakthroughs that lead to important advances in our struggles against what Columbia University Professor Frank Rose eloquently calls "the face of organized disaster and depravity."[7]

Okay, you know what I was considering telling the convention about the nature of teaching; but what was it that motivated me to devote my life to the job? Not a problem. Quite simply, nothing gave me greater pleasure in my bittersweet youth than watching movies in my neighborhood theaters. By the time I left Ohio State University, I knew I wanted to be a teacher. I came to love the life of the mind, and the incredible inspiration I received from intellectual curiosity. I prized and still do studying literature and the arts. And I wanted to share my great passion with others. It was only later that I found out I wanted to be a film teacher, not an English teacher. (Truthfully, if it had turned out otherwise, I still would have considered myself a very lucky person.) I made my decision in those days not only because it seemed the sensible thing to do, but also because my very being left me no other choice.

The next question my peers might want to know is why did film so possess me? Many of my colleagues, like me, chose our profession because they treasured the movies and wanted to spend their lives studying what they loved and admired. But unlike these wonderful teachers, I knew a lot of what I wanted to do with film teaching was connected to the disorientation, pessimism, and anger I felt, beginning in childhood, when I witnessed shocking and tragic events both on the screen and in the streets. Not only did I empathize with those who suffered and died, but also I loathed the traditional institutions and the authority figures that seemed unwilling, unable, and unconcerned with the problems. And I wasn't the only one, growing up in the fifties, who felt so moved. For example, Martin Scorsese recalls, those were the days movies "had different attitudes, different values, and seemed to emerge from a different country. Life was more complex, more complicated. People like Ethan Edwards and Shane had never been seen before. I related to their loneliness, their dreams and their frustrations, and followed a similar ethical code."[8] As I've often reminded my readers, it was the brilliant French filmmaker Jean Renoir who taught me in *The Rules of the Game*, "The tragedy of life is that everyone has a reason."[9] Well, my reason was I wanted to fight against these terrible forces and cruel monsters. What's more, I believed then and now, film has the power to change the world and us as well. It may seem corny or naïve to modern audiences; but in those days, many of us felt that way. Some of us still do.

Okay, okay, enough rhetoric. Give me some examples of the films and artists in your developing years that so influenced your decision to teach about films. Will do. But here's something fascinating to me. If I don't take time to sort through an extensive list of possible choices, but instead react immediately, three movies come quickly to mind: Carl Theodor Dreyer's *The Passion of Jeanne D'Arc*,[10] Ingmar Bergman's *The Seventh Seal*,[11] and Akira Kurosawa's *Seven Samurai*.[12] When I look at these examples I am quite taken a back. Not that the pictures aren't masterpieces, but that they are all foreign films. I've always believed my greatest love was for American films, and yet these three movies reveal another story. If I had to choose my favorite directors akin to Andrew Sarris' Pantheon of immortals, I couldn't do it; just as I could never answer the question asked most often of me in my career: "What is your favorite movie?" It depends on when you ask me, what the times are like, and the mood I'm in. It depends on what genre we are discussing, or even what I have just viewed. No one is more frustrated with that answer than my beloved children. "Just give me a film," they plead. "There must be one." Sorry, I can't do it.

These are some of the ideas I played around with before beginning to craft the convention address. Some thoughts survived in different forms; some ideas disappeared because there wasn't enough room. But there was one topic that I felt not only had to be included, but also I had ignored mentioning for far too long. It was a long overdue tribute to a teacher I felt changed my life and who was also my muse. And so to paraphrase the late, incomparable Jimmy Durante, "Here's to you Mr. Fuchs, wherever you are."

The story begins in my senior year at Midwood High School, right next to Brooklyn College. For a decade, I had gone to public school classes an angry and disruptive human being. I had no use for my teachers, and they showed no great affection for me. Then in my senior year's English class, overflowing with students eager to head to college, I came face to face with Mr. Henry Fuchs.

At first, he seemed no different from the other educators I routinely tortured. One day, as I remember it, I raised my hand in class and told him, "Mr. Fuchs, you're an anti-Semite." He paused, looked at me somewhat bemused, and said, "Why is that, Frank?" "Because," I replied, "you rarely call on the Jewish students in class." He mulled over my assertion, and then calmly suggested I sit in the back of the crowded classroom, make a seating chart, and for the next three weeks check off each of the students he called on. Then, the sage educator explained, by the end of the month we would see whether what I said was true.

I eagerly accepted the challenge. It was to be war between us. I never knew what hit me. Almost two weeks into the fact-checking experiment, I realized that Mr. Fuchs had beaten me. I was so busy with the stupid chart, I had no time to harass him. So after class that day, I sheepishly went up to see the English genius. "Mr. Fuchs," I said, "you're the only teacher that ever beat me. I really admire you." "If that's true," he said, "would you do me a favor? I know you don't read books teachers assign, but I'd like you to read this one: William Somerset Maugham's *Of Human Bondage*."

I don't remember whether he gave me a copy of the book or I bought the novel from Barnes & Noble.[13] The fact is I immediately began reading the story. I don't know if you remember what the book was about, so on the chance you don't recall the narrative, let me remind you. Maugham's Bildungsroman begins with Philip Carey, a nine-year-old child cursed with a clubfoot, losing his widowed mother, and being sent to live with his harsh and sanctimonious uncle, the Vicar William Carey. The boy grows more sad and unruly with each passing year. He comes to identify religion with his Uncle's pious, selfish, and unloving behavior. In addition, his Aunt Louisa's pity does little to offset the ridicule heaped on him by his schoolmates because of his deformity. Fortuitously, Philip, at eighteen years of age, comes into a small inheritance that allows him to study at a Berlin University. This experience results in his discovering a novel idea: "religion was a matter upon which discussion was possible."[14] This revelation leads to his rejecting religious convictions. It also becomes part of a process whereby Philip seeks to free himself from human cruelty and become master of his own fate.

After schooling is completed, the young man returns home, has an unsatisfying affair with an older woman, decides to try his talents in accounting, then turns his hand to art, and finally settles on a career in medicine. During this confusing period, he meets one of the great villainesses in literature, the vulgar waitress Mildred Rogers. Through most of his life, she will torment, betray, and bewitch Phillip. He only truly becomes free from her after she dies. Even though he realizes his attachment to Mildred is madness, he feels so strongly for her that he can not distinguish which brings him more pleasure: suffering or passion.

Once again, fate intervenes; and Philip becomes friends with Thorpe Atheny, one of his patients. Through that association, the maturing doctor meets and soon falls in love with Sally, one of Thorpe's daughters. The happy arrangement suddenly comes to a turning point. Thinking Sally is pregnant, he resolves to give up any further dreams and marry her. But when he discovers she is not expecting a child, he rapidly becomes excited at the prospect of being free for the first time in his life. By now, his clubfoot has been surgically repaired, and nothing stands in the way of his travelling anywhere and doing anything.

It's at that moment in the book's conclusion that Philip finally realizes nothing is more important in this world than the ability to love and to be loved. Up to that moment, and all through his life, "he had followed the ideals that other people, by their words or their writings, had instilled into him, and never the desires of his own heart." He now rejected that behavior. He now believed in the simplest pattern of all: "a man was born, worked, married, had children, and died...." In essence, "surrender[ing] to happiness was to accept defeat, but it was a defeat better than most victories."[15]

So it was I learned what Mr. Fuchs wanted me to understand. I wasn't so different from millions of angry and rebellious youngsters down through the ages. We each have our abnormalities; we each search for answers to the great questions. We each gain success not by never failing, but by learning from our mistakes and moving forward. Every one of us searches, like Philip Carey, for moral, spiritual, religious, and sexual values. And the hardest lesson to learn is the one most obvious. But most appropriately for those of us who presume to teach others is what Maugham took away from the great philosopher Spinoza, the alienated Jew whose ideas were once considered heretical. It was from this legendary Dutch exile that the popular British author found the inspiration for his masterpiece: Our most valuable experiences come about when we think and are resourceful.[16]

Almost four years to the date we met, April 12, 1956, Mr. Henry Fuchs, forty-eight-years of age, died of a heart attack.[17] Ironically, my oldest son Steven was born on April 12th, 1961. I never thanked my English teacher for what he did to change my life. I hope these few words indicate how much his kindness meant to me.

A Postscript. Years later, after I was blissfully married and living in Vermont, the love of my life, unbeknownst to me, took my original copy of Maugham's book and had it bound in leather. Then she placed the bound copy of *Of Human Bondage* on a table in our living room. So it is that every day of my life as I walk into that room, I am reminded of what I owe to W. Somerset Maugham, Philip Carey, Spinoza, and a teacher by the name of Henry Fuchs.

Notes

[1] Gilbert Seldes, *The Movies Come From America*. Preface Charles Chaplin. New York: Charles Scribner's Sons, 1937. P. 14.
[2] www.brainyquote.com
[3] David Holbrooke, *The Diplomat*. USA: Giraffe Partners, 2015.
[4] Rudyard Kipling, "If." Written in 1895; first published in 1910.
[5] Morton DaCosta, *Auntie Mame*. USA: Warner Bros., 1958.
[6] Matt Ridley, *The Evolution of Everything: How New Ideas Emerge*. New York: Harper Collins Publishers, 2015.
[7] Frank Rose, "Beyond Our Control," *New York Times Book Review* (November 29, 2014): 15.
[8] Martin Scorsese, *A Personal Journey with Martin Scorsese Through American Movies*. England: British Film Industry, 1995; USA, 1996.
[9] Jean Renoir, *The Rules of the Game*. France: Nouvelles Editions de Films (NEF), 1939.
[10] Carl Theodor Dreyer, *The Passion of Jeanne D'Arc*. France: Gaumont, 1928.
[11] Ingmar Bergman, *The Seventh Seal*. Sweden: Svensk Filmindustri (SF), 1957.
[12] Akira Kurosawa. *Seven Samurai*. Japan: Toho Company, 1954.
[13] W. Somerset Maugham, *Of Human Bondage*. New York: The Modern Library, 1915.

[14] Ibid., 135.
[15] Ibid., 759.
[16] Benedictus de Spinoza, *Ethics, Demonstrated in Geometrical Order*. 1677.
[17] "Rites for Henry Fuchs," Obituary, *Brooklyn Daily* (Friday April 13, 1956): 18.

Thank You, Mr. Fuchs

I have been asked to comment on the beginnings of American film education, and how those times influenced my writings and teachings over the past fifty years. I'm also supposed to comment on my new book [*Every Step a Struggle*], and then end mercifully with some advice for the future. That is quite an assignment in so short a time frame and just after a hearty lunch.

If our mutual ordeal is to be bearable, you need to cut me some slack. I am seventy-two years of age, and not in the best of health. I tend to become garrulous and ramble. Moreover, I delude myself into believing I am a disciple of the Orson Welles' school of film history. That is, in his words, "There are still a few of us who trudge alone along a lonely, rocky road...This [is what makes us who and what we are]. We don't move as fast as our cousins on the highways; we don't get as much accomplished as the wealthy and the powerful. What we come up with is not necessarily better. It is just different. If there is any excuse for us, it is that we are following the old American tradition of the maverick—a vanishing breed...."[1]

So let's get to it. The fact that I have spent a lifetime watching movies and am passionate about them should not surprise you. However, you may be curious about why I took the road I did, how my thinking about film study evolved, and what factors motivated me.

My memories take me back to a time when dress codes were in fashion, when no one dared talk back to his or her teachers, when our parents told us that the school system was always right, when we were judged by our religion, the color of our skin, and our family heritage. There were no TVs, no computers, no multiplex theaters, no DVDs, and no Internet.

You need to recall what New York City was like when my film journey began in the late 1930s: we had three major league baseball teams—The New York Yankees, The New York Giants, and the Brooklyn Dodgers—; the major studios—the people who owned the theaters—were MGM, Fox, Paramount, Warner Bros, and RKO—; they created a film distribution system in which the nation was divided into thirty-two zones. The minor companies—Columbia Pictures, United Artists, and Universal—had a "gentleman's agreement" with the majors to show films in their theaters. Each zone consisted of a clearance system—that is, a length of time for a film to run in a particular area: First-run films in New York opened at the picture palaces on Broadway; after the run was done, the film would be released to Second- and Third-run theaters.

The programs in the Third-run houses like the Loew's Delancy on the Lower-East Side, and later The Elm and The Midwood in Brooklyn, included coming attractions, a cartoon, novelty films, newsreels, double features, and on Saturday matinees, a fifteen-chapter serial like *Flash Gordon Goes to Mars*.[2] It was non-stop entertainment. Most important for my narrative, the theaters had a children's section, which was carefully watched over by a uniformed woman called a matron. Keep in mind that you could stay in the theater as long as you wanted, seeing everything over again and again for the same price of fifteen cents. Candy was a nickel.

I was just four years old when I started going to the movies two or three times a week. My father was a traveling salesman, on the road six months a year. My mother was a hard-working woman who kept the family going. She did everything possible to keep my younger sister and me happy. There were no affordable daycare centers for us. When my mother couldn't find a babysitter, she mainly used the movies and books to keep me, and later my sister, safe, occupied and entertained.

By the time I entered the first grade in September of 1941, I may not have understood what I was watching, but I knew there was a difference between the movies of Roy Rogers, Gene Autry, and Johnny Weissmuller as compared to films like *Snow White and the Seven Dwarfs, Gone With the Wind, The Grapes of Wrath, The Great Dictator, Mr. Smith Goes to Washington, The Wizard of Oz, Goodbye, Mr. Chips,* and *How Green Was My Valley*. I became familiar with the music of Irving Berlin, Rodgers and Hart, the Gershwin brothers, Cole Porter, Jerome Kern, Yip Harburg, Rogers and Hammerstein, and heaven knows how much jazz and classical scores in the adventure films and cartoons.

Social historian Paul Von Blum in his discussion of art captures the importance of these first steps in the motion picture world unintentionally. What he says about painting I believe is also true about films: "I don't believe any painter can use a mural or an easel painting to give you a precise and sophisticated analysis of the complexities of human politics. That is not the role of art. But art, on the other hand, can inform, can enflame, it can propagandize, it can make people think...."[3]

It was the magic of the movies that I experienced between the ages of four and seven that led me to the majesty of film over the last 100 years. Yet there was a time when the academic establishment ridiculed me and demanded to know how popular arts could produce great artists. I do not see many of those dinosaurs around today. At the same time, I'm thrilled to learn that two of my favorite former students—cinematographer Robert Richardson and producer Jon Kilik—are finally working together on a new Oliver Stone film about My Lai.[4]

There were many other influences on my career, including major-league baseball, public libraries, opera, classical music, Broadway, and the radio. For today, I will focus on the films, and touch only lightly on the others.

As I entered the first grade, America was engaged in an intense internal struggle over the issues of intervention vs. isolation. In addition, the nation remained confused over the relationship between the Soviet Union and Nazi Germany. The film industry was under investigation by the U.S. Senate over issues like profit, propaganda, motivation and values. December 7th, 1941 changed all that.

In 1942, Washington created the Office of War Information; and a second form of film censorship took place, the first was the Motion Picture Production Code. The bureaucrats manipulated not only the war effort but also what values were appropriate to Americans. The propagandists favored escapism over message-oriented movies. They stressed the struggle for survival by ordinary people against fascists and dictators.[5] The gatekeepers, as effectively summarized by scholars like Kathryn Kane, concluded that the American way meant supporting your government, trusting your leaders; believing that Americans were sensible, modest, clean-cut, and well behaved. The bad guys were unruly, cruel, and followed despotic leaders.[6] A basic war film consisted usually of a tough sergeant, a rich kid, an ex-con, a Jew, an African American, a Polish-American, and an Italian-American.[7] These movies dramatized the conflicts between the democratic ideals of the ordinary middle-class versus the arrogance of the rich and powerful upper class. It was not hard in those days to develop a healthy class-hatred, and I took full advantage of my opportunities.

These were the years when I learned to reject any notion of religious or racial exclusion. The War Years also indoctrinated me with a strong work ethic and a sense of social responsibility. To my eyes, these war films backed no political party but a political ideology of We vs. Them. Filled with novelty, originality, and excitement, the movies from the United States and its allies cared little about reason, materialism, or aesthetic issues. Their function mainly was to play on our emotions and unite the allies in a common cause against a common enemy of racism and fascism. At least, that's what a young, white, middle-class American Jew took away from the movies from 1941 to 1945.

In 1949, I lived about ten blocks from Midwood High School. Almost every morning I hitched to school. Often I would ask the driver where he was heading. If he said "New York," I told him I'd go with him. I played hooky from high school as often as possible, just to watch the great stage shows that took place with all the First-run movies on the Great White Way. I read almost none of the books that teachers assigned, and took my reading lists from the understanding Brooklyn librarians that daily fed my insatiable intellectual curiosity.

Because Midwood High School was so overcrowded, I—as well as my classmates like Woody Allen and Erich Segal—got out of school extremely early in the day. As a result, by age sixteen, I worked at the major ballparks selling peanuts and hot dogs. At Ebbets Field, the Dodgers didn't let the fans in until 11 AM. From 9 AM until then, the candy butchers could fungo, pitch and play ball with the likes of Jackie Robinson, Gil Hodges, Pee Wee Reese,

Carl Furillo, and Roy Campanella. Much of my writings would be developed on the playing fields of the bombers and the bums. To know more about the era, read David Riesman's *The Lonely Crowd*[8] or Charlie A. Reich's *The Greening of America*[9] to place me in my time.

But the decline of the studio system, blacklisting, the rise of art houses, and the passing of the torch to a new generation of filmmakers revealed another America, one that seriously questioned the values of the past. The times taught us to fear the possible disasters that the Cold War could produce. Every film genre in one way or another reminded us about the dangers of communism, the end of the world because of the arms race between the major powers and the stock piling of Atomic Bombs.

As if that were not enough to terrify us, we also had to deal with the racism rooted in American society. For example, in 1947, Hollywood addressed the issue of anti-Semitism with *Gentleman's Agreement* and *Crossfire*. Two years later, the film capital began an extensive look at the Negro problem with movies like *Lost Boundaries*, *Pinky*, *Intruder in the Dust*, and *Home of the Brave*. The 1950s and the early 1960s focused frequently on the issue of miscegenation and the mistreatment of people of color in America. Remember movies like *No Way Out*, *Bad Day at Black Rock*, *Broken Arrow*, *King of the Khyber Rifles*, *The Searchers*, *Island in the Sun*, *Kings Go Forth*, *The World, The Flesh, and The Devil*, *The Unforgiven*, and *Sergeant Rutledge*.

In the interests of brevity, let me cite just three events that reshaped my life just from 1947 to 1952. Naturally, because of my age, I did not know of two of these events at the time, but by the end of my undergraduate education in 1957, they were ingrained in my thinking.

First, came the 1947 pact between President Leon Blume of France and US Secretary of State James F. Byrnes. It allowed Hollywood to flood post-war French film theaters with hundreds of American movies made since the 1930s but prevented from being shown in France till after WWII. Young French rebels, a number of whom played hooky from college classes, watched these films religiously in a museum called the *Cinematheque Francaise* run by a brilliant and passionate curator named Henri Langlois. These mavericks looked to these movies to reshape not only the French cinema but also the world itself. I'm talking about youngsters like François Truffaut, Jean-Luc Godard, Claude Chabrol, and Eric Rohmer.

The key effect on me, discovered later through Andrew Sarris' dazzling work, was that Truffaut created the Auteur Theory. Simply put, the brilliant French filmmaker and his fellow mavericks insisted that the Hollywood movies made in pre-war days, movies that had been denigrated as factory-made products, should now be recognized as having been made by artists as great as any that had ever worked in the cinema. That was not news to me. Just the opposite. It was a rousing confirmation of what I already knew.

The second momentous event, again unknown to me at the time, came in 1952 when the Encyclopedia Britannica published *The Syntopican*, a revised collection of the great books of the western world. The collection's introductory volume was entitled *The Great Conversation: The Substance of a Liberal Education*. In the *Preface*, Robert Maynard Hutchins, the collection's editor-in-chief, made clear the purpose of collecting fifty-two masterpieces of western civilization. It was assumed, he asserted, that educated people knew the worth of the great books of the ages. Such works were revered, he argued, not only because they had endured but also because they contained brilliant ideas and possible answers to the problems that historically preoccupy human beings in such areas as religion, philosophy, politics, morality, education, love and death, art and beauty, and social concerns—in essence, humanity's ongoing relationship to the world it inhabits.

It was the next section that shaped my career. Hutchins pointed out that the choices in the collection were not, and could not, be permanent. How could they be? We live in a changing world, he explained, and thus venerated works must always be tested against new ideas and new discoveries as humanity evolves. Consequently, the choice of works studied always changes from era to era. In Hutchins' words, "…this process of change will continue as long as 'men' [quotes mine] can think and write. It is the task of every generation, he reasoned, to reassess the tradition in which it lives; to discard what it cannot use, and bring into context with the distant and intermediate past, the most recent contributions to the Great Conversation." I believed that then and I believe it now. Furthermore, I would spend the rest of my professional life arguing that great films deserved a role in the Great Conversation.

The third major event, and the one I understood at the time, took place during the first half of my senior year in 1952. An English teacher named Henry Fuchs took a liking to me. He gained my trust and asked me to read, as a favor to him, W. Somerset Maugham's *Of Human Bondage*. In following the journey taken by the protagonist Philip Carey from childhood to maturity, many of the questions I had being asking myself seem to be answered by Maugham's literary hero. Because of my miserable public school years, my life seemed quite fragmented. I never really felt connected to society, family, and the social issues of the day. Mr. Fuchs changed that. He made me believe that people everywhere were the same: some good, some not so good. That wealth and power were not in themselves good or bad; what mattered was how you used money and power.

In other words, the post-war period forced me to rethink everything I had learned about life from the movies. I came to believe that a careful examination of our film experiences was not only important for the mental health of nations, but also that it was important for everyone individually; and the movies were not just the private domain of artists and intellectuals.

In the fall of 1962, I tried an experiment that further shaped my career. Unlike the strategy used by Hilary Swank who played Erin Gruwell in *Freedom Writers*,[10] my experiment faced no opposition from either the administration or my peers. Because in those days, no one cared what you did with the so-called "slow learners" as long as you kept them quiet and orderly.

But a distracting myth grew up in those pre-screen education days that followed me for forty years. It was that those of us who were passionate about studying the mass media wanted to substitute the popular arts for the great works of the past. Absolutely not! We just wanted to give the mass media its proper and necessary place in a curriculum designed not only to make us better citizens, but also to make us better human beings.

Over the next five years—from 1962 to 1967— I would begin writing about film, switch to college teaching, get my doctorate at Teachers College, Columbia University, and accept a position as an Associate Professor of English at the University of Vermont.

A decade later, in 1977, UVM became part of a national movement to shift from being a community of teachers to becoming a community of scholars and teachers. The College of Arts and Sciences hired Dr. John G. Jewett, a gifted chemist and extraordinary administrator, to become Dean. A few months later, he appointed me as his Associate Dean. What I learned in the next eleven years about a standard of excellence in a world of educated men and women is the stuff of two more speeches.

One of my responsibilities was to oversee Continuing Education (CE) in the College. At the end of the first year, working with CE, I had accumulated a $75,000 surplus. The question was how best to use the money. John suggested an experiment to determine if humanists would find computers as useful as scientists did. I decided to revise *Film Study* as the subject for the experiment. Long before the ten years it took to complete the four-volume work, computers were in the hands of the humanists.

In 1990, *Film Study: An Analytical Bibliography* came out, I went back to the classroom, and began looking around for a new project. It was then I turned to my research on African American film history that I had started back in late 1969. The book was finished a decade later.

Let me conclude this talk, not with advice from an old-timer, but with a request from someone, who like Orson Welles, believes "he is happy to be with you not [because] of your kindness and generosity, but…[because] it validates my own contrariness."

My one request to you involves listening to the words of a blacklisted writer, Michael Wilson, who never received in his lifetime his Oscar for co-writing *The Bridge on the River Kwai*. Mike, however, received the Screenwriters Guild's Laurel Award in 1976, and he said in his acceptance speech the following, which I have slightly altered for us:

> I don't want to dwell on the past. But for a few moments to speak of the future, and I address my remaining remarks particularly to you, younger men and women who have perhaps not yet established yourselves in… [our profession] at the time of the great witch hunt. I feel that unless you remember this dark epoch and understand it, you may be doomed to replay it. Not with the same cast of characters, of course, or on the same issues.

But I see a day, perhaps coming in your lifetime if not in mine, when a new crisis of belief will grip this republic. When diversity of opinion will be labeled disloyalty, and when extraordinary pressures will be put on writers... [and educators] to conform to administration policy on the key issues of the time, whatever they may be.

If this gloomy scenario should come to pass, I trust that you younger men and women will shelter the mavericks and the dissenters in your ranks and protect their right to work. The Guild [and the universities] will have the use and the need of rebels if it is to survive as a union of free writers [and responsible teachers]. This nation will have need of them if it is to survive as an open society.[11]

Thank you for your patience.

Notes

[1] "American Film Institute, "AFI Tribute to Orson Welles." USA 1975.
[2] Ford I. Beebe and Robert F. Hill, *Flash Gordon's Trip to Mars*. USA: Universal Pictures, 1938.
[3] Rick Tejada-Fares, "Rivera in America," in *American Masters*, ed. Susan Lacy USA 1988.
[4] The film has yet to be made.
[5] Frank Manchel, *Film Study: An Analytical Bibliography*, 4 vols. Rutherford, N.J.: Fairleigh Dickinson University Press, 1990. 231-32.
[6] Ibid., cited on p. 233.
[7] Ibid., 273
[8] David Reisman, *The Lonely Crowd* (1950).
[9] Charles A. Reich, *The Greening of America* (1970).
[10] Richard LaGravenese, *Freedom Writers*. USA: Double Feature Films/Jersey Films/Paramount Pictures, 2007.
[11] Frank Manchel, "Sink or Swim: Hollywood After World War II," College of Arts and Sciences Dean's Lecture Award. Burlington: University of Vermont, 2000. 20-21.

25. Robert B. Richardson

Epilogue

It would be a wonderful thing for a man of many years to die with a boy's heart.[1]
Carl Sandburg

Where all men think alike, no one thinks very much.[2]
Walter Lippmann

Only by joy and sorrow does a person know anything about themselves and their destiny. They learn what to do and what to avoid.
Johann Wolfgang von Goethe

Here's the part of the book where I'm supposed to tell you I've heard the chimes at midnight; or off in the distance the incomparable Judy Holiday is singing, "The party's over; it's time to call it a day."[3] Some readers might expect me to despair over the realization that my youthful dreams have faded; and that I lament that my adolescent ambitions are no longer possible. All this is, because, as Walter Huston sang decades ago, "the days grow shorter when you reach September."[4] I'm supposed to confide to you that I am haunted by the mistakes I've made, the places I've never seen, or the things I've never done. And if I'm really honest, I'm meant to tell you, given how I feel about what man has done to man, that it's all been a tale of sound and fury, signifying nothing. In the end, you might even expect me to share with you a bucket list that I'm going to try to empty before I start on my last great adventure

Well, it ain't gonna happen. That's not my style. If anything,

I'm singing, "If my friends could see me now!" It's a tune from a 1966 show called *Sweet Charity*.[5] Lyricist Dorothy Fields unwittingly captured my feelings perfectly. From the difficult streets of New York to my beloved Vermont home in the Forest, I've lived a charmed life, had a challenging career, worked at a splendid university, married the woman of my dreams, and been blessed with a precious family. I couldn't have done it without the magic of the movies, the wisdom of poets, and the immortal music of great composers. At the same time, I have not ignored the less than perfect world around me, nor remained silent in the presence of the social injustice I witnessed around the world; and I've got the scars to show for it.

While I've known disappointment, despair, and disillusionment; I've also experienced kindness, friendship, and love. In addition, I have not taken for granted the few intellectual and spiritual gifts bestowed upon me. Rarely have I wasted those irreplaceable riches in pursuit of pointless prestige, power, or ambition. That is because I took to heart what I learned from the works of geniuses like Swift, Twain, Shaw, Cervantes, Rostand, Maugham, and Shakespeare.

When I write, as I do throughout this behind-the-scenes book, that I am an American Jew, it is because I wanted to remind you that the former taught me about rights and the later reiterated my responsibilities. From the third grade on, I've refused to robotically accept authority, so when someone told me to do something without giving a good reason why, I knew it was not going to be a good day for either of us. I have also found the courage to see myself as I am, and not as I want to be. As I said from the start, I'm nothing more than an amateur; and after sorting through my selected memories, you now understand why. Nevertheless, I remain steadfast in my opinion that the past offers as much knowledge as we hope to find in the future. With every fiber in my body, I believe that the great artists, the brilliant scholars, and the trailblazing trendsetters in each and every age are miracles given to me by a higher power that I cannot begin to understand. All I ever needed to do is to figure out what to do with this information.

Moreover, I have concluded because of our human nature and the mysterious workings of the universe that what many people see as progress, I view as change. That thought remains an important theme in *Take Two: A Film Teacher's Unconventional Story*. Consider this. As I prepare to conclude our journey together, 150 years have past since President Abraham Lincoln was assassinated; 120 years since Louis and Auguste Lumiere helped give birth to the cinema; 100 years since Professor Albert Einstein revealed his theory of relativity; seventy years after World War II concluded; fifty-five years since the Selma Voting Rights Movement took to the streets of Alabama; forty years after the Vietnam War ended; and only months since the Ferguson Report has come out.

Add this data to the mix: inventor Dean Kamen believes, "We could empty half of all the beds in all the hospitals in the world by just giving people clean water."[6] *The New York Times* reports, "Nearly 60 million people around the world have been driven from their homes by war and persecution—more than at any time since World War II. Half are children."[7] Other news agencies document more than 40% of Americans are without jobs; 1 out of every 7 people lives in poverty, and some CEO's now make more than 300 times the salary of the average worker. Only 19.8% of African American youngsters have jobs. Every night, and I mean every night; I hear how brutally and senselessly barbarians and ignoramuses treat girls and women around the world. I see pictures of men, women, and babies drowned as they fled the horror in their native lands to seek refuge in fearful and unknown places. Last but not least, ISIS is growing in strength and savagery!

Nevertheless, some intellectuals will insist there is reason to be optimistic about the future. We're making progress! Just be patient. And some politicians will argue that before we rush to open our doors to millions of helpless and demoralized immigrants, we should take a few years to see how safe it is to let these tragic refugees enter the land of the free and the home of the brave. Other pundits may well tell you I am rambling and inconsistent. That, contrary to what John Donne told us centuries ago, another's man's death does not diminish me, nor am I my brother's keeper. I'm nothing more than a bleeding heart liberal, naïve and impulsive and devoid of sense and caution.

Do I really have to spell out that today's problems are age-old predicaments that continually resurface in different shapes throughout time; that they will always remain present for every generation? Isn't it obvious those past ethical challenges Professor Hutchins discussed in 1952 "in such areas as religion, philosophy, science, politics, morality, education, economics, love and death, art and beauty, and social concerns" confront us every day of our lives; and that today's dilemmas are similar in many ways to those difficulties of yesterday, and just as likely to be the challenges of tomorrow?

That's why I'm always carrying on in this iconoclastic book about getting involved in the Great Conversation, as well as remembering blacklisted screenwriter Michael Wilson's plea that each of us needs to protect society's dissenters, anywhere, anytime, and any place. I believe, like Wilson, we won't survive as a free nation without them. And as the late Ralph Waldo Emerson has explained, we do what we must, we go where we will, and we should never expect a pat on the back if we get some things right.

That said, I know how easy it will be to mock what I write. I appreciate I am a person with limited wisdom and pretentious claims. I don't deny that I often doubt myself and question whether what I say really means anything. And if I don't admit my failings and frustrations; trust me, Sheila will point them out. But that really is who I am.

As I took you back in time to retrace from whence I came in my teacher's unconventional travels, I had a second agenda. I wanted you to see that a person can go against the status quo and still survive. There was no attempt to mislead you that the world was kind or generous or just, especially to the weak, the poor, and the uneducated. If I had adhered to conventional wisdom, I would never have survived as well as I did, let alone be as happy as I am today. Let me be absolutely clear on this point. I do not insist that my opinions are earth shattering or divine revelations. But as Professor Raul Hilberg taught me decades ago, there are tiny elements in this book's eighteen sections in which imaginative people can find useful tools for teaching and for finding hope if only they have the interest and the will to do so.

In the process, I've also learned some important lessons. For example, I discovered that I had never really appreciated how many splendid individuals had made my quirky story not only enjoyable but also meaningful. To them, I sincerely apologize for not having been more grateful for their generosity and gentleness. I'm particularly sad that there are some persons like Mr. Fuchs that I never had a chance to say thanks to while they still lived. I also regret spending so much wasted time quarreling with the Objectionables. Obviously, you can't avoid rivals; or prevent, as Kipling said, seeing "the truth you have spoken twisted by knaves to make a trap for fools." But you don't have to give them more time than is necessary.

In addition, I'm surprised by how long it took me to realize you don't bring about meaningful changes by yourself; and that no matter how smart I am, there are other ways of doing things that I haven't yet dreamt of in my philosophy. Also, people need not only have ideas, but also have help in implementing those ideas. Most importantly, they must have faith that wrongs can be righted. Another discovery: far too much of the world I have shared with others has put too much emphasis on excellence and not enough on compassion and love; too much currency on reputation and not enough on human decency. I have seen the price foolish people have paid for their poor choices. Finally, I've learned that I may be old but I'm not useless. There are still impossible dreams to chase after, unfinished tasks to get done, and useful solutions to be found for unanswered questions. I may not be able to do everything on my agenda, but I can do something. How much depends on me and on how hard I try.

Now that this chapter in my life is concluded, I'm heading back to my storied life with Sheila in the Forest. When I get settled in, I'm going to see the following films that explore many of the important cultural issues I've covered in this unorthodox book: David Gordon Green's *Our Brand is Crisis*; Danny Boyle's *Steve Jobs*, Tom Hooper's *The Danish Girl*, Sarah Gavron's *Suffragette*, Steven Spielberg's *Bridge of Spies*, John Crowley's *Brooklyn*, Tom McCarthy's *Spotlight*, Justin Kurzel's *Macbeth*, Quentin Tarantino's *The Hateful Eight* (with Richardson doing the visuals), Sylvester Stallone's *Creed*, Larry Abrahamson's *Room*, James Vanderbilt's *Truth*, Ericson Core's *Point Break*, Todd Haynes' *Carol*, Alejandro Gonzalez Inarritu's *The Revenant*, Michael Moore's *Where to Invade Next*, Frederick Wiseman's *In Jackson Heights*, Samba Gadjig's *Sembene*, Stig Bjorkman's *Ingrid*

Bergman—In Her Own Words, David Evans' *What Our Father's Did: A Nazi Legacy,* Kent Jones' *Hitchcock/Truffaut,* Spike Lee's *Chi-Raq* (with Kilik producing), Laszlo Nemes' *Son of Saul,* Craig Gillespie's *The Finest Hours,* the Coen Brothers' *Hail, Caesar!,* and Scott Cooper's *Black Mass.*[8] Then I am going to consider how much history is in and on the films, plus what hidden agendas the directors had in making these movies. Then I'm going to tell someone, anyone, what I think!

In short, I'm going to try with my last breath to make the world better for my children and grandchildren. The last thing I want when it's all over, is someone saying he quit too soon. He talked the talk, but never walked the walk!

And what of you? I hope you will think the time with me was well spent, the information valuable; and getting past my weak prose and the academic bluster was not as difficult as you first thought. That said; let me end our journey together by recalling a scene from Brad Bird's idealistic but uneven film, *Tomorrowland*:

An English teacher is lecturing his students on how literature often reflects life, and what we think impossible sometimes comes true. He reminds his impressionable audience that futurist novels like Aldous Huxley's *Brave New World,* George Orwell's *1984,* and Ray Bradbury's *Fahrenheit 451* were once considered fiction, but they are happening right now. Moreover, he laments, things seem to be getting worse.

At that moment, a student raises her hand and says, "Yes, but what are you going to do about it?"[9]

Notes

[1] Carl Sandburg, *Always the Young Strangers*. New York: Harcourt, Brace and Company, 1953.
[2] www.brainyquote.com.
[3] Betty Comden & Albert Green/Jule Styne, Broadway Musical *Bells are Ringing,* 1956.
[4] Maxwell Anderson & Kurt Weill, Broadway Musical *Knickerbocker Holiday,* 1930. Walter Huston starred in the 1938 revival.
[5] Cy Coleman & Dorothy Fields, Broadway Musical *Sweet Charity,* 1966.

[6] Paul Lazarus, *SlingShot*. USA: White Dwarf Productions, 2014.
[7] Jake Silverstein, The Displaced," *The New York Times Magazine*, November 8, 2015. 45.
[8] I indebted to the *New York Times'* Holiday Film list for 2015-16.
[9] Brad Bird, *Tomorrowland*. USA: Walt Disney Pictures, 2015.

Appendix I

Talking Pictures

Professor Emeritus Frank Manchel's love of film began in the movie houses of New York City in the 1940s, where his working parents found a reliable babysitter and Manchel got his first glimpse of the art form that would become his passion. David Franzoni '71 grew up in Rutland, Vermont, where his first foray into filmmaking was his high school project about a "Russian sniper," abandoned for lack of the cash to buy more 16mm film. The two met at the University of Vermont in the 1960s/70s, where Franzoni's interest in film drew him to Manchel's classes and a strong mentorship/friendship began to grow, one that would continue long past graduation. On a life transforming post-college motorcycle trip around the world, David Franzoni's love of film crystallized into the desire to become a screenwriter, a dream that has been realized far beyond hope. Citizen Cohn, Amistad, Gladiator, King Arthur, and the upcoming Hannibal—Franzoni has become one of Hollywood's most successful and serious screenwriters. With King Arthur on the way to video and Hannibal headed to a theater near you, Franzoni, the Hollywood screenwriter, and Manchel, the film scholar, sat down for a conversation about new movies and old times.

MANCHEL: David, one of the things I've always believed in is that when somebody writes about history, they're really using history to talk about the present. Do you agree with that?

FRANZONI: One of the things I said when I sat down with Steven Spielberg to first talk about *Gladiator* was we can't really make this about ancient Rome. Try to imagine this isn't ancient Rome as much as it is Los Angeles a thousand years from now. Mike Ovitz is a model for Proximo. Ted Turner is a model for Commodus. And this is Dodger Stadium and the CAA agents all represent the gladiators. And Ridley (Scott, *Gladiator,* director) got into thinking of it like that, too. And everyone has always remarked and always seen the movie as fresh and modern rather than like some stagy old ancient piece.

One of the best things that happened when we had the premiere is that the World Wrestling Federation had a huge camera set up there to interview us. They got it completely. I was really happy they were there. I said, "Yeah, this is about you guys. This is about the way we are consumed by the media. We are consumed by our entertainment."

MANCHEL: After reviewing your films now for two weeks, I've noticed that you are much more of a traditionalist than I thought when I started thinking about the interview. In *Amistad* and *Gladiator* and *King Arthur*, you have this father-son relationship and these strong family relationships. Unlike a lot of films I see, you don't criticize, you put something up from the past as a way of presenting a model for the present. Did you do that intentionally or am I misreading it?

FRANZONI: No, you're not wrong, *Gladiator* is a perfect example. I've always told everyone that *Gladiator* is about family. One example is the family of Marcus Aurelius, which is one of the most dysfunctional families of the time and the extension of that family is what Rome has become. Whereas the family of Maximus is probably the most perfect family you could imagine. It's not a hyperbole; I don't think his family is unreal.

MANCHEL: You seem to hammer that theme over and over again, and you do it in such a beautiful way that I'm surprised that no one talks about it.

FRANZONI: One of the reasons I do that is because I believe, as Americans in particular, that there is this core value we have—corrupted, of course—that is fashioned around the family and about love and trust in the family and that those are the pillars of this country. Besides that, I also think that allows people to get into the movie. It is not about the Prince of Persia or Ben Hur, it's about us.

MANCHEL: I think you're one of the great screenwriters of our generation because you take it seriously. To you, it's not a trivial exercise. I mean the pain and the effort is so clear in the writing. But when I watched *King Arthur*, I felt as if the film had nothing to do with the script. I spent a good deal of my life, as you know, studying the Middle Ages, studying King Arthur, and I've seen almost every movie ever made about the period. None was as fresh as *King Arthur* in terms of the originality, in terms of the script, and then when you watch the movie, it looks like they were making a comedy—-

FRANZONI: Well, they had comedy writers come in and work on it.

MANCHEL: You're kidding.

FRANZONI: No, no, no, they had five writers come in while I was there as executive producer. When we wrote the original script, it was basically supposed to be *Platoon*. The idea was this is the fall of Saigon, Arthur and his knights are this one last group of Special Forces. They can't get in the helicopter leaving from the top of the embassy. They have to go north for one last mission. Merlin is Ho Chi Min and the Sarnations are the Viet Cong. That was the metaphor for this thing and the original script was unbelievably cut. They came in and put in all of that crappy *Top Gun* dialogue and messed up the structure. The problem is that these people don't understand what they're doing. So when intuitively, they wreck the structure. Then you start out with a broken script. Then when we get to Ireland, the director began rewriting the script and we had actors writing their own dialogue. That's why every time Clive (Owen, who plays *King Arthur*) opens his mouth it sounds like he's making a speech. He wrote a lot of that because he wants to sound like he's in an Elizabethan movie.

MANCHEL: I don't understand why they hire you then, if that's what happens to the script. With your talent and stature in the field, why do you persist in the Hollywood film as opposed to the independent film?

FRANZONI: I personally believe that most independent films today are nothing more than cheap Hollywood films. I don't find them particularly good. I mean, there are some. But I haven't seen a *La Dolce Vita*. I haven't seen a *Conformist*. I haven't seen anything out there that really just knocks me out of my shoes. If I have to go the independent route, I will. But what I want to do—and I think the most subversive thing you can do—is to do what I want to do within the system, not without it. I'm trying to set up something to direct based on a script I have that, I think, in their (the Hollywood studios) minds is quirky, and commercial, and cheap enough that they'll do it. I think you have to do it in the system. I think the studio system has corrupted the independent market almost totally.

MANCHEL: I find the critics are just as corrupt as the –

FRANZONI: There are no critics; this is not the days of Pauline Kael. We're just talking about people who are going to tell you whether to go to "Magic Mountain" and which rides to go on. They're not trying to criticize films. They don't know how to criticize films. One of the new girls working for the *L.A. Times*, apparently is a big critic over there, has never even heard of the French New Wave. I was working in Paris and people would come on the set to talk to us about what we were doing, everybody knew about film. They were steeped in it. Here, they are like ex-weathermen. There's no film criticism.

MANCHEL: You couldn't be an intellectual in the sixties and seventies without film as the center of everything. That is all gone today. This is the year that the three most successful films are *The Passion of the Christ, Fahrenheit 9/11,* and *Shrek II*. That's where we've come to, it seems to me, and I don't see anyone objecting to it.

FRANZONI: They're not objecting, of course, because the money is rolling in. Look, the only reason that we had sort of—I wouldn't call it a golden moment—but *Easy Rider* came out and nobody could figure out what the hell it was and why it made money, so they kind of let people play with cameras for a while and we got some stuff.

MANCHEL: And it was also an intellectual exercise, we had the rise of the art houses in the fifties and sixties, so people thought it was like going to the opera when you went to a film.

FRANZONI: There were consumers for it. Today, what I'm looking toward right now, to sort of give us some direction is popular music. For me, hip-hop has become nothing more than angry elevator music. It has completely lost its stature in the art world. Fortunately, there's a group called Green Day and their #1 hit, and it's been #1 forever, is called "American Idiot" and it's about what you're talking about. Maybe there's some hope when kids are starting to react against this disgusting crassness that, apparently, some generation between you and me has just hammered in place. You can't get rid of it.

MANCHEL: Who were the major influences on your writing?

FRANZONI: Well, besides you, filmmakers you mean? The French New Wave. Truffaut, Fellini, Antonioni, Bertolucci.

MANCHEL: But not Americans, you don't mention Americans.

FRANZONI: I don't have any favorites.

MANCHEL: Not John Ford?

FRANZONI: I like John Ford. The problem for me with John Ford is that although I admire the movies and what he does with them, they're always predictable to me. I always know how they're going to turn out. You know what I mean?

MANCHEL: What about Sam Peckinpah?

FRANZONI: Well, off and on Peckinpah. Sure, *The Wild Bunch*, fantastic. When he was great, he was great. Other American films—*Vanishing Point, Easy Rider, Cuckoo's Nest* to a certain extent, *Badlands*...

MANCHEL: How about *The Godfather*?

FRANZONI: No *The Godfather* didn't do anything for me. I didn't dislike them...I don't know, maybe I've seen them too much.

MANCHEL: Through the years, I've always had students ask — what course should I take, where should I go, how can I get into the film industry? What do you recommend?

FRANZONI: It depends on what you want to do. If you want to be a screenwriter, you don't have to go to film school. It's better to go get a list from someone like Frank Manchel of films to see and go rent them. That's A Number One. A Number Two is read scripts. Get them on-line, anywhere. See how people write in different styles. Find movies that you admire. That's what I did. I found movies that I admired, like Alvin Sargent was at that time doing *Julia* and I wanted to see how he was writing. Because back then it was up against *Star Wars*, and everything else just seemed ridiculous. I went to the script library at UCLA and I read his scripts.

If you're going to write a spec script that you want people to respond to, don't try to write the same BS that is out there. Don't go, "I'm going to write the new...*Spiderman.*" Just don't even waste your time because everybody is always doing that all of the time. So, all of the scripts studios get across their desks are the same old stuff.

First of all, you should be writing something that you really want to say, because people will notice right away if it's an honest exercise or if it's just an exercise. And you should try, struggle, strive, to do something different. It's like art when you're trying to paint or sculpt. Well, try doing this with marble instead of trying to do the piazza, try to do…a frog with a square head or something. Just try, as an exercise, to find ways of creating scripts.

You don't need to go to school for that. You need to see films. In most cases, for most people, I think film school is a tremendous waste of time. If you want to learn a technical craft, yes, that can help. If you want to learn how to edit, or want to learn how to handle a camera, lighting…

MANCHEL: My argument has been, first of all, I think it's most important to get a liberal arts education before you even think about a professional career.

FRANZONI: Of course you've got to do that. I'm assuming that you've done that.

MANCHEL: No, most of these people say, I want to go directly to USC or UCLA. What's the point of getting a break if you have nothing to say? If you have no background?

FRANZONI: The first thing I advise is get a life. You're talking about an art form. You can't create art if you're empty. Get a life by going to college. Get a life by traveling. I know that everyone wants to run right to film school, right to Hollywood. I was 29 when I came to Hollywood. I'd traveled around the world on a motorcycle. I'd done some things. I had a lot of guns stuck in my face. I've had a life. So, I was passionate about what I was writing about. We don't need any more people writing movies about the movies they've seen, because it is a downward spiral.

My second advice is if you want to direct a film, go pick up a camera. Today, with digital stuff, it's a joke. When I was in high school I tried to shoot a film about a Russian sniper and I just ran out of money trying to shoot the film on 16 millimeter. I just couldn't finish it. You don't have that problem these days. You can go get a damn digital camera. You can edit it on your freakin' computer. You don't have to show it to anybody, but you can do it. You can get your hands dirty without spending any money.

MANCHEL: Tell me about UVM, what was it like back in the seventies for you?

FRANZONI: It was very exciting. When you went to see a movie back in the sixties and the seventies, which is the only thing I can speak for because in the fifties I was back in Rutland, Vermont watching *Godzilla*. You'd go to the cinema at the college and you saw *Breathless*, or whatever, and it was part of your conversation, it was part of your life. You'd sit down and have dinner and talk and you were talking about these films. They weren't an entertainment. It was something compelling and crucial to see.

MANCHEL: The thing that I remember about you at UVM was that you always made it a point to engage people. You weren't a passive student who went to class, took the assignment, did your paper, got your grades, and walked on. Class was not something that was separated from your life. Also, you were one of the few people I've met in my life who always tried to get me involved in some scheme—why don't you invest in this? Do you remember that?

FRANZONI: (Laughs) Probably...

MANCHEL: After UVM, you traveled to Europe and stayed for quite a while.

FRANZONI: I wanted to check it out. I felt a draw. I had been reading about it. I'm not drawn to the pueblos; the Amazon doesn't draw me. I'm drawn to Europe, the richness of the culture. The motorcycle trip was a big one. There were times I had to sell my blood for money, but that's all part of it. If you go over there and you do the elite tour you never see anything. When I got back from the trip around the world I saw this book in the UVM bookstore, *India on $50 a Day*. I was doing it on 50 cents a day. You could buy India for $50 a day. No wonder the guy had a good time.

MANCHEL: What was it about that motorcycle trip? You've said it was when you decided to be a screenwriter.

FRANZONI: Well, I was a knight. I was Don Quixote, with all that that implies on my trip around the world. I wasn't necessarily righting wrongs, but I wanted to at least see what the wrongs were. Being on a motorcycle, unlike being a hippie in a van, people responded to me in every country where I went. You came here on a motorcycle? Come have dinner with us. Stay with us. They put me up on the floor of their restaurants. It just opened up the door to everybody. I had that feeling of being a knight, of being completely free, and it actually turned out to be not just an imaginary concept. It was a real concept.

MANCHEL: If we can get back to the process of your writing, do you feel that every scene you write has to drive the story?

FRANZONI: Here's my opinion. Until you discover who your main character is, you can't write the story, which is the opposite of what Hollywood does. They want you to write the story and then we'll fix the characters later. For me, Maximus, the entire landscape of *Gladiator,* is Maximus's soul. It's all about Maximus. There isn't a scene in that movie that isn't about Maximus in some way—about what he said, about what he believed, about what he's striving for, everything is about him. None of it is disconnected from him. To me, you sit down and you take a hard look at your lead character, you try to understand everything about that man, that woman, and the movie happens from there.

MANCHEL: Do you have somebody in mind when you write a character?

FRANZONI: Never.

MANCHEL: So, I'm not in any of your films? (Laughs)

FRANZONI: Oh, you're in every one. I can't get rid of you.

MANCHEL: How do you build characterization? Your characters are complex—in *Gladiator* there are things about Commodus that you hate, but there are things that make your heart go out to him.

FRANZONI: That's against the Hollywood grain. I think what you have to do is look at Commodus; the big tragedy in his life is that he was always looking for his father's love. When I was in Austin at the film festival, a high school kid asked me, "If your parents fight all of the time, should you use it?" I told him that you've got to use that stuff. Don't use your parents, but what you feel about that, what they're saying to each other. Take a hard look at what their fights are about. Because wherever there's this kind of emotion, something is going on. You can make a king say those things, because the emotionalism is all. I think that you have to look at the people around you. That's why you have to have a life.

MANCHEL: Big question. I was recently telling someone that I think one of the greatest tragedies of the 20th century is the way the public responded to the media. They think that it's trivial, it's trite, and that it gets in the way. But we could not have had all of the major events of the past 50 years if it had not been for the media—

imagine the civil rights movement without television, imagine reading Martin Luther King's speech without hearing it or seeing it. How do you convince people of the importance of film in our lives?

FRANZONI: It's tough. I will not sit down to write unless I can find a way to make it important to me. After *Amistad*, I was introduced to a new agent who asked me to define exactly what I wanted him to do for me. I told him, "Here's what our job is, plain and simple: change the world."

Appendix II

Friendship in Film

The relationship between Academy Award winning cinematographer Robert Richardson, who is a former UVM student, and Frank Manchel, professor emeritus of English and film, is seemingly not the stuff of a Hollywood screenplay. No embrace on the stage at graduation (there was no UVM graduation, in fact, for Richardson), no annual dinners to talk over the old days, yet the two have a late-blooming bond that has opened across time and distance.

Richardson, who won an Academy Award (his third) this year for his work on Martin Scorsese's *Hugo*, enrolled at UVM in 1973 and would spend a couple of years on campus before leaving for another school. While the university can't claim him as a graduate, the transformation that set his path in life did take place here. It began with watching Ingmar Bergman's *The Seventh Seal* at a film society screening on campus.

Richardson was transfixed, entering into a "zone" where everything beyond what was taking place on the screen fell away. "I think Bergman taught me how to look through an eyepiece," Richardson recalls. "I think he taught me how to live inside of an eyepiece as if you are living in the zone. And I mean zone almost as akin to Jordan getting into the zone in basketball or anyone when they find that special place."

Struck to the core by the legendary director's artistry, the previously unfocused undergrad quickly beat a path to film courses, which led directly to Professor Frank Manchel's classroom. "Frank Manchel forced me into places I never would have walked and opened the door to extraordinary things," Richardson told journalist Susan Green in an interview for the *Burlington Free Press* in 2004.

"But he was very tough on me. His grading on my papers? Oh, Lordy! Even so, those classes were inspirational. He's the most intelligent person I've met in the film world, in terms of teaching—as brilliant as Quentin Tarantino and Marty Scorsese."

Sitting down for coffee in the Davis Center, basking in the glow of a late afternoon sun and the recent Super Bowl victory by his beloved New York Giants, Manchel laughs at Richardson's memory. The retired professor recalls that when students would ask him about his reputation for being stingy with an A grade, he would say: "A + is for God, A is for me: B+ is good enough for the rest of you."

Richardson took all the classes he could with Manchel, though he admits he audited some to spare himself the lash of the professor's red pen. A seminar on war films was among the courses in which he learned with Manchel. Some twelve years later, Richardson's breakthrough as a major motion picture cinematographer would come on a war film, Oliver Stone's *Salvador*. The genre has been central to Richardson's work, including Stone's *Platoon* and *Born on the Fourth of July*, and Quentin Tarantino's *Inglorious Basterds*, among others.

Richardson ultimately left UVM for a deeper education in hands-on filmmaking than the university could provide. He transferred to the Rhode Island School of Design for his undergraduate work and later earned a master of fine arts from the American Film Institute Conservatory.

REEL LIVES

Inspiring students to careers in film was familiar ground for Manchel during his long tenure on the UVM faculty. Among the most notable: screenwriter David Franzoni '71, best-known for *Gladiator* and other sweeping historical dramas, and producer Jon Kilik '78, who initially built his career through collaborations with director Spike Lee, has added names such as Julian Schnabel, Jim Jarmusch, Robert Altman, and Alejandro Gonzalez Inarritu to the list of leading directors he's partnered with, and just produced his first blockbuster with *The Hunger Games*.

Kilik and Franzoni have largely remained close with Manchel through the years. With Richardson, it was a different story. Manchel had no idea of his influence on the cinematographer until he read Green's article in the *Free Press* some thirty years after Richardson had left UVM. But he and his former student would soon reconnect and have stayed in touch since with emails back and forth at least once a week, though they hadn't met in person or talked on the phone over the past eight years.

That changed in February when Richardson and Manchel talked film for seventy minutes on the phone, a wide-ranging conversation excerpted in *Vermont Quarterly* online. Calling the VQ office from a longtime family home base on Cape Cod, Richardson spoke to the role the running e-dialogue with his old professor has had in his life. "I don't have an ongoing email relationship with many people in the business. Frank is rather unusual for me;" Richardson says. "So the aspects of what I share with him are a wonderful balance between personal and professional. We can communicate about anything in the industry. This is a strong comfort zone."

Their running email dialogue is usually about film, of course, and often Richardson's current and future projects. While his work has earned three Academy Awards, seven nominations, and the admiration of his former professor, it doesn't mean that the feisty professor is necessarily inclined to approve of all of his films.

Manchel had a deep disregard for Tarantino's *Inglorious Basterds* and he let Richardson know it. The cinematographer tried to bring him around, sending positive reviews and the commentary of others. Though Manchel stands his ground, Richardson hasn't given up on convincing him of the movie's worth.

Manchel recounts their exchange about *Eat, Pray, Love,* an atypical Richardson project, which he took on a desire to do something different. "He asked me what I thought;" Manchel says. "I wrote, 'The opening shot was so beautiful…it's a shame it couldn't have been a documentary.'" Richardson's quick reply: "I get your point."

No such worries with *Hugo,* a film beloved by Manchel and many, many others. As Richardson accepted the 2012 Academy Award for his cinematography at the Kodak Theatre in Los Angeles, Frank Manchel was on the other side of the continent in a setting that was less glamorous, maybe, but more comfortable—a seat on the couch in front of the TV applauding a student once lost, a friend later found.

Bibliography

Adler, Mortimer J. *What Makes a Great Book Great? Great Ideas from the Great Books.* New York: Washington Square Press, Inc., 1961.

Adler, Renata. "'The Heart Is a Lonely Hunter': Alan Arkin Starred in McCullers Story Dean Martin Western Is at Local Houses." *New York Times*, August, 1968.

AFI Tribute to Orson Welles. USA: American Film Institute, 1975.

Agee, James and Walter Evans. *Let Us Now Praise Famous Men.* Boston: Houghton Mifflin Company, 1941.

Aleiss, Angela Maria. *From Adversaries to Allies: The American Indian in American Films, 1930-1950.* Ph. D. Dissertation, Columbia University, 1991.

Aleiss, Angela Maria. *Hollywood's Ideal of Postwar Assimilation: Indian/White Attitudes in Broken Arrow.* MFA Thesis, Columbia University, 1985.

Alexander, Michelle. Introduction. *The New Jim Crow: Mass Incarceration in the Age of Colorblindness.* New York: The New Press, 2012.

Allen, Robert C. and Douglas Gomery. *Film History: Theory and Practice.* New York: Alfred A. Knopf, 1985.

Anderson, Maxwell and Kurt Weill. *Knickerbocker Holiday.* Broadway Musical, 1930.

Andrew, Dudley. *An Open Approach to Film Study and the Situation at Iowa. Film Study in the Undergraduate Curriculum.* Ed. Barry Keith Grant. New York: Modern Language Association, 1983.

Anker, David. *Imaginary Witness: Hollywood and the Holocaust.* USA: Shadow Distribution, 2004.

Ansen, David and Allison Samuels. "Amistad." *Newsweek*, December 8, 1997.

Ansen, David and Allison Samuels. "The Long Shadow of Slavery." *Newsweek*, December 8, 1997.

Apted, Michael. *Amazing Grace.* Britain: Bristol Bay Productions, 2007.

Arcand, Denys. *The Barbarian Invasions*. France: Pyramide Productions, 2003.
Ascher, Rodney. *Secrets of* The Shining *Panel Discussion, Room 237*. DVD. USA: Highland Park Classics, 2012.
Avildsen, John G. *Lean on Me*. USA: Warner Bros., 1989.
Avisar, Ilan. *Screening the Holocaust: Cinema's Image of the Unimaginable* Bloomington, Ind.: Indiana University Press, 1988.
"Backstage at the Oscars." *Variety,* March 22, 1994.
Baron, Lawrence. *The Modern Jewish Experience in World Cinema*. Waltham: Brandeis, 2011.
Baxter, John. *The Hollywood Exiles*. New York: Taplinger Publishing Company, 1976.
Beebe, Ford I. and Robert F. Hill. *Flash Gordon's Trip to Mars*. USA: Universal Pictures, 1938.
Bennetts, Leslie. "How Cicely Tyson Got to Teach in Wales". *New York Times*, August 22 1983.
Bentley, Eric. *Are You Now or Have You Ever Been, and Other Plays*. New York: Harper & Row, 1972.
Bentley, Eric, ed., *Thirty Years of Treason: Excerpts from Hearings Before the House Committee on Un-American Activities*, 1938-1968. New York: Viking Press, 1971.
Benton, Robert. *The Human Stain*. USA: Miramax, 2003.
Bergman, Andrew. *The Freshman*. USA: Tri Star Pictures, 1990.
Bergman, Ingmar. *The Seventh Seal*. Sweden: Svensk Filmindustri (SF), 1957.
Benzine, Adam. *Claude Lanzmann: Spectres of the Shoah*. USA: Jet Black Iris American, 2015.
Bernard, Emily. *Carl Van Vechten & the Harlem Renaissance: A Portrait in Black & White*. New Haven and London: Yale University Press, 2012.
Bessie, Alvah. *Inquisition in Eden*. New York: Macmillan and Company, 1965.
Bettelheim, Bruno. "Reflections: Surviving." *The New Yorker*, August 2, 1976.
Bingham, Dennis. *Whose Lives are They Anyway?: The Biopic as Contemporary Film Genre*. New Brunswick, N.J.: Rutgers University Press, 2010.
Bird, Brad. *Tomorrowland*. USA: Walt Disney Pictures, 2015.
Blair, Jon. *Schindler: The Real Story*. England: Thames Television, 1994.
Blau, Eleanor. "James Earl Jones: How Does an Actor Make his 'Statement' as an Artist." *The New York Times*, October 10, 1980.
Bogle, Donald. *Blacks in American Films and Television: An Encyclopedia*. New York: Garland Publishing, Inc., 1988.
Bordwell, David, and Kristin Thompson. *Film Art: An Introduction*. 5th Ed. New York: McGraw, 1997.

Bourne, St. Claire. *Paul Robeson: Here I Stand*. USA: American Masters, 1999.
Bradbury, Ray. *Fahrenheit 451*. New York: Ballantine Books, 1953.
Brantley, Ben. "Home Is Where the Years Disappear: 'The Trip to Bountiful' at the Stephen Sondheim Theater." *New York Times*, April 24, 2013.
Breitman, Richard and Allan J. Lichtman. *FDR and The Jews*. Cambridge: The Belknap Press of Harvard University Press, 2013.
Bridges, James. *The Paper Chase*. USA: Twentieth Century-Fox, 1973.
Brooklyn Dodgers: The Ghosts of Flatbush. USA: Major League Baseball Productions, 2007.
Brooks, James L. *Terms of Endearment*. USA: Paramount Pictures, 1983.
Brooks, Richard. *The Blackboard Jungle*. USA: MGM, 1955.
Brooks, Richard. *The Professionals*. USA: Columbia Pictures, 1966.
Brown, Jim and Steve Delsohn. *Out of Bounds*. New York: Zebra Books, 1990.
Brown, William Wells. *The Black Man: His Antecedents, His Genius, And His Achievements*. Boston: James Redpath, 1863. Kraus Reprint Company, 1969.
Buob, Jacques. *L'honneur de Herr Schindler (The Honor of Mister Schindler)*. *L'Express* February 24, 1994.
Burns, Ken. *Unforgivable Blackness: The Rise and Fall of Jack Johnson*. 3 Episodes. USA: WETA, 2004.
Burns, Ken. *Jackie Robinson*. USA: PBS, 2016.
Cable, Mary. *Black Odyssey: The Case of the Slave Ship Amistad*. New York: Penguin Books, 1971.
Caine, Michael. "Interview with James Lipton." *Inside the Actor's Studio*. Bravo. Film and Arts Network: New York, 1997.
Canby, Vincent. "Milestones Can Be Millstones: They Call Me Mr. Tibb." *New York Times*, July 19 1970.
Carabello, Marlene. *The Great Indian Wars: 1540-1890*. USA: Dan Dalton Productions, 1991.
Carpenter, Susan. "Hartford High School." *The La Mancha Newsletter*, ed. Littleton Long. Vol. 1. May 1969.
Carr, Ian. *Miles Davis, the Definitive Biography*. Emeryville, CA: Thunder's Mouth Press, 1999.
Carr, Jay. "Bold and Brutal, *Amistad*, a Powerful and Compelling Work." *Boston Globe*, December 26, 1997.
Cawelti, John. *The Six-Gun Mystique*. Bowling Green: Bowling Green UP, 1970.
Cayton, William. *Jack Johnson*. USA: Big Fights, 1970.
Chaikin, Judy. *Legacy of the Hollywood Blacklist*. USA: One Step Productions, 1987.

Champagne, Duane, ed. "Chapter 13: Media." *The Native North American Almanac: A Reference Work on Native Americans in the United States and Canada.* Detroit: Gale Research Inc., 1994.

Chaplin, Charles. *The Great Dictator.* USA: United Artists, 1940.

Chase-Riboud, Barbara. *Echoes of Lions.* New York: William Morrow, 1989.

Chazelle, Damien. *Whiplash.* USA: Sony Pictures Classics, 2014.

Cheadle, Don. *Miles Ahead.* USA: Bifrost Pictures, 2015.

Chomsky, Marvin J. *Inside The Third Reich.* USA: The History Channel, 1982.

Christensen, Bonnie. Obituary. *Burlington Free Press,* January 24, 2015.

Cieply, Michael and Brooks Barnes. "Oscars Less White? There's No Shortage of Black Fims in 2016," *New York Times.Com* (May10, 2016).

Ciment, Michel. *Kubrick.* New York: Holt, Rinehart and Winston, 1980.

Clavell, James. *To Sir, With Love.* USA: Columbia Pictures, 1967.

Coates, Ta-Nehisi. "The Black Family in the Age of Mass Incarceration." *The Atlantic* Vol. 316, No. 3. October 2015.

Cocks, Jay. "A Battle Over Justice." *Time,* May 12, 1975.

Cocteau, Jean. *Sunday, the 28th, Beauty and the Beast: Diary of a Film.* Adapted by George Amberg. Mineola, New York: Dover Publications, 1946.

Cogley, John. *Report on Blacklisting: 1 – Movies.* New York: The Fund for the Republic, 1956.

Cohen, Alan. "The Collapse of Family and Language in Stephen King's *The Shining.*" *The Shining Reader,* ed. by Anthony Magistrale. Mercer Island, WA: Starmont House, 1990.

Cohen, Roger. "The Cruelty and the Depravity: A Historian Depicts the Concentration Camps Where Many of the Holocaust's Millions Died." *New York Times Book Review,* July 12, 2015.

Coixet, Isobel. *Elegy.* USA: Lakeshore Entertainment, 2008

Coixet, Isobel. *My Life Without Me.* Netherlands: El Deseo, 2003.

Cole, Lester. *Hollywood Red: The Autobiography of Lester Cole.* Palo Alto: Ramparts Press, 1981.

Coleman, Cy and Dorothy Fields. *Sweet Charity.* Broadway Musical, 1966.

Collins, Shirley S. "Champlain Valley Union High School." *The La Mancha Newsletter,* ed. Littleton Long. Vol. 1. May 1969.

Comden, Betty and Albert Green/Jule Styne. *Bells are Ringing.* Broadway Musical, 1956.

Comolli, Timothy. "South Burlington High School." *The La Mancha Newsletter,* ed. Littleton Long. Vol. 1. May 1969.

Cook, Bruce. *Dalton Trumbo.* New York: Charles Scribner's Sons, 1977.

Crabtree, Susan. "Afghan Pic Reels in D.C. Pols." *Variety,* March 1-7, 2004.

Cropper, Steve. *Soul Man.* USA: New World Productions 1986.

Crouch, Stanley. *Always in Pursuit: Fresh American Perspectives.* New York: Vintage Books, 1998.

Crouch, Stanley. *Considering Genius: Writings on Jazz.* New York: Basic Civitas Books, 2006.
Crouch, Stanley. *The All-American Skin Game, or the Decoy of Race.* New York: Vintage Books, 1995.
Custen, George F. *Bio/Pics: How Hollywood Constructed Public History.* New Brunswick, N.J.: Rutgers University Press, 1992.
DaCosta, Morton. *Auntie Mame.* USA: Warner Bros, 1958.
Daves, Delmer. *Broken Arrow.* USA: 1950. Twentieth Century-Fox, 1950.
Daves, Delmer. *Kings Go Forth.* USA: MGM, 1958.
Davis, Miles. *The Complete Jack Johnson Sessions.* USA: Sony Music Entertainment, Inc., 1971.
Dayton, Alison M. and Jean M. Minotti. "Ninth Grade General Program in Mass Communication (Revised Curriculum)." *The La Mancha Newsletter* II: 1 July 1970.
Debonne, Yann and Craig Haffner. *The Real West.* Arts & Entertainment Network documentary series, 1993.
Deloria, Vine, Jr. *Custer Died for Your Sins.* New York: Avon Books, 1969.
Denby, David. "Cry Freedom." *New York Magazine,* December 15, 1997.
Denby, David. *Do The Movies Have a Future?* New York: Simon & Schuster, 2012.
Dibb, Mike. *The Miles Davis Story.* USA: Channel Four Television Corporation, 2001.
"Die Ganze Wahrheit Schwarz auf Weiss" (The whole truth in black and white). *Der Spiegel.* February 21, 1994.
"Diego Rivera: Rivera in America." *American Masters*, Season 3, Episode 5. USA: Eagle Rock Entertainment, August, 1988.
DiOrio, Carl. "Valenti Valedictory View an Eye-Opener." *Variety,* March 29-April 4, 2004.
Donen, Stanley. *Interview with James Lipton. Inside the Actor's Studio.* New York: Bravo Film and Arts Network, 1998.
Donnelly, Ann and Elizabeth Woledge. *Shakespeare: Work, Life and Times.* London: Jigsaw Design and Publishing, 2012.
Dreyer, Carl Theodor. *The Passion of Jeanne D'Arc.* France: Gaumont, 1928.
Driscoll, F. Paul. "Opera Queen." *Opera News,* March 2016.
Duke, Bill. *Hoodlum.* USA: United Artists, 1997.
Dunne, Philip. *Take Two: A Life in Movies and Politics.* New York: McGraw-Hill Book Company, 1980.
Dworkin, Martin. "Clean German and Dirty Politics." *Film Comment,* Winter, 1965.
Early, Gerald. *This is Where I Came in: Black America in the 1960s.* Lincoln: University of Nebraska Press, 2003.
Egoyan, Atom. *Remember.* USA: Serendipity Point Films, 2015.

Eliot, T. S. *The Complete Poems and Plays 1909-1950*. New York: Harcourt, Brace and Company, 1950.

Elisberg, Robert J. "E-Mail Interview with David Franzoni." *WGA*. 1997.

Eller, Claudia and James Bates. "Company Town: Despite 'Serious Questions' Judge to Let 'Amistad' Open" *Los Angeles Times*, December 9, 1997.

Emerson, Ralph Waldo. *'Self-Reliance: Essay II,' The Collected Works of Ralph Waldo Emerson*, Volume II. Cambridge: Harvard University Press, 1979.

Evan, David. *My Nazi Legacy* USA: PBS Independent Lens, 2016.

Fein, Bruce. "As the Amistad Edict Evolved." *Commentary*, December 31, 1997.

Feldstein, Ruth. *How It Feels to Be Free: Black Women Entertainers and the Civil Rights Movement*. New York: Oxford University Press, 2013.

Fellini, Federico. *La Strada (The Road)*. Italy: Dino de Laurentiis Distributions, 1954.

Fenin, George N. and William K. Everson, *The Western from Silents to the Seventies*. New York: Grossman, 1973.

Ferber, Edna. *So Big*. New York: Doubleday, 1924.

Ferreira, Patricia. *Jack's Nightmare at the Overlook: The American Dream Inverted. The Shining Reader*, ed. by Anthony Magistrale. Mercer Island, WA: Starmont House, 1990.

Ferro, Marc. "Film as an Agent, Product and Source of History." *Journal of Contemporary History*, July, 1983.

Fincher, David. *The Social Network*. USA: Columbia Pictures, 2010.

Flemyng, George. *The Split*. USA: MGM, 1968.

Ford, John. *Sergeant Rutledge*. USA: Warner Bros, 1960.

Ford, John. *The Searchers*. USA: Warner Bros, 1956.

Foster, Norman and Sam Wanamaker. *The Legend of Custer*. USA: Twentieth Century-Fox Film Corporation, 1968.

Fraser, C. Gerald. "John Bright, 81, a Screen Writer." *New York Times*, September 16, 1989.

Fuchs, Henry. Obituary. *Brooklyn Daily*, Friday April 13, 1956.

Gabbard, Krin. *Jammin' at the Margins: Jazz and the American Cinema*. Chicago: The University of Chicago Press, 1996.

Gabler, Neal. *An Empire of Their Own: How the Jews Invented Hollywood*. New York: Crown Publishers, 1988.

Gardner, Elysa. "Driving Miss Daisy Down Memory Lane with a Ghost." *USA Today*, Oct. 22 2010.

Garris, Mick. *The Stand*. USA: Greengrass Productions, 1994.

Gavin, James. *Stormy Weather: The Life of Lena Horne*. New York: Atria Books, 2009.

Gennari, John. *Blowin' Hot and Cool: Jazz and Its Critics*. Chicago and London: The University of Chicago Press, 2006.

Giannetti, Louis. *Understanding Movies*. 7th ed. Englewood Cliffs: Prentice-Hall, 1996.

Gilbert, Lewis. *Educating Rita*. USA: Columbia Pictures, 1983.

Gilmour, David. *The Film Club*. New York: Twelve, 2008.

Glasrud, Bruce A. and Alan M. Smith. *Promises to Keep: A Portrayal of Nonwhites in the United States*. Chicago: Rand McNally, 1972.

Glenville, Peter. *The Comedians*. USA: MGM, 1967.

Goethe, Johann Wolfgang von. "Wilhelm Meister's Apprentice." Translated by Eric A. Blackall. *Goethe's Collected Works* Vol. 9. New York: Suhrkamp, 1989.

Goldstein, Warren. "Bad History is Bad for a Culture." *The Chronicle of Higher Education*, April 10, 1998.

Goldworthy, Joan and Sara Pendergast. *Cicely Tyson*. Contemporary Black Biography, Gale Cengage Learning, 1992.

Gomery, Douglas. "Hollywood, the National Recovery Administration, and the Question of Monopoly Power." *Journal of the University Film Association* 31:2, Spring 1979.

Goodman, Barak. *American Experience: My Lai*. USA: WGBH/PBS, 2010.

Gourevitch, Philip. "A Dissent on Schindler's List." *Commentary*, February 1994.

Graves, Robert. *Greek Gods and Heroes*. New York: Dell Laurel-Leaf, 1960.

Gray, Thomas. *Elegy Written in a Country Churchyard*. 1751.

Gregory, Don. *James Earl Jones as Paul Robeson*. USA: Kultur, 2005.

Griffith, James. *Adaptations as Imitations: Films from Novels*. Newark, Delaware: University of Delaware Press, 1997.

Grindon, Leger. *Shadows on the Past*. Philadelphia: Temple University, 1994.

Gross, John. "Hollywood and the Holocaust." *New York Review of Books*. February 3, 1994.

Grove, Martin A. *Hollywood Report:* Schindler *Global Hit*; Maverick *Sneaks Well*. *Hollywood Reporter*, April 6, 1994.

Gunther, Lenworth. *Black Stereotypes*. Encore, July, 1973.

Gutierrez, Eric. *News Analysis: The Politics of Filmmaking*. New York Times, December 25, 1997.

Haidt, Jonathan. *The Righteous Mind*. New York: Pantheon Books, 2012.

Hala, James. *Kubrick's* The Shining*: The Specters and the Critics*. The Shining Reader, ed. by Anthony Magistrale. Mercer Island, WA: Starmont House, 1990.

Hallenbeck, Brent. "UVM Debate King 'Tuna' Snider Dies." *Burlington Free Press*, December 12, 2015.

Hanson, Curtis. *Wonder Boys*. USA: Paramount Pictures, 2000.
Heckerling, Amy. *Fast Times at Ridgemont High*. USA: Universal Pictures, 1982.
Hellman, Lillian. *Scoundrel Time*. Boston: Little, Brown and Company, 1976.
Herek, Stephen. *Mr. Holland's Opus*. USA: Buena Vista Pictures, 1995.
Hilberg Raul. "Is it History or is it Drama?" *New York Times*, December 11, 1987.
Hilberg, Raul. *Perpetrators Victims Bystanders: The Jewish Catastrophe 1933-1945*. New York: HarperCollins, 1992.
Hilberg, Raul. *The Destruction of the European Jews*. London: W H. Allen, 1961.
Hilberg, Raul. *The Politics of Memory: The Journey of a Holocaust Historian*. Chicago: Ivan R. Dee, 2001.
Hilberg, Raul. *The Warsaw Diary of Adam Czerniakow: Prelude to Doom*. New York: Stein & Day, 1978.
Hilger, Michael. *Native Americans in the Movies: Portraits from Silent Films to the Present*. London: Rowman & Littlefield Publishing Group, 2016.
Hiller, Arthur. *Love Story*. USA: Paramount Pictures, 1970.
Hoberman, J. "Parting Glances." *Village Voice,* January 11, 1994.
Hoffman, Michael. *The Emperor's Club*. USA: Beacon Communications, 2002.
Hofsess, John. "Kubrick: Critics Be Damned." *Soho News,* May 28. 1980.
Holbrook, Hal. *Mark Twain Tonight in the CBS Television Network Special*. New Jersey: Kultur Video, 1999.
Holbrooke, David. *The Diplomat*. USA: Giraffe Partners, 2015.
Holmes Jr., Oliver Wendell. "The Path of the Law." *Harvard Law Review*, 1897.
Holmes Jr., Oliver Wendell. *The Common Law*. Boston: Little, Brown and Company, 1881.
Horne, James W. *College*. USA: United Artists, 1927.
Horsman, Reginald. "American Indian Policy in the Old Northwest, 1783-1812." *The William and Mary Quarterly* Vol. 18, No. 1, Jan 1961.
Howard, Ron. *A Beautiful Mind*. USA: Universal Pictures, 2001.
Hughes, John. *Ferris Bueller's Day Off*. USA: Paramount Pictures, 1986.
Hughes, John. *The Breakfast Club*. USA: Universal Pictures, 1985.
Huston, John. *The Unforgiven*. USA: MGM, 1960.
IBE 2011 Living Legend Award Winner—Cicely Tyson. USA: Indiana Black Expo Youth Video Institute, 2011.
Ifell, Gwen. "Conversation with Gwen Ifell." *PBS News Hour*. October 14, 2015.
Iles, Alexandra. *Scandalize My Name: Stories from the Blacklist*. USA: Unapix Home Entertainment, 1998.

Insdorf, Annette. *Indelible Shadows: Film and the Holocaust*, 2d ed. New York: Cambridge University Press, 1989.
Jacobovici, Simcha and Stuart Samuels. *Hollywoodism: Jews, Movies and the American Dream*. USA: Associated Productions, 1997.
Jacquot, Benoit. *The Disenchanted/La désenchantée*. France: Centre National de la Cinematographie, 1990.
James, Steve. *Life Itself*. USA: Magnolia Pictures, 2014.
Jewison, Norman. Interview with James Lipton. *Inside the Actor's Studio*. Bravo Film and Arts Network: New York, 1997.
Jobes, Gertrude. *Motion Picture Empire*. Hamden: Archon Books, 1966.
Joffe, Lawrence. "Raul Hilberg: Historian prepared to risk his career to expose the Holocaust." *The Guardian*, September 19, 2007.
Johnson, Jack. *Jack Johnson—In the Ring—and Out*. Chicago: National Sports Publishing Company, 1927.
Johnson, Lamont. *One on One*. USA: Warner Bros, 1977.
Johnson, Wally. "La Mancha Project Is a Hit, According to Students." *The Burlington Free Press*. September 27, 1969.
Jones, Howard. *Mutiny on the Amistad: The Saga of a Slave Revolt, and Its Impact on American Abolition, Law, Diplomacy*. Revised Edition. New York: Oxford University Press, 1987.
Jones, James Earl and Penelope Niven. *James earl Jones: Voices and Silences*, 1st ed. New York: Charles Scribner's Sons, 1993; repr., 2002.
Joseph, Peniel E. *Dark Days, Bright Nights: From Black Power to Barack Obama*. New York: Basic Civitas Group, 2010.
Kael, Pauline. "Sugarlands and Badlands." *Reeling*. Boston, 1976.
Kael, Pauline. "The Current Cinema: Cicely Tyson Goes to the Fountain." *The New Yorker*, 1974.
Kael, Pauline. "Whipped." *Taking It All In*. New York, 1984.
Kael, Pauline. *Hooked*. New York, 1989.
Kagan, Jeremy. *The Chosen*. USA: Chosen Film Company, 1982.
Kagan, Norman. *The Cinema of Stanley Kubrick, New Expanded Edition*. New York: Continuum, 1993.
Kahn, Gordon. *Hollywood on Trial: The Story of the 10 Who Were Indicted*. New York: Boni and Gaer, 1948; Rpt. New York: Arno Press, 1972.
Kaminsky, Stuart. *American Film Genres*. 2nd ed. Chicago: Nelson-Hall, 1985.
Kanew, Jeff. *Revenge of the Nerds*. USA: 2oth Century-Fox, 1984.
Katz, Ephraim. "James Earl Jones." *The Film Encyclopedia*, 5th Edition. Revised by Fred Klein & Dean Nolen. New York: HarperCollins, 2005.
Kaufman, Deborah, and Alan Snitow. "Blacks and Jews." *American Documentary, Inc.*, ed. Marc Weiss. USA: Snitow-Kaufman Productions, 1997.

Kazan, Elia. *Gentleman's Agreement*. USA: Twentieth Century-Fox, 1947.
Kazan, Elia. *On the Waterfront*. USA: Columbia Pictures, 1954.
Keeler, Greg. "*The Shining*: Ted Kramer Has a Nightmare." *Journal of Popular Film and Television*, Winter, 1981.
Keen, Andrew. *The Cult of the Amateur: How Today's Internet Is Killing Our Culture*. New York: Doubleday, 2007.
Keneally, Thomas. *Schindler's Ark*. Austria: Hodder and Stoughton, 1982.
Kennedy, John F. *Address in the Assembly Hall at the Paulskirche in Frankfurt*. June 25, 1963.
King, Henry. *Beloved Infidel*. USA: Twentieth Century-Fox, 1959.
King, Henry. *King of the Khyber Rifles*. USA: Twentieth Century-Fox, 1953.
King, Stephen. *Doctor Sleep: A Novel*. New York: Scribner, 2013.
Kipling, Rudyard. "If." *Complete Poems of Rudyard Kipling*. Hertfordshire, UK: Wordsworth Press, Ltd. 1991.
Kitses, Jim. *Horizons West*. Bloomington: Indiana University Press, 1969.
Klarer, Alain. *American Cinema: Film in the Television Age*. Episode 6. USA: A New York Center for Visual History Production, 1995.
Koch, Howard. *As Time Goes By: Memoirs of a Writer*. New York: Harcourt Brace Jovanovich, 1979.
Konkle, Lincoln and David Garrett Izzo. *Stephen Vincent Benet: Essays on His Life and Work*. New York: McFarland & Co. Inc., 2002.
Kramer, Stanley. *High Noon*. USA: United Artists, 1952.
Kramer, Stanley. *Judgment at Nuremberg*. USA: United Artists, 1961.
Kramer, Stanley. *R.P.M.* USA: Columbia Pictures, 1970.
Kroll, Jack. "Stanley Kubrick's Horror Show." *Newsweek*, May 26, 1980.
Kubrick, Stanley. *Dr. Strangelove: or, How I Learned to Stop Worrying and Love the Bomb*. USA: Columbia Pictures, 1963.
Kubrick, Stanley. *Paths of Glory*. USA: United Artists, 1957.
Kubrick, Stanley. *The Shining*. USA: Warner Brothers, 1980.
Kunhardt, Peter W. *Nixon by Nixon: In His Own Words*. USA: HBO Documentary Films, 2014.
Kurosawa, Akira. *Seven Samurai*. Japan: Toho Company, 1954.
LaGravenese, Richard. *Freedom Writers*. USA: Double Feature Films/Jersey Films/Paramount Pictures, 2007.
Landis, John. *National Lampoon's Animal House*. USA: Universal Pictures, 1978.
Lanzmann, Claude. *Tashal*. Germany: Bavaria Film, 1944.
Lazarus, Paul. *SlingShot*. USA: White Dwarf Productions, 2014.
Leder, Mimi. *Pay It Forward*. USA: Warner Bros, 2000.
Lee, Spike. *School Daze*. USA: 40 Acres and A Mule Filmworks, 1988.
Lehman, Peter. "Texas 1868/America 1956: The Searchers". *Close Viewings: An Anthology of New Film Criticism*. Ed. Peter Lehman. Tallahassee: Florida State UP, 1990.

Leibowitz, Flo and Lynn Jeffres. "The Shining." *Film Quarterly,* Spring, 1981.

Leigh, Mike. *Mr. Turner.* Britain: Film4, 2014.

Lewis, Jerry. *The Nutty Professor.* USA: Paramount Pictures, 1963.

Lewis, Joseph H. *7th Cavalry.* USA: Columbia Pictures Corporation, 1956.

Lichtblau, Eric. *The Nazis Next Door: How America Became a Safe Haven For Hitler's Men.* Boston: Houghton Mifflin Harcourt, 2014.

Lippman, Jr., Theo. "Trial was longer in movie, *Amistad.*" *Baltimore Sun Journal,* December 18, 1997.

Litvak, Anatole. *Confessions of a Nazi Spy.* USA: Warner Bros, 1939.

Lovell, Hugh G. and Taisle Carter. *Collective Bargaining in the Motion Picture Industry.* Berkeley, California: Berkeley Institute of Industrial Relations, University of California, 1953.

Luketic, Robert. *Legally Blonde.* USA: MGM, 2001.

Lumet, Sidney. *Twelve Angry Men.* USA: United Artists, 1957.

Lumet, Sydney. "Interview with James Lipton." *Inside the Actor's Studio.* Bravo Film and Arts Network, New York. 1995.

Luzer, Richard. "Fair Haven Union High School Media Center, VT." *School Library Journal,* September 1, 1980.

MacDonald, Fred J. *Blacks and White TV: Afro-Americans in Television since 1948.* Chicago: Nelson-Hall Publishers, 1983.

MacDougall, Ranald. *The World, the Flesh, and the Devil.* USA: MGM/Har-Bel/Sol C. Siegel, 1959.

Macklin, F. Anthony. "Understanding Kubrick: *The Shining.*" *Journal of Popular Film and Television,* Summer, 1981.

Madigan, Mark. "Orders from the House." *The Shining Reader,* ed. by Anthony Magistrale. Mercer Island, WA: Starmont House, 1990.

Magistrale, Anthony. "Sutured Time: History and Kubrick's *The Shining.*" *The Shining: Studies in the Horror Film.* Ed. Daniel Olson. Lakewood, CO: Centipede Press, 2015.

Magistrale, Anthony. *The Shining Reader.* Mercer Island, WA: Starmont House, 1990.

Major League Baseball, *Brooklyn Dodgers: The Ghosts of Flatbush.* USA: Major League Baseball Productions, 2007.

Mamet, David. *Oleanna.* USA: Samuel Goldwyn Company, 1994.

Manatu, Norma. *African American Women and Sexuality in the Cinema.* Jefferson: McFarland & Company, 2003.

Manchel, Frank. "A War Over Justice: An Interview with Marcel Ophuls." *Literature/Film Quarterly* 6, no. I, Winter 1978.

Manchel, Frank. *Cameras West.* Englewood Cliffs, N.J.: Prentice-Hall, 1971.

Manchel, Frank. *Conference on Teaching the Slow Learner.* Metropolitan School Study Conference: The English Committee of the Metropolitan School Study Conference, 1964.

Manchel, Frank. *Every Step a Struggle: Interviews with Seven Who Shaped the African American Image in Movies*. Washington: New Academia Publishing, 2007.

Manchel, Frank. *Exits and Entrances: Interviews with Seven Who Reshaped African American Images in Movies*. Washington, D.C.: New Academia Publishers, 2013.

Manchel, Frank. *Film Study: An Analytical Bibliography*. 4 vols. Rutherford, N.J.: Fairleigh Dickinson University Press, 1990-1.

Manchel, Frank. *Great Sports Movies*. New York: Franklin Watts, 1980.

Manchel, Frank. "Interview with Raul Hilberg." *Vermont Reports*. Vermont Public Television, June 1985.

Manchel, Frank. "Movies and Man's Humanity." *Teaching the Humanities: Selected Readings*, Ed. by Sheila Schwartz. New York: Macmillan. 1970.

Manchel, Frank. "Sink or Swim: Hollywood After World War II." *College of Arts and Sciences Dean's Lecture Award*. Burlington: University of Vermont, 2000.

Manchel, Frank. "What Does It Mean, Mr. Holmes? An Approach to Film Study." *LFQ* Volume 31:1, 2003.

Manfull, Helen, ed. *Additional Dialogue: Letters of Dalton Trumbo, 1942-1962*. New York: M. Evans and Company, 1970.

Mann, Daniel. *The Last Angry Man*. USA: Columbia Pictures, 1959.

Margolis, Jeff. *Oscars Greatest Moments*. USA: Columbia TriStar Home Video, 1992.

Marsden Michael T. and John G. Nachbar, "The Indian in the Movies, "Wilcomb E. Washburn, ed. *History of Indian-White Relations*, Vol. 4. Washington: Smithsonian Institution, 1988

Maslin, Janet. "Flaws Don't Dim Kubrick's *The Shining*." *New York Times*, June 8, 1980.

Maslin, Janet. "Imagining the Holocaust to Remember It." *New York Times*, December 15, 1993.

Maslin, Janet. "Pain of Captivity Made Starkly Real." *New York Times*, December 10, 1997.

Mason, B.J. "The New Films: Culture or Con Game?" *Ebony*, 1972.

Matviko, John W. *The American President in Popular Culture*. Westport, Connecticut: Greenwood Press, 2005.

Maugham, W. Somerset. *Of Human Bondage*. New York: The Modern Library, 1915.

McCall, Mary. "My Name Isn't Costello." *Screen Guilds' Magazine*, February 1937.

McKitrick, Eric. "JQA: For the Defense." *New York Review*, April 23, 1998.

Mencken, H. L. "On Truth" in *Damn! A Book of Calumny*. New York: Philip Goodman, 1918.

Mencken, H. L. *The Philosophy of Friedrich Nietzsche*. Boston: Luce, 1908.
Mencken, H. L. *The Smart Set: A Magazine of Cleverness*. New York: Ess Ess Publishing Company, 1919.
Menendez, Ramon. *Stand and Deliver*. USA: Warner Bros, 1988.
Meryman, Richard. *Mank: The Wit, World, and Life of Herman Mankiewicz*. New York: William Morrow and Company, 1978.
Milestone, Lewis. *The Purple Heart*. USA: Twentieth Century-Fox, 1944.
Miller, Robert Ellis. *The Heart is a Lonely Hunter*. USA: Seven Arts/Warner Brothers, 1968.
Mintz, Steve. Conversation, H-NET List for Scholarly Studies and Uses of Media, University of Houston. Tue. Feb. 17, 1998.
Morsberger, Robert E., et al., eds. "Dictionary of Literary Biography." *American Screenwriters*, Vo. 26. Detroit: Gale Research Company, 1984.
Mulligan, Robert. *Up the Down Staircase*. USA: Warner Bros, 1967.
Murray, Albert. *The Omni-Americans: Some Alternatives to the Folklore of White Supremacy*. New York: De Capo Press, 1970.
Murray, Donald M. "Give Your Students the Writer's Five experience." *The La Mancha Project: Proceedings of the University of Vermont's First Annual Model School Conference*, eds. Frank Manchel and Tom Devine, Burlington, Vermont: May 31- June 2, 1968.
Nagorski, Andrew. "Spielberg's Risk: The Director Takes a Chance with a Holocaust Drama Shot in Black and White." *Newsweek*, May 24, 1993.
Navasky, Victor. "Honor the Blacklistees." *The Nation*. April 3, 2000.
Negulesco, Jean. *Humoresque*. USA: Warner Bros, 1946.
Nelson, Thomas Allen. *Inside a Film Artist's Maze*. Bloomington: Indiana University Press, 1982.
Nemes, László. *Son of Saul*. Hungary: Laokoon Film Arts, 2015.
Newell, Mike. *Mona Lisa Smiles*. USA: Sony Pictures Entertainment, 2003.
Newmeyer, Fred C. *The Freshman*. USA: The Harold Lloyd Corporation, 1925.
Nichols, Mike. "Interview with James Lipton." *Inside the Actor's Studio*. Bravo Film and Arts Network: New York, 1997.
Nichols, Nichelle. *Beyond Uhura: Star Trek and Other Memories*. New York: G. P. Putnam's Sons, 1994.
Norment, Lynn. "Ebony Interview: Cicely Tyson." *Ebony*, February 1981.
Novick, Peter. Introduction. *The Holocaust in American Life*. Boston: Houghton Mifflin Company, 1999.
Nugent, Elliott. *Mr. Belvedere Goes to College*. USA: 20th Century-Fox, 1949.
Ohlheiser, Abby. "How Martin Luther King Jr. Convinced Star Trek's Lt. Uhura to Stay on the Show." *The Washington Post*, July 31, 2012.
Osagie, Iyunolu. "Historical Memory and a New National Consciousness: The Amistad Revolt Revisited in Sierra Leone." *Massachusetts Review* 38, Spring 1997.

"Our Views: Studying Genocide." Editorial. *Montreal Gazette*. February 12, 2016.

Owens, William A. *Black Mutiny: The Revolt on the Schooner Amistad*. New York: Plume Book, 1953

Pakula, Alan J. *The Sterile Cuckoo*. USA: Paramount Pictures, 1969.

Palma, Brian De. *Carrie*. USA: United Artists, 1976.

Paskaljevic, Goraan. *When Day Breaks*. Serbia: Nova Film, 2012.

Pasquier, Sylvaine. "Raul Hilberg: Un Acte Majeur (Raul Hilberg: A Major Act)." Trans. by Dennis Mahoney and Eileen Riley. *L'Express*. February 24, 1994.

Payne, Alexander. *Election*. USA: Paramount, 1999.

Peerce, Larry. *Goodbye, Columbus*. USA: Paramount Pictures, 1969.

Peerce, Larry. *One Potato, Two Potato*. USA: Bawalco Picture Company, 1964.

Penn, Arthur. *Little Big Man*. USA: National General Pictures, 1970.

Penn, Leo. *A Man Called Adam*. IUSA: Embassy Pictures, 1966.

Perry, Louis B., and Richard S. Perry, *A History of the Los Angeles Labor Movement, 1911-41*. Berkeley: University of California Press, 1963.

Petrie, Daniel. *A Raisin in the Sun*. USA: Columbia Pictures, 1961.

Pitkethly, Lawrence. *The Western. American Cinema*. New York Center for Visual History. PBS. KCET, Los Angeles, January, 1994.

Plante, Caroline. "Make genocide studies part of high school curriculum: petition." *Montreal Gazette*, February 11, 2016.

Poitier, Sidney. *A Warm December*. USA: First Artists, 1973.

Pollack, Sydney. *The Way We Were*. USA: Columbia Pictures, 1973.

Poussaint, Alvin F. "Blaxploitation Movies: Cheap Thrills that Degrade Blacks." *Psychology Today*, February 1974.

Preminger, Otto. *Exodus*. USA: United Artists, 1960.

Puig, Claudia and Andy Seiler. "In Hollywood, ideas are worth fighting for; Amistad suit just one of many disputes." *USA Today*, December 9, 1997.

Pursell, Michael. *"Full Metal Jacket:* The Unraveling of Patriarchy." *Literature/Film Quarterly* 16:4, 1988.

Quart, Leonard. "Frank Capra and the Popular Front." *CINEASTE* 8:1. Summer 1977.

Rapf, Maurice. *Back Lot: Growing Up with the Movies*. Latham: The Scarecrow Press, 1999.

Rashke, Richard. *Useful Enemies: John Demjanjuk and America's Open Door-Door Policy for Nazi War Criminals*. New York: Delphinium Books, 2013.

Ray, Man. *Source/Notes: To Be Continued, Unnoticed*. 1948. Izquotes.com.

Reich, Charles A. *The Greening of America*. USA: Random House, 1970.

Reid, Mark A. *Redefining Black Film*. Berkeley: University of California Press, 1993.

Reisman, David. *The Lonely Crowd*. Yale University Press, 1950.
Reisz, Karel. *The Gambler*. USA: Paramount Pictures, 1974.
Renoir, Jean. *The Rules of the Game*. France: Nouvelles Editions de Films (NEF), 1939.
Ricciarell, Giulio. *Labyrinth of Lies*. Germany: Naked Eye Filmproduktion, 2014.
Rich, Frank. "Extras in the Shadow." *New York Times*, January 2, 1994.
Rich, Frank. "Who Stole History?" *New York Times*, December 13, 1997.
Richard, Jacques. *Henri Langlois: The Phantom of the Cinematheque*. France: Les Films Elementaires, 2004.
Richardson, John N. "Steven's Choice." *Premiere* 7, no. 5, January, 1994.
Ridley, Matt. *The Evolution of Everything: How New Ideas Emerge*. New York: Harper Collins Publishers, 2015.
Riley, Stevan. *Listen to Marlon*. USA: Passion Pictures, 2015.
Ritt, Martin. *The Great White Hope*. USA: Twentieth Century-Fox, 1970.
Roach, Jay. *Trumbo*. USA: Groundswell Productions, 2015.
Robe, Mike. *Son of the Morning Star*. USA: Preston Stephen Fischer Company, 1991.
Roberts, Randy and Johnny Smith. *Blood Brothers: The Fatal Friendship Between Muhammad Ali and Malcolm X*. New York: Basic Books, 2016.
Robinson, Louie. "Cicely Tyson: A Very Unlikely Movie Star." *Ebony*, May, 1974.
Roffman, Peter and Jim Purdy. *The Hollywood Social Problem Film: Madness, Despair, and Politics from The Depression to the Fifties*. Bloomington: Indiana University Press, 1981.
Rollins, Dean Alfred B., Jr., and Samuel N. Bogorad. "Introduction." *The La Mancha Project: Proceedings of the University of Vermont's First Annual Model School Conference*.
Rollins, Peter C. and John E. O'Connor. *Hollywood's Indian: The Portrayal of the Native American in Film, Expanded Edition*. University Press of Kentucky, December 14, 2003.
Romano, Andrew. "How Ignorant Are Americans?" *Newsweek*, March 20, 2011.
Romanowski, William D. "Oliver Stone's JFK: Commercial Filmmaking, Cultural History, and Conflict." *Journal of Popular Film and Television* 21, Summer, 1993.
Rose, Frank. "Beyond Our Control." *New York Times Book Review*. November 29, 2014.
Rosen, Peter. *God's Fiddler: Jascha Heifetz*. USA: Kultur International Films 2011.
Rosenberg, Harold. "The Shadow of the Furies." *The New York Review of Books*, January 20, 1977.

Ross, Gaylen. *Killing Kasztner: The Jew Who Dealt with Nazis*. France: GRFilms Inc., 2008.
Ross, Murray. "Labor Relations in Hollywood." *Annals of the American Academy of Political and Social Sciences* 254. November 1947.
Ross, Murray. *Stars and Strikes: Unionization of Hollywood*. New York: Columbia University Press, 1941; Rpt. New York: AMS Press, 1967.
Rossen, Robert. *Island in the Sun*. USA: Twentieth Century-Fox, 1957.
Rostand, Edmond. *Cyrano De Bergerac*. A New Prose Translation by John Murrell. Canada: Talonbooks, 1995. Kindle edition.
Rothschild, Hannah. *The Charlie Rose Show*. PBS. S24 EP 229, Nov. 12. 2015.
Russell, Bertrand. *A History of Western Philosophy*. London: George Allen & Unwin LTD, 1945.
Sackler, Howard. *The Great White Hope. A Play*. New York: The Dial Press, 1968.
Sainte-Marie, Buffy. "Now That the Buffalo's Gone." Lyrics Published by Kobalt Music Publishing Ltd., Universal Music Publishing Group.
Salkow, Sidney. *Sitting Bull*. USA: United Artists, 1954.
Sandburg, Carl. *Always the Young Strangers*. New York: Harcourt, Brace and Company, 1953.
Sanders, Charles L. "Cicely Tyson: She Can Smile Again after a Three-Year Ordeal." *Ebony*, January, 1979.
Sands, Pierre Norman. *A Historical Study of the Academy of Motion Picture Arts and Sciences 1927-1947*. New York: Arno Press, 1973.
Sarandon, Susan. "Interview with James Lipton." *Inside the Actor's Studio*. Bravo Film and Arts Network: New York, 1998.
Sargent, Joseph. *The Man*. USA: ABC Circle Films, 1972.
Schaefer, Christien Harty. "Ship of Slaves: The Middle Passage." *The History Channel*. US: DreamWorks, 1989.
Schaefer, Christien Harty. "The Making of Amistad." Supplementary Materials, *Amistad* DVD, 1999.
Schatz, Thomas. *Hollywood Genres*. Philadelphia: Temple University Press, 1981
Schickel, Richard. "Amistad." *Time*, December 15, 1997.
Schickel, Richard. "Heart of Darkness: Ghosts in Their Millions Haunt Steven Spielberg's Powerful *Schindler's List*." *Time*, December 13, 1993.
Schickel, Richard. *Gary Cooper: American Life, American Legend*. USA: Turner Network Television, 1991.
"*Schindler's List*: Myth, Movie, and Memory." *Village Voice*. March 29, 1994: 30.
"Schindler's Wife 'Lists' Stake." *Daily Variety*, February 10,1994.
Schmidt-Garre, Jan and Marieke Schroeder. *Aida's Brothers & Sisters: Black Voices in Opera and Concert*. Germany: Pars Media, 2009.

Schnabel, Julian. *The Diving Bell and the Butterfly*. France: Pathe, 2007.
Schon, Jeffrey. *American Cinema*: *Film Noir*. Episode 7. USA: A New York Center for Visual History Production, 1995.
Scorsese, Martin. *A Personal Journey with Martin Scorsese Through American Movies*. England: British Film Industry, 1995; USA, 1996.
Seldes, Gilbert. *The Movies Come from America*. New York: Charles Scribner's Sons, 1937.
Shakespeare, William. "Henry IV." *Shakespeare: Major Plays and the Sonnets*, ed. G. B. Harrison. New York: Harcourt, Brace and Company, 1948.
Shapiro, Harold T. *A Larger Sense of Purpose: Higher Education and Society*. Princeton, N.J.: Princeton University Press, 2005.
Shapiro, Laurie Gwen. "My Lower East Side Neighbor Caught Adolf Eichmann," *Forward.com*. April 28, 2016.
Shaw, Bernard. *Saint Joan: A Chronicle Play in Six Scenes and an Epilogue*. Definitive Text. New York: Penguin Books, 1951.
"'Shoah' Filmmaker Claude Lanzmann Talks Spielberg, 'Son of Saul,'" *Hollywood Reporter.com*. May 5, 2016.
Short, Kenneth R. M. "Introduction." *Feature Films as History*, ed. Kenneth R. M. Short Knoxville: University of Tennessee Press, 1981.
Sieving, Christopher. Soul Searching: Black-Themed Cinema from the March on Washington to the Rise of Blaxploitation. Middleton, Connecticut: Wesleyan University Press, 2011.
Silber, Glenn. *The War at Home*. USA: Catalyst Media, 1979.
Silverstein, Jake. "The Displaced." *The New York Times Magazine*, November 8, 2015.
Singleton, John. *Higher Learning*. USA: Columbia Pictures, 1995.
Skinner, B. F. "Skinner Tells His Strategies for Handling Old Age." *The New York Times*, August 24, 1982.
Sklar, Robert. "Historical Films: Scofflaws and the Historian-Cop." *Reviews in American History*, June, 1997.
Smale, Alison. "Oscar Groning, Ex-SS Soldier at Auschwitz, Gets Four Year-Sentence." *The New York Times*, July 15, 2015.
Smiley, Jane. "The Bluecoats Are Coming: William T. Vollmann's Novel Looks to the 1870s as Westward Expansion Ignites the Nez Perce War. *New York Times Book Review*, August 2, 2015.
Smith Jr., Claude L. "*Full Metal Jacket* and the Beast Within." *Literature/Film Quarterly* 16:4, 1988.
Smith, John N. *Dangerous Minds*. USA: Buena Vista Pictures, 1995.
Sobchack, Thomas, and Vivian C. Sobchack. *An Introduction to Film*. 2nd ed. Boston: Little, 1987.
Soderbergh, Steven. *Erin Brockovich*. USA: Universal Pictures, 2000.
Sontag, Susan. "Regarding the Torture of Others." *The New York Times*, May 23, 2004.

Spielberg, Steven. *Amistad*. USA: DreamWorks, 1997.
Spielberg, Steven. *Schindler's List*. USA: Universal Pictures, 1993.
"Spielberg's Crusade." *Atlanta Journal Constitution* [online], December 12, 1993, NEXIS Library, NEWS File: CURNWS.
Spinoza, Benedictus de. *Ethics, Demonstrated in Geometrical Order*. 1677.
Staples, Brent. "Black Characters in Search of Reality." *New York Times*, February 12 2012.
_____. "To Hollywood, Blackness Is Just a Special Effect," *Editorial Observer, New York Times* (March 20, 2016).
Stedman, Raymond William. *Shadows of the Indian*. Norman: University of Oklahoma Press, 1982
Stephani, Frederick and Ray Taylor. *Flash Gordon*. USA: Universal Pictures, 1936.
Stevens Jr., George. *George Stevens: A Filmmaker's Journey*. USA: Castle Films, 1984.
Stevens, George. *The Diary of Anne Frank*. USA: Twentieth Century-Fox, 1959.
Stone, Oliver. *Untold History of the United States*. USA: Ixtian Productions, 2012.
Sturges, John. *Bad Day at Black Rock*. USA: MGM, 1955.
Suber, Howard. *The 1947 Hearings, or, The House Committee on Un-American Activities into Communism in the Hollywood Motion Picture Industry*. M.A. thesis: U.C.L.A., 1966.
Suber, Howard. *The Anti-Communist Blacklist in the Hollywood Motion Picture Industry*. Unpublished Ph.D. dissertation: U.C.L.A., 1968.
Sweeney, Edwin R. *Cochise: Chiricahua Chief*. Norman: University of Oklahoma Press, 1991.
Sweeney, Edwin R. *Cochise: Firsthand Accounts of the Chiricahua Apache Chief*. Norman: University of Oklahoma Press, 2014.
Sweeney, J. K. "Book Review of James Earl Jones: Voices and Silences." *Magill Book Reviews*, 2009.
Swift, Jonathan. *The Correspondence of Jonathan Swift*. 1725. London: G. Bell and sons, Ltd., 1951.
Szwed, John. *So What: The Life of Miles Davis*. New York: Simon & Schuster Paperbacks, 2004.
Taylor, John Russell. *Strangers in Paradise: The Hollywood Émigrés'. 1933-1950*. London: Faber and Faber, 1983.
Taylor, Tate. *The Help*. USA: Dream works, SKG, 2011.
Teachout, Terry. *Pops: A Life of Louis Armstrong*. Boston: Houghton Mifflin Harcourt, 2009.
Tejada-Fares, Rick. "Rivera in America." *American Masters*, ed. Susan Lacy. USA: Eagle Rock Entertainment, 2006.

Terrace, Vincent. *Fifty Years of Television: A Guide to Series and Plots, 1937-1988.* Cranbury, N.J.: Cornwall Books, 1991.
Terry, Joseph C. *Oprah 'Amistad'*. USA: Harpo Studios, 1997.
"The Economist." *Spielberg List* [online], December 25, 1993; available from NEXIS Library, NEWS File: CURNWS.
"The Great Jewish Exodus." *The New York Times*, February 21, 2015.
"The Memory of Justice: An Exchange." *The New York Review of Books*, March 17, 1977.
Thorpe, Richard. *The Adventures of Huckleberry Finn*. USA: MGM, 1939.
Titterington, P. L. "Kubrick and *The Shining*." *Sight and Sound*, Spring 1981.
Toback, James. *Harvard Man*. USA: Cowboy Pictures, 2002.
Toplin, Robert Brent. "Film and History: The State of the Union." *Perspectives*, April, 1999.
Toplin, Robert Brent. *History by Hollywood: The Use and Abuse of the American Past*. Champaign: University of Illinois Press, 1996.
Trial of Adolf Eichmann. Narrated by David Brinkley. USA: ABC News, 1997.
Trilling, Lionel. "Introduction." *Homage to Catalina*. George Orwell, ed. New York: Harcourt Brace Jovanovich, 1980.
Trotta, Margarethe von. *Hannah Arendt*. Belgium: Heimatfilm, 2012.
Truffaut, François. *Fahrenheit 451*. Britain: J. Arthur Rank, 1966.
Trumbo, Dalton. *The Time of the Toad: A Study of Inquisition in America and Two Related Pamphlets*. New York: Harper and Row, 1972.
Twain, Mark. *Huckleberry Finn*. Milano: Radici, 2014. Kindle edition.
Tyldum, Morten *The Imitation Game* USA: The Weinstein Company, 2014.
Ulin, David L. "Celebrating the Genius of *Huckleberry Finn*." *Los Angeles Times*, November 14, 2010.
Ullman, Michael. "The Jazz Column." *Fanfare*, November/December 2009.
Ulmer, James. "In Transit: Schindler Dodges Unkindest of Cuts." *Hollywood Reporter*, April 8-10, 1994.
Underwood, Tim and Chuck Miller. *Feast of Fear: Conversations with Stephen King*. New York: Carroll and Graf, 1992.
Ushpiz, Ada. *Vita Activa: The Spirit of Hannah Arendt*. USA: Zeitgeist Films, 2016.
Van Sant, Gus. *Finding Forrester*. USA: Sony Pictures Entertainment, 2000.
Van Sant, Gus. *Good Will Hunting*. USA: Miramax, 1997.
Vaughn, Robert. *Only Victims: A Study of Show Business Blacklisting*. New York: G. P. Putnam's Sons, 1972.
Wachsmann, Nikolaus. *KL: A History of the Nazi Concentration Camps*. New York: Farrar, Straus & Giroux, 2015.
Wagner, Andrew. *Starting Out in the Evening*. USA: Little Film Company, 2007.

Walker, Elsie M. and David T. Johnson. "Introduction." *Conversations with Directors: An Anthology of Interviews from Literature/Film Quarterly*, Ed. By Elsie M. Walker and David T. Johnson. Lanham: The Scarecrow Press, Inc., 2008.

Walsh, Raoul. *They Died with Their Boots On*. USA: Warner Bros, 1941.

Ward, Brian. *Just My Soul Responding: Rhythm and Blues, Black Consciousness, and Race Relations*. Berkeley: University of California Press, 1998.

Warren, Mame, ed. *Johns Hopkins: Knowledge for The World*. Baltimore: John Hopkins University Press, 2000.

Washington, Denzel. *The Great Debaters*. USA: The Weinstein Company, 2007.

Weatherford, Elizabeth. *Native Americans on Film and Video*. Washington, DC: National Museum of the American Indian, 1981.

Weaver, Thomas. "Voices from the Past." *Vermont Quarterly*, April 14, 2014.

Weinraub, Bernard. "Islamic Nations Move to Keep Out *Schindler's List*." *New York Times*, April 7, 1994.

Weinstein, Julius and Tyler Measom. *An Honest Liar*. USA: Left Turn Films, 2014.

Weir, Peter. *Dead Poet's Society*. USA: Buena Vista Pictures, 1989.

Weiss, Alan J. *James Earl Jones Biography*. USA: Alan J. Weiss Productions, 1995.

Welkos, Robert W. "Company Town: Another Author Challenges Spielberg." *Los Angeles Times*, December 18, 1997.

Welles, Richard. "North Country Union High School." *The La Mancha Newsletter*, ed. Littleton Long. Vol. 1. May 1969.

Wenders, Wim and Juliano Ribeiro Salgado. *The Salt of the Earth*. France: Decia Films, 2014.

Wheaton, Christopher Dudley. *A History of the Screen Writers Guild (1920-1924): The Writers' Quest for a Freely Negotiated Basic Agreement*. Unpublished Ph.D. dissertation: University of Southern California, 1974.

White, Armond. "Against the Hollywood Grain." *Film Comment* 34:2, Mar/Apr 1998.

White, Susan. "Male Bonding: Hollywood Orientalism, and the Repression of the Feminine in Kubrick's *Full Metal Jacket*." *Arizona Quarterly*, Autumn, 1988.

Whitney, William. *The Adventures of Captain Marvel*. USA: Republic Pictures, 1941.

"Why Criticism Matters." *The New York Times Book Review*, January 2, 2011.

Wiesel, Leon. "Washington Diarist: Close Encounters of the Nazi Kind." *New Republic*, January 24, 1994.

Wilkerson, Isabel. *The Warmth of Other Suns: The Epic Story of America's Great Migration*. New York: Random House, 2010.

Williams, Michael. "Spielberg Adds DGA to 'List': Helmer Wins Friends on Euro Tour" *Variety,* March 7, 1994.
Williams, Paul. *The Revolutionary*. Australia: Pressman-Williams Productions, 1970.
Williams, Todd "Troubled History." *Premiere,* January 1998.
Wilson, Michael. *A Trip to Bountiful.* TV Movie. USA: Ostar productions, 2014.
Wilson, William. "Riding on the Crest of the Horror Craze." *New York Times Magazine,* May 11, 1980.
Wise, Robert. Odds against Tomorrow. USA: United Artists, 1959.
Wood, Sam. *Goodbye, Mr. Chips*. USA: MGM, 1939.
Wrathall, Nicholas D. *Gore Vidal: The United States of Amnesia*. USA: IFC Films, 2013.
Wright, Will. *Six Guns and Society*. Berkeley: University of California Press, 1975.
Youngblood, Denise J. "The Master of the Movies: A Tribute to Frank Manchel." *Film & History: An Interdisciplinary Journal of Film and Television Studies,* Spring, 2006.
Yvonne. "Cicely Tyson." *Ms.* August, 1974.
Zaillian, Steven. *Searching for Bobby Fisher*. USA: Paramount Pictures, 1993.

Index

1941 (1979), 260
2001: A Space Odyssey (1968), 437
400 Blows, The (1959), 29
7th Cavalry (1956), 331
Abe Lincoln in Illinois (1940), 28
Abraham, Arthur, 309
Abrahamson, Larry, 549
Academy Awards, 104, 139, 140, 150, 363, 368, 483, 491, 561, 563
Academy of Motion Picture Arts and Sciences (AMPAS), 18, 197, 205, 207, 212, 261, 276, 352, 357, 362, 370, 372, 398, 421, 466
Action in the North Atlantic (1943), 206
Actors' Equity Association, 208
Adams, John Quincy, 304, 308, 310, 378, 403, 444
Adderley, Cannonball, 475
Adler, Mortimer J., 149, 152, 154, 158
Adler, Renata, 495
Adorno, Theodor W., 257
Adventures of Huckleberry Finn, The (1939), 402
Adventures of Marco Polo, The (1938), 9
Aeneid, 13
Affair to Remember, An (1957), 420
African Queen, The (1951), 366, 420

Agamemnon, 2
Agee, James, 20, 26
Aida, 1
Air Force (1943), 442
Alamo, The (1960), 444
Alamo, The (2004), 446
Aldrich, Robert, 86, 327
Aleiss, Angela Maria, 347, 349, 351
Alexander, Michelle, 457, 464
Algiers (1938), 206
al-Husayni, Mohammad Amin, 229
Ali, Muhammad, 104, 510, 513
Alice Doesn't Live Here Any More (1974), 445
All About Eve (1950), 416
All Quiet on the Western Front (1930), 30, 442
All the King's Men (1949), 29, 299, 416
All the Pretty Horses, 159
Allard, Jessica, 433
Allen, Debbie, 302, 306-309, 315
Allen, Jay Presson, 94
Allen, Jeanne Thomas, 191
Allen, Robert C., 191, 205
Allen, Robert L., 84, 86
Allen, Woody, 10, 16, 86, 388, 538
Allied High Command, 135
Altman, Robert, 332, 562
Amberg, George, 158

Ambrose, Stephen E., 295, 297
American Federation of Labor, 199
American Film Institute, 93, 437, 543, 562
American History X (1998), 273
American Library Association, 90
American Madness (1932), 208
American Missionary Association, 305
American Red Cross, 473
American Tail, An (1986), 260
American Tail: Fievel Goes West, An (1991), 260
Amistad (1997), 37, 277, 278, 285, 287, 293, 300-303, 306-316, 318, 378, 403, 444, 552, 553, 560
An American Tragedy (1931), 29, 389
Anderson, Lindsey, 134
Anderson, Marian, 467
Anderson, Maxwell, 550
Andrew, Dudley, 191, 385, 425, 429
Andrews, Dana, 370
Andy Hardy Meets Debutante (1940), 9
Angelou, Maya, 476
Angels With Dirty Faces (1938), 8, 9
Anker, David, 521
Ansara, Michael, 349
Anschluss, 221
Ansen, David, 317, 318
Antonioni, Michelangelo, 86, 556
Apache (1954), 327
Apache Territory (1958), 327
Apocalypse Now (1979), 442
Apted, Michael, 492
Aquinas, Thomas, 3
Arcand, Denys, 427, 434
Archard, Army, 362
Arendt, Hannah, 231, 233, 243
Aristotle, 3, 191, 281
Arkin, Alan, 483
Arlen, Harold, 458

Armstrong, Lance, 102
Armstrong, Louis, 9, 458, 475, 479, 480
Armstrong, William H., 485
Army Signal Corps, 124
Arnheim, Rudolf, 281
Arnold, Elliot, 339, 349
Arnold, Matthew, 429
Arns, Robert G., 184, 190
Around the World in Eighty Days (1956), 29
Arrindell, Helene, 45
Arrow Cross, 289
Arrowhead (1953), 327
Arsenic and Old Lace (1944), 30
Ascher, Rodney, 151, 155-158
Asphalt Jungle, The (1950), 366
Assault, The (1986), 261
Associated Actors and Artists of America, 208
Astaire, Fred, 437
Atanarjuat: The Fast Runner (2001), 332
Atherton, William, 488
Au Revoir les Enfants (1987), 261
August, Benjamin, 296
Auschwitz, 140, 141, 142, 228, 230, 239, 248, 250, 251, 256, 262, 264, 266, 309, 367
Austin, Bruce A., 191
Authors League of America (ALA), 199
Autobiography of Miss Jane Pittman, The (1974) (CBS), 486, 487, 491
Autry, Gene, 10, 322, 536
Avalanche (1978), 105
Avenue of the Righteous, 248
Avildsen, John G., 20, 26
Avisar, Ilan, 270, 273
Avos, Pirke, 382

Babes in Arms (1939), 9

Index

Bacon, Francis, 375
Bad and the Beautiful, The (1952), 356
Bad Day at Black Rock (1955), 327, 511, 539
Bad News Bears, The (1976), 108
Bad Seed, The (1956), 30
Badham, John, 109
Badlands (1973), 556
Baker, Josephine, 468
Balazs, Bela, 92
Baldwin, Roger Sherman, 303
Balio, Tino, 191
Ballard, Lynn, 182
Barbara Watson Modeling School, 473
Barbarian Invasions, The (2003), 427
Barbour, Shelley, 316, 422
Barnes, Brooks, 463
Baron, Lawrence, 232, 244, 272, 273
Barry Lyndon (1975), 161
Barry, Don 'Red', 322
Barry, Jack, 236, 244
Barry, John, 458
Bascom, George, 325, 344
Basehart, Richard, 153
Bataan (1943), 442
Bates, James, 318
Battle of Apache Pass (1951), 327
Batty, Roy. *See* Hauer, Rutger
Baxter, John, 422
Baxter, Warner, 322
Bazin, Andre, 85, 281
Beatty, Warren, 86
Beau Geste (1939), 9, 30
Beautiful and the Damned, The (1922), 356
Beautiful Mind, A (2001), 39, 44
Beauvoir, Simone De, 244
Because of Winn-Dixie (2001), 488
Becker, Lutz, 125, 134, 135, 136, 137
Beebe, Ford I., 543

Beethoven, Ludwig von, 213
Begin, Menachem, 242
Bellush, Bernard, 201, 203
Ben Hur (1959), 29
Benet, Stephen Vincent, 97, 364
Ben-Gurion, David, 229, 230, 242
Benigni, Roberto, 368, 369
Bennett, Lerone, Jr.,, 309
Bennett, Leslie, 490, 495
Bennett, Luke, 45
Benteen, Frederick, 331
Bentley, Eric, 204
Benton, Robert, 39, 44
Benzine, Adam, 244
Berger, Ludwig, 9
Bergerac, Cyrano de, 6, 75, 379, 404, 405, 469
Bergman, Andrew, 43
Bergman, Ingmar, 86, 420, 530, 533, 561
Berkeley, Busby, 9
Berlin, Irving, 9, 458, 537
Berlinale Camera Award, 112
Bernard, Emily, 473, 493
Bertolucci, Bernardo, 556
Bessie, Alvah, 204
Best Years of Our Lives, The (1946), 416, 442
Betrayed (1988), 287
Bettelheim, Bruno, 142, 146
Bible, In the Beginning, The (1966), 366
Biddle, Francis, 144
Big Parade, The (1925), 442
Big Wednesday (1978), 105
Billy the Kid (1941), 208
Billy the Kid (William H. Bonny), 323
Bingham, Dennis, 522
Bingo Long Traveling All-Stars and Motor Kings, The (1976), 109, 517
Bird, Brad, 550

Birth of a Nation, The (1915), 306, 368
Birth of the Blues, The (1941), 9
Biskind, Peter, 446
Bismarck, Otto von, 213
Bjorkman, Stig, 549
Black Elk, 325
Black Hawk, 325
Black Hawk Down (2001), 432
Black Kettle, 325
Black Mass (2015), 550
Black Nationalism, 452
Blackall, Eric A., 25
Blackboard Jungle, The (1955), 20
Blacks: A Clown Show, The, 476, 482, 508
Blade Runner (1982), 391
Blair, Jon, 241, 269
Blair, Wayne, 359
Blake, Robert, 322
Blanco, Pedro, 302
Blankfort, Michael, 349
Blaustein, Julian, 339, 348
Block, Bertram, 198
Blockade (1938), 206
Bloff, Willie, 202
Blume, Leon, 539
Boat is Full, The (1981), 114, 261, 364
Boetticher, Budd, 327
Bogart, Humphrey, 365, 437
Bogle, Donald, 484, 486, 495
Bogorad, Samuel N., 61, 63
Boles, Robert, 134
Bond, Ward, 392
Bone, Robert A., 84, 86, 87, 89, 91
Boone, Daniel, 326
Bordwell, David, 191, 388, 389
Born on the Fourth of July (1989), 299, 442, 562
Bosnian War, 294
Bourke-White, Margaret, 201
Bourne Ultimatum, The (2007), 431

Bowie, James "Jim", 326
Bowser, Leroy, 501, 517
Bowser, Pearl, 501
Boy's Town (1938), 9
Boyd, William, 322
Boyle, Danny, 549
Bradbury, Ray, 57, 63, 550
Bradley, Tony, 190
Bramley, Raymond, 343, 349
Brancato, Chris, 488
Brando, Marlon, 372, 394, 453
Brandon Films, 47, 53
Brandon, Henry, 392
Brantley, Ben, 491, 496
Brauner, Arthur, 269
Breakfast Club, The (1985), 20
Breitman, Richard, 217, 241
Brethren's Kaleva Norman Dickson High School, 506
Brian's Song (1971), 105
Bridge of Spies (2015), 549
Bridge on the River Kwai, The (1957), 420, 421, 542
Bridger, Jim, 326
Bridges, James, 39, 44, 408
Bright, John, 198, 206
British Air Force Intelligence, 134
British Broadcasting Company (BBC), 124, 125, 128-132
British Royal Academy, 57
Broadcast of 1936 (1936), 207
Broadway Bill (1934), 208
Broadway Melody of 1940 (1940), 9
Broken Arrow (1950), 320, 327, 334, 338-340, 343-349, 416, 511, 539
Bronte, Anne, viii
Brooklyn (2015), 549
Brooks, Cleanth, 281
Brooks, James L., 427, 434
Brooks, Mel, 86
Brooks, Richard, 20, 26, 43, 60, 327, 335

Brooks, Van Wyk, 429
Brown Girl, Brown Stones, 474
Brown, Jim, 364, 365, 454, 461, 487, 495, 501, 505, 513
Brown, Nacio Herb, 9
Brown, Patricia Leigh, 457
Brown, William Wells, 318
Browne, George E., 202
Browne, Roscoe Lee, 454, 476, 482, 490, 501
Brubeck, Dave, 475
Buccaneer, The (1937), 207
Buccaneer, The (1958), 29
Bugsy Malone (1976), 125
Bundy, McGeorge, 127
Buob, Jacques, 270
Burke, Edmund, viii
Burke, Jack, 289, 291
Burlington Free Press, The, 61, 62, 363, 459, 561
Burns, Ken, 332, 441, 512, 522, 523
Burns, Tommy, 509
Burstyn, Ellen, 468
Burton, Richard, 28, 482
Bush, George H., 455
Bush, George W., 439
Bustin' Loose (1981), 488
Byrnes, James F., 539

Caan, James, 367, 394
Cabaret (1972), 261
Cabin in the Sky (1943), 9
Cable, Mary, 317
Cagney, James, 365, 437
Cahan, Abraham, 8
Cahiers Du Cinema, 420
Cain, James M., 355
Caine Mutiny, The (1954), 442
Caine, Michael, 388
Calling Bulldog Drummond (1951), 208
Calloway, Cab, 458

Cambridge, Godfrey, 476
Camera Three's Between Yesterday and Today, 474
Cameraman, The (1928), 356
Cameron, James, 300
Campanella, Roy, 539
Camus, Albert, 124
Canby, Vincent, 522
Cannes Film Festival, 444
Cannon, Jimmy, 151
Canterbury Tales, The, 13
Capra, Frank, 9, 85, 208, 210
Captain Marvel, 22
Captains Courageous (1937), 9, 208
Carabello, Marlene, 335
Carmichael, Stokely, 475, 481, 515
Carnaby Street, 129
Carol (2015), 549
Carpenter, John, 440
Carpenter, Susan, 63
Carpetbaggers, The (1964), 356
Carr, Ian, 478, 494
Carr, Jay, 314, 318
Carrie (1976), 20
Carrigan, Anna, 136, 137
Carroll, Diahann, 470, 484
Carroll, Vinnette, 474
Carson, Kit, 326
Carter, Benny, 481
Carter, Taisle, 204
Casablanca (1942), 442
Case of Lena Smith, The (1929), 207
Case, Arthur E., 297
Cassavettes, John, 86
Castellano, Richard S., 394
Castle, William, 327
Catch 22 (1970), 38, 98, 102, 442
Cawelti, John, 386
Cayton, William, 512, 522
Cazale, John, 394
Ceplair, Larry, 191, 201, 204, 210
Cervantes, Miguel de, 13, 58, 282, 546

Cezanne, Paul, 352
Chabrol, Claude, 540
Chaikin, Judy, 422
Champagne, Duane, 335
Champlain Valley Union High School, 61, 78
Chandler, Jeff, 320, 349
Chandler, Raymond, 355
Chanina, Rabbi, 111
Chaplin, Charles, viii, 2, 9, 79, 221, 241, 367, 369, 398, 411, 412, 421, 437
Chapman, James, 190
Charade (1963), 387
Charles Evans Hughes High School, 473
Charles, Ray, 489
Chase-Riboud, Barbara, 309, 312, 316, 318
Chaucer, Geoffrey, 13, 17, 57
Chazelle, Damien, 20, 26
Cheaper by the Dozen (1950), 29, 30
Cheshire High School, 46, 87
Chevalier, Maurice, 19
Chief Joseph, 325, 350
Chief Looking Glass, 350
Chi-Raq (2015), 550
Chisum, John Simpson, 323
Chomsky, Marvin J., 241
Chosen, The (1982), 39
Christensen, Bonnie, 59, 63
Christie, Julie, 83
Churchill, Winston, 124, 143, 144
Chutkow, Paul, 289, 296
Cicely Tyson School of Performing and Fine Arts, 490
Cieply, Michael, 463
Cieply, Stefan, 431, 434
Ciment, Michel, 177
Cincinnati Kid, The (1965), 209
Cinematheque Francaise, 85, 420, 539

Cinque, Joseph (Sengbe Pieh), 302, 309-312, 314
Citadel, The (1938), 30
Citizen Cohn (1992), 552
Citizen Kane (1941), 299, 436
Civil Rights Movement, 11
Clark, Virginia, 175, 190, 269
Claude Lanzmann: Spectres of the Shoah (2015), 244
Claudine (1974), 517
Clavell, James, 20, 26
Clemmons, Jack, 190
Cleven, Nels, 354
Clift, Montgomery, 366
Clinton, William Jefferson, 254
Cloak and Dagger (1946), 209
Close Encounters of the Third Kind (1977), 250, 391
Coach (1978), 105
Coates, Ta-Nehisi, 399, 457, 464, 493, 521
Cobb, Humphrey, 153
Cobb, Lee J., 228, 242
Cochise, 320, 325, 339, 340, 342-350
Cochran, Robert, 72
Cocks, Jay, 123, 126, 146
Cocteau, Jean, 151, 158, 420
Cody, William F. "Buffalo Bill", 326
Coen, Ethan, 550
Coen, Joel, 550
Cogley, John, 204, 206
Coglin, Bertram, 311
Cohan, George M., 19
Cohen, Alan, 162, 176
Cohen, Roger, 243
Coixet, Isobel, 39, 44, 428, 434
Colbert, Claudette, 437
Cole, Lester, 198, 200, 204
Coleman, Cy, 550
College of Arts and Sciences, 90, 98-100, 179, 181, 182, 373, 399, 401, 473, 542

Collins, Audrey, 312
Collins, Marva, 468, 488
Collins, Shirley S., 63
Color Purple, The (1985), 260, 308
Coltrane, John, 458, 459, 478
Columbia Pictures, 33, 38, 64, 78, 84, 149, 197, 198, 204, 411, 419, 420, 536
Columbia University, 33, 38, 64, 78, 84, 149, 204, 541
Comden, Betty, 550
Comedians, The (1967), 482, 509
Communist Party of the United States (CPUSA), 196, 201-203, 209, 210, 216
Comolli, Timothy, 62, 63
Confessions of a Nazi Spy (1939), 220, 241, 283
Conformist (1970), 554
Congress of Racial Equality, 475
Connolly, Maggie, 504
Connolly, Maureen Catherine, 106
Conquest of Cochise (1953), 327
Conrad, Joseph, 13
Contempt/Le Mepris (1963), 356
Cook, Bruce, 204, 210
Cooper, Gary, 224, 328, 437
Cooper, James Fenimore, 322
Cooper, Scott, 550
Coppola, Francis Ford, 249, 367, 372, 390, 394, 522
Corbett, "Gentleman Jim", 108
Core, Ericson, 549
Corliss, Richard, 191
Corn is Green, The, 490
Corsitto, Salvatore, 394
Cory, David, 322, 335
Cosby, Bill, 484
Costa-Gavras (Gavras, Konstantine), 276, 287, 290, 291, 296
Costner, Kevin, 332
Coughlin, Father Charles, 220

Court Martial of Billy Mitchell, The (1955), 443
Courtney, Susan, 511
Covey, James, 304
Coy, Walter, 392
Crabbe, Buster, 22
Crabtree, Susan, 447
Cranston, Bryan, 507
Crawford, Joan, 437
Crazy Horse, 325, 331
Creed (2015), 549
Crockett, Davy, 326
Crook, George, 331
Crosby, Bing, 437
Crossfire (1947), 416, 539
Crossland, Alan, 8
Crothers, Scatman, 175
Crouch, Donald, 505
Crouch, Stanley, 19, 25, 313, 478, 494
Crowley, John, 549
Cry, The Beloved Country (1951), 29, 439
Culbert, David, 191
Curtis, Tony, 357
Curtiz, Michael, 8, 9, 209, 323, 328, 412
Custen, George F., 512, 523
Custer, George Armstrong, 325, 331, 344, 350
Cyrano de Bergerac (1950), 13, 16, 29

Dachau, 226
DaCosta, Morton, 533
Dance Theater of Harlem, 490
Dandridge, Dorothy, 306, 467, 469, 472
Dangerous Minds (1995), 20
Daniels, Victor, 322
Danigelis, Nick, 348
Danish Girl, The (2015), 549
Darrow, Clarence, 201

Dartmouth College, 5, 120, 209
Daves, Delmer, 320, 327, 334, 339, 348, 522
David and Lisa (1962), 29
Davis, Baron, 103
Davis, Bette, 437
Davis, Evelyn, 473
Davis, Miles, 459, 477-479, 489, 491, 512, 513, 522
Davis, Ossie, 479, 501, 507, 519, 523
Davis, Sammy, Jr., 479
Day for Night/Lu Nui americaime (1973), 356
Day of the Locust, The (1975), 356
Day, Martha, 269, 348
Dayton, Alison M., 63
De Gaulle, Charles, 124
De Mille, Cecil B., 86
De Niro, Robert, 357, 370
Dead End (1937), 8, 9
Dead End Kids, 8
Dead Poet's Society (1989), 20
Dead, The (1987), 366
Deadliest Season, The (1978), 108
Dean, James, 445
Dean, Phillip Hayes, 518
Dee, Ruby, 451, 454, 461, 476, 501
Defiant Ones, The (1958), 29
DeKnight, Freda, 473
Deloria, Vine, Jr., 348, 351
Delsohn, Steve, 495
DeMille, Cecile B., 323
Demjanjuk, John, 240, 288
Denby, David, 11, 14, 16, 83, 90, 310, 318, 430, 434
Dennis, Sandy, 21
Desert Fox, The (1951), 223
Desire (1936), 207
Detective Story (1951), 30
Devine, Tom, 63, 72
Dewey, John, 201
Diamond, Neil, 335

Diary of Anne Frank, The (1959), 29, 226, 227, 261, 273, 283
Dibb, Mike, 495
Dickens, Charles, 13
Dickerson, Glenda, 311
Dickinson, Emily, 13
Didion, Joan, 355
Dieterle, William, 352, 369
Dilling, Elizabeth, 201
Dippie, Brian W., 349
Disney, Walt, 513
Divided We Fall (2000), 273
Dixon, Berlie Ray, 42, 449
Dixon, Ivan, 36, 42, 45, 449, 454, 461, 476, 484, 501
Do The Right Thing (1989), 437
Doctor Sleep, 156
Doctor Zhivago (1965), 84
Doenitz, Karl, 135
Don Quixote, 13, 57, 558
Donat, Robert, 25, 26, 404
Donen, Stanley, 387
Donnelly, Ann, 381
Donnelly, Catherine, 190
Donner Party, 172
Donovan, James, 513
Doolan, James, 323
Dostoyevsky, Fyodor, 3
Double-Headed Eagle: Hitler's Rise to Power (1918-1933) (1973), 134
Douglas, Kirk, 153
Douglas, Lawrence, 245, 296
Douglas, Suzanna, 485
Dr. Jekyll and Mr. Hyde (1941), 30, 208
Dr. Strangelove Or: How I Learned to Stop Worrying and Love the Bomb (1964), 437, 442, 508
Dramatists Guild (DG), 198, 199
DreamWorks, 308, 312, 313, 316
Dreiser, Theodore, 389
Dresden, 134, 135

594 Index

Dreyer, Carl Theodor, 530, 533
Drums Along the Mohawk (1939), 29
DuBarry was a Lady (1943), 9
Duke, Bill, 488, 495
Dunaway, Faye, 468
Dunne, Philip, 204, 208
Durante, Jimmy, 530
Durham, Delcie R., 295
Duvalier, François ("Papa Doc"), 482, 509
Duvall, Robert, 394
Duvall, Shelley, 170, 175
Dworkin, Martin, 223, 242
Dylan, Bob, 400

E. T.: The Extra-Terrestrial (1982), 250, 269
Early, Gerald, 511, 522
Earp, Wyatt, 326
East of Eden (1955), 357, 445
East Side, West Side (CBS), 476, 477, 478, 508
Eastabrook, Howard, 208
Eastwood, Clint, 332, 442, 443
Easy Rider (1969), 172, 555, 556
Eat, Pray, Love (2010), 563
Eban, Abba, 237
Ebert, Roger, ix, 10, 22, 289, 296, 353, 362, 381
Educating Rita (1983), 39, 44
Egoyan, Atom, 296
Eichmann, Adolf, 229, 230-233, 236, 286
Einstein, Albert, 298, 455, 547
Eisenhower, Dwight D., 12
Eistein, David, 241
Ejdus, Predraj (Belgrade Rabbi), 425
El Cid (1961), 29
Elder, Leone, III, 485
Election (1999), 20
Elegy (2008), 39, 44

Elephant (2003), 445
Elephant Boy (1937), 9
Eligon, John, 457
Eliot, T. S., 13, 87, 375, 379, 382
Elisberg, Robert J., 318
Eller, Claudia, 318
Ellin, Abbey, 457
Ellington, Duke, 9, 458, 475
Elm, The, 8
Emerson, Ralph Waldo, ix, 19, 25, 57, 83, 90, 462, 499, 521, 548
Emperor Jones, The (1964), 508
Emperor's Club, The (2002), 20
Empire of the Sun (1987), 260
Empty Mirror, The (1996), 273
Enemy Below, The (1957), 223
Englund, Steve, 191, 201, 204, 210
Erens, Patricia, 191
Erin Brockovich (2000), 427
Escape from Sobibor (1987), 256
Eszterhas, Istvan, 293
Eszterhas, Joe, 287, 293, 296
ET the Extra-Terrestrial (1982), 307
Europa, Europa (1990), 273
Evans, David, 297, 550
Evans, Mark, 458
Evans, Walter, 26
Everson, William K., 335
Exodus (1960), 29, 227, 228, 283
Eyre, Chris, 332

Fadiman, Regina K., 191
Fahrenheit 9/11 (2004), 443, 555
Fairbanks, Douglas, Sr., 79, 411
Faragoh, Francis Edward, 198, 207
Farley, Dick, 335, 336
Farrakhan, Louis, 481
Farrow, John, 327
Fast Times at Ridgemont High (1982), 20
Fat City (1972), 366
Father of the Bride (1950), 445

Faulkner, William, 124, 298, 299, 306
Fein, Bruce, 318
Feldman, Jan, 269
Feldstein, Ruth, 470, 492
Fellini, Federico, 1, 16, 86, 153, 158, 367, 420, 556
Fenin, George N., 335
Ferber, Edna, 378, 382
Ferguson, Niall, 399
Ferreira, Patricia, 162, 176
Ferris Bueller's Day Off (1986), 20
Ferro, Marc, 283, 295
Fetterman, William J., 325
Field of Dreams (1989), 517
Fields, Bert, 312
Fields, Dorothy, 546, 550
Fiennes, Ralph, 253
Fincher, David, 39, 44
Finding Forrester (2000), 20
Finest Hours, The (2015), 550
Fishburne, Laurence, 488
Fisher, Lucy, 191
Fishkin, James, 336
Fitzgerald, Ella, 458
Fitzgerald, F. Scott, 165, 356
Five Easy Pieces (1970), 172
Flash Gordon, 22, 536
Flashdance (1983), 287
Fleming, Victor, 9, 389
Flemyng, George, 521
Fletcher, Louise, 442
Fonda, Henry, 437
Fonda, Jane, 490
For Me and My Gal (1942), 208
For Whom the Bell Tolls (1943), 443
Ford, Aleksander, 271
Ford, Henry, 220
Ford, John, 9, 85, 323, 327, 332, 336, 371, 388, 390, 522, 556
Ford, Paul, 482
Forever Amber (1947), 209

Forman, Carl, 328
Forman, Milos, 8, 86, 150
Forrest, Frederic, 289
Forsdale, Louis C., 78, 84, 86, 87, 90, 102
Forsyth, John, 304
Foster, Gloria, 36, 45, 482
Foster, Norman, 331, 336
Fountainhead, The (1949), 443
Four Feathers, The (1939), 9
Franco, Francisco, 94, 201
Frank, Michael, 431, 434
Frank, Nikas, 297
Frankenheimer, John, 86
Franklin, John Hope, 309
Franzoni, David H., 13, 54, 59, 115, 117, 294, 301, 308, 309, 312, 314, 316, 552, 562, 563
Fraser, C. Gerald, 206
Freed, Arthur, 9
Freedom Riders, 475
Freedom Writers (2007), 20, 541
Freeman, Morgan, 188, 312, 378
Freshman, The (1925), 39
Freshman, The (1990), 39
Freud, Sigmund, 201
Freundlich, Hans, 298
Friendly Persuasion (1956), 443
From Here to Eternity (1953), 420, 442
Front, The (1976), 417
Frost, Robert, 23
Frye, Northrop, 66, 281
Fuchs, Henry, 530, 533, 534, 541
Furillo, Carl, 539

Gabbard, Krin, 481, 494
Gable, Clark, 26, 366, 437
Gabler, Neal, 411, 422
Gadjig, Samba, 549
Gaines, Ernest, 486
Gallipoli (1981), 299

Gambler, The (1974), 39
Gandhi, Mahatma, 3
Gangs of New York (2002), 446
Garcia, Andy, 488
Garden of Stones (1987), 442
Garden of the Finzi-Continis, The (1971), 261
Gardner, Elysa, 521
Garfield, John, 24
Garland, Judy, 437
Garrett, Oliver H. P., 208
Garrett, Pat, 323
Garris, Mick, 148, 149, 156, 158
Gary Cooper: American Life, American Legend (1989), 442
Gates, Henry Louis, Jr., 309, 457
Gavin, James, 469, 492
Gavron, Sarah, 549
Geer, Will, 349
Genet, Jean, 476, 508
Gennari, John, 277, 295, 458, 464
Gentleman's Agreement (1947), 18, 25, 29, 30, 222, 283, 327, 357, 416, 539
George Foster Peabody Awards, 186, 189, 237
German American Bund, 220
Geronimo, 325, 339, 342, 344, 346, 349
Gershwin, George, 9, 458, 537
Gershwin, Ira, 9, 537
Get Shorty (1995), 356
Gettysburg (1993), 444
Ghislanzoni, Antonio, 1
Ghosts of Mississippi, The (1996), 307
Gibson, Mel, 444, 446
Gigi (1958), 19, 420
Gilbert, Lewis, 39, 44, 158
Gillespie, Craig, 550
Gilmour, David, 158, 359
Giry, Stephanie, 270
Gish, Lillian, 453, 454, 455, 482, 501

Gladiator (2000), 115, 552, 553, 559, 562
Glasmon, Kubec, 198
Glasrud, Bruce A., 351
Glenville, Peter, 482, 495, 509, 522
Glory (1989), 299
Godard, Jean-Luc, 540
Godfather Saga, The (1981), 394
Godfather, The (1972), 367, 372, 390, 394, 556
Godzilla (1954), 558
Goebbels, Joseph, 213
Goeth, Amon, 253, 254, 262, 264, 265, 266
Goethe, Johann Wolfgang von, viii, 19, 25, 545
Goldberg, Joel, 158, 190
Golden Globes, 301
Goldstein, Warren, 283, 295
Goldworthy, Joan, 492
Goldwyn, Samuel, 411
Gomery, Douglas, 205
Gone With the Wind (1939), 9, 299, 306, 536
Good Morning, Miss Dove (1955), 29
Good Will Hunting (1997), 39
Goodbye, Columbus (1969), 20
Goodbye, Mr. Chips (1939), 9, 20, 25, 29, 30, 536
Goodman, Barak, 113, 122
Goodnight, Charles, 323
Gorcey, Leo B., 8
Gordon, Chad, 103
Gordon, Edward, 69, 523
Gordone, Charles Edward, 454, 476, 501, 516, 517
Goring, Hermann, 136, 213, 223
Gossett, Lou, Jr., 476
Gourevitch, Philip, 262, 271
Graduate, The (1967), 388, 445
Graff, Christopher, 244
Graham, Sheila, 356

Grand Illusion (1937), 437
Grant, Ulysses S., 345
Grapes of Wrath, The (1940), 9, 28, 437, 445, 536
Graves, Robert, 41, 44
Gray, Thomas, 153, 158
Great Debaters, The (2007), 39
Great Dictator, The (1940), 9, 221, 283, 369, 536
Great Expectations, 46
Great Gatsby, The (1926, 1949, 1974), 356
Great White Hope, The (1970), 510, 511, 513, 517
Great White Hope, The (play), 455, 509, 523
Greatest, The (1977), 89, 105
Greek Gods and Heroes, 44
Green Day, 555
Green, Albert, 550
Green, David Gordon, 549
Green, Susan, 561
Greene, Gary, 463, 464
Greene, Graham, 482, 509
Greene, Matthew, 462
Greene, Stanley, 45
Greening of America, The, 12
Gregg, Don, 72
Grey, Zane, 322
Griffin, John, 47, 51, 52
Griffith, David Wark (D. W.), 79, 271, 411
Griffith, James, 434
Grinde, Don, 317
Grindon, Leger, 285, 296, 511
Groning, Oskar, 239
Gross, John, 270
Grove, Martin A., 271
Grubin, David, 241
Guess Who's Coming to Dinner (1967), 445, 483
Guiding Light, 484

Guilty by Suspicion (1991), 417
Guinness, Alec, 482
Gulag Archipelago, 132
Gulliver, Lemuel, 2
Gulliver's Travels, 13
Gunfight at the OK Corral (1957), 390
Gunga Din (1939), 9
Gunning, Tom, 191
Gunther, Lenworth, 447
Gutierrez, Eric, 318

Haas, Lukas, 289
Hackman, Gene, 467
Haidt, Jonathan, 470, 493
Hail, Caesar! (2015), 550
Hair (1979), 442
Hala, James, 160, 175
Haley, Alex, 307, 488
Hall, Huntz, 8
Hallenbeck, Brent, 190
Hamlet, 2, 28, 379, 453
Hammerstein, Oscar, II, 9, 537
Hammett, Dashiell, 200
Hannah Arendt (2012), 229, 231, 232, 239
Hannibal (2013), 552
Hansberry, Lorraine, 447, 476
Hanson, Curtis, 39, 44
Harburg, Yip, 9, 537
Hardy, Thomas, 12
Harlan County U.S.A (1976), 140
Harlem Globetrotters, The (1951), 439
Harman, Fred, 322
Harpole, Charles H., 191
Harmonists, The (1997), 274
Harris, Julius, 36, 45
Harris, Sir Arthur Travers, 134
Harrison, William Henry, 305
Hart, Lorenz, 9, 537
Hart, William S., 79
Hartford High School, 61

598   Index

Harvard, 39, 115, 158, 307, 428, 486
Harvard Man (2002), 39
Harwood, Ronald, 233
Haskell, Molly, 437
Hassett, Marilyn, 106
Hateful Eight, The (2015), 549
Hathaway, Henry, 323
Hawking, Stephen, 2, 513
Hawks, Howard, 86, 328
Haworth, Jill, 228
Hawthorne, Nathaniel, 13, 282
Hayes, George "Gabby", 322
Haynes, Lloyd, 484
Haynes, Todd, 549
Hays, Gregory, 16
Hearst, William Randolph, 299
Heart is a Lonely Hunter, The (1968), 482-484, 491
Hearts and Minds (1974), 131
Heaven Can Wait (1978), 105
Heaven Knows, Mr. Allison (1957), 208, 366
Hecht, Ben, 208, 355
Hecht-Hill-Lancaster Company, 419
Heckerling, Amy, 20, 26
Heifetz, Jascha, 381
Heller, Joseph, 38
Hellman, Lillian, 200, 204, 417
Hello Dolly (1969), 480
Help, The (2011), 491
Hemingway, Ernest, ix, 11, 39, 119, 124, 376, 402
Henry, John, 504
Henry, O. (William Sydney Porter), 322
Hepburn, Katharine, 437
Herbert, Anthony, 136
Herek, Stephen, 20, 26
Hero Ain't Nothing but a Sandwich, A (1978), 488
Herrmann, Bernard, 458

Hess, Rudolph, 136, 213, 223
Hester Street (1975), 8, 299
Heston, Charlton, 447
Hiawatha, 325
Hickok, Wild Bill, 326
High Noon (1952), 29, 224, 328, 443
Higher Learning (1995), 39, 44
Hilberg, Raul, 15, 144-146, 156, 157, 189, 213-216, 228, 231-234, 236-241, 243, 244, 250, 259, 270, 273, 291, 432, 502, 548
Hilger, Michael, 335
Hill, George Roy, 86, 522
Hill, Robert F., 543
Hillel, Rabbi, viii, 225
Hiller, Arthur, 39, 43
Hillier, Larry, 191
Hilton, Brian, 432, 434
Hilton, James, 25
History Channel, 241, 333
Hit Parade, The (1937), 207
Hitchcock, Alfred, 86, 388, 412
Hitchcock/Truffaut (2015), 550
Hitler, Adolf, 201, 203, 213, 220, 221, 229, 252, 285, 364, 481
H-Net List for Scholarly Studies and Uses of Media, 282
Hobbes, Thomas, 57
Hoberman, J., 264, 271
Hobson, Laura, 25
Hodges, Gil, 538
Hoffman, Michael, 20, 26
Hofsess, John, 175
Holbrook, Hal, 23, 122, 190, 403
Holbrooke, David, 533
Holbrooke, Richard, 525
Holder, Geoffrey, 178, 188, 190
Holiday, Billie, 459
Holiday, Doc, 326
Holiday, Judy, 545
Holly, Ellen, 477
Hollywood Code, 199

Hollywood on Trial (1976), 140
Hollywood Ten, 198, 209, 224, 417, 507
Hollywood Ten, The (1950), 224
Holm, Celeste, 18
Holmes, Oliver Wendell, Jr., 373, 381, 425, 434
Holmes, Sherlock, 28, 362, 390
Holocaust, 57, 117, 126, 141, 142, 145, 156, 157, 215, 216, 223, 227-239, 246, 247, 249, 250, 251, 254, 255, 256, 257, 258, 259, 260, 261, 262, 263, 264, 266, 267, 268, 272, 273, 286, 288, 290, 292, 298, 309, 313, 364, 367, 369, 425, 521
Holocaust (1978), 226, 256, 273
Home of the Brave (1949), 416, 439, 539
Homer, 13, 28
Hondo (1953), 327
Hoodlum (1997), 488
Hooks, Kevin, 485
Hooper, Tom, 549
Hoover, J. Edgar, 210
Hope, Bob, 437
Hopkins, Anthony, 378
Horace, 281
Horne, James W., 39, 43
Horne, Lena, 467, 468, 469, 470, 472
Horse Soldiers, The (1958), 208
Horsman, Reginald, 348
Hotel Terminus: The Life and Times of Klaus Barbie (1988), 110, 113, 120, 261
Hounsou, Djimon, 308
House Un-American Activities Committee (HUAC), 206, 207, 209, 224, 328, 357, 413, 416-418, 506, 519
Houseman, John, 404
Houston, Beverle, 191
Houtenmouser, Charles, 32

How Green Was My Valley (1941), 9, 536
Howard, Oliver Otis, 334, 345
Howard, Ron, 39, 44
Howard, William K., 9
Howe, Irving, 241
Howell, David, 72
Huckleberry Finn, 13, 28, 30, 402
Hud (1963), 29
Hughes, John, 20, 26
Hughes, Rupert, 200
Hugo (2011), 561, 563
Human Stain, The (2003), 39, 44
Humoresque (1946), 24
Hunger Games, The (2012), 562
Hunnicutt, Arthur, 349
Hunter, Jeffrey, 392
Hurricane, The (1999), 389
Hustler, The, 40
Huston, John, 86, 365, 366, 388, 522
Huston, Walter, 545, 550
Hutchins, Robert Maynard, 436, 437, 438, 443, 444, 540, 548
Hutton, Paul Andrew, 349
Huxley, Aldous, 550
Hyman, Earle, 187

I Can Hear It Now (Edward R. Morrow), 27
I Married an Angel (1942), 9
I Remember Mama (1948), 29
Ichikawa, Kon, 86
Ida (2013), 239
Ikiru (1952), 6, 16, 437
Iles, Alexandra, 507, 522
Iliad, 13
Imhoof, Marcus, 364
Imitation Game, The (2014), 55
In Jackson Heights (2015), 549
In the Heat of the Night (1967), 389
Inarritu, Alejandro Gonzalez, 549, 562

Indiana Jones and the Last Crusade (1989), 250, 269
Inglorious Basterds (2009), 562, 563
Ingrid Bergman—In Her Own Words (2015), 550
Insdorf, Annette, 191, 270, 273, 499
International Alliance of Theatrical Stage Employees (IATSE), 196, 198, 202
Interstellar (2014), 381
Intruder in the Dust (1949), 29, 307, 416, 439, 539
Iqbal, Mohammad, 373
Isherwood, Christopher, 355
Island in the Sun (1957), 539
It Happened One Night (1934), 208, 216, 219, 241
Izzo, David Garrett, 103, 371

Jackie Robinson (2016), 523
Jackson, Andrew, 304, 329
Jacobovici, Simcha, 241
Jacquot, Benoit, 359
Jagged Edge (1985), 287
James, Caryn, 290, 296
James, Frank, 323
James, Jesse, 323
James, Steve, 16, 359, 382
Jameson, Frederick, 155
Jarmusch, Jim, 4, 562
Jarvis, Merrill, 114, 364
Jaws (1975), 250, 269
Jazz Singer, The (1927), 8
Jeffords, Thomas Jonathan, 320, 339, 340-349
Jeffres, Lynn, 162, 163, 166, 176, 177
Jeffries, James J., 509
Jewett, John G., 181-185, 189, 473, 542
Jewison, Norman, 389
JFK (1991), 300, 339, 444
Jim Thorpe-All American (1951), 328

Joadson, Theodore, 310, 378, 403
Jobes, Gertrude, 210
Jodl, Alfred, 223
Joe Kidd (1972), 390
Joffe, Lawrence, 234, 244
Johnson, David T., 122
Johnson, Diane, 165, 175
Johnson, Jack, 509, 510, 512, 513, 522
Johnson, Lamont, 39, 43
Johnson, Lyndon B., 455, 513
Johnson, Wally, 61, 63
Jones, Howard, 309, 315, 317
Jones, James Earl, 13, 109, 454-456, 476, 482, 493, 498, 501, 504-507, 509, 510, 514-523
Jones, Kent, 550
Jones, Robert Earl, 504, 506, 507, 522
Jones, Ruth (Connolly), 504
Jones, Stan, 392
Jordan, Dorothy, 392
Joseph, Peniel E., 475, 493
Jowett, Garth S., 4, 191, 268, 331, 446
Judenrat, 251, 265
Judgment at Nuremberg (1961), 27, 142, 224, 261
Jules and Jim (1962), 437
Julia (1977), 556
Jurassic Park (1993), 250, 269

Kadar, Jan, 86
Kael, Pauline, 5, 10, 16, 39, 85, 249, 269, 270, 281, 282, 376, 429, 480, 485, 487, 494, 555
Kafka, Franz, 161
Kagan, Jeremy, 39, 43
Kagan, Norman, 160, 175
Kahan, Abraham, 241
Kahn, Gordon, 204
Kahn, Michael, 269

Kalaelola, Luuialuanna "Mama", 501
Kamen, Dean, 547
Kaminski, Janusz, 233, 269, 308, 311
Kane, Kathryn, 538
Kanew, Jeff, 39, 44
Kanfer, Stefan, 201, 203, 204
Karel, Russ, 241
Kasztner, Rudolph, 243
Katz, Ephraim, 122, 296, 521
Kauffmann, Stanley, 123, 281
Kaufman, Bel, 20
Kaufman, Deborah, 482, 494
Kazan, Elia, 18, 222, 224, 242, 327, 357, 362, 368, 370
Kazin, Alfred, 281
Keach, Stanley, 483
Keaton, Buster, 398, 437
Keaton, Diane, 394
Keeler, Greg, 172, 176
Keen, Andrew, 11, 16
Keitel, Wilhelm, 223
Kelly, Gene, 437, 480
Keneally, Thomas, 214, 241, 248
Kennedy Center, 468, 492
Kennedy, John F., 12, 55, 63
Kennedy, Joseph P., 220
Kennedy, Kathleen, 115, 233, 259
Kennedy, Robert, 80
Kern, Jerome, 9, 458, 537
Key Largo (1948), 366
Kilik, Jon, 13, 113, 115, 117, 226, 227, 233, 424, 524, 537, 550, 562, 563
Killing Kasztner: The Jew Who Dealt With Nazis (2008), 242, 243
Kinder, Marsha, 191
King (1978) (NBC), 488
King Arthur (2004), 552, 553
King Herod, 446
King of the Khyber Rifles (1953), 511, 539
King of the Newsboys (1938), 207
King Philip, 325
King, Coretta Scott, 468, 488
King, Henry, 359, 522
King, Martin Luther, Jr., 3, 301, 362, 371, 475, 481, 513, 560
King, Morgana, 394
King, Stephen, 148, 150, 151, 154-156, 158, 159, 171
Kings Go Forth (1958), 511, 539
Kingsley, Ben, 212, 252
Kinmont, Jill, 106
Kipling, Rudyard, 37, 533, 549
Kirk, Wilbur, 45
Kissinger, Henry, 455
Kitses, Jim, 336
Kitt, Eartha, 474
Klarer, Alain, 422
Klein, Fred, 296
Knute Rockne: All American (1940), 9
Koch, Howard, 204
Kohl, Helmut, 237
Konkle, Lincoln, 103, 371
Korda, Zolton, 9
Korty, John, 486
Kotto, Yaphet, 45, 509
Kracauer, Siegfried, 281
Kramer vs. Kramer (1979), 445
Kramer, Stanley, 39, 43, 86, 224, 242, 261
Kroll, Jack, 172, 176
Krugelis, K., 26
Ku Klux Klan, 220, 481
Kubrick, Stanley, 86, 134, 153-172, 174-177, 242, 367, 389, 508, 517, 522
Kuizenga, Donna, 399
Kunhardt, Peter W., 91
Kunuk, Zacharias, 332
Kurosawa, Akira, 6, 16, 86, 367, 420, 530, 533
Kurzel, Justin, 549

Kyle, Chris, 513

L'Avventura (1960), 29
La Dolce Vita (1960), 554
La Strada (1954), 153, 154, 437
Labyrinth of Lies (2014), 242
Lacombe, Lucien (1974), 142
Ladri di Biciclette (Bicycle Thieves) (1948), 85
LaGravenese, Richard, 20, 26, 543
Lambert, Gavin, 355
Lancaster, Burt, 224, 419
Landis, John, 39, 43
Landrum, Larry, 191
Lang, Fritz, 412
Lange, Jessica, 276, 288, 292
Langlois, Henri, 85, 373, 539
Lansbury, Angela, 502
Lanzmann, Claude, 220, 232, 237-240, 244, 261, 263
Lardner, Ring, Jr., 200, 209, 210, 224
Lardner, Ring, Sr., 209
Last Angry Man, The (1959), 492
Last Hunt, The (1956), 327
Last of the Mohicans, The, 70
Last Samurai, The (2003), 444, 446
Last Tycoon, The (1976), 357, 370
Laura (1944), 209
Laval, Pierre, 124
Lawford, Peter, 227, 479
Lawrence of Arabia (1962), 29, 437
Lawson, John Howard, 198, 200, 206, 224
Lawson, Tad, 224
Lawson, William Henry, 206
Lazarus, Paul, 551
Le Morte d'Arthur, 13
Leab, Daniel J., 191
Lean Elk, 325
Lean on Me (1989), 20
Lean, David, 83, 86, 91, 271

Leary, Lewis, 64
Leder, Mimi, 20, 26
Lee, Canada, 507
Lee, Spike, 39, 44, 314, 424, 550, 562
Legally Blonde (2001), 39
Legend of Custer, The (1968), 331
Leibovitz, Liel, 245, 296
Leibowitz, Flo, 162, 176
Leigh, Mike, 57, 63
Leonard, Robert Z., 9
Leone, Sergio, 8, 391
Lesson Before Dying, A (1999) (HBO), 488
Letter from an Unknown Woman (1948), 416
Levi, Primo, 230, 256
Lewis, Anthony, 204
Lewis, Jerry, 39, 44
Lewis, Joseph H., 331, 336
Library of Congress, 437
Lichtblau, Eric, 242, 244, 245, 288, 290, 296
Lichtman, Allan J., 217, 241
Lieberson, Sanford, 125, 129
Life and Times of Judge Roy Bean, The (1972), 366
Life is Beautiful (1997), 368, 369
Life Itself (2014), 16
Life of Emile Zola, The (1937), 29, 352, 369
Lifton, Robert Jay, 213
Light in the Forest, The (1958), 30
Limelight (1952), 398, 417, 523
Lincoln Center, 476
Lincoln, Abbey, 42, 45, 470, 476
Lincoln, Abraham, 514, 547
Linton, James M., 191
Lion King, The (1994), 517
Lipinsky Institute, 272
Lipman, Maureen, 149
Lippman, Theo Jr., 317
Lippmann, Walter, 258, 380, 525, 545

Index   603

Little Big Man (1970), 331
Little Caesar (1930), 207
Little Miss Sunshine (2006), 483
Little Nellie Kelly (1940), 9
Little Orphan Annie (1932), 207
Litvak, Anatole, 220, 241
Livingston, Robert, 322
Lloyd, Danny, 175
Locke, Sondra, 483
Loeterman, Ben, 241
Loews Delancy, 8
Lone Ranger, 10, 322
Lonely Crowd, The, 12
Long, Huey, 299
Long, Littleton, 61, 63, 175, 269, 348
Longest Day, The (1962), 27, 442
Looking Glass, 98, 325
Lord Jim, 13
Losey, Joseph, 86
Lost Boundaries (1949), 327, 416, 439, 539
Lost Horizon (1937), 9, 30, 208
Lost World: Jurassic Park, The (1997), 308
Lounck, Helen, 45
Love is a Many-Splendored Thing (1955), 420
Love of the Last Tycoon, The (1976), 356
Love Story (1970), 39
Lovell, Hugh G., 204
Loving, Al, 190
Loving, Oliver, 323
Lubitsch, Ernst, 369, 412
Lucas, George, 249, 391
Luketic, Robert, 39, 43
Lumbly, Carl, 485
Lumet, Sidney, 261, 388, 474, 493
Lumiere, Auguste, 547
Lumiere, Louis, 547
Lumumba, Patrice, 475
Lupton, John, 349

Luzer, Richard, 103
Lyne, Adrian, 287
Lyons, Timothy J., 191

M*A*S*H (1970), 209, 442
Macbeth, 23, 188, 489
Macbeth (2015), 549
Macdonald, Dwight, 281, 429, 431
MacDonald, J. Fred, 487, 493
MacDougall, Ranald, 522
Macklin, F. Anthony, 167, 177
Macksey, Richard, 449, 463
MacLachlan, Janet, 476, 514
Madam Curie (1943), 28
Madigan, Mark, 161, 175, 176
Magistrale, Anthony, 154, 155, 158, 160, 162, 175, 177
Magnificent Obsession (1954), 30
Magnificent Seven, The (1961), 390
Mahin, John Lee, 200, 208
Mahler (1974), 125
Mahoney, Dennis, 269, 270
Mailer, Norman, 355
Majdanek, 288
Malcolm X, 475, 481, 515
Malcolm X (1992), 314, 339, 494
Malle, Louis, 142
Malory, Thomas, 13, 41
Maltese Falcon, The (1941), 366
Mama Flora's Story (1998) (CBS), 488
Mamet, David, 39, 44, 403, 408
Man Called Adam, A (1966), 479, 480, 481, 482
Man in the Glass Booth, The (1975), 274
Man of La Mancha, The (1972), 368
Man Who Fell to Earth, The, 40
Man Who Would Be King, The (1975), 366
Man, The (1972) (ABC), 498, 514, 515, 517

Manatu, Norma, 485, 495
Manchel, Olga, xviii, 322, 360, 377, 536
Manchel, Rose, 536
Manchel, Sheila, 15, 41, 43, 56, 120, 121, 152, 188, 233, 278, 282, 379, 399, 424, 428, 450, 451, 460, 461, 548, 549
Manchurian Candidate, The (1962), 417
Mandela, Nelson, 97, 513
Mandingo (1970), 306
Manfull, Helen, 204
Mankiewicz, Herman J., 200
Mann Act, 509
Mann, Daniel, 474, 493
Mann, Michael, 332
Marathon Man (1976), 274
Margaret Herrick Library, 18, 212, 276, 352, 370, 372, 398, 466
Margolis, Jeff, 422
Marie, Julienne, 515
Mark of Zorro, The (1940), 209
Marlowe, Brian, 198
Marquand, Richard, 287
Married Woman, A (1982), 445
Marsden, Michael T., 335
Marsh, James, 16
Marshall, Bande, 474
Marshall, William, 454, 501, 518, 523
Marty (1955), 431
Masina, Giuletta, 153
Maslin, Janet, 161, 175, 251, 254, 270, 300, 317
Mason, B.J., 492
Massachusetts Institute of Technology (MIT), 158
Master and Commander: The Far Side of the World (2003), 446
Masterson, Bat, 326
Matewan (1987), 517

Mathieson, F.O., 429
Matilda (1978), 105
Matthau, Walter, 108
Matviko, John W., 515, 523
Maugham, William Somerset, 13, 282, 531, 533, 541, 546
Mauthausen, 287
Mayer, Edwin Justus, 198, 206
Mayer, Louis B., 197, 357
Mayor of Casterbridge, The, 12
McCall, Mary, 202, 210
McCann, Chuck, 483
McCarthy, Cormac, 159
McCarthy, Joseph, 86, 417, 506
McCarthy, Tom, 549
McConaughey, Matthew, 381
McCoy, Horace, 355
McCrea, Joel, 22, 323
McCrorey, H. Lawrence, 190, 448, 459
McCullers, Carson, 482
McDaniel, Hattie, 468
McDougald, Worth, 186
McGovern, George, 205
McGuinness, James Kevin, 200
McKinney, Nina Mae, 468
McKitrick, Eric, 318
McLaughlin, Fran, 47, 50, 51, 52
McLuhan, Marshall, 33, 62, 87, 353
McNamara. Robert, 127
Meacham, Jon, 434
Measom, Tyler, 407
Medea, 2
Medicine Lodge Treaties, 349
Meditations of Marcus Aurelius, 1
Meet John Doe (1941), 9, 208, 443
Mein Kampf (1960), 29
Mekas, Jonas, 359
Melies, George, 79
Melior, William C., 226
Mellon, Joan, 191
Melville, Herman, 13

Memory of Justice, The (1976), 110, 119, 120, 123, 124, 127-129, 135, 139-142, 146, 232, 260, 261, 283
Mencken, H. L., 12, 16, 93, 179, 189, 190, 405, 408
Mendes-France, Pierre, 124
Menendez, Ramon, 20, 26
Menjou, Adolphe, 153, 224
Mercer, Mae, 454, 501
Merchant, Ismail, 86
Meredyth, Bess, 200, 209
Merrill's Nickelodeon Theater, 317
Meryman, Richard, 211
Metro-Goldwyn-Mayer (MGM), 197, 198, 209, 411, 440, 536
Mexican War, 350
Middle Passage, 302, 309, 310, 311
Middleton, Ray, 22
Midnight (1939), 207
Midnight Cowboy (1969), 363
Midwood (theatre), 8, 536
Midwood High School, 225, 506, 530, 538
Miles, Nelson A., 331
Milestone, Lewis, 9, 222, 241
Mill, John Stuart, 57
Milland, Ray, 357
Miller, Arthur, 366
Miller, Chuck, 177
Miller, Robert Ellis, 482, 495
Milloy, Courtland, 314
Milton, John, 57
Mineo, Sal, 228
Miner, Steve, 39, 43
Mingus, Charles, 475
Minnelli, Vincente, 9, 19
Minotti, Jean M., 63
Mintz, Steven, 285, 296
Miracle on Main Street (1939), 207
Miracle Woman, The (1931), 208
Miracle Worker, The (1962), 29
Misfits, The (1960), 366

Mississippi Burning (1988), 300, 307
Mister Roberts (1955), 30, 442
Mitchell, Greg, 205
Mitchum, Robert, 357
Moby Dick, 13
Moffat, Donald, 289, 291
Moffett, James, 74
Mona Lisa Smiles (2003), 39
Monaco, James, 191
Monk, Thelonious, 477
Monroe, Marilyn, 366
Monster (2003), 445
Montana, Lenny, 394
Monuments Men, The (2014), 239
Moonstruck (1987), 389
Moore, Michael, 443, 549
Moreau, Jeanne, 357
Moriarty, Michael, 108
Morris, Wright, 355
Morsberger, Robert E, 204
Mossad, 229
Mother Teresa, 513
Motion Picture Association of America (MPAA), 440
Motion Picture Players Union, 208
Motion Picture Production Code, 101, 258, 537
Moulin Rouge (1953), 366
Moyers, Bill, 237
Mr. Belvedere Goes to College (1949), 39
Mr. Deeds Goes to Town (1936), 208, 443
Mr. Holland's Opus (1995), 20
Mr. Smith Goes to Washington (1939), 9, 443, 536
Mr. Turner (2014), 57
Mueller-Stahl, Armin, 276, 289, 291
Mulford, Clarence E., 322
Mulligan, Robert, 20, 22, 24, 26
Muni, Paul, 352, 369
Munk, Andrzej, 271

Murnau, Friedrich, 412
Murphy, Laurence, 323
Murray, Albert, 484, 495
Murray, Donald M., 60, 63, 72, 74
Murray, Elizabeth, 297
Muse, Clarence, 82, 454, 501
Muse, Ena, 501
Music Box (1989), 274, 276, 287-290, 292, 293, 296
Music Corporation of America (MCA), 130, 248
Musser, Charles, 191
Mussolini, Benito, 94, 201
Mutiny on the Bounty (1935), 29
My Friend Flicka (1943), 207
My Lai, 113, 116, 126, 127, 140, 537
My Nazi Legacy (2016), 297

Nachbar, John G. (Jack), 191, 335
Nagorski, Andrew, 270
Naked City, 474
Nasty Girl, The (1990), 261
National Association for the Advancement of Colored People (NAACP), 362, 468
National Board of Film Critics, 140
National Broadcasting Company (NBC), 33, 226, 235, 488, 518
National Industrial Recovery Act (NIRA), 196, 200
National Labor Relations Act (Wagner Act), 200, 203
National Lampoon's Animal House (1978), 39
National Recovery Administration (NRA), 196, 199, 205
Navasky, Victor S., 204, 418, 422
Nazarro, Ray, 327
Neame, Ronald, 94
Neeson, Liam, 212, 250
Negulesco, Jean, 24, 26
Nelson, Barry, 175

Nelson, Ralph, 488
Nelson, Thomas Allen, 163, 176
Nemes, László, 242, 550
New Deal, 196, 199-202, 220, 413, 417
New Line Cinema, 123
New Moon (1940), 9
New Rochelle High School, 15, 19-21, 25, 37-39, 56, 89, 97, 114, 333, 377
New York Film Critics, 140
New York Film Festival, 131
Newell, Mike, 39, 43
Newman, Alfred, 458
Newman, Paul, 227, 228
Newmeyer, Fred C., 39, 43
Nicholas, Denise, 484
Nichols, Bill, 192
Nichols, Claude, 449
Nichols, Dudley, 200, 208
Nichols, Mike, 86, 388
Nichols, Nichelle, 362, 371
Nicholson, Jack, 171, 172, 175, 177, 357
Night and Fog (1955), 234, 259, 261
Night of the Iguana, The (1964), 366
Nilsen, Vladimir, 387
Nineteen Eighty-Four (1954), 30
Niven, Penelope, 493, 504, 521, 523
Nixon (1995), 444
Nixon, Richard M., 86, 491
No Way Out (1950), 416, 439, 539
Nolan, Christopher, 381, 382
Nolen, Ronald Dean, 296
Nolley, Ken, 434
Norment, Lynn, 493, 495
North Country Union High School, 61
North Dallas Forty (1979), 105
North to Alaska (1960), 208
Northwest Passage (1940), 9
Nothing But a Man (1964), 36, 42, 45-47, 51, 53, 283, 483

Novick, Peter, 213, 232, 241
Nugent, Elliott, 39, 43
Nuremberg Trials, 124, 126, 127, 132, 136, 140, 223, 229
Nurses, The, 474
Nutty Professor, The (1963), 39, 44

O'Connor, Glynnis, 106
O'Connor, John E., 335, 336
O'Donnell, Pierce, 313
O'Hara, John, 355
O'Hara, Scarlett, 13
O'Neal, Frederick Douglass, 454, 501, 507
Obama, Barak, 515
Odds Against Tomorrow (1959), 474
Odysseus, 38
Odyssey, 13
Of Human Bondage, 13, 531, 533, 541
Of Mice and Men (1939), 9
Off the Edge (1976), 140
Office of Special Investigations, 293, 294
Office of War Information, 537
Ohio State University, 12, 41, 180, 287, 360, 529
Oleanna (1994), 39, 44, 403
Olson, Daniel, 158
Omalu, Bennett, 513
On the Beach (1959), 431
On the Town (1951), 387
On the Waterfront (1954), 29, 224, 357
Once Upon a Time in America (1984), 8, 391
Once We Were Warriors (1994), 332
One Flew Over the Cuckoo's Nest (1975), 150, 172, 556
One in a Million: The Ron LeFlore Story (1978), 105
One on One (1977), 39, 105
One Potato, Two Potato (1964), 511, 522

Opatovsky, David, 228, 242
Operation Paperclip, 286
Ophuls, Marcel, 13, 86, 110, 112, 119, 122-124, 232, 261, 263, 274
Ordinary People (1980), 445
Ornitz, Samuel, 198, 207
Orphee (1950), 151
Ort, Dan, 47
Orwell, George, 210, 550
Osagie, Iyunolu, 317
Osama (2003), 439, 440
Oscar Presents: The War Movies and John Wayne (1977), 441
Oscars, 261, 301, 362, 421
Osceola, 325
Othello (1964), 508
Other Side of the Mountain, The (1975), 105
Our Brand is Crisis (2015), 549
Our Winning Season (1978), 105
Overfield, James H., 353
Ovitz, Mike, 552
Owen, Clive, 554
Owens, Jesse, 513
Owens, William A., 307, 317, 318
Owre, Ed, 190
Ox-Bow Incident, The (1943), 29, 30

Paasche, James Calvin, 432, 434
Pacino, Al, 372, 394
Paget, Debra, 349
Paillard Corporation, 31, 32
Pakula, Alan J., 39, 43, 261
Palance, Jack, 37, 321
Palevsky, Max, 139
Palma, Brian De, 20, 26
Palmer, Ernest, 349
Palmer, Keke, 491
Paper Chase, The (1973), 39, 44
Papp, Joseph, 508
Paramount Decision, 418
Paramount Pictures, 123, 128, 139, 197, 198, 208, 411, 536

Parker, Alan, 125, 300
Parker, Charlie, 458, 459, 478
Parker, Dorothy, 14, 200
Parker, Leonard, 45
Parker, Quanah, 325
Parks, Donald, 190
Parks, Larry, 224
Parks, Rosa, 468
Pascal, Ernest, 208
Paskaljevic, Goraan, 434
Pasquier, Sylvaine, 270
Passion of Jeanne D'Arc, The (1928), 530
Passion of the Christ, The (2004), 444, 446, 555
Passos, John Dos, 355
Pasternak, Boris, 46, 83
Paths of Glory (1957), 153, 154, 389, 420, 437, 442
Patriot, The (2000), 444
Patton (1970), 339, 442, 446
Patton, George S., 242
Pawnbroker, The (1964), 261, 388
Pay It Forward (2000), 20
Payne, Alexander, 20, 26
Pearl Harbor, 221, 525
Peck, Gregory, 18, 25
Peckinpah, Sam, 86, 332, 391, 556
Peerce, Larry, 20, 26, 522
Pendergast, Sara, 492
Penn, Arthur, 331, 336
Penn, Leo, 479, 494
People of the Wind (1976), 140
Perkins, Jack, 349
Perkins, Millie, 226
Perry, Gerald, 43
Perry, Louis B., 204
Perry, Richard S., 204
Petain, Marshal Philippe, 124
Peters, Brock, 454, 461, 501, 507, 510, 512, 522
Petrie, Daniel, 476, 493

Pfefferberg, Leopold, 247, 253
Phenix, Philip, 64
Piaget, Jean, 76
Pianist, The (2002), 233, 274
Pickford, Mary, 411
Pike, Lipman, 108
Pilate, Pontius, 446
Pine, Lester, 479
Pinkville (2009), 113, 114, 115, 524
Pinky (1949), 357, 416, 439, 539
Pinter, Harold, 357
Place in the Sun, A (1951), 389
Plante, Caroline, 122
Plaszow Forced Labor Camp, 250, 251, 254
Plato, 57, 123, 262, 264, 271, 279, 281
Platoon (1986), 442, 554, 562
Player, The (1992), 356
Playing for Time (1980), 256, 260, 274
Please Don't Eat the Daisies (1960), 29
Pleasence, Donald, 357
Plummer, Christopher, 28, 296
Pocahontas, 325
Podgorze Ghetto, 250
Point Break (2015), 549
Poitier, Sidney, 416, 439, 476, 486, 495
Polanski, Roman, 86
Polk, James K., 329
Pollack, Sydney, 39, 44
Polytel International, 125, 130
Pontiac, 325
Pope Pius XII, 239
Pope, Alexander, 44
Popper, Nathaniel, 243
Popular Front, 201, 203, 210
Porsche, Ferdinand, 135
Porter, Cole, 9, 458, 537
Porter, Edwin S., 79

Portman, Natalie, 490
Portrait of Dorian Gray, The (1945), 30
Postman, Neil, 33
Potter, H. C., 9
Poussaint, Alvin F., 486, 495
Powell, Michael, 86
Powwow Highway (1989), 332
Preminger, Otto, 86, 227, 242, 412
Prichard, Marian von Binsbergen, 226
Pride of the Yankees, The (1942), 443
Priest, Martin, 45
Prime of Miss Jean Brodie, The (1969), 94
Princeton, 128, 134, 143, 192
Prisoner of Zenda, The (1937), 30
Prizzi's Honor (1985), 366
Professionals, The (1966), 60
Pronay, Nicholas, 192
Provenzano, Nicholas, 26
Public Broadcasting Service (PBS), 113, 236, 237, 333
Public Enemy, The (1931), 206
Puig, Claudia, 317
Purdy, Jim, 336
Purple Heart, The (1944), 222
Purple Rose of Cairo, The (1985), 10
Pursell, Michael, 176
Puttnam, David, 125, 129, 133

Quantrill, William, 323
Quart, Leonard, 210
Quebec Conference, 144
Queen Elizabeth I, 55
Queen Isabella, 304
Queen Victoria, 304
Quinn, Anthony, 153
Quo Vadis (1951), 208

R.P.M. (1970), 39
Racklin, Martin, 208

Radio Writers Guild, 199
Radio-Keith-Orpheum Pictures (RKO), 192, 197, 220, 411, 536
Ragtime (1981), 8
Raiders of the Lost Ark (1981), 250, 260
Raisin in the Sun, A, 476
Raisin in the Sun, A (1961), 29, 30, 445, 447
Randi, James "The Amazing", 399
Rapf, Harry, 209
Rapf, Maurice, 5, 16, 200
Raphaelson, Samson, 198
Rashke, Richard, 242, 245, 296
Ratoff, Gregory, 9
Ray, Man, 374, 381
Ray, Satyajit, 86, 420
Reagan, Bernice Johnson, 468
Reagan, Ronald, 86, 162, 224, 237
Reagans, The (2003), 444
Rebel Without a Cause (1955), 29, 445
Red Badge of Courage, The (1951), 366
Red Cloud, 325
Red Dust (1932), 208
Redford, Robert, 43, 332
Reds (1981), 299
Reed, Carol, 86
Reese, Pee Wee, 538
Reflections in a Golden Eye (1967), 366
Rehrauer, George, 192
Reich, Charles A., 12, 16, 539, 543
Reid, Mark A., 480, 494
Reisman, David, 543
Reisz, Karel, 39, 43
Remember (2015), 296
Reno, Marcus, 331
Renoir, Jean, 86, 361, 388, 529, 533
Resnais, Alain, 234, 260, 261, 263
Return of Martin Guerre, The (1982), 299

Revenant, The (2015), 549
Revenge of the Nerds (1984), 39, 44
Revolutionary, The (1970), 39
Reynolds, Jean, 99
Ricciarell, Giulio, 242
Rice, Henry Grantland, 97
Rich, Frank, 89, 91, 262, 271, 297, 318
Richard, Jacques, 381
Richards, I. A., 281, 429
Richards, Lloyd, 476, 517
Richardson, John N., 270
Richardson, Ralph, 227
Richardson, Robert B., 13, 113, 115-117, 524, 537, 544, 549, 561-563
Ridley, Matt, 528, 533
Riefenstahl, Leni, 369
Riesman, David, 12, 16, 539
Riley, Eileen, 270
Riley, Stevan, 464
Rio Bravo (1959), 328
Riskin, Robert, 200
Ritt, Martin, 466, 482, 485, 510, 511, 513, 517, 522
Ritter, Thelma, 366
River Niger, The (1976), 488
Rivera, Diego, 453
Rivkin, Allen, 208
Roach, Jay, 242, 507, 522, 549
Road to Singapore (1940), 9
Robards, Jason, III, 59
Robards, Jason, Jr., 453, 455, 516
Robe, Mike, 331, 336
Robe, The (1953), 419
Roberts, Randy, 494
Robeson, Paul, 458, 506, 507, 518-520, 523
Robeson, Paul, Jr., 518, 519
Robinson, Edward G., 221, 365
Robinson, Jackie, 513, 519, 538
Robinson, Louie, 493
Rocky (1976), 61, 96, 104-106, 405
Roddenberry, Gene, 363

Rodgers, Richard, 9, 458, 537
Rodrigues, Percy, 483
Rodriquez, Alex, 102
Roemer, Michael, 36, 45
Roffman, Peter, 336
Rogers, Howard Emmett, 200
Rogers, Roy, 10, 322, 536
Rohmer, Eric, 540
Rolle, Esther, 476
Rollins, Alfred B., Jr., 61, 63
Rollins, Peter C., 335, 336, 450, 525
Roman Opera House, 1
Romance (1930), 207
Romano, Andrew, 336
Romanowski, William D., 247, 269
Rome, Tina, 479
Romero, Cesar, 322
Rooker, Michael, 289
Room (2015), 549
Room 237 (2012), 155, 156, 157
Room at the Top (1959), 29
Rooney, Mickey, 402, 442
Roosevelt, Franklin Delano, 143, 144, 196, 197, 199, 201, 205, 216, 217, 220, 223, 239
Root, Well, 208
Roots (1977) (ABC), 307, 488
Roper Organization, 262
Rosa Parks Story, The (2002), 488
Rose of Washington Square (1939), 9
Rose, Elliot Joseph Benn, 134
Rose, Frank, 529, 533
Rosen, Peter, 382
Rosenberg, Harold, 142, 143, 146
Rosenblatt, Sol, 199
Rosenstrasse (2003), 273
Rosenthal, Alan, 241
Ross, Gaylen, 242, 243
Ross, Murray, 204, 205, 206, 208
Rossen, Robert, 40, 522
Rostand, Edmond, 13, 16, 282, 382, 404, 405, 408, 546

Rostow, Walt, 127
Roth, Philip, 20
Roth, Tim, 488
Rothschild, Evelyn, 125
Rothschild, Hannah, 434
Roundtree, Richard, 510
Royal Scandal, A (1945), 207
Rozsa, Miklos, 458
Rubin, Robert, 45, 46
Rugheimer, Gunnar, 130, 132
Rules of the Game, The (1939), 361, 437, 529
Russell, Bertrand, 455, 464
Russell, Ken, 125
Russians are Coming, The Russians are Coming, The (1966), 483
Russo, Gianni, 367
Rustin, Bayard, 481
Ruth, Roy Del, 9
Ruysdael, Basil, 349
Ryan, Bonnie, 190
Ryan, Thomas C., 483

Sacagawea, 325
Sackler, Howard, 509, 510, 514, 523
Sagalle, Jonathan, 253
Sahara (1943), 206
Sahl, Mort, 213
Saigon, 136, 554
Saint Joan, 13, 405
Saint, Eva Marie, 227, 228
Sainte-Marie, Buffy, 335, 336
Sakharov, Andrei, 132
Salgado, Juliano Ribeiro, 335
Salgado, Sebastião, 321
Salkow, Sidney, 331, 336
Salvador (1986), 562
Samuels, Allison, 317, 318
Samuels, Stuart, 241
San Quentin (1937), 206
Sandburg, Carl, 545, 550
Sanders, Charles L., 493

Sandoval, Dolores, 190
Sands, Diana, 476
Sands, Pierre Norman, 205
Sandusky, Jerry, 102
Sarandon, Susan, 389, 468
Sargent, Alvin, 556
Sargent, Joseph, 498, 514, 523
Sarris, Andrew, 85, 86, 249, 281, 530, 540
Sartre, Jean Paul, 124, 244
Saunby, Sir Robert, 135
Saving Private Ryan (1998), 308, 442
Scarface (1932), 208
Scarlet Letter, The, 13
Schaefer, Christien Harty, 317
Schaffer, Linda, 445
Schama, Simon, 241
Schary, Dore, 208
Schatz, Thomas, 192, 335
Schenck, Joseph M., 202
Schenk, Bill, 190
Schertinger, Victor, 9
Schickel, Richard, 249, 269, 277, 295, 315, 318
Schiller, Friedrich, 213
Schilo, Harriet, 47, 50, 51, 53
Schindler, Emilie, 254, 270
Schindler, Oskar, 212, 215, 221, 247-250, 252-254, 262-267
Schindler's List (1993), 15, 156, 212, 214, 217, 227, 233, 238, 246-250, 254, 255, 258, 259, 262, 263, 267, 268, 274, 279, 283, 285, 294, 299, 308, 309, 313, 314, 339, 432, 437
Schindlerjuden, 248, 264, 266, 267
Schirk, Heinz, 235
Schlesinger, John, 363
Schmidt-Garre, Jan, 492, 521
Schnabel, Julian, 233, 244, 562
Schon, Jeffrey, 422
School Daze (1988), 39, 44
Schroeder, Marieke, 492, 521

Schulberg, Budd, 200, 206, 209, 355, 356
Schwartz, Nancy Lynn, 204, 206
Schwartz, Sheila, 26, 72
Schweitzer, Albert, 360
Scorsese, Martin, 21, 26, 83, 90, 115, 214, 241, 249, 321, 333, 335, 529, 533, 561
Scott, George C., 476
Scott, Oz, 488
Scott, Pippa, 392
Scott, Randolph, 22
Scott, Ridley, 391, 553
Screen Actors Guild (SAG), 199, 206, 208, 224
Screen Actors of America, 208
Screen Playwrights (SP), 200
Screen Writers Guild (SWG), 196-200, 202, 203, 206-208, 210, 211, 294, 357, 542
Sea Around Us, The (1953), 28
Sea Chase, The (1955), 223
Searchers, The (1956), 327, 390, 392, 511, 539
Searching for Bobby Fisher (1993), 20
See, Carolyn Penelope, 355
Segal, Erich, 538
Seiler, Andy, 317
Seitz, George B., 9
Seldes, Gilbert, 525, 533
Selznick, David O., 411
Sembene (2015), 549
Seminole (1953), 327
Sennett, Mack, 79, 412
Sense of Loss, A (1973), 113, 123, 124
Sergeant Rutledge (1960), 332, 336, 511, 539
Sergeant York (1941), 442, 443
Serling, Rod, 514
Serpico (1973), 388
Servant, The (1963), 29
Seven Beauties (1975), 142, 234, 369

Seven Samurai, The (1954), 437, 530
Seventh Seal, The (1957), 437, 530, 561
Shaft (1971), 469
Shah, Krishna, 488
Shakespeare, William, 13, 28, 57, 155, 282, 353, 359, 453, 546
Shane (1953), 30, 529
Shapiro, Harold T., 494
Shapiro, Joshua, 244
Shapiro, Laurie Gwen, 243
Shaw, George Bernard, 11, 13, 80, 149, 282, 405, 408, 438, 546
Shawcross, Lord Hartley, 143
She Done Him Wrong (1933), 206
Sheinberg, Sidney, 248, 249
Shepherd, Alan, 175
Sheridan, Philip H., 331, 341, 344, 349
Sherin, Edwin, 509, 510
Sherman, Barry, 186
Sherman, George, 327
Sherman, William Tecumseh, 331, 344, 350
Shimura, Takashi, 6
Ship of Fools (1965), 261, 273
Shire, Talia, 367, 394
Shoah, 225, 232, 235, 238-240, 260, 261, 285, 286, 290-294, 482
Shoah (1985), 237, 260
Shop on Main Street, The (1965), 260, 261
Short, Kenneth R. M., 282, 295
Show Boat (1951), 208
Shrek II (2004), 555
Sica, Vittorio De, 85, 86, 91
Sieving, Christopher, 481, 494
Sigurd, Jacques, 190
Silas Marner, 23, 70
Silber, Glenn, 39, 44
Silent Movie (1976), 356
Silkwood (1986), 388

Silverheels, Jay, 349
Simon, John, 281
Simone, Nina, 459, 464, 470
Simons, G. A., 220
Simpson, O. J., 102
Sinatra, Frank, 437, 492
Sinatra, Frank, Jr., 479
Since You Went Away (1944), 442
Singer, Aubrey, 132
Singin' in the Rain (1952), 356, 387
Singleton, John, 39, 44
Sirk, Douglas, 327
Siskel, Gene, 22
Sister Kenny (1946), 28
Sisyphus, 38
Sitting Bull, 325, 331
Sitting Bull (1954), 331
Skinner, B. F., 428, 434
Sklar, Robert, 115, 192, 284, 296, 315, 318
Slap Shot (1977), 105
Slater, Joseph, 90
Slaughter (1972), 365
Slave Ship (1937), 306
Slaves (1969), 306
Slesinger, Stephen, 322
Slide, Anthony, 192
Smale, Alison, 239, 245
Smiley, Jane, 334, 336
Smith College, 33
Smith, Alan M., 351
Smith, Bradley F., 142, 143
Smith, Joan, 421
Smith, John N., 20, 26
Smith, Johnny, 494
Smith, Liz, 362
Smith, Maggie, 94
Smithsonian Institution, 330, 335
Smoke Signals (1998), 332
Snitow, Alan, 482, 494
Snow White and the Seven Dwarfs (1937), 536

So Dear to My Heart (1949), 209
Sobchack, Thomas, 192, 385
Sobchack, Vivian C., 192, 385
Sobibor, 240, 288
Social Network, The (2010), 39, 44
Society for Cinema and Media Studies, 90, 526
Soderbergh, Steven, 427, 434
Sokoloff, Vladimir, 352, 369
Solzhenitsyn, Alexandr, 132
Son of Saul (2015), 243, 550
Son of the Morning Star (1991), 331
Song of the South (1946), 209, 306
Sontag, Susan, 440, 447
Sophie's Choice (1982), 260, 261, 367
Sorlin, Pierre, 192, 338
Sorrow and the Pity, The (1969), 110, 113, 120-125, 141, 260, 261
Soul Man (1986), 39
Sounder (1972), 455, 466, 482, 485-488, 492
South Burlington High School, 62, 67, 71, 78
Southern Connecticut State College, 38, 41, 42, 56, 87, 89, 97, 99
Soviet Union, 201, 223, 285, 537
Spaatz, Carl Andrew, 135
Spacek, Sissy, 468
Spark, Muriel, 94
Spartacus (1960), 29
Speer, Albert, 125, 135, 144, 223
Spiegelman, Art, 254
Spielberg, Steven, 43, 156, 212, 214, 215, 246, 247, 249-252, 254-261, 263-267, 269, 278, 285, 294, 300, 301, 307-316, 378, 391, 431, 549, 552
Spinks, Leon, 104
Spinoza, Benedictus de, 534
Spotlight (2015), 549
Spotted Elk, 326
Spy Who Came in from the Cold, The (1965), 274

St. Jacques, Raymond, 476, 482
Stagecoach (1939), 9
Staiger, Janet, 192
Stalin, Josef, 143, 144, 201, 202, 203
Stallone, Sylvester, 96, 106, 549
Stand and Deliver (1988), 20
Stanwyck, Barbara, 437
Staples, Brent, 464, 479, 494
Star is Born, A (1937), 9, 209, 356, 420
Star Wars (1977), 391, 517, 556
Staron, Stanislaw, 235
Starting Out in the Evening (2007), 39, 44
Stavis, Gene, 432, 434
Stedman, Raymond William, 335
Steinem, Gloria, 38
Steiner, George, 257
Stephani, Frederick, 26
Stephens, James, 16
Sterile Cuckoo, The (1969), 39
Stern, Itzhak, 212, 252, 265
Steve Jobs (2015), 549
Stevens, George, viii, 9, 86, 111, 122, 179, 226, 242, 261, 273, 389
Stevens, George, Jr., 122, 190, 226
Stewart, Donald Ogden, 200
Stewart, James, 320, 340, 348, 437
Stewart, Melvin, 45
Stoler, Mark A., 242, 417
Stone, A. Harris, 99
Stone, Oliver, 113, 269, 300, 334, 336, 524, 537, 562
Stone, Philip, 175
Story of Louis Pasteur, The (1936), 28
Story of Vernon and Irene Castle, The (1939), 9
Strebel, Elizabeth Grottle, 192
Streep, Meryl, 367, 490
Street Scene (1931), 8
Streetcar Named Desire, A (1951), 357

Streicher, Julius, 223
Streisand, Barbra, 43
Strode, Woody, 332, 454, 501, 505
Sturges, John, 327, 390, 522
Styne, Jule, 550
Styron, William, 260
Suber, Howard, 204, 312, 349
Suffragette (2015), 549
Sugarland Express, The (1947), 249
Sugarman, Richard, 232, 244
Sukowa, Barbara, 231
Sullivan, John L., 108
Sullivan's Travels (1941), 356
Sunrise at Campobello (1960), 29
Sunset Boulevard (1960), 356, 416
Super Fly (1972), 469
Susskind, David, 477
Swank, Hilary, 541
Swastika (1974), 125, 134
Sweeney, Edwin R., 350, 351
Sweeney, J. K., 521
Sweethearts (1938), 9
Swift, Jonathan, 6, 13, 16, 41, 44, 59, 282, 297, 374, 380, 382, 546
Swing Kids (1993), 274
Szwed, John, 475, 478, 489, 493

Taking Sides (2001), 274
Tale of Two Cities, A (1935), 23, 29
Talent Associates, 477
Tamahori, Lee, 332
Tamango (1959), 306
Tappan, Arthur, 303
Tappan, Lewis, 303
Tarantino, Quentin, 549, 562, 563
Tarza, 325
Tarza, Son of Cochise (1954), 327
Tarzan, 22
Taurog, Norman, 9
Taylor, Elizabeth, 482, 490
Taylor, Philip, 192
Taylor, Ray, 26

Taylor, Tate, 491, 496
Taylor, Telford, 124, 136, 137, 138, 139
Teachers College, 33, 37, 64, 78, 84, 541
Teachout, Terry, 480, 494
Tecumseh, 325
Tejada-Fares, Rick, 277, 295, 543
Tender is the Night (1962), 356
Tennyson, Alfred Lord, 550
Terms of Endearment (1983), 427
Terrace, Vincent, 351
Terrett, Courtney, 198
Terry, Joseph C., 317
Tevis, Walter S., 40, 41
Thalberg, Irving, 357
That Night in Rio (1941), 209
The Longest Yard (1974), 104
The Red Network 1934, 201
The Shining (1980), 151, 154, 156-163, 174, 177
The Stand (1994), 156
The Way We Were (1973), 37, 39, 44, 417
They Died With Their Boots On (1941), 331
They Made Me a Criminal (1939), 9
Thief of Bagdad, The (1940), 9
Thin Red Line, The (1998), 432
Third Reich, 126, 135, 214, 215, 223, 230, 232, 272, 274, 285
Thirteen (2003), 445
Thirteen Days (2000), 444
Thirty Seconds Over Tokyo (1944), 442
This Side of Paradise (1991), 356
This Sporting Life (1963), 29
Thomas, Dylan, 13, 23
Thompson, Kristin, 192, 388, 389
Thomson, David, 296
Thoreau, Henry David, 492
Thorpe, Richard, 402, 407

Three Kings (1999), 442
Till We Meet Again (1936), 207
Tin Drum, The (1979), 261
Tiomkin, Dimitri, 458
Titanic (1997), 300
Titsch, Raimund, 251
Titterington, P. L., 161, 176
To Be or Not to Be (1942), 207, 369
To Kill a Mockingbird (1962), 29, 307
To Sir, With Love (1967), 20
Toback, James, 39, 43
Tocqueville, Alexis de, 57
Tolstoy, Leo, 6, 13
Tom Jones (1963), 29
Tomorrow the World (1944), 209
Tomorrowland (2015), 550
Top Gun (1986), 554
Toplin, Robert Brent, 283, 284, 295, 317, 336
Tora, Tora, Tora (1970), 442
Tracy, Spencer, 224, 437
Treasure of the Sierra Madre, The (1948), 366, 416
Treblinka, 288
Tree Grows in Brooklyn, A (1945), 445
Trial (1962), 29
Trial of Adolf Eichmann, The (1997), 229
Tribute to Dylan Thomas, A (1961), 29
Trilling, Lionel, 210, 281
Trip to Bountiful, A (film), 496
Trip to Bountiful, A (play), 491
Triumph of the Spirit (1989), 273
Trotta, Margarethe von, 229
Troy (2004), 441, 446
Truffaut, François, 57, 63, 86, 116, 388, 540, 556
Truman, Harry S., 131
Trumbo (2015), 242, 507, 549
Trumbo, Dalton, 86, 200, 204, 209, 210, 224, 227, 507, 513

Truth (2015), 549
Tubman, Harriet Ross, 468, 472, 488
Tucker, Julia, 501
Tucker, Lorenzo, 454, 501, 513, 517, 523
Turing, Alan, 513
Turkel, Joe, 175
Turner Classic Movies, 441, 442
Turner, J.M.W., 513
Turner, Ted, 552
Twain, Mark, 13, 23, 28, 111, 121, 122, 179, 282, 361, 402, 403, 405, 408, 546
Twelve Angry Men (1957), 29, 388, 474, 493
Twentieth Century-Fox, 94, 197, 209, 338, 348, 411, 419, 536
Twist, Oliver, 8
Twister (1996), 313
Tyldum, Morten, 16, 63
Tyler, John, 305
Tyler, Tom, 22
Tyson, Cicely, 13, 454-456, 461, 466-470, 476-478, 480, 482, 484, 485, 487, 488, 490-493, 495, 501, 505
Tyson, Theodosia, 471, 472
Tyson, William, 471

Ugly American, The (1963), 29
Ulin, David L., 408
Ullman, Michael, 475, 493
Ulmer, James, 269
Uncle Tom's Cabin, 70, 306
Under Two Flags (1936), 209
Underwood, Blair, 491
Underwood, Tim, 177
Unforgiven, The (1960), 511, 539
United Artists, 158, 192, 411, 419, 420, 536
United Nations, 227, 475

Universal Pictures, 27, 35, 197, 411, 419, 420, 536
University of California in Los Angeles, 192
University of Southern California, 192
University of Vermont, 43, 53, 56, 58-60, 62, 66, 67, 73, 74, 89, 90, 97, 99, 100, 111, 112, 114, 118, 120, 121, 124, 148, 156, 158, 180, 181, 185, 188, 226, 233, 237, 274, 277, 294, 333, 353, 354, 356, 390, 400, 401, 407, 424, 433, 458-461, 473, 520, 541, 552, 557, 558, 561, 562, 563
University of Wisconsin, 192
Unsuspected, The (1947), 209
Up the Down Staircase (1967), 20, 22, 23
Urie, Ester J., 72
Uris, Leon, 227
Ushpiz, Ada, 243
Ustinov, Peter, 482

Van Buren, Martin, 304, 329
Van Dyke, W. S., 9
Van Sant, Gus, 20, 26, 39, 43
Van Wert, William F., 192
Vanderbilt, James, 549
Vanishing Point (1971), 556
Vaughn, Robert, 205
Verdi, Giuseppe, 1, 374, 489
Vermont Reports (PBS), 236, 245
Vernon Rice Award, 476
Victorio, 325
Vidal, Gore, 41, 44, 330, 355
Vidor, King, 8, 9, 323, 454, 501
Vietnam War, 11, 113, 126, 136, 142, 162, 256, 452, 491, 547
Vigoda, Abe, 394
Virgil, 13, 507
Visual Programmes Systems Ltd., 125

Volcano (1976), 140
Vollman, William T., 334
von Blum, Paul, 453, 537
von Papen, Franz, 223
von Sternberg, Josef, 412
Voyage of the Damned (1976), 274

Wachler, Horst von, 297
Wachsmann, Nikolaus, 245
Wacks, Jonathan, 332
Wagner, Andrew, 39, 44
Wagner, Honus, 108
Wajda, Andrzej, 86, 271
Walker, Elsie M., 122
Wall, Max, 473
Wall, The (1982), 256
Wallace, Irving, 514
Wallach, Eli, 366
Wallenberg: A Hero's Story (1985), 256, 260
Waller, Fats, 458
Walsh, Raoul, 323, 331, 336
Walt Disney Company, 192, 250, 414, 551
Wanamaker, Sam, 331, 336
Wang, Wayne, 488
Wannsee Conference, 231
Wannsee Conference, The (1992), 235
War and Peace (novel), 13
War and Remembrance (1988-89), 256
War at Home, (1979), 39
Ward, Brian, 492
Wardour Street, 126, 129, 131
Warm December, A (1973), 486
Warner Brothers, 192, 197, 198, 209, 369, 411, 536
Warren, Charles Marquis, 327
Warren, Mame, 463
Warsaw, Robert, 429
Washburn, Wilcomb E., 335, 336
Washington, Denzel, 39, 43
Washington, Fredi, 468

Washington, George, 348, 455
Washington, Wilcomb E., 330
Watanabe, Kanji, 6
Watch on the Rhine (1943), 28
Watergate Investigation, 11, 162, 491
Waters, Ethel, 467, 468, 472, 487
Waugh, Evelyn, 355
Waxman, Sharon, 293, 297
Wayne, John, 328, 392, 441
Weatherford, Elizabeth, 335
Weaver, Thomas, 463
Webb, Robert D., 327
Weill, Kurt, 550
Weinraub, Bernard, 254, 270, 297
Weinstein, Julius, 407
Weir, Peter, 20, 26
Weiss, Alan J., 521, 522
Weissmuller, Johnny, 10, 22, 536
Welch, David, 192
Welkos, Robert W., 318
Welles, Orson, 86, 271, 367, 535, 542
Welles, Richard, 63
Wellman, William A., 9
Weltzenkorn, Louis, 198
Wenders, Wim, 335
Werker, Alfred L., 327
Wertheimer, Alan P., 269
Wertmuller, Lina, 142, 234, 369
West, Nathanael, 355
Westmoreland, William, 127, 136
What Our Father's Did: A Nazi Legacy (2015), 550
Wheaton, Christopher Dudley, 205
Where to Invade Next (2015), 549
Whiplash (2014), 20
White Feather (1955), 327
White, Armond, 317
White, Josh, 458, 519
White, Lucille, 72
White, Susan, 162, 176

Whitfield, Stephen, 220
Whitmore, James, 454, 461, 501
Whitney, William, 26
Who's Afraid of Virginia Woolf? (1966), 388
Widmark, Richard, 224
Wiesel, Elie, 237, 257, 290
Wieseltier, Leon, 262
Wilberforce, William, 467
Wild Bunch, The (1969), 391, 556
Wilder, Billy, 85, 412
Wilder, Thornton, 201
Wilkerson, Billy, 349
Wilkerson, Isabel, 477, 494
Wilkins, Roy, 481
Willard, Jess, 510
William Tell Overture, 10
Williams, Billy Dee, 109, 476
Williams, Clarence, III, 484
Williams, Emlyn, 490
Williams, Michael, 269
Williams, Milton, 45
Williams, Paul, 39, 43
Williams, Todd, 297, 318
Williams, Vanessa, 491
Wills, Garry, 204
Wilson (1944), 28
Wilson, August, 517
Wilson, Edmund, 429
Wilson, Michael, 421, 491, 496, 542, 548
Wilson, Walter, 45
Wilson, William, 177
Winfield, Paul, 485
Winkler, Irwin, 287
Winslett, Kate, 490
Winter Carnival (1939), 209
Wise Blood (1979), 366
Wise, Robert, 474, 493
Wiseman, Frederick, 549
Wizard of Oz, The (1939), 9, 389, 536
Woledge, Elizabeth, 381
Woman in Gold (2015), 239

Woman of the Year (1942), 209
Wonder Boys (2000), 39
Wonder of Women (1928), 209
Wood, Lana, 392
Wood, Sam, 9, 20, 408
Woods, Tiger, 102
Wordsworth, William, 6, 16, 57
World, The Flesh, and The Devil, The (1959), 511, 539
Worth, Harry, 22
Wouk, Herman, 237
Wovaka, 326
Wrathall, Nicholas D., 44
Wright, Will, 335
Writers Guild, 208, 309, 413, 421
Writers Guild Arbitration Board, 309
Wuthering Heights (1939), 9
Wyler, William, 8, 9, 85, 412
Wynn, Tracy Keenan, 486

Yad Vashem Museum, 248
Yale University, 69
Yalta Conference, 144
Yeats, W.B., 13
Yoseloff, Julien, 90
You Can't Take it With You (1938), 208
Young at Heart (1954), 445
Young Lions, The (1958), 223
Young, Robert, 45
Young, Victor, 458
Young, Whitney, 481
Youngblood, Denise J., 175, 269, 348, 360, 450, 463
Yvonne, 492

Zaillian, Steven, 20, 26, 214, 267, 269, 294, 309
Zanuck, Darryl F., 339
Zinnemann, Fred, 328
Zola, Emile, 352, 369
Zoma, Ben, 381

www.ingramcontent.com/pod-product-compliance
Lightning Source LLC
Chambersburg PA
CBHW021822220426
43663CB00005B/103